BATTLE FOR HURUNGWE:

A SPECIAL BRANCH VICTORY IN AN UNWINNABLE WAR

RHODESIA 1965 ~ 1979

John Padbury

To ALAN.
Something to remind
you about Africa.
J Padbury
15/06/23

TSL Publications

First published in Great Britain in 2022
By TSL Publications, Rickmansworth

ISBN / 978-1-914245-34-3

Cover image by John Padbury: The Regional Commander and author

Cover design by Corvus-Design.co.uk.

Document images courtesy of Peter Stiff's widow, unless otherwise stated

To those who lost their lives, or limbs, or minds, or dreams,
and those who wonder why.

CONTENTS

SOUTHERN RHODESIA
1965

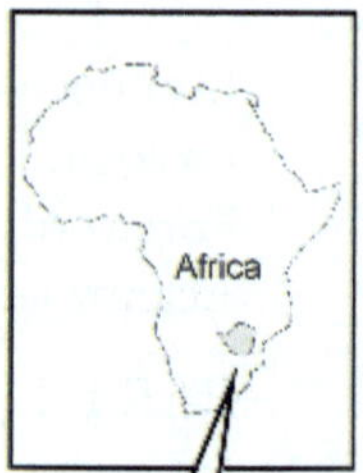

INTRODUCTION

This book discusses Special Branch operations in Rhodesia conducted in the course of the liberation struggle against white minority rule during the years 1965 to 1979. It is based on diaries compiled by former British South Africa Police (BSAP) Detective Inspector John Padbury, supported by Rhodesian Air Force Pilot logbooks and personal statements from those involved in the various operations during the time of the actions. Top secret Rhodesian military reports, archived secret and confidential British records, political documents and diaries were also scrutinised in the production of this work.

Part 1 covers counter-insurgency operations during the period 1973-1978 mainly in the Makoni and Manyika Tribal Trust Lands. Here, insurgents from the Zimbabwe African National Liberation Army (ZANLA),[1] based and trained mainly in Mozambique, had successfully penetrated these areas mobilising the masses and brutally assaulting, maiming and killing "sellouts" as they imposed, what was to all intents and purposes, martial law. ZANLA then commenced strikes against Rhodesian forces, planting landmines, attacking white-owned farmsteads and strategic targets. Unprepared and untrained Special Branch officers had to learn counter-insurgency strategies which grew rapidly in sophistication and effectiveness but failed to stem the revolutionary tide, as insurgents continued to flow into the country, increasing their areas of control en route to their ultimate goal, Salisbury, the capital.

In Part 2, the book moves on to discuss counter-revolution and mass-mobilisation operations in Hurungwe Tribal Trust Land. The destruction of two civilian Viscount airliners shot down by insurgents from the Zimbabwe People's Revolutionary Army (ZIPRA),[2] and subsequent murders of some of the passengers surviving the crash, are also discussed. By 1978, ZIPRA insurgents had crossed the Zambezi River into Rhodesia from Zambia, successfully occupying the Hurungwe Tribal Trust Land. ZIPRA put a stop to Rhodesian civil administration services and established their particular form of military rule.

In September 1978, former Special Branch Detective Inspector John Padbury was deployed to Hurungwe district with a handful of specially selected and trained elite men to develop a Special Branch strategy with the intention of recapturing Hurungwe, in order to counter the invading ZIPRA forces and re-establish civil administration. This was the commencement of the battle for Hurungwe. The key to this operation was the mobilisation of the masses. This was a strategy completely overlooked and resisted by the Rhodesian Front Government and the Security Forces throughout the war. Accounts of the struggle for the occupation and repossession of Hurungwe recorded in Padbury's diaries reveal how these brave men risked their lives for a more prosperous future for all Rhodesians, black and white, that they might live together in peace and harmony.

Fire Force operations are discussed in detail along with various ground force operations, including one SAS operation. These deployments were all planned by Padbury. ZIPRA insurgents and their collaborators are identified and their base locations pinpointed by original sketches, which help complete a picture of what happened throughout the area. For the first time, the experiences of the rural African population living in their kraals, along with those operating ZIPRA's intelligence organisation, are brought together with the Security Forces of the Salisbury Government. Consequently, this account of strategies and tactics deployed and the insights gained by Padbury and his comrades, as well as his enemies, will provide insight to those considering how best to confront and defeat contemporary insurgencies around the world.

[1] Military wing of Zimbabwe African National Union (ZANU). Founded in 1963, headed by Ndabaningi Sithole and later Robert Mugabe.

[2] Military wing of Zimbabwe African People's Union, (ZAPU). Founded in 1961, headed by Joshua Nkomo.

Finally, this book questions why, as early as 1972, when Government politicians in Salisbury acknowledged the extent and nature of the political impasse, and knew the war could not be won, did the Rhodesian Front Government keep the armed forces fighting for a further seven years to maintain white minority rule? Why was a lost cause pursued which would lead to the destruction of what was commonly known as the "jewel in Africa" and its population?

John Padbury.
May 2021

PROLOGUE

For many years, I contemplated documenting the diaries I kept while operational in Hurungwe Tribal Trust Land, but never did it. With the appearance of some memoirs containing questionable accounts about events in Hurungwe, I felt compelled to set the record straight. I am grateful for the challenges I faced during the writing of this book, as it forced me to verify and authenticate my records, with reference to those of friends and comrades, and those against whom we waged war.

Little has been written about Special Branch operations and how intelligence officers operated in Rhodesia during the civil war. I believe my account will help clarify crucial aspects of the history of the war. Although strategies and tactics varied in each theatre of conflict, I have recorded the specific techniques we developed and brought to bear during the struggle. My thinking led me to organise the material in the book chronologically, to assist the reader in following the development of our methods as we operated in the field. In several places, I have brought together the intelligence gathered over a period of time, including a description of the resulting military action, to present a compelling account rather than a monotonous log of diarised events.

In order to understand this book, it is essential to grasp that "politics is war without bloodshed and war is politics with bloodshed".[1] The link between political agendas, the military and the people, the process of the three becoming one, is vital to comprehending successful counter-revolution and mass-mobilisation strategies. In other words, the political precedes the military. Special Branch work is intrinsically embroiled with political manoeuvring, so I have delved into aspects of significant relevant political issues of the day. As the war escalated, I became increasingly aware of the political failures of the then Rhodesian Government and the impact these had on the military. This knowledge was vital to our success in Hurungwe, where we could address the people's political aspirations and bring them into unity with the military. In Chapter 1, I discuss some of the important African nationalists' political grievances. To include them all calls for a separate project. This is not a forensic examination of a political standpoint as this will follow in future publications. The political thoughts and opinions expressed here are my own and are not the responsibility of the many authors and contributors I have cited throughout the book. Indeed, it is likely many of them will be uncomfortable with my outlook at the time or with my reflections 40 years after the events described. I also discuss my early childhood as this might give the reader an idea of the wonderful and privileged colonial lifestyle we lived. We were generally isolated and diverted from and, therefore, unaware of the reality of the plight of the African people.

As I delved into this project, and realised the wealth of oral and recorded history now available, I have aspired to authenticate my work, as far as possible, by including contributions from those men involved in the same battles and incidents. It has been an enlightening journey, taking me back to the war days by meeting up with numerous Security Forces personnel with whom I fought, many of whom were simply faces at the time. In my search for the pilots and crew involved in a controversial SAS contact, I realised I could link the pilot's logbook details to contacts recorded in my diary. This revealed a fascinating area of research. I have included many contributions as they explain, in detail, the dedication, commitment and resolve of the Security Forces to fight and, in many cases die, for their country, despite overwhelming odds. Also explained are the strategies and tactics used which can be compared to those I developed and utilised in the battle for Hurungwe.

On 5 May 2015, I received the following email: "I am writing a PhD thesis on SFAs in Hurungwe. I have some unanswered questions. Can we interact? Joshua Chakawa." Such is my suspicious Special Branch mind that I hesitated, taking a couple of months to reply while I researched his background. Dr Chakawa's thesis, which he began in 2010, was on ZIPRA operations in Hurungwe

[1] Zedong, M. (1976), pp. 58-59.

district as well as the SFA's operations. With an interest in military history, he could not understand how or why the operation we conducted was such a success and why a white operative would have been so actively involved. His research included extensive interviews with former ZIPRA insurgents, contact men, *mujibhas*, resident ZIPRA collaborators and residents of Hurungwe intrinsically involved in the conflict. The thesis confirmed many of my diary entries and it was enlightening to cross-reference entries with Joshua's work. Such was the interest in Joshua's work that it made its way to former Zimbabwe President, Robert Mugabe, for analysis. His thesis was accepted and, at his graduation ceremony, he received his doctorate from Robert Mugabe on 25 November 2015. Joshua also carried out research for me in Hurungwe: I was "operational" again. We decided that I would give him sufficient information to locate the areas I wanted researched and he would carry out oral interviews to establish the facts. His independent research could then be used to corroborate my diaries. Through this process Dr Chakawa identified and interviewed people documented in my diaries who had lived through the war, including contact men, *mujibhas*, ZIPRA collaborators and residents involved in specific incidents detailed in my diaries. He confirmed some of these locations by GPS to authenticate my diaries. For the first time the reader will learn in detail from both sides engaged in the conflict. Joshua and I finally met when, with my brother, Maj. David Padbury, we attended the International Conference on History Education in Africa convened by the University of KwaZulu-Natal in December 2015.

Two years later, in July 2017, I contacted Lord David Owen, the British Foreign and Commonwealth Secretary during 1977-1979. To my surprise, Lord Owen replied and sent me recently declassified secret, confidential and personal documents relating to his time in office. I interviewed him at his home on 19 March 2018. A great deal of what Lord Owen had to recount was a revelation to me, bringing a degree of clarity I had not anticipated but which confirmed many of the thoughts and observations detailed in my diaries.

My diaries contain a considerable amount of detail about ZIPRA combatants, their collaborators, base camps and locstats which I have, in the main, left out of the text and condensed into logs and maps. Likewise, details of contacts between SFAs and ZIPRA. In some cases, I have retained this detail as it helps explain the extent of our intelligence confirming the overwhelming support we enjoyed among the people of Hurungwe. There is much conjecture regarding atrocities committed during the war. All parties (including the Security Forces, Selous Scouts, ZANLA, ZIPRA, Special Branch, and so on), deny or deflect blame. After much soul searching, I decided to present events as accurately as possible, as I understood them at the time, in order to leave the reader in no doubt as to the facts and consequences of this tragic war in my field of operations. Therefore, generally the names of those involved have not been changed. The names of girls who were forcibly or voluntarily sexually involved with ZIPRA combatants have been changed or removed. Details of some of the people supporting the United African National Council (UANC), headed by Bishop Abel Muzorewa, have in places been changed unless it is confirmed they are deceased. I have liaised closely with Dr Chakawa on this matter. Similarly, most former Security Forces members did not object to their names being mentioned. Some requested anonymity which I have respected. Dr Chakawa has corrected all the African names and rural places, amending some of my spelling from the original diaries. To avoid confusion, I use the correct African names in the text and maps and the white cities, towns and places are named and spelt at the time of the event being described. It should be noted at this stage that Dr Chakawa agreed it was in order to publish the photographs and names of UANC officials, SFAs and civilians mentioned in my diaries. Likewise Maj. Gavin Rawstron with members of the Rhodesian African Rifles.

The truth of this war is that we faced insurmountable odds. The Rhodesian Security Forces fought bravely winning the military battles when the enemy was located, but ultimately losing the war. This book attempts to provide not simply a narrative about the aspects of the conflict I directly experienced but also reflects upon why we were unable to win.

Apologies for the atrocities committed upon all sides are entirely self-serving and inappropriate. All wars are atrocious which is reason enough for doing all we can to avoid them. But, in setting out the record of my role and contribution in the war we fought for Rhodesia, I have attempted to provide as honest and thorough an account as my diaries, later research and subsequent reflection would allow.

The reader will note I consistently quote Mao Zedong[1] throughout this book. As our enemy adhered to Zedong's revolutionary military strategies, I decided the only way to counter the revolution was to adopt, refine and develop Zedong's methodology in the battle for Hurungwe. In my opinion this was the only way to counter the revolutionary forces we faced. I need to emphasise, I strongly condemn violent oppression of people for political gain on both sides of the conflict.

With the emergence of religious fundamentalist insurgencies in Africa, and worldwide, there is no doubt the strategies and tactics developed and deployed in Hurungwe district are relevant in the struggle, to hold the ground and defeat an enemy committed to ensnaring entire populations with terrorism. It is my hope that reflection on the principles, strategies and tactics of counter-revolution and mass mobilisation developed in Hurungwe during the latter stages of the bush war will prove useful to the process of rethinking military responses to extremist insurgency and dictatorships.

This book covers events which occurred some 40 years back. Therefore, fading memories merge battles and incidents, and timescales are elusive. However, I have researched numerous resources to confirm the facts. Invariably I have relied on more than one source to verify incidents, thereby using the method of triangulation.[2] This of course was only a difficulty in Part 1, not Part 2, where I have relied on my diaries which have been authenticated by numerous researched resources. Because of my extensive research around the world, I believe I have presented the facts accurately. Should there be errors outside of my diaries, they are my responsibility completely. There have been numerous contributions to the writing of this book comprising miscellaneous accounts, both military and civilian, and official reports pertaining to the Rhodesian civil war. In order to preserve their authenticity, these contributions have been published in their original format. This principle has also been adopted for certain footnotes. My personal diarised accounts, and selected extractions thereof, have been modified and adapted for the purposes of fluency and comprehension.

Finally, I quote Dr Joshua Chakawa who, in my view, aptly summarised the success of our operations in Hurungwe in his thesis: "In Hurungwe for example, auxiliaries were reported to have flushed out ZIPRA from most parts and were enjoying almost widespread power. Under pressure, ZIPRA had been compelled to retire to the perimeters of the TTL reportedly thrust back by the hostility of the people and the aggressive efficiency of the auxiliaries as the Rhodesians would have preferred to say." Dr Chakawa continues: "When Maumbe Primary School was closed, all teachers were severely beaten and compelled to sing a song called *Pasi Pamera Ziso*. (The earth has developed eyes. The meaning is the earth which contains the dead and ancestors, has developed eyes which can see those passing information about ZIPRA activities or supporting the Rhodesian Government.[3]) One teacher, Mr Dabengwa, bled profusely all over. It was at the beginning of 1978 when the school was closed only to be opened later in the same year by SFAs. An interesting component of this version is the failure of ZIPRA to put up resistance against SFAs who came to re-open the school. It is still mind-boggling to explain, how SFAs, some of whom hurriedly trained for 3 weeks, could be tactical enough to easily beat seasoned guerrillas."[4]

How was this possible against such overwhelming odds? What were our strategies and tactics? What obstacles did we overcome to succeed? What prevented the implementation of this strategy from the outset of the war? This book, *Battle for Hurungwe*, is a compelling account of the secrets of an African revolution.

John Padbury

[1] Mao Zedong 1893-1976, Chinese communist revolutionary, founding father of the People's Republic of China, Chairman of the Communist Party of China. He wrote extensively on revolutionary military strategies, and political policies.

[2] Validation of data through cross-verification from two or more sources.

[3] Dr J. Chakawa WhatsApp discussion 24/7/2019.

[4] Dr Chakawa, J. (2015), pp. 186-187.

FOREWORDS

Lord David Owen

Your book in my judgement has a lasting value. You have a lot of information about building a people's army that is very interesting. What is important is that your writing will contribute hugely to an overall understanding of what was actually happening on the ground in Rhodesia from 1973-79.

Lord David Owen was British Foreign Secretary, 1977-1979.

***

Doctor Joshua Chakawa

My PhD thesis focused on Security Force Auxiliaries in Zimbabwe's war of liberation. I was frantically trying to talk with some whites who had commanded them and thus I took a lot of time trying to connect. It was at this critical time when John responded to my email and we began to discuss his own experiences during the war of liberation in Zimbabwe. We finally met in December 2015 in Durban when I attended the International Conference on History Education. He wanted some further clarification with regards to the war of liberation in Hurungwe district while I also became a student learning about his wartime experience. From our discussions, we then continued to interact by mail and phone calls with a view of trying to understand the war better.

Throughout his fieldwork, John paid particular attention to details. Therefore, at times he had to request me to go to specific wartime battle sites so as to authenticate the information he had. Some of the trips needed verification from the National Archives of Zimbabwe, former combatants, *mujibhas* and civilians in war zones. He was also eager to have correctly written names of people and places and as much as possible sought the correct versions. As a result of his desire for precise information, on his part, he travelled widely to interview people with information of some of the details of Zimbabwe's war of liberation. Primarily, he also relied on his war diaries which had day-to-day detailed information on his wartime encounters.

In this book, John wrote honest opinions about his experiences in Makoni district and then Hurungwe district where he operated as a member of the Rhodesian Special Branch. It was in the former that he began a process of turning captured *mujibhas* and other young men with military skills as well as the ability to gather intelligence information against ZANLA guerrillas. When he was transferred to Hurungwe district in 1978, he had perfected the art and became key to the creation of Security Force Auxiliaries from among local young men and some captured guerrillas. Research on these forces has remained a grey area in Zimbabwe's history because often that work is considered divisive, counterproductive and as an attempt to open wounds that had already healed. Those who fought as auxiliaries are defined in Zimbabwe as traitors hence Africans who fought in this capacity choose to remain quiet for fear of stigmatisation. John's book represents an effort to bring in varied experiences of the war and enable researchers to understand Zimbabwe's liberation war better.

This book sets in motion further debates on the war of liberation. It is key to guerrillas and other stakeholders who were involved in the battles and places identified. As they answer back and provide clarifications, the war is understood better. This work is also a challenge to former guerrillas to begin pencilling their experiences. I urge readers to acknowledge the fact that John wrote about the war as he saw it then. Over time, some of these opinions have also changed. The book is not about celebrating counter-insurgency, but understanding it better particularly from political and military perspectives.

Doctor Joshua Chakawa (DPhil, MA in African History, PGDE, BA),
Head of the Department of History, Midlands State University, Gweru, Zimbabwe.

Edward Sheriff

Battle for Hurungwe is a reliable, accurate and true account of people and events by a former Special Branch Security Officer who served in the British South Africa Police. This book has been written without fear of disfavour. It promotes a theory that in a terrorist war the capture or killing of a terrorist alone would not defeat the revolutionaries. A programme designed to secure the safety of the masses for all time was essential.

The author has, in writing this account of events adopted an analytical approach and logical reasoning. He has shown an unwillingness to make concessions and maintained a bold and shameless approach when deciding events of both terrorists and security force members.

The book can be classified as a study of history, undisputed in the stating of events that circumnavigated the events of the terrorist war in the Hurungwe Tribal Trust Land in Rhodesia.

Edward Sheriff, former Senior Assistant Commissioner, British South Africa Police.

***

Vernon Loker

John has produced a monumental work on the Rhodesian war of the 1960s to 1970s. His meticulous recording and attention to detail makes for a riveting read. John also shows an insight into the political affairs of his day, allowing the reader to reach an informed opinion and decision on matters as they unfolded in the demise of the Ian Smith Government and the inevitable climax of majority rule in Zimbabwe. In addition, John allows the reader to glimpse into his psychological and emotional state as the war wore on taking its toll, not only personal relationships, but also his outlook to life. He has also gone to scrupulous lengths to verify the content and facts of *Battle for Hurungwe* which, in my view, will ensure it stands the test of time. I highly recommend this work to former Rhodesians as well as those interested in the subject of war, revolution and counter-revolution.

Vernon Loker is the editor of this book.

ACKNOWLEDGEMENTS

With a book of this magnitude there are inevitably a considerable number of people who have contributed and supported me throughout the process. A team of fine men and women emerged who were determined to see the end result, often unwittingly carrying me through the difficult times of authorship. In no order of merit I would like to specifically mention some people who helped me.

Notwithstanding, first and foremost I need to acknowledge my wife Lynette who has been back at war for seven years. Her patience and understanding gave me the liberty to dedicate considerable time to writing. She was a front-line warrior who often took "direct hits from the K-Car" but survived, recovered and marched on. I hope we can move into the present now. Likewise, my immediate family who provided background support. They encouraged me for many years to pen my diaries and remained interested in my life and history. My brother, Maj. David Padbury, stood by my side and literally carried me through some really difficult times. He is a solid trustworthy inspiration who is not afraid to speak the truth. Similarly, Dr Don Milligan who patiently guided me through the process of writing a book. Dr Joshua Chakawa reached out to me in search of the truth. He is a man of integrity, a committed dedicated historian and friend. His independent research prior to our meeting and subsequent research on my behalf has proved invaluable. Keith Samler regularly reminded me to write "my book". He was close at hand and always available to chat. Phil Wright meticulously produced all the maps. Remarkably, we have remained friends despite the numerous alterations and corrections I requested. Lord Owen "reopened a chapter in his life" and allowed me to interview him on 19 March 2018, for this I am most grateful. Andrew Field connected me to many of the police contributors.

There are too many contributors to thank individually. They opened their hearts to write their stories. Many gave documents, reports, personal logbooks and provided statistics which have brought a unique touch to the book and authenticated it. The Rhodesian civil and military organisations and associations, in particular the BSAP Regimental Association and Rhodesian Air Force Association were of, and remain, considerable assistance and motivation. Training staff at a computer store in Plymouth helped me develop my computer skills. Their "never critical, everything is possible, and you can do it" approach was an incredible help and encouragement. On several occasions they rescued and recovered the book. The BSAP Historian Paul Brewster helped in providing ballistic evidence from the "Peter Stiff Archive" which was very generously donated to the BSAP Regimental Association UK by Fran Stiff. This new source of material will hopefully help others in telling their story while in the BSAP. Dudley Wall provided information regarding the Ministry of Internal affairs and African customs and traditions.

To help with costs, I found volunteer editors who have given freely of their time. I am indebted to the input of Dr Don Milligan (political), Dr Joshua Chakawa (historical), David Padbury (military) and Keith Samler (CID/SB). I also need to record a thank you to my editor, Vernon Loker.

I have quoted numerous sources and obtained permission from the copyright holders. In some cases, I was unable to contact the copyright holders and have proceeded on the principle of fair-use. I have cited all contributions. This includes the three Google maps. I quote United Kingdom Parliamentary information licensed under the Open Parliament Licence v3.0.

PART 1

MAKONI:

THE BLOODING GROUND

The military don't start wars. Politicians start wars.
William Westmoreland

1 ~ Origins

The people, and the people alone, are the motive force in the making of world history.
Mao Zedong

Early Rhodesia: The Seeds of African Nationalism

The earliest known people to live in Zimbabwe were the San hunter-gatherers (Bushmen), who were either relocated or absorbed into the farming and cattle-herding culture of the Bantu groups who migrated from the north around 1200 CE. Present-day Shona[1] were one such group who have lived for about 2,000 years in a region of the southern plateau which includes most of Zimbabwe and parts of Mozambique. Between the 11th and 15th centuries, the Shona Kingdom was wealthy and powerful, engaging in gold production and in trading with Swahili people along the Mozambican coast. Historians are unsure of the causes of the decline of Zimbabwe.

In 1838, Mzilikazi (the great road), an Ndebele ruler[2] (Ndebele: men of long shields, also known as Matabele), invaded Zimbabwe from the south and established his capital at Bulawayo. The Ndebele were a faction of the Zulus living in Natal, South Africa, who fled north during King Shaka's militant reign, settling in western Zimbabwe. Mzilikazi died in 1868 and was succeeded by King Lobengula. Lobengula crushed rebels opposed to his reign and, at the time of his coronation in 1869, his army comprised 15,000 men in 40 regiments. He was a ruthless leader.

Cecil John Rhodes (5 July 1853 ~ 26 March 1902), was a British businessman, mining magnate and politician in southern Africa. He was Prime Minister of the Cape Colony from 1890~1896. In 1888, he orchestrated the colonial occupation of Zimbabwe when he secured mining rights to Lobengula's kingdom in what was known as the Rudd Concession. In return, King Lobengula was offered 1,000 Martini-Henry breech-loading rifles, 100,000 rounds of matching ammunition, a steamboat on the Zambezi River (if Lobengula preferred, a lump sum of £500) and £100 a month in perpetuity. Lobengula received the rifles and the stipend, paid regularly until 30 June 1893, when the British South Africa Company (BSAC) suspended payments on account of the impending Matabele War. The steamboat was not delivered.[3] This concession enabled Rhodes to persuade Lord Salisbury, the British Prime Minister, to grant him a Royal Charter after which he established the BSAC on 29 October 1889. This chartered company was an association formed by investors or shareholders for the purpose of trade, exploration and colonisation. It avoided a drain on Imperial finances. Rhodes organised the Pioneer Column, which brought white settlers in search of gold and arable land.

To organise, equip and lead the column, Rhodes appointed an adventurer, 23-year-old Frank Johnson, who acquired 62 wagons for transportation and signed up 180 civilian colonists. In accordance with the Charter, 200 paramilitary volunteers were signed up to protect the settlers during the trek and occupation of Rhodesia. This was the forerunner of the British South Africa Police. All volunteers were offered 3,000 acres of land and 15 gold-mining claims for their services. The column was commanded by the Irishman, Lt. Col. Edward Pennefather, and was equipped with Martini-Henry rifles, revolvers, seven-pounder field guns and Maxim recoil-operated machine guns, as well as an electric searchlight. The well-known hunter, Frederick Courtney Selous, guided the column to the location later named Fort Salisbury, arriving on 12 September 1890. Despite pioneer

[1] Shona is the collective name given to about 80 per cent of the Zimbabwean population. It was given to them by the Ndebele. Before that, they were known by areas they occupied or their chief, for example, people of Makoni.

[2] Sibanda, M. (1992), *passim.*

[3] Rotberg, R. (1988), p. 269; Palley, C. (1966), p. 32; Cary, R. (1970), p. 34.

avowals that the country was a British possession, the pioneers were unauthorised agents to acquire territorial sovereignty for Britain, nor did Britain subsequently ratify the unauthorised annexation.[1] Rhodes imposed a border around Rhodesia forcing the co-habitation of rivalling Matabele and Shona tribes.[2] This forced integration would inevitably end in a struggle for dominance.

The Ndebele nation were largely opposed to this invasion and in October 1893 rose against the white settlers. However, they were defeated by 700 BSAC Police who, with their Maxim guns, overwhelmed 3,000 Ndebele fighters, killing around 1,500 for the loss of four of their own men.[3] Sororenzou Murenga was a leader of the Ndebeles.

As the white colony continued to prosper and grow, the early pioneers realised the necessity for a system of administration for the country. The BSAC Charter permitted the Company to administer and govern the country with minimal British Government involvement. A chief native commissioner was appointed in Bulawayo. Under his command were several native commissioners and assistant native commissioners. These appointments were the forerunner of an administration managed later by the Ministry of Internal Affairs (Int.Aff.). In 1894, the Matabele Native Police (MNP) was inaugurated and placed under the command of the Chief Native Commissioner of Bulawayo. The responsibility of the MNP was to act as the "eyes and ears" of the authorities and was also responsible for law enforcement, the recruitment of labour and the collection of the hut tax. This revenue was a colonial method of collecting finance to cover the costs of the BSA Company's administrative expenses and helped in maintaining the supply of labour that was much in demand for the farms and mines, by binding the people into the financial economy of the white settlers. The income, an amount of 10 shillings per hut, was assessed on the number of wives a man had married. Each wife had her own hut so these wife-huts were indicative of the man's wealth. Taxation was collected in the form of cash or market related values in crops or livestock in accordance with the Matabeleland Order in Council of 18 July 1894. The first yearly payments for Mashonaland was due on 1 October 1894.[4] This was in fact a levy for occupation of their own lands.

Those who failed to pay the monies suffered confiscation of cattle, loss of land and imprisonment. This imposition was a direct attack upon tribal institutions. Land chiefs who protested against these demands were arrested and spirit mediums, who served as guardians of their social order, were also arrested.[5] "Rhodes and his fellow prospectors did not find communities of Africans anxiously waiting for opportunities for wage labour presented by their operations. Far from it. Forced labour, dispossession of land and livestock, taxation, fines and imprisonment became key weapons in the struggle to convince Africans that they should leave their village communities for the world of European wage labour and the whip."[6]

The First *Chimurenga*

This issue of land acquisition, mineral exploitation, hut tax and compulsory labour continued to sow the seeds of revolution. In March 1896, the Ndebele spirit medium, Mlimo, convinced Ndebele and Shona forces that the white colonists were responsible for the devastating drought, plagues of locusts, and outbreaks of rinderpest, a contagious viral disease. Over 2,000 Ndebele started the revolution known as the first *Umvukhela* (Ndebele) or *Chimurenga* (Shona) and in the first week 141 white settlers in Matabeleland were murdered. BSA Company forces, assisted by Imperial forces led by Col. Robert Baden Powell, were sent to quell the Ndebele uprising. A settlement was secured in July 1896 when Rhodes agreed to address the Ndebele grievances.

Colonial forces that included the mounted infantry led by Sir Edwin Alfred Hervey Alderson then concentrated on quelling the Mashonaland uprising which had commenced in June 1896 at Mazowe

---

1 Palley, C. (1966), p. 40.

2 Queen Victoria in 1888 had, through her ministers, recognised Lobengula as Sovereign over the Matabele and the Shona.

3 Ferguson, N. (2004), pp. 224-225.

4 Keppel-Jones, A. (1983), *passim*; Pakenham, T. (1992), pp. 497-498. Kindle Edition Location 11885.

5 Isaacman, A. (1977), pp. 7-8.

6 Johnson, D. (2002), p. 4.

with an attack on Alice Mine. This was followed by the capture and murder of the Mazowe Native Commissioner, Mr H.H. Pollard, ostensibly at the instruction of the spirit medium Nehanda Nyakasikana. Other participating chiefs included Mashayamombe, Makoni, Seke, Mangwende and Mapondera. Nehanda Nyakasikana, Makoni and Kaguvi Gumboreshumba were captured and executed by the colonial authorities. Nehanda's dying words, "My bones will rise again", predicted the Second *Chimurenga* where she was of considerable influence. Many ranches, homes and mines were burned and 103 settlers were killed.

Although both rebellions had been defeated, the war never ended but was placed on hold as the discontent simmered beneath the surface of smiling, apparently happy Africans. In the meanwhile the whites were back in control.

The spirit mediums also played a significant role during the Second *Chimurenga* that started in the mid-1960s. Interestingly, in the Makoni district near Rusape, the hilly terrain and numerous caves made it difficult for the settlers, unfamiliar with the lie of the land, to confront Chief Makoni's fighting men.[1] I would experience similar difficulties in the Second *Chimurenga* war when stationed at Rusape during 1974-1978.

The BSA Company reasoned that the rebellion had two principal causes: "Firstly, the incompleteness of the conquest of the Matabele Nation in 1893 and secondly, the incapacity of a warlike and aristocratic race to relinquish their old habits and accept their 'natural place' in the peaceful and industrial organisation of a settled 'civilised community'."[2] In 1879, when eliminating American Indian opposition to settler occupation of America, an army officer, Richard H. Pratt, put it this way: "Kill the Indian and save the Man." He introduced education to uplift and assimilate Indians into mainstream American culture: "He trimmed their hair, required them to speak English, and prohibited any displays of tribal traditions such as Indian clothing, dancing or religious ceremonies."[3]

The Shona and Ndebele were fighting to defend their land, way of life, social institutions and culture. Prior to the arrival of European colonists, African societies had their own economic, social and political systems.[4] These were coherent, complex, dynamic and, in their minds, worth fighting and dying for. Both the Ndebele and Shona relied heavily upon cattle and land as primary sources of wealth. Cattle were important in linking communities and families together through trade and *lobola* (the price a prospective son-in-law needs to pay his future father-in-law for his daughter). When white settlers arrived in greater numbers and began occupying the land, imposing a hut tax to force indigenous people to work for cash wages paid by white farmers and mine owners, the Ndebele and Shona revolted. However, these African communities were not simply unified against the whites, they were often divided internally with some people benefiting from colonial arrangements through trade and employment, while others were impoverished and oppressed.[5]

In 1898, the Southern Rhodesian Legislative Council was empowered by the British Crown to make laws for the "peace, order and good government of Southern Rhodesia". The Crown retained certain powers, including those relating to natives, to ensure their interests were protected. Executive control over the military and police force was also retained by the United Kingdom.[6] In 1922, a referendum of mainly white voters decided to become a self-governing colony independent of South Africa. A year later, on 30 July 1923, Britain annexed the territory and Southern Rhodesia became known as the self-governing British colony of Southern Rhodesia, 33 years after the unauthorised raising of the British flag by the pioneers at Fort Salisbury.[7]

---

[1] Alderson, E.A.H. (1971), *passim.*

[2] British South Africa Company (1975:5).

[3] Richard H. Pratt, Digital History ID 3505: *Kill the Indian and Save the Man.*

[4] Dawson, S. (2011), pp. 144-145.

[5] Ibid.

[6] Palley, C. (1966), p. 133-134, 148.

[7] Ibid., pp. 213-214. High Commissioner's Proclamation No. 41 of 1923 announced colonial status as from 12/3/1923; Papenfus, T. (2010).

Land Apportionment Act

In 1930, the Legislative Assembly passed the Land Apportionment Act which allocated 51 per cent of the land for exclusive white use. Thirty per cent was allocated for the African Reserves and for private African purchase, while most of the remainder was unallocated.[1] Two per cent of the population was white with the remaining 98 per cent indigenous. Moreover, the land allocated to the white population was prime property and favourably located in relation to transport, infrastructure and urban markets, while the African Reserves were situated in remote areas which were prone to drought.[2] This skewed distribution, combined with high population growth-rates over time, translated into ever deepening poverty among Africans in the rural areas.[3] State agricultural policy and legislation strongly favoured white agriculture and undermined and marginalised African production. While there were amendments to this Act, the disparity between the distribution of land remained, which fanned the flames of discontent. The other issue ignored by legislators was that land for European distribution and farming was, in the mind of the African, "holy land"; home to ancestral spirits residing in caves and mountains making this rearrangement unacceptable to them.[4]

There were other factors that contributed to the Africans' general discontent that had built up over the years. Issues such as The Maize Control Act of 1930, which established the Maize Control Board, forced African maize growers to subsidise white farmers reducing African maize sales. White farmers received prices 40 per cent higher than the world market prices, while the African farmers were paid the local market price which was much lower.[5]

Compulsory Native Labour Act

By November 1942, some 12,855 Africans had been conscripted, in terms of the Native Affairs Act, to build aerodromes required to support the World War II effort through the Empire Air Training Scheme. Native commissioners were given district quotas and the chiefs and headmen from the reserves were required to produce the labourers. Tribal messengers acting as policemen rounded up African labourers.[6]

The Compulsory Native Labour Act was passed in June 1942 and came into effect on 1 August 1942. This Act legitimised the procurement of reluctant African labour for a colony desperate for labour on the mines and railways and, in particular, white farmers whose interests were supported by the Rhodesian Farmers Union. In the process, chiefs and headmen who were required to round up the labour, lost the respect and control of their people and were considered puppets of the government. However, Africans were adverse and antagonistic to compulsory labour which made state intervention more direct and confrontational. Africans not working were regarded as lazy, despite the fact that many of them were living self-sufficient lives in the reserves and surviving outside of the economic stream. In describing the failure of chiefs and headmen to provide adequate assistance for compulsory labour recruitment, the Native Commissioner for Makoni reported in 1944: "Chiefs and headmen have little control and though most of them have done their best, it is a poor best." The Native Commissioner of Hurungwe reported in 1946: "Chiefs and headmen … do not command enough obedience or respect which should fit in with their status. I suppose we must blame our methods of colonialism for this."[7] My police duties would, in time, take me to Makoni and Hurungwe.

A total of some 33,145 labourers were conscripted into the system which continued until well after World War II, finally being repealed in August 1946.[8] Gradually, the Africans' traditional ways

---

1 Esterhuysen, P. (2004), *passim;* Johnson, D. (2002), p. 2.
2 Esterhuysen, P. (2004), *passim*; Austen, R. (1975), pp. 34-45.
3 Esterhuysen, P. (2004), *passim*; Stocking, M. (1978), p. 133.
4 Ranger, T. (1985), Chap. 5, pp. 198-200.
5 Mazungu, E. (2005), Chap. 22; Johnson, D. (2000), p. 3.
6 Johnson, D. (2000), p. 92; *Moving Images of the British Empire-Outpost at War:* www.colonialfilm.org.uk/node/5580, 1944.
7 Johnson, D. (2000), Chaps. 3-4, pp. 99-100.
8 Ibid., p. 106.

were interfered with by the imposition of colonial rule which necessitated them helping to fulfil a huge labour requirement throughout the country.[1] In 1943, compulsory destocking regulations were passed to prevent overstocking livestock in the reserves, causing much discontent and concern among the Africans, while to the contrary, their white counterparts flourished.[2] This African discontent was eventually expressed in a general strike in April 1948.[3] Of interest, 9,000 whites and 15,000 blacks fought for the Allied Forces during the Second World War.[4]

Resistance to white supremacy grew and gradually intensified, inflamed by the absence of meaningful reform. Sir Reginald Stephen Garfield Todd was Prime Minister of Southern Rhodesia from 1953 to 1958. He introduced moderate gradual African advancement with the emphasis on education and voting, where he increased eligible African voter per centages from 2 per cent to 16 per cent. This was unacceptable to his Cabinet Ministers opposing significant African advancement, thereby forcing him to resign. He was replaced by Sir Edgar Cuthbert Fremantle Whitehead, who continued the road to African reform. Whitehead's policies disturbed the white population and he was ousted from power in 1962 by Winston Field, the first Prime Minister from Ian Smith's newly formed Rhodesian Front party.

In the early 1960s, two African political organisations, the Zimbabwe African People's Union, led by Joshua Nkomo, and the Zimbabwe African National Union, headed by Ndabaningi Sithole, were formed. In response the Colonial Office in London, which had retained a veto on Southern Rhodesian legislation concerning native affairs, began to insist that the country guaranteed racial equality.

On 3 February 1960, during a sitting of the South African Parliament, Harold Macmillan made his famous "Winds of Change" speech. He had delivered the identical talk in Ghana a month earlier:

> It is, as I have said, a special privilege for me to be here in 1960 when you are celebrating what I might call the golden wedding of the Union. At such a time it is natural and right that you should pause to take stock of your position, to look back at what you have achieved, to look forward to what lies ahead. In the fifty years of their nationhood the people of South Africa have built a strong economy founded upon a healthy agriculture and thriving and resilient industries.
>
> No one could fail to be impressed with the immense material progress, which has been achieved. That all this has been accomplished in so short a time is a striking testimony to the skill, energy and initiative of your people. We in Britain are proud of the contribution we have made to this remarkable achievement. Much of it has been financed by British capital.
>
> As I've travelled around the Union I have found everywhere, as I expected, a deep preoccupation with what is happening in the rest of the African continent. I understand and sympathise with your interests in these events and your anxiety about them.
>
> Ever since the breakup of the Roman Empire one of the constant facts of political life in Europe has been the emergence of independent nations. They have come into existence over the centuries in different forms, different kinds of government, but all have been inspired by a deep, keen feeling of nationalism, which has grown as the nations have grown.
>
> In the twentieth century, and especially since the end of the war, the processes which gave birth to the nation states of Europe have been repeated all over the world. We have seen the awakening of national consciousness in peoples who have for centuries lived in dependence upon some other power. Fifteen years ago, this movement spread through Asia. Many countries there, of different races and civilisations, pressed their claim to an independent national life. Today the same thing is happening in Africa, and the most

[1] Johnson, D. (2002), p. 99.
[2] Alexander, J. (2006), p. 25.
[3] Johnson, D. (2002), Chap. 6.
[4] British Parliament Hansard: HL Deb 15/11/1965 vol 270 cc 228-413.

> striking of all the impressions I have formed since I left London a month ago is of the strength of this African national consciousness. In different places it takes different forms, but it is happening everywhere.
>
> The wind of change is blowing through this continent, and whether we like it or not, this growth of national consciousness is a political fact. We must all accept it as a fact, and our national policies must take account of it.
>
> Well, you understand this better than anyone, you are sprung from Europe, the home of nationalism, here in Africa you have yourselves created a free nation. A new nation. Indeed, in the history of our times yours will be recorded as the first of the African nationalists. This tide of national consciousness which is now rising in Africa, is a fact, for which both you and we, and the other nations of the western world are ultimately responsible.
>
> For its causes are to be found in the achievements of western civilisation, in the pushing forwards of the frontiers of knowledge, the applying of science to the service of human needs, in the expanding of food production, in the speeding and multiplying of the means of communication, and perhaps above all and more than anything else in the spread of education.
>
> As I have said, the growth of national consciousness in Africa is a political fact, and we must accept it as such. That means, I would judge, that we've got to come to terms with it. I sincerely believe that if we cannot do so we may imperil the precarious balance between the East and West on which the peace of the world depends.
>
> The world today is divided into three main groups. First there are what we call the Western Powers. You in South Africa and we in Britain belong to this group, together with our friends and allies in other parts of the Commonwealth. In the United States of America and in Europe we call it the Free World. Secondly there are the Communists, Russia and her satellites in Europe and China, whose population will rise by the end of the next ten years to the staggering total of 800 million. Thirdly, there are those parts of the world whose people are at present uncommitted either to Communism or to our Western ideas. In this context we think first of Asia and then of Africa. As I see it the great issue in this second half of the twentieth century is whether the uncommitted peoples of Asia and Africa will swing to the East or to the West. Will they be drawn into the Communist camp?
>
> Or will the great experiments in self-government that are now being made in Asia and Africa, especially within the Commonwealth, prove so successful, and by their example so compelling, that the balance will come down in favour of freedom and order and justice? The struggle is joined, and it is a struggle for the minds of men. What is now on trial is much more than our military strength or our diplomatic and administrative skill. It is our way of life. The uncommitted nations want to see before they choose.[1]

The British Government's recognition of the reality that the time was ripening for inevitable change, and that the way this was recognised and dealt with, would determine the success of this transformation regarding the well-being of Africa, was made quite clear to southern African politicians. It was the time for meaningful change, to negotiate from a position of strength and remain connected to the resources of Britain, the Commonwealth and its allies in the West, including America. Much against the opinions of many, the "Winds of Change" speech was deeply profound and, in my opinion, prophetic. History would record which allies the Rhodesian African nationalists were directed to.[2] Mao Zedong had already made China's position clear in 1956: "We must give active support to the national independence and liberation movement in countries in Asia, Africa and Latin America as well as to the peace movement and to just struggles in all the countries of the world."[3]

---

[1] Website: http://africanhistory.about.com/od/eraindependence/p/wind_of_change2.htm. Accessed 18/3/2017.
[2] de Meneses/McNamara (2018), Chap. 1.

A Brief History of the Federation of Rhodesia and Nyasaland

In 1953, a British initiative led to the formation of the Federation of Rhodesia and Nyasaland that joined the self-governing colony of Southern Rhodesia and the British protectorates of Northern Rhodesia and Nyasaland. The capital was Salisbury, from where the appointed governor general and Federal Government ruled. Growing nationalistic aspirations, especially in Northern Rhodesia, led to African unrest between 1960 and 1961, and the eventual dissolution of the Federation on 31 December 1963. Northern Rhodesia and Nyasaland gained their independence from Britain, becoming Zambia and Malawi respectively. However, Southern Rhodesia was denied independence.

Southern Rhodesia was governed by the 1961 Constitution negotiated by the then Prime Minister Edgar Whitehead, with the British Government. As a result, Legislative Assembly membership was increased to 65 seats. Voters could be enrolled on either the "A" or "B" roll according to their qualifications including standard of education, property and income. "A" roll voters required higher qualifications and voted for 50 members representing constituencies.[1] "B" roll voters, the majority of whom were Africans, elected 15 members for electoral districts. The aim of the constitution was to bring about African majority rule within 10 to 15 years.[2] There was no provision for sovereign independence in the advent of the dissolution of the Federation. Sir Edgar Whitehead made it quite clear in an address to Parliament on 25 August 1964, that the 1961 Constitution guaranteed internal independence not sovereign independence. He stated: "I am saying this authoritatively because I made the bargain; I know, and therefore we would not give it (UDI) support." Ian Smith was informed by Whitehead, the British Government and the Salisbury High Commissioner that he was misguided in repeatedly stating the 1961 Constitution contained the basis of independence should the Federation be dissolved.[3] Ian Smith was convinced that independence was the only solution to stem the rising threat of African nationalism.

On 5 November 1965, having been assured by Ian Smith and his Cabinet that they were not contemplating declaring a unilateral declaration of independence,[4] the Governor, Sir Humphrey Gibbs, on the advice of the Southern Rhodesian Government, proclaimed a State of Emergency, in terms of the Emergency Powers Act.[5] Under Section 4 of the Act, further regulations[6] were made with more following on 10 November 1965.[7]

These regulations were comprehensive but essential to understand as they shaped Rhodesian policies, attitudes and thinking. I discuss the road to UDI in Chapter 8. The Lord Chancellor, Lord Gardiner, summed up the situation in the House of Lords on 15 November 1965:

> The situation in Southern Rhodesia is one in which there is an illegal Government; a state of emergency has been declared, and regulations have been made under it which provide powers, inter alia, to control the movement of persons, to detain persons, to place cordons around designated areas, to prohibit the possession, sale or distribution of newspapers; to control or prohibit printing or publishing of any designated book, newspaper, pamphlet, et cetera; to prohibit the possession of arms within designated areas; to prohibit gatherings or classes of gatherings; to designate protected places or areas and to control access to them; to impose curfews; to deny access to restrictees and

---

3 Zedong, M. "Opening Address at the Eighth National Congress of the Communist Party of China" (15/9/1956).

1 A group of voters in mainly white areas who elected a representative to the Legislative Assembly.

2 Palley, C. (1966), p. 316; Smith, I. (2008), Chap. 9; Loc 2798.

3 Rhodesian Legislative Assembly records 25/8/1964, pp. 1210-1211 and 1216-1217. Later confirmed by the Lord Chancellor (Lord Gardiner) and Lord Alport in the House of Lords on 15/11/1965 and a letter from Sir Alec Douglas-Holme in September 1964 to Ian Smith. (British Parliament Hansard: HL Deb 15/11/1965 vol 270 cc 228-413); Smith, I. (2008), Chap. 6; de Meneses/McNamara (2018), Loc. 1144.

4 Palley, C. (1966), p. 749; Flower, K. (1987), pp. 52-55.

5 Proclamation 51 of 1965.

6 The Emergency (Maintenance of Law and Order) Regulations 1965, R.G.N. No. 736; Palley, C. (1966), p. 749.

7 *Government Gazette* Extraordinary, 10/11/1965 R.G.N. Nos. 737 A-M; Emergency Powers (Dissemination of Information) Regulations 1965 and the Emergency Powers (Censorship of Publications) Order 1965, R.G.N. Nos. 737 J & K; Emergency Powers (*African Affairs*) Regulations R.G.N. 737 M; Palley, C. (1966), p. 750.

> detainees or any communication with them; to arrest persons on suspicion without warrant and to detain them for up to thirty days, and to detain a person in any place, including a dwelling, flat or room; that is to say, a power of house arrest. In addition, there is provision for detention camps.
>
> It is an offence punishable by imprisonment or fine to publish or distribute information, statements, et cetera, likely to cause alarm or despondency. By further regulations nearly all civilian employees, including judges, can be directed to stay at their posts indefinitely on conditions fixed by the Minister, and can be directed to perform any act deemed necessary by the Minister. Employees can be suspended indefinitely, and other persons drafted into public service.
>
> Failure to comply with, or hindrance of, regulations incurs penalty of fines up to £500 or imprisonment up to two years. Censorship operates through the Director of Information or censorship officers, to whom any article must be submitted before publication. The Government have powers to take over, intercept or suspend telegraph, telephone or telex services, and to take over or control any radio station, service or apparatus. Employees of printing and publishing firms or communications services can be directed to stay at their posts and must obey directions given. There are wide powers also as to goods and services, as well as financial provisions.
>
> In addition, a new Constitution, which is of course quite invalid, has been promulgated, and under that Constitution if the Queen does not appoint a Governor General on the advice of the illegal Ministers of Rhodesia within fourteen days a Regent will be appointed. Section 128 of the illegal Constitution provides that the Chief Justice and other judges may be required to accept the illegal Constitution on pain of automatic dismissal without compensation. The Governor has been ordered to leave Government House, and regulations provide that civil servants and judges can be directed to stay at their posts indefinitely. The entrenched clauses of the Constitution are now safeguarded merely by a two-thirds vote of Parliament.[1]

Furthermore, the regulations provided for controlling the movement of persons. The Minister of Law and Order was empowered to authorise the taking over of printing or publishing firms, to control and direct their business for so long as the minister considered expedient, and to require persons employed in such firms to continue their labours. Despite the view of the government that it enjoyed the support of the chiefs, it also took powers to suspend chiefs, to appoint acting chiefs, to remove chiefs from the tribal areas, and to order them to remain in places specified by the Minister of Internal Affairs. Matters relating to import and export control, the tightening of exchange control, control of goods and services, and price control were introduced.[2]

Having carefully planned and implemented the groundwork for rejecting majority rule and having been denied independence, in defiance of British policy, by self-proclamation, the Southern Rhodesian Government declared its Unilateral Declaration of Independence (UDI) on 11 November 1965, thereby assuring the ongoing subordination of the African population. The Declaration essentially emulated the American Declaration of Independence, although omitted was the assertion that all men are created equal and governmental power was derived from the consent of the governed. The 1961 Constitution had been amended and was replaced by the 1965 Constitution which remained in place until the 1969 Constitution was promulgated. Changes included the erosion of legal provisions that the British Government could legislate and act on behalf of Southern Rhodesia, renamed Rhodesia. Legislation provided for an Officer Administering The Government (OAG) to replace the Governor.

The OAG was the ostensible Commander in Chief of the Armed Forces, while the Prime Minister, Mr Ian Smith, served as the de facto Commander in Chief.[3] Most military activities were

---

[1] British Parliament Hansard: HL Deb 15/11/1965 vol 270 cc 228-413.

[2] Palley, C. (1966), p. 750.

conducted after Mr Smith had been briefed while some were only brought to his attention once concluded.[1] The country was geared for war: politics with bloodshed.

White voters were to elect 50 members to the House of Assembly, the Lower House of Parliament, African voters would elect 8, and 8 seats to be indirectly elected representing chiefs and tribal interests. The Senate, the indirectly elected new Upper House was to be composed of 23 senators, of whom 10 were to be elected by white members of the House of Assembly and 10 were African chiefs. Half from Mashonaland and the remaining half were from Matabeleland. They were selected by an electoral college composed of members of the Council of Chiefs and three appointed by the President. The ratio of blacks to whites was approximately 20:1.

This process ignited a guerrilla war known as the Second *Chimurenga*. It entailed military action which was seen by the African nationalists as the only viable route to bring about change. It was a commonly accepted fact that China and Russia, seizing the opportunity to expand their influence in Africa, supported ZANLA and ZIPRA respectively. Political, moral and limited military support was provided by the neighbouring states of Zambia and Mozambique, who also provided bases for the training of the growing number of recruits leaving Rhodesia. Botswana provided similar low-key support. The Organisation of African Unity (OAU)[2] focussed the attention of African nations on a Rhodesia isolated from the world and surrounded by hostility. This provided the African nationalists with funding, training, bases and international support. Britain sought a negotiated settlement while South Africa supported the Rhodesian Government on an ad-hoc basis.

Rhodesia's Economy

Interestingly, during this period of instability, Rhodesia's economy flourished. Between 1901 and 1956, the annual gold output increased from £610 to £2,526,000. Farming (tobacco, maize, cattle and citrus), mining (particularly gold and chrome) and industry increased significantly, enabling investment into education, hospitals, clinics, communications, infrastructure and African development programmes. In 1960, the Gross Domestic Product per Capita was 60 per cent of world average. By 1970, it was 50 per cent. The white population increased to approximately 250,000 by 1970 and the economy continued to grow. The country had a stock exchange, merchant banks and most aspects of a developed first-world society.[3] Rhodesia had become economically powerful and independent in the fields of agriculture, mining and industry. Hydropower was provided by Kariba Dam, completed in 1959. In December 1966, Britain and the United Nations imposed international sanctions on Rhodesia. A highly sophisticated international trade operation, headed by the Rhodesian ministries of Foreign Affairs and Finance, the Reserve Bank and Special Branch, ensured that Rhodesia's economy survived and, for some years, prospered.

Pesonal Background

During World War II, while stationed in India, my father, Maj. Percy Eric Padbury, from Kent in England, serving with the British Army, met Lt. Elizabeth Larmour Kempson. She was a "feisty lady" from Bangor, Northern Ireland, serving as a nurse in Queen Alexandra's Imperial Army Nursing Corps. They married in Kent on 11 June 1947. Initially, they emigrated to Cape Town in South Africa but subsequently relocated to Southern Rhodesia where they settled.

While heavily pregnant with me, my mother returned to Bangor by sea on the *Stirling Castle* to visit her ailing father, docking at Southampton on 1 June 1951 and continuing her journey to Belfast to

3 Rhodesian Constitution 1965, Chapter II, 3 (1); J.R.T. Wood email 8/10/2018.

1 J.R.T. Wood email 8/10/2018.

2 Organisation of African Unity (OAU) was founded in May 1963. Its basic principles were co-operation between African nations and solidarity between African peoples. Another important objective of the OAU was an end to all forms of colonialism in Africa.. The OAU established a committee based in Dar-es-Salaam, with representatives from Ethiopia, Algeria, Uganda, Egypt, Tanzania, Zaire, Guinea, Senegal and Nigeria to support African liberation movements. The support provided by the committee included military training and weapon supplies. Wikipedia: https://en.wikipedia.org/wiki/African_independence_movements.

3 Smith, I. (2008), Loc 295.

be with him. She brought with her my brother David (3 yrs) and sister Moira (1 yr). Subsequently, I was born at the Belfast City Hospital on 24 September 1951. My mother, David, Moira and I sailed for home to Salisbury Southern Rhodesia, leaving Southampton on 22 November 1951 on the *Cape Town Castle* when I was 59 days' old.

Our family lived at 5 Seagrave Road, Avondale, a plush suburb of Salisbury. We were surrounded by middle-class residents with our home situated on an acre of land. My eldest brother, David, and I shared an outside cottage which had two large bedrooms a toilet and shower. Moira and Michael (13 years my junior) shared the main house with our parents.

We were fortunate to be able to afford an African cook and general labourer, Frank. He lived in a *kia*[1] at the bottom of the garden as did the various "garden boys" whom we employed from time to time. My mother was not very good with servants, she was a hard taskmaster and regularly hired and fired them. Frank, however, proved resilient and in time we viewed him as part of the family and not merely an African employee.

When in trouble, Frank was a comfort to us children and we often shared his meal of sadza and relish.[2] He would frequently entertain us and was a constant companion. Such were our childhood years. It never crossed our young minds that he might have his own family, culture or home. Periodically, he would ask to visit his family, but this request mostly annoyed my parents who rarely granted him leave to visit his rural home. Little did we realise that Frank wished to attend a wedding, funeral service, attend to matters of sowing, ploughing or harvesting his crop. Sadly, my parents viewed Frank's requests to visit friends and family as merely an excuse to laze about and not work. In our minds, Frank had no other life beyond being our cook, servant and playmate. When eventually he could return home for brief spells, we as a family were forced to do our own cooking, tidying up, and other mundane routine household chores. We considered his time off as an inconvenience.

In time, David and I went to Mount Pleasant Boys' High School which taught the British General Certificate of Education (GCE) examination syllabuses. Moira went to the Salisbury Roman Catholic Convent, with Michael attending Marlborough High School. The history we were taught had mainly to do with Great Britain, Europe, America, and the colonies. The conquests of Cecil John Rhodes and the benefits he brought to the "uncivilised" Africans were also part of our curriculum. We were subjected exclusively to government and white public opinion and propaganda that insisted on the inferior capabilities and status of Africans. I was raised with the belief that Africans in Rhodesia were a "warlike and aristocratic race that needed to give up their old habits and accept their natural place in the peaceful and industrial organisation of a settled civilised community".[3] The educational system appeared to pay scant attention to the history of Africa or the lives and experiences of Africans. The syllabus excluded Shona or Ndebele languages, or anything about African history, politics or culture. African aspirations were seemingly ignored. It became my assumption, largely as a result of the prevailing educational setting, that white Rhodesians were more civilised, better educated and had superior moral values than those of their native counterparts. To me, and along with many of my acquaintances, it was evident that only whites were the most competent, best suited and capable leaders within the country. It was only they who should occupy seats of rulership and government. My opinion would change dramatically as my life progressed.

In my youthful mind, early schooling was about sport and outdoor adventures. Education as such took a secondary role in my life. During my first year at high school, I contracted either polio or meningitis, the actual disease was never diagnosed. I spent several months in St Anne's Hospital and considerable time at home recuperating. Thus there was a year's gap in my education which added to my problems. I was fortunate to play First XI cricket and First XV rugby at high school. My brother, David, was my athletics' coach and, on that front, we excelled as together we held all the

[1] Small outbuilding for servants with a room, toilet and fireplace for cooking, usually at the rear of larger houses.

[2] *Sadza*: African staple food. Ground maize cooked in water to form a thick pulp which is rolled into a ball, held in the right hand and dipped into gravy or meat and eaten. Relish: Cooked vegetables and meat.

[3] British South Africa Company Reports on the Native Disturbances in Rhodesia, 1896-1897 (1975), p. 5.

school hurdles' records. Following David's footsteps, I joined the cadets and thoroughly enjoyed the youthful uniformed military organisation. We were taught foot drill, musketry and fieldcraft.

The stern voice of Mr Louis Lecler, our Latin and English teacher, still rings in my ears after some 50 years: "You have not done your homework, Padbury!" "No sir," I would reply. Thereafter, I would watch as he opened his right-hand drawer, remove a sheet of paper and neatly, using a ruler, tear off a section, write on it, fold it and send me on my way to the headmaster. I never did read the note but was always caned for my misdemeanours. Little changed during those lessons despite Louis Lecler's tireless repetition of: "It would be far easier for you if you listened and did your homework."

These exchanges exemplified my attitude to learning in the first two years of secondary education. In my third year of high school at 15 years of age, having learned little, Mr Lecler directed a question at me while reading the poem The Pylons[1] during an English lesson. "So, Padbury, what do you think about The Pylons?" To my and Mr Lecler's profound surprise, I articulated thoughts on the poem. From deep within I gave voice to my notions for the first time. My English teacher was astonished. That event proved a watershed in my life. From that day on, the day Mr Lecler had patiently and unwaveringly waited for, I began to pay attention during lessons, to take notice and more importantly to respond with interest. Mr Lecler became a mentor not only at academics but also at sport. He taught me the intricacies and finer aspects about cricket. In particular he gave me insight into the art of captaincy. On the education front he sparked in me a desire to learn and accurately express myself. He passed on to me a genuine love for the English language.

My 16th year was eventful. Firstly, I passed my driving licence test which entitled me to drive the family Land Rover for as long as my weekly pocket money, which bought 10 shillings' worth of petrol, lasted. Secondly, at school, a retired district commissioner, Arthur Pendred, offered to teach students Shona from his newly written curriculum. By that age, I had decided on a rural outdoor career and was the sole volunteer from the entire school. This showed the little importance the local African language and culture played in our white colonial lives. Arthur Pendred was a model gentleman. He taught me to speak Shona fluently and helped me gain some understanding of Shona culture and traditions. I took the GCE "O" Level[2] Shona exam but failed. However this Shona education would prove invaluable when I joined the BSAP.

Our father was an adventurer and took us on safaris to the remote wilds of the African bush, creating in David and me a deep desire to become a part of the unspoiled African wilderness. These trips also gave us glimpses of my father's military past. I recall the first camping outing when he took twelve-year-old David and me, aged nine, to an extremely remote area of the Zambezi River where we had to transport our own provisions by Land Rover. At night from our camp we would look up at a canopy of stars which sparkled and glowed, lighting the dark, magical skies. It was a fascinating environment dominated by the sounds of beetles, crickets, frogs, the occasional roar of a distant lion and the splashing of the mighty Zambezi River[3] as it flowed through the channels of basalt rock as high as 250m. These surroundings were in stark contrast to regular city life. To David and I it was like being in a zoo, except we humans were being viewed by inquisitive animals supplied with night vision watching and observing us in our camp. I spent a good part of the night making sure the campfire had plenty of wood to burn, in the hope the fire would keep the beasts at bay.

On the first morning of our camp, my father gave David and me half a mug of water and walked off to make tea. When he returned he asked if we had brushed our teeth and washed our faces. "No," we replied. "Well what did you do with the water then?" he asked. "We drank it," was our answer. "That water was to brush your teeth, wash your face and drink what was left," he replied sternly. Our bush training had begun. One evening our father excitedly woke us and pointed out a lone fast-moving "star" called Sputnik. This was the first man-made satellite ever to leave Earth. It

[1] Spender, S. (1933), *passim*.

[2] British General Certificate of Education "Ordinary" Level.

[3] The Zambezi River is the fourth longest waterway in Africa (2,700km). During its course to the Indian Ocean delta either crosses or forms the international borders of six countries: Zambia, Angola, Namibia, Botswana, Zimbabwe and Mozambique.

was launched by the Russians on 4 October 1957 and circled the earth at regular one-and-a-half-hour intervals. Countless technological advances have been made in space travel beginning from this singular event. Not least of all, Neil Armstrong being the first man to walk on the moon on 20 July 1969. In addition, scores of space exploration journeys, including the possibility of inhabiting Mars, together with the proliferation of satellites orbiting earth with innumerable known and secret agendas, have been launched.

On other occasions, my father, David and I went camping and fishing on the banks of Lake Kariba[1] and Mana Pools on the Zambezi River where the wild life was abundant and remarkably varied. This proved to be a fantastic introduction to the wilds of the African bush. There were no toilets or such like conveniences, just rough camping ground. Survival depended on what one transported into the camping locality and, hopefully, the fish one managed to catch. Naturally we took Frank along to do the cooking. At Mana Pools once, when looking for a bush toilet, Frank was surrounded by buffalo and took refuge up a tree for the entire day. Dad was furious when we returned from a day's fishing to find no "cook boy" and no evening meal prepared. As dusk set in, Frank gingerly made his way from the safety of his lookout and cautiously returned to the camp and, to our combined delight, prepared our meal.

In our early camping experiences, we discovered that hippopotamuses have an aversion to campfires, when one attacked us in an attempt to put out our campfire. A local game ranger added to our outdoor adventures when he taught us to stand our ground when charged by a raging, ear-flapping, trumpeting elephant. The menacing elephant ground to a halt some 15m ahead of us. Dust enveloped the scene as we breathed a sigh of relief. Courage, I instantly learned, is easily gained from the security of a position behind a game ranger and an older brother. One night we heard a lion make a kill of some hapless animal close to 100m from our tents. The satisfied purr and occasional grunts of the predators, eager to eat their fill before sunrise and the onslaught of opportunist hyenas and vultures, drifted through the dark of night. This silence was periodically interrupted by screeching piercing shrieks that broke the deathly hush of the dark. Gradually, hours later, normal life in the wilds returned. The day was greeted by a nocturnal symphony courtesy of a host of wild life: a communal declaration that a new day was to commence.

Elephants often walked through our camps at night, leaving behind their large circular footprints embedded into the dusty soil. Most amazing was watching the African Fish Eagles as they sat majestically upright in dead, leafless trees, scanning the lake waters for fish. With a cry they would launch themselves, gliding down towards their unsuspecting prey, lunging their talons forward at the last minute before virtually stepping on the fish with wings thrust outward. Magnificently, these supremely agile birds would spring forward with a simultaneous downward thrusting wing and grasp the unsuspecting fish from the water. Wriggling and gasping in the eagle's claws, in a futile struggle to escape, the fish would gradually succumb to its fate as the eagle completed its mission, settled on a branch and began its meal.

It was in this environment that I was raised a proud colonial Rhodesian. I successfully completed four British GCEs and three Matric[2] examinations. All too soon, my high school days came to an end. Now was the time to consider a future career and all that accompanies the termination of initial education. As to a career, I had not given the matter the slightest thought until the final days of my matriculation. As examinations loomed, I found myself in a state of mild shock. I had worked part-time during school Christmas holidays for several years at Greatermans, a general dealer store in Salisbury. This low-key occupation had provided valuable and much-needed pocket-money on many occasions. However, following matriculation, a permanent career was now to be sought. To my distress, I was ill-prepared for what lay ahead.

---

[1] Lake Kariba is the largest artificial lake in Africa, created between 1958 and 1963 by damming the Zambezi River, and provides hydroelectric power to Zambia and Zimbabwe, where it narrows at the Kariba Gorge. It is 238km long, and 32km wide in places, covering an area of about 5,439km^2.

[2] Matric: South African university entrance examinations.

Early Police Career

While I was drawn to the African bush way of life, it was quite difficult with my level of educational achievements to find a suitable occupation with future prospects of advancement. I attempted to gain entry to the Department of National Parks for a game ranger position. I applied to the Ministry of Water Development as a field officer and even considered training as a pilot. These applications, together with a batch of others to various organisations, all came to nothing as I did not have the necessary educational qualifications, and I had no chance of improving my academic achievements due to my family's financial position.

At 17 years of age, I found myself limited in the choice of a career. I had no precise direction in life nor was I particularly passionate about any future occupation. By chance I came across the enthusiastic BSAP recruiting officers in Salisbury where I also watched the annual police displays at the police grounds. For many years the annual police displays were very popular entertainment events nationwide. They featured various aspects of the historic and ceremonial traditions of the BSAP, together with modern-day techniques in combating criminal activity. These displays enhanced public relations and were supplemented by exhibition stands at the numerous agricultural shows held throughout the country. Suddenly, the police service seemed an attractive prospect. For an adventurous young man such as myself, zealous for the outdoors, keen to ride horses and motor bikes, drive police cars and power-boats on Lake Kariba, and play rugby and cricket. The BSAP seemed to fit the bill. Adventure, excitement and the thrill of the chase filled my mind with heady thoughts. Several of my friends were also enlisting with the BSAP which propelled my desire to become a policeman.

On 9 January 1969, I attested in the BSAP as a cadet.[1] I was stationed at Avondale[2] Police Station where I served for three months. While I attended various accident and crime scenes with my senior officers, my primary responsibility was to monitor the House Under Supervision (HUS) files, to ensure that the African constables had checked various vacant white residential properties at scheduled times when their occupants were on leave. Strange as it may seem, an important daily duty was to cycle down King George Road to the local bakery and collect cakes and buns for the white staff at the station. The greater challenge on the return journey, was to cycle back up the intimidating steep hill without stopping before serving tea for all white staff on duty. My task was to match tea-and-bun orders for each individual officer. My newly acquired title was "Cadet", which was for strange reasons, the source of merriment among the white officers. I was made good-natured fun of at every opportunity by men who took me under their wing and mentored me. Under these circumstances, it came to me early on in my career with the BSAP that, as far as possible, I should not leave myself open to criticism.

Soon on arrival, I joined the police rugby team. In time I was selected captain of the BSAP under-20 team. I represented Mashonaland and the Rhodesian under-20 team for two consecutive years. My rugby playing days ended in 1971 with a serious knee injury while playing for the senior Police First XV. I had been pressured into playing for the Police First XV rather than captaining the under-20 team which was playing at the Salisbury police grounds the same day. After the injury, I struggled for some time as rugby had been my purpose and major activity in my life. More positively though, I learned not to be pressured into doing things against my own better judgment.

After my initial happy three months at Avondale, I was transferred to the Police Reserve Hard Square Station, Morris Depot, Salisbury. It was there that I met S/O Mike Plant who taught me to shoot accurately while out on training exercises. My primary duties included the management of the armoury and the safekeeping and usage of firearms and ammunition. BSAP Standing Orders, Chapter 7 provided strict control measures for the security and usage of weapons and ammunition throughout the police force at all stations. My role included ensuring that all weapons in the armoury were clean, safe and in working order. They needed to be chained, locked and secured. Every

[1] Cadets joined the BSAP between the ages of 16-18 years.

[2] Avondale: A Salisbury suburb.

weapon and all the ammunition needed to be safely stored and accounted for. I was responsible for preparing the monthly Arms and Ammunitions Return (BSAP Form 42), an administrative procedure that accounted for all hardware in the armoury, including ammunition expended.

C/Insp. Eric Kennelly, the Chief Musketry Instructor, stationed at Morris Depot and located at the main BSAP Armoury, Hard Square, Salisbury, clarifies the matter: "The members in charge of all stations throughout the country were required to account for every weapon and all ammunition every month by physically checking them and submitting an Arms And Ammunition Return, to reach the Central Armoury by about the middle of each month. These returns were consolidated by Police Reservist Reg Eastes into a single return which was submitted to Police General Headquarters for the attention of the Commissioner of Police. It was a full-time job for Reg, the figures had to be accurate. Inaccuracies and shortfalls were severely dealt with. These high standards were maintained in the face of the pending war and continued throughout its peak until its conclusion."[1] Supt. Maurice Power states: "The high standards of weapons safekeeping were maintained throughout the war. Certainly I recall no raids at Police stations in the Salisbury District, where ammunition or arms were stolen, the consequences were most severe and their safekeeping was a high priority for the members in charge of each station who were held accountable for any loss."[2]

BSAP Standing Orders were specific, simple to follow and did not tolerate deviation from laid-down procedures. This regimentation was frustrating to begin with, but I soon learned that adhering to laid-down procedures served as protection to all concerned, civilian as well as police personnel. These Standing Orders created accountability, induced discipline and simplified day-to-day life. I gained much experience in this situation and spent most of my days in the armoury cleaning weapons and counting ammunition. Periodically, the member in charge despatched me on my Velo Solex moped to pay his personal bills in Salisbury.

For training and demonstration exercises, Central Armoury, a short walk away, issued us one RPD, an AK-47 and an SKS with a small quantity of 7.62mm intermediate ammunition. These weapons and ammunition were supplied to insurgents entering Rhodesia from, in the main, the Soviet Union and China. After training, the weapons, unused ammunition and expended cartridge cases were returned to Central Armoury. Police stations in the urban suburbs and rural areas were not authorised nor did they keep these types of firearm and ammunition. Hence, I was privileged to be in the rare position of learning to strip, fire and take care of them in the early stages of my career.

During this time, I contracted measles and spent several weeks in a hospital isolation ward. At one stage, concerned that I might not survive, my mother called our priest to my bedside. I pulled through and spent several weeks at home recuperating.

Morris Depot Training

Being posted to Morris Depot, the BSAP Training Depot in Salisbury, was a life-changing, enjoyable experience that enhanced every aspect of my life. Continued adaption to the police lifestyle required little effort. As a cadet I joined Training Squad 6/69 and took up residence in Bodle Block. On 24 September 1969, my 18th birthday, I became a patrol officer in the BSAP and began an enjoyable career as a policeman. I enjoyed the training at Morris Depot, where routines and discipline had enduring and long-term positive outcomes.

The curriculum for new recruits of the BSAP included physical and endurance training, unarmed defence, swimming and lifesaving, foot drill and various weapons manoeuvres while at the march or

---

1 C/Insp. Eric Kennelly email 29/9/2017.

2 In 1978, Supt. Maurice Power was Supt. Suburban for the northern 11 stations and carried out monthly inspections of these stations. Email confirmation 26/1/2015 from Maurice Power. C/Supt. (5610) Nigel Roche, Officer Commanding Crime, Salisbury South District (1978-1979) carried out similar inspections in his district. Telephone call 19/5/2018. These two officers (Power and Roche) covered the entire Salisbury district and confirm no ammunition or weapons were stolen in raids from the Salisbury district. Also confirmed by (1) C/Insp. Eric Kennelly email 29/9/2017; (2) Supt. (6319) Chris Looker, SB Officer Commanding Salisbury Operations (SALOPS) 1978 - 1980, (Operations around Rhodesia's capital, Salisbury), email 25/10/2017.

stationary. We were also versed in aspects of law and policing, first aid, typing and musketry. We learned to groom the most aggressive horses I had yet come across in my young life during equitation. One doesn't soon forget those animals who were gifted with the ability to identify and sniff out the raw recruits during basic training. They would pucker their lips to reveal menacing teeth, divulging an over-eagerness to bite any recruit at close quarters. In my view, their rear legs were like spring-loaded weapons waiting to attack the faint-hearted such as me.

In addition to the normal tasks and responsibilities, I was also a keen rugby player. We had access to the police club where we could buy favourably priced meals and ice-cold beer. Along with personal transportation, which consisted of a Honda 50cc motorcycle, I was well satisfied with my life.

Our instructor was Mel O'Brien, a strict disciplinarian who had his limits, and one knew when one was close to, or about to cross them, which was not on the "recommended list". Mel had previously done six months in the Police Training School in Lusaka, and then several years as a platoon commander in the Northern Rhodesia Police Mobile Unit, the equivalent of the BSAP Support Unit. He has commented: "I really did enjoy my time as a squad instructor. There was a great deal of personal pride in trying to get the best out of each recruit and having the best squad in terms of all of the topics that we, as squad instructors, were required to lead. I seemed to follow the military 'beasting' approach which was to push recruits as far as I could over the first few days to show that I 'meant business'. Most of you youngsters were ready for it though. As an instructor I did have pride in the achievements of the squad."[1]

In my mind, there is little to rival the camaraderie which develops between a group of men brought together for the purposes of police paramilitary training. Cramped in confined space with all of the dynamics which accompany close-quarter living, these circumstances make for life-long friendships. In a figurative sense it could be compared to being stuffed into the washing machine, tumble dried, pressed and ironed. The final step finding expression in the "passing-out parade", after which one is a trained, equipped and recognised policeman prepared for duty. Many of those friendships formed during that period have continued until today.

We were woken in the morning by the bugler sounding the *Reveille* (wake up call), at 5.20 a.m. This was followed by *Warning for Parade* at 5.45 a.m., when we started making our way to the parade square. At 5.55 a.m. the *Quarter Call* was sounded and our squad formed up and the roll-call was taken. Then at 6 a.m. the *Fall In* (for parade) was sounded and thus began the day's events. There were various other calls and announcements throughout the day which ended with the *First Post* at 10 p.m., warning of the close of the day, and the *Last Post* at 10.15 p.m. which ended the day. *Lights Out* was announced at 10.30 p.m. These calls formed memories that have lasted a lifetime.

Once our basic training had been completed, our squad was transferred to the Police Driving School at Cranbourne Barracks on the outskirts of Salisbury, where I obtained a police driving licence for both motor vehicles and motor bikes. On completion of driving school, I was posted to Salisbury Central Charge Office on 9 January 1970. It was here that I took up residence in police accommodation at Fife Avenue Hostel, room 19. As in my previous location, the surroundings were comfortable with meals provided, a swimming-pool and bar. My favourite waiter was Calib who was full of fun. As our relationship developed, he would serve me with extra portions of food which was most welcome. I soon learned, throughout the country at the various police stations, there was always accommodation and a meal. Somehow we policemen were connected through our training at Morris Depot, sport, our police experiences and as friends or friends of friends. Rhodesia was a small country and our police "brotherhood" unique.

My First Brush With Death

One early morning, the duty inspector asked me if I had ever seen a dead person. "Only at the mortuary, sir, while training at Depot," I answered. "Get your cap and come with me," he instructed.

---

1 Staff S/O Mel O'Brien email 19/8/2015.

Shortly after our exchange, we set off on the Umtali road some 32km from Salisbury. On arrival, we were greeted by the horrible scene of a motor accident. A vehicle carrying three Portuguese men on their way to a football match across the Mozambique border at Vila de Manica, had ploughed into a trailer towed by a tractor. The trailer was loaded with long telephone poles which extended well beyond the tail gate. Unfortunately, an early-morning mist had settled in the valley, concealing the tractor and, as the motor vehicle struck the trailer, the poles ploughed through the windscreen crushing and instantly killing two passengers on the left-hand side of the vehicle. Miraculously, the driver survived. The duty inspector directed investigations while I assisted when instructed. I was shocked at first but in time adjusted and was able to carry out the duties required of me, which pleased me as I was sure there would be more cases involving death in my career. However, my first visit to observe a post-mortem while in depot training proved to be a more traumatic experience. So overpowering was the stench of decaying human flesh, that I lit a cigarette and held it to my nose to remove the stink. That disgusting odour lingered with me for days to follow. It felt to me that it had stuck to my skin and clothing.

One of a policeman's duties at the charge office was the security of the Prime Minister's Residence (PMR). We were also required to guard the Prime Minister's Offices (PMO) as well as the Governor's Residence. There was once a threat at the PMR, so the normal number of guards was doubled for the night duty. We were instructed to conceal ourselves in the grounds and be at the ready in the event of an attack. I duly followed instructions. Some hours later I was awakened by the footsteps of the duty inspector as he walked past my position at dawn. "Good morning, sir," I said. "Well camouflaged," he replied. Well camouflaged indeed, I thought.

Assistant Commissioner Robin Harvey, Special Branch (SB), was in charge of Ian Smith's personal Close Security Unit. He recalls: "The Close Security Unit consisted of a total of 21 men drawn from uniform branch but under the command of SB. These men were armed with concealed sidearms and required to pass a monthly firearms test. His office and residence, like the President, were guarded by Uniform Branch under the command of Officer Commanding Salisbury Urban. When the PM returned to his farm then the local Member i/c Selukwe was responsible for organising his security. Close Security was not provided for any other Government Minister. When travelling to South Africa one member of the close security team accompanied him. On arrival in South Africa the Special Branch representative attached to the Diplomatic Corp also travelled with him. When travelling in other countries he was accompanied by an SB Officer and number of uniform men depending on prevailing circumstances. On rare occasions the PM was seen to ride his bicycle."[1]

I soon relished the life of a policeman and felt I had stumbled on a wonderful career. It felt to me I was being paid to have fun and enjoy myself. On 4 September 1970, I was politely informed, by a note pinned to my door by S/O Barry Tiffin, the Member in Charge of the Hostel, that I was to be transferred. "P/O PADBURY – 19 (my room number) Report in uniform to S/O Wilhelm at Licence Insp. Office at 2 p.m. sharp. You have been transferred to Licence Insp. W/E/F[2] NOW", the note read. With no prior notice I had been transferred to Licence Inspector. This section dealt with liquor-licensed premises and offences relating to the consumption and selling of drugs. A few months later on 8 February 1971, I was attached to the CID Drug Section when the section was taken over by them, and was then posted to Avondale Police Station on 10 May 1971, where the member in charge was Insp. Bill Linfield.[3]

On reporting to my new posting, I was accommodated in a comfortable and pleasant house which served as quarters for single men. In no time I was involved with routine police duties which included attending crime scenes, road traffic accidents, general observation patrols and docket work.

[1] Robin Harvey oral interviews 10/6/2019 and 25-27/2/2019. I never saw the Prime Minister riding a bicycle at his residence or office.

[2] W/E/F: With effect from. Tiffin was injured during Op Nickel on 13/8/1967. He was awarded the Police Decoration for Gallantry.

[3] Insp. William (Bill) Linfield achieved the rank of C/Insp. before retiring on 7/7/1977.

All investigations into criminal activity were diarised to show the course of events, to establish the identity of perpetrators with a view to prosecution. The investigation diary, evidence, statements from witnesses and those accused, affidavits, forensic evidence and all relevant information was filed in a docket. Dockets were submitted to the public prosecutor for prosecution, or closed because the accused had not been identified or insufficient evidence had been gathered.

Periodically we carried out roadblocks on the main road from Kariba to Salisbury. It was our function to inspect long-haul heavy-duty trucks to ensure insurgents were not concealed in them. In my time with these duties, we never came across any. This was, in a small way, my first involvement, with anti-insurgent operations. Insurgents had attempted to use these vehicles to travel to Salisbury in 1966 but their efforts had been thwarted. In May 1967, four insurgents, hiding in a furniture van attempted to make their way to Salisbury. Special Branch had information about the group and they were attacked and killed with the help of the SAS in a roadblock 30km outside Karoi.[1]

In order to conceal a routine roadblock, I positioned them in the long valleys found in the main road from Salisbury to Kariba in my territory. One morning well before sunrise, while searching a heavy-duty truck, I heard the engine roar of a motor vehicle some distance away which, to my mind, was travelling at excessive speed. As the vehicle began the descent down the valley towards us, its momentum increased as did the whine of the engine. I warned the African policemen with me to move off the road and I moved to the rear of the truck I was inspecting. While standing in the road, I attempted to slow the oncoming vehicle down but to no avail. My torch and luminous gloves did not produce the desired effect. About 30m from our position the driver of the vehicle suddenly began to apply the brakes. In haste I dashed behind the truck, sprinting for my life. There was a thunderous crash of metal as the vehicle swerved to the right and struck the stationary truck. I ran around to the vehicle and, as I approached it, the front passenger door swung open and a body fell out. The remaining three occupants in the vehicle did not move. I found myself in a state of panic.

My first instinct was to flee the scene, but this was not an option as I was the senior police officer in charge at the incident. I promptly radioed Salisbury Central Police Station, explained the situation and requested assistance. To my dismay, this was denied me as all the vehicles at the station were in commission. However, an ambulance was available which I welcomed. While it made its way to the scene, I remained anxious to depart the crisis, such was the carnage of the collision. The four occupants of the vehicle were alive but in a serious condition. Prior to the arrival of the ambulance, we removed them carefully and placed them safely on the side of the road for fear of a repeat occurrence. A follow-up with Salisbury Central revealed still no possibility of additional assistance. My sole recourse was to complete the Traffic Accident Report Book, mark up the position of the vehicles, and call for breakdown vehicles to remove the wrecks. Gradually I took control of the situation realising the uniform I wore carried authority and expectations I was required to fulfil. Authority in these instances was not a choice, the situation imposed it. In time, the ambulance arrived and removed the injured to hospital where they miraculously recovered and survived their ordeal. This event served a sharp increment on my learning curve and remained with me throughout my career and later life. The driver causing the mayhem was in time charged and later successfully prosecuted.

As I progressed in my police career, I began to find investigational work of any description fascinating. One docket I was investigating involved a hit-and-run incident in which a vehicle had knocked down and killed an African pedestrian. We received information that led us to impound a vehicle which had damage to the front left headlight. The S/O in charge of investigations accompanied me to inspect the vehicle where we took samples of glass and paint and sent them to the Forensic Science Laboratory for examination. Later I sent items from the deceased's clothing to the laboratory and they were able to link the various fragments of clothing, glass and paint which resulted in a successful prosecution. This process intrigued me, and I knew I had found the right career. I began to thrive on putting all the pieces of the crime scene together.

[1] Ellert, H. and Anderson, D. (2020), pp. 106-107.

In 1972, I was transferred to CID Southerton where D/Insp. Keith Samler was in charge. On 20 May 1973, I passed the written promotion examination from detective patrol officer to detective section officer and was promoted shortly afterwards. On 31 May 1973, I was transferred to CID Crimes of Violence where our investigations included serious assaults, attempted murder, murder and rape.

It was while serving in the CID and carefully watching experienced detective inspectors meticulously investigating murder and crime scenes, that I began to learn the art of police investigations. This process fascinated me. Patience, careful observation, detailed written, photographic and crime scene evidence were key requirements to achieving successful conclusions. Open mindedness, avoiding assumptions and not jumping to hasty conclusions were additional aspects these experienced and expert investigators taught me. Thus my skills and experience and insight in policing matters continued on the upward trend.

On 18 February 1974, I attended the CID Detectives Training Course 1/74, passing the written examination at the end of the week. Course content included administration, finance, scenes of crime and questioned document examination procedures, pathology and fingerprints. We also studied legislation relevant to police work, investigational procedures including interrogations and the taking of statements, warned and cautioned statements and charge sheets. During the latter part of the week we covered practical photography, identity parades, informers and sources. A lecture on the CID work relevant to the operational areas was delivered.

It was the CID who sent me on two deployments in the operational area, these being Chiweshe Tribal Trust Land and Mukumbura, both in 1973.

First Operational Deployments

The first deployment I went on was to the Chiweshe TTL where I was based at Bari Mountain. I have three clear recollections of this deployment. The first being the magnificent view from the "long drop",[1] which was situated on the side of Bari Mountain overlooking the rural African bush. The second memory occurred late one Friday afternoon. An hour before sunset, I took the unit's Land Rover for a drive into the remote area of the TTL. As I travelled, I found myself in a magnificent setting. Msasa trees dotted the countryside. Kopjes jutted into the clear blue sky while African villages lay scattered throughout the region. The fading orange sunset flooded the countryside. I felt as though I was looking through a tinted lens when I came across a Shona village with thatched roofs, circular mud-walled homes in what seemed like the middle of nowhere. The thought went through my mind that these people were hardy, resilient and ingenious. It seemed to me they were a people at one with their environment. They appeared peaceful and content. Peasants by any worldly standard yet there was a harmony and tranquility about their way of life which captivated me.

My third recollection is that of my first ride in a helicopter to a contact scene. This proved an abrupt contrast to the previously mentioned pastoral scenes. I was summoned by radio from those in the vicinity who had made contact with a group of insurgents. They had arrested an elderly African male whom they thought could provide information regarding a suspected insurgent group. I was collected from Bari Mountain and flown to the contact area with my African CID detail. Not one of us knew what to do other than carry out direct and aggressive interrogations. Mostly such exercises were in vain. After some time, we released our captive and walked from the hut. We proceeded as confidently as possible and told the awaiting soldiers that the suspect knew nothing about the suspected terrorists. Later that afternoon I was flown back to Bari Mountain with the helicopter journey the highlight of the day. Other than that, I had little to show for the day's activities.

My second deployment came in June 1973. This was to the region of Mukumbura, a magnificent base camp on the Mukumbura River that bordered Mozambique and Rhodesia. This base was under

[1] Long drop: An outside toilet. A 2-3m deep hole serving as a lavatory. Commonly known as a PK (*piccanin kia:* small house).

threat by both FRELIMO[1] and ZANLA as the war of liberation in both countries gathered momentum. There were regular attacks and landmines constantly planted in the surrounding roads of both Mozambique and Rhodesia. This was to prove a memorable camp environment. We had our own police canteen, while across the Mukumbura River in Mozambique, was "Abu's Place", a typical rural Portuguese African bar-cum-restaurant that served Portuguese beer, cool drinks and food. A pleasant continental break, reminding me of family holidays in Beira. These were the only good things about Mukumbura. The initial three-week patrol that stretched to eight weeks was monotonous and more of an endurance test rather than an active or positive contribution to the war effort.

However, it was here at Mukumbura that I learned to deal with what is commonly referred to among soldiers as "war nerves". The drive from Bindura to Mukumbura was in a military convoy led by a Ferret scout-car, armed with a single .303 (7.62mm) machine gun. This was a two-man vehicle, which was intended for light reconnaissance. Resupplies of military equipment, fuel, food and Security Forces personnel travelled in the convoy over the hazardous Mavhuradonha Escarpment that at first overlooked but later descended into the Zambezi Valley. I was the passenger in the front seat of an RL, a general-purpose five-ton truck. We literally laboured up the mountain gravel road in first gear. No hope if we get ambushed, I thought.

Enjoyment of the magnificent and unique scenery was absolutely spoiled by the threat of ambush by insurgents. Fresh in our minds was a recent attack on a convoy that occurred on 23 April 1973, when four soldiers, L/Cpl. M.B. Cockroft, Rifleman J.T.V. Forbes, Cpl. B. Davison, 4RR, and a driver, Private Matangira of the 10 Supply and Transport Platoon, were killed and several others slightly injured in an ambush on a truck in the Mukumbura tribal trust area. Three insurgents were also reported killed, and an undisclosed number captured. An African civilian was seriously injured in the incident.[2]

My life continued as a surreal journey. In the morning I left behind the security of Salisbury City, the police canteens, night clubs, sporting activities, my daily routine in the CID offices at Salisbury Central Police Station and safety of my flat in Avondale. I travelled through the day via "ambush alley", ending up on the northern border of Rhodesia in a war zone. As I journeyed, the realisation came to me that I was not a war hero, nor did I have any intention of such aspirations. Several cold beers in the police pub commonly known as "Mukumbura by the Sea" settled my nerves on the first evening. As a group of us policemen sat around the bar drinking beer that evening, the discussion inevitably moved to the plans for the following morning. This was to be a roving vehicle patrol along the border road to try and find some locals and gather intelligence.

Later that night, without warning, I began to experience nervousness while trying to get some sleep. In addition, I was gripped by stomach cramps and nausea throughout the night. In the morning, I awoke fearful, sick in the stomach and reluctant to participate in the patrol. I struggled with this quandary for some time but later recognised that I was frightened for my life and what might transpire should we make contact with the enemy. Early in the morning, I made up my mind to join the patrol, although I was still gripped by a paralysing, unexplainable fear. The skilful propaganda machinery of the government demonstrated, to my mind, blatant hypocrisy. The motive was to mask the escalating war with an "all-is-well" mentality.

Following the success of the patrol without incident, I was to gain further insight into the matter of everyday life. In essence, the principle I took from the experience was: "Do the thing you fear, and you conquer fear." It transpired I enjoyed the patrol. More so the camaraderie, the socialising and in typical police fashion, even more, the cold beers in the evenings which followed. It was at this time I learned a second valuable principle which was: "Perfect beer casts out all fear." I felt myself wonderfully liberated. Not from fear itself but from being ruled by fear. It was an important personal victory which set me on a journey to becoming obsessed and consumed by the war in my country.

1 FRELIMO: Front for the Liberation of Mozambique, the African nationalist movement fighting for the removal of Portuguese colonialist occupation.

2 Adrian Haggett email 30/5/2015; J.R.T. Wood email 30/5/2015.

There was a clear distinction between Special Branch and CID. Special Branch was involved in intelligence matters while the CID investigated and documented the criminal aspect of the war. Acts of terrorism were deemed criminal. However, the escalating war would soon narrow this division. While at Mukumbura there were minimal actual detective undertakings to conduct. We had no contacts with insurgents. We merely engaged in several vehicle patrols and collected locals for interrogations. However, as I was not involved with Special Branch, I was unaware of the overall "intelligence scenario" of the area and was not familiar with the information-gathering mechanisms of the country.

One morning, following a meeting with Portuguese military commanders, D/S/O "Ken" Stewart, the senior Special Branch officer in charge, announced that there were rumours that FRELIMO were planning to attack the Mukumbura base with weaponry that included a 75mm recoilless rifle. The next day, the report continued, the Portuguese military were going to initiate patrols, to begin clearing their access roads which had been heavily mined. Ken Stewart had also received intelligence reports that an insurgent would be travelling on a bus to a local store. In the light of this information, a group of us were deployed in the afternoon to wait at the bus stop. This was some 16km south of the camp. Once parked at the bus stop, we started to enjoy the pleasures of the African sunset. Without warning, we heard an explosion from the direction of our camp. "Portuguese detonating landmines," was our immediate consensus. However, the explosions continued at regular intervals. "Our base is being attacked," said Ken as he, with us in tow, raced towards our vehicles and sped off in the direction of our base.

That drive home resembled scenes from a war movie. Intermittent exploding shells landed around us as we sped along. FRELIMO forces were firing towards the camp from their position in Mozambique, their initial attack overshooting by some considerable distance, as they were adjusting their sights. On arrival at the camp, we leapt from our vehicles and took shelter in a bunker. Two uniformed policemen and I landed in the same bunker. With little to do we drew straws to see who would crawl into the nearby house and return with a pack of cold beers. One of the uniformed men lost the draw and, after a short while following his return, we were together sipping our first cold beer. As the ineffective attack died down, an army officer, while on his rounds, came across the three of us enjoying our beers in the security of our bunker. We noted his disapproval but continued to enjoy our drinks.

In the morning, during the follow-up operation, military firearms experts confirmed that a 75mm recoilless rifle and mortars were indeed used in the attack. Unfortunately the culprits escaped.

Another time, in a remote spot close to the Mozambique border, we collected a Selous Scouts operator who had returned from a long-range reconnaissance mission in Mozambique on his own. I could but only admire this man's bravery, military skills and bushcraft that enabled him to penetrate deep into enemy territory, carry out his mission and return safely.

The most successful operation I experienced at that stage of the conflict was when Ken Stewart received an intelligence report that a ZANLA section had paid a visit to a local storekeeper to demand supplies as well as a radio. Ken organised for a radio to be set up as a booby trap when it was switched on and, when tuned to a certain frequency, it would explode. These devices were code named "road runners." Strict instructions were given to the informant to ensure the safety of his family and relatives prior to the radio being deployed. A day later we established that several ZANLA had been killed and one injured when the radio exploded at the prearranged frequency.[1]

Late afternoon on 4 July 1973, I was ordered to go and clear the local gravel airfield with a team of men because a pilot, shot and wounded, would be making an emergency landing. He didn't have time to frighten onlookers and animals from the runway by flying over the landing strip at an exceedingly low level prior to landing. This practice is commonly referred to as "buzzing" with the deafening roar of the plane's engines causing fear in idle bystanders and chasing off animals. Thus our task became a matter of urgency.

1 Confirmed by Ken Stewart email 20/3/2017.

We sped from our base in two Land Rovers and on arriving, immediately cleared the airfield and waited anxiously for the plane to arrive. Let Air Lt. Pete Simmonds tell the story:

> Early in July 1973 I was based in Centenary at FAF 3 flying a Percival Provost T52. For a few days I had been getting up before first light each morning and flying down to Mukumbura to be on stand-by there from sunrise to sundown. We could not stay there overnight as there were no guards for the aircraft and Mukumbura was right on the Mozambique border close to very unfriendly terrorist territory. Each evening I would fly back as the sun set and do a night landing in Centenary. I had been tasked to do top cover duty in support of one of the Rhodesian African Rifles (RAR)[1] Companies who were based in Mukumbura and were conducting anti-terrorist operations both inside Rhodesia and in Mozambique at the time.
>
> A good friend of mine, Lt. Mike Wilson, of the RAR had been following terrorist tracks from the site of a landmine in Rhodesia. The landmine had been detonated by an African bus on the border road a few days earlier, causing ghastly casualties. Following the terrorist tracks from the landmine incident he found that they went straight over the border into Mozambique. Once he had been tracking in Mozambique for only a day, he had walked off his map with his stick of 10 men and neither he nor his Boss in the Mukumbura Operations tent were too sure of where he was. After two days he had only a very general idea of his position, so if he caught up with the terrorists, the plan was that he would guide me overhead from high level in order for me to support him with my guns and napalm. Each day he got closer to the enemy and then fell behind again while he and his stick of men slept on the tracks during the night. His Commanding Officer, Major Roy Gardener (OC E COY 1RAR) in Mukumbura, was in a dilemma about whether or not to send me over the border to find him and at the same time drop him some new maps. We didn't want the enemy to know that we were following them by letting them see my Provost, but the further he tracked away from Rhodesia, the more pressing it became that we should know exactly where he was. This went on for three days and on the fourth it was decided that since he was running out of radio batteries as well, I would have to find him at last light and drop him both maps and batteries. It was 4 July 1973.
>
> At about 5 p.m. a package of maps wrapped around batteries and personal mail for the men in the bush was tied up and I set off to find them in the Provost with Leading Air Craftsman Mike Guy, my very trusting technician. I flew east into Mozambique for about 20 minutes at over 2500 ft. above ground level until Mike Wilson could see me whereupon he directed me overhead his position. He told me that his tracker estimated they were about 12 hours behind the terrorists at that stage and he was around 30 miles from the Rhodesian border. He had obviously been tracking hard for the previous few days. When I found him, I pulled out the correct map and put a large X on it with 'YOU ARE HERE' written next to the X. I then used this map to wrap around the package before tying it all up with another layer of string. We descended to 50 ft. above the trees and I lined up with Mike Wilson on the ground, put down full flap and slowed down to just above the stall with the cockpit canopy wound back. As he and his troops disappeared under the nose of the aircraft, I was just about to chuck the package out of the cockpit when there were two very loud bangs as if the engine had back-fired. I was sure it was the aircraft engine and looked at the engine instruments while pushing the throttle forward. I was always very worried about having to force land in Mozambique and therefore tended to watch the

[1] RAR: Formed in 1940. Comprised one battalion of African non-commissioned officers and soldiers with white officers. At the dissolution of the Federation, Army HQ asked the RF Government to authorise an additional RAR battalion. Both battalions to have three rifle companies instead of four. It would be far easier to add a fourth rifle company than a new battalion. The RF declined. RAR Depot (training) and a second battalion, 2RAR, were eventually formed in 1975. 3RAR was formed in 1979. Brig. Heppenstall email 4/6/2019 and telephone call 30/6/19.

engine instruments of the single engine Provost constantly whenever I was far from home. I was surprised then when I saw the engine instruments performing perfectly well and heard the engine responding normally to the throttle. I looked at Mike Guy quizzically next to me in case he had the answer to the bangs. His eyes were firmly focused on my legs, with a very surprised look on his face. I was wearing the usual khaki shorts and veldskoens[1] and as I looked down realisation hit me that I had been shot through the left thigh. My left femur was broken and the bullet had stopped in my right leg leaving thick dark-red blood all over my legs, seat and parachute. The second bang was another bullet going through the fuselage behind the cockpit. Mike Wilson was as surprised as we were that he had caught up with the terrorists who had in fact been watching him from their resting place on higher ground before I arrived. I turned the Provost back to Mukumbura and told them what had happened to me. I then asked my tech, Mike Guy, to fly the aircraft straight and level while I tried to sort myself out. There was little pain and a lot of adrenaline but I could do no more than block the holes in my left leg with my thumb and middle finger. I was terrified that the loss of blood would cause me to faint and I knew if that happened, Mike Guy would not have been able to stand a fighting chance of landing the aircraft on his own with me hanging all over the control column and rudders. I am sure it was the adrenaline that was brought on by this thought that kept me awake and flying. As we flew back towards Mukumbura, I remember willing the Mavuradona Mountains in the distance to come closer, faster. It took 20 minutes to fly back to Mukumbura and by then the RAR major had organised a reception party for me at the airfield with a medic.

I may have had bad luck in being shot that day, but I was very lucky in other ways. I was unable to get my broken left leg off the rudders but my right leg was still functioning and I was able to pull and push the rudders a little due to the toe strap across the top of each rudder pedal. The toe strap made the difference in being able to land the aircraft or crashing it onto the ground without the ability to stay straight on the runway. The Percival Provost is the only aircraft I have flown that has these toe straps on the rudders and a brake handle on the control column. The rough rubble surface of the runway at Mukumbura was also in my favour as it was ideal for sliding sideways in a ground loop. I landed gently and was able to keep the Provost straight on the runway while slowing down and braking with my hands until the tail touched the ground at about 50 knots. I then squeezed the brake hard locking the wheels and we ground looped through 270 degrees. The Provost lurched to a stop facing 90 degrees off the runway but still in the centre of the airfield.

The flight was over. The priority of landing safely was now behind us and a tremendous wave of immense pain hit me even before the dust had settled. I managed to switch off the engine. There is no point in trying to describe the level of pain I felt as I don't believe words can express it. There was another problem though. I was unable to get out of the cockpit on my own and was stuck there. One of the biggest RAR soldiers I had ever seen volunteered to fix this. He thrust his hands underneath me with one arm underneath the broken bone and the other around my waist. He then hauled me out of the cockpit in a second and carried me off the wing onto a stretcher while I screamed and yelled. My broken leg seemed to have a mind of its own as it flailed about in the air until I was settled on my back. I always remember how calmly Mike Guy took his predicament while with me in the aircraft and while, as frightened as he may have been, he never showed it. Air Lt. Pete Wilcox flew a chopper from Centenary without a horizon that dark night to get me back to Centenary. Dr Griffiths the Army doctor accompanied him. By the time I arrived in Centenary, I was as high as a kite on Pethadine and time meant very

[1] A shoe manufactured from leather sewn to a rubber sole.

> little to me. My squadron friend, Air Lt. Alf Wild, took me in a Trojan to New Sarum and an ambulance delivered me from there to the Salisbury General Hospital. The doctors fixed my leg up and six months later, I returned to operations, but this time for four and a half years on helicopters and a very nasty escalating war. I have always been grateful to Pete Wilcox, Dr Griffiths and Mike Guy.[1]

I watched the unfolding of the scenario in awe. This was my first experience of the reality of war. People died and were injured: there would be many more. I would be in action with Pete Simmonds again in the Makoni TTL on 25 August 1976.

When I finally left Mukumbura at the end of July 1973, I was as ignorant of intelligence-gathering matters pertaining to the terrorist threat as when I first arrived. In addition, I had no insight and was not aware of the political manoeuvring which was taking place regarding the impending war the country was facing. Little was known regarding the strategies and tactics of the enemy. We were ill-informed as to their commitment to the war, their intentions, the role of the local peasants, their unmet political grievances and aspirations. In my ignorance, I viewed insurgents as isolated renegade groups who could be hunted down and killed. I held the view that this was a war confined to our borders and remote TTLs which was far removed from our cities and had no influence on our daily lives. My opinion was no more than something is going on out there. At least I was gaining operational experience.

However, life takes on an entirely different perspective when you face an enemy whose sole intent is to kill you. Confusion further inflames the situation when you have no real understanding of why the foe is prepared to carry out total destruction. These conditions felt to me similar to a game in which I did not know the rules or the consequences of victory or defeat. On my return to Salisbury, I found it difficult to settle into routine duties at CID Crimes of Violence.

I can honestly say I did not enjoy the war at this stage. Although I enjoyed the adventure of being in the bush, the idea of being killed was not appealing. However, the time away from Salisbury helped me reflect and appreciate what a wonderful career the police force was and the amazing facilities we had. The Salisbury Police Club was a delightful venue for a drink and meal on the verandah overlooking the sports grounds. The main fields hosted many club, provincial and international games of rugby as well as good quality cricket at local, provincial and international level. There were bowls, tennis, squash, a great swimming-pool where I played water polo and underwater hockey and trained for the sub-aqua section. Our diving trips to Sinoia Caves were an exhilarating experience. The club hosted the Annual Police Display, the drawcard for many a recruit and was available for use by members for wedding receptions, dances and annual general meetings for the various organisations within the police force. Talking of dances reminds me of the New Year's Eve dinner dances at the club and at Fife Avenue Hostel. Like the war, the rising nationalistic stirrings were "out there" and it was a situation that did not affect our way of life. Government propaganda ensured the Rhodesian public were kept ignorant of the facts of the war as its momentum increased. So effective was this propaganda and psychological campaign that we lived on merrily, unaware and unprepared for the growing threat.

Rusape: Early Days

In July 1974, two rural CID vacancies arose. One for Sinoia, the other for Rusape. My friend, D/S/O Lawrie Mabin, applied for the Sinoia vacancy and I applied for Rusape. I liked the eastern districts of Rhodesia which, in my ignorance, I thought would be free from terrorist activity. There was a revolutionary war raging in Mozambique between the Portuguese colonial administration and the FRELIMO revolutionary army who were fighting to overthrow their Portuguese colonial masters. This was another war I considered remote. However, I was soon to learn otherwise.

On Saturday, 5 October 1974, Lynette and I were married at the BSAP Chapel in Salisbury. The following morning, we left for Chileka International Airport, Malawi, for an eight-day all-inclusive

---

1 Pete Simmonds emails 31/5/2015, 8/9/2015 and 24/11/2018; Petter-Bowyer, P. (2005), pp. 192-193.

Flame Lily Holiday that cost R$88 per person. To us newlyweds that price was a bargain. At Chileka airport, while waiting for the departure of our flight to our resort on Lake Malawi, we had a few beers at the bar and inevitably met up with other Rhodesian couples on the same holiday. Finally, our group was summoned for the next leg of the journey. In good spirits, we all boarded a 10-seater twin-engine airplane for our destination, Club Makokola. This resort was situated along a stretch of the shores of Lake Malawi.

When we were seated, joking with each other and excited about our forthcoming adventure, we all saw an African dressed smartly in a white uniform with a cap on. We started joking about the possibility of him being our pilot, and so on ... He walked up to the plane, opened the pilot's door, sat down and said, as he buckled up: "Good afternoon ladies and gentlemen, I am your pilot." We were astonished! You see, with our minds narrowed by our limited colonial experience, Africans could not be pilots. However, we had a comfortable flight in the hands of a competent pilot. His competence and expertise posed a real challenge to my colonialist prejudices. We had a wonderful time fishing, snorkelling, sailing and swimming at this idyllic African resort. The same pilot flew us back to Chileka for our connecting flight home to Salisbury. A month later I was transferred to Rusape CID where the member in charge was D/Insp. Dan Stannard.[1]

Rusape had an interesting history, particularly regarding the town's roots which were firmly entrenched in the First *Chimurenga.* The English translation of Rusape is "may it never dry". This is a reference to the Rusape River. Rusape was originally a British South Africa Company settlement established on the river's banks in 1894. During the First *Chimurenga*, Chief Chingaira Makoni, incensed that his lands had been pegged out for farms and gold claims, joined the Matabele rebellion in 1896. In the early days of the uprising, he, along with several followers, hid in a large cave at the sacred Gwindingwi Mountain, 20km north-east of Rusape. It was here that British troops besieged him and his loyal supporters. This took place towards the end of August 1896. Chief Makoni was finally captured on 4 September, tried, executed and legend has it, beheaded in full view of his subjects.[2] In terms of oral African history, these were "recent" events. They had occurred in living memory and in their minds were but one or two generations past. Hence the stories would be told and retold in meetings and discussions around the evening fires, thereby ensuring these events would never be forgotten.

In 1974, the war was gaining momentum. Rebel African recruits were exiting Rhodesia for training camps in Mozambique. Dan Stannard had been liaising with the Portuguese Army in Mozambique and built good relations with the Portuguese military and the administration at Vila Gouveia. He acquired significant and useful intelligence reports that related to FRELIMO and the movement of Rhodesian Africans into Mozambique where they joined ZANLA. Initially, he flew by helicopter from the military base at Inyanga to Vila Gouveia, located some 90km north-east from Vila de Manica and contiguous to Inyanga.

Thereafter, Stannard would drive the Special Branch Peugeot car through Umtali[3] to Vila de Manica before branching off to Vila Gouveia. These road trips became increasingly useful as he could spend more time in Mozambique. Through this military liaison he began meetings with various FRELIMO personnel nearby Vila Gouveia. To make them more relaxed he used to take gifts of shoes. This tough bush footwear was commonly known as *veldskoens.* Stannard also provided handouts of shirts and other items Africans valued. Gradually, over time, he built a firm and trusting relationship with these FRELIMO. On one occasion he provided transport to a FRELIMO cadre

[1] D/Insp. Dan Stannard joined the BSAP in 1957 and served in the CID then SB where he was the PSBO Salisbury and Mashonaland shortly before Independence in 1980. After Independence, he served as Director Internal (DIN) of the CIO. He retired in 1992.

[2] Executed today.com 1896, *passim; The Sunday Mail,* Zimbabwe, 16/11/2014; Ranger, T. (1988), pp. 29-30.

[3] Umtali: At the time, the third largest city in Rhodesia, 272km from Salisbury and 324km from the Mozambique port of Beira. The town was served by road, rail and an air service that operated from Grand Reef, Umtali's airport, 27km west of the town. It was an important trade link for landlocked Rhodesia, although the British mounted a naval blockade of Beira throughout the period of Rhodesia's Unilateral Declaration of Independence and the war that followed.

armed with an SKS rifle. Some distance from Vila Gouveia he indicated that Dan needed to leave the road they were travelling on and drive him to his home. Stannard relates the story: "I drove along the route he pointed out and after quite a few miles, on a dirt road, we suddenly came upon a very big ZANLA camp and were instantly surrounded by a hostile group of terrs toting RPGs, A/Ks and other such weaponry." Fortunately, the passenger spoke to them and explained that Stannard was liaising with FRELIMO and was known to them. "While the FRELIMO cadre was jabbering to them in Portuguese I very quietly and slowly turned around and drove off gradually increasing my speed until I was well shot of this camp. I have no idea what or exactly where this camp was but whatever and wherever it was it was full of ZANLA terrs. I had a quick change of underwear en route back to Umtali!"[1]

The Flechas

Dan Stannard recalls:

> On these trips to Mozambique I was accompanied by Lt. David Padbury whose role was to travel with me on our regular visits by helicopter to Vila Gouveia, one of the Military Headquarters of the Portuguese Army based in the area. Lt. Padbury would take part in the briefings from the Portuguese Army, and then stand in for me by taking part in various military discussions on strategies, deployments and inspections of their military hardware. This break gave me the opportunity to engage with sources that I had established over the course of about 4 years. It also allowed me the time to engage with the leaders of the Flechas movement. The Flechas (Arrow in Portuguese), were sections of mainly Bushmen and locally recruited and trained men with Portuguese Officers, that specialised in tracking, reconnaissance, intelligence gathering and pseudo-terrorist operations. This unit was established by the Directorate-General for Security (DGS), the Portuguese Secret Police.[2]
>
> These operations were reasonably successful but came to a rapid end because of the military coup in Portugal on the 25th April 1974. A ceasefire was declared in Mozambique on 8th September 1974. Subsequent Independence was granted to the country on the 25th June 1975. Some of the Flechas joined FRELIMO but in liaison with the Portuguese Army and with the assistance of Lt. David Padbury, we arranged a covert operation and safe passage for thirty to forty Flechas with their leader, Alvaro Manuel Alves Cardoso, to cross the Rhodesian border and join 'our' security forces.[3]

David Padbury continues:

> I was deployed to the Katiyo Tea Estates to organise deployments of 3 Independent Company to secure the border for the crossing of the Flechas. This was planned to take place by night and vehicles were positioned for transporting them were concealed in the bush. The plan was that Dan Stannard would fly by fixed wing the day before to Villa Gouveia to co-ordinate the final movements and liaison for the crossing. When all was set, I was contacted by radio and informed that the Flechas were on the way. Sections from 3 Independent Company were strategically deployed to ensure that there would be no interference. The crossing was executed without incident during the night as planned, and the Flechas transported to the Selous Scouts. However, during the operation, a callsign that was deployed to watch the house of one of the managers of the Estate had observed a small group of FRELIMO being entertained in the house. This they reported to me. I knew that Dan Stannard was going to be flying back during the afternoon after the crossing, passing overhead to ensure that all had gone to plan. This he did, and I

1 Dan Stannard letter and telephone discussions on 20/4/2017 and 12/5/2017.

2 Emerson, S.A. (2014), pp. 33-35.

3 Dan Stannard letter and telephone discussions on 20/4/2017 and 12/5/2017.

> reported what we had observed. Dan landed on the Tea Estate airfield and debriefed the troops involved and flew on to Rusape.[1]

Dan Stannard recollects:

> As a result of this intelligence I organised an operation that resulted in the arrest of Matata Bombada Tembo who was a high-ranking FRELIMO guerrilla operating in the COREMA sector which included the Katiyo Estate. When we concluded our interrogations, and through *Servico Nacional da Seguranca Publica*[2] (SNASP) the Mozambique intelligence service, I organised for Tembo to be returned to FRELIMO at Vila Gouveia. In exchange we were given two high ranking FRELIMO liaison officials, including Viega Junior, who were to keep us informed regarding ZANLA operations in Mozambique. I visited these two men regularly at Maputo and gleaned important intelligence from them. Meetings were held with various FRELIMO personnel in and around Vila Gouveia and I gradually built up a very good liaison which continued until the border closure in 1975. All intelligence I received was forwarded to the Provincial Special Branch Officer (PSBO) based at Umtali for onward transmission to SBHQ Salisbury. One of the side benefits of these trips was my ability to smuggle back cashew nuts and wine for one of the local Hotels.[3]

General CID District Work

Until mid-1975, district work in the CID became a dream come true. We went on regular fishing trips to Lake Lesapi. Often we went camping, played tennis, rugby and golf on Saturday afternoons and were only an hour's drive from the magnificent Inyanga area where there was a police holiday cottage that was extremely cheap to rent. In 1975, I captained the Rusape rugby team and we beat our Afrikaans-speaking rivals from Inayzura for the first time in many years. I went on to captain the Manicaland team in a provincial tournament against Matabeleland and Mashonaland. To my disappointment we lost the games. Sadly, by 1976, full-scale war had set in, bringing our rugby-playing days to an end. Fortunately, entertainment continued at the Rusape police canteen. Snooker games were a regular feature of police life as was our inimitable barman, Rukweza. He was a colourful character and I don't believe I ever saw him sober. Amazingly, he always remembered one's favourite beer, while his stocktaking and cashing-up generally balanced.

I shan't forget the famous annual Rusape river-boat race. Participants from across the country made their way down the Lesapi River in all forms of river craft. Inflated tyre-tubes, barrel rafts and canoes, as well as many other innovative designs, made their appearances at this event. Essentially there were two goals to this annual river-boat race. The first was to finish the course and, secondly, to consume as much beer as possible while competing. My brother, David, and I took part in the 1975 event in an inflated-tyre contraption but with no success to boast of.

After a community show in 1975, three of us formed a band and started playing at weddings, other social functions and parties. The lead guitarist sang, I played the piano and we had a drummer. In time, Martin and Rose Stander, owners of the Balfour Hotel, invited our band to play at their establishment. One evening at the hotel, during a refreshment break, the three of us went through to the bar area for a drink. To my misfortune, I found myself involved in a game of bok-bok.

In many respects bok-bok was not so much a game but rather an activity during which supposedly adult men would attempt to display and gain physical superiority in a somewhat primitive exercise of running, jumping and landing on the backs of other adult men. One individual would lean his back against a wall while two or three men would bend forward at roughly 90 degrees, clasp each other about the waist to form a line of exposed backs onto which others would dive following a short run-up. At the discretion of the man serving as the anchor against the wall onto whom the

---

[1] David Padbury email 18/4/2017.

[2] Mozambique Intelligence Service. Confirmed by D/Insp. Henrik Ellert email 12/8/2017.

[3] Dan Stannard letter and telephone discussions on 20/4/2017 and 12/5/2017.

others had positioned themselves, he would cry out "bok-bok". Those wishing to participate, which was invariably a large number, would position themselves in an extended line-up and begin the process of leaping onto the exposed backs of those serving as a landing platform. The game had essentially two purposes. The first being an attempt by those serving as a platform not to collapse, while those landing on the backs of the others had the intention of collapsing the extended human structure. One by one fresh arrivals would charge at the bok-bok team to jump, dive, ramp, leap and attempt by any means possible to reduce the line-up to a crumpled heap on the floor. Inevitably, those serving as landing mats would collapse producing much good-natured mirth, laughter and ridicule. Needless to say, often slight injuries were incurred during such robust sessions and, on this occasion, I found myself nursing a few cuts and bruises and a ripped shirt. When I returned to the band half-way through the next session, I was greeted with: "What the hell happened to you?"

All told, the Rusape district area was at peace. Life was comfortable and relaxed: those stationed at the base were living in ideal rural conditions. The armed struggle launched by ZANLA and ZIPRA was confined to the north and north-eastern regions of Rhodesia and had not yet reached the Rusape district. Our thinking was, it never would!

Pleasant and peaceful though Rusape was, there was still work to be done. A detective inspector member in charge headed up two sections. There were Special Branch and CID units, both ably assisted by a complement of African staff. A D/S/O oversaw each section and managed a number of African detectives.

CID Duties

During my first year at Rusape, I attended an in-depth "scenes of crime course" at CID headquarters in Salisbury. These courses included fingerprints, forensic science, scenes of crime and ballistics. Ron Blackmore, the Questioned Document Examiner, taught me a lot. I also attended a police heavy-duty vehicle driving course and obtained the appropriate licence. There was a CID photographic laboratory in our offices and I learned how to develop photographs which was extremely interesting and beneficial. These skills enabled me to create our own scenes of crime service and laboratory, and develop a basic fingerprint bureau for the quick identification of local criminals, which helped speed up investigations. My duties at Rusape included the attendance of crime scenes to gather evidence, the investigation of all serious crimes, such as murders, rape, serious assaults, fraud and drug-related crime. I carried out licensed premises checks, and general rural patrols. In each case we dealt with, all investigations were methodically recorded in a log and filed in a docket. The docket would include affidavits and statements taken from witnesses, accused persons and the investigating officer, fingerprint matches to previous crimes, photographic evidence or evidence from the crime scene. Dockets were reviewed regularly by the member in charge who would check progress, make corrections and recommendations ensuring the crime was thoroughly investigated and reached the required standards before submission to the office of the public prosecutor.[1] These skills that were imparted to me by highly professional and experienced men would play a very important part in my future career and would be invaluable in future police and intelligence work.

Most importantly, I passed the detective inspector's written examination on my first sitting, which cleared the way for promotion. This was the last written police promotion examination I would have to take.

British South Africa Police Special Branch

A brief history of the BSAP Special Branch would be in order at this point. It dated back to the Federation of Rhodesia and Nyasaland, also known as the Central African Federation, which was formed on 1 August 1953, and comprised Northern Rhodesia, Southern Rhodesia and Nyasaland. The Federal Intelligence and Security Bureau (FISB), was responsible for external intelligence

1 At some rural stations, the public prosecutor was an appointed member of the BSA Police. At Rusape, this was S/O Dave Pattinson.

matters and was manned with staff from Northern Rhodesia, Southern Rhodesia, Nyasaland and the United Kingdom. In Southern Rhodesia, internal intelligence gathering was the concern of the British South Africa Police Special Branch.

At the dissolution of the Federation on 31 December 1963, the Central Intelligence Organisation (CIO), was formed under the command of the Director General, Mr Ken Flower, retired deputy commissioner of the BSA Police. A contract was drawn up between the Prime Minister and Flower in which the most important clause was that he, Flower, would be directly responsible to the Prime Minister and a new organisation, namely the CIO. This department was camouflaged as the Department of the Prime Minister. Its finances would be controlled by the Secretary to the Prime Minister, the Secretary to the Treasury and Mr Flower.[1]

Operationally, the CIO comprised two sections, namely Branch I and Branch II. Branch I remained an autonomous unit within the BSAP called Special Branch and was responsible for internal intelligence matters, headed by the OC SB, who was generally known as Director Internal (DIN). Branch II, headed by Director External (DEX) was responsible for external intelligence, including liaison with foreign services and was staffed by civilian members. Often these were former high-ranking police, military and service personnel, and others from the original FISB. DIN and DEX reported to the Deputy Director General (DDG) who reported to DG Flower. DIN also reported to Deputy Commissioner (Crime and Security) and the Commissioner. The staff composition of Branch II worked alongside Branch I in the same building and shared the same registry.[2]

As previously mentioned, Dan Stannard was transferred to CID Fraud Section, Salisbury, with my new member in charge being D/Insp. John (Jock) McCallum. Like Dan, he was a fair man, gracious and taught the importance of meticulous documentation that eventually earned me a commendation in my annual efficiency report from the Provincial Criminal Investigation Officer (PCIO), C/Supt. Vic Sidnell. My newly developed scrupulous recording procedures were to be of great importance in later operations.

D/Sgt. Herbert (pseudonym) was assigned to work with me in 1974 and was my right-hand man. We became friends and spent a great deal of time together, often in extremely difficult circumstances. Herbert was a Shona, 28 years old and five years my senior. He had a wonderful memory and the uncanny ability to assess circumstances and situations which initially seemed complex and complicated. Being a Shona, his command of the language and traditional customs helped him develop into a competent intelligence officer. He was able to piece together a myriad of leads and suggestions, accurately interpret a mass of information and present a logical reasoned picture of the actual situation on the ground. We worked as equals without considerations of rank. Our strengths and weaknesses complemented each other. It worked. Herbert was the first of several African friends I would make through the course of my career in the police.

Christmas 1974 was a memorable time for me as it was our first Christmas as a married couple. I asked D/Sgt. Chiwasha[3] where we might find a Christmas tree. "I will sort it out," he said before departing from my office. Some 30 minutes later I glanced out of my window to see him wandering back, smile on his face, to the office with a Christmas tree over his shoulder. "Where did you get that from?" I asked. "The top of the member in charge's tree," he replied. Sure enough, he had climbed the tree in the uniform branch member in charge's garden, lopped off the top and merrily carried it into my office. Covertly and in great haste we took it home in the back of our Land Rover.

However, it was the area of African staffing that concerned me. I found myself as a 23-year-old D/S/O with just over five years of experience in charge of a complement of senior African staff who were more experienced, older and wiser than I, yet I held the senior rank and they were expected to address me as "sir". I was continually ill at ease with this practice and it caused me

[1] Flower, K. (1987), pp. 13-14.

[2] Ellert, H. & Anderson, D. (2020), pp.173-201; Robin Harvey WhatsApp discussion 18/10/2019. CIO included Branch III (Military Intelligence), Branch IV (Government Telecommunications Agency), Branch V (Close Security) and Branch VI (Government Protective Security). Flower, K. (1987), p. 17.

[3] Pseudonym.

considerable discomfort. I felt it to be unethical and sensed the discontent among these senior men who patiently accepted me and taught me a great deal about criminal investigations and the culture of those we were policing. Consequently, I did not allow these men to call me "sir" outside of the office. They were loyal and reliable members of staff and we shared meaningful times together as a unit. An ingredient to many of the difficulties we encountered was that African policemen had an entirely separate rank structure and were not permitted to enter into the mainstream ranking system of white police officers. These included salary structures, uniforms and general conditions of service.[1]

Matters of Moment

I was not alone with these concerns. I would like to draw attention to some matters I was not aware of at the time. There were, indeed, rumblings among the African members of the police force which were shared by some of the senior white members.

A high-ranking policeman, Snr. Asst. Comm. Ted Sheriff, makes the comment:

> I inspected stations run by well-educated African policemen who were as equal to the task as their white colleagues. Their stations were maintained at a high overall standard. Furthermore, I visited an African Secondary School in Highfields African Township in 1961 when I was Member in charge of Harare Police Station and saw the high level of education being achieved by the African students. I realised that if a way was not made for African advancement and development they would join the growing nationalist movements. As a result of this experience, I wrote to Police General Headquarters (PGHQ) and enquired why Africans were not permitted to embrace the white ranking structures. After writing about eight letters over a six month period, PGHQ eventually replied that it was not Government Policy. Politicians merely stopped the process. Recruiting educated Africans needed to be supported by evidence that they were capable and competent to advance in rank. Should the country's leadership have adopted my recommendations and amended their policy of advancement for Africans serving in the forces, this could have been a watershed proving the government's intention of advancing Africans and drawn support away from discontent African nationalists. Instead, I fell out of favour with the hierarchy.[2]

Further concerns were expressed by a colleague, Dennis Anderson.[3] He recalls an SB course in Salisbury in 1972, around June, attended by senior detective inspectors during which he, and several others, asked Deputy Commissioner Peter Sherren if, and when, African members of the police force, with the educational and service qualifications, were to be integrated into the white rank structure and given the opportunity to command a station. They were concerned about the inequality of the rank structure and felt it was time for change. Sherren stated: "It was not the policy of the Rhodesian Front Government to advance African members beyond the present rank structure."[4] This reinforced the decision by the Government who rejected proposals for African advancement and integration proposed in the Packard Report in 1962.[5] This policy remained entrenched until 8 August 1978, when a confidential report from the BSA Police General Headquarters entitled *Accelerated Advancement of African Policemen: Promotions and Recruitment* was circulated.

The intention was to promote 12 African members to the rank of inspector from the Uniform Branch, the CID and SB before the end of 1978. In my view, this was clearly a panic response in light of the past RF policies that had now finally backfired to the detriment and future of the country.

1 Stapleton, T. (2011), pp. 5-6 and 85-86.

2 Ted Sheriff oral interview 16/12/2017.

3 At the time, D/Insp. Dennis Anderson was in charge of CID/SB, Marandellas (from 1971-1974). He then moved to CID Salisbury for three months before being transferred to Umtali as the District Criminal and Special Branch Officer.

4 Dennis Anderson email 27/1/2016.

5 Packard, Charles Douglas: *Report of the Survey of the British South Africa Police, 5 May 1962*, pp. 22-26; Assistant Commissioner Mike Edden's unpublished memoirs, Chap. 8; Stapleton, T. (2011), pp. 162-166.

Sherren himself was in favour of African advancement in the BSAP. Former Special Branch Officer for JOC Mt Darwin, Robin Harvey recalls: "In 1977, during open discussions with members of Nat.JOC. who flew into Mt Darwin on regular visits, the subject of African Advancement was raised. Commissioner Sherren stated: 'It was high time there was African Advancement within the BSAP.' This got the nod of approval by those attending."[1]

After Ian Smith addressed parliament on 29 June 1973, making it clear that a settlement with Britain was remote, Supt. Brian Chalk from Special Branch, Salisbury, submitted a top secret report to SB Headquarters under reference XYS 70002/23 the same day. He recommended various courses of action to resolve Rhodesia's political problems which included adequate opportunities for Africans to advance in all spheres. The alternative he suggested was a bloody conflict in the coming years.[2]

For some years the army had been facing similar problems. On 2 December 1967, the Army Chief of Staff, Maj. Gen. R.R.J. Putterill, proposed to commission Africans from the RAR who had previously served with distinction in Malaya and initial military operations in Rhodesia. However, the RF Minister of Defence, Lord Graham,[3] in the light of prevailing racial attitudes within the governing Rhodesian Front, refused the request.[4] Subsequent RAR personnel persisted in this matter. COs of 1RAR, David Heppenstall (1974~1976) and Mike Shute (1976~1978), both state: "We pressed for better service conditions for the RAR African soldiers. These included pay, promotion and accommodation. At that stage there was no hot water in the African soldiers' accommodation. These efforts were thwarted by Rhodesian Front policies."[5] In his annual report to the Regimental Association on 7 October 1977, Lt. Col. Mike Shute, CO 1RAR, raised the issue of African soldiers' (AS) pay and allowances as had his predecessors. This had been a bone of contention for many years. He said:

> The terrorist war really started in 1967. That certainly is the first time we suffered casualties against the CTs. This means that all our African soldiers with over ten years' service had been continually on operations except for leave, R & R and courses for ten years, and I think it goes without saying, really, those African soldiers have given ten years of damned fine soldiering yet what is their reward? After ten years they cannot re-engage with a gratuity like their ES (European Soldiers) counterparts. They are just expected to soldier on with no rewards or inducements. The pay for AS is quite dreadful and although promised a pay review two years ago, no change to pay and conditions has been forthcoming. [Author Shute's note: The following year's pay rise of 15% across the board, though welcomed by all AS, simply increased the differences in pay between ES and AS.]
>
> There are also many areas in trade pay and allowances, where for the same skills as ES – for example trackers – they receive a smaller allowance. [Author Shute's note: The advent of the non-discriminatory Selous Scouts allowance boosted the take-home pay of an African private soldier by over 35% and was the largest single inducement persuading RAR soldiers to apply for Selous Scout selection].
>
> The AS are also suffering, as many of you will know, by terrorist actions against their families in the TTLs. When this happens they just cannot afford, from their own resources, to move their families to a new TTL or urban area.[6]

Ultimately, the first African army officers were commissioned in 1977, another panic move and case of "too little, too late".[7]

---

[1] Robin Harvey oral interviews 25-27/2/2019.

[2] C/Supt. Brian Chalk: Unpublished memoirs.

[3] Lord Graham 7th Duke of Montrose. Later became Minister of Agriculture.

[4] Wood, J.R.T. (2012), Loc 20415.

[5] Dave Heppenstall and Mike Shute confirmation emails 15/7/2019 and 17/7/2019.

[6] Binda, A., Heppenstall, D. & Hopkins (2007), pp. 315-316.

[7] Stapleton, T. (2011), p. 182; Dave Heppenstall and Mike Shute email 15 and 17/7/2019.

The Rhodesian Special Air Service[1] had the identical difficulty. Maj. Brian Robinson[2] emphasises the point:

> During my command of the SAS, and around 1975~1976, I realised that I could not operate effectively without a "black" face under certain conditions and circumstances. Even with our "black is beautiful" makeup we used to use, it was impossible to mimic a black, we walk and behave differently in all our mannerisms. Our missions were consistently frustrated by the part played by the local population. Our groups crossing the Zambezi in the middle of the night would often be reported by local fishermen who would alert the local authorities. Parachute entries often ended in failure thanks to teenage herd-boys coming upon tracks they did not recognise. In among a hostile populace we were effectively fish out of water. I felt it vital to recruit blacks for the SAS so discussed the issue with Brigadier John Hickman who was at the time my Brigade Commander, probably about 1975/76. Brig. John Hickman agreed with me and the matter was discussed at Army/Prime Minister level. I was politely informed that Prime Minister Smith had turned down the suggestion as a nonstarter. I believe Smith said: 'I have got to have one unit I can trust completely', he wanted his SAS to remain white. No further discussion! Coincidently, at that very time I had allowed a coloured[3] to attend the SAS selection course. I recall him passing part of the course. However, I remember having to invent an excuse for not accepting him into the SAS which was very unfair. I cannot remember what excuse I gave the poor bloke. Without the support of the people the war was lost from the start, we lost the war and our country.[4]

As the war escalated during 1973, the OCC/JPS[5] considered forming an African militia to enable the rural population to defend themselves against terrorist attacks. However, this outlook was unpopular with both the military and the politicians, neither favouring the arming of the African population, while those serving in the army refused to seriously consider them a legitimate fighting force.[6] The RF Government already had some difficulty trusting their own African soldiers but were forced to increase their numbers with the closure of the Mozambique border and escalation of the war. This intentional lack of African advancement by the country's government was exploited by African nationalists as early as the 1950s.[7] ZANLA and ZIPRA directed propaganda to undermine the subservient position of African policemen and African Security Forces members in general.

During discussions with British Prime Minister, Edward Heath, in November 1971, Ian Smith's approach to African advancement in the police, army and civil service was made clear: "As far as the police and army were concerned there was no one in the ranks who was considered to be suitable material. With regard to the civil service, he would be far happier if more Africans would come for the more senior posts, but their veneer of civilisation was very thin and would need time to improve things."[8]

---

1 During the Rhodesian conflict, the SAS carried out 254 external operations (operations outside of the Rhodesian borders). Confirmed by Sgt. Colin Prain, C Sqn 22 SAS email 8/12/2016.

2 Commanding Officer, SAS from December 1972 to June 1978. Email 3/12/2016.

3 Coloured: A person of mixed race.

4 Brian Robinson email 8/12/2016.

5 Operations Co-ordinating Committee (OCC): Ian Smith's war council. The Joint Planning Staff (JPS) comprised men from the army, air force and CIO. Smith appointed one of his ministers in charge of the Nat.JOC which was staffed by his SF commanders or their deputies. "There was a daily meeting which started at 07h00 every day. First with the internal situation, and from this the planning team was tasked. This usually ended by 07h55 as Walls would be in his office to listen to the 08h00 SA News. This was followed by the special operations brief, a closed group of selected command officers, usually done by me. During these briefs, tasks would be given to the special operations planning team, if necessary. Conferences and planning briefs would then be scheduled as and when necessary." David Padbury emails 3/1/2019 and 31/3/2020.

6 Mike Edden's unpublished memoirs, email 30/11/2016.

7 Stapleton, T. (2011), *passim,* p. 159.

8 de Meneses & McNamara (2018), pp. 71-72.

In a speech to the House of Lords on 15 November 1965, Lord Gardiner revealed the root of the problem. He stated: "When Mr Smith was over here, we asked him whether, if there was United Kingdom help, he would increase the amount of African education. And he said, No. We believe in education for its own sake, because the African who is to some extent educated is more use to us economically than one who is completely uneducated. But we do not believe in bringing African majority rule nearer, and we certainly should not agree to African education being expedited for that purpose. The Rhodesian Government would think it wrong to accelerate the educational advance of the Africans simply in order to improve their political status in the community. Mr Smith said he must make it clear that the Government Party in Rhodesia did not believe in majority rule."[1]

Ironically, at a public meeting in Salisbury on 29 August 1976, Ian Smith finally conceded that there was indeed unjust racial discrimination in Rhodesia which offended the dignity of the people, and that this should not be tolerated. Discrimination which inferred that some of the people, because of their race or colour of their skin, were superior to others and entitled to enjoy certain privileges. He warned Rhodesians that failure to adapt to changes to their previous ways of life would be disastrous. (Associated Press SYND 29.8.76)

Patrols

As a unit, we engaged in two forms of rural CID/SB patrols. Those made by the African staff and others in my vehicle. The TTLs were inhabited by the Shona who were friendly, and we were always made welcome.

African detectives were deployed in the rural areas on foot or bicycle patrols for periods ranging between one to two weeks. Occasionally, the detectives would be armed with a .38 revolver, which was easy to conceal. His duty was to visit well-established informers, attempt to gain new recruits, visit the local chief, headmen and kraalheads and also mingle with the local people in their kraals to solicit information. Experience taught us that for the detectives to live among the local tribe was the most efficient method of obtaining various forms of information. This would include details concerning specific or general criminal activity, domestic issues, general gossip, and security intelligence. This was our method of maintaining contact with the local population.

On the other hand, my rural patrols, also an integral part of my duties, were carried out in a Land Rover accompanied by an African detective. These patrols were enlightening as we explored the remote regions of the country and l learned to understand the fascinating African culture in its undisturbed setting. This knowledge would prove invaluable in the war days that lay ahead. We conducted general patrols and combined the work of carrying out criminal investigations with enjoyable jaunts through the bush and visits to many business centres. These centres were dotted around the rural areas. Here cold beer in quart bottles could be bought and enjoyed to the sound of traditional music. What a pleasant way to end a day's patrol, rumbling along dusty roads, watching the golden sun set on a spectacular African evening, as country folk ambled home to kraals void of electric lights, yet peacefully ordered.

Everywhere I went on patrol was an expedition into unknown territory. I explored the vast area under our administration. This included the Makoni, Manyika and Chiduku Tribal Trust Lands, Buhera and Inyazura, across to Inyanga, including Ruda. An adventurer's paradise. Travelling along rural dirt roads was always a challenge, particularly in the rainy season, when often the rivers flooded making crossings treacherous or even impossible. I was to learn there are not many places a Land Rover could not be driven. These roads were well used by buses once or twice a week and by owners of business centres who generally owned a vehicle to transport their goods. Some school teachers, missionaries and wealthier locals also owned private motor vehicles. In this "traffic" were the various government service vehicles, including those of medical clinics and Internal Affairs with their numerous administration programmes. However, the general population, composed largely of poor peasants, either walked or used scotch carts, two-wheeled wooden carts hauled normally by a donkey or some other beast of burden.

---

[1] British Parliament Hansard: HL Deb 15/11/1965 vol 270 cc 228-413

One such patrol I made to the Honde Valley in 1974 was to investigate a spate of crimes at the Mtarazi Falls car park. These falls, the second highest in Africa and sixth highest in the world, are perched on the edge of the Eastern Highlands. Here the Mtarazi River plunges off the edge of the escarpment, falling powerfully, particularly during the summer rains, 762m down a two-tiered granite waterfall system to the Honde Valley below, where it joins the Pungwe River.

Mtarazi Falls is a tourist's attraction, drawing sightseers from around the world. However, as is often the case, foreign holidaymakers also attracted criminals lurking in the surrounding bush, waiting to take advantage of unsuspecting visitors who left their vehicles unattended and laden with valuables at the car park some 600m from the falls. All too frequently, impoverished local criminals would smash the car windows, plunder the contents of the vehicle which often included clothing, jewellery and personal belongings conveniently packed in "get-away" suitcases. Wallets stacked with local and foreign currency were also looted. However, it was fortunate that passports and other personal documents that had no value to criminals in the back-of-beyond were abandoned in this remote African setting.

My investigations identified the mastermind as living in a village on the banks of the Pungwe River which ran close to Rhodesia's eastern border with Mozambique in the valley below the falls, a distance of about 24km from the base of the falls. Access to the suspect's village was difficult. However, this and many similar obstacles were part of the adventure and privilege of being in the BSAP. One morning we set off on patrol in a Land Rover. I was accompanied by two African constables. We were determined to apprehend the suspect regardless of his whereabouts. Yet again, an adventurous journey into the wild African bush. In almost every respect I found myself reflecting on the thought that I was living the dream.

We set off on our journey following the road from the Inyanga highlands into the Honde Valley. This was a 20km tarred road which wound its way to our destination, dropping some 761m down the slopes of Mount Inyangani. The hot, humid climate supported abundant tropical vegetation, quite different from the lush grassy open spaces and pine-clad hills of the Inyanga district. As we reached the valley floor, the tarred road gave way to a familiar dusty route.

Eventually, we called in at Ruda Police Station. It was a small outpost situated near a gravel airfield. We introduced ourselves to the local authorities, announcing our intentions and then carried on with our journey. The route we followed was the picturesque Pungwe Scenic Road which meandered alongside the Pungwe River close to the Mozambique border.

Eventually, we arrived at our destination and parked the Land Rover along the side of the road. Our enclosed light-grey, long wheelbase Land Rover was covered with official police lettering and insignia which served as a deterrent against theft and break-ins. However, due to the declining security situation in the country this was to be the last time I would leave an official police vehicle unoccupied along the roadside nearby the Rhodesia/Mozambique border. Within a short space of time, I was to gain in wisdom in the nuances of war and this experience greatly altered my outlook and approach to future such journeys.

On this occasion we had to cross the 30m-wide Pungwe River on an arched rope swing footbridge. Two, two-inch thick ropes were suspended from tall trees on either side of the river, supporting a carefully woven rope net that stretched down to a gangway made from wooden planks cut from nearby trees. Clutching the shoulder-high main ropes, I cautiously entered the bridge. Gradually, I established my rhythm and, with each step, swayed and bounced to the other side 10m above the gently flowing river. Satisfied the bridge was safe, the two constables followed. We then walked about 8km in search of the suspect's village. Wearing shorts, long socks and *veldskoens* proved to be the appropriate apparel for the heat of the Honde Valley.

We had no difficulty in identifying the suspect's house, as we had prior information regarding its location. It was a double-storey brick home with a galvanised iron roof, in sharp contrast to the surrounding mud-and-thatch kraals. Although the suspect was absent on our arrival, we recovered much identifiable stolen property. Once we had gathered our evidence, we made our way back to our vehicle and returned to Rusape. Having identified the suspect, his details and description were circulated throughout the district and he was eventually arrested, charged and convicted. Our actions and subsequent conviction never stopped the thefts at the Mtarazi car park, but this outing proved yet another adventure in my career as a policeman. It was not too long before I returned to the Honde Valley under completely different circumstances.

Sergeant Bikiri: Attempted Murder

In 1975, an African man in a local beer hall accosted Sgt. Bikiri of the BSAP stationed at Buhera, while on a routine patrol. During the confrontation, the assailant wrestled Sgt. Bikiri's .38 service revolver from him and fired off two shots, before absconding. No one was injured in the shootings. Jock McCallum was keen to establish that the incident was not linked to insurgents. I was in the BSAP Rusape canteen with Lynette on a peaceful Sunday afternoon when Jock called me to say that a Police Reserve Air Wing (PRAW) flight had been arranged to convey me to Buhera early Monday morning in order to investigate this case. Bill Linfield, a former PRAW pilot and Commander of the Air Wing, clarifies the role of the PRAW: "The PRAW were a specialist Unit of the BSA Police utilised to perform basic support in the performance of Police duties. During the conflict they were adapted to a more active roll which included amongst other duties, that of transporting personnel, casualty evacuation, air reconnaissance, supply drops and providing top cover for civilian and Police vehicle convoys. The majority of aircraft in the PRAW were flown by the owners, however, other aircraft were from Charter companies and Flying Clubs. Contracts were signed between the Police and aircraft owner. Aircraft hire rates were paid according to aircraft make and size and pilots received their normal Police Reserve daily rate of pay. In the latter stages of the conflict PRAW aircraft were equipped with weapons for defence and aerial response."[1]

Although Buhera Police Station was only some 144km south-west from Rusape, a trip of about three hours on the dirt road that serviced Dorowa mine, flying was a more reliable means of transportation. The gravel road crossed a ford at the Sabi River which periodically flooded in the rainy season and was often impassable. It was frustrating getting to the river and being unable to cross.

Monday morning dawned and I was flown to Buhera. On landing, I was met by the duty patrol officer and driven to the police station. Jock McCallum had also arranged for a team of detectives to travel down to assist in the investigation and at midday we met together. While awaiting their arrival, I obtained statements from Sgt. Bikiri and the witnesses to the crime. Soon the accused was identified together with the kraal where he lived. When the team arrived, we drove to the beer hall in the attempt to gather additional evidence. The accused, it transpired, had made his way home. The following day we set off on foot patrol to find him. We walked from kraal to kraal, following the accused's journey home. We discovered that he had passed through each kraal. At this stage of the war, the locals assisted the police with their investigations. What proved interesting was that the further we walked into the TTL, the more suspicious the locals became of us. In due course, we found the accused's kraal, but he had been informed of our pursuit and fled. This was a fruitless yet enlightening walk of close on 24km in total, before our return to the beer hall.

Once our initial investigations were completed, we returned to Rusape. The magistrate at Rusape issued an arrest warrant for the suspect. Soon afterwards, we distributed the identity and description of the accused using the BSAP Uniform Branch, CID, SB and Ground Coverage, as well as the Internal Affairs networks, including the chief and his messengers, headmen and kraalheads. All stores in the district were alerted. Over and above their normal functions, rural stores were a gathering point for locals. They served as bus terminals while also operating as the local post office. Information of the whereabouts of individuals, movements of persons, local events and the likes filtered down to the local store. These venues served as a wealth of information. We relentlessly pursued the accused and were rewarded four months later when Jock McCallum called me one evening to inform me that the culprit hand been arrested at Gutu. We collected the accused the following day and brought him back to Rusape where he was detained in the police cells. When he

1 Bill Linfield email 8/5/2020.

appeared at court two months later, he was convicted of the attempted murder of Sgt. Bikiri and sent to prison.

It was this investigation that taught me the importance of keeping a regular up-to-date and accurate investigation diary. As a result, I proceeded to record every incident in this diary as they occurred. Jock McCallum demanded a high level of record keeping and I was to gain the benefit of his standards. I kept the diary current and ensured that no investigation or clues went missing as a result of a cluttered mind. In fact, this investigation and others I conducted resulted in my receiving a favourable annual efficiency report. Maintaining a daily diary became a habit and a natural part of my life. The investigation also helped me understand the communication systems in the rural area which were unique.

My normal criminal investigation work in our district meant that I spent a great deal of time in rural areas, particularly the Makoni TTL. I learned much about the local culture and traditions. It was intriguing observing the hive of activity around the remote business centres that was often a focal point of rural life. Once or twice a week the bus would arrive bringing family and friends from the city and towns, as well as provisions for the store, and mail which was held at the store for later collection. A distant cloud of dust announced the bus's arrival as it rambled along dusty, corrugated dirt roads, roof racks laden with all manner of property: bicycles, mattresses, beds, furniture, suitcases and other household items. In fact, if it was transportable, it would be secured to the bus's roof rack. Generally, the buses were late on arrival and often they would fail to arrive at all. This, however, seldom dampened the enthusiasm of the welcoming parties who would make merry either way, accepting life as it was. This was a local celebration, not limited to those expecting family, friends or mail. Everybody joined in.

With the buses came news from the towns that would soon be shared around an evening meal. It was traditional for families to sit around a fire at the feet of the elders and discuss events of the day. News from the local area, nearby villages and towns was relayed as was their oral history, traditions, spiritual matters, and forthcoming events. Births, deaths, sickness, the killing of a goat or cow, upcoming beer parties, domestic disputes and gossip were all eagerly related and shared. People told stories of events in their daily lives as information flowed, first among the family then, during the coming days, to neighbours and acquaintances. In this manner the information was blown, similar to that of a gentle breeze which blew to and fro, enflaming periodically like wildfire, when important news raced across the entire area.

Later, when the buses departed, taking with them friends and relations, mail, and maybe small gifts, they also took verbal stories freighted with the taste and panorama of home to distant towns and cities. I learned that this was the main channel for the distribution of news as there were very few phones and, of course, no mobile phones. Sending and receiving mail was a major and treasured event, much celebrated, and announced with glee to the recipients. These rural people were remote yet connected, isolated from Western culture, estranged from white Rhodesians but firmly bound together when family or communal disaster struck, help was needed or celebrations called for. News flowed freely around the TTL and to and from the cities. This stark contrast remains with me to this day.

Another significant impression that was implanted in me was that, when an individual or family came into possession of money, often by the hand of a traveller returning from the city, news soon spread that a person was "wealthy". Some time was spent broadcasting this fact to all and sundry, and the individual would visit the store on numerous occasions, to investigate the purchasing possibilities. The poor rarely had money for clothes, consequently they were inevitably shabbily dressed, often wearing the same threadbare clothing. These well worn items would need to serve as clothing for sometimes years on end. Thus, the purchase of new clothing was a significant event that called for announcement. Following this communication was the assurance that the purchaser was buying good-quality items, as they could ill afford to purchase items that would not last. I found the thrift and resourcefulness of these people quite simply inspiring. This process also removed suspicion that any new items had been stolen. In the same vain, Africans often spoke in a loud voice to ensure passing friends or strangers would not think they were being spoken about.

I would watch barefoot African children running and walking to school and other destinations and, on most occasions, they would need to cover considerable distances on foot. It amazed me that they were happy. They talked and sang as they made their way to their early-morning chores. Often, these tasks included toiling in schoolyard vegetable and flower gardens. Schools were frequently housed in the most primitive of buildings with the ratio sometimes one teacher to 30 or even 40 eager-to-learn children. As I saw it, the African children's singing was a natural and confident expression of their lives. Breaktimes were spent playing in barren, dusty fields where the boys played football with balls made from plastic bags and any other material that would take the shape of a rounded ball. To me it was a privilege to witness their fortitude and good humour. One evening, during a routine patrol, I came across a student studying by a candle's flickering light which danced in harmony with his breathing and the slightest change of the direction of the wind. It was a humbling sight which left its mark on me.

I could not reconcile the contrasts between the African's and white's way of life. The enormous disparity troubled me. For example, one day when on a police patrol we came across a Western-style wedding in a remote region of Makoni TTL. The bride was dressed in a beautiful white wedding outfit, the groom in a suit with the guests suitably attired. It was difficult to bring together that such a costly European tradition had spilled over into remote Africa. This was a celebration of note. I learned a great deal about the Shona culture in those early days at Rusape and often thought how fortunate I was to have been taught the Shona language and customs by Arthur Pendred while at school. It was beneficial and the African staff appreciated it.

I found that the Shona peasants had peace, joy, strong communal affiliation and fun despite their abject poverty and lack of the most basic requirements of electricity, running water and sanitation. They accepted their circumstances readily, and seemed to be in touch with life in a noticeably leisurely fashion. Their lives were unhurried, they had time at hand which was an elusive quality that evaded our busy cluttered Western minds. In my view, they were care-free people and, on occasions, I was envious. Working in remote Africa, I felt, was an honour and a privilege. The rural areas seemed unaffected by the war. On the other hand, we whites were living in a "dreamland". Unwittingly, we were about to be dragged into a revolutionary war that would know no bounds. Our role as policemen would change significantly.

My experiences in these rural areas helped mould me into a person who could easily relate to the African rural people. It did not change my love for my own culture or race but certainly helped me to understand how African culture operated. I learned first-hand how to work within it. This is what helped me achieve success in the BSAP, particularly operational work as the war arrived. While on patrol, I was able to keep contact with Lynette as she was employed as the radio operator in the police control room.

The family cottage David and I shared at Avondale, Salisbury.

COIN training, Horse Shoe Block, 1969. (L-R) Brian Perkins, author surveying a map and Rob Riedy.

Our full section, author 2nd left.

Author's pass-out parade, June 1969.

Receiving the Charl Viljoen Memorial Trophy and Canada Dry Shield for winning the Mashonaland U20 League, 1970.

B.S.A. Police Under 20 Rugby XV – 1970

Winners of the Canada Dry Shield and Charl Viljoen Memorial Trophy

Back Row (left to right): S. O'Donnavan; M. van Rensburg; A. Silva; F. Cleary; J. Dodd.

Centre Row (left to right): M. Thomas; ‡E. Robinson; ‡D. Lambourn; B. Pitt; G. Readings.

Front Row (left to right): ‡F. Varkevisser; Commissioner S. F. S. Bristow; *‡J. Padbury (Captain); Asst. Commissioner P. J. Robinson (Commandant Depot); ‡V. Roach.

Absent: ‡P. Little; ‡L. Howie; ‡M. Rees; ‡P. Schult; A. Sims; G. Janks; A. Furia; D. Bayley; J. Vorster.

* Rhodesia U/20. ‡ Mashonaland U/20.

BSAP U20 Rugby Team, 1970.
Author (captain), seated centre.

Sgt. Chiwasha with the Christmas tree 'stolen' from the member i/c.

CID investigations Inyanga district, 1975.

The author inspecting a flooding river prior to crossing in the Makoni TTL.

CID vehicle patrol 1976. Land Rovers were now mined-proofed.

River crossing. The Land Rover is not mine-proofed.

Armed CID rural patrols Rusape district 1976.

2 ~ ZANLA LIBERATES THE MAKONI

All the guiding principles of military operations grow out of the one basic principle: to strive to the utmost to preserve one's own strength and destroy that of the enemy.
Mao Zedong

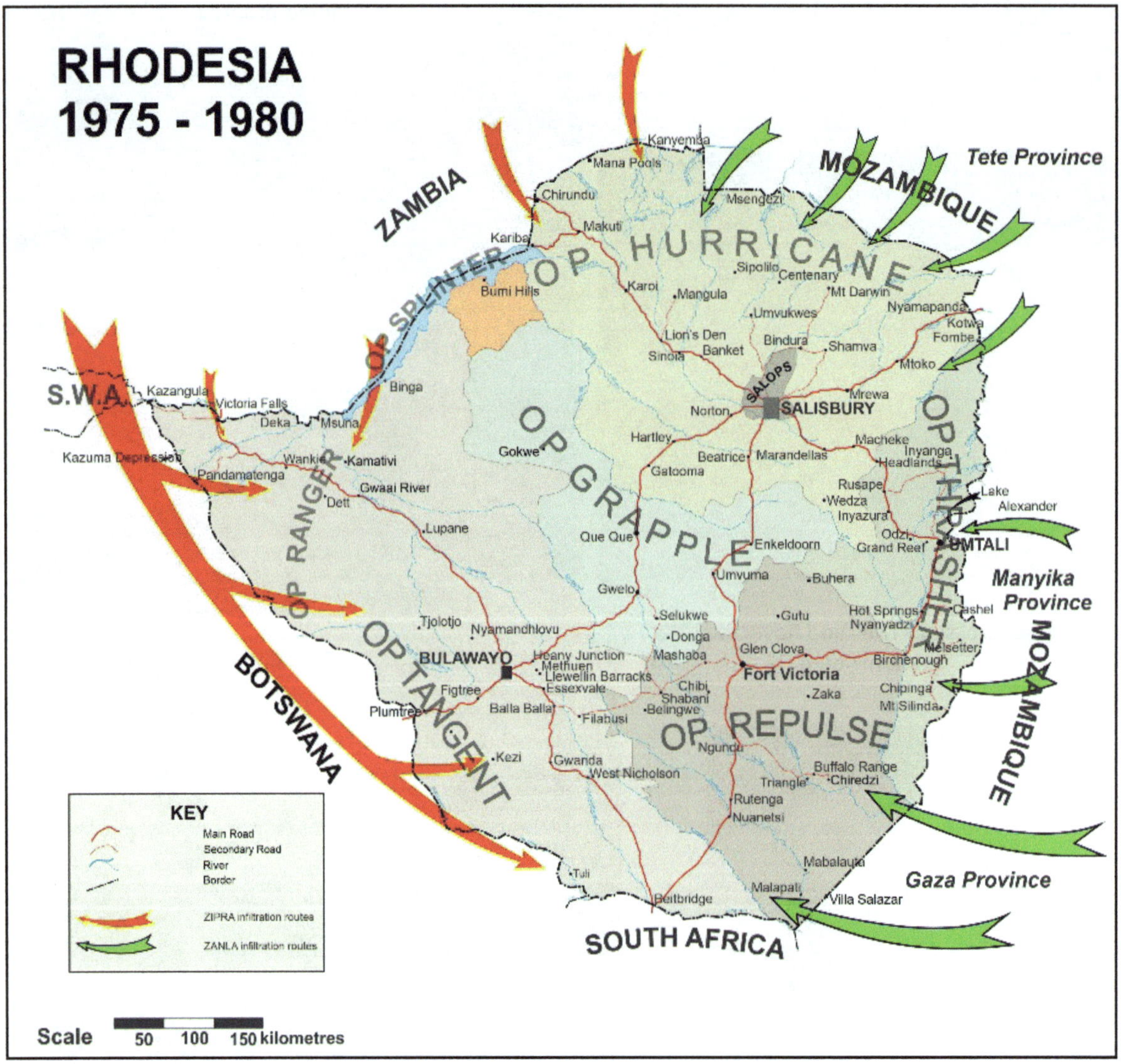

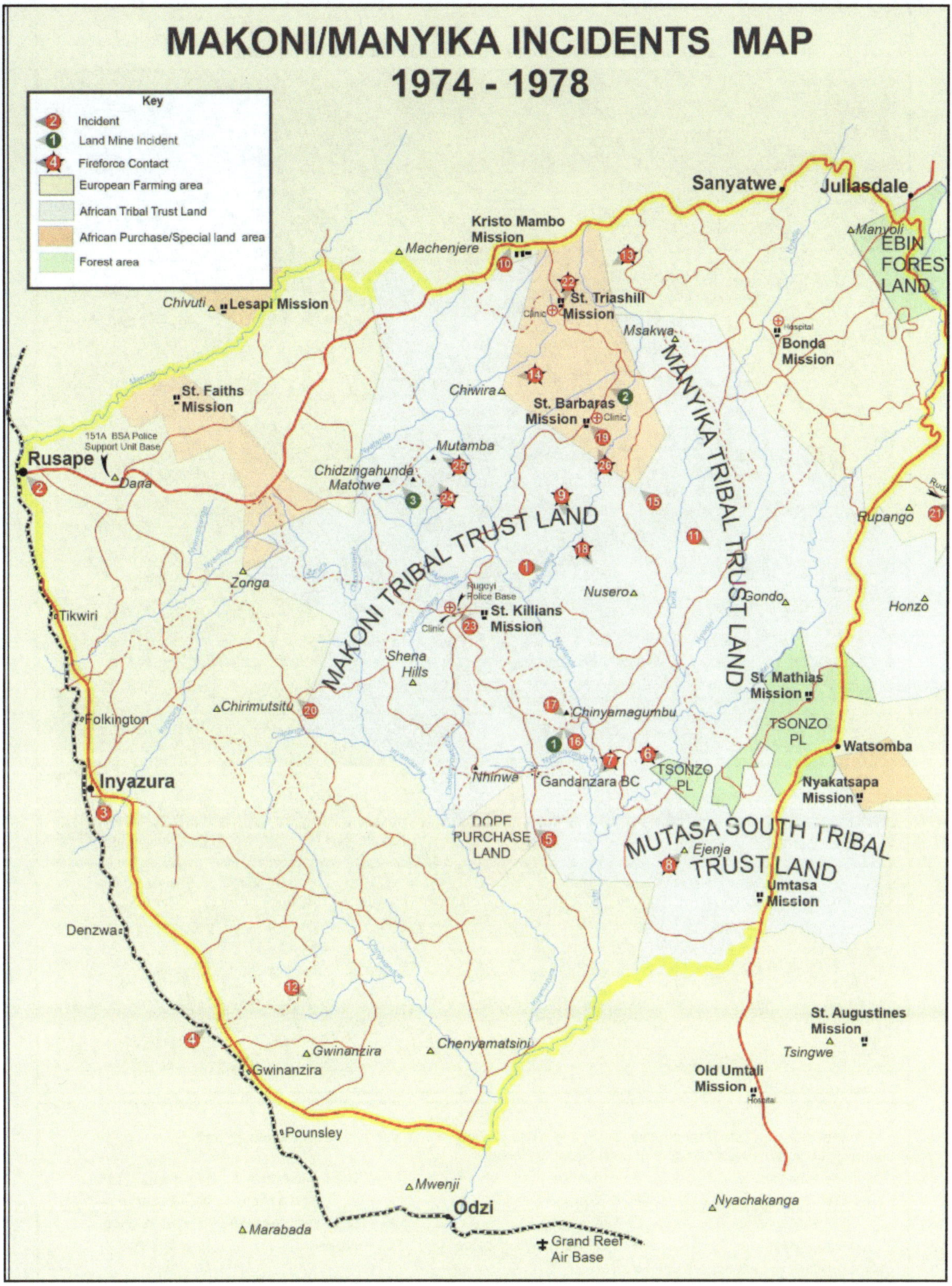

Note: This only reflects incidents discussed in Padbury's book, there were considerably more.

OP THRASHER
Salisbury Central Armoury - Ballistics Incidents Map - 1977

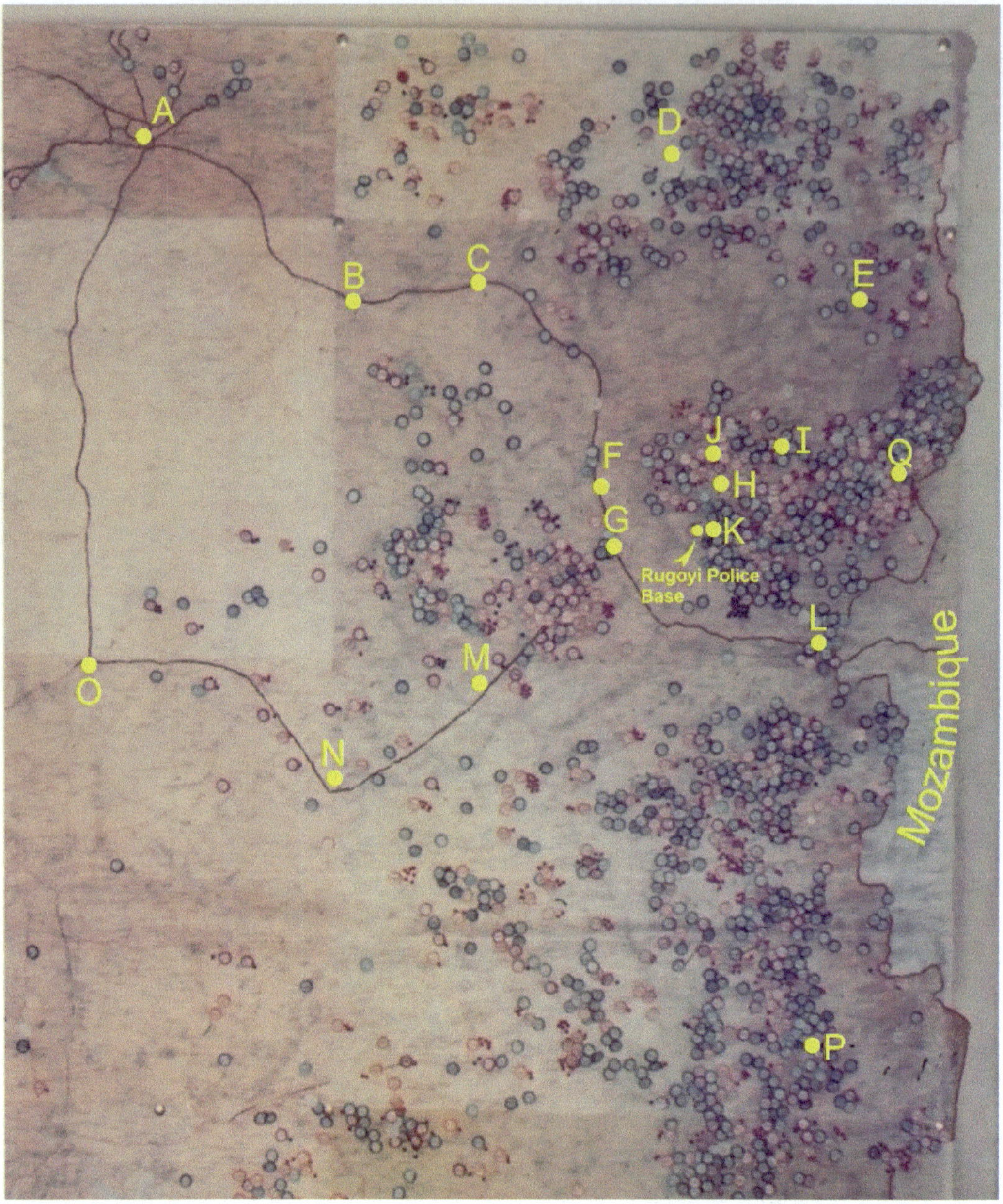

KEY

Incidents include white farm attacks, black and white civilian murders, civilian and Security Force ambushes, landmines and contacts with Security Forces.

A - Salisbury	E - Inyanga	I - Bonda Mission	M - Dorowa Mine
B - Marandellas	F - Rusape	J - St. Triashill's Mission	N - Buhera
C - Macheke	G - Inyazura	K - St. Killian's Mission	O - Enkeldoorn
D - Mayo	H - St. Barbara's Mission	L - Umtali	P - Chipinga
			Q - Ruda

Maps provided by ballistics expert Paul de Mattos.

Understanding the Tribal African

To understand how ZANLA intelligence networks functioned during the war, it is important to have a basic understanding of the traditions and culture of the rural African, as well as the system that was in place to administer and control them. In Chapter 1, I discussed how most of the African population ended up in the less arable, less accessible areas of diminished fertility when the seeds of discontent were sown. Relocated to regions called Tribal Trust Lands, they continued their culture and traditions.

Ministry of Internal Affairs[1]

Internal Affairs (Int.Aff.) was the intermediary between the Rhodesian Government and the African people. As such, Int.Aff. carried out their duties under instructions from the Rhodesian Government who gleaned their decisions from senior Int.Aff. officers. Success or failure of government policies lay squarely in the hands of the Government. Int.Aff. men on the ground were generally working diligently despite operating under very difficult circumstances.

The Rhodesian Government administered African affairs through the Ministry of Internal Affairs and divided Rhodesia into 54 districts, each administered by a district commissioner (DC) with his staff consisting of an assistant district commissioner, district officers, cadet district officers and African district assistants. These districts were in turn grouped under seven provinces which also had a governmental structure led by provincial commissioners. The provincial commissioners reported to the Secretary of Internal Affairs and then to the Minister.

The DC was considered a senior government official and ranked above all other officials in his district. Other members of staff included agricultural officers, co-operative officers, primary development officers, irrigation managers and sundry specialists. The DC was responsible for co-ordinating all of the government effort in his designated district.

Int.Aff. members were formally taught the customs and language of the people. Unfortunately, this did not translate to the rest of the Security Forces, who generally remained uninformed: a euphemism for ignorance. This was as I observed matters.

i. Responsibilities of the district commissioner and his staff

Int.Aff. was considered the eyes, ears and mouthpiece of the Rhodesian Government. When staff members were on patrol, they had the responsibility of making contact with the local African population, to determine their overall well-being, and to build up their confidence in the country's government. The DC's duties included:

1. Promotion of African local government through community boards and councils.
2. Ensuring that traditional leaders and courts functioned efficiently.
3. Registration of births, deaths and marriages. Once a person was appointed as a district officer, they became marriage officers.
4. Promotion of African agriculture through the Agricultural Development Fund.
5. Chairmanship of the district Civil Defence Organisation.
6. Presiding over African civil courts.
7. Attending white farmers' meetings.
8. Attending rural council meetings.
9. Attendance of other Government meetings as senior Government advisor.

Agricultural affairs were an integral part of the daily life of the DC's staff. Agricultural officers' and primary development officers' duties included developing effective contour-ridge systems,[2] good

[1] Main contribution taken from the Rhodesian Internal Affairs Website (https://dudleywall.webs.com/customsandbeliefs.htm) by permission of Dudley Wall, a former district officer in the Ministry of Internal Affairs, who served from 1972 to 1979 as a senior district officer. Dr J. Chakawa and I have made certain comments and observations from our own knowledge and experiences. Email 23/5/2015

[2] Contour ridges are small ridges, 15-20cm high, dug on a hillside to control soil erosion.

farming practices and cattle dipping.[1] The practice of contouring was resented by the locals in some areas of the country.

Serving as the "eyes and ears" of the government, the DC's staff also had a responsibility for collecting ground coverage information in conjunction with the BSAP Ground Coverage, which was a natural extension of the effort by the Rhodesian Government to obtain intelligence for security purposes. Int.Aff. fitted into this role. This responsibility increased as the war escalated. District commissioners and staff worked diligently at ground coverage, complemented by ceaseless patrolling by foot, bicycle and vehicle patrols to counter the efforts of the insurgents. Many district assistants died while on GC patrols collecting information on insurgent activities as did many BSAP members.

ii. ***Traditional tribal setting***

The rural African and their families, occupied what is commonly referred to as a traditional kraal. It is built with mud walls and thatched with savannah grass roofs. Normally one family with extended members would live in one kraal surrounded by a stockade for the animals. Animals kept in this area included cattle, goats and chickens. A communal kitchen occupied the central position in the kraal and nearby was a granary to store the maize harvest. A village is a conglomeration of households under the supervision of a kraalhead known, in Shona, as *sabhuku*. However, close relatives can also constitute a village of their own. For example, Gasura village in Hurungwe near Mahwada is made up of people with the same surname.

Stepping into rural areas was like entering another world. The people were, it seemed to me, more in touch with each other and aware of local current events. Little went unnoticed by the locals. They carried out daily chores with seemingly monotonous routine yet had an uncanny ability to remain peaceful and content. An approach to life achieved by facing reality, accepting one's lot, being present to the moment and realising things were unlikely to change. All news rippled throughout the TTLs.

Customs and beliefs had been established by the people over many years and passed down from generation to generation by word of mouth. Village elders would sit around the evening fire in the centre of the village, or at a *dare* (men's gathering), and share stories of ancestors and the ways in which they conducted themselves. Families and relatives from the village listened and absorbed this information. Since almost all of the stories were never written down, the next generation added some embellishments to suit the situation. Customs that developed from this communal gathering became customary law for the African. If individuals, or groups, deviated from these laid-down customs, the ancestral spirits would take offence with ominous consequences for the offenders.

Africans, generally speaking, were bound together by strong family bonds that were enhanced by customary law and the spirits of the ancestors who possessed the elders. Even following death, it was believed the ancestors had a direct influence over the day-to-day happenings of village life.

In tribal/communal areas the chief (sometimes known as *mambo*, *changamire* or *ishe* in ChiShona or *iNkosi* in SiNdebele) is the most important person. He is appointed by birthright as well as the approval of the people and also the spirit mediums of the local area. The chief has three main roles to play within the community: spiritual, judicial and administrative.

Shona chieftainship is based on a hereditary system known as "collateral succession" whereby the appointment is passed on to the firstborn son. When the firstborn son of the serving chief dies, the position of chief is inherited by the oldest male of the chief's youngest brother. Following his death, the position is inherited by the next oldest surviving male of the next brother and so on. In time, it is sometimes difficult to determine the next chief in succession, hence the intervention of tribal spirits. The spirit of the first chief will be consulted and his advice followed in determining the succeeding male chief.

While, culturally, chiefs inherited their positions from their fathers and held the office in perpetuity, to their chagrin they still required governmental sanction in terms of Section 4 and 17 of

[1] Dipping prevented tick infestations and tick-borne diseases in Rhodesia.

the African Affairs Act by the Governor. Following this appointment, they were considered government officials. They held office at the pleasure of the Governor and contingent on good behaviour and general fitness. Between 1928 and 1965, 32 chiefs were deposed by the government for various reasons, including unsuitability, drunkenness or criminal convictions. In 1951, 89 out of approximately 323 chieftainships were abolished. Of the 217 appointed chiefs in 1965, 188 of them, with a following of over 500, received an annual salary of £420. The remaining 29, with lesser followings, received an income of £240 annually. Fifty-four chiefs received personal allowances ranging from £6 to £240 per annum. Allowances depended on whether they co-operated with the government and had a satisfactory record. For each court case heard in their tribal courts they received five shillings. In 1961, the Council of Chiefs was created and the Provincial Assemblies of Chiefs formalised, enabling the government to consult them on legislative measures affecting the African people. Edgar Whitehead's government policy was to build the chief's position to offset the growing threat from African nationalist leaders. In 1965, the government's view was that, despite the absence of any institutionalised consultation with their people or any formal device parallel to the "vote", the chiefs did not express personal views, but only expressed views after consultation with their people. Chiefs were charged with duties of tax collection, prevention of crime in their tribal areas and oversight of the general good conduct of Africans under their charge.[1]

Shonas believed it necessary for a leader to reach maturity. With age comes wisdom and respect, so older people are often appointed as leaders. In the hierarchy of tribal life, the next most senior leader is known as the headman (*sadunhu*). He oversees a smaller segment of the chief's people living in his vicinity. Their appointment was approved by the Secretary for Internal Affairs acting on "chiefly" advice.[2] Under his authority were the village kraalheads. Some headmen were formerly chiefs and later demoted by the colonial administration. Chiefs and headmen were charged with ensuring good conduct of Africans under their care and with the duty of notifying all crimes in their area to the district commissioner. Kraalheads' responsibilities included the reporting of crime, the arrival of newcomers in their area and the unauthorised construction of buildings and farming activities. Messages between people and chief were carried by the chief's messenger. These African messengers were government "non-traditional" employees charged with conveying messages to chiefs and headmen from the DC.[3] They also conveyed messages from the chief to his people.

iii. ***Spiritual Affairs***

It was my observation that spiritual awareness and worship are two of the most powerful influences on indigenous Africans. It is through these mediums that Africans regulated their daily lives and by which tribes, clans and villages are controlled. It is also through the dominating factors of superstition and suspicion that many Africans are governed. Regrettably, few white Rhodesians understood this, which was to their disadvantage as they soldiered in the war.

Regarding religious deities, Shona people believe in a "supreme being" which they refer to as *Mwari*. Among the Ndebele, this being is known as *Mlimo*. There are "important spirits" who are subordinate to *Mwari* and occupy the bodies of human beings (mediums) on occasions. These "important spirits" include Chaminuka, Nehanda, Nyamuswa and Nehoreka and are all capable of producing rain. These spirits have never taken on human form. Tribal spirits however are ancestral and were human in the past. The spiritual world is a vital aspect of African life. Many still contact their family members and other deceased through spirit mediums. These interactions are selected based on the appropriateness of their relationship. A spirit medium is known as a *svikiro/swikiro/mhondoro* (depending on dialect). Where insurgents operated in an area, they placed great importance on having a good relationship with the spirit mediums and sought them out for their blessing and approval to operate in their area. If they could get the spirit mediums "on side", the general support of the locals would follow. This was partly due to fear of retribution from the spirits

[1] Palley, C. (1966), pp. 476-482.
[2] Ibid.
[3] Ibid.

who could be invoked by the mediums if they failed to support the insurgents. Nehanda's spirit played a role in the same way. The spirit of a person was believed to be passed on from family member to family member down the generations and, because Nehanda was a powerful medium, this was a focus of the uprisings in the early days. The medium possessed by Nehanda's spirit in the bush war held significant power as far as the insurgents were concerned and they did invoke the spirit to gain support of the people. In my opinion the Rhodesian SF did not understand the significance of gaining the support of spirit mediums.

When consulting the spirits, the *svikiro* falls into a state of trance. The *mhondoro* will then communicate through the *svikiro* to family members at a special gathering. This spell is induced by concentrating on the matter needing to be dealt with in a small gathering of those who wish to either pass on or receive a message from the ancestral spirits. The use of tribal medicine or other items of sacred value may be used in this ceremony. This would include the "throwing of bones" (*kukanda hakata*) which empowers the medium to diagnose the problem.

Family spirits, *mudzimu* (singular)/*midzimu* (plural) are important in daily life because they are responsible for making sure that the family are in good health and are not struggling with emotional, material, relational and spiritual issues incurred through daily living. In turn, the family must appease the spirits. This placating would entail regularly consulting with them in matters requiring decisions and communicating on all family affairs. On an important occasion, the family would sacrifice an animal to celebrate the favours the spirits provide. The tribal spirit is responsible for the welfare of the tribe and must not be neglected. This being is powerful and could send bad fortune to those who displease him. These ancestral spirits are worshipped by their followers and are consulted on a regular basis on all aspects of daily living. The vital link in African spiritual matters is the spirit medium.

In fact, there are numerous spirits that play a role in the everyday life of the African. One such spirit is known as a *shave*/*shavi*. This spirit is a lost soul who has not had the customary tribal rites at death. Collectively, they wander around until such time as they find a suitable human being in which they can reside. A *shave* spirit may inhabit a host's body leading to that person performing deeds which may be quite out of their ordinary behaviour. An example is where such a host displays extraordinary mental and physical skills which they, in the normal course of life, do not possess. For example, should an individual be normally shy and withdrawn he or she would suddenly become an excellent storyteller. Many of the stories will be from the *shave* lifetime. It could be the person begins to speak in a totally different language because he or she is possessed by the spirit of a person of a different tribe. Such incidences will be noticed by the people and the claim made that the haunted person is possessed by a *shave* spirit, which allows them to perform a skill which may be extraordinary. Some *shave* spirits may not necessarily be human as they may have origins in an animal. At times, special gatherings are held where they are given the liberty to take possession of the host's body. At these events vigorous dancing and trance-like behaviour takes place.

Another African spirit which is given attention and respect is the *ngozi*. This is the spirit of a person who may have been badly treated while alive or may have some grievance and wishes to take revenge. Such spirits can be dealt with by diviners who will undertake a ceremony to exorcise the *ngozi*, at a price. Diviners are empowered to perform these rituals, thanks to their knowledge of the spiritual world. They may also be possessed by a more powerful yet benevolent spirit.

iv. ***Witchcraft***

An additional influence which is closely allied to the African spiritual world, is that of witchcraft. Witches and wizards *muroyi* (singular)/*varoyi* (plural) are powerful people and may be considered an enemy of the local African tribe, as they have the ability to cast spells and inflict evil on an individual or even a group. They are also known to travel on the backs of hyenas at night and to eat corpses should they so desire. Protection from the *varoyi* may be obtained by undergoing a consultation with a *svikiro* to invoke the protection of ancestral spirits.

African spirituality views any form of perceived bad luck, death or sickness or other disaster as not simply a matter of chance. For the African, there is mostly a reason to the set-back with the tendency being that of aggrieving the ancestors by neglecting to conduct a specific tribal ritual. Thus, the afflicted spirit would need to be appeased. The view could also be that an evil spell has been cast by an individual with malicious intent requiring the services of a *muroyi* to remove the wicked threat. A *svikiro* may conduct a ritual to identify the witch. In such instances, once the individual has been determined, punishment invariably follows.

In African tradition, identifying a guilty individual involves a process of three customs. These are known as *Muteyo*, *Nyikisa* and *Rupadza*. *Muteyo* finds the accused drinking a potion made from poisonous bark and roots. If he or she survives consuming this concoction, they are pronounced innocent. *Nyikisa* takes place when the suspect is required to retrieve a small stone from the bottom of a pot of boiling water while still placed on a fire. The accused must retrieve the stone without being scalded to establish innocence. *Rupadza* comprises placing one's tongue on the metal blade of a *badza* (hoe) which has been heated over a fire. If the individual's tongue is not burnt, the accused is declared innocent. Interestingly, there is a similar Biblical procedure to establish guilt in adultery: Book of Numbers, Chapter 5, verses 11~31.

v. ***Herbs and Healing***

Generally, Africans believe illness is due to those still alive upsetting the *midzimu*. The *nganga* is a central member of the community. He or she is able to cure many ailments and diseases by means of superior knowledge passed down the generations. They are also considered protected by an ancestral spirit who possesses them in a trance and provides the necessary recipe when called on to blend a concoction of herbs to treat a patient. Such *nganga* can also banish evil spirits or provide a charm which will protect the wearer from various evils and mishaps.

vi. ***Marriage***

Marriage is essential for Shonas as they believe it is only in marriage and having children that they can continue the family lineage. It guarantees the ancestral spirits continue to exist and have the living worship them. In the view of the Shona, this is the sole means of continuing a peaceful life. Women possess the mysterious means necessary to ensure life continues but, despite this, they have no say in tribal politics or any other serious matters. The woman's power lies in her ability to encourage, persuade or to sometimes goad men into action.

Marriage also ensures that two separate families become a closer unit. The marriage contract is between both families and not just the individual newly-weds. Should a husband and wife quarrel, both families will intervene to end the dispute and ensure mutual agreement.

When a man decides on marriage, he will begin his search for a suitable partner. This relationship will be initiated by open public meetings. These encounters will possibly occur on occasions such as cattle-dipping day or visits to the local market. Once the man decides on his marriage partner, he will inform his family so that arrangements may be made for the two families to commence negotiations which will make the relationship official. The first step is the appointment of an intermediary (*gwevedzeri*) who will visit the young lady's family to establish whether her feelings are mutual. A small gift, considered a "love token", may be taken by the intermediary when the first visit takes place. The bride-to-be indicates her approval by touching the token (a procedure known as *ruvunzo*). She may also accept it as a preliminary wedding-day gift (*rubvumo*). Once done, both families will be aware of the future bride's view of the proposed marriage. The future son-in-law (*mukuwasha*) and his family then negotiate an amount to be paid for the bride. This is commonly known as *roora/lobola*. The amount could be a combination of cattle, other livestock and cash. Once the final amount has been settled on, the woman joins her husband's family. The *roora* is paid on the understanding that the wife bears children.

In more recent years, modern marriage customs have been embraced and Western-style weddings fully accepted and practised. The most important duty of the new wife is to produce children, thus ensuring the family line may continue and the ancestral spirits remain for generations to come. This is a brief description of the premarital procedure and does not include the wedding day itself. I have not dealt with other matters related to married life, such as the naming of children, settling of family disputes, divorce and so on.

vii. ***Births and Deaths***

Children are a vital component of the Shona family unit. Among other duties, sons bear the responsibility of continuing to settle their fathers' debts, while daughters till the land, fetch and carry water. Should a young wife be unable to bear children, both families are cast into a state of calamity. When a married woman becomes pregnant for the first time, she returns to her home as the firstborn must be born at her parents' home. Once the child is delivered, word is sent to the father who is then called upon to visit the first arrival of his family. He then travels to his father-in-law's home but, on arrival, may need to wait a day or two before permission is granted for him to see his first child. However, as the biological father, he has custody and full rights over the child from the onset.

Should a married woman commit adultery and have a child by another man, it would not be considered such a disaster. These children are often deemed to belong to the husband as he and his family have paid *roora/lobola* for the woman. The Shona believe it is "cattle and not men who beget children". In their view, this justifies the *roora/lobola* system. Notwithstanding, the father of the illegitimate child is traditionally expected to meet certain expenses related to his child. A further payment may be made to the husband of the woman which then indicates that the husband acknowledges the parental rights of the third party. This does not mean that the child leaves its mother. The child remains with the mother until it is old enough to leave the home. Another payment must be made by the biological father to the husband as compensation for rearing the child. A husband seldom acknowledges that his wife had taken a lover and that the liaison produced a child, unless he was absent from home and wife at the time of conception!

Sons remain the responsibility of their parents until they marry and establish a home of their own. Daughters also remain within the family until they marry. If a daughter has a premarital physical relationship with a man, her father is entitled to sue for reimbursement whether a child is born or not. The father of the daughter is, in the view of the Shona, entitled to compensation following this out-of-wedlock bond. If a marriage follows this relationship, the traditional *lobola* needs to be negotiated and agreed on by both families.

Dr Chakawa comments on Shona deaths: "When a child is born, the community celebrates. Women in particular bring presents. Death is not quite welcome. It is a worrisome enemy who visits uninvited. Whenever a person dies, there are procedures to be followed. The cause of the death has to be established. Usually the body is examined by elders in case there was foul play. Two to four days are spent mourning. Relatives and friends come to bid farewell to their departed colleague. The dead is then buried in a grave among relatives. Ancestors are informed and if not a natural death, they are pleaded with. If that person was killed, revenge is requested. After a year, a ceremony is undertaken to bring the spirit of the dead person to protect the family. That is done only for the married. In relation to the war, burial was not done properly if at all. The spirits of the dead continue to plague their families. They are demanding decent burials and ceremonies."[1]

viii. ***Parentage***

In the family hierarchy, there exists close ties between children and their father (*baba*) and his siblings. If there are three sons in a family and the middle son marries and has children, those children will consider all three brothers as their father. This is due to the Shona male believing the bloodline from father to son is pure and not connected to the lineage of the mother. Each of the three sons is addressed as "father". *Baba mudiki* will be the youngest of the three and *baba mukoma* the eldest.

---

1 Dr J. Chakawa WhatsApp discussion 10/3/2019.

ix. General Behaviour and Manners

Everyday courtesy and politeness are governing principles of the Shona and Ndebele. Common civility was, during my years in Rhodesia, to some extent different from that of European cultural norms. Some minor examples are as follows. Africans fit into a hierarchy of seniority. If one considers another senior to him or herself, being junior he will sit without being invited, however at a level in which the more senior is elevated. This is a mark of respect showing the more senior within the community the respect due and that he has command over the subordinate.

It is the view of the African that, during a general discussion, a junior-ranking individual, whether by youth or status, does not make eye-contact when addressed by one considered senior or superior. To make eye-contact with one considered in higher standing, is inappropriate. The lower-ranking individual directs his gaze downwards in a deferential manner.

When receiving a gift, both hands will be extended in a cupped fashion to receive whatever is passed on from one to the other. Alternatively, the right hand will be supported at the wrist by the left hand. This serves to indicate that what is being received is valuable, whether in fact this is the case or otherwise. The gesture is that both hands are required to accept the gift. Men will clap their hands in a cupped fashion with fingers extended forward prior to extending their hands to receive a handout (*kuita gusvi*). Women cross their hands to form a hollow in the palm when they clap their hands (*kuita nondo*).

When men sit around the communal fire at mealtimes, they will partake from a communal pot of *sadza*. Hands are washed before and after the meal in a container of water provided by the young girls. The meal will also include a pot of gravy and relish (*usavi*). The right hand is used to take some *sadza*, roll it into a ball, and then make a small indentation allowing the diner to dip it into the *usavi* to scoop some gravy before consuming it. Africans consider the left hand to perform unclean tasks. It would be an insult to use the left hand during a meal or the giving and receiving of gifts or hand-outs.

For the African, litotes and hyperbole are also aspects of communal life. For instance, if one asks the distance from a particular village, one will be told it is "not that far". This standard response is made even in the event of the destination being over 50km ahead. This anomaly is due to the African believing it is polite to tell a person what they want to hear, not what is factual. Alternatively, when livestock meanders into a vegetable garden, the individual who witnessed the incident will report to the garden owner that the entire patch of vegetables has been consumed. When the owner investigates, he may discover that only one or two vegetables have been eaten. The rationale behind this reasoning is that the garden owner will be relieved to learn that the damage is less than initially feared.

Africans consider it polite when passing two individuals engaged in a conversation, not to walk on the outside of the two but rather between the individuals. This is considered civil as it shows that the passer-by has no malicious intentions towards either of the two.

x. Routine and Chores

For the rural African, there is a disciplined, ordered routine of daily chores for which each member of the family is responsible. This pattern of life became essential to understand because when insurgents were in either a specific kraal, or in the neighbourhood at large, we detected subtle nonconformities to these patterns. Recognising these deviations, helped discern whether insurgents were present in an area or not.

A standard routine in an African village is that elders in the kraal are usually first to awake before sunrise. Younger boys and girls usually arose shortly after sunrise. They would linger longer in the comfort of beds if it was the rainy season. The mother would rise early to prepare food and warm water for the children who were school-going. At times these preparations included catering for the father either leaving or returning from work.

Daughters-in-law, *muroora* (singular)/*varoora* (plural) assisted by the girls, would sweep the kraal area in the mornings. This duty would rarely be undertaken by the mother as she had other chores to attend to. This discipline also helped establish if any SF had visited the kraal or surrounding area during the night, or at any other time. It also ensured that visiting insurgents' spoor was swept away once they left the village. Often, footprints leading into a kraal would disappear, confirming the kraal's inhabitants' complicity with insurgents.

Preparing meals was generally the responsibility of the more mature women. Young girls (*vasikana*) did not typically cook often because the men preferred to eat meals prepared by their women. Elder women infrequently cooked unless living alone. Firewood was collected by the girls who also ensured pots were clean and the firewood was readily available for their mother's cooking. However, when the scotch cart was used, the boys and young men participated.

Most meals were cooked over an open fire with various pots in use: one for *sadza*, the other for meat, with another used for relish. Traditionally, *sadza* was served on a plate and eaten by hand. Meat, on average, was eaten twice a week. Goat and other livestock were eaten as well as mice during the dry season, along with other small rodents. When slaughtered, cattle would be shared among the entire community. Many Africans living near game parks would also poach animals such as pigs (*nguruve* or *njiri*), elephants (*nzou*), buffaloes (*nyati*) and duikers (*mhembwe*).

In African custom, young boys were mostly despatched to the nearby business centres to collect provisions. These business centres were often a considerable distance from the kraal unlike the modern city convenience stores which are frequently a short distance from home. Young girls, as a common practice, did not run errands but rather assisted their mothers with routine household chores. Fathers were generally not sent on errands as they were much slower and might not return in time.

In most African rural areas, it was the father's responsibility to prepare the garden for his wife (or wives), buy provisions for the farming season and pay for his children's education. He was also in control of the construction of huts and supervising everyday family affairs. When necessary, he dug the family well to provide water and participated in communal activities such as funerals, general political affairs and other social functions.

In addition to cooking, the mother's responsibilities included weeding, sweeping, cleaning and fetching water. Younger girls generally collected water from boreholes (*zvibhorani*), wells (*matsime*) and rivers in the mornings and evenings, using buckets (*migomo*). The girls were also responsible for watering the gardens. The women were responsible for washing clothes.

The boys' main responsibility was shepherding cattle and livestock. In addition, they hunted for small game such as mice (*mbeva*), birds (*shiri*) and hares (*tsuro*) for the pot. In this way, they developed excellent natural bushcraft skills, particularly tracking. These skills were utilised in the search of evidence, such as footprints left by Security Force patrols and OPs, when they drove their cattle and goats over the mountains and kopjes specifically in search of the SF.

Among the Africans, elders would preside over communal courts and assist with herding cattle, treating the ill, building huts and weeding. One of their most important functions was that of serving as custodians of their culture.

From a social point of view, African beer was brewed purely for the sake of enjoyment while, at the same time, raising some funds and the important function of appeasing the spirits. In most cases, Africans retired to bed at an early hour.

xi. ***Conclusion***

In my view, the customs of a person make them what they are. These customs define one's world view, shapes and moulds one's character and moral code. They establish core values of society and need to be respected. Over the years, customs are changed and adapted to suit the circumstances. The basic values, however, remain the same. Today, in my opinion, modern Africans have adopted many Western ways and have incorporated them into their traditions. At one time, African women would never wear trousers or short skirts. Today such Western dress is the norm among the younger generation.

The chief's court settled affairs of the tribe. On occasions he met with his headmen and kraalheads, particularly when important social, economic and political issues affecting the tribe were to be discussed. Criminal matters were handed over to the police. Chiefs' messengers carried news and information across the TTL, either on foot or bicycle. These paid messengers formed part of the Rhodesian intricate intelligence networks. African district assistants knew their areas intimately and provided an effective network of informers. The staff of Int.Aff. stations became increasingly valuable as an early-warning system and were often called on to provide information on an area and its local population. They also served as guides and interpreters for various units of the armed forces.

This unique way of life was disrupted and changed as ZANLA insurgents returned to Rhodesia from their training camps in Mozambique, and infiltrated and occupied the TTLs. Insurgents politically motivated the various populations to reject white authority in their quest to achieve civil disobedience and the breakdown of law and order. This destabilisation of local inhabitants was necessary and created an environment in which to impose their authority (martial law) over the tribal system, thereby disempowering the authority of the chiefs. In the process many chiefs, headmen and kraalheads were beaten and often put to death by ZANLA (and ZIPRA). Internal Affairs found it increasingly difficult to function as the war escalated. At stake was the decay of the traditional African culture.

ZANLA Operational Strategies Change

In 1971, it became clear to ZANU national chairman Herbert Chitepo[1] that direct confrontation with the Rhodesian forces would not be a successful military strategy. The Commander of ZANLA, Josiah Tongogara, had been trained in 1966 at Nanking Academy, Peking. He became an expert in mass mobilisation, strategies and tactics.[2] It was clear to Chitepo and Tongogara that the Rhodesian armed forces were militarily better trained, disciplined and organised to withstand an armed invasion. In addition, Smith's Government had the decisive advantage of airpower and support. Their intelligence networks were also vast, organised with well-placed informers in the rural and urban African societies. In rural areas, Special Branch and Ground Coverage duties were performed on foot and bicycles by African policemen who kept close contact with informers. These patrols were well structured and all information documented on return to the BSAP Stations. The BSAP were capable of detecting any change in the political views and attitude of locals, so we thought at the time. At this stage of the developing war, insurgents entering Rhodesia were eliminated by the SF's overwhelming superior military strengths and mobility. These early successes ensured that the general support of the rural African people was maintained.

Chitepo introduced the classical Maoist strategy of rural mobilisation using political motivation[3] which would have a lasting effect on the tribal system. Political motivation used the method of creating the awareness of grievances among the African population and assuring them that removal of white colonialists would open the gates for nationalist empowerment when their grievances would be addressed.[4] To a large percentage of the country's African population, the inequality maintained by the existing regime was obvious, dating back to 1894. Chitepo had learned that political support of the people was vital and preceded military operations. Once the support of the people had been achieved, the insurgents could safely, as Mao Zedong states: "move among the people as a fish swims in the sea,"[5] protected from the SF. ZANLA recruits were, first and foremost, indoctrinated politically. This inspired them to fight and possibly die for these political objectives.[6] The battle for Rhodesia would be fought from the TTLs where ZANLA (and ZIPRA) established a permanent presence. In military terms, the TTLs became operational areas which I later considered to be the Ground of Tactical Importance (see Chapter 11).

---

[1] Chitepo: The first African barrister in Southern Rhodesia, leader of ZANU until assassinated by a car bomb in Lusaka, Zambia, 18/3/1975.

[2] Martin, D. (1981), p. 11.

[3] Sadomba, Z. (2011), pp. 11-12; Flower, K. (1987), pp. 121-122 and 136-137; Martin, D. (1981), p. 13.

[4] Ranger, T. (1985), Chap. 5, pp. 178-179.

[5] Zedong, M. (2010), p. 49.

[6] Ranger, T. (1985), Chap. 5.

At the time, there was considerable political and military experience among African nationalist movements spread across the African continent opposing colonialism. Knowledge gained from these revolutions was being passed on to Rhodesian nationalists. These countries included the Congo, Kenya, Algeria, Mozambique, Angola, Guinea-Bissau, Eritrea, Tanzania and, as was to be expected, the unfailing support of the Organisation of African Unity. Countries such as China (ZANLA) and Russia (ZIPRA) also provided military advisers and armaments. ZANLA and ZIPRA were not alone!

In keeping with Chitepo's changed strategy, when entering new operational areas in the TTLs, political meetings and movements from one area to another were undertaken under the cover of darkness, to avoid detection. ZANLA political commissars laboured tirelessly in these areas, their pre-eminent work being preparation for a classical Maoist People's Revolution. ZANLA Political Commissar, Comrade Zeppelin, made the point: "We get into an area, study the problems in that particular area, and then teach those people about their problems, how we can solve them by fighting the enemy."[1] ZIPRA used similar strategies as stated by Comrade Colin Matutu: "The simplest way was to learn their grievances…when you are dealing with the masses you have to talk about relevant issues on the ground."[2] Land ownership was one of the central issues.

In order to avoid detection, ZANLA would establish concealed bush-bases in safe areas that were difficult to access and some distance from supporting kraals. Local bases nearer kraals were also established as this would give access for those people who provided meals and attended political meetings. Meals were generally prepared by the young girls known as *chimbwidos* who would form "feeding parties".[3] These occasions would take place early morning and late afternoon. ZANLA slept in base camps in the bush as they did not know who were trustworthy in the villages. This strategy made it difficult for intelligence organisations to detect the insurgents' movements and for SF to observe during patrols, or from OPs. As the war progressed, some ZANLA started sleeping in the kraals. Insurgents were not uniformed and favoured denim clothing and boots or *veldskoens*, bead necklaces and bracelets given by witchdoctors for their protection. They often had long, carefully twisted locked hair.

In the attempt to establish themselves in the TTLs, ZANLA had to wrest power and control from the established authorities, initially from traditional tribal and parental authority followed by government authority, in attacking and destabilising civil administration. Tribal and parental authority were gradually eroded and successfully replaced with a strong nationalistic, socialistic political party agenda. *Vatengesi* ("sellouts"), supportive of "the cause" or not, were beaten and often summarily executed. I attended many of these incidents.[4] For this reason generally, ZANLA (and ZIPRA) did not deploy in their home areas. Their violent campaign was easier to impose in the absence of families, relatives and friends. This was a significant weakness waiting to be exploited.

Local store owners, politicians and missionaries were recruited as ZANLA gained momentum and control in a carefully planned and executed strategy. Authority was imposed by ZANLA and their intelligence networks. Inevitably, this well-intentioned "liberation" transitioned to martial law. Essential traditional values were eroded with far-reaching, ongoing consequences. ZANLA's violent oppression of the people made it clear to me that they intended to rule by the "barrel of a gun" and the people were merely pawns in the process. This was a sure sign of intent, regime change as opposed to attending to the people's grievances, needs and aspirations (GNA). ZANLA's mass mobilisation, propaganda and intimidation policy altered the infrastructure of communities. Political power achieved in this manner violates human dignity and order, according to Dr Howard Halpern: "When our shared humanity with those with whom we disagree is stripped away, it becomes acceptable to blow them up."[5] Once a human being has been dehumanised and branded an enemy,

---

1 Ranger, T. (1985), pp. 178-179.

2 Ibid.

3 Ibid, Chap. 5, p. 207.

4 Flower, K. (1987), p. 121.

killing becomes a matter of course. This was relevant to both sides of the conflict, who were trained in military operations and, through events of the war, to hate each other as enemies and not to consider one another as human beings. The enemy and their supporters were considered targets for elimination once the human element was removed.

Chitepo's strategy transformed the war. Politicising and mobilising the masses, gaining their support voluntarily and with the use of intimidation, when it was considered expedient, enabled ZANLA to penetrate deep into Rhodesia without detection.

On 25 June 1975, Mozambique achieved independence from Portugal. This rendered its entire eastern border of approximately 1,231 kilometres with Rhodesia vulnerable to insurgent infiltration and attack. Up to this point, ZANLA, a close associate of FRELIMO, had only been able to operate from Tete Province in northern Mozambique. However, with the departure of the Portuguese colonial authorities, ZANLA could move freely between the two countries. This resulted in a significant escalation of the Rhodesian conflict. Recruitment and training of revolutionary cadre was forthwith simplified with the consequence of an intensification of the war. Infiltration routes were established along the frontier as a result of easier, quicker and more reliable paths through the Manica and Sofala provinces of the central Mozambican region. This led to the increasing flow of arms and ammunition into Rhodesia, where they were distributed and cached.

Unfortunately, the peace we had experienced in Rusape district since our arrival was short-lived, ending abruptly in 1975 when insurgents started to show their hand.[1] Little did we realise that ZANLA had been active in Makoni for some time. They had done a significant amount of political work with the local population and considered the area liberated and safe enough to carry out hit-and-run attacks. The idea of mass mobilisation of the people by ZANLA committed to the mode of guerrilla war favoured by Mao Zedong never crossed our minds. We were unaware of these tactics. We were oblivious that they had completed Phase 1 of their strategies:

Phase 1: ZANLA Strategies

1. Commence covert operations in order to mobilise and politicise the people, including traditional leaders, local politicians and missionaries.
2. Mobilise businessmen for material and financial support.
3. Ensure an overall majority of locals in an area support the revolution (voluntarily or forcibly).
4. Identify, turn or eliminate existing Security Forces intelligence networks and suspected "sellouts" (informants for the BSAP Special Branch and Ground Coverage, and Int.Aff. Ground Coverage).
5. Break down the traditional tribal system and impose a new political social order enforced by martial law.
6. Establish and maintain intelligence networks.
7. Identify and remove recruits for external training.
8. No overt operations such as deliberate attacks on enemy targets, civilians or Security Forces.
9. Build arms caches. Arms caches included AK-47s, SKSs, 7.62 intermediate ammunition, RPG-2s/RPG-7s launchers and projectiles, landmines, including detonators and hand-grenades.

The Rhodesian Security Forces found Chitepo's new political strategy extremely frustrating. Although we were considered militarily superior, particularly with air cover and support, we had to hunt for a most elusive enemy who chose to carry out random hit-and-run attacks on our patrols, farms, and any "soft" target as and when it suited them. According to Mao Zedong's philosophy, time is immaterial in guerrilla warfare.[2] "When the enemy advances, withdraw; when he stops, harass; when he tires, strike; when he retreats, pursue."[3] In Fire Force deployments (see Chapter 3), ZANLA sensibly ran and took cover. It did not make sense to stand and fight overwhelming odds, including complete air dominance. Based on our early successes, Rhodesians were led to believe that

[5] *The New York Times,* 2/5/1995.
[1] Ranger, T. (1985), Chap. 5.
[2] Ranger, T. (1985), Chap. 5, p. 209.
[3] Zedong, M. "A Single Spark Can Start a Prairie Fire", *Selected Works:* Eng. ed., FLP, Peking, 1965, Vol. I, p. 124.

terrorism was purely a military threat of isolated acts of banditry. Conventional military strategies and tactics were suitably and successfully adapted and a "kills-win-wars" mentality adopted which persisted throughout the war, unwittingly forcing the military onto the back foot.[1] While this was part of a vital necessary strategy, it isolated the SF from the African people and was a complete misunderstanding of history and counter-revolutionary warfare. Politically, the RF appeared intransigent, perpetuating their unachievable agenda, despite the growing threat.[2] According to D. Lowry in his *Cold War in Southern Africa*: "There was thus no military 'silver bullet' to end the insurgency, but the RF remained a prisoner of its own ideology and cherished world view."[3]

As ZANLA gained control of rural areas, SB and GC foot patrols became hazardous and ceased; informers were eliminated, went to ground or joined the insurgents' cause, giving them greater control of the rural areas. In Makoni they moved swiftly into Phase 2 of their operations:

Phase 2: ZANLA Strategies

1. Continue to penetrate and eliminate Security Forces intelligence networks, including those in African townships.
2. Break down the civil administration through civil disobedience including non-payment of taxes, destruction of, or prevention of attendance to, livestock dips, schools and clinics, in order to ensure that they are unsafe to staff.
3. Infiltrate with additional sections in order to increase manpower.
4. Commence strategic landmine campaign in order to prevent, restrict, deter or harass Security Force movements into and within Makoni. Landmines also used to restrict and control movements of locals to and from Makoni.
5. Commence widespread hit-and-run attacks against vulnerable and isolated targets, e.g. white farm attacks. Attacks spread out across a wide area in order to extend Security Forces manpower and resources.
6. Cause Security Forces to react to incidents and manoeuvre them into vulnerable positions in order to attack them.
7. Avoid the Fire Force and develop escape strategies when attacked.
8. Commence basic military training for locals.
9. Open new operational fronts in order to increase areas of control and stretch enemy manpower and resources.
10. Establish liberated areas.
11. Increase recruiting which is a natural consequence of successful, seemingly achievable political propaganda, growing ZANLA activity and control of the masses.

Having achieved control in liberated areas, civil disobedience was orchestrated and local government cattle dips, schools and clinics were either destroyed or rendered unsafe to attend. Some missionary schools remained open. Increasingly, taxes were not paid and it became difficult for Int.Aff. to collect monies due in accordance with government legislation. The requirement to contour on hills was ignored.

Once the area was considered liberated, insurgents travelled about more freely, confident their intelligence networks would support them and identify SF in the area. Movement in late afternoon did not immediately concern them as they had learned, once detected, the Fire Force would have little reaction time. Often, these insurgents would randomly open fire on overhead helicopters. Helicopter pilots were generally restricted to fly with a visible horizon and could do little against an evasive enemy sheltered by fading dusk.

As hostilities progressed, insurgents would only strike when satisfied they had the support of people in their defined operational area and when it was to their advantage. Our duty as policemen

---

[1] Smith, I. (2008), Loc 4566, 4786; Ranger, T. (1985), Chap. 5, p. 209.

[2] Cilliers, J. (2003), pp. 60-61.

[3] Lowry, D. (2009), p. 100.

was to respond to reports of ZANLA activity as they strengthened their grip on the locals. Main strategic access roads into Makoni were mined thus announcing an intense landmine campaign. ZANLA's plan was to obstruct, prevent, deter and restrict Security Force access to the TTL. In this way they sustained their liberated areas while aiming for total freedom of movement, as well as complete support from the people. Many mines were detonated by civilian vehicles causing numerous deaths. One Peugeot pick-up overloaded with passengers struck a landmine killing some five occupants and maiming the rest. It was carnage. Only in advantageous circumstances were SF vehicles ambushed, and patrols and white farmsteads attacked. Theirs was a carefully orchestrated strategy.

Noticeably, ZANLA attacks and incidents spread rapidly across Makoni, placing pressure on our limited manpower and resources, thus demonstrating their acute military strategic awareness. ZANLA sections covered considerable distances as they attacked their targets, creating the impression there were several sections in the area. This carefully planned approach to guerrilla warfare stretched our resources. Locating the sections was the problem and our success depended on infiltrating their intelligence networks. However, elimination of a section, or even a portion thereof, did not interrupt their operations. It remained largely intact with some minor adjustments in which fresh personnel or replacement sections merely took their place.

The police base at Rugoyi was securely fenced and permanently guarded. A permanent BSAP Ground Coverage unit was deployed which began patrols to gather information about insurgents from locals. Mine-proofed vehicles were deployed and all vehicle patrols were accompanied by an armed escort vehicle.

Almost overnight, "peaceful" Makoni had been turned into a fully fledged military operational area and with that, my thoughts of escaping the war vanished. The people were no longer receptive to our friendly approaches. They were fearful and suspicious of us. I could understand this as our sole purpose in calling in on them was for the gathering of information and intelligence which would help locate insurgent sections and identify their supporters. Inevitably, the well-being of the local African population became a lesser priority than in earlier times. In effect, all local people were considered supporters, voluntarily or under threat of death. This was an unenviable position. ZANLA gained the people's support through a cleverly orchestrated aggressive propaganda programme. They carried out atrocities including murdering those known or suspected not to support them. Voluntary field intelligence and information from the TTLs became rare and sporadic as previously reliable informers were either killed or switched loyalties. The stage was set for a war located on our doorstep.

I was issued with a new mine-proofed vehicle, Registration No. G-LL1442 (fondly referred to as 1442). Troops were based at Rusape on a permanent basis and our radio station was manned 24 hours of the day for seven days of the week. Our sole objective was gathering information and a strategy to locate and eliminate ZANLA fighters. As far as I was concerned, regarding the gathering of intelligence, we were in the dark. It was difficult to know where to begin. My only experience in this matter was gained from two deployments to Chiweshe and Mukumbura where I learned very little.

The ability of ZANLA to change their political and military strategies was carried out throughout the war enabling them to stay ahead of the SF whose political leadership remained stagnant and intransigent, believing naïvely, that kills brought success and victory.

ZANLA Launch their First Attacks

In February 1976, Operation Thrasher was established[1] in response to ZANLA's threat from the entire Mozambique border. Joint Operations Centre (JOC) Headquarters were at Umtali and various

1 Cilliers, J. (2003), p. 65. The start of Operation Thrasher was documented on BSAP Form 36 dated 9/2/1976 after four incidents in the Chipinga area: two SF ambushes on 3/2/1976 and 4/2/1976, and three landmine detonations on 4/2/1976 and 7/2/1976. On the form it was stated: "This was the start of Thrasher, you can use this in brief for general background."

Sub.JOCs were opened. Sub.JOC Rusape was officially opened by Maj. Garth Barrett who remained in charge until relieved by Maj. John Peirson in May 1976.[1] Col. Henry Dunn replaced Maj. Peirson in July/August 1976. Sub.JOC Rusape comprised the OC BSAP Rusape, Supt. Ken MacDonald; SB officers, Supt. Dave Sloman and Brian Thomas from Salisbury who operated on a six-week rotational basis; a military representative, Maj. Barrett and DC Ian Bickersteth. I was transferred to Special Branch, attached permanently to the Sub.JOC and was responsible for operations in the Makoni and Manyika TTLs. The war was escalating rapidly although Ian Smith was "satisfied that our terrorists had come to the conclusion that they desired a settlement".[2] This was not in keeping with reality.

As time moved on, our operational duties increased exponentially. We spent most of our time in the operational area reacting to incidents instigated by ZANLA and gathering intelligence from unwilling residents. Without specific SB counter-insurgency training, we were forced to learn from operations as we came across them: in a sense we learned "on the run". Notwithstanding, we applied ourselves fully to the task at hand.

However, we did have many successes in the course of time as we adjusted to our circumstances. Maj. Garth Barrett makes the point: "During my stay we had a good success rate, Colonel Ron Reid-Daly reminded me of this when he commented that JOC Rusape had the highest 'kills' in the country, partly due to the Special Branch team of D/S/O's Milne, Cutting and Padbury."[3]

Inyazura Petrol Station Attack

At 7.45 p.m. on 14 May 1976, ZANLA carried out a night attack at Inyazura situated on the main road, 20 kilometres from Rusape towards Umtali.[4] D/Insp. McCallum made the following report on the Application For Scientific Examination (BSAP Form 36), dated 15 May 1976 (see appendix): "Two armed men in possession of AK rifles (Terrorists) came to Bi-Pass Welders Garage, Inyazura Village (Just on main road Rusape to Umtali) with the obvious intention of robbing the Night attendant who was attending to stock records and cash proceeds involving nigh on R$88. The Terrorists claimed to be from a local Haulage firm and enticed the Attendant out from his locked room. However, upon seeing them with AK rifles he made off with the 2 terrorists firing at him, luckily missing him. Through his line of flight the 18 expended cartridge cases were recovered. The 2 petrol pumps and 1 Oil rack were blown up and this thought to have been by stick grenades being used to effect the explosions etc. The building was also shot at with very noticeable holes on the walls. However, a check to locate expended cartridge cases in this connection was negative." Beryl Rheeder, manageress of the business at the time recalls: "The fuel pumps on a centre island in the forecourt were both blown up and completely demolished, just bits of metal were left lying around. Windows of the workshop and the front plate glass window of the office were blown out, leaving the office itself in disarray. Fortunately, the blast went up in the air; had it gone down into the ground, the underground tanks would have exploded and there wouldn't have been much left of either the business or, Inyazura the local town!"[5]

On 31 May 1976, D/S/O Cutting and D/Cst. Ganga carried out further investigations at the scene. Thirty-seven AK-47 doppies and an AK-47 magazine were found in a vlei 56 yards from the scene. D/Insp. McCallum reported on BSAP Form 36 dated 31 May 1976 (see appendix): "This area was alleged to have been cleared by SAS and these exhibits were found in a further routine check of the area."

---

[1] John Peirson email 5/6/2016 and SMS 14/7/2017. Col. Henry Dunn then took over the military post. Confirmed by Garth Barrett, although he was not sure of the precise dates as per email 15/7/2016. Makoni/Manyika Incidents Map: Incident 2.

[2] Smith, I. (1997), pp. 199, 202.

[3] Email 13/11/2015. D/S/O Ken Milne served from 9/2/1965 to 31/5/1980. D/S/O Cutting served from 14/11/1968 to 3/5/1980.

[4] Makoni/Manyika Incidents Map: Incident 3.

[5] Beryl Rheeder remarried becoming Beryl Smorenburg, email 8/4/2017.

The duty policeman at Rusape Police Station, P/O Graham Brand, also recalls the event: "I was instructed to set up a roadblock on the main Salisbury/Umtali road just outside of Rusape. This was an attempt to ambush the escaping terrorists and prevent traffic travelling towards the incident. Seven men were tied up (involved) in the necessary but fruitless operation."[1]

It was interesting to note how many Security Forces details were involved in this one incident. The Officer Commanding the District, members in charge BSAP Inyazura, as well as men from CID and SB, Rusape including myself, attended the scene which was approached and secured by SF personnel. Follow-ups by trackers and a BSAP Dog Section team would attend at first light in an attempt to track down the enemy. Roadblocks on both sides of Inyazura were carried out. Approximately 24 men were attached to this incident.

We were taken completely by surprise by this attack and at a loss as to where the ZANLA fighters had come from and how they managed their escape. Our conclusion was that an expeditionary group of insurgents had randomly decided to attack the petrol station to see what reaction it would provoke.

On the same evening, insurgents attacked the railway line near Inyanzura, about 64 kilometres from the Mozambique border. As a result of these two attacks, it was announced that night-time passenger traffic on the Salisbury/Umtali railway line was being suspended.[2]

Detective Constable Ganga

D/Cst. Ganga was deployed by the SB Office into Makoni district on a routine SB patrol. He was principally tasked to gather intelligence to establish the political climate in the light of the recent Inyazura attacks. This would include visits to established informers. The date was 25 July 1976, and on this pleasant sunny day, Lynette and I were hosting a braai (barbecue) in our garden. From our elevated position, we had a wonderful view of the open country of low-lying bush which swept down to the local African township of Vengere, some two miles away. Many of the African population migrated to towns in search of work and these townships were built to accommodate this labour force. Prime Minister Godfrey Huggins clarifies the matter: "Towns were the white man's kraals (villages), and the natives were only there as visitors, if they wished to come and offer their services to the legitimate inhabitants."[3]

Lynette and I lived in quite a luxurious house although once the war gained momentum, we found ourselves in the line of fire as ZANLA insurgents on two occasions fired their AK-47s from Vengere Township over Rusape. It was disturbing watching tracer bullets fly over our house. They were never a threat but one of the memories which remains lurking in the back of my mind. The smell of freshly baked bread from a cast-iron oven heated with charcoal drifted through the air as I cooked the last of the lamb chops and sausages on our skottle braai. A skottle braai is a plough disc heated over the coals of a fire. The great advantage of this set-up is that tomato-and-onion gravy is cooked in the juices of the meat. Add to that small red chillies and one has a delicious gravy for the *sadza*. Copious quantities of beer had been consumed. Thus we found ourselves eagerly anticipating our meal when the phone rang with a message from Jock McCallum. He informed me that D/Cst. Ganga had been abducted by ZANLA in Makoni TTL. The informant, an elderly man, was prepared to take police to the kraal where the group were holding Ganga captive. It would be true to say that the abduction of Ganga took us all by complete surprise.

Without thought, I hastily grabbed my webbing and FN rifle and drove to the charge office. There I was met by D/Insp. Jock McCallum, P/O Graham Brand, S/O Richard Davis, the police public prosecutor,[4] D/Sgt. Danda and the informant. After a brief discussion, we established that ZANLA had abducted Ganga while he was visiting a local kraal. He was being held captive at Mutwiro Kraal, not too far from Rugoyi Police Base.

After planning our strategy to rescue Ganga, we set off in two vehicles arriving at Rugoyi Police

1 Graham Brand: Summary of email 7/4/2017.

2 Makoni/Manyika Incidents Map: Incident 4.

3 Stapleton, T. (2011), p. 92; Johnson, D. (2000), pp. 142-143.

4 At some rural police stations, the public prosecutor was an appointed member of the BSA Police. At Rusape this was now S/O Richard Davis.

Base at sunset. We parked the vehicles and started out for the kraal. The walk took about three hours. It followed a footpath which wound its way through kopjes until we heard, in the distance, merry sounds of a lively party. Night had fallen but fortunately we had clear skies with a full moon, making visibility good. As we drew close to the kraal, Graham and I tried to crawl nearer to the huts to establish what was going on. However, we were thwarted by a wire fence and returned to the rest of our section who were keeping guard.

A brief discussion followed and we decided to follow the path leading directly into the kraal. We advanced in single file, commonly known as "Indian file", with Graham leading. I followed him with Richard, Jock and Danda in tow. We made our way cautiously towards the settlement. The party was at its peak with music blaring, loud singing and energetic dancing. Little did we know, we were walking into a deathtrap. Ignorance in situations of war results in death or injury with only the fortunate surviving. However, there is an essential difference between ignorance and risk. Ignorance or a lack of information brings about death, whereas risks are calculated from which soldiers generally survive. About 20 metres from the kraal someone cried out, "*Ndiani*?" (Shona for who is it?). I instinctively started firing at a hidden sentry who was lodged in a small cave to our right.

Graham Brand picks up the story:

> I heard the call of the sentry, "*Ndiani*?" to our right and John just started firing at the concealed "voice", which was about five meters away. I immediately joined in the firing and went to ground, the terr fired back at us and an intense fire fight developed. There was an explosion and John was knocked unconscious. The firefight continued. Suddenly John regained consciousness and joined in the firing. The sentry kept calling I'm Blue Boy, I'm Blue Boy – he suddenly rushed us as we continued to fire. There was a second huge explosion as an RPG7 projectile he was carrying exploded and he dropped dead.
>
> We were then fired upon by the rest of the terrs from a position further down the path next to the kraal. After returning fire the fighters withdrew. As John and I tactically withdrew a pig ran past scarring the living daylights out of us. We moved up the slopes of a rocky outcrop (kopje), regrouped with the rest of our section who had taken a defensive position further up the hill. After a quick discussion we set off away from the contact area, took up defensive positions and settled down for the night.[1]

We were poorly equipped and did not have radios, maps or warm clothes, very little ammunition or water, and we had no idea of our location. Later, I became aware of blood streaming from my head but there was nothing we could do about that. At dawn, we started walking to safety and managed to find our way back to Rugoyi Police Base. Not too long after our arrival at the base camp, some helicopters flew in searching for us. Richard Davis volunteered to identify the contact area to the pilots. The kraals were deserted. One deceased ZANLA insurgent was found and a number of 7.62mm (intermediate) spent cartridges from various firing positions recovered.

During the contact, I had been hit with shrapnel on the left side of my body from my head down and was despatched to Salisbury Central Hospital. X-rays revealed shrapnel lodged in the bone of my skull and was not to be removed. Beyond doubt, Graham saved my life that night.[2]

That experience was a stark "wake-up call". We gained insight into the business of war but what struck me was that "someone" wanted to deliberately kill me. It dawned on me, I was engaged in a full-scale war. I was intimately involved in a matter of life and death in a real way. Deploying single, unarmed African detectives proved far too dangerous and was abruptly ended. Naturally this change of approach played into the hands of ZANLA as it weakened our intelligence-gathering methods giving them more control of the locals. Clearly ZANLA were now established in Makoni TTL and were generally enjoying the support of the population. Only members of the older generation, those like the initial informant, were to some extent resisting ZANLA. But that was not to last.

From this event, it was obvious we policemen were not thoroughly trained soldiers, so I

1 P/O Graham Brand email 13/3/2015. Confirmed by S/O Richard Davis email 21/3/2017.

2 Makoni/Manyika Incidents Map: Incident 1.

immediately adopted the policy of never deploying without professional military backup. I learned to take the right equipment, radios, maps, food and warm clothing, and to always let our authorities know of our destination. As I replayed the events of that night in my mind, it struck me that we were fortunate to have survived. ZANLA were at war with us, meaning we were no longer engaged in routine police work. The enemy were at an advantage, fully mobilised, committed and dedicated to their cause. Their intent clearly was to eliminate us. We had grown complacent. Sadly, we never received news of D/Cst. Ganga. He was presumed "killed in action".

Everitt Murder: Roads Department

Later in the year, on 4 August 1976, ZANLA attacked a Government Roads Department works party in the south of the Makoni, killing a white contractor, John Everitt. The incident was logged on the Operation Thrasher Incidents Log (No. 413: see appendix) and D/P/O Charles Atkinson made the following report on the BSAP Form 36 on 4 August 1976 (see appendix): "Mr Everitt was working in the Makoni TTL when he was fired upon by terrorists, at the time he was in possession of an F/N rifle which he attempted to use in retaliation before his death. The rifle has since been stolen by the terrorists who had attacked Mr Everitt. The F/N is a Police Reserve Rusape weapon, Number 5865 for which 2 magazines and 40 rounds were issued to the deceased. Mr Everitt fired 25 rounds prior to his death. 50 AK doppies were collected."[1] Everitt's daughter, Angie Wynne recalls: "My father was working on the roads in the Makoni TTL when he was ambushed by terrorists. In the fire fight he managed to get his men to safety before he was killed. I was led to understand that in the follow up the security forces killed the terrorists who attacked my Dad, one of them had my father's watch."[2]

On 18 August 1976, Fire Force made contact with ZANLA insurgents, approximately 6 kilometres East of the Everitt murder, 11 of whom were killed. I was not involved in this deployment. Exhibits recovered were five AK-47s (Nos. 332805, 2006226, 20076563, 140204 and 18130441), two folding-butt AK-47s (Nos. 1971 DD 21356 and 1975 948381), three SKSs (Nos. 18003678, 10295997 and 18003797), one flare pistol (No. 120171), 23 Chinese stick-grenades, 110 doppies, remnants of a mortar bomb and two unidentified tops.[3]

Later we learned that the attack on the Inyazura railway line and petrol station were far from being random acts. They were attacks on carefully selected targets on the main railway line and highway from Salisbury to Umtali which insurgents knew would attract local, national and international interest. ZANLA had publicised their capacity to strike at will, to disrupt transport and communication networks and other infrastructure, and to further extend the "overstretched" Security Forces. They had escalated their campaign in Makoni TTL to a more deadly level. We were gradually drawn deeper into responding to various ZANLA attacks and incidents without realising the extent of the threat.

It was a bleak picture. Our troops were eager for action but we did not have any information on ZANLA's whereabouts to assist them. D/S/O Ken Milne was transferred from SB Inyanga to SB Rusape. Ken was a welcome addition to our staff as he had previous operational experience. He had a wonderful dry sense of humour which relieved tension at times. Importantly, he was also an adept snooker player which, on occasions, provided welcome relief from the harsh realities of war. Ken taught us the current Security Forces operational tactics, but my growing concern was that we would always be reacting to ZANLA and not taking the initiative.

In the face of these attacks, we were forced to rise to the occasion, with the BSA Police Support Unit taking on a central role. With the growing number of incidents in the district, Support Unit was

---

1 Makoni/Manyika Incidents Map: Incident 5.

2 Contributed by Angie Wynne, John Everitt's daughter, Messenger 3/11/2018; Lewis, A. (1992), pp. 219-220.

3 Makoni/Manyika Incidents Map: Incident 6; Geldenhuys, P. (2014), Air Strike Log Entry 447; Application For Scientific Examination (BSAP Form 36) dated 20/8/1976; Operation Thrasher Incidents Log 458; Central Armoury Forensic Ballistics reference FB(T) 1077/76.

sent to establish a base and offer permanent troops for deployments. It became critical that we no longer operated on a "reactive" mode of approach but rather became "proactive" towards the enemy and took the fight to them. However, this approach was not possible without reliable and accurate intelligence. We had lost the confidence of the local population and could no longer effectively work in or control the area.

British South Africa Police Support Unit

Men of the BSAP Support Unit were well-trained, disciplined soldiers who carried out their duties stoically. It is my opinion that on occasions they out-performed other branches of the Security Forces I had engaged with. They had the added advantage of having mainly African members and, once again, in my view, an adaptable police-trained mind. I believe these factors helped us understand each other. The Support Unit did not elevate themselves to a superior role. Rather they merely accomplished the job at hand. Their understanding of the Shona language, culture and traditional environment of the TTLs was an added benefit.

I considered it a pleasure and privilege to work alongside them. We seldom had disagreements and they always listened to our advice and deployed on our intelligence, despite the inevitable periodic "lemons".[1] They brought with them experience gained from deployments in war theatres in the north and north-east of Rhodesia.

Barry Woan[2] explains:

> A troop base was set up by Superintendents Fred Mason and Tom Naude on a farm 17km from Rusape in mid-1976. Their main areas of responsibility were the Chiduku, Makoni and Manyika Tribal Trust Lands but were not restricted to these areas. Mason and Naude took an active part in commanding the effective base called Mantle 151A. This concept allowed the Support Unit to operate in numbers with full support from each other and in particular with the effectiveness of Fire Force. Thereafter bases were established near Wedza, Shabani, Plumtree with satellite bases at Wankie and Lupani.
>
> The Support Unit was able to operate in four man teams (callsigns) which enabled them to be deployed and redeployed during Fire Force actions. Each callsign would have a Section Leader, supplied with a radio, a MAG Gunner, Medic and one additional member. Apart from the gunner, the remainder would carry FN Rifles with a minimum of eight magazines with a capacity of 20 rounds each, grenades and smoke grenades. The Section leader would be in possession of extra medical kit, map and a shackle code (one of the many codes used to protect SF radio communications). Binoculars were carried by at least two men in the callsign. The gunner would carry extra belts for his gun and in some instances, others would carry additional belts. A60 radios were on issue in the late 60's to be replaced by the A63 and A73 radio on VHF and the cumbersome and heavy TR28 for use on SSB frequency. (See Chapter 14: Strike 2 for descriptions of these radios.) Capable and well equipped, these troops could remain in the operational areas for up to seven days without requiring assistance.[3]

We were set for action!

---

1 Lemons: Failure. Refers to intelligence that did not lead to a contact, was incorrect and reminiscent of the sour bitter taste left after eating a lemon.

2 L/Insp. Barry Robert Charles Woan, MLM, BSAP Support Unit.

3 Barry Woan email 31/5/2015. During the war the Support Unit lost 118 members KIA; many more were injured.

3 ~ A DRAMATIC LEARNING EXPERIENCE

The man who creates, establishes, and maintains patterns, makes himself predictable and vulnerable.
John Padbury

Security Forces Tactics

General infantry tactics in the Rhodesian War were based on classic counter-insurgency strategy. Intelligence was gathered by Special Branch and Ground Coverage patrols and passed on to the military for action, which varied according to the nature of the intelligence. The military carried out general patrols, ambushes, observation posts, attacks on insurgent bases and pseudo-operations. Clearly, accurate intelligence was key to these operations where the objective was simply to defeat the enemy. Political propaganda of the day emphasised that "all is well" and the successful SF kill-rate justified their agenda. By adopting this approach, they emphasised and confirmed, so they believed, the principle "kills win wars". However, we faced an already well-established enemy and we were an unsuspecting establishment. There was much to learn as we set our minds to finding an elusive enemy. My mindset had to change by entering the mind of the enemy in order to penetrate his strategies, tactics and methodology. It required a rapid transition from peace to war. Among our successes were failures. However, we learned quickly. We adopted various strategies and tactics and gradually gained momentum. There were a considerable number of insurgent activities and incidents in Makoni, but I have chosen a few to illustrate how we developed.

Special Branch Ground Patrols

ZANLA focused on politicising the people, gaining popular support and breaking down the traditional system of informers in the TTLs. They aimed to control the population primarily by maintaining a perpetual presence among them. Even after the initial attacks, we were still unaware of the extent of the growing threat as we began patrolling the area in mine-proofed vehicles. Both doors were removed which allowed for quick escape if necessary and enabled us to direct our weapons outwards in order to return fire in the event of an ambush. A patrol consisted of two vehicles, driver and passenger in each, a total of four men armed with FNs that would protect each other in the event of an ambush or detonation of a landmine. It was my principle to always drive the front vehicle as this would theoretically show positive leadership and a disregard for mines and ambushes. There was another reason: I didn't want to travel in the trail of dust raised by the first vehicle which was like following a desert sandstorm. It was always hilarious looking at the escorts in the second vehicle after a drive through the rugged terrain of the African veld, their eyes beaming like twin searchlights out of faces covered with rich, brown dust.

We rarely drove along the main tracks of the corrugated, potholed roads, electing to drive with one wheel in the centre of the road, the other just off the road, alternating from side to side. This method worked and certainly I am here today to tell the tale. Naturally, we tried not to set patterns. We alternated departure times and routes trying to avoid returning by the same roads when and wherever possible. Our watchwords became: "Never establish or follow a set pattern, be alert and unpredictable."

Travel had been restricted by ZANLA's landmine campaign. It was always a challenge travelling on these roads and remaining alert to ambushes. Mindful of the threat, I learned to "read the signs". When there was little or no local traffic, no tyre tracks on the dirt roads, it became my assumption that the road had been mined and I called in engineers responsible for detecting and lifting landmines.

However, there were lapses in our attention to caution when we raced each other home. Our Land Rovers were weighted down by steel-plated mine protection but, notwithstanding, could hold the road well which helped negotiate corners at considerable speeds. In these situations, there was only one speed, flat out. The advantage generally going to the rear vehicle travelling in the slipstream of the lead vehicle, attempting a last-minute overtake close to base or Rusape. This didn't always work but was worth a try. Fortunately, we were neither ambushed nor hit a landmine, although twice, while in convoy, military vehicles behind our two vehicles detonated landmines. It really was the luck of the draw.

We started holding meetings with the chief, his headmen and kraalheads, as well as meetings in the general kraal areas. This was our attempt to win the hearts and minds of the locals, assuring them that our weapons were superior, our forces stronger, and that we would take care of them far better than ZANLA. Our message was unequivocal. We were here to stay and committed to winning the war. It was likely that some ZANLA comrades were in the crowds listening to our propaganda, observing our tactics and strategies, and learning how to counter them. On completion of these meetings, we drove off into the sunset to our comfortable base or home, leaving the people to the perpetual presence of ZANLA who would invariably set about reversing our efforts. With the benefit of hindsight, we were naïve.

Initially, we adopted a system of randomly selecting kraals in areas we suspected were involved in collaborating with ZANLA. Descending on the unsuspecting villagers, we would select a few for interrogations and take them back to our base camp. It was difficult to extract information from people whose very lives depended on their maintaining secrecy. While we would return to the safety of our base camp, the villagers had to return to their homes to the inevitable visitation of resident ZANLA comrades. Any inkling that a person had co-operated with the SF carried the death penalty. It was difficult to get to grips with our evasive foe. Thus our frustrations, understandably, increased as did the severity of our interrogation.

In the early part of 1977, I started mapping incidents such as landmines, contacts, ambushes, OPs, Fire Force deployments, ballistics evidence, murders, beatings and atrocities on our ordnance survey maps in my office. As insurgent activity increased, I began to establish patterns of incidents which indicated the presence of permanent ZANLA sections in and around specific kraal areas. While it was clear that all kraal dwellers in Makoni were exposed to ZANLA politicisation, a pattern began to emerge which revealed that some kraals had a more intimate involvement with our enemy. In this way, I started to get a "feel for the enemy". I focused our interrogations on these areas and began confirming their more direct involvement and support of ZANLA insurgents. This all formed a picture of ZANLA's activities and helped me strategise deployments.

Information from the old informers' network trickled through to me but, in conditions of intensified armed conflict, it soon ceased. A serious problem facing our SB operations was that our intelligence networks and procedures were well known to the locals and, therefore, to ZANLA. I recall driving to the edge of Makoni TTL to meet one such informer who provided the last bit of information I received in this manner. This was an increasingly dangerous process as I was uncertain whether ZANLA were using the informer to "set me up". However, he confirmed a permanent presence of several ZANLA sections in Makoni who were forcing the people to follow their instructions. Generally, the people were unhappy about this situation. Many of them were beaten and some murdered for refusing to assist insurgents. The failure and inability of the SF to protect these people from insurgents left ordinary civilians no choice but to obey ZANLA. My informer did not pass on any specific information but at least I gained an understanding of the overall situation and paid him for the information he provided. A week later he was murdered by ZANLA.

In our scramble to obliterate the enemy, it became evident that this was not going to happen overnight. I had to define my role and purpose. After some thought, I settled on the following resolve: "To understand the mind of the enemy, his goals, purpose, strategies and tactics in order to predict his actions, patiently waiting to strike hard and eliminate him."

We spent a growing amount of time reacting to ZANLA incidents, yet the people continued to support the occupying ZANLA comrades rather than our periodic and fleeting presence. Without doubt, as our interrogations grew in intensity, the people became puppets in a game which favoured our enemy.

It was also important to assess the people, distinguishing between normal activity and patterns of behaviour which revealed the presence of insurgents. In time, I was able to detect the difference. Understanding the people was beginning to help understand the war. When the insurgents were in the area, locals were alert, mindful of our actions rather than continuing with their daily routine. Conversely, when ZANLA comrades were not in an area, the people generally carried on with life and their daily routine. They were not perplexed by our presence and less attentive to our actions. There was a distinct difference and over time I learned to sense these changes. We had much to learn about ZANLA's intelligence networks and the nature of their work with the people. We were still unaware of the extent to which they had established themselves. Every form of traditional police investigational procedure was used in pursuit of a cunning, unconventional enemy who had no rules. In these early days, ballistics played a significant role.

Ballistics

Ballistics examinations and evidence identified insurgent actives during the course of the conflict reflecting where a particular weapon was fired, such as in contacts with SF, farm attacks and murders of civilians. These details indicated activities of a particular individual weapon, defining an area of operation, as well as providing evidence for criminal prosecution of a captured insurgent carrying a weapon linked to ballistic evidence. Hence the importance of collecting doppies from incidents, as well as ensuring all captured weapons were collected and sent for examination. The Forensic Science Laboratory at CID Headquarters, Morris Depot, handled this work. N/S/P/O Paul de Mattos[1] explains the standard ballistics procedures in place at the Armoury, BSA Police Depot, Hard Square:

> Exhibits, normally AK's, RPK's, RPD's SKS's or any other CT weapons, Fired Cartridges Cases (FCC) or landmine and grenade fragments would arrive with an SB/CID detail accompanied by a BSAP Form 36: Application For Scientific Examination. Exhibits would be received by a ballistics detail, logged in and given a Forensic Ballistics (Terrorist) [FB(T)] number. Weapons would be labelled and racked for later examination. FCCs would be stored in date order by operational area. Cases would only be examined in date order to ensure that all previous possible matches would not be missed by examining them before older scenes had been examined.
>
> Once a ballistics detail collected a case for examination, recovered weapons from the scene were stripped and the barrels pulled through with "4x2" cleaning cloth to establish whether they had been previously fired. Thereafter they would be test fired at a 25m mini rifle range in the police grounds and 5–10 FCCs sealed in plastic bags from each weapon. These bags would previously have been tagged with the FB(T) number and the weapon serial number for all the weapons being test fired. All recovered firearms had their serial numbers entered in a master log and were then stored in the main Armoury store. When these weapons were issued to other approved units such as SAS, Selous Scouts, or SB, the date, name and force number of the detail to whom they were issued, were recorded in the master log. Firearms were also issued to armourer's workshop for use as anti-ambush weapons in Police Land Rovers and for Police launch boat armament.
>
> The bags containing the Test Fired Cartridge cases were then placed in trays with FCCs from the scene. Where there were limited numbers of FCCs, they would then be cleaned by the ballistics technician as they were initially examined under a binocular microscope.

[1] N/S/P/O Paul de Mattos: Served from January 1974 to December 1974 at Morris Depot, then as BSAP Field Reservist from January 1975 to May 1980 in the Ballistics Section, Armaments Branch, Hard Square, Morris Depot.

The initial examination was performed in order to separate the FCCs into groups fired by the same weapon. This was established using the extractor marks on the rim of the FCC, the ejector mark on the head of the FCC, any marks on the FCC neck resulting from chamber imperfections, and striker marks. Any indistinct cases not immediately recognisable were put to one side and re-examined once the initial sort had been completed. Re-examination could take place several times until virtually all cases had been allocated to an individual weapon. It was normally possible to allocate all the cases to individual weapons within a relatively short time period. Any completely indistinct cases that could not be positively allocated were bagged and labelled as such. In the instance where there were many hundreds or thousands of FCCs as was frequently the case, they would be manually cleaned using cloths dipped in petrol before being examined. This was necessary as they were normally greasy with powder residue.

It was possible to distinguish the different weapon types such as AK/AKM/RPK, SKS, RPD, PKM and Gorynov as each weapon left typical distinguishing marks on the FCCs. It was frequently possible to establish the origin of AK/AKM as being from China, East Germany or Russia. The majority of ZANLA weapons originated from China and East Germany with weapons from other Eastern Bloc countries also being utilised. Such countries included Yugoslavia, Romania, North Korea and North Vietnam.

The FCCs from each weapon at the scene were then photographed in black and white on a comparison microscope. Two cases were photographed on each of the viewing stages with the ejector marks position at right angles to one another in order to highlight distinctive features. If there were distinctive neck marks these would also be photographed separately.

A log was made of the negative numbers on each film with the relevant FB(T) log number of the scene. Once films, normally 36 exposures in length, were complete they were developed in the ballistics dark room and dried quickly using cloths liberally soaked in methylated spirits. This reduced the emulsion drying time from 6–8 hours to around 30 minutes with the aid of an electric fan. Quarter plate prints were made from each negative, dried and were annotated on the back with the FB(T) number. Normally the time required to prepare these prints was close on 6–8 hours from the start of the FCC examination. Generally, FCC prints from a scene examined on one day would be ready for searching the following day. Where there were hundreds of FCCs this process could take several days.

Once the scene prints were available, they would be searched against previous photographs from the same operational area, or from 2 or more operational areas if the scene map co-ordinates were close to one or more area boundaries. Potential matches were made by sight and experience of the previous scenes in the vicinity of the map reference. With experience it was often possible to accurately identify matching FCCs before using a comparison microscope. Some ejector marks were so distinctive that one weapon from the Op Hurricane area had been identified at least 13 times and the individual carrying it was known by his Chimurenga name of Solomon Hondo. There was however some suspicion from SB/CID that weapons were exchanged between individuals on occasions. All matches were confirmed by comparing current scene FCCs with previous scene FCCs on the comparison microscope. This included FCCs from captured weapons in order to remove their photographs from search stock and hence reduce search time. This whole operation was entirely manual with no digital imaging, matching or information storage available in the 70's. By comparison to what would be possible with modern technology now it was extremely time consuming.

Confirmed matches were based on 8–12-point comparisons of individual characteristics which was acceptable and admissible as evidence for investigations and prosecution.

Supt. Don Hollingworth set the standard at twelve points comparisons where possible. The probability of there being another exact same 8 points of comparison in the same order is to one chance in 16,777,216, calculated from 8 to the power of 8. All matches were checked by a more experienced technician and re-confirmed by either CI(T) Dave Perkins or D. Hollingworth.

There would normally be 5–6 technicians searching and matching plus another 2–3 cleaning and test firing weapons, developing film and producing prints. They would in addition test fire, record and issue captured weapons to SAS, Selous Scouts and SB details. There were two full time typists maintaining the FB(T) logs and preparing reports.

Ballistics technicians would often process 20–50 matches per day and would examine in a month more than most civilian technicians in any other police force would achieve in many years or possibly even their careers. The quantity and standard of work in the BSA Police Forensic Ballistics section was of an exceptionally high standard unlike any in the world before or since. The following statistics indicate the work performed by the Forensic Science Laboratory from January 1979 to December 1979:

Total number of cartridge cases examined.	417,029
Total number of weapons examined, and test fired.	3,939
Total number of scenes recorded.	4,665
Total number of photographs taken and processed.	22,659
Pages of schedule typed and posted weekly.	1,008
Total number of civilian scenes dealt with.	335

All ballistic examination cases were recorded on 1:250 000 ordnance survey maps. I took photographs of the same maps for Op Hurricane and Thrasher in 1977.[1]

First Fire Force Scene: Maxwell's Escape[2]

We started deploying SF foot patrols and setting up observation posts based on this early intelligence and began recording successes. We were gradually beginning to understand the enemy. However, it was a measurable learning experience.

Maxwell was a ZANLA man, trained in Mozambique and deployed into Gandanzara Province in Makoni TTL. He was one of an eight-man section operating in the southern area of Makoni. In 1976, this region was part of the liberated areas with much support for ZANLA. This was identifiable by the fact that insurgents were operating during the day, secure in the protection of their intelligence networks and support of the people. The war was going well for them but this was about to change. We subsequently captured Maxwell in a Fire Force action and he confirmed details of this battle (see Chapter 4).

A Support Unit ground patrol from Delta Troop came across the tracks of Maxwell's eight-man section at about 10 a.m. on 25 August 1976 and commenced tracking them. Some two hours later, radio communication with 151 Alpha, the Support Unit Headquarters was lost, causing concern for their safety.[3] Support Unit HQ was stationed in an abandoned post office wireless repeater tower which resembled the outer shell of a rocket. It was about 20 metres high, round, painted white and was a distinct feature clearly visible for many miles. Prior to the arrival of Support Unit, this relay station was called "Skylab". Situated some 17 kilometres from Rusape on the Juliasdale road, the building served as their ops room and communication centre. The base was home to three Support Unit troops at any one time and had Police Reserve radio operators and drivers also working on a rotational basis. Sub.JOC Rusape had allocated the Chiduku, Makoni and Manyika Tribal Trust Lands for Support Unit operations. Selous Scouts from time-to-time would also deploy in these areas.

1 Paul de Mattos emails 8/12/2017 and 14/2/2020.

2 Makoni/Manyika Incidents Map: Incident 7; Geldenhuys, P. (2014), Air Strike Log Entry 452; Flt. Lt. Pete Simmonds (from the Mukumbura incident) was involved in this contact.

3 Incident confirmed by email 10/2/2016 and oral conference in Durban, South Africa, 3/12/2015, with Fred Mason, Barry Woan, Winston "Sakkie" McKay, and David and John Padbury.

From the top communications room there was a splendid view of the scrubby vegetation of Makoni, with its mountains and kopjes bordered by lush white farmlands. In keeping with the "rocket setting", I had adopted the callsign Apollo 2 and my support vehicle was called Apollo 1. I was on patrol when the radio in 1442 (my Land Rover) crackled into life as we bounced along the dusty, corrugated TTL tracks.

"Apollo 2, 151 Alpha."

"151 Alpha, Apollo 2, go ahead," I replied, recognising the voice of Sunray Mantle, Officer in Charge of the Support Unit.

"Mantle Zulu 2 has been following tracks of eight terrs and we have lost communication with them. Are you anywhere near the road leading to the Nyatanda River?"

"I'll get there in about 20 minutes," I said and set off towards the Nyatanda River, followed closely by Apollo 1, ever on the lookout for adventure. Sunray Mantle advised us that Fire Force was on standby and available if required.

We had been on a routine patrol close to the "follow-up" and were familiar with the area. It was low-lying terrain, sloping gently towards the Nyatanda River and behind Gwidza and Munyeziwa mountain ranges. While the mountains provided excellent terrain for ZANLA base camps and good observation positions for the SF, they interfered with SF radio reception when they were operating in low-lying areas. In these situations, we depended on relay stations to communicate with our HQ.

This was one of those situations when we threw caution to the wind and sped along to see if we could find the missing troops on patrol. After about 20 minutes and several calls, we finally made contact with them, with the following conversation ensuing:

"Mantle Zulu 2, Apollo 2," I called.

"Apollo 2, Mantle Zulu 2, go ahead, reading you strength 5."

"Good to hear you. Where are you?" I asked.

"About a mile from you. We can see you," confirmed Mantle Zulu 2.

"We can't see you," I relayed, as we scanned the area for the patrol.

"If you drive down the road about 200 metres, we will be on your right. We are very close to the terrs, just minutes," crackled the radio.

I cautiously eased 1442 forward, scrutinising the recently ploughed fields until I spotted MZ 2 about 500 metres to my right, spread out in a wide arrowhead formation heading directly towards us. The tracker had his head down, focused on spoor and flanked by seven camouflaged troops, weapons at the ready. Impressive I thought, particularly the MAG gunner. The Support Unit had many fine trackers, certainly among the best in the country. N/S/P/O Mike Stewart (a Support Unit member) recalls: "We once tracked a group over 15km with them doing every thing possible in anti-tracking. We spent from about 9.00 a.m. (they were spotted at 6.30 a.m. by Int.Aff.), until making contact at about 5 p.m.. When we made contact they were about 3km from where they were first spotted, so spent the whole day anti-tracking. That gives you an idea how good my two trackers were. Between the two of them, the terrs had no chance."[1]

Suddenly it dawned on me that, if MZ 2 were to my right following spoor heading towards me and they were a couple of minutes behind the insurgents, we must be right in the middle. "Where are the terrorists then?" I asked. "On the other side of your position," replied MZ 2.

I spun my head towards the kraals about 20 metres to my left. Assessing the situation, I concluded that the insurgents must be in ambush waiting to attack MZ 2 who were vulnerable in the open field. At that moment, eight ZANLA insurgents wielding their AK-47s broke cover from the kraals and sprinted towards the sparsely vegetated tributary that flowed into Nyatanda River 150 metres east of the kraal. They were closely followed by the Support Unit callsign in hot pursuit. I radioed Sunray Mantle and gave him the map reference (locstat), VQ410358. He called in Fire Force while D/Sgt. Herbert and I sat on the Land Rover's bonnet and watched the unfolding drama. We could not move as our responsibility was to act as a relay station between Sunray Mantle and MZ 2.

1 N/S/P/O Mike Stewart email 2018.

The village seemed deserted but Herbert told me the locals would be hiding, afraid of both terrorists and the SF. What a dilemma: dammed if you win, dammed if you lose. I did not consider there to be any innocent parties in this war. One either supported the insurgents or the SF. It was a close-quarters, bloody conflict fought out amidst people's homes, farms and surrounding bush. Civilian casualties on either side were unavoidable and inevitable.

MZ 2 reported they were still on the tracks of eight insurgents as they regrouped heading down to the Nyatanda River,[1] which had thick vegetation and substantial tree cover. A secure venue to camouflage in but not enough to disappear, which was ZANLA's preferred strategy.

Mantle Sunray reported that Fire Force from Grand Reef was on its way. Fl. Lt. Mark McLean explains:

> At Grand Reef near Umtali (FAF 8), the hooter blasted, and the Fire Force scrambled. The helicopters were on standby, fuelled, armed and ready for take-off. On occasions, technicians would start the helicopters, so the aircraft were idling by the time the pilots arrived but this procedure was not the usual practice. Everyone ran to his station. There was excitement all around. Intelligence staff distributed maps while the intelligence officer briefed the K-Car commander and pilot on the essentials. The in-flight brief would give the details. It was all go and speed was of the essence. No time to waste. Efficient concurrent activity all round was essential to ensure a successful deployment.
>
> Walking toward the chopper the pilot routinely ran his eye over the machine looking for anything amiss. He checked the surrounds for loose articles, wind direction and blade clearance. At the door he reached in and picked up his flak jacket, shrugged it on then pulled himself up with the grab strap, swung a leg over the cyclic[2] and settled into the hard armoured seat. He strapped into the harness and, reaching up, lifted his sweat stained helmet off the hook on the cabin roof, pulled on his gloves, slipped on the helmet and clipped the chin strap. The radio "pigtail" multi-plug connection for radio and intercom, connecting the helmet to the radio apparatus, was plugged in. His movements were practiced, habitual, as he gripped the cyclic with his right hand giving it a slight "stir" to check friction and centralised so that the rotor disc would be level during the start. With his left hand he checked "collective down and locked". He placed his feet on the pedals and adjusted to neutral position. A glance around the cabin, out over his right shoulder and left, across to the technician standing outside the chopper. Satisfied he ran through his pre-start checks. Rotor brake off, fuel flow back, fingers and eyes running through the sequence. Reaching for the start selector he called "Clear start", and the technician responded, "Clear start".
>
> As the switch is flipped three start sequence indicators light up, the igniters sound their quiet clacking and the turbine started spinning. With a whoosh the fuel ignited in the combustion chamber and the engine howled into life, sending a shimmering plume of hot gasses out of the tail pipe. The N1, (turbine speed) moved up in response to the rapidly climbing Tail Pipe Temperature gauge (TPT). The acceleration steadied and the start sequence lights went out in turn. The engine was steady at ground idle. Another quick run-through of the engine gauges and the pilot started the rotor engagement by moving the fuel flow lever forward with his left hand, carefully monitoring the TPT, and rpm. The blades began to move, the pilot pressed the stopwatch, and with practiced movements synchronised rotor acceleration with the stopwatch sweep hand to ensure centrifugal clutch engaged in the specified time. Too fast or too slow would result in damage. The machine is ready for flight.

---

[1] Nyatanda River: VQ4532.

[2] Cyclic is the cyclic control which is the approximate equivalent of an airplane's control column/yoke/stick which controls lateral flight direction by altering each blade-pitch angle cyclically, thus changing the distribution of lift over the rotor and exerting a force in a lateral direction.

The whole pre-flight sequence had taken about one and a half minutes during which time the crew remained almost motionless but alert to every sequence and sound associated with the start-up. Watching for any anomaly, listening for a change in the familiar sounds. Now that the helicopter was ready, the crew went through their own procedures. The technician swung up behind his gun and strapped himself in, the pilot adjusted the collective friction,[1] giving a little "bump" up and down to check it and adjusted the cyclic friction to his personal "feel"; a touch on the pedals would give the chopper a slight waggle of the tail.

For those who have experienced this moment, the memory will never fade as the characteristic whine of the Alouette as it "spooled up" and the smell of the exhaust Avtur[2] from the ever-increasing energy from the engines saturated the arena for furious action. Radios were turned on to a preset frequency; troops scrambled aboard their pre-assigned choppers. The leader pilot called Ops[3] to get the heading and distance to target then radioed "Formation check-in," at which each helicopter called their formation number "2, 3, 4 . . . Lead lifting." Airborne the pilot turned onto the track passed to him from Ops and pressed his stopwatch. The formation followed strung out in a loose line astern, listening to the briefing from Ops to the "K" Car Commander.

As information came in from the troops on the ground this was relayed to the Fire Force as it raced to the location of the sighting. Flying low to minimise any possible compromise by the sound of the engines from the aircraft, the helicopters flew at tree-top level. The Lynx[4] was available and flew at a height creating "covering sound" to deceive the terrs.[5]

2 Commando RLI was the Fire Force commanded by Maj. John Dawson.[6] We heard the distant sounds of their approach. Periodically, a distinctive blade clatter could be heard as they flew through turbulence. Clatter is the sound of a blade stalling under high-load conditions.

The Fire Force Commander had many things that had to be done simultaneously: orientation, map reading, ground assessment and formulating a preliminary battle plan, all while the strike force raced into the target area, with essential liaison with the ground forces.

As the K-Car approached the target area, it climbed to 1,000 feet, contacted the ground forces and the Fire Force began to "shake out" into combat orbit circulating anticlockwise around the target area. The ground troops gave out their information.

"Apollo 2, K-Car."

"K-Car, Apollo 2, go ahead," I replied.

"I have your Land Rover visual. Where is Mantle Zulu 2?"

"Mantle Zulu 2 are in pursuit about a mile to our north," I responded.

"Mantle Zulu 2, K-Car, what is your position?"

"We are about a mile north of the Land Rover in a small river line, still on the tracks of four gooks who seem to have split up."

Indeed, the original eight insurgents had split up. The commander of the insurgents told Maxwell to take three men and head north up the Nyatanda River, while he would take the remaining three and head south down the river, where there was better cover and a gum-tree thicket.

"Throw smoke," instructed the Fire Force Commander as the four G-Cars settled into a wide, left-handed orbit, circling the contact area enabling the guns to be trained on the ground below. The

[1] The collective: The pilot's connection to all three blades through multiple levers and hydraulic actuators. By having a mechanical adjustable friction built into the system, the pilot is able to adjust the amount of effort it takes to move the lever. Hence his preferred "feel". Additionally, it ensures that the lever remains in the same position if he takes his left hand off the collective to do something else. Mark McLean email 9/11/2018.

[2] Avtur: A type of aviation turbine fuel. Actually paraffin, better refined and with some anti-freeze additives.

[3] Ops: Operation Centre. Each FF would have an operation room.

[4] Lynx: A twin-prop fully armed Cessna 337.

[5] Mark McLean email 1/6/2015.

[6] Geldenhuys, P. (2014), Air Strike Log Entry 452.

K-Car leading the attack had figurative "feet" like an eagle, floating, searching, ready to swoop in an instant while holding a central flight pattern above the four G-Cars. In the haze of the river line red smoke floated up above the tree line.

"Got you visual Mantle Zulu 2. Stay on the tracks," instructed the Fire Force Commander as he assumed control and started to implement his battle plan.

"Mantle Zulu 2 stay where you are, K-Car is firing," said the K-Car pilot calmly. There followed a series of violent explosions as the K-Car unleashed the full force of its 20mm cannon, firing high-explosive incendiary rounds at a rate of 700 rounds per minute. The insurgents had made it to the Nyatanda River but had been spotted by the K-Car. Thus, the battle developed. "Stops", were four-strong groups of soldiers, ferried in by helicopter. On landing, they were strategically and hastily despatched. The land-tail trucks, carrying mainly troops and Avtur, arrived bringing reinforcements and fuel closer to the battleground. This reduced flight time and helped the commander maintain momentum as he deployed reinforcements to help contain the enemy. These troops were uplifted by helicopters and ferried into battle.

This was the first time I had watched the Fire Force in action. I was mesmerised. Witnessing gunfire from the troops on the ground, the K-Car firing its 20mm cannon and the smell of gunpowder all blasted through my mind and nostrils, fuelled by elevated levels of adrenalin.

There was more to come as the high-pitched drone of the Lynx drifted into the battle zone. The Fire Force Commander directed the Lynx to drop Frantan (Napalm). Once the target area was defined, the Lynx made its strike. Air Lt. Chris Tucker, a Lynx pilot, explains: "Diving at 185mph, two .303 Brownings, mounted on the dorsal fuselage blazing away, and at about 100 feet the Lynx delivered its Frantan. The bomb exploded, laying down an inferno that covered an area of almost 700 square meters. On a low level or level run the Lynx could deliver the Frantan at 50 feet, always selecting a line that ran parallel to the 'Stop groups' to prevent bombing our own troops. Frantan had a blast effect and as a quick burning chemical, similar to phosphorous, it did literally 'suck in' all oxygen in the immediate area, some terrs were found with their lungs hanging out of their mouths; it was a particularly useful weapon when the enemy were in rocky terrain or holed up in caves. The bomb was shaped like an elongated 500lb standard Nato bomb. Its casing was made of fibreglass to reduce weight and provide frangibility,[1] hence Frantan – 'Fran' (gibility) – 'tan' for the burns. The bomb's detonator was a crude but failsafe device. It had a ball-bearing in a circular housing with a detonator pin at the base. On impact the ball-bearing shot round the circular ball race until it struck the pin, triggering instant detonation. Each bomb weighed approximately 50kgs and contained about 40kg of petrol, and a chemical mix, thought to be of detergents plus other cheap household items, which ignited on impact. It was a terrifying weapon which the terrs feared above all else."[2]

"On target," said the Fire Force Commander as the Lynx climbed out of the dive and resumed its circular left-handed flight path around the perimeter formed by the circling Fire Force choppers high above the battle. This was followed by resumed firing from the K-Car and troops on the ground, as they engaged the enemy, followed by a procession of helicopters back to the land-tail to refuel from the drums of Avtur. The Lynx was called in to deliver another strike, which was once again on target.

Shadows began to creep across the valley as the Fire Force completed their mopping-up operations. One G-Car delivered the bodies of four dead insurgents to 1442, together with their AK-47s and webbing.[3]

On searching the bodies and webbing, I discovered a copy of Mao Tse-Tung's little red book, *Quotations from Chairman Mao Tse-Tung* which became my "war bible". The book contained quotations of Mao's political and military statements. I started studying it daily throughout the conflict in order

1 Frangibility: A material that breaks up into pieces through deformation.

2 Air Lt. Chris Tucker email 25/4/2015.

3 Details of this contact confirmed by Barry Woan and "Sakkie" McKay at a conference in Durban, South Africa, with Fred Mason, Barry Woan, "Sakkie" McKay and David and John Padbury, 3/12/2015, and email 10/2/2016.

to understand the thoughts, strategies and tactics of our enemy. I also found a large bundle of cash and advised one of the FF pilots who returned to collect the booty.

Once the battle was over, recovery of ground troops began under the watchful and protective eye of the K-Car. The land-tail left the area and the Support Unit men regrouped and began their elated journey back to base. We also made our way back to Rusape Police Station, in time for celebrations in the police canteen, but not before handing over the captured weapons to CID for onward transmission to the BSAP Armoury for ballistics examination.[1]

On reflection, I realised the potential for success by the SF, particularly the Fire Force. Reading the documents recovered from the contact, I became aware that ZANLA had a sound command structure, they were efficiently organised and well entrenched and accepted in the area. Locating them was our difficulty. Once found, killing was not difficult. It was also clear that ZANLA had a presence in Makoni and our great weakness was that the SF did not. We would meet Maxwell in battle a year later: on 17 July 1977 to be precise.

The good news for 1976 was that I passed the written exams from detective section officer to detective inspector, which meant that my career was well set. I was a D/S/O at the age of 25 years. I had succeeded at the last written exams to detective inspector and, all being well, would be promoted in 1978, when I would be permitted to sit before the Promotions Board. Promotion thereafter was on merit.

On 28 November 1976, Fire Force engaged ZANLA, killing four insurgents and one civilian, and injuring two civilians.[2] There was a further Fire Force deployment on 1 February 1977, but the results were not recorded.[3]

Fire Force

In time, following each contact, it became clearer to me that once the enemy had been located, Fire Force was the most effective "killing machine".

My brother, Capt. David Padbury, who had experience both on the ground and from periodically commanding Fire Force deployments for a period of about three years in the RAR explains:

> This aerial attack force was made up of a combination of the light and versatile Aerospatiale Alouette 111 helicopters and troops specially trained for the role of being delivered directly into the fight with the enemy. The helicopters were configured for two main roles, that of the Gun Ship, commonly known as the K-Car (command) and the troop transporters which were commonly called G-Cars (general duty). The K-Cars were generally armed with the devastating French Matra MG151 20mm cannon, while the G-Cars were armed with twin 303 browning machine guns. As the war developed, the Dakota[4] was introduced to deliver troops by parachute, greatly enhancing the capability of the Fire Force, making it by far the most effective killing machine developed by the Rhodesian security forces. Tactically, it was a concentrated effort and carried with it maximum force and devastating surprise. With it, we had complete air superiority because the insurgents had no air support at all, but as the war progressed it transpired that they had a much more potent weapon, the resilient support of the people.
>
> The K-Car pilot was responsible for the air co-ordination of the aircraft while the deployment of the ground forces and the ground battle was under the expertise of the army commander in the K-Car. In reality, this was often a joint effort with great co-operation between the pilot and the army commander who was designated the Fire Force Commander. Once the follow-up callsign's position was identified by the K-Car, he would overfly the enemy and seek to establish their whereabouts. Usually they would

---

1 Binda, A. (2014), eBook Location 5525 of 16593.

2 Makoni/Manyika Incidents Map: Incident 8; Geldenhuys, P. (2014), Air Strike Log Entry 544.

3 Makoni/Manyika Incidents Map: Incident 9; Geldenhuys, P. (2014), Air Strike Log Entry 609.

4 Dakota: C 47 is a twin-engined transport aircraft flown by No. 3 Squadron, Rh.AF.

have gone to ground and be hiding. He would assess the area, identify the likely escape routes and instruct choppers 2, 3, and 4 where he wanted them to position their troops in formations known as Stops. There was no standard operational format for a Fire Force unit. This could comprise, 3 choppers, 2 G-Cars and 1 K-Car, or 4 choppers, a Lynx and a Dakota or more, depending on availability of men and aircraft.

The Fire Force countered the main tactic of the insurgents which was referred to as the classic guerrilla "bombshell". They would immediately suspend contact and disperse in several directions to escape the security forces. They would then choose their targets for maximum effect carrying minimum risk, as and when it favoured them. However, with the advent of the Fire Force this frustrating tactic was largely thwarted, especially by the K-Car as it delivered its deadly firepower.

In order to make our impact even greater, many different tactics were developed as the deployment of Fire Force evolved. One of the more effective tactics was the "Dummy Drop", where G-Cars would simulate the dropping of troops into key locations. This would help to slow the dispersal tactic of the insurgents, allowing time for our ground troops to contact the enemy.

As this key strike force progressed, another aspect was to become critical; that of Intelligence. Intelligence was vital in two key aspects. Firstly, it was needed in the form of sightings or information from the ground which pinpointed the enemy's location. This required the deployment of reliable observation-post troops that were able to infiltrate the area and remain undetected while they kept watch in the hills and from other vantage points. One of the crucial skills they possessed was the ability to interpret the various scenarios unfolding in the daily lives of the local population together with observing a building up of suspicious activity.

The second aspect that grew in significance was the accurate post de-briefing of the Fire Force action. This became significant if the Fire Force was deployed to the same general area because good de-briefing would enable flight directions to be identified and trends established that could be passed to Fire Force commanders for consideration as the battle developed. Good intelligence and knowledge became vital. This is what provided the body count at the end of the day, and proved the Fire Force effectiveness when all this came together.[1]

Wick Farm Store Robbery[2]

As the war progressed, it became increasingly difficult to distinguish between ZANLA involvement in incidents, as opposed to insurgent-inspired or simple lawlessness. I was convinced the criminal element were taking advantage of the deteriorating security situation in the TTLs and were increasingly influenced by ZANLA propaganda.

It was my policy to treat all incidents as terrorist until proved otherwise, in order to ensure our lives were not at risk. All investigations were carried out with an armed escort and, when necessary, with a tracking unit such as dog section.

One such incident occurred on Sunday, 20 March 1977. Here's the text of the memorandum acknowledging the performance of good work:

> During the early hours of Sunday, 20 March 1977, the premises of Wick Farm Store, situated 42.4km North East of Rusape, were broken into. Certain items of property were stolen and thereafter the remaining contents of the building were set on fire. Property was found outside, and the initial assessment was that the damage had been caused by terrorist elements.
>
> A team from Sub.JOC Rusape 8674 PO Davis, 9297 PO Howard (two dog section

[1] David Padbury email 28/5/2015.

[2] Makoni/Manyika Incidents Map: Incident 10.

details), 18494 Det. Cst. Matimba, two army trackers, and DSO Padbury was formed to investigate the incident. (Author's note: the trackers were both game rangers from the National Parks.)

With the aid of dogs and trackers, the team was able to follow the spoor of between eight and ten suspects from the scene into the adjacent Makoni TTL, for a distance of approximately 10km, where a resting place was located. It was established that this was the spot where the stolen property had been shared among the culprits. Directed by DSO Padbury the team initiated an extended line sweep through a kraal line some 549m away, and during the course of this exercise, two African males were located and apprehended after a chase of 92m. When questioned they admitted that they knew the identity and whereabouts of ten local tribesmen whom they claimed to be responsible for the incident. (Author's note: we withdrew back to base.) At 1900 hours the same evening the team moved back into the Makoni TTL, and following indications by one of the persons previously arrested, they apprehended one accused who was prepared to indicate the whereabouts of the remainder of the gang. At this stage, it was raining heavily forcing the team to suspend operations until first light the following day. (Author's note: we took shelter in a local kraal hut, warmed by a smouldering fire.)

At 0500 hours on 21 March 1977, the team carried on for a further 7km, where four African males were observed in thick bush carrying bundles of property. Before they could be apprehended the suspects spotted the Police team and ran off. They were called upon to stop and when they did not, Detective Section Officer Padbury instructed his team to open fire. This resulted in the arrest of two of the suspects and the recovery of further property identified as having come from Wick Farm Store. (Author's note: we walked a total of approximately 54km on the two deployments.)

On 18 May 1977, the three accused were convicted of house breaking, theft and arson, and each received 5 years IWL (Internment with Labour). Efforts to locate the remainder of the gang continue.

The Commissioner is most pleased to learn of the initiative, tenacity of purpose and devotion to duty displayed by these members under adverse weather conditions, and he directs that a copy of this memorandum be placed in their respective records of service in recognition of their efforts.

While on the subject of supply stores, during one of my patrols into the Makoni, we stopped at a local shop for refreshments: quarts of beer to be precise. When the storekeeper went to get our change, I noticed he had a large trunk loaded with cash. I told him that the terrorists would steal the money from him if they found out about it, but he was not concerned in the least. However, the matter concerned me, and I subsequently confiscated the container and invited the storekeeper to return to Rusape with me. D/S/O Cutting and I spent hours counting the money. I then took the storekeeper with his stash to the Standard Bank, where we opened an account in his name. Here the principles of banking were explained to him. He was most grateful as, prior to that, he was convinced he was about to lose his life's savings. We had no such intentions but I was aware the insurgents would not hesitate to rob him of his earnings.

Observation Posts (OPs) Strategies and Successes

As I have explained earlier, the TTLs were liberated areas where ZANLA had gained the support of most inhabitants now opposed to the SF and their operations. They were required to assist ZANLA in every conceivable way. This included supplying food, clothing and beer for parties, as well as sexual pleasures. At a military level, locals were required to search out and identify any SF movements, patrols and OPs, reporting back to ZANLA through their intelligence networks. It was my contention we faced a community favouring ZANLA and opposed to us. Therefore, we were operating in enemy territory behind enemy lines. This reality raised our level of awareness, ensuring we were constantly alert to possible attacks and threats.

The purpose of our observation posts was to infiltrate an area of suspicion covertly and then remain undetected while observing the locals' activities, in order to gather intelligence and identify patterns of behaviour which would help us locate and identify insurgents. Thereafter, we would initiate military action against them. The most effective method in this regard was a combination of the OP and Fire Force.

OPs would generally be positioned following intelligence gathered by Special Branch and Ground Coverage units and would usually be situated overlooking kraals, missions, schools and stores. A great deal of bushcraft was required to successfully penetrate rural areas and set up an OP position without being compromised. This included anti-tracking methods to ensure locals did not identify "foreign" footprints, while also remaining concealed in the OP position for the duration of the deployment.

Two critical elements needed to be established for a successful OP. Firstly, understanding the people and their ways and, secondly, understanding the enemy and his ways. Initially, these two elements were absent. The only method of identifying ZANLA fighters was by visually identifying the weapons they carried. We assumed if no weapons were sighted, no ZANLA fighters were in the vicinity. This proved a serious mistake as ZANLA fighters could be present in the area and simply moving among the people unarmed. We, of course, could not do so as we were the dominant colonial force and did not have the numerical strength or capacity to become one with the people over whom we ruled. What we needed to learn was how to interpret events on the ground.

When one examines the above, it becomes obvious that success is largely about intelligence. While the skills of the OP operators grew in these vital areas over time, there were factors which were overlooked until it became "too little, too late". The first was the potential of African troops who would naturally have a better understanding of rural activity and the second was the use of "turned" *mujibhas* and insurgents. The size of the *mujibha* resource and its potential was not fully realised until it was too late. Despite these weaknesses, we encountered successes, notably by units including African troops.

Don Peacock's Observation Post[1]

There was no specific Special Branch coverage of Manyika TTL which bordered the Makoni, so I was asked to oversee intelligence operations in Manyika. I promptly agreed. This would bring continuity of intelligence input between the two TTLs making sense, as the Manyika was also a ZANLA liberated area. It was a picturesque environment filled with huge granite mountains and outcrops, colourful Msasa trees, rivers and reasonable dirt roads that wound around the TTL. The only disadvantage was the roads were vulnerable to ambushes and in several places there was only one access road. This was a concern. However, it was not long before we had our first successes in Manyika as we continued to use OPs in an area well suited to them. Naturally, we also encountered setbacks.

Police Anti-Terrorist Unit (PATU) deployments usually lasted a week commencing on a Monday. These four- to five-man sticks normally included one or two African policemen in the team which helped their effectiveness by interpreting events on the ground and assisting in interrogations when necessary. They were very dedicated and effective units that proved extremely efficient in OPs. Thus, when Insp. Don Peacock[2] arrived at Sub.JOC Rusape with his four-man stick for briefing, it was pleasant to be reacquainted, as he was a good friend from Salisbury. Don was well known. He was particularly tall which opened himself to much good-natured banter. His first words surprised me: "I have to be back from deployment by Friday as we have a big party coming up. Could you arrange that for me?"

His request was totally against my policy. I was opposed to short deployments as these meant fewer men in the field, decreasing our killing potential. However, Don was a long-standing friend

[1] Makoni/Manyika Incidents Map: Incident 11.

[2] Insp. Don Peacock served from April 1975 to June 1981. He died on 4/5/1995 in Durban, South Africa.

which made my decision difficult. I agreed that he could return home once he killed some insurgents or at least called the Fire Force in on a deployment. This would require the section to at least make a sighting of ZANLA and I knew he would make the most of the opportunity. That pleased Don, so we continued with the usual briefing and arrangements. He was to be deployed into the eastern mountain ranges of Manyika TTL. It was a forested area with substantial rugged granite outcrops which concealed many caves on the mountainous slopes. This was always extremely difficult terrain to work in with good radio communications when high up, but poor reception in the valleys. However, the difficulties worked in the OP's favour as it made being compromised by locals less likely.

I chose this area for two reasons. Firstly, ease of deployment and, secondly, the remoteness of the region. It was difficult and dangerous to access by vehicle as there was only one entry and exit road. We referred to this hazardous scenario as "ambush alley" but, as we didn't often visit the area, I reasoned the chances of success to be favourable. I hoped the minimal Security Forces activity would have caused the insurgents to be less vigilant. Don was to be deployed off the main tar road which linked Umtali and Inyanga. It was a long, difficult walk to the target area. He and his team were deployed under the cover of dark and bashed their way through the bush until he thought he was in the vicinity I had pinpointed overlooking Bethana Kraal.

He decided to wait until morning to verify his location and ensure they were in a position that provided adequate protection. Dawn was approaching and, along with it, a noticeable drop in temperature that preceded the sun's arrival which warmed the day. As matters transpired, Don's section had found an ideal position from which to launch their operation. He despatched one of his men to scout for water in the river some distance away before sunrise. The arrival of a new day would wake the locals and thus set in motion their normal day-to-day activities. As it was, crowing roosters along with intermittent barking dogs were making vain attempts to rouse sleeping residents. Despite these early rousings of the locals, finding a nearby source of water along with good cover, was the priority for an OP in a new position. Each man carried his own food rations, sleeping bag and clothing, but water had to be obtained locally. Spare ammunition, grenades and radio with spare batteries were also shared among the stick. While scouting the area, the reconnaissance man overheard snoring. Alerted by this, he crouched, scrutinised the terrain ahead then, in painstaking silence, carefully avoiding disturbing twigs and stones, he inched his way forward until he had sight of four insurgents sleeping in a cluster. Dawn was beginning to break but there was an unusual calm. A stillness that precedes a conflict. Birds were quiet. A deathly silence prevailed. Eventually, the scout was satisfied there were no other insurgents in the immediate vicinity. Stealthily retreating, with rifle at the ready, he carefully retraced his steps. He moved extremely slowly, gently placing his rubber-soled boot onto the soil, to avoid breaking twigs or causing stones to rattle. He methodically made his way back to Don and the rest of the stick.

In a hushed whisper he delivered his astonishing news to the section. Don decided to act rather than risk calling in Fire Force. The team hatched a hasty plan. Odds were even: four on four. Don decided to attempt to capture one insurgent and shoot the remaining three. He whispered his instructions. Fortunately, the team's weapons were already cocked, so safety-catches were released and trigger fingers at the ready. Each man was to focus on one enemy while Don would aim to apprehend one of the insurgents. Don would initiate the attack with a downward motion of his head. Furtively, they made their way to the sleeping group, quietly identifying the individual to be captured. A seemingly eternal, motionless and apprehensive moment passed while they waited in anxious anticipation. Don gestured with a curt nod. The African dawn was shattered by three bursts of automatic gunfire which eliminated three insurgents instantaneously. Simultaneously, Don attempted to capture his startled foe. However, with remarkable strength and agility, the insurgent freed himself and slipped through his grasp. Another burst of automatic fire killed him instantly. Don was relieved he had prepared his section to take this action should he be unable to overpower his adversary. Even capturing a sleeping terrorist proved a daunting and impossible task.

Don radioed for me to attend the scene and I was air-lifted to it by helicopter. On arrival at the contact site, I collected the bodies and weapons. From documents found on the bodies we ascertained that this was a command group that had come to establish communications with the rest of the comrades under their command. We recovered two Russian Tokarov pistols and four AK-47s. Don's report read as follows: "Deployed Monday evening. 4 terrorists killed Tuesday morning, choppered back to base. Tuesday afternoon and evening celebrate our success. Home on Wednesday."[1]

Pete Cutting recalls: "I joined the Special Branch and was posted to the Joint Operational Command at Rusape, together with a couple of other chaps including John Padbury. We were allocated various areas of responsibility and I well recall the incident described by John where Don was responsible for the killing of four insurgents. While the outcome of Don's deployment was excellent, the security forces had yet to overcome the fact that ZANLA had created a permanent presence on the ground and were collaborating with the people. Our strategy essentially depended on confirmed visual weapons sightings from OPs and Selous Scout deployments. Getting captures was not as simple as it might have seemed to some at the time. The reality was that while a capture was invaluable, it would always prove extremely difficult."[2]

Dog Section Follow-Up[3]

A successful technique of tracking down insurgents after incidents was the use of the BSAP Dog Section, a fine, dedicated and highly skilled unit which adjusted well to the war. I respected their courage as they were always, as with any tracking unit, at the forefront of any search, the point of greatest risk. They were invariably keen and never complained.

A two-man dog section team was based at Sub.JOC Rusape. I used them frequently and enjoyed their company, especially in the police canteen. P/O George McLennan[4] tells the story:

> Being woken up in the dead of the night with the phone ringing meant only one thing for the dog section detail, you are being called out to a "terr" incident. Patrol Officer Hugh "Jabs" Temple,[5] the search and attack dog handler came through and said that there had been a farm attack and that they required us to attend. Still pitch black outside we got dressed and collected our dogs; my dog "Alexis", a pure bred black and tan Bloodhound who was rated as one of the best tracker dogs in the Police Dog unit, being able to track scent over 24 hours old. Jabs' dog, "Major", was a German Shepherd who disliked anything that was human and was able to walk on two legs.
>
> We proceeded to the JOC Ops room where we met Detective Section Officer (D/S/O) Padbury – from Special Branch who briefed us; Rebeuni farm in the Inyazura area, had been attacked with small arms fire and ransacked, and he asked us to accompany him in order to try and track down the terrorists involved.
>
> John Padbury led the way, we followed, accompanied by about six police reservist "shotgun riders", whose duties were to escort us and assist with fire power should we be attacked or ambushed while driving to the scene of the attack. Most of them were not equipped with backpacks and did not carry the equipment necessary for a follow up as this was not their role.

---

[1] Confirmed by D/S/O Pete Cutting, SB Sub.JOC Rusape, oral interview and telephone discussions March to May 2015. The events are told as described to me by Don in the debrief.

[2] Pete Cutting email 16/3/2015.

[3] Makoni/Manyika Incidents Map: Incident 12.

[4] P/O George McLennan joined the BSAP in 1969 as cadet C628. He passed out as a patrol officer in 1970 and was posted to Gatooma. In 1971, he joined the Dog Section, passing the six-month course as a patrol dog handler, and later the tracker unit. He did numerous stints as a patrol dog handler and was involved in numerous contacts. In 1978, just prior to his release from the police force, he was awarded the Bronze Baton for bravery and dedication to duties.

[5] P/O Hugh Temple joined the BSAP in February 1971. He served at Salisbury Central Charge Office and Traffic Section. He then did a B-Car course, was posted to the Information Room before finally transferring to Dog Section in 1976 until he left the force in May 1980.

As first light came up, we arrived at the scene and while John Padbury investigated the scene, Jabs and I started to look for the terrorist's spoor. After a short while we found the spoor of a large group of at least 20 terrorists heading away from the farm.

They had attacked the farmhouse from outside the security fence with small arms fire and had put an RPG 7 into the house, which hit a 40KG gas cylinder. The resultant explosion had damaged the walls, and also set the roof on fire. Fortunately no one was at home at the time.

DSO Pete Cutting arrived with the JOC Officer, Supt Sloman. John was in the meantime trying to get some members to act as follow up for us but there were no PATU sticks available, they were all deployed on other scenes. His only option was the Police Reservists who were drivers and lookouts, and he asked if they could be our follow up group along with himself!

Jabs and I looked at each other, amazed; John was not dressed for the occasion as he was Special Branch and dressed in civilian clothing, and the reservists were fairly old 45-years plus with very little ammunition on them, no food, no water. We were not about to put our lives in their hands! I told John that when doing a follow up you went at the dogs' speed, you could not go around thick undergrowth but straight through it and trust me, you move at speed. We did not want to be rude and tell John that as a Special Branch man he did not look like a "mean machine" and was not really as fit as we dog handlers were.

We had known John for a long time and knew he was game to come with us for the possibility of a fire fight, so he organised another 5 reservists and D/S/O Cutting as our follow up team. The tracking harness was put on "Alexis" which had a 30-foot rope attached to it and pointed out the scent to her which she very quickly picked up, and off we headed. The tracker dog handler is always reading his dog by visually watching the dog when not in thick undergrowth to see how he is tracking, when in thick bush you read your dog by the tension on the rope. You are also checking the ground in front of you to confirm that you are still on the terrorists' tracks, watching for foot-prints, scuff marks in the sand, grass bent over, any disturbances on the ground that indicates the direction of flight.

The patrol dog handler is there to act as the tracker's eyes and warn of any dangers that might crop up; he would also use his patrol dog "Major" to clear any area where we thought there might be an ambush. Jabs was my guardian angel, and my life depended on him.

This was an extremely efficient method of tracking. We tracked for a number of hours, stopping every now and again so that our follow up group could take a break, at every water point or river we let them soak themselves and have a drink. In the Rhodesian bush the temperature is very high and you need to drink plenty of water; we were not going a normal walking pace but at a pace very close to breaking into a trot.

Our tracking started at around 7.30 a.m. in the morning and by late afternoon, after covering a distance of approximately 18 kilometres, we were all very tired and worn out when Alexis stopped and started to circle, keeping her nose to the ground at all times, she would then turn around and go the other way.

I informed John that we were close and to tell the follow up members to be wide awake. John radioed the JOC, gave them our position and the JOC advised the Fire Force who were now standing by. Alexis led us to the base of a kopje and started to walk up the fairly steep face with thick vegetation and lots of loose stones around, so going up holding onto the lead and carrying my rifle was making it very difficult. All of a sudden, the tracking rope went slack, I stopped and was waiting for the rope to get taught again which would indicate to me that she was back on the spoor. Nothing happened. I was busy looking for spoor and trying to see where Alexis was when I heard the sound of a weapon being cocked and, knowing that all of us on the follow up had our weapons cocked and ready, it only meant one thing!

I looked up, and approximately 30 feet away I saw one insurgent pointing his AK-47 in my direction; this seemed like a slow-motion picture and before I could drop to the ground my "eyes behind me" had also seen what was going on and immediately opened fire, the rest of our support group joined in.

A huge firefight erupted and I was constantly pulling on the rope to get Alexis back to me but with no luck, my immediate thought was that she had been shot. After what seemed like ages, Jabs called "cease fire"; we all stopped shooting and it was dead quiet, you could hear a pin drop, Jabs immediately sent "Major" in to clear the area. Jabs constantly shouted instructions to his dog and then instructed the follow up group that he was going in to "clear" the contact area and they were not to open fire.

Jabs set off and John got hold of JOC Rusape on the radio informing them that we had made contact and requested Fire Force attend. Eventually, after what seemed to be another eternity, Jabs came back and said that we had walked into the terrs base camp, there was a lot of equipment left behind including clothing, ammunition, food and what we first thought was ground to air missiles. John informed JOC Rusape of our find and the helicopters carrying the Fire Force came in to the contact sight from a very high altitude!

We cleared the camp, gathered all the equipment together and made our way down to a rendezvous point to be picked up while the fire force was deployed along likely escape routes, and also to follow the spoor when they abandoned their camp. Our job was over.

On going through the camp we estimated that we had made contact with a group of 26 terrs, verified by the number of places where they had been sleeping, the kit they had left behind and the way they had been scattered around the kopje. Unfortunately, no terrs were killed in the contact or during the Fire Force follow up. Back at the rendezvous site it was apparent that this was the first time the reservists had been on a follow up, let alone been in a punch up.

That night back at the pub John bought the drinks for all the members involved in the punch up and trust me we really drank, because it was not often that Special Branch bought you drinks.

The total distance that we tracked was around 18 Ks, with eight security force personnel against 26 terrs.[1]

The skills of the dog-tracking section were remarkable. Once their dogs smelt a scent, they rarely lost it. I considered them among the best in Rhodesia. Not only were the police handlers excellent trackers but they had the added advantage of the dogs, an incredible combination. Watching a bloodhound as its rear bobbed from side to side, tail wagging, nose to the ground, while periodically looking up for a moment, then resuming the search, was an exhilarating experience.

During the follow-up, George was convinced we were going to make contact with insurgents and I passed on this information to Sub.JOC Rusape several times, regularly updating them with our locstat. We were tracking in a white farming area some distance from the TTL. In retrospect, the Sub.JOC Rusape should have called for the Fire Force, as it was not deployed and geared for action. I had suggested their use at the time and I remain convinced that we would have achieved better results had they done so. Hindsight, as is commonly noted, is a precise teacher. Another interesting aspect of this engagement was our discovery, while searching the camp, of a British 3.5-inch high-explosive anti-tank bazooka and a rocket with the word "HEAT" inscribed on the body of the projectile. Initially, we thought it was a heat-seeking missile, but Fire Force Command corrected us, as this was not the case.

---

1 George McLennan email 18/5/2015. Confirmed by Pete Cutting email 20/7/2015.

Ambush

Another strategy we developed was to ambush paths that linked kraals we knew supported ZANLA. This monotonous operation did from time to time, pay dividends. On occasions, we received good intelligence regarding the movement of ZANLA sections and set up ambushes accordingly.

N/S/P/O Michael "Mike" Stewart recalls: "I remember being deployed by John Padbury who had intelligence that a group of 15 to 20 ZANLA insurgents were going to be at a specific kraal in the central Manyika TTL. We walked south into the area and then at about 3 a.m. walked to just behind the kraal. We were sitting in the shadows next to a major path, by a hedge grove with the kraal to our south, waiting for first light. Suddenly we heard soft voices coming up the path from the east. The lead was a young *mujibha*,[1] about 15 years old and the gooks were about 20m behind him. He stopped right next to me as I think he saw our shadows. He then tried to run back down the path when I was forced to kill him. We followed up immediately, dropping our packs and had a fleeting contact with the fleeing gooks, but those gooks had run! It was most frustrating. We did find some of their packs, a stick grenade and a few magazines and stayed in the area for a few more days without any further successes. I never thought myself to be in charge. I always led through consultation and firmly believe we were successful due to this fact. I had two very close constables, Charles Chibi and David Zimba, who I bonded with. We ate together and drank together when back in town. I hated the racial crap that other units showed, especially the all white units. I always thought it very unfair the separate rank structure, although I did not know about the different pay scale. Every time we came back to town, I always went and drank Black Label (strong beer) with the lads in their canteen, although this was frowned upon, but then I never was conventional and hated rules"[2]

Selous Scouts

Pseudo-operations were organised Security Forces teams disguised as insurgents and deployed to penetrate enemy sections. Captured insurgents formed part of these pseudo-teams. They were very successful operations in the conflict and worth a mention, as accurate intelligence provided by Special Branch was essential for successes in the field. The OC Special Branch, Selous Scouts Internal Operations until 1979 when he was transferred to JOC Hurricane, was Supt. Keith Samler. He explains:

> Nationalist inspired uprisings and terrorist infiltrations commenced in Southern Rhodesia subsequent to the break up of the Federation of Rhodesia and Nyasaland in 1962. During the early 1960s the African townships, particularly in the capital city, Salisbury, were a hotbed of Nationalist inspired incidents, secret meetings, setting up of arms caches, riots, petrol bombings, murders and every other conceivable law breaking enterprise they could think of. The BSAP were in the front line to combat this. During some riots the army was called upon to assist to mount cordons and provide manpower but were never ordered to discharge their firearms. The first cross border incursions commenced in 1967/8 in the North East of Rhodesia and the Rhodesian Military was totally unprepared to mount offensives against forces conducting true guerrilla warfare.
>
> The Special Branch of the BSAP was tasked to infiltrate and suppress this upsurge. These self taught counter insurgency operators undertook what any right thinking "Detective" would do and that was to commence an "undercover" operation to infiltrate and eliminate the scourge of terrorism, undertaking numerous "undercover" and "pro-active" pseudo operations in the African townships during the 1960's political upheavals. In the Salisbury area this later became a full blown operation involving the military and named operation Hurricane. To assist the BSAP (SB) senior military commanders were approached and asked to identify suitable army personnel who could combine together

[1] See Glossary.

[2] N/S/P/O Stewart email 10/7/2015.

and create an "iron fist and sharp point" of the small SB unit. As policemen trained in upholding the law of the country and serving the citizens through investigations, protection etc. (also helping old ladies across the road), we were not trained like military personnel, although a few prior operations were conducted by us which the army would have considered "inappropriate". Army personnel of high calibre such as Andre Rabie, Stretch Franklin, Pete Clements, Basil Moss, Jerry Strong to name but a few, together with Game Department personnel, were seconded to SB leading to very favourable results.This small SB/Army operation was the precursor for future thinking necessary to establish a combined Unit which was to lead to the formation of the Selous Scouts Regiment in 1974 under the command of the legendary Lt. Col. Ron Reid-Daly.

This combination of the military and Special Branch gave the operation considerable impetus and punch. It can assuredly be said that Special Branch wrote the script and the military "operators" were "he actors that presented and ensured that the play was a resounding success." As a result of these successes involving the two arms of the Rhodesian Security Forces, BSAP Special Branch and Army, Senior Police and Army Officers created a new Special Forces Unit to be called the Selous Scouts which was to be used to counter Nationalist terrorists both infiltrating and already established inside the country. This new unit would operate in a "pseudo" role internally. Later a small number of Selous Scout personnel, the "Recce Group" would carry out external reconnaissance to provide intelligence for attacks to be mounted on terrorist training camps in adjoining countries. Many of these external attacks would also be conducted by Territorial Army (TA) members of the Selous Scouts Regiment.

However, in the initial stages of its formation in 1974 the Regiment was tasked in the pseudo role only with a small unit of Special Branch officers attached directly to the Regiment to provide the Intelligence to enable the pseudo callsigns to make contact with terrorist groups within Rhodesia. Once having successfully established the CT groups position the Fire Force would be called in to make contact and eliminate the group without compromising the pseudo callsign. This allowed these clandestine pseudo operations to continue making ongoing contact with other terrorist groups.

Army personnel transferring to the Unit from other regiments such as the SAS, RLI, RAR were volunteers and put through an extremely rigorous selection course at the training camp on the shores of Lake Kariba called Wafa Wafa – literally translated meaning "You're dead, You're dead"! Every Selous Scout "operator" black and white, had to undergo the course and the dropout rate was very high indeed. After the gruelling physical selection course the new Selous Scouts were to go through the last part of the course known as the "Dark Phase". This was designed to introduce the new members to the ways of the real ZANLA and ZIPRA terrorists; how to emulate them in the bush, how to pass off as the real thing to the locals in the area of operation, and to eventually make contact with the real terrorists and by various methods of communication bring in Security Force Fire Force units to annihilate them.

Initially, most of the black members of the Regiment were drawn from the Rhodesian African Rifles (RAR) with a few from the BSAP Support Unit (a para-military force within the BSAP). It was vital to support the callsign personnel with members of the terrorist organisations to give credibility both to the Army members individually and the callsign as a unit. For this purpose captured terrorists were given a thorough background check and put through a selection process by the members with whom they would be deployed. It is testimony to these selection procedures that there were a mere handful of captures who took an opportunity to defect.

It was for the simple reason of anonymity that captured terrorists in all theatres of the war in Rhodesia were held incognito and generally handed over to the SB Selous Scouts personnel for interrogation and debriefing. Thereafter a decision was made whether the capture would be good material for induction into a callsign. For example, once selected the capture would be introduced to other members of the callsign and generally showed shock at seeing many of his erstwhile comrades now belonging to "*Skuze apo*" (African slang for Selous Scouts). He would slowly over a period mostly of a couple of weeks but sometimes due to exigencies only days, be inducted. Around a campfire he would be presented officially with his AK-47 which he had been carrying around with a loaded magazine for some days. Now reunited with his AK he would be allowed to point it in the air and discharge the magazine at which he would do so but with only a loud click from the firing mechanism. Perplexed, he would look at the callsign commander who would then present him with his firing pin! A few minutes later he would proudly discharge his magazine and with congratulations all round immediately take part in the beerfest to follow.

Good Intelligence was the key word for the deployment of Selous Scout callsigns. Throughout the country Special Branch personnel attached to the Selous Scouts in the various Joint Operational Command (JOC) areas would interrogate captured terrorists in particular. Local terrorist contact men (usually clandestinely uplifted), local tribespeople, Government Departments such as the Dept of Conservation and Extension, Internal Affairs etc. would be tapped for any information which might assist in putting a picture together for the benefit of the callsigns ready to be deployed into a particular area. Importantly, and because of the ability of BSAP personnel to knock on anybody's door and be met with complete trust intelligence was readily obtained and updated on an ongoing basis.

Prior to deploying a Selous Scouts callsign into any operational area the local JOC Commander would be notified to "freeze" the particular area. This was absolutely necessary to avoid conflict between friendly forces as had happened previously resulting in the deaths of Selous Scouts personnel as had happened to Andre Rabie.

The briefing prepared by the SB Selous Scouts operator would be as detailed as possible with what known facts were available. To deploy a callsign usually comprising 17 black soldiers and three white soldiers without some information regarding the terrorist group they were likely to meet, their names, ranks, type of weapons, passwords, identifying symbols would probably result in compromise and withdrawal of the callsign from the area without any positive results being achieved. It was a never ending task of the SB man to acquire the right clothing, usually blue denims, and weaponry with which to arm the troops. Many AK-47s, for example, recovered after a contact with security forces Fire Force would be minus the bayonet, kept as a souvenir, or a RPD without its magazine also kept as a souvenir. To deploy a callsign with such items missing would spell immediate compromise.

The most important piece of intelligence, of course, was a terrorist captured during a fire fight. Information obtained from captures would add enormously to establishing the bona fides of the Selous Scouts callsign. Letter writing between terrorist groups was their preferred way of making contact with other groups in the same area. To be able to communicate by rank and name etc. was a sure way to establish bona fides and result in the terrorist group being contacted by the Fire Force called in by the Selous Scouts callsign commander, usually perched on top of a hill who was in direct radio communication with Selous Scouts HQ.

The areas selected for callsign deployments rested primarily on the amount of useful intelligence to hand allied to the threat level posed in any particular area of the country. Deployments would last for perhaps two or three weeks and then the callsigns were recalled to barracks for retraining or a period of R & R. During this period the SB men would be seeking out and putting together briefings on known infiltration routes, espe-

> cially along the Eastern Border with Mozambique in which country the ZANLA organisation had large training camps.
>
> It is testimony to the efficiency and dedication of both the white and black members of the Selous Scouts Regiment that the Regiment was credited with having been directly involved in 68% of all terrorist casualties between 1974 and 1979.[1]

The Scouts were paid a bonus based on kills which was an added incentive.[2] Much to the detriment of other sections of the Security Forces, the Selous Scouts normally had priority regarding the deployment of the Fire Force. Ringo was one of the most infamous insurgents we sought in the Chiduku TTL. He was finally shot and killed during a Selous Scouts Fire Force call-out. Late the same afternoon as we celebrated his demise the song Ringo, by Lorne Greene, beamed from the radio adding to our frivolities.

Operations became progressively more difficult as ZANLA learned how to counter our Selous Scouts' tactics. Incidents involving so-called "tame" terrorists greatly hampered operations. One such individual was Habakuku Gumbo in April 1975. Gumbo, a ZANLA section commander, was captured and thought to be an "onsides" Selous Scout. This, despite the advice of SB operator D/P/O Ed Bird, who did not trust Gumbo. One night, while Gumbo was on patrol, he shot and killed his six sleeping comrades (two African SB detectives, three African Selous Scouts and one "turned" insurgent), and made his way back to Mozambique. Thereafter, he started training insurgents at bases in Tanzania and Mozambique on current Selous Scouts' tactics which did much harm to their operations.[3]

In time, our tactics proved effective. Our kill-rate was increasing and we were disrupting the ZANLA fighters in a cat-and-mouse hunt. We stalked, found and eliminated the enemy. However, in my view, we had no progressive political message to deliver and showed no desire to change the material circumstances or living conditions of the African population. Our inability to remain with the locals isolated us, creating an ever-increasing barrier as we abandoned them to the wiles of ZANLA who continued to enforce their martial law. I considered the people as an instrument of finding and eliminating insurgents. Nothing more.

As matters transpired, ZANLA were more organised than we imagined and continued to advance on us with relentless momentum. They had clearly defined strategies, laid landmines, continued to promote civil disobedience and attacked only when it favoured them, thereby avoiding detection and confrontation as much as possible. Granted, they were at our mercy when we did locate them, but therein lay the difficulty. They were an elusive enemy. Frequently, it crossed my mind that there had to be a more effective way of confronting our adversary. Fortunately, at that stage of the war, I had learned not to react in an anticipated manner. On the contrary, in hostile situations, I always learned to react unpredictably.

---

[1] Supt. Keith Samler emails 10/6/2015 and 28/11/2019.

[2] Ellert, H. & Anderson, D. (2020), p. 205.

[3] Bird, E. (2014), Chap. 1.

4 ~ BREAKING ZANLA STRATEGIES

A man presented with a factual account of his history, his colleagues and his associates frequently capitulates under interrogation.
John Padbury

We had numerous successes using *mujibhas* as we wrestled to formalise an overall strategy and understanding of ZANLA's intelligence operations. The following authenticated contact serves to help understand the potential of the *mujibha* intelligence networks waiting to be unleashed.

Mission *Mujibhas*: Presuppositions Challenged[1]

At this junction, I wish to acknowledge and emphasise my hitherto ignorance of African intellect and ability, until one fateful day in Makoni when, on patrol, I visited Kriste Mambo Mission. How bizarre I thought. Here in the middle of a TTL, at a Catholic mission school, are young African students, smartly dressed in their uniforms, following the British GCE curriculum. Wandering around the classrooms, I discovered students were studying subjects which included mathematics, science, English and geography, which included map reading. I stored this observation in my mind. Map reading? I pondered in disbelief, but the revelation struck a chord. Having been raised in a British colony, the Africans I knew were cooks, house cleaners, gardeners, made deliveries or were simply menial labourers. These were the tasks reserved for them and I believed they were happy with their lot. At least they had regular work, I reasoned. Even with our African staff, while I acknowledged their valuable experience and respected their age and rank, I was still conditioned to think they needed our expertise to manage and execute the more intricate and significant matters such as docket work. I do not believe I was alone in this mindset. Many, if not most, of the white population of my generation were raised with this presumption. As I became more involved in the war it appeared that no apparent paradigm shift was made by my peers. This view persisted even towards the end of hostilities.

The day after my visit to the mission, we drove a further 8 kilometres beyond it and parked our vehicles alongside of the road. I said to Herbert that we should walk into the TTL. Usually, we patrolled in two mine-proofed Land Rovers. Periodically we walked on patrols always fully armed with FN rifles. A patrol would normally consist of four armed policemen dressed in full camouflage outfits with webbing.

I loved walking. There were such beautiful views of the multicoloured, often variegated leaves of msasa trees, kopjes, each one rugged and unique, occasional kraals and, naturally, locals with whom I would converse. It was, in my view, the best way to get a feel for the TTL and to observe the people in their natural environment. With some care and luck, one could surprise them but, generally, this was their homeground. They were alert, astute and knew of our presence well before we had an inkling they were in the vicinity. If ZANLA were in the area, the kraals were deserted well in advance of our arrival, to prevent being interrogated or in any way being associated with the SF.

There was a freedom to walking, despite the threat of compromise and attack. Vehicle patrols made one vulnerable, whereas on the ground odds for survival were better. We carried a rifle and our webbing contained all the resources we required for the immediate situation. Four extra magazines loaded with live rounds, hand-grenades, maps, water bottles, enough food (commonly referred to as "rat packs") for a one- or two-day patrol and a gas cooker. The hiss of a gas cooker

[1] Makoni/Manyika Incidents Map: Incident 13. The map locstat is estimated. This was contact confirmed during oral and telephone discussions with D/S/O Pete Cutting (March to May 2015), and Supt. Fred Mason (December 2015 and June/July 2017).

brewing tea in the bush remains an unforgettable memory for me. I found myself completely satisfied in these circumstances. What more does a man need in life, I asked myself! A combatant carries the necessities for life in the moment. These, together with a few additional personal treasures, such as photos of loved ones, lucky charms and identity tags known as "dog tags" are all a soldier requires. When a soldier dies in combat, all that is vital for his survival, and those precious possessions, lie with him. To my mind, that is the tragedy of witnessing a soldier killed in action. Such are the veteran's battle-scarred memories.

D/Sgt. Herbert and I left an armed guard with the vehicles and set off following a path through a forest leading down towards a steep valley. After a short while, we surprised two young Africans walking towards us. Herbert remarked that we had spoken to them the previous week when visiting their kraal and that they should have been in school. The two drew alongside us and we searched them and found a note from a ZANLA section addressed to a kraalhead demanding he attend a meeting with them.

After a brief interrogation, the two admitted that they were *mujibhas* and ready to talk. They had little choice as they had been caught red-handed. The speed with which they co-operated was noteworthy. Little did I realise what an important key this was for the future.

The two confirmed there were eight ZANLA insurgents in a nearby base camp. The commander of the group had sent them to collect the kraalhead as they suspected he was a *mutengesi*. They were to return to the base camp with the kraalhead as soon as they had found him, for the purpose of eliminating him.

I asked them what route they would follow to reach the ZANLA base camp. They replied that they would walk to the business centre (BC), then follow a path down the valley, cross a river, pass their kraals and proceed into the hills. The base camp was apparently at the lower part of some hills in thick bushes and numerous trees quite close to a river. The two *mujibhas* were around 16 years old.

Based on our experience at the mission, knowing that map reading was part of their syllabus, I asked if they could find the base camp on a map. They answered in the affirmative. First, we asked them to explain how they would walk to the base camp from our current position. Herbert drew a rough sketch of the route, noting significant landmarks such as the business centre, the river crossing, kraals, valleys, paths and the position of the base camp on the hill.

When satisfied with the sketch, we opened the map, showed our current position to orientate them and asked where the BC they had mentioned was. We then asked them to show us on the map where the ZANLA base camp was.

Without hesitation, the two *mujibhas* worked out the route to the base camp. Remarkably, to my mind, it all tied up. Their description, the sketch and their directions on the map all tallied. The base camp was pinpointed at the foothills of a mountain. We asked them if we put them in a helicopter, could they direct us to the base camp. This was a strategy we had not tried before and would be controversial. If I was struggling to believe the young men's ability to lead us to the ZANLA base, what would it take to convince Fire Force and Security Forces personnel? Despite my ponderings, the two *mujibhas* were confident they could find their way from a helicopter. Herbert reassured me that they had lived in the area all their lives, therefore were intimately familiar with their environment. His logic made sense.

What a daunting thought. Standing before us were the educated "eyes and ears" of the people, a fact of which I had hitherto been oblivious. With the help of the *mujibhas*, we worked out the map reference for the base camp VQ468636[1] then radioed Sub.JOC Rusape giving them a full sitrep. After a brief wait, we were advised that the Fire Force based at Grand Reef was willing to react to our intelligence. We were instructed to rendezvous at the Support Unit Base, 151 Alpha, which was some distance from the location of the ZANLA base camp. Shortly after making our arrangements, we set out, ensuring the two *mujibhas* would not be compromised.

The challenge of our situation mounted in my mind. We were deploying FF on the directions of

1 This is an estimated locstat.

two young local African males merely on information they had provided. This was unheard of. When we arrived at the RV, while waiting for the FF, we checked the *mujibhas'* sketches and let them "talk us" along the route, scrutinising the directions and base camp locstats repeatedly. I wanted the route and locstat to be accurate and firmly fixed in all our minds, to ensure we would not get lost when leading the FF into action. We selected one *mujibha* to direct the FF into battle.

From a distance, the familiar beat of helicopter rotor-blades clattering intermittently could be heard, signifying that the might of Rhodesian airpower was approaching and prepared to unleash its arsenal. I experienced an amazing adrenalin "rush" as the FF closed in. Ever optimistic, we were concerned yet convinced our enthusiasm and confidence would be shared by the FF Commander. Our operation required his acceptance and approval.

We watched as the FF comprising four G-Cars and a K-Car approached the landing zone (LZ). The K-Car took the shortest route for a safe and efficient landing while allowing space behind for the remaining helicopters to also make trouble-free touchdowns. This reduced flight time and the risk of collision. The technicians kept a watchful eye for overhead power cables across the LZ, tree stumps which could damage the chopper rotor-blades and other loose articles, thus ensuring the tail-rotor was clear. They assisted the pilot with in-flight observations, approaching hazards and dense vegetation which improved flight safety, thereby reducing accidents. These technicians faced a multitude of responsibilities apart from firing on-board weapons and addressing chopper "snags". In my estimation, they presented a formidable team. One by one the choppers settled, blowing up a dust storm in the process caused by the downwash of the blades. Once stationary, the turbines screamed but soon idled for a short while before finally being shut down by the pilot. This winding-down process lasting some 35 seconds.

I was immediately impressed by these men. They exhibited confidence, were relaxed and in control of not only their aircraft but the situation itself. I felt it a privilege to enter their world.

The briefing that followed went well, although the FF Commander was understandably sceptical of this young *mujibha's* ability to direct the FF onto a ZANLA base camp from the air. Our trump card was that there were no other options for the FF to deploy, so it was worth having a go.

A G-Car was designated to carry the *mujibha* along with Herbert and I. We were to direct the FF into the contact zone. Our agreed plan was to fly over the BC to orientate the *mujibha*, who would then indicate the route to follow to the base camp. I was to follow the route drawn on the sketch and the G-Car pilot would follow the route on a map. We would fly just above treetop level. Once the base camp was identified, the K-Car would take command of the ensuing action. Support Unit troops would stand by to be deployed as required when the insurgents were engaged.

We embarked in the G-Car. The *mujibha* was seated in front next to Herbert and I squatted behind them. Herbert and I were both handed a headset. I hoped I looked as impressive as Herbert. He displayed a commanding presence. The pilot went through "start procedures" carefully nursing the chopper into "flight idle" before gently lifting it from the ground. He nudged the nose down and, with that, we were off to battle. I found this experience exhilarating. Once the technician/gunner had completed his take-off duties, he sat behind the twin side-mounted .303 Brownings and strapped himself in. These Brownings fired .303mm rounds fed by a belt at a rate of 1,200 rounds per minute.

Pressure intensified as we flew just above the treetops following river valleys and low-lying ground. This tactic reduced the time the enemy on the ground had to see our approach. Valleys and hills were used to muffle the sound of our approach and allow for maximum surprise. Trailing choppers were strung out in a loose-line formation. We travelled at speed, yet the *mujibha* seemed to recognise his surroundings.

The pilot identified the business centre, pointing towards a brick building with a galvanised roof reflecting the bright African sun. Visibility was good as it was a clear day. Herbert pointed out the BC to the *mujibha* who had already seen it and turned beaming and pointing excitedly. With an outstretched arm he started directing the G-Car, which banked from right to left, over the river crossing, down a path that led along the river valley then excitedly pointed down and shouted "*Apo*" (there). There, I repeated into my headset and pointed to the base camp. The G-Car pilot banked sharply to the left and performed a spiral manoeuvre over the target area making us feel we were pivoting on an invisible axis. There was no movement in the dense bush below. The trailing FF choppers gained altitude and enveloped the area.

During the helicopter's extreme banking, the *mujibha* became disorientated and, in fact, so did I. He was not certain that he had identified the correct location. The K-Car Commander instructed us to rerun the route from the BC while the rest of the FF orbited the original position indicated. We banked sharply as we retraced our incoming flight path. The *mujibha* regained his sense of direction and quickly identified the BC, following which he redirected the pilot back to the same target area. The tension and pressure mounted. A cloud of doubt tried to claw its way into my mind, but that assurance of confident, positive, assertive urgency held as I focused on the mission at hand. The G-Car pilot banked, gained altitude and joined the orbit of the other three G-Cars. "K-Car is firing," announced the pilot. Beneath, the ground erupted with explosions from the 20mm cannon. I saw no movement.

Perched expectantly behind the twin Brownings, the on-board technician/gunner scrutinised the ground below. Without warning, bursts of automatic fire blazed from their barrels as he jerked the Brownings into action. I could still not see movement on the ground, but the firing continued. Suddenly, I caught sight of an insurgent darting behind a tree. The technician/gunner continued firing. As the tree splintered, I noticed a body fall to the ground. Alert and knowing what to look for, I could now detect several insurgents dashing from one position to another followed by exploding 20mm rounds fired from the K-Car before, in time, they fell limp to the ground. Our technician/gunner kept firing.

Yet again I found myself in a surreal zone. All too soon the FF Commander instructed our G-Car pilot to return us to the Support Unit Base and collect a stick to deploy. "You have done your job, we are taking you home," he said. As we left the area, I could hear the FF Commander deploying his "stops" on the ground as he prepared to attack the base camp.

On landing at 151 Alpha, the pilot kept the turbines at "flight idle", rotor-blades spinning at about 350rpm as the technician/gunner walked us from the chopper, ensuring we leaned forward to prevent being struck by the overhead blades. A thumbs up from the pilot signalled the awaiting four-man Support Unit stick to board the chopper. He lifted the collective-power lever while the tilt of the blades created downwash. The pilot then gently eased the chopper into flight and, with nose down, returned to battle.

Thus, the relays began. G-Cars arriving to refuel, collect awaiting Support Unit sticks and airlift the men into battle. It was a long, hard battle that lasted until mid-afternoon. As the operation wound down, the seven insurgents killed in the operation were transported by the helicopters to 151 Alpha. We searched the bodies for relevant documentation and I organised the bodies and their weapons to be conveyed to the CID offices at Rusape for routine investigations. The Support Unit troops were returned to base and the choppers flew back to Grand Reef. In the ensuing silence, I paused for reflection.

Significantly, I had learned and tested a new tactic for a deployment of FF which would prove invaluable in future operations. Most importantly, I was learning how involved *mujibhas* were with ZANLA sections, as well as the insurgents' strategic and tactical abilities. The two captured *mujibhas* were housed in police quarters.

Col. Dunn congratulated me on the success of the strategy and operation. While he was keen to listen and learn, Supt. Sloman remained silent. Milne, Cutting and I discussed the developing *mujibha* scene, in particular, the problem of *mujibhas* being compromised and unable to return to their homes, as ZANLA would certainly kill them. Therefore, a solution was needed for their dilemma.

How effective would ZANLA be if they had control of the FF was a question which frequently crossed my mind. Our air dominance and ground support were comforting and reassuring. Along with this, my understanding of African educational standards increased exponentially. We were learning how to infiltrate the *mujibha* intelligence networks and utilise their vast hitherto untapped incredible potential.

Maxwell Captured

The regular Support Unit presence at Rusape was reassuring and essential to our war efforts. They were competent para-military soldiers and particularly skilled in their role on OPs. I enjoyed working with them as we were all policemen. This bond made for genuine camaraderie.

In July 1977, we started to receive intelligence that a group of ZANLA were operating in the north of the Makoni TTL. A calculated network of Support Unit OPs was promptly deployed to survey the scene. On 17 July 1977, the unit confirmed a sighting of insurgents and called in Fire Force which made contact with them at Chiwira Mountain.

Winston "Sakkie" McKay[1] picks up the story: "We were contacted by the Fire Force Commander who requested an additional stick as a Stop Group. We already had callsigns in the vicinity and to the north of the contact area and were told to leave those alone, so they could observe any further movement. I gathered a Bravo callsign together and we were uplifted at mid-morning and dropped as a Stop. The running contact was in progress and I was directed towards a small brick building from where we came under heavy fire. I relayed this to the K-Car Commander who instructed all callsigns to standby as K-Car would be firing. He then blasted the house with 20mm cannon fire and I heard one of the RLI callsigns radio 'K-Car You Beauty'. The Commander announced that my problem had been solved and I was to continue. K-Car Commander then advised that a Support Unit callsign to the north had spotted movement and I was uplifted and dropped next to a Bravo Troop stick commanded by Peter Allanby. We located tracks of two men and at a distance we opened fire killing one and recovering an AK. We were then uplifted by our 'Lima' callsign trucks and returned to base. I am not certain how many (ZANLA) were killed during this Fire Force engagement."

During the contact, Herbert and I were airlifted into the battle zone to carry out interrogations where we met the capture, Maxwell, who had a gunshot wound to his left leg which he received in the Fire Force action. Fortunately, it was not serious. A second uninjured captive was conveyed to the Selous Scouts to avoid compromise. He would be used in their immediate operations.

The first words Maxwell spoke were: "Do you want to see the arms cache?" As the Fire Force action was still ongoing with the odd skirmish only about 100 metres from our position at a kraal, I asked the FF Commander for permission to recover the arms cache. He agreed and, after identifying our callsign and position, Maxwell, Herbert and I, supported by a handful of FF soldiers, walked into a nearby mealie (maize) field to unearth the arms cache. After walking in the field for about 15 metres, a contact broke out ahead of us and the FF Commander told us to return to the kraal area as there were insurgents in the mealie field a short distance ahead of us. That was an instruction to obey immediately.

We returned to the kraal and waited for matters to settle before the Fire Force Commander gave us permission to proceed and collect the arms cache. We recovered a landmine, AK rounds, spare magazines and several hand-grenades. While this was not a sizeable cache, however, it did prove Maxwell's credibility. In the battle, seven ZANLA were killed and two captured.[2]

On our return to Rusape, I established that the Selous Scouts did not wish to utilise Maxwell, as his injuries would hamper deployments. I duly arranged to retain him in my service. We discovered that Maxwell had been involved in the Support Unit/Fire Force contact in Makoni TTL when his section leader and three other insurgents were killed. (See Chapter 3.) As he needed time for his

[1] Insp. Winston "Sakkie" McKay: Posted to the Support Unit Base at Rusape (callsign 151A) to work as second in command and relief to Supt. Tom Naude September 1977. Email 10/2/2016; conference in Durban, South Africa with Fred Mason, Barry Woan, "Sakkie" McKay, and David and John Padbury, December 2015.

[2] Makoni/Manyika Incidents Map: Incident 14; Geldenhuys, P. (2014), Air Strike Log Entry 710 could refer to this incident. Dates, events, locstat and details tie in with the Air Strike Log Entry as confirmed by Supt. Mason, D/S/O Cutting and myself.

injury to heal, we focused on debriefing him regarding ZANLA's operational strategies, tactics, field intelligence and the workings of the *mujibha* system. He also identified ZANLA's regional and detachment commanders and the number of sections in the area.

After a short period, Maxwell became a loyal friend. It astonished me what little time was required for former enemies to bond and thenceforth remain inseparable. Following his recovery, we deployed him with Support Unit callsigns. Maxwell and the Support Unit adapted well to our changing strategies and tactics. He was the first externally trained insurgent we were permitted to retain and proved to be a key in unravelling the *mujibha* networks.

Mujibha Tactics Unveiled

At the forefront of ZANLA's political process of mobilising the masses was the *mujibha* system. This was strategy aimed at politicising and empowering young unarmed African males, aged on average between 10-18 years. They were the ultimate political and military intelligence network and superseded traditional authority.

Mujibhas acted as the intelligence sources, the "eyes and ears" of ZANLA. Their primary role was to discover the location of Rhodesian forces, identify *vatengesi*, including family members, and carry messages for ZANLA. Giving such power to the youth, opened the door for abuse and many innocent people were falsely accused, beaten and killed, often for the most trivial reasons, including the settling of old and new feuds. As is so often the case, these violent young men also frequently abused their exalted authority for personal gain, demanding food and supplies for "ghost" insurgents.

These young *mujibhas* operated within a cell structure, modelled, as were all ZANLA strategies and tactics, on Maoist principles. A group of *mujibhas* resident in a localised kraal area reported to a senior *mujibha* who in turn reported to a contact man who co-ordinated intelligence and organised events, including political meetings, feeding parties, social events and female companionship. These contact men could include, but need not have been, a kraalhead or headman. Normally, only senior *mujibhas* knew the identity of a neighbouring *mujibha* cell network leader and contact men. Hence, if one *mujibha* or person connected to an intelligence network was captured or compromised, the web would remain intact with limited information revealed during interrogations. Notably, captured contact men, *mujibhas* or locals might be able to provide a breakdown of ZANLA sections. This would include information about those involved in the intelligence networks and their support structures. However, they would not necessarily be able to accurately divulge the current location of insurgents. Furthermore, the death of a contact man or a *mujibha* would not bring about a breakdown of ZANLA's intelligence networks. No intelligence network is ever reliant on a single individual.

ZANLA's means of securing control was through fear, intimidation and violence, most notably through the "barrel of a gun". Brutal beatings and murders were considered justifiable practices in the interests of "the cause" which always took precedent over reason and justice. Locals feared *mujibhas*. They ruled and overpowered the tribal leadership system, allowing ZANLA to establish military rule by dictatorship. Chiefs, headmen and kraalheads opposed to ZANLA were eliminated. Parents and elders living in isolated rural villages now feared their sons and daughters, as ZANLA gave authority and power to the youth. Isolated from traditional authority, representation and protection by government agencies, the people feared both ZANLA and the SF, trapped in a world of fear and terror by day and night. To control the people, ZANLA needed to undermine the tribal system by "ruling" the areas themselves and empowering their *mujibha* networks, the youth.

When in base camps, the *mujibha* networks would protect insurgents who also remained vigilant with their own OP systems in place. Ever alert to air attacks, they would move to cover if helicopters were heard. Senior *mujibhas* underwent weapons training and often joined the insurgents, as they lost men in battles with the SF. Following a contact with the SF, or where a *mujibha* or contact man went missing in action, ZANLA went on high alert. Prearranged rendezvous were always organised and carefully approached. Communication with the local *mujibha* network was carefully reinstated in case it had been penetrated or compromised by the SF. Names of missing insurgents and *mujibhas* suspected as either being killed or captured were quickly circulated throughout their intelligence networks and the people, to thwart SF and pseudo-Selous Scouts operations. There was limited confusion among ZANLA. They were more difficult to locate as they re-established contact with their intelligence networks, identifying missing comrades, *mujibhas* and taking reprisals on locals to enforce their authority. Insurgents were at home in the TTLs. They were not threatened by locals but, once established, integrated with them. This was a different experience to that of the SF who were isolated from the people and generally received no volunteered information.

Thus, information filtered through the *mujibha* networks to senior *mujibhas* and on to contact men who were in touch with the local insurgents when in their area. Should they not be in his area and a senior *mujibha* had intelligence to report, such as an SF presence, he informed the nearby *mujibha* network, ensuring that such information reached the senior *mujibha* for onward transmission to the nearest ZANLA section, normally six to eight men.

The networks of intelligence that flowed in the TTLs were extremely efficient, organised and controlled. Few, if any, occurrences went by without notice. The *mujibhas'* normal routines included caring for cattle and sheep, which required them to walk on the footpaths and surrounding areas to and from their traditional grazing fields. All told, *mujibhas* were excellent trackers. They knew the footwear and footprints of family, surrounding kraal dwellers and visiting friends. They read the ground on which they trod like a book, remembering all the details while readily identifying "foreign" footprints and reporting these, through the networks, to the senior *mujibha* for onward transmission to the nearest ZANLA section. Hills were scanned and scrutinised while seeking grazing pastures for cattle and goats, often compromising SF OPs. Their environment was a picture-book story and a primary method of communication: their living news broadcast.

When ZANLA forces were in their area, young girls, *chimbwidos*, from neighbouring kraals, aged on average between 12 and 18 years, would gather together and take responsibility for feeding, washing laundry and performing other general chores, including sexual pleasures, for the insurgents. Food was prepared and carried to the base camps along footpaths which were easily distinguishable from traditional paths. On occasions ZANLA were fed in the kraals. Traditional footpaths are a network of various trails leading to nearby villages, stores, rivers, fields, schools, clinics, cattle dips and livestock-grazing areas. These daily used ancestral paths were noticeably older and well worn, whereas feeding paths from kraals to ZANLA base camps, generally located in nearby kopjes, mountains and river valleys, were fresher, less travelled and ended abruptly in base camps. Identifying these tracks by air surveillance became a useful SF strategy to locate and pinpoint ZANLA base camps.

Identifying *mujibhas* and *chimbwidos* in a kraal complex, particularly those "foreign" to the kraals, and observing and interpreting their activities, was to become a key factor in locating insurgents. Because of their close links with ZANLA, many *mujibhas* and *chimbwidos* were killed in contacts with the Security Forces.

Clearly, we, the Rhodesian forces, were facing a sophisticated enemy with disciplined strategies and tactics. They had well-established intelligence networks and were confident, dedicated and committed to fight to the end, no matter what their losses were. Insurgents were not deployed to their home areas but positioned in different TTLs primarily, as they were required to carry out, when necessary, violent oppression of the people who opposed them and failed to collaborate, even after politicisation. It was unlikely that they would murder family or friends when their security was threatened or breached. Therefore, operating in "foreign" TTLs was the safest strategy. In this way, insurgents could not be placed in subordinate positions by elders because of their youth. Insurgents only used Chimurenga names so that they could not be traced back to their homes.[1] *Mujibhas* were ZANLA's link to the people. When a section of insurgents was moving to a new location, usually a *mujibha* walked 10~15 metres ahead in order to detect any SF ambushes. These *mujibhas* were invariably shot and killed first.

ZANLA had no R & R, no helicopter support and minimal medical assistance, although some missionaries provided access to their hospitals and clinics.[2] They depended on the local people for

[1] Ranger, T. (1985), p. 207.

information, food, sexual favours, local and international news. They had few home comforts and were not concerned by the economics of the conflict. The longer the war endured, so much the better. They were free from everyday pressures of paying bills, house maintenance, education and school fees, the difficulties of family life and the many everyday stresses facing the man-in-the-street. Their priority was "the cause" and war, to which they were totally committed. Their task of politicising the people was never-ending. In the process, they were provided entertainment, many alcohol-drinking parties, together with the company of numerous young women. As areas were liberated, they began living in kraals, always leaving elements of the section in the open to protect those within.

ZANLA *mujibhas* were a formidable intelligence force. By 1979, ZANLA claimed at least 50,000 operational *mujibhas*.[1]

It was not all about war. Insurgents attended local celebrations and parties where beer was brewed from millet in 44-gallon drums. As can be expected, beer-brewing became an indicator of a possible ZANLA presence. These activities became worth monitoring and ambushing. Both ZANLA and ZIPRA insurgents enjoyed the social privileges and lifestyle awarded to revolutionary soldiers.

Mujibhas and the Security Forces

As I referred in Chapter 2, rural people lived a consistent, regular, everyday pattern and routine way of life. Their behaviour was ordered and disciplined. This conduct was decidedly different when ZANLA were present in the area. *Mujibha* activity increased. Young girls gathered from surrounding villages at a central kraal to prepare and carry meals to our enemy's base camps. Political gatherings were held during the evenings whereas this had not been the case prior to ZANLA arriving in a region. In the more remote and liberated areas, ZANLA would sweep through villages greeting and "policing" the local population. Generally, this took place during late afternoon, with the insurgents knowing full well that SF action, if any, would be limited due to bad light.

Rhodesian SF traditional counter-terrorism strategies were producing positive results but failed to stem the stream of insurgents into the country, thus allowing them to penetrate deep into the central areas of Rhodesia. Once the well-established SF informers' system had been fragmented and various areas liberated, we depended on a method of gathering locals and interrogating them, with the hope of extracting intelligence that would help locate insurgents. This was generally a slow, arduous and unreliable process with limited success. A further frustration was that SF had been forced into the process of reacting to ZANLA actions such as landmine incidents, ambushes, murders, farm attacks and so on. We failed to recognise that we faced an all-out war, believing the government propaganda of "all is well".

The primary method of locating ZANLA was the deployment of OPs as discussed in Chapter 3. The aim of the OP was to locate insurgents. They could only be accurately identified when seen bearing weapons. Generally, Fire Force would only deploy on visual sightings of insurgents carrying weapons: there were a few exceptions. Understanding the people was the key to locating the enemy. The difficulty facing our OPs and intelligence systems was that we could not identify locals and distinguish between legitimate residents and visitors or strangers. Furthermore, we could not interpret the day-to-day activities and events in the villages and surrounding areas. Consequently, SF OPs found it difficult to distinguish between normal daily kraal social behaviour, activities and patterns with those when insurgents were in the vicinity. They were confronted with the struggle of correctly identifying and understanding activities and events on the ground, along with trying to discern the nature of the insurgents' intelligence systems and strategies. Additionally, the problem with positioning troops in OPs was that once a callsign had been compromised, the insurgents would merely retreat undercover or relocate to another area. On occasions, and generally from some distance, ZANLA would attack compromised OPs with mortars, RPG-7s and small arms.

---

[2] There was a hospital at Bonda Mission and medical clinics at St Barbara's and St Triashill's.

[1] Moorcraft, P. (2011), p. 54.

By contrast, a *mujibha* deployed onto an OP overlooking his home village could instantly identify locals and intuitively interpret their behaviour and living patterns, and ascertain whether their activities were consistent with everyday life or otherwise. Hence, they could accurately determine whether ZANLA were in the area or not, saving an OP valuable time. If insurgents were not in the area, the OP could safely change locations in pursuit of their enemy. However, if they were in the area, the *mujibha* would be able to glean valuable intelligence based on his knowledge of the local scene. This would lead to pinpointing the location of the insurgents, enabling the SF to attack, normally by calling in Fire Force. Simply put, a *mujibha* could observe an individual and, as a result of their communal lifestyle, identify a stranger, male or female, and conclude whether he/she belonged in the area, and whether his/her activities were consistent with that kraal's normal conduct. Should the *mujibha* detect any deviation from the norm and identify *mujibha* or *chimbwido* activity, it was certain ZANLA were in the area. As a general rule, *mujibhas* and young girls located outside of their home areas created suspicion and were closely observed, raising the question, were ZANLA close at hand? Our difficulty was to link this knowledge to SF operations.

Our strategy developed, firstly, by identifying members of *mujibha* networks. This information was initially gleaned from our interrogations of locals who found it easier to provide names of *mujibhas*, rather than identify insurgents and their whereabouts. We would then locate and arrest the *mujibhas* and, through a process of interrogations, allow them to reconsider their approach and affiliation to the SF. Once accomplished, we would deploy them into the field with Support Unit to OP positions in their home operational areas, to locate ZANLA as swiftly as possible, acting on immediate intelligence. Prolonged delays could alert the occupying ZANLA sections that their intelligence network had been breached. As a precaution, they would change locations and, as the term has it, "go to ground" until they were assured of safety.

Mujibhas could be useful in future operations as the local population with their normal behavioural patterns seldom changed. Nor did their operational conduct deviate when ZANLA deemed it safe to return to areas where their intelligence network had been breached. They were required to return in order to maintain their presence and continue the work of politicising the local population, as their very existence depended on the support of these people. To abandon an area with its people was not an option as this would be interpreted as defeat. Success was determined by "swimming with the people", and maintaining a perpetual presence. *Mujibhas* were also useful in operational areas outside of their home locations. They could observe and interpret local behavioural patterns based on their understanding of ZANLA's strategies, tactics and modus operandi, thereby confirming a ZANLA presence or not.

Another benefit of operating with *mujibhas* was that they could lead the callsign into favourable OP positions without our SF being compromised. As *mujibhas* knew their areas intimately, they were aware of safe routes to avoid kraals. They knew well-travelled paths and areas which would alert residents and remaining *mujibhas* of their having passed through, or their mere presence in the area. As these new recruits were able to readily locate the SF, it followed they were equally adept at avoiding detection. Once an SF callsign trusted our *mujibha* system and overcame the fear of being led into an ambush, they came to realise their incorporation into the SF was the most efficient method of ensuring success and progress in the war. Ironically, the local population were the key element to both ZANLA and the SF. While ZANLA occupied the land and were one with the people (see Part 2), should the SF correctly identify and interpret the activities of the locals, the location and elimination of ZANLA sections was achievable. In both cases, the support of *mujibhas* was vital.

During SF patrols, *mujibhas* provided vital additional intelligence by identifying fellow *mujibhas* and assisting in the interrogation and reorientation process. I kept records of known *mujibhas* and contact men in their various cell networks which increased the efficiency of their identification when we met, making interrogations strategically accurate and less onerous. A man presented with a factual account of his history, his colleagues and his associates frequently capitulates under interrogation.

Mujibhas were the new-found link to our SF success.

Once a *mujibha* was compromised, or became known, suspected, or it was fabricated that he had given information to the SF, he could not return to his home as he would be killed by the remaining insurgents or *mujibhas*. This presented a problem for the growing number of *mujibhas* we were recruiting, either voluntary or involuntary, serving as collaborators with our forces. Among them was Maxwell, with more of his story to follow.

D/S/O Ken Milne from SB Rusape filed a report to SBHQ, documenting our breakthrough and the successes we achieved in the field of having identified the *mujibha* networks as the backbone to ZANLA's intelligence. Following Ken's report, a farm close to Rusape was rented which became the first *mujibha* farm in the country. Similar-styled farms across the country followed in quick succession. The rationale to securing the farm, other than providing safe housing for compromised *mujibhas*, was to train, arm and deploy them with SF to assist in operational areas. This new strategy greatly increased our kill-rate in the armed conflicts, as *mujibhas* became the "eyes and ears" of the SF. I was given command of this unique *mujibha* farm with additional aid from resident policemen, police reservists and N/S/P/Os. They assisted with the training of *mujibhas* and the construction and maintenance projects situated within the farm.

Our focus was to teach the *mujibhas* discipline, safe weapons handling and accuracy in shooting a firearm. It was not necessary to instruct them in bushcraft, tracking, anti-tracking or any covert skills they were competent at and familiar with. The farm became home to these young men and a unique esprit de corps developed among them. Living together, sharing life's experiences soon formed a safe and secure bond within the group. Successful field deployments and battles were topics of fervent discussion around the campfire. It is important to understand that, from a *mujibha's* perspective, a successful deployment was one where he/they had led the SF into an OP position without having been compromised. Thereafter, local conditions were quickly interpreted and, in conjunction with the military base commander and SB, decisions made whether to remain in the area or relocate. It was a team effort with the *mujibha* being the key.

Interestingly, our interrogation methods evolved from extracting information involuntarily from an individual, into discussions between equals. We had learned the hard way. We could now identify a captured *mujibha*, place him in his "*mujibha* network", identify the rest of his network and place him with his associates who had been compromised and now lived at the farm. New *mujibhas* quickly changed their thinking and we immediately deployed them with one of their "friends" from the farm. Barry Woan comments: "The gathering of information and the utilisation of captured *mujibhas* were critical to the success of ground Support Unit Troops."[1]

There were pleasant aspects to life on the farm. It was not all war. A most memorable contact occurred near the farm late one afternoon. A patrol armed with two RPDs, two FN Browning shotguns and six FNs opened fire on the enemy. The firepower was immense, and the contact area erupted into a cloud of dust. When visibility had improved and, while sweeping through our most recent battleground, we found the enemy had escaped. To our mirth, we discovered a clutch of terrified guinea fowl had miraculously survived the shoot-out.

Knowing the enemy's tactics, strategies and intelligence networks eased the difficulty of locating him. The people were the key in this, a people's war. Insurgents are totally dependent on the local population for their survival. Contrariwise, without the support of the people, the military is isolated, directionless and virtually defeated from the outset of hostilities. This is a political truth. Maxwell, the *mujibhas* and Mao Zedong's *Little Red Book* had taught me a great deal concerning revolutionary warfare.

We were progressing with our understanding of guerrilla warfare. Locating the enemy became less cumbersome but we still generally operated on a search-and-destroy, uplift- and-regroup basis. Furthermore, we failed to "occupy and possess the land". Frequently, I pondered, there had to be another way. We could no longer view the people as a means and vehicle to locating insurgent

[1] Barry Woan email 10/2/2016.

groups in our attempts to eliminate them. It was necessary to consider the people's humanity and to identify with them. Clearly, it seemed to me, to date we had failed in our approach while ZANLA were filling, or at least promising to satisfy, the void in the enemy's life with futuristic ideology which may have sounded possible and plausible, although in my view, unlikely.

I felt a growing notion that we had no progressive political message to offer the local population. Therefore, we would secure no long-term military solution other than "kills win wars". The RF political message to the majority of Africans, in particular those living in the TTLs who were directly involved in the war, was in fact (my words): "You stay where you are, we will stay where we are and never in a 1,000 years will you be capable of changing the status."[1] Ian Smith delivered a televised speech on 20 March 1976, when he stated: "I don't believe in majority rule ever in Rhodesia…not in 1,000 years. I repeat that I believe in blacks and whites working together. If one day it is white and the next day it is black, I believe we have failed and it will be a disaster for Rhodesia." Smith was advocating a continuum of white-empowered rule with shared African participation but failed to implement progressive steps to support his statement or reform to remove racial prejudice from the outset of his leadership. The first sentence "stuck" in the minds of his worldwide audience. This outlook is difficult to defend. By contrast, the white minority were led to believe that "all is well". The RF had everything under control and "never in a thousand years" would matters change. This approach was only worth fighting for, if one believed it to be true. I, for one, began to doubt this belief.

In the words of Zedong: "War is the continuation of politics. In this sense, war is politics and war itself is a political action; since ancient times there has never been a war that did not have a political character…When politics develops to a certain stage beyond which it cannot proceed by the usual means, war breaks out to sweep the obstacles from the way…When the obstacle is removed, and the political aim is attained, the war will stop. Nevertheless, if the obstacle is not completely swept away, the war will have to continue until the aim is fully accomplished…It can therefore be said that politics is war without bloodshed while war is politics with bloodshed."[2]

Meanwhile, during a drive through Salisbury, past the golf courses, cricket fields, rugby grounds and other sports clubs and nightclubs, I found evidence of a general lack of understanding among white Rhodesians regarding the gravity of the situation facing the country. The "well-oiled" Rhodesian Front propaganda machinery was keeping the white population misinformed while trumpeting "all is well". Their ignorance and what amounted to contempt for the enemy was nakedly displayed and astounded me. On 27 September 1976, I submitted a report questioning why able-bodied men in our own Police Staff Branch were not being called up for operational duties. Snr. Asst. Comm. Ted Sheriff agreed: "As the war progressed I realised that we were fighting a full time war as part time soldiers; 6 weeks on call-up then 6 weeks off. The country should have been put on a war footing. Except for duty staff, weekends were off with people golfing, sailing, braaing (BBQ) and socialising. Policemen were, except for the Support Unit, required to do a soldiers' job which we were not trained for. Police Reservists aged 40-60 yrs could not fight insurgents. Businessmen were making money (some a lot) and were not interested in fighting the war. PGHQ staff worked alternate Saturday mornings and had the rest of the weekend off. They were not dedicated to fighting the war. Some senior Police Officers did not get involved with the war and were not dedicated to winning it. Part of my work involved the procurement of mine proof vehicles, we had to fight for every penny."[3] I noted that members of the Jehovah Witness sect were being prosecuted for not going to war as they were conscientious objectors. One Police Reservist in Rusape did road patrols and radio station duties despite having a wooden leg.

It was from these early beginnings that SB strengthened its case for the creation of Security Force Auxiliaries, drawing local *mujibhas* from their home areas, training, arming, and then deploying them

---

1 Flower, K. (1985), p. 101.

2 Zedong, M. (1976), pp. 58-59.

3 Oral interview 23/10/1978.

in their own areas to occupy the land and protect their own people from ZANLA and ZIPRA.[1] This was an issue Premier Ian Smith and his RF party emphatically resisted, until it became "too little, too late". In guerrilla warfare, one doesn't capture the territory, rather one must occupy and possess the land, and live among the people which requires a different strategy. The SF were isolated from the people. This will be examined in Part 2.

[1] Cilliers, J. (2003), p. 48.

River crossing in "1442" on a Special Branch patrol deep into the Makoni TTL. Land Rover now mine proofed.

Special Branch foot patrol Makoni TTL, 1977. Author front right.

Camouflage for all seasons. Nyatanda River, Makoni TTL.

Rusape *mujibha* farm. Maxwell second row standing (L), dressed in a denim jacket with author standing behind him.

ZANLA attack on two vehicles near Dorowa Mine, Inyazura.

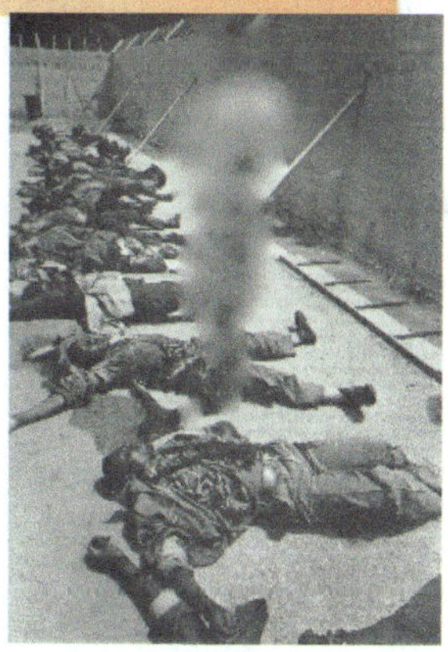

A successful Fire Force action. Picture from local newspaper report.

5 ~ GETTING TO GRIPS WITH THE NATIONAL THREAT

The object of war is not to die for your country,
but to make the other bastard die for his.
George S. Paton

The war was escalating and we knew we were engaged in a major political and armed conflict. Wide-ranging ZANLA activity compelled us to rapidly adjust our approach to the war. Makoni became a liberated area. Cattle dipping had ceased, and dip tanks either destroyed or attendance at these venues made impossible. In addition, ridge-contouring and tax collection halted. Most government schools and clinics closed but the Roman Catholic mission hospital, clinics and schools remained open throughout the war. Public and private transport came to a virtual standstill but those venturing onto rural roads were dependent on clearance from ZANLA, because the dirt roads were regularly mined. As the locals were now supporting ZANLA, it became clear to me that we were operating in enemy territory, behind enemy lines. I viewed this as a positive revelation, vital to survival as it kept us vigilant and alert. Our strategies and tactics needed to be adapted. It became important to constantly approach the war in an unconventional manner, for that is the nature of guerrilla warfare. Neither soldier nor civilian sit around waiting to be killed. Makoni was also a transit TTL for ZANLA's penetration to central Rhodesia en route to Salisbury. There was no respite as insurgents streamed into and across Makoni.

Fortunately, our strike-rates increased as our intelligence became more accurate. *Mujibhas* were deployed with Support Unit troops as their "eyes and ears". They could covertly lead sections to good OP positions, quickly interpret the "picture" on the ground and decide whether the area contained a ZANLA presence or whether the callsign should continue to new OP positions. The questions, where were the enemy, when would they attack and how do we combat them, continually occupied our minds. The key factor was that our *mujibhas* had, when working for the insurgents, learned to discover Security Forces movements and positions. This skill in turn equipped them to remain undetected by opposing ZANLA *mujibhas*. They could use this ability to conceal themselves and the soldiers with them and locate insurgents. This became a team effort that required trust between the callsign and *mujibhas*, along with close liaison between the callsign, OC Support Unit (Sunray Mantle) and Special Branch. Supt. Fred Mason, Sunray Mantle at 151 Alpha, had good insight of the *mujibha* concept and deployed his men with measured skill.

Our altered approach to the war developed into an interesting "about turn" in thinking: one that required courage. Fortunately, the Support Unit readily adopted this initiative. Other white troops did not generally do so, leading to frustration and disappointment among many engaged in the war. They had difficulty in trusting an African civilian, now soldier, carrying a firearm with live ammunition. For that matter, neither did our white government. As our kill-rate increased so did ZANLA reprisals on the locals. They were beaten and murdered as Security Forces collaborators. These hapless locals found themselves in a hopeless situation. Sadly, that is the nature and brutality of war. Notwithstanding, we persevered with our strategy. We were, committed, dedicated and resolved to win the war, while ZANLA increased their activities in an effort to restrict and control our movement in the TTL.

Landmine Patterns

As the war intensified, ZANLA's ruthless landmine campaign escalated and virtually halted civilian motor traffic in Makoni. Government vehicles were the main road users and always travelled in convoy with either their own or a military escort vehicle. We were vulnerable yet alert when travelling the roads. In the final analysis we had no alternative but to persevere.

One morning, as some troops were travelling to a deployment through the Gandanzara area, situated at the southern end of Makoni, into Manyika TTL, the leading vehicle detonated a landmine. Fortunately, there were no injuries. We were nearby, at Rugoyi Police Base, and decided to accompany the recovery vehicle team and investigate the scene. Taking the lead and using our usual landmine evading tactics, we led the recovery team to about 200 metres from the incident when there was a massive explosion. The rear army vehicle had detonated a second landmine. Providentially, both our Land Rovers had driven over it. Fortunately, there were no injuries.[1] Fire Force had been called to assist with the follow-up after the first landmine had detonated but their efforts, unfortunately, came to nothing.

While the Fire Force was flying about, a Support Unit stick situated in the middle of rugged, mountainous terrain in Manyika TTL called for assistance. They had killed one insurgent. I had deployed that callsign two days earlier on an OP assignment and recalled that the leader was a soft-spoken, unassuming man. A chopper was despatched to assist and it was suggested SB accompany the pilot. Thus, Herbert and I flew off on another airborne sortie. Another exhilarating experience.

After a short flight, while gaining height, the G-Car contacted the callsign to establish directions to their location. They were situated in a remote valley, surrounded by high mountains with vertical cliffs towering to heights of 400 metres. The only access to the valley was a narrow footpath which passed through a few kraals found about 1.5 kilometres from the contact area. The kraals were deserted.

I watched enthralled as the callsign threw a smoke-grenade to draw attention to their location. The chopper pilot selected a suitable landing zone as close to the troops as possible. On touchdown, Herbert and I stepped down from the chopper and walked off to survey the scene. We were requested to complete investigations as quickly as possible. Rather than remain stationary on the ground and vulnerable to attack, the pilot circled overhead, affording us protection from the air as Herbert and I proceeded.

We soon established that, during the previous evening, the callsign had detected a ZANLA presence in the kraal line and decided to attack as they could not make radio contact with their base. Overnight they had taken up their positions and lay in ambush until first light when they moved in, killing one insurgent. I viewed this as a brave and courageous decision and commended the troops on their initiative and achievement. We called for the chopper, collected the body and an AK-47, and lugged both to the landing zone.

As we lifted off the ground, I could not help but admire the courage, commitment, dedication and bravery of the callsign as they prepared to continue their patrol in what was clearly an enemy-inhabited area, bearing in mind they had been compromised. ZANLA and the locals knew their position. They now faced the daunting task of defending themselves before finding cover further from the contact area under cover of dark, which was hours away. They stood by watching in silence as we flew from their position. The thought crossed my mind: these men are the silent heroes.[2]

We returned to the landmine scene and deposited the body in 1442. A small victory in the light of losing two vehicles to landmines. At least no SF lives were lost which gave us the upper hand, I thought. This, in my estimation, was the appropriate approach to such matters.

There was a great deal of activity at the landmine explosion scene as army engineers set about removing the wreckage from the vicinity. Around 3 p.m. our job was done, not that there was much to achieve in that locality. It was time to leave. I instructed our team to prepare to move and informed the remaining callsigns of our departure. There were sufficient men to defend themselves from further attack and our role as intelligence officers was over.

---

1 Makoni/Manyika Incidents Map: Landmine LM 1.

2 Makoni/Manyika Incidents Map: Incident 15.

As we arrived back at base, we received information via the radio that the callsign from which we had departed had been subjected to a long-range mortar and small-arms attack. No injuries were reported on either side. There was no doubt the war was intensifying and this was one of the few times I was lured into directly responding to ZANLA who, in my mind, were becoming increasingly brazen and aggressive. Noticeably, this was their first daylight follow-up attack after an incident they had instigated.[1]

Mujibhas Deployed with Support Unit to Chinyamagumbu[2]

I assume ZANLA must have been pleased with their success that day. Two vehicles destroyed by landmines and one mortar and small-arms attack on a disabled convoy. I was confident they would not leave the area but rather celebrate and use the successful landmine incidents to politicise the locals, thereby increasing their acceptance and momentum once we returned to our bases. I felt it was time to act decisively. A few days later, I resolved to deploy troops into the same area in an attempt to "flush out" the insurgents. The only worthwhile protection was the 400-metre-high hill, Chinyamagumbu, which overlooked the densely populated 5-kilometre-long Gandanzara Kraal line. We decided on Support Unit callsigns being transported by vehicle and dropped off at night, some distance from the target area. From then on, they could walk to their destinations. One callsign was to position itself as an OP and a relay station on Chinyamagumbu Hill. The other callsigns would sweep through the kraals at first light, watched carefully by the OP.

This was a difficult deployment into a densely populated area, requiring extreme vigilance on the part of the callsigns. They needed to exercise great skill in order to avoid being compromised. There was little natural concealment other than Chinyamagumbu Hill, leaving our men exposed throughout the operation and as a result, making them vulnerable. Sweeps through kraals were always a treacherous procedure, exposing the men to considerable danger. Needless to say, the Support Unit accepted the challenge. We had two *mujibhas*, David and Mike, who were intimately familiar with the area. In addition, both were well-trained RPD gunners. They deployed with the OP and led them into position.

All went according to plan. The OP secured its position and the sweep lines waited for sunrise before beginning their search of the kraals, achieving in my opinion, the impossible, arriving uncompromised.

At daybreak the sweep lines began their task. Insurgents were sleeping in the kraals who, when alerted, ran towards Chinyamagumbu Hill (seemingly their rendezvous position) straight into the line of fire of the Support Unit OP. In the ensuing battle, four insurgents were killed. However, the most rewarding aspect of this engagement was the active participation of our two *mujibhas*. They were fully engaged in the firefight as they blazed away with their RPDs, alongside the callsign, on the fleeing enemy, thus chalking up their first direct battle. This proved a turning point for our operations with Support Unit troops. There was much celebration and joy at their triumph. The *mujibhas* had been successfully integrated into our battle arsenal.

Back at the *mujibha* camp one would have thought the two *mujibhas* had just won the war. In a way we gained a major victory as David and Mike had proved their loyalty, commitment and capabilities and, in so doing, earned the respect and acceptance of the Support Unit.

Our understanding of the enemy was increasing. As we confronted a growing number of ZANLA incidents, carried out interrogations and deployed troops and *mujibhas*, the more experience we could draw from. This enabled us to provide increasingly accurate intelligence. To many of us, the war was becoming second nature. We were beginning to operate often by discerning the correct course of action and, on other occasions, by intuition: essential ingredients for surviving a war.

On the subject of survival, without being fully watchful of it, I had departed the so-called civilian world by means of a subconscious metamorphosis which was initially thrilling, audacious and challenging. It was exhilarating pursuing the enemy and masterminding their destruction. Killing

---

[1] Makoni/Manyika Incidents Map: Incident 16.

[2] Makoni/Manyika Incidents Map: Incident 17.

became my way of life. I found the process of outwitting the enemy stimulating, particularly while in the company of men with similar outlook and disposition. Together we commiserated our failures: together we celebrated our victories. In our minds, there were only two categories of people, us and them. They were either for us or against us. There was no middle ground. Join us and live or oppose us and die. If a direct kill was not an immediate option, an alternative means of annihilation would be sought, regardless of the cost or process.

Recognition of the areas ZANLA had liberated and accepting this reality required a rejection of government political propaganda that emphasised the SF were winning the war. If the truth be told, we were not. This attitude was a dangerous, negative state of mind which elevated the ego rather than embracing the immediate dangers we faced. Notwithstanding, we pressed on, developing our strategies and tactics, learning to pinpoint areas for OP deployments which were proving increasingly successful.

PATU "Cave Man" Observation Post[1]

It was approximately 2 a.m. when the phone rang on Sunday, 7 August 1977, rousing me from a deep sleep. At the other end of the line was the voice of a charge office constable informing me that the PATU callsign, Oscar Victor 10, which I had deployed on 5 August, had sighted a large group of insurgents in the St Killian's Mission area, Makoni TTL. My thinking became disjointed. Why was this happening at 2 a.m.? I pondered. Hastily, I made my way to the charge office, a drive of no more than three minutes. This was the first OP in that area for some time and, on reflection, I was convinced there was a ZANLA section nearby. We had confirmed evidence that the local Roman Catholic mission, St Killian's, was sympathetic towards ZANLA. Several murders of "sellouts" had been reported in this remote and inaccessible region.

I promptly deployed callsign Oscar Victor 10, a four-man PATU stick led by Allan Johnston and included Field Reservist Jon Pimm. Allan recalls:

> I was conscripted as a N/S/P/O in 1974 and posted to Support Unit for a year. I was then called up again for general PATU for another year. On my first 6 weeks call-up with JOC Rusape in 1977 I was invited by John Padbury to work on the *mujibha* farm outside Rusape. I left my job in Salisbury and joined the team.
>
> It is important to note that this area was also a well-known transit route for gooks entering and exiting the country from Mozambique. Honde Valley, a well-worn path route known to SF and CTs alike, was not far from our location. A network of *mujibhas* in this area kept a very vigilant eye on movements and regularly herded their cattle into inaccessible areas so that they could assess SF presence while maintaining innocence.
>
> We were briefed by John Padbury and deployed by vehicle after dark on 5 August 1977 with the objective of setting up an OP in the general area listed.
>
> The walk-in started at around 21h00 at locstat VQ452436. Our plan was to walk in from a south-westerly direction and head through the "gomos"[2] in a north-easterly direction following the river line. I had seen from the map that we would be walking in classical ambush terrain, the foot path we decided to follow into the target area was surrounded by mountains, so we maintained an extended line. Visibility was poor, it was a half moon, I was grateful for the darkness.
>
> At approximately VQ465453 around 23h30 we started hearing voices emanating from the north east in the same direction as the path we were walking on. It seemed as if the voices were approaching in our direction although we did not know if they were static up ahead.
>
> At this point I made the decision to climb up the high granite boulder hill on our left in a northerly direction to get a better fix on the bearing of the voices. It seemed very

1 Makoni/Manyika Incidents Map: Incident 18; Geldenhuys, P. (2014), Air Strike Log Entry 716

2 Gomos: Granite outcrops and or hills generally with a lot of cover, ideal for base camps and OPs alike.

strange to be hearing this amount of noise at close to midnight and it quickly became evident that the group was moving along the same footpath we had just left in the opposite direction from the north east. We sat about 100m above the path and listened as the group made its way in a long-extended line talking freely and oblivious to any SF presence that may have been in the area.

I decided to continue up to the top of the hill as far as we could so that we could set up an OP position with a view down into the valley in the vicinity of VQ455454. Our position was set as VQ462455. At first light we started observing the valley running in a north/south direction and tried to make radio contact at 07h00 to report what we had encountered but with no joy.

We were fairly high up on an exposed granite mountain which like all of them in the eastern highlands lacked vegetation and cover, we had to maintain a very low profile throughout the day. At the same time, we positioned ourselves in a spot where we could have a good view of the valley below.

Throughout the day we started noticing women carrying pots and food into a thicket against the opposite hillside to where we were. On exiting the thicket, they were empty handed which led us to believe that there was a gook presence at VQ452454 but who and how many we had no idea.

I figured out that if there was indeed a presence, they would not remain there for the night but would enter the village immediately below us which consisted of maybe six huts and a grain stand. We started discussing what actions we could take, the most likely being to make contact with the group at first light as they emerged from the villages after having spent the night in the huts. We even had individual positions marked out so as to maximise our cover and kill zone.

Towards early evening of Saturday 6 August, and to our absolute astonishment Jon Pimm noticed gooks filing out of the bush and we were unexpectedly treated to an open line extended march into the mealie fields from the dense bush at the base of the mountain opposite us. Leading the group of at least 30 terrs was a tall man wearing a long black leather jacket and carrying an RPD. It seemed as if this was a display for the locals as they remained in open ground until it was dark. I estimate that they must have been about 800m away from our position.[1] At this point and with 500 rounds of ammunition between us and no radio comms it became very evident very quickly that we could not attack the group as it far exceeded our expectations in terms of numbers.

Under the cover of dark I moved away from our OP position and tried again to make comms, but with no luck.

We decided to wait until later that evening and descend the mountain the way we had climbed it onto the path below and exit the area the way we had come in. I was very conscious that there was only one route out for us and it was the way we walked in, through classical ambush alley! There was a high risk of ambush if, at any time, we had been seen by the locals.

The plan was to walk out and hit the main district road to Rugoyi Police Base and advise John Padbury on the situation before first light so that he could activate, hopefully, a FF action. I can remember thinking that it seemed too good to be true if our plans would in fact align themselves and that there would still be gooks in the area by the time SF had arrived.

It was a very tension filled walk out along the path as we needed to avoid making contact with anyone let alone the group of terrs. We reached the Police base at around 0200 a.m. Sunday 7 August, identified ourselves to the camp guards to ensure we were not shot by our own men, and entered the base camp. I called John Padbury, gave him a

1 Allan Johnston believes there were as many as 80 insurgents, many of whom dispersed during the night. Email 31/3/2016.

PATU "CAVE MAN" OP - VQ452452 - ST. TRIASHILL

KEY

PATU "CAVE MAN" OP - VQ452452 - ST TRIASHILL

(A) At approximately 21h00 PATU call sign Oscar Victor 10 is moving north east along a path from the distant BSAP Base at Rugoyi.

(B) They reach this point and hear a lot of voices to their front at point "C". Realisng that it was likley insurgents ahead, they leave the path and climb the feature to their left with the intention of observing.

(C) Point from which voices can be heard.

(D) They establish an OP in this position.

(E) After dawn breaks they observe feeding parties from local kraals moving backwards and forwards to a position at point "E" which is a thicket of bush on a riverline just below a rocky ridge across the valley to their west. However they lose communications with their base and cannot report the sightings.

(F) They watch for the rest of the day and eventually at last light they observe at least 30 insurgents walking westwards in an extended line formation. They disappear into the bush near point "E".

(G) Having no communications, the call sign waits for cover of darkness and, following their route in, they head back towards Rugoyi, some fifteen kilometres distant, arriving there at about 02h00. Padbury is advised and arrangements are made for one of the PATU members to guide a Fire Force to the scene.

(H) Just after first light a heliborn and paratroop Fire Force, consisting of the RAR supported by elements of 5 Independent Company and the BSA Police Support Unit, pay the area a visit where the camp (E) is indicated by a member of the PATU stick. Contact is made and some insurgents fled eastwards down the river, whilst others try to hide in caves. One insurgent is extracted from a cave by Special Branch using teargas. 6 ZANLA are killed, 2 are captured, whilst 3 civilians in the camp are killed and 4 are injured. 2 members of the SF are slightly injured.

> sitrep and he made arrangements for a vehicle to transport me to the JOC at Rusape, I took the maps of the area with me. On arrival John advised me that the FF at Grand Reef were keen to deploy on the intelligence and we immediately set off in his mine proof vehicle which had no doors, it was freezing, and I was oblivious as to what was about to transpire. En route we discussed the deployment in great detail, John wanted to ensure that I would deliver a good quality sitrep, particularly regarding the map reference, which would be vital for a successful engagement. I was confident that I could lead the Fire Force into the attack.[1]

On arrival at Grand Reef, there was a hint of dawn on the horizon. We went straight into the conference room and met the FF Commander, Maj. Andre Dennison, of the Rhodesian African Rifles. This was a RAR Fire Force with 5 Independent Company also involved. Dennison was focused as he listened intently to Allan's account of the sighting. Once he had satisfied himself that the location and events were correct, and there were no contradictions in Allan's detailed presentation, Dennison methodically drew his conclusions that the FF would deploy with the K-Car, three G-Cars and Paradak. Allan was to fly in the Lynx and indicate the target area. His estimated time of departure (ETD) was 0600hrs. Dennison made it clear that if they deployed and it was a "lemon", Allan would be "history". Allan nodded while a tangible air of resolution and determination settled across the room as the weight of the entire operation fell on his shoulders. I confirmed that sufficient Avtur was available at the Rugoyi Police Base.

I left Allan with the Fire Force, raced back to Rusape, collected Herbert and headed for Rugoyi, some 13 kilometres from the contact zone, a short flight for choppers.

A lone vehicle travelling through the TTL was not a wise decision but I knew Herbert could drive if I was injured in an ambush. Detonating a landmine of course would be an entirely different matter. Three weeks earlier, while Herbert and I were at a local store drinking ice-cold quarts of Castle Lager on the veranda, I asked him whether he could drive. I felt he should learn in the event of an emergency. He asked me for the keys for 1442 and I reluctantly handed them over. He climbed into the vehicle, started the engine and drove off, disappearing behind a cloud of dust. Five minutes later, a long five minutes for me, he reappeared, to my significant relief. He declared proudly that he could indeed drive. We celebrated with another quart of Castle Lager. I resolved to send him on a police officer driving course as soon as possible. This would take place months later.[2] Allan Johnston continues:

> With the array of air borne inventory in tow, the Lynx arrived in the target area and I directed the pilot into an orbit above the base camp, moments later the FF helicopters and the Dakota arrived a thousand feet or so below us.
>
> The FF commander impatiently asked where the hell the "gooks" were, and I suggested to him that I was sure they would break cover any moment. Excitement started to turn to nervous anticipation especially when I was told over the airwaves that I had led them into a lemon. At that moment I saw a gook running down the river line away from the base camp which was nestled in between the dense bush and steep walls of the granite cliff as the backdrop. Dennison had also seen this movement and with a puff of dust on the ground the K-Car fired and stopped him, and this initiated the larger breakout of the remaining terrs.

Dennison strategically deployed his "stops" on the ground and instructed the Dakota pilot to despatch the paratroopers. The Dakota, with the rear door removed prior to departure and a wind-deflection plate fitted on the forward section of the door-frame to stop buffeting by diverting the airflow away from the door, could carry 20 men, five sticks of four men each. The aircraft

1 Allan Johnston email 31/3/2016.

2 All white policemen automatically went to the driving schools at Salisbury and Bulawayo after passing out (completing their training course at Morris Depot), and completed motor vehicle and motor cycle courses to achieve their driving licences. This was not the case for the Africans who went on a selection basis only.

required a minimum 600 metre runway to take-off. Lift-off was achieved at 3,000rpm and a speed of 80 knots with quarter-flaps and 65 knots with half-flaps when taking off on a short runway. Cruising height was normally around 1,500 feet, sufficient to avoid small-arms fire. Maximum flying time with full tanks, no cargo or troops on board at 1,980rpm and 90 knots was 14 hours. Fully loaded, flying time was some four hours.

There was no radio altimeter fitted to the Dakota, making the despatch of paratroopers onto rising ground extremely dangerous. In fact, some men lost their lives as a result of not having this instrument on board. In order to counter this problem, a K-Car would overfly the drop zone, note the altitude and pass the information on to the Dakota pilot who would select his despatch height, run in, and drop the troops safely.

When approaching the drop zone, the pilot would illuminate the red warning light above the exit door to alert the paratroopers of their upcoming deployment. He would then fly at approximately 90 knots at a minimum height of 500 feet above ground level (AGL), 1,500 feet AGL on static-line practice and, when over the drop zone, trigger the green light signalling for them to jump from the plane. Approach to the drop zone depended on various factors including wind direction, terrain, the relative position of the insurgents to the SF on the ground and the location of anti-aircraft weapons or ground fire, to mention a few.[1]

Two sticks were dropped in high-gusting, windy conditions. Platoon Warrant Officer Wilson broke a bone in his foot on landing, thus suspending the remaining drops. Wilson was casevaced by chopper and flown to hospital. Dennison had worked with the Support Unit at 151 Alpha, so he requested two sticks be deployed to Rugoyi Police Base. Supt. Tom Naude despatched N/S/P/O Mike Stewart and seven men to Rugoyi. Allan Johnston continues:

> Effectively there were only three escape routes out of the valley. The northerly route which was now cut off with a stop group. The easterly and westerly routes were some distance away and would be difficult to reach unless cover was maintained against the granite cliff face. Sweep teams started to make their way up the river line and many skirmishes took place. At this point I felt vindicated and effectively was relegated to a spectator with a prime seat vantage point.
>
> After what seemed like an hour or more Dennison instructed the Lynx pilot to come in and drop snebs[2] into the cave where the gooks were holed up. It seemed a fierce fire fight was taking place at the entrance to the cave. The gooks were repelling each attempt to enter it, the pilot suggested I place my flak jacket under the seat in case of any ground fire being directed at the aircraft. The pilot brought the Lynx in at a very steep angle following the river line vegetation up into the cave against a steep granite wall of rock. He released the snebs which impacted against the rock wall and was confirmed as a direct hit on the cave from the ground troops. Unaware of the forces of gravity that were about to be exerted I blacked out and regained consciousness seconds later. Repeated attempts to enter the cave were repulsed and if memory serves me correct the Lynx pilot conducted a second strike against the cave with similar effects.
>
> Tensions on the ground were rising as the frustration of not being able to dislodge the gooks increased. By this stage we had taken some casualties while those gooks that were on the run were being cut off. There was a lull in the action on the ground and the pilot requested leave of the action as his fuel reserves were running low and he had to return to Grand Reef to refuel and rearm. On landing back at Grand Reef, the pilot asked if I would like to join him on the mopping up operations which I declined as the lack of sleep was taking its toll.

The battle raged on, with fierce resistance from the insurgents. Choppers buzzed to and from

---

1 All the information regarding the Dakota was supplied by an Rh.AF Dakota pilot who wished to remain anonymous.

2 Snebs: Rockets fired from pods mounted on the wings of the Lynx.

Rugoyi as they refuelled and re-entered the battle. In a series of skirmishes, troops under the command of Lt. Shrag killed four insurgents. They then moved up the river line to join N/S/P/O Mike Stewart from the Support Unit. Stewart was 19 at the time. He picks up the story:

> My stick comprised my trusty 3 amigos, Wilson, David and Amos (pseudonyms) the medic and we had positioned at Rugoyi Police Base where John Padbury and his Special Branch team were also waiting. I remembered John well because he had given a few briefings in my time at Rusape, mainly 1977, and his Intelligence was always good. The Fire Force commander called us in and we were uplifted by chopper and dropped into the area slightly north of the other RAR stop groups. The K-Car had already eliminated some CTs. We had just hopped off the chopper so were exposed and moved towards the river line where there were lots of boulders and cover, when we came under fire from about 15m. We killed the culprit and then another just near him, who had been wounded in the initial contact.
>
> Sweeping through the contact area we came across another wounded CT who kept saying he was a recruit. We secured him and attended his wounds before taking him back to the Landing Zone (LZ) where he was uplifted. I was told to move up the river line as that was where the CTs had initially been spotted. We found two more bodies, one being a very fat female CT; she was wearing communist webbing and had an AK.
>
> As we continued to move up the river line, we came under fire again from several CTs; I tried flanking their position, but they were up the side of the kopje and it was difficult terrain. We were joined by an RAR stick led by Lieutenant Schrag who decided on a direct approach. I warned him that the gooks had a good position, but he carried on, and was shot through the shoulder and casevaced by chopper.[1] We discovered that the intensive fire had come from a pillbox type cave.
>
> I was instructed to bring the dead bodies to the LZ which was quite a mission especially the rather large woman. After this we were choppered back to the forward base at Rugoyi.[2]

The captured injured insurgent was casevaced to Grand Reef and from there, to the Special Branch at Bindura. Under interrogation, he revealed there was an arms cache concealed in the manure near a kraal complex that was nearest to the contact area. This arms hoard was lifted. The captured man revealed that the group comprised two sections from Wedza and Chiduku TTLs and were returning from a resupply mission which confirmed Allan Johnson's initial thoughts. This efficient procedure enabled skilled SB officers to glean intelligence for immediate action, mainly by Selous Scouts, as well as longer-term deployments regarding matters of internal and external intelligence.

There were still unknown numbers of insurgents holed up in the cave as dusk set in. Dennison ordered his men to surround the cave so that the operation would be finished off in the morning. The helicopters returned to Grand Reef for the night.

On my return to Rusape, Supt. Cy Hartley[3] announced it was Special Branch's responsibility to remove the insurgents from the cave. I called for dog section backup and organised the issue of tear gas guns and canisters, tear gas smoke-grenades, gas masks and a megaphone from the armoury. These were issued by Insp. John Wilkins[4] who also joined the team with another police reservist. My thinking was that the dog section handler would send his dog into the cave and determine whether insurgents were present. If that was the case, we would tear gas the cave and force the occupants out. This plan made sense to me and had the advantage of avoiding the need to enter the cave. We were prepared for an early start.

Three mine-proofed Land Rovers rolled out from Sub.JOC Rusape at 3 a.m., allowing enough

---

[1] Schrag was decorated with the Military Forces Commendation on 15/3/1978 for this action.

[2] Mike Stewart email 10/7/2015.

[3] Supt. Cy Hartley was the SB Sub.JOC Rusape officer from 1/8/1977-30/9/1977. Confirmed by original Sub.JOC Rusape duty roster which I initiated on 16/11/1976.

[4] Insp. (T) John Wilkins: Member in Charge, Police Reserve, Rusape.

time to reach Rugoyi Police Base by first light, thus coinciding with the Fire Force's arrival. Dennison gave instructions that we would be airlifted in on the first flight, as the G-Cars were empty. His troops were still in the field. The dog section detail, led by Gary Tudor-Jones, was uplifted and deployed to the contact scene.

Chopper flights at treetop level always excited me as it took me into the heart of the war where I felt a part of the killing machine. As the chopper flew over the contact zone, I could see the large area that had been part of the battleground. "Stops" were clearing the area and the radio periodically announced findings of weapons, ammunition and dead bodies.

As the chopper landed, we made our way to the dog section detail who had positioned itself at the cave entrance. John Wilkins, who later entered the cave, takes the story further: "The cave resembled a World War Two bunker set under a large rock formation. Two massive granite rocks supported the roof above a gap about four meters wide and one meter above the ground. It sloped slightly downhill. There were two entrances on either side, one of which I was told the Fire Force had tried to use to put grenades into the cave without success. To the right-hand side was the entrance that dropped down about three meters to the cave floor; it looked quite formidable and impenetrable. Inside there was a large entrance chamber, in which people could stand and move around, and a passage leading from one side of the cave to the other connecting the entrances on both sides."

The Fire Force stick leader informed us that there had been no movement around the cave all night and he was uncertain whether the insurgents were still occupying the cave. Soldiers walked to-and-fro across the entrance to the cave, confident the insurgents had fled during the night. The Fire Force was wrapping up their actions, and the choppers began to ferry the soldiers out of the contact zone. One "stop" remained at the cave, armed and ready for action, but looked on as the police teams positioned themselves. Tudor-Jones made his way self-assuredly to the cave entrance and released his German shepherd dog. A short while later the animal came bounding back, indicating a presence of some kind, but Tudor-Jones considered that "it was dead!"

Based on the assumption the cave was unoccupied, Dennison, armed with a Smith and Wesson .44 Magnum, entered the cave, closely followed by Wilkins and Tudor-Jones. A brief silence prevailed, only to be shattered by a short burst of automatic gunfire. The escort group dived for cover, moving away from the bunker-like entrance of the cave. Cy and I moved speedily to the side entrance. As the seconds ticked by and with weapons at the ready, we heard scuffling coming from the cavern. The dog handler appeared, crawling backwards on his rear-end. He had been shot in the leg. Since the cave was meant to be "clear", Cy and I thought Tudor-Jones had had an accidental discharge. However, Tudor-Jones painfully confirmed that he had been shot by an insurgent. Hartley instructed me to rescue him. I leapt into the cave and hauled the shocked man out. Once it was realised there was no way of reaching the insurgent, Dennison and Wilkins decided to exit the cave through another entrance. As Wilkins followed, another burst of automatic fire erupted, narrowly missing him.

Dennison organised Tudor-Jones's evacuation while the medic carried out first aid treatment. The K-Car Commander passed on instructions from Grand Reef to Dennison that they were to withdraw and risk no further casualties.

Taking command of the scene, Hartley was determined to capture the insurgent(s) in the cave. The FF departed but Dennison decided to remain. As the Fire Force departed and the whirl of the chopper's rotor-blades faded in the distance, an eerie calm settled over the area. I studied the cave entrance thinking what a lonely, isolated and vulnerable position we were now in. When a battle is imminent, time, it seems, does indeed stand still. Creation is rendered silent, emptiness lingers, nature is stilled in the face of her displeasure, seemingly aware of the impending killing, as men focus upon venting their misplaced anger on slaughtering each other.

There were three entrances to the cave. One directly ahead of us, one to the east and the third to the west. Dennison and Herbert were positioned to cover the west entrance. Hartley and the police reservist covered the east entrance. Wilkins and I scrutinised the front bunker entrance and would be responsible for firing tear gas into the cave. Cy instructed all details to put on their gas masks. Thumbs up from all concerned indicated we were ready. With that, Wilkins and I began firing tear gas into the main bunker entrance.

Herbert started calling out to the insurgent(s) using the megaphone but there was no response. More tear gas, more cajoling. No insurgents appeared. The Police Reservist, fluent in Shona, also called out but to no avail. It didn't take long for the tear gas to start drifting out the east and west exits. We gained the impression that a draught was drifting through the main bunker entrance circulating the tear gas through the cave and rising through the east and west exits. No tear gas smoke was seen leaving the cave from other openings, leaving me to believe, confidently, we had all the exits covered. Drifting tear gas began to smother us, making it difficult to see through the haze. More propaganda, more tear gas and no sign of insurgent(s): total silence!

John Wilkins comments: "The tear-gas found a 'tear' alright, Dennison who was guarding the lower cave entrance was overcome by it and cried out that he could not see; he had not removed the hair from his forehead allowing the tear gas to enter the mask. Padbury pulled his hair to one side, tightened the straps of the gas mask up to seal the rubber sides against his clear facial skin, and sat him out of the way in the fresh air; he could observe the rest of the action, and help with a fire fight if necessary."[1] And that is exactly what happened.

More tear gas, more propaganda and still no hint of the enemy. After an hour, a loud call was heard from within the cave:

"*Ndapera.*" (I am finished.) The extraction party tensed up at the ready.

"Do you want to come out?" asked Herbert.

"*Hongu.*" (Yes) answered the insurgent.

"How many are you?" Herbert enquired.

"*Mumwe chete, asi mukadzi wangu aripo,*" (One only, but I have my girlfriend) answered the insurgent.

"How many guns do you have?" Herbert called out.

"*Imwe chete,*" (One only) replied the insurgent.

"You come out first and your girlfriend is to follow. Leave the gun behind," instructed Herbert, ensuring that the extraction party were aware of what was going on.

"*Hongu,*" called the insurgent, now clearly in distress.

After about another minute, through the haze of tear gas, the insurgent appeared at the east exit which was now covered by Hartley and Herbert. He walked with his hands held high, closely followed by his girlfriend. Some party she had been to, I thought. This scene played through my mind: never allow yourself to be lured into a cave by an insurgent. Herbert established that the insurgent's gun was in the cave. As a precaution, the insurgent's hands were securely bound, and he was led back into the cave to collect his firearm. The police extraction group still had their gas masks on but the captive did not, providing an incentive for ensuring he did not make a false move. Tense moments followed as the extraction group was mindful this could be another trap or, secondly, the prisoner may attempt an escape. Lying on the ground behind a large stone was his AK-47 and webbing, along with four magazines. There were no other occupants in the cave. With the cave cleared, we withdrew for the final time. The captured man was delivered to Selous Scouts for immediate follow-up in the field. Ken Milne later confirmed that, while on deployment with the Scouts, the capture attempted to escape and was shot dead.[2]

The final tally of the two-day operation was six ZANLA killed, one wounded and one unharmed captured. Two African females and one African male were killed. Four African females were injured and casevaced to Umtali Hospital. Two SF personnel were injured in battle and one SF parachutist was injured on landing. The materials we recovered included three SKSs, three AKMs, six MK 20 rockets, six hand-grenades and 1,300 x 7.62mm intermediate rounds.

---

1 John Wilkins email 22/11/2016, various discussions.

2 This overall account is confirmed by John Wilkins emails and discussions, 19/11/2016 and 22/11/2016.

Dennison was awarded the Military Legion of Merit for capturing the terrorist in the cave, which was in fact a BSA Police operation. I found this award surprising.[1] This cave siege was reminiscent of the capture of Chief Chingaira Makoni almost 100 years earlier. Not all that long ago and still within the confines of oral history. The extreme dangers of this type of cave operation were exemplified in a similar incident in the Bikita area on 28 September 1977 when Lt. Jeremy Fisher (22), from A Company, First Battalion, Rhodesian African Rifles, was killed in action. Jeremy's patrol was with another Security Force unit when they discovered terrorists holed up in a cave. After efforts to flush them out had failed, Jeremy threw a grenade into the cave to clear it, went in but was shot and killed. L/Cpl. Russell Phillips entered the cave to recover Fisher, armed with a 9mm pistol. He was shot at by a group hiding within the cave and emptied his clip before exiting to collect more ammunition. On re-entering, he gave covering fire which enabled Cpl. Sandro Mazella, the troop medic, to recover Fisher. In the ensuing battle, Phillips killed three terrorists and wounded one.[2]

Arms Cache, Makoni TTL[3]

It was generally from captured insurgents that we successfully located arms caches, as well as other essential intelligence. A captured insurgent's information was authenticated in the field by his level of co-operation which included the location and removal of weapon hoards. *Mujibhas* did not usually know the location of stashed arms. Uplifting caches, particularly landmines, was important to protect Security Forces vehicles and personnel. The removal of hidden weaponry also damaged ZANLA morale. Transporting arms over distances was cumbersome, requiring much effort. Subsequent removal of the munitions by the SF created uncertainty as to the loyalty of the locals. Cpl. Cliff Rochester recalls two operations he was involved with:

> During the conflict I served as a conscriptee Corporal in 3 Engineer Squadron. Life during the war in Rhodesia as a conscriptee was a schizophrenic type of existence spending every alternate six weeks in the operational area as a soldier, and then back home to one's job and family for six weeks. There were compensations however with the amazing camaraderie existing among all arms of the security forces and the long-standing friendships made.
>
> It was standard procedure for Sappers to be attached to Infantry Battalions to provide mine detection and lifting expertise including explosives and booby traps. At the time, four of us Sappers were allocated to 8th Battalion Rhodesia Regiment based at the Joint Operation Command Centre (JOC) in the small rural farming town of Rusape.
>
> Also based at the JOC was the BSAP Special Branch who were responsible among many other tasks for the collation and interpretation of the intelligence information extracted by various units on the ground and from captured insurgents. Based on information, and with a capture as a guide, John Padbury from Special Branch at the JOC, set about organising a mission to locate an arms cache.
>
> Members of Special Branch fortified by a platoon of 8th Battalion infantry and supported by the Sappers assembled on the particular day ready to embark when unannounced Army Public Relations brass appeared with a cameraman from the BBC who was to record this story for BBC News. I distinctly remember John being highly annoyed at the intrusion of this civilian and remonstrated adamantly that he didn't want him on the mission. Army brass however outranked him, and the cameraman joined us but was told by John in no uncertain terms to keep well out of his way. Keith Samler was based at Rusape with the Selous Scouts and accompanied us with two of his men. He recalls the incident and the name of the BBC man as Francois Marais.
>
> The convoy set off travelling stressfully through areas where getting ambushed was always a threat and the frequent craters of previous mine detonations in the road were a

[1] Wood, J.R.T. (1989), pp. 128-131; Moorcraft, P. (1981), p. 193; Shaw, B. (2018), pp. 316-318.

[2] J.R.T. Wood email 7/4/2020

[3] Dates are not confirmed..

continual reminder of that real possibility. On our arrival at the area and guided by the prisoner we set off climbing up what seemed never ending hills. The physical exertion coupled with the constant possibility of being led into a trap by the prisoner was stressful and tiring. Our unwanted cameraman trudged up those hills carrying a really big, heavy TV camera.

Eventually, way up in the clouds, we arrived at the suspected location and started to search for the cache. One of Keith Samler's men took a break, sat on a boulder and was scuffing the ground with his foot when he unearthed a TM46 landmine. With the comfort of the infantry perimeter defence the sappers set about probing the indicated cache area for booby traps. None were found but a considerable amount of supplies and weaponry was subsequently unearthed.

It was a mission accomplished. We got the cache and the BBC got their footage which was I believe, aired on BBC Prime Time News. The cameraman even got John's respect at the end of the day for his strenuous effort keeping up with us.

There was a snooker table in the BSAP next to the JOC and John and myself enjoyed many a game and more than a few beers! Having the benefit of the small Rusape Country Hotel in the town which was frequented by the off-duty military and BSAP much bonding was enjoyed among the local farming community and the security forces.[1]

Eastern Highlands Murders[2]

Cpl. Cliff Rochester continues:

I remember well when as Sappers we were called out to accompany Special Branch to the scene of the murder of an elderly white farming couple on a farm in the Eastern Highlands of Rhodesia which was a spectacularly beautiful mountainous region. We cleared the access roads finding no mines and made our way onto the property. The bodies of the deceased had already been removed by the authorities. We were however there to look for information which would assist Special Branch in the following up of the culprits.

An inspection of the buildings and grounds revealed no booby trapping, however in the outbuilding workshops which were partially damaged by fire we found the badly burnt body of one of the culprits who was still barely alive. It was obvious that in his attempt to torch the buildings the container of petrol had exploded in his hands. The terrorist was moved to a mission hospital in the area and a few days later we accompanied Special Branch to interrogate the badly burnt survivor who was in a bed under a tunnel keeping the bed linen off his burns. An attempt to extract useful information from the insurgent was fruitless due to his advanced disablement and he died a few days later.[3]

African village as seen from a Security Force Observation Post. Photo Barry Woan.

1 Cpl. Cliff Rochester email 18/12/2017.
2 Date not confirmed.
3 Cliff Rochester email 30/3/2017.

Kraals were often burned after contacts or on suspicion that the villagers were enemy collaborators. Photo Barry Woan.

Frustrations of hunting an elusive enemy. Photo Barry Woan.

RPG-7 attack on a police mine-proofed Land Rover, Mayo, 10/11/1976.
Cst. Zacharia Dongo killed and Police Reservist Cooper Smit seriously injured but recovered. Photo by Dawn Smit.

Remains of N/S/P/Os Pod Hurd's and Charlie Hand's Land Rover after landmine incident. Photo by Charlie Hand.

Hurd (L) and Hand survived! Photo by Charlie Hand.

Bus landmine incident attended by Hurd and Hand 15 minutes after their landmine incident. Photo by Charlie Hand.

Members of Charlie Troop, BSAP Support Unit with an army pookie. Picture provided by Barry Woan taken by Rob McCrea.

A typical African rural village. Photo by Rod Hein.

6 ~ REVOLUTION AND THE CHURCH

Opinion and truth carry the same weight today
which is a grave injustice.
Vernon Loker

The Carmelite Order of the Roman Catholic (RC) Church was an integral part of the Makoni, Manyika and Mutasa TTLs and it was becoming clear to me that they were actively supporting ZANLA. The following summary briefly describes their arrival, intentions, development and involvement in the Rhodesian conflict. Gallagher in his book *The Catholic Church in Manicaland* makes the comment: "In 1895 Abbot Francis met Cecil John Rhodes at Mount Ayliff and secured 1000 morgen of land in the Inyanga District for mission purposes. The title deeds were dated 10th December 1895. 1896 saw six RC missionaries arrive at the land which they named Triashill and on it built a primitive hut. Shortly after their arrival they got news of the outbreak of the First *Chimurenga* and hastily made their way to Umtali before returning to Natal. In 1907 St Triashill was finally occupied by missionaries who opened St Barbara's Mission, St Killian's and Kriste Mambo."[1]

The missionaries' vision was to bring the Roman Catholic faith to the people through proclaiming the Christian belief, the building of schools and hospitals, and training the indigenous folk for vocations. They identified with the people through the study of their language, customs and traditions. These Catholics were indeed one with the people. They were accepted openly, treated as their own and served the people well. At the outbreak of the Second *Chimurenga* Fr Edward (Ned) Ward was at St Triashill's and oversaw Kriste Mambo Mission, run by the Dutch Sisters of Charity, specialising in nursing and education. Fr Michael Kenny was at St Barbara's and Fr Joseph Neville oversaw St Killian's. There was a hospital at Bonda Mission and clinics at St Triashill's and St Barbara's, the latter two remaining open for the duration of the war. There was no clinic at St Killian's as a government health centre was nearby.

During the Second *Chimurenga*, the missionaries were assumed to be part of the struggle and, in general, advised by the people not to fraternise with the SF as this would be misinterpreted as supporting them, which would lead to reprisals from ZANLA. All told, these missionaries had close contact with insurgents and were well informed regarding ZANLA activities, notably when they laid landmines. Some missionaries did report to the SF but were then advised by the church to leave the area for fear of reprisals.

These missionaries were directed to assist insurgents by their bishop as is made clear in the following article by the Carmelite priest, Leo Gallagher:

> Bishop Lamont[2] told his priests and sisters that he himself would be entirely responsible for their actions, both in giving medicine to the terrorists and in not reporting their presence. The freedom fighters told the missionaries not to report their presence in the area. The security forces usually visited the missions during the day and the freedom fighters normally came in the evening time.
>
> It was a time of great tension, but the clear unequivocal leadership of Bishop Lamont helped the individual missionary to do the correct thing. Bishop Lamont said: If the Christian missionary is the informer, the whole community understandably blame him,

[1] Gallagher, L. (1996), Chap. 1. St Triashill's, St Killian's and St Barbara's were entrusted to the Roman Catholic Carmelite Order between 1948-1949. Kriste Mambo School was established in 1963.

[2] Donal Lamont (1911-2003), Bishop of the Diocese of Umtali (Mutare) which included Makoni, Manyika and Mutasa TTLs, and Rusape.

> and they blame not only him but the whole organisation to which he belongs. Not only the church gets the blame but Christianity itself is condemned as afraid, as an agent of oppression, and is accused of preaching the brotherhood of all men in creation and in redemption, and of contradicting it in practice - even becoming the willing accomplice in the bombing and destroying of villages and in the killing of innocent women and children.
>
> He told his priests to support, as best they could, those who required their help. The priests lived in the midst of the people. They knew many of the leaders of the freedom fighters and had taught many of them in their schools and the sisters had attended them in their clinics. The people stood by their priests, advised them in certain difficult situations, informed them of possible impending dangers and spoke up for them at various *Pungwes*.[1]

The missionaries and their assistants, including the teaching staff, openly and actively supported ZANLA and their *mujibhas*. Their backing continued to escalate from the inception of the war. I would, on occasions, make social calls to the mission posts for a chat and tea but that ended once ZANLA arrived in the area. Thereafter, priests were reluctant to be seen with me. I recall an incident where a bus detonated a landmine in the Makoni TTL near the missions. The human and vehicle carnage was gruesome and catastrophic. Many civilians were beaten, maimed and killed by ZANLA insurgents in Makoni and Manyika TTLs. Leo Gallagher continues: "Fr. Ward once went to St Barbara's to celebrate Christmas with Fr. Kenny although he knew that the freedom fighters were staying with Fr. Kenny. He did not know what kind of mood they were likely to be in so his visit was a brave act of kindness. Yet again he was protected from harm."[2]

In my opinion, these missionaries and their staff, including the teaching staff, were collaborators with the enemy. I viewed this as particularly heinous, especially when the decision to co-operate and assist ZANLA was reasoned, deliberate, and the facts and consequences of their actions made known. During the years 1974-1978, our policy was to treat the missionaries and their staff with respect. We did not harass them despite our intelligence confirming their collaboration and involvement with the enemy. I made no request of them nor did I expect support or assistance from them. At no stage of the war did I question them regarding their involvement with ZANLA. I understood and was aware of their position, yet was troubled by it. It was within the law to arrest and charge them, but I chose against it. I knew full well they harboured the enemy and that we could use this knowledge to our advantage and locate the ZANLA groups they were assisting. In any event, if the priests or staff were prosecuted and removed from the area, it was likely they would soon be replaced. To appease their consciences, these missionaries shifted blame to the SF and Selous Scouts for atrocities I knew ZANLA were responsible for. There were notable occasions when they refused to assist the SF requiring help, which I found astonishing.[3] I am aware of one occasion when the priests refused to help an injured member of the SF and turned him away from their mission station. I was unable to fathom a wounded soldier's personal safety being further jeopardised by a Carmelite priest's partiality to ZANLA. While I understood their predicament, especially as the SF were unable to sustain a presence in the areas, I did not consider them, as the term has it, a "Christian witness". I did not regard their actions as congruent with the spreading of the Gospel and considered their position farcical. In my opinion, their voluntary support of ZANLA was directly responsible for the deaths of countless African civilians and several Security Forces personnel in the area. I personally consider the blood of those victims on their hands and consciences. Several German Roman Catholic priests were murdered in Matabeleland during the war.[4] In a post-war interview I had with

---

1 Gallagher, L. (1996), Part D. *Pungwes*: Political meetings.

2 Ibid.

3 Ranger, T. (1985) p. 215.

4 J.R.T. Wood email 23/3/2018. There were three separate incidents: (1) Lupane: Former Roman Catholic Bishop of Bulawayo, the Rt. Rev. Adolf Schmitt with Father Possenti Weggarten, priest, and Sister Maria Francis van den Berg were ambushed and killed on a lonely dirt road on 5/12/1976. (2) Lupane: St Paul's Mission: Roman Catholic missionaries, German Dr Johanna Maria Decker (59) from Munich and Sister Ann Ploner, Austrian-born but

one of the Makoni Carmelite priests who wished to remain anonymous, he stated: "Their (the Carmelites in Makoni) attitude to the murder of fellow German Roman Catholics in Matabeleland who had associated with the security forces was that they 'got' what they deserved."

One venture into the south of the Makoni illustrates the extent of the support afforded ZANLA by the Roman Catholic missionaries.

St Triashill's and St Barbara's Missions

Following up on information received, we exhumed the body of a local kraalhead accused by *mujibhas* of being an informer. He had been brutally beaten and killed by ZANLA. This brutality occurred close to St Barbara's Mission. St Triashill's and St Barbara's missions were located in the area generally referred to as St Triashill's. Tragically, it transpired that there had been a domestic dispute which *mujibhas* decided to settle by means of fatal "justice". It is not possible to lightly brush aside such an incident. Coming to terms with the utter desolation of a grieving rural, tribal people bereft of their leader, husband and father was virtually unfathomable. These emotionally aching human beings, bedraggled, isolated (for who would wish to associate with alleged traitors with the fear of retribution lurking), scantily dressed and with clothing in tatters, stood mourning, stunned and pathetically lost in their grief, sorrow and abandonment.

We arrested a *mujibha* during the investigations and removed him to Rusape. Once there, he passed information on to us about the insurgents operating in the vicinity of St Triashill's and St Barbara's areas, in particular the location of their base camps.

The next day I took the *mujibha* on an aerial reconnaissance with the PRAW, an increasingly successful strategy. He pointed out base camps around his local area and the nearby St Triashill's and St Barbara's missions. To a keen and trained eye, these base camps were easily identifiable. One base camp was situated at the foot of an enormous granite rock that projected high above the mountaintop overlooking St Barbara's Mission. It was clearly visible from both the air and ground. The *mujibha* informed us that the outcrop was used as a reference point for ZANLA making their way to the base camp located at the foot of the rock. Insurgents travelling from Mozambique to central TTLs, close by the outskirts of Rhodesia's capital city, Salisbury, transited through the Makoni TTL. This rock was a useful beacon as well as a rendezvous point should they come under the attack of our SF. There were numerous meeting points in the TTLs, this being possibly the most prominent. With the base camps identified and positioned on my survey map, we went on patrol to not only gather intelligence but also to establish the feel and the mood of the local population in the area, particularly among the Catholic missionaries.

When we arrived at St Triashill's Mission, I noted the resident priest's car parked in the shade of the Msasa trees. I asked one of the mission station's novices where Father Ward was. He informed me that he was at St Barbara's Mission. I pondered as to how he travelled there as his car was parked nearby. The novice informed me that he had walked and implied that he often did. I wondered why he had walked when he had a motor vehicle at his disposal. In addition, I had never known him to do so and concluded the novice would venture no further worthwhile information. Yet again, I was made aware that knowledge of local conditions, the people, their movements and their habits, were critical to survival, not only during a war, but including the everyday business of life. I radioed the Sub.JOC at Rusape and requested a Pookie with an escort to be sent to clear the roads, as I suspected they had been mined.

The Pookie was a locally designed VW Beetle-type, armour-plated landmine-detector vehicle. It travelled about 100m ahead of the convoy. The driver sat up high above the ground in a V-shaped explosion-resistant hull that deflected the blast away from the operator. To distribute the weight of the vehicle as widely as possible, giant Formula One (F1) tyres were fitted to the wheels, thus ensuring minimal pressure being exerted on the road, preventing detonation of the mines. These

South African, were shot dead on 10/3/1977. ZIPRA were active in the area. (3) Embakwe Mission School: Roman Catholic Brothers, German Pieter Geyermann (36) and Swiss Andrew von Arx (45), were killed by gunfire at the mission on 2/6/1978.

features allowed the sensor "pans", resembling rectangular wings, to be lowered and positioned perpendicular to the road under the cab. The sensors were able to pinpoint the location of a landmine.

On arrival of the Pookie and army escort vehicle at St Triashill's Mission, we set off along with our two vehicles on the dirt roads of the Makoni TTL heading towards St Barbara's Mission.

Visibility was always poor on rural roads as dust lingered in the air when disturbed by the Pookie, its escort vehicle, 1442, and my backup Land Rover. There was great excitement in hunting for landmines and psychologically defeating ZANLA. I was also keen to confirm the Catholic missionaries' involvement with the enemy. After a drive of about 40 minutes, the Pookie came to a sudden stop. Its warning lights flashed as the driver reversed the vehicle and halted. Escort soldiers scrambled to take up sentry positions, securing the immediate area from attack. Calmly the Pookie driver reported that he had found a mine and the process of removing and disarming the explosive with grappling hooks began. Brave man, I thought. What further impressed me was how this soldier was first and foremost concerned for the safety of his fellow troops and not that of his own. As I had done on many previous occasions, I marvelled at the mind of the loyal, dedicated combatant. I noted the mine was in the middle of one of the tracks, the route we generally avoided. Once the TM 46 was removed and rendered safe, the convoy continued towards St Barbara's Mission with no further incident.[1]

There was little to say to the two Catholic priests, Fathers Ward and Kenny,[2] on arrival. We informed them of the landmine we had lifted. They knew of it and they were involved with ZANLA, of that I was convinced. There comes a time to reveal knowledge of local goings-on but, in my view, this situation was inappropriate for such disclosure. I did not want the priests or ZANLA to know the extent of our intelligence. It was time to formulate an attack.

At the JOC meeting the next day I briefed Col. Dunn on the recent events and won his approval of a plan I was considering. I was seldom invited to attend JOC meetings. Present were Col. Dunn, OC Uniform Branch, OC Special Branch and OC Support Unit. Col. Dunn briefed the meeting and outlined the intelligence to hand, including the confirmed location of ZANLA bases in the area. He decided to deploy Support Unit OPs in the area accompanied by *mujibhas* from the same district. Once a ZANLA presence had been established, the plan was to deploy Canberras to bomb the base camp. The camp at the base of the granite rock was particularly easy to identify from the air and, therefore, an easy target. The mission of the OPs was to identify suspicious movement, thereafter the Canberras would do the work.

The OP positions were then discussed, identified and the deployment arranged. We would send *mujibhas* familiar with the area to assist the callsigns. Col. Dunn reviewed the plan, making sure those attending understood their instructions and promptly closed the meeting.

On 11 August 1977, Juliet Troop, under the command of S/O Lee Le Crerar with stick leaders P/O Ray Hughes,[3] Sgt. Mashimbwe, N/S/P/O Cary Hughes and N/S/P/O Derek Kotze were deployed in and around St Triashill's and St Barbara's areas. It did not take long for one of the OPs to report that several locals were observed moving around suspiciously, indicating a possible ZANLA presence in a nearby base camp. As the Fire Force was not available, Lee Le Crerar was instructed to lead his section to investigate the suspicious activity but were ambushed by 10 to 15 insurgents. Sgt. Mashimbwe was killed and one constable slightly injured. A member of one of the OPs observed a considerable number of ZANLA fleeing down the hill from the contact. During the follow-up the following day, two insurgents were killed.[4] To my mind, any daytime attack by ground forces without air cover, handed the advantage to the enemy. I was annoyed that the original plan was discarded. These are the harsh realities of war!

---

1 Makoni/Manyika Incidents Map: Landmine LM 2.

2 Ranger, T. (1985), pp. 211, 215 confirms Kenny and other missionaries were co-operating and linked to ZANLA.

3 He later joined the Rhodesian Air Force as a pilot and was killed while serving with the SAAF in Angola.

4 Confirmed by Barry Woan, "Sakkie" McKay emails, 10/2/2016 and Lee Le Crerar telephone call, 10/10/2017. Makoni/Manyika Incidents Map: Incident 19.

This exercise produced a mixed result. The missionaries were aware I knew they were involved with ZANLA and the enemy became cognisant that we had neutralised their lethal landmine. The novice at St Triashill's Mission would be panic-stricken, anticipating ZANLA would accuse him of alerting us to the planted mine. Tragically though, one of our soldiers had been killed in this skirmish. In my view, his blood was on the hands of the missionaries.

Makoni Bridge Vehicle Ambush

Sometime later, we once again found ourselves patrolling the central Makoni area. While visiting a rural school, I was quietly called aside by one of the teachers to be informed that two days previously, he had been woken at night by a group of six insurgents. Possibly his conscience had gotten the better of him and he was under the impression that we had come to investigate that incident which, in fact, was not the case. The entire population's legal responsibility was abundantly clear. It was mandatory for all people to report as soon as possible and reasonably practical and, in any event, within 72 hours, any information people had concerning the presence of terrorists.[1]

He continued, telling me the insurgents had demanded he drive them, in his private vehicle, across Makoni TTL through the white-owned farm lands to the neighbouring Chiduku TTL. In fear of his life, he naturally obliged. This was the first report we had received that ZANLA were prepared to use a civilian vehicle to travel in Makoni TTL.

The incident was unusual as in 1977 government had imposed a 6 p.m. to 10 a.m. curfew in Makoni TTL to prevent the people, insurgents and their collaborators moving under the cover of darkness.[2] This legislation had curtailed insurgents' movements to some extent, but also brought about a number of civilians killed by SF on the assumption that, in ignoring the curfew, they were either insurgents or assisting them. Under the Indemnity and Compensation Act (1975), civil or criminal proceedings could not be instituted or continued in any court of law against anyone believed to have acted in "good faith" and for the purposes of, or, in connection with, the suppression of terrorism.[3] In effect, this law justified the killing of curfew breakers. There was no question of conscience in this conduct. It was purely a legal matter, a case of following the letter of the law to survive.

As can be expected, the teacher, who had caught my attention, drove the insurgents across Makoni TTL to Chiduku, paying the costs of the journey from his own earnings. In my thinking, this was another incentive for drawing me into his confidence. Teachers were not well paid, and every penny counted. Normally, when rural people needed to be transported by vehicle in an emergency, they themselves had to meet the cost of fuel. Petrol was in short supply in Rhodesia at the time and only sold on production of petrol coupons. The Petrol Rationing Office, a government department, calculated one's basic monthly petrol requirements and issued sufficient coupons to cover that mileage. Naturally, this additional journey demanded by the insurgents would severely curtail the teacher's future journeys.

There was little we could do about the incident, other than give the teacher some petrol coupons as a reward for informing us of the event, and I duly arranged for his extra ration of fuel. A few months later, a Support Unit callsign had a fleeting contact with a group of insurgents in the same area with no casualties on either side. When analysing the situation, I decided to place an ambush on the road through the TTL at a river crossing on the boundary along the white farming area. There was a steep drop into the riverbed where there was a concrete base and an equally steep climb out on the opposite side. As I saw it, an ideal ambush locality. It was a hunch on my part but I felt it worth the effort. We called that location The Devil's Pass Bridge.

---

[1] Law and Order (Maintenance) Act (1974), Chapter 65, Section 51, Subsections (1), (2) and (3); Mushonga, M. (2000), pp. 171-185.

[2] The Law and Order (Maintenance) Act (1974), Chapter 65, Section 53, subsections (1), (2) and (3) dealt directly with curfews; Mushonga, M. (2000), pp. 171-185.

[3] Mushonga, M. (2000), pp. 171-185.

I made my way to the Support Unit Base and discussed the plans with the OC who, as always, was zealous for action. One could never doubt the enthusiasm of the Support Unit, as well as their ability to adjust to the unconventional. The brief was straightforward. It was suspected a green Toyota[1] would be conveying a group of insurgents through the TTL after the 6 p.m. curfew. The callsign was to ambush this motor car at the riverbed. An attempt was to be made to prevent, if possible, the vehicle's passage by placing a rock or some other obstruction in the road. This would allow opportunity for identifying potential insurgents before attacking.

The ambush unit needed to be in position by 6 p.m., curfew time and, thereafter, making it legitimate to shoot the passengers/enemy. Deployment was to take place in the white farming area some distance from the river crossing. This would allow the callsign to journey along the road and hopefully avoid being compromised by locals. As our movements were to take place approaching the travel restriction period, we anticipated the locals would have made their way home by that hour.

The callsign was duly deployed as prearranged. While taking up their positions and trying to find a rock or some other obstruction to place on the road to coincide with the 6 p.m. curfew hour, suddenly they heard a vehicle travelling through the TTL towards them. They took up ambush positions and waited. As expected, a vehicle drove down into the riverbed and the callsign opened fire on the vehicle which travelled wildly into and out of the riverbed, only to stall some 30 metres further along the road. Unfortunately, the Support Unit did not have time to block the road.

At the time, I was in the Rusape police canteen when I received a radio call that the ambush had been sprung. In order to avoid unnecessary delays, Herbert and I promptly departed and sped to the location without an escort. The nagging thought of civilians being killed crossed my mind but these I dispelled as any military action was considered legitimate once a curfew had been initiated.

When we arrived at the ambush scene, we were informed that, after the shoot-out, the SF had pursued the vehicle, only to discover it abandoned. By that hour, it was too dark to execute a follow-up operation. The vehicle contained AK rounds, two hand-grenades and fully loaded AK magazines. Our intelligence had been accurate. We had recovered insurgent equipment. The vehicle was badly damaged but we had not achieved enemy deaths. It was unlikely ZANLA would risk this route in the near future.[2]

The informant reported to our offices the following day, visibly concerned by the whole incident, especially his ruined vehicle. He confirmed that he had once more been forced to drive a section of insurgents through Makoni TTL and had been ambushed at the riverbed. We assisted with the repairs to his vehicle but it was now abundantly clear ZANLA were confident travelling through the operational area at will. I found this realisation disturbing.

Matotwe Mountain: Communication with the Enemy

By this stage of the war, I decided it was time to meet with Chief Makoni, his headmen and kraalheads, as well as gathering together as many of his people as possible. We had previously held irregular meetings in various parts of the TTL but I believed the time had arrived to bring together all the people under the chief's authority, in an attempt to demonstrate his support for our SF. A date was set with the chief who also agreed to put out the word through his messengers, thus employing the tribal communication network to its best advantage. The messengers were loaded with information and useful in carrying messages to and from the local population. During the "peaceful days", prior to the war, I had met the ageing Chief Makoni on several occasions. He was receptive, friendly and generally assisted us where and when he could. However, our relationship changed once ZANLA's grip on the people tightened. I had also prearranged for a Support Unit section to give a weapons and firepower display on the day. About 500 people arrived to attend the meeting: more than I had anticipated. I held little regard for the chief's position as I considered myself senior in rank and authority. As I interpreted the situation, the people had no alternative but

1 Changed to protect the identity of the teacher.
2 Makoni/Manyika Incidents Map: Incident 20.

to submit to our orders and support the government and its SF. Securing their backing was not an invitation, rather it was a demand!

Rural African meetings seldom, if ever, start on time. In many instances, people are required to walk vast distances, sometimes for days on end, to attend assemblies, making punctuality a much-desired luxury and not a reality. This fact also explains the unusual length of get-togethers of any description, be they celebrations, weddings, burials, church services, political gatherings or even family reunions and related special occasions such as the birth of a child. These times could be prolonged for days, rather than minutes or hours. Mostly, due to the distances travelled, these protracted times together often delay the return journey.

In light of the above, the meeting eventually commenced and, once proceedings finally began, I opened the meeting with my usual political address, emphasising the strength of the Rhodesian SF, our dominant airpower, greater numbers of highly trained troops, more capable and efficient fighting skills, and our vastly superior weaponry. I spoke of the evil conduct of the terrorists by beating, mutilating and killing their own people and their planting of landmines, often detonated by buses transporting innocent men, women and children. I drew their attention to the fact that frequently civilian vehicles, including scotch carts, pedestrians and military vehicles, were the victims of these landmines. In passing, I mentioned these explosives did not overly concern the military (although in reality we were anxious), as we had mine-proofed vehicles. At a social level, I highlighted that the terrorists were abusing their daughters by literally stealing their virginity and, in so doing, demeaning them and reducing young women to the status of objects. I continued that this downright rape was disrespectful towards parents, greatly jeopardising the African *lobola* custom and undermining the African family-value system, particularly towards young girls. I went further, directing my listeners' minds to their rapidly deteriorating education system, the elimination of schools, dips, clinics and general social benefits, and concluded by drawing attention to the good work the government was doing in the TTLs.

However, the main reason for the meeting was to demonstrate the superior power of our Security Forces weapons. When I had finished my address, we cleared the people from harm's way and prepared a safe line of fire directed at an old large tree. The Support Unit callsign took up a position ready to fire when a panic-stricken chief called for a halt to the proceedings. He sent a messenger to find out what we were doing. I explained that we were going to fire our weapons at the tree. This was not to be. Unbeknown to us, the tree had important ancestral connections. We duly repositioned ourselves and, on agreement with the chief, now content with our altered line of fire, the Support Unit opened fire. At a personal level, I was suitably impressed but I am unable to comment on behalf of the spectators that day. When the MAG was fired, I found it terrifying, and was pleased that I would not be on the receiving end of that weapon. The conclusion of the display marked the end of the meeting. Later, those in my party and I mingled with the locals and thanked the chief for arranging the events of the day.

During the afternoon, Herbert told me that Matotwe Mountain, situated close to the chief's kraal, was also considered a sacred mountain: a haven for the ancestors.[1] Herbert was adamant he would not venture up the mountain under any circumstances and doubted if the insurgents traversed it either. This made me realise that ZANLA could well use these superstitions to their advantage and take refuge on it. Nevertheless, unfortunately, the Support Unit also knew the locals considered Matotwe Mountain as sacred and would be reluctant to climb it.

While considering the information to hand, I decided to wait until there was a changeover of Support Unit troops and then organise a sweep up the mountain. The replacement sections would be unaware of the spiritual complications and I would keep Herbert from the exercise. At the same time, I would visit the people on the eastern side of the mountain.

Two weeks later, when the Support Unit changeover was completed, I organised a sweep of

1 Ranger, T. (1985), Chap. 5.

Matotwe Mountain by three sections. We deployed before first light, climbing the steep side in about two hours, ascending from 1,400 metres to 1,650 metres. Lush green grass carpeted the plateau. From that height the trees appeared stunted, not unlike a bonsai plantation. Granite pools, refreshed by morning dew, reflected the African sun. Scaling granite mountains was always hazardous. Outcrops often concealed caves that were suitable venues from which to launch an ambush but that day we were fortunately safe. However, we did find several areas that had been used as base camps, confirming my suspicions. The great advantage of this mountain's situation was it gave an excellent view of the main roads below, making for a clear observation of Security Forces movements.[1]

I did not often have the opportunity to enjoy these unique African views. Cattle and goats roamed the countryside searching out scant patches of grass while under the custody of half-naked young boys carrying knobkerries[2] and sticks for protection, while their faithful, skinny mongrel dogs lay close by. Young girls jovially washed clothes and pots in trickling streams that also provided drinking water. Children played games boisterously around the kraal areas under the watchful eye of the elderly. Superficially, life appeared serene and peaceful but there was always the underlying uneasy feeling of death loitering, should one let one's guard down.

The return to our vehicles was equally uneventful. However, the exercise had taken longer than I anticipated, therefore I decided to visit the kraals on the eastern side of the mountain the following day. I would have the added advantage of Herbert's company. Early that morning, we set off to visit the kraals. However, this was not a straightforward matter as only one road led to and from the kraal. Not a favourable setting but there was no alternative to reaching our destination. My reasoning was that ZANLA would not expect us to revisit an area the day after an operation, as this was not our regular pattern. On the contrary, it was more their modus operandi as they would despatch *mujibhas* to establish our movements prior to their making an appearance, and re-establishing their presence and control.

Accompanied by my usual Land Rover escort, we headed for the kraals. The scenery in these more remote parts of the TTL, accessed only by less-travelled back roads, was magnificent. Africa at its best. Rarely, if ever, did we come across another vehicle on these dirt roads which wound their way around the high, steep-rising mountains and kopjes, observed by distant locals who heard, but seemingly never took notice of visitors. They apparently ignored us but, in fact, were well aware of our presence as they went about their daily routine. Time stood still in these isolated havens inhabited by people distant from morally bankrupt politicians and the lure and clutches of capitalism. By no doings of their own, the war had introduced uncalled for tensions in their peaceful lives but, through it all, they continued living one day at a time.

Ever on the alert, for there was little more we could do than respond to an attack, we drove the 12 kilometres along the isolated road, unable to appreciate the scenery and calm as the intensity of the drive mounted. Rifles cocked, and safety-catches off, we were trapped in a setting totally out of our control. Our drive was not lengthy but, to Herbert and I, it felt like a lifetime before we reached the kraals. Most of the locals ran away leaving the young and elderly to fend for themselves. There was no one in the kraal suitable for interrogation so we gathered the few remaining locals, gave a short political speech, and told them that we would return the following day. They were to tell the absent residents to be present for a 10 a.m. meeting.

Herbert was not impressed with the advance notice of the morning meeting and asked why I had announced our plans which would surely be relayed to the insurgents. According to Herbert, ZANLA were likely to react, ambush and attack us. I explained to Herbert that if tomorrow we were attacked, we would know if these people were collaborating with the insurgents and how quickly they were getting our messages. If they attacked, we would know that we were indirectly talking to them, which would help us in the future. A silence followed as we both found the thought unsettling.

After a short while we left, apprehensive, but readily prepared to respond to any attack. Our

---

1 Moyes H. (2012), Part IV, p. 22; Ranger, T. (1985), Chap. 5. My suspicions were confirmed in this research.

2 Knobkerry: A short wooden club with a heavy knob on one end, usually thrown with great accuracy as a weapon.

return drive seemed longer and it felt as if we faced more hazardous obstructions and potential ambush positions than we noticed on the way to the kraals. Eventually to our considerable relief, we returned safely to the main road leading back to base. On our return to Sub.JOC Rusape, I arranged for a Pookie and its two escort vehicles for the next day's expedition. Departure time was set for 9 a.m. Later, a few beers in the canteen calmed the nerves and swelled the ego. I was anticipating yet another day's adventure.

We met at the Sub.JOC on time the following morning. I drove to the base in my Renault, reversed it next to the Avtur drums, left the key in the ignition and found the Pookie driver and the escort details. An unofficial arrangement prevailed, allowing part-filled drums of Avtur, which were of no use to the Air Force, being siphoned into selected private vehicle fuel tanks, a decided benefit in the face of petrol rationing. Herbert was prepared to move out, as were our two Land Rover escorts. At 9 a.m., as planned, we made our departure. As we travelled, I found myself more comfortable and confident with the army escort vehicles and additional troops supporting us. Our instructions were that the Pookie would lead the convoy, followed by the two army vehicles with our two Land Rovers bringing up the rear.

As we reached the half-way mark at the rear of Matotwe Mountain, the column stopped behind the halted Pookie. The driver had located a landmine and proceeded to remove it as the escort troops defended our position. Herbert and I walked to the stationary Pookie, curious to see what the indications of a hidden landmine in situ were, before it was removed. We wished to familiarise ourselves with the details for future reference. The landmine was a TM 46. Another victory, I thought, but ahead of us lay the remainder of our journey to the kraals, not to mention our safe return to base, before we could claim a victory.[1]

After a delay of about two hours, we set off again for the kraals, arriving once more to a handful of elders. I announced that we had lifted the landmine in the road. It was now obvious the kraal dwellers had informed the insurgents that we would be travelling on the road that day. Confidently, I told the small audience that we were invincible and wanted the terrorists to come and fight us, so much so that we would return to the kraals again the following morning. Bravado came easy while securely surrounded by so many troops. Herbert was shocked and stated openly that I was asking for trouble.

In fact, I had no intention of returning the following morning but I wanted the locals to think we were unafraid. Most importantly, I now knew we could disseminate propaganda to the insurgents through the locals. This was my first success at luring ZANLA to react to our plans, providing a breakthrough in our war effort. The insurgents had been quickly informed regarding our visit the previous day and of our intentions for the following day. They had acted speedily, decisively and deliberately. This told me that they considered themselves close to the people who were on their side and informed them of Security Forces movements at short notice. Furthermore, they had the capability to strike the SF at will. They were nearby and observing us. They could find us but we could not find them. More importantly, these developments allowed me to view the war from their perspective. Significantly, they had exposed their hand which was a psychological victory for us. I was certain they would anticipate our presence in the area the following day. However, unbeknown to them, we would not appear. I decided to deploy troops into this area in due course.

While this strategy of communicating with ZANLA, through the local population, did not greatly assist our operations in Makoni TTL, we were at least aware that ZANLA knew our every move and understood the words we spoke. I was aware we faced a capable enemy. We returned to the Sub.JOC without incident. On my drive home, I checked my Renault petrol gauge and the needle registered full. The army engineers had assured me that Avtur would do no harm to the engine, jesting it would "jet us along". However, the most important feature in my estimation was that the fuel was free.

Now that we could direct communication to ZANLA, through the local population, I started a propaganda campaign by dropping leaflets from a PRAW aircraft targeted at locals we had identified

1 Makoni/Manyika Incidents Map: Landmine LM 3.

as enemy supporters. In the leaflets, we thanked them for their assistance which had led to specific contacts, to the lifting of landmines and other useful information they had passed on to us. We also dropped flyers thanking the population in general for their help and assured them that the war would soon be won. The overall commander of the Makoni/Gandanzara detachment was Lameck Tembo and I used pamphlets to target him as well.

The Catholic Commission for Justice and Peace (JPC) did not view our pamphlet drops in a favourable light, compelling me to submit an explanation to the Officer Commanding, Special Branch, which I submitted on 7 November 1977, a copy of which is found in the appendix. As far as I was concerned, the enemy were perturbed and, in my mind, that was of utmost importance. I also felt that the battle lines were clearly drawn between the JPC and SF. I cannot recall the JPC addressing ZANLA's wanton beating, mutilation and murders of the local population nor their increasing landmine campaigns, affecting civilians and the SF alike, nor their attacks on farmsteads and the SF. It was my opinion, the insurgents were using the JPC to communicate their anti-SF propaganda. I became incensed and increased the leaflet campaign.

This was to be my second brush with the JPC. The first being on 14 December 1976, when the Support Unit were engaged in a follow-up with Fire Force and the Reverend Kuwana and his wife were caught in crossfire and killed. Bishop Abel Muzorewa issued a statement claiming that he had personally visited the scene, declaring the couple had been murdered by the Security Forces. My investigations confirmed that the couple had been involved in feeding and assisting a local group of ZANLA, who had a base camp a few hundred metres from their house. Ian Smith understood the predicament the SF faced and commented: "It was explained to me forcibly that it was impossible to separate them (women and children from the terrorists), that they were all terrorists, and that part of the communist teaching was to use women and children as a means of protecting the fighting men. It was pointed out that terrorists had no compunction about killing women and children; indeed, that they seemed to show a preference for doing so as part of their trade that made them better terrorists."[1]

Supt. Edward (Ted) Painting from the CID in Umtali carried out a full investigation and the inquest was held on 12 January 1977 at Umtali. The SF actions were found to be legitimate and a verdict of "not guilty" was passed on 17 January 1978. Little did I know that I would soon meet Bishop Muzorewa under completely different circumstances when I moved to Hurungwe.

Consequences of Reacting to Incidents

Difficulties to the immediate response of a reported insurgent incident were considerations such as the possibility of ambush or detonating a landmine. It was clear that ZANLA created incidents, knowing we would respond in a well-established pattern. Usually, we drove in convoy (two mine-proofed Land Rovers) to an incident, risking ambush, detonating landmines, or both. The protection of a Pookie was infrequent, but a blessing when available. This was the primary method ZANLA employed to attack the SF, requiring us to be astute, diversifying responses, avoiding patterns and assessing when, where and how to respond, thus ensuring we took the initiative, not the insurgents.

My return to Honde Valley was initiated by a decision to meet a colleague from the Salisbury CID Fraud Section, D/S/O Rick Hardy. He had been called up to serve a period at Ruda Police Base. I first met Hardy when I was a cadet at Avondale Police Station in 1969.

As the war continued its momentum, more CID staff were deployed into the field to assist with intelligence gathering and criminal investigations associated with the war, such as murders, landmine incidents, terrorist attacks, atrocities, contacts and so forth. Hence Hardy's deployment to Ruda Base Camp. He contacted me to discuss his deployment to what was for him unfamiliar territory. We arranged to meet at Ruda. There was no war-time training for these city policemen. This was through no fault of their own. Men such as Hardy typically found themselves in a foreign environment which placed not only themselves in grave danger but also their comrades.[2]

[1] Smith, I. (2008), Loc 5069.

On 2 September 1977,[1] I decided to patrol through Manyika TTL which bordered Honde Valley. This would get me to Ruda for the night, although, if the truth be known, our scheduled meeting was more along celebration lines and less about the present hostilities. I enjoyed keeping in touch with colleagues from Salisbury and Hardy was among those men.

This was to be a very different setting from the trips I'd made on arrival at Rusape. My Land Rover, 1442, was now completely mine-proofed. It had been professionally fitted with roll bars and anti-ambush AK-47s. One weapon was mounted under the bonnet facing forward, and two in the rear of the vehicle facing either side. They were triggered by a switch connected to a starter solenoid which pulled wires attached to the triggers. While on our travels, we were fully harnessed to prevent injury in the event of detonating a landmine. Alert and vigilant, we constantly checked the dirt roads for evidence of landmines while simultaneously watching for ambush positions. When passing African peasants, we scrutinised their clothing, gestures and conduct for indications suggesting the presence of insurgents or *mujibhas*. This perpetual state of tension became a regular way of life which at the time, I thought, was exhilarating, exciting, thrilling and to be envied.

As we turned off the main Juliasdale to Umtali road, beginning our descent to the Honde Valley, we were stopped by a routine police roadblock and, after a brief chat, cleared to proceed. It was about 3.30 p.m.. My plans to reach Ruda when the pub opened at 4.30 p.m. were on schedule. Engaged in second gear and steadied by the foot brake, 1442's engine whined as we commenced the steep 761-metre descent on a tar road, akin to a horse wanting to bolt for home after a long ride. Just before a sharp left-hand curve on the steeply descending road, we encountered a Lobels Bread delivery van.[2] It had broken down under the strain of climbing out of the valley or so it appeared. The bonnet was raised and the vehicle surrounded by six or seven denim-clad African men. I decelerated, changed into first gear and reduced speed to snail's pace. Herbert and I agreed that these individuals looked like either terrorists or *mujibhas*.

Drawing up virtually alongside the Lobels van, I noted the high ground above the stranded vehicle was exposed, due to the road having been cut into the side of the mountain. I thought, ominously, that it was a classic ambush position. Tension mounted as the group stared intently at us. However, there was no sign of weapons and the truck driver made no request for help.

I lifted my foot off the brake, changed into second gear and continued our journey. Unconcerned, I announced to Herbert that it was not our area of responsibility. I can offer no explanation for not wishing to stop at this scene. Under normal conditions, I would have savoured the opportunity for action, gathering and piecing together clues in order to kill and destroy the enemy. The draw of the Ruda pub prevailed. In due course I discovered why I did not stop.

It was 4 p.m. when we arrived at Ruda Base Camp: perfect timing, I thought. Herbert made his way to his colleagues and I scouted for Hardy in the CID office. He was completing some work and, together, we made our way to the police canteen, arriving at 4.30 p.m.. Eager to quench our thirst, we each gulped down an ice-cold beer. I was looking forward to a fun-filled evening until Hardy received information of a terrorist attack. The police roadblock at the top of Honde Valley reported that the driver of a Lobels Bread delivery van had been robbed by insurgents.

Hardy sprang into action. He announced that he had to attend the scene and invited me to accompany him. I emphatically refused and told him that when I passed that van on the way down it was surrounded by either terrorists or *mujibhas*. I told him this was obviously a setup and the incident was at an ideal ambush position. Hardy was determined to proceed and made a further attempt to entice me to accompany him. I sensed danger. My policy was to build intelligence and strike when victory was assured, not expose myself to unnecessary danger. He was determined to recover "vital" evidence from the scene such as spent cartridge cases and any other equipment abandoned by the terrorists in the attack. Hardy felt the robbery was in retaliation to the arrest and interrogation of a local insurgent commander's girlfriend who was supporting the group.

[2] Mike Edden's unpublished memoirs, pp. 41-43.

[1] Confirmed by original Sub.JOC Rusape duty roster.

[2] Lobels were the main bread manufacturers and suppliers in Rhodesia, and are still in business today.

I asked him what he hoped to achieve as it was dusk and he had no idea where the robbery had taken place. The Lobels van had already passed through the police roadblock at the top of the escarpment. As the night was closing in, he would not have time to find and follow the terrorists' tracks. Furthermore, there was no dog section detail at Ruda. My concern was that he was putting his own life and the lives of accompanying men at unnecessary risk.

Hardy was determined to "show the flag" and made one final attempt to secure my presence on this sortie which I had refused repeatedly. I suggested he forget "the flag" and promptly ordered another drink while Hardy joined the men preparing to escort him to the scene. He set off in a 2.5l Mercedes Unimog, a military troop carrier driven by an army intelligence soldier, Sgt. Frazier. An armed escort of four army personnel and Special Branch African details accompanied him. Sipping my beer and pondering in the canteen, I realised how much I had grasped regarding military strategies in this war. My mind was ingrained with strategies and tactics of both the enemy and our own. Recognising Hardy's obvious inexperience in this war theatre was the catalyst for my considerations. Experience in these matters had impressed on me to avoid unnecessary risks.

Survival in a hostile environment requires adaptation to ever-changing conditions far removed from "civilised moral conduct". Failure to adapt and recognise the dissimilarities between civilian conduct in peacetime and military action during warfare will lead one to either serious injury or untimely death. Compassion is eroded in a war zone in which the rule of the gun and uncontrolled violence holds sway. War and violence create other bonds of moral understanding arising between soldiers locked side-by-side in battle. A gulf is inevitably exposed between the peacetime morality of politicians and city dwellers, and those in the direct line of fire in the immediate combat zone, where solidarity among the Security Forces takes precedence over all commonplace ethical considerations and everyday moralities. This division is conspicuous when a civilian, with little military training or experience, is thrust into the line of fire. Consequently, attempts to impose peacetime morality in war can, and often does, result in men falling prey to the enemy. It is both preposterous and fatal to attempt to efface the difference between these vastly separate worlds. Subsequently, survival in war requires entry into a zone of instinct which eliminates normal, civilised social interaction, abandons conscience and embraces a unique comradeship cemented in principles that justify the defeat and slaughter of the enemy. My definition of enemy is any armed combatant, and their supporters, attempting to destabilise or overthrow a government using any means, including intimidation and violence. In my view, I am justified in killing the enemy who attempts to kill me, any member of my family or countryman.

As I began to mellow while draining my third pint in the canteen and allowing myself to be lulled into alcohol-induced merriment, I was summoned by the army commander who informed me that Hardy and his escort had been ambushed and that there were casualties. This news incensed me. Granted my relaxed evening was instantly ruined but, most importantly, my life was suddenly at risk. The army commander organised another two vehicles with troops to escort me to the ambush scene. He also instructed the PRAW pilot to prepare for the evacuation of the casualties to Grand Reef airfield near Umtali. Added to the complexity of the hastily planned operation, was the absence of landing-lights on the local airfield, resulting in the improvisation of strategically placed vehicle lights to guide the aircraft along the runway.

Rick Hardy picks up the story: "Sunset drifted into dusk as we slowly wound our way up the Honde Valley escarpment leaving behind the Pungwe River that separated Mozambique from Rhodesia; kraals became ever diminishing impersonal circular clusters. My apprehension ruined what should have been a beautiful evening; I was alert, expecting the worst, but not wanting it to happen! Frazier was driving the left-hand drive Unimog up a steep gradient in second gear when we came to a sharp right-hand bend and suddenly came under heavy fire from some high ground to our left; it was a well-chosen ambush position, we were 'sitting ducks'. Frazier was shot several times and stalled the vehicle in the 'killing ground'. I was carrying an RPD and returned fire, emptying the full magazine of 100 rounds towards the ambush position. Frazier managed to restart the vehicle and drive it to safety some 30 meters further up the road before collapsing. Fortunately, the terrorists did not pursue their clear advantage and our radio was not damaged; I called our base for assistance."[1]

Back at Ruda Base Camp, Herbert and I scampered into 1442 and followed the troop carriers as they began the slow journey, mostly in the lowest gears, up the escarpment. As evening set in, visibility deteriorated with the likelihood of an ambush increasing. My short-lived mood of cheerfulness elevated from annoyance to grave apprehension. Solemnity settled over the party. Little was said. An acute alertness as to the inevitability of what lay ahead dominated our minds. Nestled across my lap, pointing out of the door-less vehicle, my FN rifle, "815", imprinted on the butt, lay ready for instant action; cocked with safety-catch released. Likewise, to my left in the passenger's seat, Herbert clutched his FN, pointing it out and forwards. We were unsure of what to expect, besides casualties, of which we had been notified. Fear was never discussed openly. We simply soldiered on in muted silence, projecting necessary courage, essential in the face of imminent attack and death, yet masking inner anxiety. Leaders are duty-bound to display bold fearlessness while leading dutiful subordinates into armed conflict. We convinced ourselves that we could handle all situations effectively.

Drawing near to the ambush location, the road gradient increased, 1442 slowed to walking pace. I engaged first gear. As we entered a sharp, right-hand bend, the ambushed vehicle was spotted about 30 metres further on. Chaos greeted us. Sgt. Frazier lay seriously injured in the back of the vehicle and Hardy, shot through both legs, was seated close to him. Amazingly, Hardy sustained only flesh wounds, the bullets miraculously not damaging the bones of his skinny legs. One African soldier had also been seriously injured and lay in the rear of the truck. The army officer deployed guards around the ambushed vehicle and despatched a patrol to search the perimeters for terrorists and render it safe.

Reaching for my medical pack, I located a saline drip and inserted the needle into a vein in Hardy's arm before they receded due to shock or loss of blood. The pitch-black night, stressful conditions and the urgency of our situation made this life-saving treatment difficult. An army medic handed me a syringe with morphine, which I administered through the drip, causing Hardy to relax. I then dressed his wounds to stem the flow of blood. Army medics attended to the African soldier and Frazier who, through his driving skills and conduct under fire, had courageously saved the lives of the troops in the vehicle. We were acutely aware of the possibility that the insurgents were watching and preparing to attack us at any moment. The cautious stalking of a perimeter guard provided me a brief moment of comfort in our most profound surreal setting.

After what seemed an eternity, we transferred the wounded African soldier, Frazier and Hardy into our vehicles and set off to Ruda. Once on the move, 1442's headlights brightened the road and verges ahead, making danger zones visible. My bravado returned as my mind leapt forward to the awaiting frivolity in the canteen. Anticipation of pleasantries gripped me yet again.

I radioed the base to advise the PRAW pilot that we were returning with three serious casualties requiring casevac to Grand Reef. Thirty minutes later we settled the casualties into the aircraft. Strategically parked military vehicles lit the perimeters and full extent of the runway, ensuring pilot, crew and passengers' safety on take-off. Anxiously, we watched as the single-engine Cessna taxied from us toward the threshold of the gravel runway with its red tail light flashing. Gradually, it was swallowed up by the African night with a train of dust from the forward thrust of the propeller. As the plane swung round to face the runway, its bright headlight pierced the darkness. The pilot prepared for take-off. He gently eased the throttle forward, allowing the light aircraft to gain momentum. Engaging full throttle, with engine revs mounting, he eased the plane forward in an elegant dash along the runway. Gently, the pilot eased the plane's nose to the correct flight "attitude" for lift-off and gracefully the plane ascended into the night sky. The Cessna climbed, banked gently to the right on a bearing to the airfield at Grand Reef, to the awaiting doctors, ambulances and rescue team. Soon, only the sound of the Cessna's engine was to be heard as it, pilot and all on board, were

[1] D/S/O Rick Hardy email 11/3/2016.

absorbed by the black African sky and its myriad of stars.

Job done! We returned to the pub with bluster to celebrate our survival and our pride in the unerring ability to outwit the enemy. Our gusto always reached its zenith towards "closing time". In the morning, AK-47 doppies were recovered from the scene for ballistic examination. Hardy recalls: "The following morning an army callsign located doppies and blood spoor at the site of the ambush. The blood spoor was followed which resulted in a contact the details of which are not known."[1] Fortunately, the African soldier, Hardy and Frazier all made full recoveries.[2]

In 1978, when attending the Detective Inspectors Board, I used this incident as part of my presentation. Candidates were required to give a talk on a subject to prove their presentation skills and knowledge of the particular subject. I had chosen to talk about a field saline drip for two reasons. Firstly, it was a practical audio-visual aid and would assist me in the talk and, secondly, enable me to direct discussion onto my homeground, namely the present war. I spoke about the application, uses and benefits of the saline drip in the field. I identified the need to find a vein before it collapsed after serious injuries. It was an assistance in cases of shock and an administration point of access for any additional drugs should they be required. A drip prevented dehydration in cases of heatstroke. It could serve as a pillow and an emergency water supply, and more. My presentation was positive, brief and direct that went according to plan. It was quite unusual for a promotions board presentation. When I had finished, I placed the drip on my lap and sat quietly, waiting for a response.

The board chairman asked if I had ever used a drip. I outlined the occasion when I used it on D/S/O Hardy, stating that he was lucky to survive. The chairman agreed, indicating that he knew about the incident. After a brief silence, the chairman offered the three remaining board officers the opportunity to pose questions to me. The silence continued so the chairman asked me if there was anything I wanted to say. I informed the board that I believed my officer in charge, Supt. Sloman,[3] had not recommended me for promotion. There was an audible silence in the room. The chairman enquired how I knew and I told him that I was a member of the Special Branch and expected to know such matters. In truth, our secretary, Margot, had informed me as I went to say goodbye, prior to leaving Rusape for the interview.

In reply to the chairman's question as to why Supt. Sloman had not recommended my promotion, I advised him that we had a personality clash. I added that the issue had not affected our work. I believe it was this reply that helped me through the board presentation and my promotion to detective inspector. Leaders in any sphere will always have difficulties with people under their command or, indeed, their superiors. It is the management of these difficult situations that is important. When my promotion was confirmed, I thanked Supt. Sloman for his "recommendations" to the board which obviously helped me through. His reply was short: "You'll never know." I knew!

Rugoyi Police Base Attack

On 25 November 1977, Fire Force deployed to the St Triashill's area, contacted a ZANLA section, killing one insurgent.[4] By late 1977, the war continued its increasing impetus. Large-scale invasions occurred in the Inyanga North area that resulted in lengthy Fire Force battles. There was an increase in sightings and contacts in Makoni and Manyika TTLs and the Support Unit continued its sterling work under difficult conditions.

At the Rugoyi base, I was supplied with my own caravan as, at this stage of the war, I was spending a considerable amount of time in the field. It was a remarkable experience living among the various branches of the SF. We shared a unique camaraderie and trusting relationships peculiar to war. Warm evenings were spent in our swimming-pool, where we enjoyed reminiscing on its acquisition. The story unfolds: One day, on impulse, we decided to do a "swan"[5] through Manyika and Makoni TTLs. We headed south, crossed into Manyika TTL at the Nyatanda River near

[1] Rick Hardy email 11/3/2016.
[2] Makoni/Manyika Incidents Map: Incident 21.
[3] Supt. Sloman died on 4/11/2011. While writing this book, I spoke to him twice on the phone.
[4] Makoni/Manyika Incidents Map: Incident 22; Geldenhuys, P. (2014), Air Strike Log Entry 740.
[5] "Swan": Colloquial term for a general patrol with no specific purpose.

Nyamusamba Business Centre and cattle dip, and then travelled north. It was a warm, sunny day. As usual, no other vehicles were on the roads, making us alone on a reasonably well-kept dirt road. A feature of Manyika TTL was the dominant high, granite-cropped mountains which in places were well vegetated. When passing an abandoned district commissioner's camp, we noticed a huge, round galvanised water tank. We promptly reached an unanimous decision: a swimming-pool for the Rugoyi base.

Relocating the water tank was a large undertaking requiring considerable effort from the four of us to load it onto 1442. We found some rope and tied it down and continued on our way. By our calculations, it was quicker to return to Rugoyi by motoring through the Manyika, rejoining the main tar road from Rusape to Inyanga. Thereafter, turning south into the Makoni and on to the Rugoyi base, a trip of close on 60 kilometres, driving on landmined roads swarming with insurgents.

Our progress was slow and dangerous. We were hampered not so much by the insurgent threat but by the size of the "swimming-pool" which hung well over the sides of 1442, causing it to roll from side to side. When we reached the main tar road, we occupied the whole road and had to deal with passing traffic from time to time, which was amusing. We finally arrived back at base in the late afternoon and, with help from the rest of the men, managed to position the "swimming-pool" on one side of the camp overlooking the TTL. The view from the pool was magnificent. An ideal location for "sundowners". It took a full night for the pool to fill from the slow trickle of our water source but it was ready for the first swim the next day. At the end of that day, our pool was commissioned with a swim, evening braai and, naturally, ice-cold drinks.[1]

On my return to Sub.JOC Rusape, I was surprised when Supt. Sloman told me that the district commissioner had reported that a water tank had been stolen from the Manyika DC Camp and asked whether I knew of its whereabouts. I denied any knowledge of the incident, ending the discussion. Sloman and I clashed on occasions. He was unappreciative of my dress code which had progressed from standard-issue military outfits, to Hawaiian-style camouflage shorts, shirt and communist webbing adjusted to carry FN magazines. Included in my gear was an Irish flat cap and a .38 revolver slung around my hip, attached by a ZANLA belt. I considered my "uniform" vastly improved following the arrest of the local tailor at Gandanzara BC. This man was required to provide clothing for the insurgents at his own expense, as his contribution to their war effort. Naturally, this was an expensive business, placing his life at risk should he fail to provide a prompt and efficient service. On the strength of this, we arrested him, conveyed all his equipment and material back to Sub.JOC Rusape, where he continued his occupation on the verandah of the building. From his new premises, he plied a prosperous trade. Most importantly, he tailored my fashionable camouflage outfits. In addition, he fitted me with denim safari suits which were "state of the art" during the 1970s.[2]

That pool served us well until early 1978. One evening that year, while a group of us were in our base enjoying a few beers after supper, I spontaneously decided to return to Rusape against the advice of my colleagues. To travel at night was inviting trouble, greatly increasing the likelihood of ambush, with frightening consequences should one detonate a landmine. However, I was determined to leave, beckoned Herbert and together we made off into the night. Motoring through the Makoni was risky. I knew no other vehicles were legitimately permitted to travel at night and our lights would beam a clear signal to ZANLA that an SF vehicle was mobile.

Two factors dominated my decision. The first being our venture was by no means a regular SF pattern, therefore it was unexpected. Secondly, on the occasions the SF did travel through the TTL it was normally in convoy, thus ZANLA might think there was more than one vehicle on the move, dissuading them from attack. In any event we made it to Rusape without incident and it was, for some reason, good to be home.

Just after midnight, I received news that Rugoyi Police Base had been subjected to a heavy attack. To my relief there were no serious injuries and my caravan was not damaged. There was bad news

[1] D/S/O Pete Cutting recalls this incident discussed on a field trip and telephone discussions March to May 2015.
[2] Ibid.

though. When Herbert and I made our way back to the camp the following morning, we discovered our recently installed "swimming-pool" had been severely damaged by small-arms fire and resembled an empty sieve. The base camp had been subjected to a prolonged attack with 82mm mortars, a 75mm recoilless rifle, as well as small-arms fire. However, there was little damage and essentially the attack was ineffective. At stake, nonetheless, was our morale, as this attack opened up a new theatre in the war as ZANLA intensified their impetus, moving into Phase 3 of their strategies.[1]

Phase 3: ZANLA Strategies

1. Increase flow of recruits for training.
2. Increase return of trained and armed insurgents.
3. Increase arms caches.
4. Increase flow of weapons and ammunition in order to train local recruits.
5. Introduce sophisticated weaponry such as 75mm recoilless rifles, 82mm mortars and 12.7 heavy machine guns.
6. Increase aggressive hit-and-run attacks against Security Forces using experience gained from successes and failures learned in previous battles.
7. Avoid the Fire Force and continue to develop escape strategies.
8. Continue hit-and-run tactics against vulnerable and isolated civilian targets.
9. Consolidate governance of the people by martial law in liberated areas.
10. Open new operational fronts en route to Salisbury.
11. Commence hit-and-run attacks on Security Forces bases.
12. Commence hit-and-run urban attacks aiming for economic strategic targets in order to destroy enemy morale. Disrupt major communication links using landmines and ambushes.
13. Extend government and military resources beyond their limits, thereby forcing political and military capitulation.

While our understanding of the war was increasing, we had yet to overcome ZANLA's one great advantage: a continuous presence in the TTL.

However, despite the war, we did have periods of light-heartedness. We would shoot at, but never hit, rabbits with our anti-ambush AK-47 concealed under the bonnet of 1442 during night sorties on TTL roads. We swam in rivers during expeditions and regularly played snooker in the canteen. There was seldom a dull day. I wasn't bogged down by mundane, routine office procedures and administration but was active in the field in search of the enemy. I thrived in this life of the outdoors and can proudly announce, I was "bush happy". This term says it all. The statement implies one has spent an excessive amount of time in the bush to the extent that it is difficult, if not impossible, to readjust to civilian and family life. "Bush happy" is when you can't contain frustration in large volumes of motor traffic. City talk and conversations that are trivial and devoid of relevant content seem meaningless. This experience is complete when one feels entirely at home in the operational area surrounded by like-minded men. In times of silence, one feels integrated with the sounds, smells, atmosphere, together with the flora and fauna of the wilds. The only tension with this idyllic life was that the enemy spent some 10 per cent of our time attempting to kill us.

The Ultimate *Mujibha* Deployment[2]

My days at Rusape were drawing to a close as my promotion to detective inspector was imminent. One of my final foot patrols took place when we deployed with Support Unit in the attempt of locating *mujibhas* in a kraal line to the east of Makoni. This was rugged terrain, dominated by high mountains. We left early in the morning in order to reach the kraal by first light. However, about 5 kilometres from the kraal, we came across tracks of eight insurgents heading towards the very kraals we were en route to. We followed the tracks right into the deserted kraal, at which point they petered

[1] Makoni/Manyika Incidents Map: Incident 23.

[2] Makoni/Manyika Incidents Map: Incident 24; Geldenhuys, P. (2014), Air Strike Log Entry 789.

out. As had become the pattern, the locals had swept the ground removing any evidence of their spoor. The Support Unit trackers carried on through the village and started to search for the continuation of the tracks.

On impulse, I decided to burn the main kitchen hut in reprisal for the kraal dwellers assisting the insurgents. As I struck the match, I heard a strange, silent inner voice at the centre of my being, asking: "What are you doing?" I was jolted to my core and immediately abandoned my efforts to raze the kraal, despite the pleadings of the accompanying men. With the kraal still intact, we moved on. About three years later, while living in the Strand, Cape Town, South Africa, I would learn the origin of that still, small voice. I genuinely believed that I had considerable intuition until I came to realise that my intuition is limited by my knowledge. I became aware that predictions and prior warnings of events had their derivation from a Higher Source. On that patrol, we did not make contact with the elusive insurgents.

The success of the *mujibha* system was epitomised on 2 March 1978 when I briefed Supt. Fred Mason and L/Insp. Barry Woan with information indicating the presence of a group of about 10 insurgents at the base of the Musere Mountain range. After studying the terrain and establishing that the FF would be available in the morning, they decided to deploy on the intelligence. Barry Woan, Troop Commander of Zulu Alpha Troop, who had a callsign available in the camp, continues: "Later that evening we deployed Sergeant Major Wilson Moyo and his callsign with the *mujibha* from the area with instructions to climb a nearby kopje and clandestinely observe the kraal and river line. Early next morning we received a call from ZA 2 that he had at least ten armed insurgents visual and expected more hiding in the thick bush. The information was deadly accurate, the Fire Force was called and precisely directed over the insurgent's camp. Stop Groups deployed, and a fierce fire fight developed ending with 12 insurgents killed, one captured and thirteen weapons recovered. Sergeant Major Wilson was congratulated by the Fire Force Commander for his accurate indications and was later to be awarded the Police Medal For Meritorious Service for this incident and others."[1]

This skirmish occurred nearby the landmine incident reported earlier in this Chapter (Matotwe Mountain: Communication with the Enemy). It is possible the group that laid the mine were eliminated in this contact. Epitomised in this deployment was the potential of the *mujibha* system. The Support Unit, comprising Mason and Woan, assessed and trusted the intelligence, researched the resources, the availability of FF, studied the terrain and deployed the callsign accordingly. The *mujibha* led them into a secure, well-positioned OP, interpreted events on the ground and helped identify the ZANLA section. A successful deployment depended not only on having accurate, immediate intelligence. Success was, in the final analysis, determined by the skill of the men on the ground. The Support Unit were highly trained men, adapting extremely well to functioning behind enemy lines.

On 29 March 1978, Fire Force deployed into a ZANLA section which was feeding at the kraals. Two ZANLA insurgents and four civilians were killed. Four additional civilians were injured.[2] After my departure from Rusape and on 26 September 1979, a K-Car piloted by Air Lt. Paddy Bate and with technician/gunner, Sgt. Gary Carter, carrying Maj. Bruce Snelgar (OC 3Commando RLI), struck power lines killing all on board.[3]

Conclusion of Rusape Operations

The *mujibha* system was gaining in strength and fully entrenched in the Support Unit's strategies and deployments. As Barry Woan comments: "The gathering of information and utilisation of captured *mujibha's* [sic] were critical to the success of ground Troops. We were soon to realise this valuable facet of operations and would always seek out *mujibhas* for capture and hand over to Special Branch. In the Rusape area we were extremely lucky to have a well-organised and experienced team of SB/CID Operatives who we worked with closely when identifying areas of operation. They

1 Barry Woan emails 24/10/2016 and 28/10/2016.

2 Makoni/Manyika Incidents Map: Incident 25; Geldenhuys, P. (2014), Air Strike Log Entry 799.

3 Makoni/Manyika Incidents Map: Incident 26; Geldenhuys, P. (2014), Air Strike Log Entry 1045.

provided valuable intelligence as well as captured *mujibhas* to make accurate indications. In particular the work, under dangerous conditions, of John Padbury, Peter Cutting and Ken Milne (Selous Scouts attachment) usually ended in success for the relevant Fire Force and ourselves."[1]

It became my practice to sit in my office and study ordnance survey maps marked with all the incidents including contacts, landmine explosions, vehicle ambushes, sightings of ZANLA, known enemy-supporting kraals, murders and ballistic reports within my area of responsibility. Deployments of the SF were pin-pointed and results recorded. Having spent much time in the operational areas, along with my involvement with captured insurgents and *mujibhas,* I could often sense the movements of ZANLA sections and anticipate deployments which would locate them. I pieced together intelligence, formed a pattern of likely movements and deployed men accordingly. The accuracy of our intelligence was uncanny. I was continually anticipating the current deployment and planning follow-ups, which could be adjusted according to the results of the current operation. It was a process akin to building a jigsaw or playing a game of chess and employing a strategy which remained one step ahead of the enemy. In fact, I sought to occupy his mind, predict his thinking, his movements and the desired consequences of his actions. I found myself forever on the look-out for tell-tale signs of the enemy's presence, his planning, his most recent activities and, naturally, his impact on local communities. Logically, one needed to respond directly to immediately available intelligence which we most frequently did. However, needless to say, on occasions we met with failure.

It interested me to note my brother, David, employed a similar approach to the war while serving as the Battalion Intelligence Officer for 1RAR in Mtoko. David referred to this pondering as "map gazing": quiet times during which he would, in the tranquility of the intelligence office, focus his mind on all the activities occurring around and about him. This reflection became a necessary component to the intelligence-gathering process, especially considering we had access to valuable, highly skilled *mujibhas.*

Our primary source of intelligence was gathered from *mujibhas* captured in the field who were "turned" and, on reorientation, provided residence in the *mujibha* farm for safekeeping, training and later deployments. From captured and deceased insurgents, we gathered documentation that gave a breakdown of ZANLA detachments operating in Makoni, Manyika or other areas if the section was in transit. This information included their names, rank, position, weapons, operational area, important local individuals or groups, propaganda and general operational information. Occasionally, documentation would record operational incidents such as ambushes, farm attacks, murders, landmine explosions or contacts with SF. This information was specifically useful when interrogating captured insurgents or *mujibhas.* It helped with the interrogation process as well as authenticating their stories.

Intelligence was used primarily in the deployment of OPs and ambushes which would operate in conjunction with Fire Force. Our strategy was based on the principle "kills win wars". OPs continued to identify insurgent presence in the kraals and bush-bases, but the more successes we had, the more ZANLA operatives moved into the area. It was impossible to surround the TTLs with OPs and it became increasingly difficult to deploy resources (Fire Force) based on the growing numbers of insurgent sightings. We simply lacked the manpower as our resources were stretched beyond limits. A Ground Coverage team was located in Manyika and one in Makoni. I was the sole white SB officer among a small team of African SB men. The odds of winning this war in my area were rapidly fading. Blindly, however, we soldiered on.

In a short period of time, ZANLA had subverted and liberated both Makoni and Manyika, gaining the support of the masses, destroying our intelligence networks and isolating us from the locals. We were operating behind enemy lines. This was the general situation throughout the country. ZANLA were hard at work mobilising the masses, teaching them about their historical and current grievances which they "promised" to rectify. ZANLA developed cunning intelligence

1 Barry Woan and "Sakkie" McKay emails 10/2/2016.

networks and strategies in their pursuit of victory over a dominant and committed enemy. They were alert, vigilant and repeatedly altered their tactics, making it difficult for us to locate and engage them. They remained absorbed in their mission, not deviating despite heavy losses in battle, particularly with Fire Force. While SF celebrated their victories, still believing "kills win wars", ZANLA plodded on politicising and "governing" the masses, striking when it suited them, reinforced with an endless supply of insurgents and armaments. Rather than being diminished in battles, their numbers were increasing exponentially, as they opened up new fronts in rural areas closer to the capital city of Salisbury, the occupation of which was their ultimate goal, and now within their sights. They had secured a plan and were well on the way to achieving it. It became apparent that the SF could do little to curtail or hinder their ambitions.

While we had developed strategies and tactics to locate, engage and eliminate ZANLA, we had no strategy to gain the people's support and protect them. Traditional Internal Affairs operations had all but ceased. Civil administration had broken down and no RF politicians visited the field to speak to the African population. How could they when they were elected to power by a minority white population? The government's voice was previously heard through the district commissioner and his men but the people had been abandoned to martial law and governance by ZANLA. Co-operation of the masses was virtually non-existent. What incentive did they have for assisting the government when SF offered no protection nor political assurances? Gathering chiefs and headmen together for talks (*indabas*) in the cities hardly represented the reality of the dire situation in their homes which were no less than combat zones.

The RF Government offered no meaningful political alternative to counter ZANLA's rhetoric other than as terrorists, they were brutal, violent murderers incapable of ruling, as witnessed across the changing political landscape of Africa as colonial powers capitulated in one way or another. The ensuing chaos of African governance, evidenced by dictatorship, corruption, tribalism and nepotism, was deemed sufficient reason to stand against a majority African population that was increasingly joining the revolutionary military campaign against the ruling minority. Government policy, in my opinion, was to defeat the enemy by militarily action. They had lost touch with the people and failed to address their grievances. The problem was gazing us directly in the face, yet we failed to recognise it. Lacking was a political aim with clear objectives and goals that allowed for a comprehensive national strategy to be formulated for the benefit of the nation as a whole, in which the entire population, black and white, could embrace, believe in and give allegiance to. We were unwittingly rushing towards self-destruction and defeat brought about by political ineptitude. The only policy the military could implement was "kills win wars" which completely excluded a peaceful solution to a rapidly deteriorating dilemma. I saw the people as the necessary ally to ferreting out the insurgents to be eliminated once found. That to my mind was the solution. How naïve I was proven to be!

As matters progressed, I was gaining considerable operational experience with the assistance of loyal, dedicated and competent men. We built an accomplished team. Without the support of the local population, our cause was a lost one and with restricted Security Forces personnel, it became impossible to create a permanent presence on the ground. Seeds of dissension and discontent took root as I gradually realised that government and Security Forces propaganda did not match the unfolding reality of the struggle manifesting itself in front of my eyes in the TTLs. Captured ZANLA documents highlighted the blatant disparities between Africans and whites, emphasising the extreme contrast between vast white farmlands and the meagre fields of a large African population in the TTLs. The legitimate grievances of the blacks were not being addressed by the RF. An abundance of cheap labour ensured low wages, while their masters in the agricultural, mining, business and in the general workplace, routinely chalked up vast profits.

Strange as it may seem, up to this stage, the war was exhilarating and had developed into a unique lifestyle. We were constantly in the company and presence of like-minded combatants. There seemed to be no end to the war but the sophisticated RF propaganda machine continued to propagate "all is well", aided and abetted by the SF ever-increasing kill-rate. The RF maintained their strategy of keeping white Rhodesians "in the dark" as the overall security situation in the country rapidly deteriorated. Skilful manipulation of statistics kept the ratio of insurgents killed well above the growing number of SF deaths. However, white Rhodesian morale was beginning to ebb as they inevitably began to face reality.

There was also the increasing political and economic pressure on the tiny landlocked southern African country, naïve enough to believe they could oppose the world. We were isolated strangers in a hostile environment and the African people had been abandoned to ZANLA's control. There had to be a better method of winning this war. A political solution needed to be formulated to move the entire Rhodesian population forward but ignorance and prejudice prevented the exploration of these possibilities. Hurungwe was to provide the theatre in which I, unimpeded, would implement and employ the experience I was gaining in the initial stages of the war and, in so doing, address the shortcomings I saw emerging.

Ian Smith on his propaganda campaign at the entrance to his offices on the corner of Jameson Avenue and Third Street, Salisbury. Photo from Associated Press.

Geneva Conference, 1976.
1. P.K. van der Byl; 2. Deputy Prime Minister, David Smith; 3. Member of the British Secretariat; 4. Secretary to the Prime Minister and Cabinet Minister, Jack Gaylard; 5. Member of the Rhodesian Information Service; 6. Robin Harvey; 7. Member of Attorney General's office; 8. Ian Smith; 9. and 10. Members of the BSAP Close Security Unit. Information and photo by Robin Harvey.

Conference at Durban, South Africa 3/12/2015 with senior members of the BSAP Support Unit. (L-R) the author, Fred Mason, Barry Woan and Sakki McKay.

Chief Makoni (right) attending the Freedom of Makoni granted to the BSAP Support Unit by the rural council 14/10/1978. He was expected to attend government functions but offered no protection at his residence. Photo from *Blue and Old Gold* and *The Outpost,* October 1978, p.18.

Lord Owen and the author, 19/3/2018.

Propaganda meeting with Chief Makoni (seated) and his people. Note the sacred tree.

Lynx, Cessna 337. Photo by Chris Tucker.

Phil Archenoul loads a casevac into a G-Car piloted by Terence Murphy.
Photo by Phil Archenoul.

Alouette 111 helicopter deploying assault troops.
Photo by Rob McCrea.

Alouette 111 with SAS troops crossing into Mozambique. Photo by Beaver Shaw.

7 ~ TRANSITION

Sooner or later a false belief bumps up against solid reality.
George Orwell

The Path to the "Internal Settlement": A Case of Missed Opportunities
Virtually from the outset of UDI, Prime Minister Ian Smith was involved with negotiations with Britain. Robin Harvey comments: "CIO head Ken Flower, together with his Deputy Derrick Robinson, maintained contact with British and international intelligence and diplomatic organisations. This communication was essential as it provided Ian Smith access to worldwide intelligence and retained diplomatic channels with both Britain and the African Nationalists. CIO and SB carried out skilled, professional, overt and covert operations, reporting daily to Jack Gaylard, the hard line right-wing Secretary to the Prime Minister and Cabinet. In highly sensitive operations, they were privy to intelligence from members of Joshua Nkomo's hierarchy. This information was relayed to government placing the RF in a privileged position. Instead of utilising the information to manoeuvre a political solution Smith used it to remain a step ahead of Nkomo and out manoeuvre him. I believe Muzorewa was reluctant to join the Rhodesian Government as he was concerned he would merely be a "puppet" to white rule. This would isolate him from International and Nationalist support, weaken his "power base" and marginalise him as a leader. In time this was the case when he participated in the March 3rd 1978 agreement.[1] Dr David Owen agreed: "My own judgement is that the Bishop was always necessary for an internal settlement but that he was not at ease in being presented as the leader when in his heart of hearts he realised that Smith was still in control."[2] Joshua Nkomo would face the same dilemma which possibly explains his reluctance to join the Rhodesian Government in 1978 during the secret David Owen initiative. In the course of time, it has become clear that Smith did not always heed the advice of his CIO.[3]

Numerous conferences and talks were held between Britain, America, South Africa, the Rhodesian Front, African nationalists, Front Line States, including Angola, Botswana, Mozambique and Zambia. Regular diplomatic shuffles occurred between all parties, including the Organisation of African Unity and the Liberation Council of Tanzania (Julius Nyerere), Mozambique (Samora Machel) and Zambia (Kenneth Kaunda).[4] Every effort was being made to end the Rhodesian political impasse and prevent the escalating war and needless casualties on both sides. Rhodesia had been thrust onto the world stage with the major stakeholders all now seeking a political settlement. With the political discrepancies and manoeuvrings in progress, two facts began to emerge. Firstly, NIBMAR (No Independence Before Majority Rule) became the nationalists' plumb line, forcing Ian Smith to accept majority rule as inevitable. The second fact to reveal itself was that Rhodesian forces could not contain the ZANLA and ZIPRA onslaught and, with this revelation, Ian Smith's bargaining position steadily weakened. He should have followed his own advice to listen to both sides of an argument.[5] Alongside these realities, the nationalists gained strength and resolve.

In 1977, Dr David Owen, in agreement with Cyrus Vance,[6] launched the Anglo-American Peace

[1] Robin Harvey email 11/9/2019, WhatsApp discussion 16/9/2019.
[2] Dr David Owen served as British Foreign Secretary (1977-1979); was appointed a life peer in 1992. Email 28/11/2019.
[3] Flower, K. *passim;* Ellert, H. & Anderson, D. (2020), pp. 115, 118, 170, and 201; Robin Harvey oral interviews 25-27/2/2019.
[4] These included the Pearce Commission (1972), SA Detente Exercise (1975), Geneva Conference (1976) and Malta Talks (1978).
[5] Smith, I. (1997), p. 26.

Proposals (AAP) which laid the foundations for the Lancaster House Agreement.[1] The AAP presented a powerful, united front which sought to bring about a political solution to the war. This strategy was the brainchild of Dr Owen and it sought to establish an agreed constitution through informal consultation with all involved parties. Once the constitution was agreed on, the participants would gather to formally accept it. The international community fervently sought to end a bloody, violent war which the country simply could not win.

The "Internal Agreement"

On 3 March 1978, the "internal agreement" was signed by Ian Smith, Bishop Muzorewa, Ndabaningi Sithole and Chief Chirau, forming the Executive Council which governed the country in the lead-up to the referendum. A new constitution was drafted and approved in a whites-only referendum which took place in January 1979. An overwhelming majority of 85 per cent voted "yes".

This was a step in the right direction provided there was a genuine transition of power evidenced by political changes. Two weeks after the settlement was put into effect, weaknesses were exposed when Byron Hove, Co-Minister of Justice and Law and Order was sacked after he had called upon the government to make significant political changes. He complained about the slow progress of Africanisation in the government and called for changes in the judiciary and career opportunities for blacks in the police. He accused the police of brutality and supporting RF policies. Hove clashed with his Co-Minister, Hilary Squires, and the Executive Council demanded he withdraw his remarks. Hove returned to his legal practice in London.[2] The problem with the "internal settlement" was that Ian Smith maintained control of the military, police, civil service, and judiciary by insisting these departments should remain professional and not be subject to political interference.[3] This was an obstacle to international acceptance. Ian Smith, obdurate as ever, continued in failing to recognise the need to meet the expectations of the African majority of the country and that his internal initiative could not stop the war.

Rhodesian politicians were finally paying some attention to warnings given by the commanders[4] at Combined Operations on 20 July 1977, when Ian Smith and his Cabinet were advised in a secret document and meeting that ZANLA and ZIPRA military capacity was increasing and the inadequate Security Forces levels were no longer capable of withstanding their threat. The white-controlled government's war was unwinnable, making a political settlement a matter of urgency.[5] The wider Rhodesian community, including the Security Forces, were unaware of the political and military realities and were led to believe that they held the upper hand. Dennis Anderson recalls: "The situation facing Ian Smith was presented by Military Intelligence in a series of map overlays revealing that in at least eighty per cent of the Tribal Trust Lands, administration had broken down or did not exist. The whole country was a JOC, white farming areas were surrounded by insurgent elements, the main rail and road link to the south and the east from Salisbury was under threat, shades of the First *Chimurenga* where a similar situation existed on the roads to the south and east from Salisbury."[6]

With Robert Mugabe and Joshua Nkomo denouncing the "internal settlement", the war dragged on, with no international recognition forthcoming because both parties chose not to be included in the process. David Owen addressed the British Cabinet on 16 February 1978, stating: "Our criteria must be the Six Principles which formed the basis of our policy. If these were genuinely fulfilled, then we should perhaps be prepared to support the settlement…If Mr Smith went ahead with the settlement and all the Principles were put into effect, our responsibilities would have been fulfilled."[7]

---

6 American Secretary of State 1977-1980.

1 Lancaster House Agreement was signed by all parties on 21/12/1979, ending the war.

2 Flower, K. (1987), pp. 201-202; Martin, D. (1981), pp. 293-294.

3 Mitchell, T.G. (1993), pp. 49-50; Flower, K. (1987), p. 211.

4 Including Lt. Gen. Walls, G.L.M., D.C.D., M.B.E. (Commander Com.Ops.), Peter Sherren (Commissioner of Police), Lt. Gen. Hickman (Commander of the Army), AM Frank Mussell (Commander of the Air Force) and Ken Flower (Director General, CIO).

5 Flower, K. (1985), pp. 308-310.

6 Dennis Anderson emails 2016.

In a confidential memorandum to the Cabinet on 4 April 1978, David Owen noted: "With great difficulty we persuaded the other four Western Security Council members[1] to abstain and not to condemn outright the internal settlement but in the Council debate they were very critical of the internal settlement terms."[2] However, the United Nations Security Council Resolution 423 of 1978, declared unlawful any "internal settlement" in Southern Rhodesia. On 29 June 1978, David Owen commented in a Cabinet meeting that: "It was extraordinary that the Smith regime had failed to make at the start the changes, such as the reform of the Land Tenure Act, which would have helped make the internal settlement stick."[3] The civil war Ian Smith hoped to stem when working out the "internal settlement" continued unabated.

This "internal agreement" paved the way for a group of notable politicians to participate in the Interim Government. Ndabaningi Sithole formed the ZANU (*Ndonga*) Party and James Chikerema joined Bishop Muzorewa's United African National Council Party before forming the Zimbabwe Democratic Party on 29 June 1979. James Chikerema, Robert Mugabe's nephew, was the vice president of the banned Southern Rhodesia African National Congress and was appointed acting president of ZAPU while in exile in Zambia (1963-1964), when Joshua Nkomo was detained in Rhodesia. Some externally trained insurgents were released from prison, while others returned to the country under the ceasefire agreement and were filtered into the Security Force Auxiliaries under the auspices of Operation Favour to assist in the political, military and intelligence spheres (see Part 2). A number of these men were extremely well-trained political and military revolutionaries in Russia, China, Cuba and various African states. In most cases, this expertise was underestimated and underutilised by the SF.

Special Branch, Salisbury: Operation Hurricane

I spent four years at Rusape (1974-1978) and, on promotion to detective inspector, was transferred to SB Salisbury. My officer in charge, Supt. Dennis Anderson,[4] recalls:

> The first *mujibha* farm was established just outside Rusape and was the result of intelligence work done by Detective Section Officers Milne, Cutting and Padbury who were Special Branch officers at Sub.JOC Rusape. They had identified that *mujibhas* were the key players in ZANLA's intelligence network and, once captured and "turned", were able to impart vital information regarding ZANLA operations and their supporters in the local area.
>
> When a *mujibha* was compromised, it was impossible for him to return to his local kraal as the ZANLA forces, or his own "friends" in the *mujibha* network, would kill him for "selling out". So, the *mujibha* farm was established to accommodate them as well as give military training for deployments to assist with security forces' operations. It was a very successful operation and John Padbury oversaw the farm, tasked with developing the project and putting it to work as a reliable strategy to employ against the terrorist forces.
>
> The problem with the *mujibha* concept was that generally, the security forces did not understand the significance and principles of ZANLA intelligence operations that were centred in the *mujibha* network. They were also reluctant to trust an armed local African

---

7 Extract marked "Secret" from Cabinet meeting on the "internal settlement", Ref. 128/63/5; Oral interview with Lord Owen 19/3/2018.

1 There were five permanent members of the Security Council known as P5:United States, China, Russia, France and the United Kingdom.

2 Confidential Memorandum by the Secretary for State for Foreign and Commonwealth Affairs to the Cabinet, 4/4/1978, Ref. CP (78)40.

3 Confidential Memorandum by the Secretary for State for Foreign and Commonwealth Affairs to the Cabinet 29/6/1978. Oral interview with Lord Owen 19/3/2018.

4 Supt. Dennis Anderson was Special Branch officer at JOC Hurricane in Mrewa and Mtoko, alternating with Supt. Dan Stannard (1974), JOC Thrasher at Chipinga and Umtali (1976-1977), SBHQ Terrorist Desk (1977), Op. Hurricane from late 1977 to December 1978, when he was transferred to Combined Operations until April 1979. Supt. Keith Samler took over his position at Op. Hurricane.

> from the TTL who could potentially turn on them at any moment – despite the growing successes of the operation! Yet this was the key to internal military operations.
>
> Following the success of the Rusape Operation, the concept was adopted at Mtoko and Marandellas, into the Mangwende North TTL, and also Salisbury Urban. A unit was deployed to Borrowdale where a young P/O, Roy Bennett, who spoke Shona fluently, was the cog in this operation. *Mujibhas* were deployed in a spotting role in the Bus Termini and shopping centres in the townships with considerable success. A similar scheme was initiated in Sinoia where our Special Branch men were also made to open a *mujibha* farm. This Sinoia operation was overtaken by Hurungwe operations under John Padbury when he was to be tasked to take over the farm and establish the Hurungwe SFA operation based in Karoi.
>
> On promotion to Detective Inspector, John Padbury was transferred from SB Rusape to SB Salisbury in 1978 where his role was to visit military operations in Operation Hurricane and brief them on the workings of the *mujibha* intelligence networks and the development and principles of the SFAs.[1]

I was back in familiar territory, Operation Hurricane, but actions had become more volatile since I left in 1974, evidenced by the Operation Hurricane ballistics map 1977. Paul de Mattos comments: "The photograph of the Operation Hurricane map shown is that of the map in Supt. D. Hollingworth's office, Armaments, Hard Square, Morris Depot where all ballistic examination cases were recorded on 1:250 000 ordnance survey maps. I took photographs of the attached Op Hurricane map sometime in 1977. In fact, there were two maps, one for Operation Hurricane which is the map in question, and one for Operation Thrasher. The pins represented incidents where ballistic evidence was collected starting from the Altena and Whistlefield Farm attacks in December 1972. I placed many of the pins in the map during the course of my work. The incidents mapped included white farm attacks, black and white civilian murders, civilian and security force ambushes, landmine incidents and contacts with security forces."[2] (see p.180)

Part of my role was to brief military and police personnel (SB/GC) throughout Operation Hurricane on current ZANLA strategies, emphasising the role and benefit of the *mujibha* system and, for a short while, Security Force Auxiliaries.

One of the problems I encountered was that, generally speaking, intelligence officers did not understand the *mujibha* system. I repeatedly stressed that it was a foundational key to understanding ZANLA operations: vital to counter-insurgency. I suspect they failed to understand we were fighting a classic Maoist People's Revolution, where all strategy was rooted in engagement with the masses. It is virtually impossible to succeed against such an ideologically motivated enemy, while employing a Western colonial mindset in which the opposition is viewed as ignorant, inferior and nothing more than peasants fit for very little save locating the whereabout of insurgents. Many of the senior officers I was attempting to convince about the *mujibha* system failed to recognise the intellect, loyalty and dedication of these *mujibhas*. This lack of understanding would prove to be a fundamental problem with management of the SFAs.

From the inception of the war, I had always believed we were opposing communism, a "dirty" word in the then Western world. However, as matters progressed, it gradually dawned on me that our enemy was, in fact, fighting with success for their political emancipation from an entrenched colonial power. Their principal weapon was Mao Zedong's revolutionary military principles, strategies, tactics, arms and advisors.[3] Notice should be taken of the statement emanating from the BSAC (British South Africa Company) in Chapter 1: "The BSAC reasoned that there were two causes for the rebellion: Firstly, the incompleteness of the conquest of the Matabele Nation in 1893 and secondly, the incapacity of a warlike and aristocratic race to give up their old habits and to accept

---

1 Dennis Anderson email 05/01/2016.

2 Paul de Mattos mails 15/3/2015 and 15/04/2015.

3 Lowry, D. (2009), Chap. 4.

their natural place in the peaceful and industrial organisation of a settled civilised community."[1] Eighty odd years on, had our outlook changed? I think not!

We were fighting a sophisticated enemy who swiftly gained control of the Ground of Tactical Importance, the local population and their rural habitat. They approached the war and engaged us on their terms, except when compromised. In addition, they had gained the support of the people and the international community. Militarily, there was no disputing the Rhodesian forces were among the finest in the world when deployed on the enemy. However, the enemy were under the influence of Zedong, who once commented: "Weapons are an important factor in war, but not the decisive factor; it is people, not things that are decisive. The contest of strength is not only a contest of military and economic power, but also a contest of human power and morale. Military and economic power is necessarily wielded by people."[2] It goes without saying, military superiority is enhanced with the advantage of a lethal Air Force. ZANLA and ZIPRA had no airpower, allowing us Rhodesians to rule the skies.

Maxwell, from the *mujibha* farm in Rusape, accompanied me to Salisbury. He was based in a "safe house" in the urban area. His role was to travel with me and provide backup when required and assist teams being deployed, and instruct them in *mujibha* strategies and tactics. He also demonstrated the assistance *mujibhas* could provide SF in detecting insurgents. Maxwell was a highly competent soldier, directing numerous callsigns into contacts and, in so doing, earning a good reputation among the SF. He enjoyed life immensely and I was often called to extract him from police custody after a night of revelry.

We were soon back in action. In time, I introduced Maxwell to a Police Special Investigation Section operating in Chinamora, Masembura and Msana communal lands. Their leader was P/O Roy Bennett,[3] one of the few men I met that fully understood the role and potential of *mujibhas*. He comments:

> As a Patrol Officer in the BSAP being fluent in the Shona language, traditions and customs, I was posted to Ground Coverage duties in Chinamora, Masembura, and Msana Communal Lands.
>
> A Special Investigation Section was formed, and I was placed in charge. During most of this period I operated with mainly black captures and other black members of the BSAP identified as able to do the work assigned to us. The section comprised myself, another white patrol officer and four black members from Support Unit of the BSAP and captured insurgents.
>
> We were attached to Special Branch one of whom was D/Insp. John Padbury. Our brief was to operate with captures and *mujibhas* to infiltrate the communal areas identifying and locating insurgent groups operating in these areas.
>
> Most of the work was deploying clandestinely in a pseudo manner where the modus operandi and dress was the same as the insurgents. My two closest operatives whom I treated as equals after getting to know them were Maxwell, a capture managed by John Padbury, and John Sango from Support Unit whose entire family had been butchered by insurgents. These men were incredible people with strong characters and great sense of humours, afraid of nothing.
>
> Our successes were numerous. Most of the time the three of us deployed with fresh captures or identified *mujibhas* which we would snatch from their homes and immediately be led by them to insurgent groups in the area. Once we had confirmed an insurgent presence, we moved into observation points and called in the fire force. The work was extremely dangerous as at any time any of the captures or *mujibhas* could have compromised us and we would have been killed as we were always severely out numbered. Many of these *mujibhas* we released back into their villages and we maintained regular meetings

1 British South Africa Company (1975), (5).
2 Zedong, M. (1976), p. 139.
3 P/O Roy Leslie Bennett, (16/2/1957-17/1/2018).

with them. They helped us identify and cultivate others into a large community network able to feed information as soon as fresh insurgents entered the area. At all times, as a white, I never felt uneasy or threatened and was always fully confident of the trust and friendship of my black colleagues. In fact, we never saw each other as white or black, we were colleagues in a war and did what we could to the best of our ability. I truly believe the many successes were not attributed to us but more to our relationship and total support of the people we worked with in the areas concerned. It is far easier to beat off insurgency and terrorism when you can identify with and get the support and trust of the people who are the target.

Max and John were both subsequently killed, Max in a beer hall brawl in Chipadze Township Bindura and John who was ambushed and killed in Chinamora. I never knew braver and more committed friends who were fighting for what they believed in. To this day I believe that they were never given the recognition, respect or status that they had so deservedly earned. The Rhodesian Police and military completely underestimated their work and potential. I was fluent in Shona and extremely well versed in African history, traditions and customs. I left the BSAP in 1978, disillusioned, and saddened that my black colleagues were never treated as equals, despite discussing the matter with my superior officers to no avail. I was also convinced that had the understanding of African history, languages and cultures been the norm, integration would have been achievable, and the country could have avoided the terrible dilemma of war.[1]

As Maxwell lived, so he died, beaten to death by some district assistants at Bindura. What the argument was about, what he was doing there and how he arrived there I never established. I became concerned, should we have investigated and identified the culprits, we would most certainly have taken retribution, thus exacerbating matters. Hence, wisely, I believe, we left the circumstances of his death to rest. We buried Maxwell at Warren Hills Cemetery, Salisbury. A sad day and an occasion which brought tears to my eyes. I had lost both a companion and loyal fellow soldier.

End of an Era

On 8 June 1978, I was awarded a Silver Baton Special Commendation by the Commissioner of Police and granted the right to wear the insignia of the Silver Baton. The award was: "In recognition of the zeal, energy and devotion to duty displayed by him while engaged on anti-terrorist operations in the Rusape Sub-JOC area. While stationed at Rusape, Detective Inspector Padbury was, through his own initiative and devotion to duty, responsible for initiating many successful engagements against terrorists."

Surprisingly, the insignia was the result of a recommendation by Col. Henry Dunn, OC at Sub.JOC Rusape. He informed me that my commanding officer, Supt. Sloman, opposed the award but he submitted the proposal notwithstanding. However, glorious as any award is, the reality was otherwise. I consulted Standing Orders and discovered that the laid-down procedure for award recipients was as follows: "BSAP Standing Orders Chapter 2 Discipline, Section 8, Medals, commendation and awards. Subsection (7) Special Commendations and Commendation Certificates will always be presented at a parade by an officer or such other person as may be arranged by the Commissioner."

Despite legislation, my presentation never occurred. Sometime later, I phoned the BSAP Quartermaster only to be told that the insignia was there awaiting my collection. The award was the least of my expectations, but common police courtesy and protocol demanded it be presented to me at an official parade. I felt slighted. Col. Dunn was aware of, and acknowledged, the good work we were doing despite my immediate superior's objections. SB and GC operational district policemen were called upon to work extremely long hours: weekends were non-existent. Even when not on official duty, we remained on standby. We had no objections to these arrangements. In our minds,

[1] Roy Bennett email 6/4/16.

these were the duties expected of devoted policemen. Rest and recreation, in our thinking, were luxuries, especially as hostilities escalated. The only means of securing time for relaxation was to apply for authorised leave of absence. While at Sub.JOC Rusape, between 27 June and 7 November 1977, I worked 134 consecutive days without time off. Following that period, I was granted leave.[1] I never did get to wear my insignia. I simply never saw the value of doing so but, with the benefit of hindsight, it would have been fitting and appropriate to display it on appropriate occasions. Looking back, it seems to me, I was overly consumed by the war.

As matters continued, these and analogous scenarios, added to a growing hopelessness that I and many colleagues were beginning to experience regarding the overall situation in Rhodesia. In my view, we were losing the war rapidly and, as I saw it, there was no political direction from the government's leaders. In fact, I felt the politicians were totally out of touch with the realities of African aspirations, the declining military morale and a lack of resolve to conclude the hostilities peacefully. We were defending the indefensible. Only one politician visited Rusape Police Station to address the police and military community. We were warned not to say anything adverse regarding the present political and military situations. As can be expected, we did not refrain from doing so. For the record, to the best of my knowledge, no white politicians campaigned in Makoni or Manyika districts.

The war began to sap me of my resources. I became detached and distant, as was evidenced by one comment of my two superior officers in my 1977 Annual Efficiency Report: "His zeal, enthusiasm and leadership in the field far outweigh any deficiencies he may have in the over-all outlook on plainclothes work. He may well find it difficult to settle down to a more routine function in the future, but if he can master this when the time comes, he should shape into an experienced and competent senior member. His conduct on and off duty is well up to the standard expected of a man of his rank. Being on full-time operational duties, sartorial elegance is not his strong point."

If the truth be known, I had significant altercations with my two superior officers, one especially, and made it my business to irritate him at every opportunity. It was a by-product of an all-out war. However, the "fun" neither hindered my functioning as a policeman in an armed, hostile environment nor did it curtail my career development. I suspect a contributory factor to this disharmony was that we were the frontmen at the cutting edge of day-to-day battle lines, while my officers, in my view, were merely administrators wearing camouflage outfits in the office. We were worlds apart. Appropriate dress codes and routine military parade-ground conduct was alien to us but those occupying higher ranks failed to come to terms with this gulf. They simply, in my view, could not understand the divide. I was not able to conceive how they believed that there would be a return to "routine function" as the war increased in hostility.

I believed the Rhodesian Front Government's political strategy of maintaining white minority rule, supported by moderate Africans through the auspices of the Interim Government, was destined for failure. Notwithstanding my sound relationships with moderate Africans[2] and my opinion that by no stretch of the imagination could I be branded a racist, there was the question of the majority African nationalists. They were defined as the enemy, CTs, to be feared and defeated.

I began to examine every aspect of my personal outlook and involvement in the situation in which I found myself. Repeatedly, I pondered how I had come to be involved in this lop-sided war. Regularly, I asked of myself why I was taking such an active role in the war? How did I get here? Who is the enemy? What is the purpose of this war? Why are "they" risking life and limb to oppose us? What were "they" fighting for? Questions such as these, and many others, flooded my mind. I had met face-to-face with many so-called "nationalist communists" in the form of captures, *mujibhas* and scores of the local population in operational areas, and I enjoyed their company. Their customs and practices I respected and, generally, found myself on solid footing with most of those with whom I made contact. In short, the Africans I met and knew, I liked. I began to reflect more deeply

[1] Confirmed by original Sub.JOC Rusape duty roster.

[2] Moderate Africans included the Security Forces, our garden and house labourers and delivery men, etc.

on matters political, military, economic and related social issues. I recalled my youth and swimming days at the MacDonald Pool, Avondale, Salisbury, where only whites were allowed access. The unequal rank structures in the SF, segregation of schools and hospitals, the disparity of land ownership and a host of social inequalities began to gnaw away at me at a previously undetected psychological level. These matters rose to the forefront of my thinking.

We had brave, dedicated, committed soldiers and Security Forces personnel skilled at the highest level yet embroiled in a rapidly failing political strategy that was causing death and mayhem. "The characteristics of the kingdom emanate from the character of the king."[1] Ian Smith was not about to change, therefore, nor would his people. "Where change is necessary, it must come voluntarily from the top, or it will come involuntarily from the bottom. Revelation is always better than revolution."[2] It was clear the RF political policies were the obstacles to be removed: the sooner the better! The more Ian Smith protracted his negotiations for a transition in government, the weaker his position became, edging him and all the country towards inevitable capitulation. The seeds for an armed people's revolution had been sown when political grievances remained unresolved, despite prolonged consultations. By addressing political grievances, the reasons for revolution are removed.

It was my opinion that Rhodesia's leaders had failed abysmally in addressing the Africans' grievances, needs and aspirations (GNA) while in a favourable negotiating position. This was the road to chaos and war. As a consequence to their inaction, Salisbury's politicians were eventually forced to negotiate from a position of weakness and failure. It became apparent to me that popular and likeable characters did not necessarily produce wise leadership. At considerable personal expense, I had mindlessly been following inadequate leaders. The SF were isolated from the African locals, rendering them politically and militarily weak. We had been locked into fighting a "no-win war", but had rapidly regressed to being embroiled in a "losing war".[3]

I had been convinced by Ian Smith's statement at a Rotary Club luncheon in Salisbury on 21 December 1972: "Rhodesia is inhabited by the happiest Africans in the world."[4] Africans, I mistakenly believed, were incapable of social, moral and educational advancement and that there was no racial tension in the country. My thinking at the time was that we were protecting our white lifestyle from "primitive" Africans who were incapable of being educated and were, therefore, incompetent in the matter of applying good governance. I had been persuaded to believe that I was not fighting a racial war but rather a war pitted against communism. A war in which the inferior Africans were challenging the superiority of the Europeans. Essentially, the prevailing outlook among many was that white rule was the sole pathway into the future. This is the way it was and this is the way it was going to stay.[5] This view was supported by Ian Smith's statement: "I don't believe in majority rule ever in Rhodesia... not in 1,000 years." Smith and his government wished us to believe we were fighting for the very preservation of justice, civilisation and Christianity in Africa. Sadly, many were drawn into this incoherent rhetoric.[6]

When I reflected on my days in the Rusape district, I can't recall political messages addressing Africans' needs. The African engagement and co-operation we sought was viewed merely as an instrument in locating and eliminating the enemy. We gave these very people no tangible reason to support us other than "the *magandanga* (terrorists) are evil and we are good"; "we are strong, they are weak"; "you will be happy and content while we rule and govern." As policemen, our chief end was to uphold the rule of law. We could make no positive political appeal or statement. Let me repeat myself. At the outset, we were fighting for a lost cause. As the tide turned and the insurgents gained momentum, the stark reality revealed itself, that they were strong and we were weak. The enemy, in

[1] Dr Ed Cole: "Coleisms" from the Christian Men's Network (USA).
[2] Ibid.
[3] Flower, K. (1985), p. 175.
[4] Ibid., p. 173; Smith, I. (2008), Loc 185; Martin, D. (1981), p. 1.
[5] Cilliers, J (2003), pp. 60-61.
[6] Smith, I. (1997) p. 106; Gibbs, P., Phillips, H. & Russell, N. (2009), p. 317; Ellert, H. & Anderson, D. (2020), pp. 36-56.

fact, had the support of the majority while the whites did not. They held sway in the rural areas while we were isolated. This isolation was compounded by the international community's vigorous support of African nationalism and the demand for one man one vote. In the final analysis we were alone, supported by the goodwill of the South African Government who were under ever-increasing international pressure to cease their support for Rhodesia.

Successful counter-revolution requires the political mobilisation of the people which results in an exchange of information between the political authorities, the people and the military. Progressive visible steps that address the expressed grievances, needs and aspirations of the people must be in place to validate commitment to the consequences of military action, not empty words, thoughts and vain imaginings. Ours was a political approach, resulting in failure to be identified with them. Consequently, the opportunity of establishing genuine, active co-operation between the African population and the military was lost.

In the matter of war, it is important to understand the term strategy. Generally, it is defined as "a comprehensive way to try to pursue political ends, including the threat or actual use of force, in a dialectic of wills in a military conflict, in which both adversaries interact".[1] Dr Vladimir Kvint defines strategy as "a system of finding, formulating, and developing a doctrine that will ensure long-term success if followed faithfully".[2] In my opinion, the RF Government adopted the incorrect strategy in its solution to the war, with the march of time proving this to be so. There appeared to be no overall and well-structured plan to bring the hostilities to a peaceful conclusion. If there had been a strategy, it seemed irrelevant to the long-term, eagerly desired outcome for the well-being of the entire country's population. In fact, we Rhodesians were reacting to the political whims and fancies of a political vessel wedged in the doldrums of a politically confused ocean, attempting falsely to reassure the passengers "all is well".

What particularly disturbed me was that city dwellers in Salisbury seemed to be unaware, even nonchalant, of a war raging in the country. Life with all its pleasures and comforts merely continued unabated at its comfortable and pedestrian pace.[3]

I no longer believed in "the cause" for which I was initially prepared to lay down my life. I could not convince myself of a valid reason to continue in the war, other than the belief that terrorists, and their supporters, were evil and we, on the other hand, were the righteous human beings. The wider claims of the Salisbury politicians were no longer convincing me. If the truth be known, I came to recognise the inequalities that prevailed in our society and the injustices of our political system. If anything, I found myself aligning with the bulk of the African people's cause. The government's intransigence and its inability to bring about meaningful transformation in the country unnerved me. I had reached saturation point and sought a way out. Discontent with the government's ineptitude, the inability of the SF to radically redirect strategies, and concerned about ZANLA reprisals when inevitably they won the war, I resigned from the BSAP on 14 September 1978, planning to emigrate to South Africa. The Commissioner of Police requested I see him to discuss my resignation. I did so. During our discussion, he assured me of a secure future in the police force should the unavoidable transition to African majority rule take place and that, should I have a change of heart, I would be welcome to withdraw my application for discharge. In return, I said that I would reconsider the matter, despite having firmly made up my mind to leave the country. I did not think that Commissioner Allum saw me for any reason other than to try and hold the British South Africa Police together. There were growing numbers of my colleagues leaving.

With my discharge pending, my superior officers enquired when I would leave the country. I advised them I was in the process of applying for permanent residence in South Africa and had no fixed plans or dates in mind. They asked whether I would continue in the operational area as SB were facing a shortage of skilled manpower. I would take command of the Special Force Auxiliaries

---

1 Freedman, L., https://en.wikipedia.org/wiki/Strategy.

2 Dr Vladimir Kvint, economist and strategist, President of the International Academy of Emerging Markets. Ibid.

3 Mitchell, N. (2016), p. 306.

(SFAs) at Karoi in an operation known as Operation Favour. I replied that I was interested as I had no desire to leave my home, Rhodesia. When I left the police force, I would have the freedom to leave the country at a moment's notice if necessary. D/Insp. (later Supt.) Geoffrey (Geoff) Burton Price was to be my immediate superior officer and he offered me a salary to match my current one, to join the Police Reserve and retain my rank. I decided to join the Police Reserve as a Special Constable (38820). Rank was not an issue to me. One could either undertake the task or not. Geoff agreed to arrange for the transfer of my team of Police Reserve Special Branch details with a handful of trained *mujibhas* from Rusape to join me. I agreed to a six-month contract, much to the annoyance of Lynette, as she felt we should leave Rhodesia immediately, correctly believing the country's situation was plummeting out of control.

To my way of thinking, my final months at war were to be "the last throw of the dice". There was no room for half-measures even more so for those of us involved in the training and co-ordinating of the SFAs. This approach called for a paradigm shift in thinking. Indeed, it could be maintained, that it was a swing for the entire nation. Africans and Europeans would have to reconcile and unite for the welfare and future of the country. All was now at stake! It was critical that those involved with the SFAs totally embraced the strategy.

The battle for Hurungwe was to develop into a proper all-round strategy encompassing the political, military and the local population, a strategy that was sadly lacking to date. History would show that few would understand and embrace the new initiative. Of the many tasked to bring about success, all but a few fully understood the undertaking and, fewer still, dedicated themselves to ensuring its accomplishment.

8 ~ MATTERS OF MOMENT

A lie doesn't become truth, wrong doesn't become right,
and evil doesn't become good just because it's accepted by a majority.
Booker T. Washington

I would like to draw attention to certain facts and realities of daily life prevailing in Rhodesia at that time. Some of these truths I observed, others I sensed, but in the main was unaware of the overall degree of the destructive political background influences. The country was at war, of that there was no doubt. Civilians, our soldiers and the enemy were being killed and mutilated, but certain facts were selectively withheld from the general public. At no time, as a Special Branch detective inspector, was I meaningfully briefed on the overall dire circumstances facing the country. Understanding these facts and how we overcame them makes our success in later operations in Hurungwe more remarkable. It became clear to me, I had unwittingly supported the RF which had created an authoritarian, manipulative, dictatorial government, suppressing black-and-white opposition through censorship, imprisonment, house arrest and deportation. I frequently speculated what the blank spaces in our censored newspapers would have read. In time, I questioned the devious, covert government propaganda campaign which had successfully influenced my mind in preparing the ground for me and, maybe others, to take up arms in the full understanding that I may well die. This all for the sake of a hopeless cause!

The Rise of African Nationalism

On 5 February 1965, Special Branch HQ produced a confidential document entitled *A brief outline of the Growth of African Nationalism in Rhodesia* for a training course that outlined the attempts to silence the voice of African nationalism. The following is a direct transcript of the notes:

1934 Formation of original Southern Rhodesia African National Congress (S.R.A.N.C.) (of little consequence – became moribund).

1947 Emergence of British African National Voice Association (B.A.N.V.A.) under leadership of Benjamin Burombo. Not so much a political organisation as a "mouthpiece" for African grievances in Matabeleland. Burombo had no national status as leader, had no external contacts, and the B.A.N.V.A. collapsed on his death in April 1958.

1956 Formation of African National Youth League (A.N.Y.L.). A vocal organisation mainly preoccupied with the discriminatory legislation and "apartheid" in Rhodesia. Activities centred in and around Salisbury.

N.B. The above organisations were not Nationalist Parties as we know them today.

1957 Formation of Southern Rhodesia African National Congress (S.R.A.N.C.) as a result of the merger between old S.R.A.N.C. (resuscitated by Nkomo) and A.N.Y.L. The first subversive Nationalist Party in Rhodesia. Banned on 26 February 1959. James Chikerema was a member of this party.

1960 Formation of National Democratic Party (N.D.P.). Aims and objects same as S.R.A.N.C., although became much more subversive and was first Nationalist Party to organise violence on large scale. (1960 – a particularly violent year). The N.D.P. created large countryside sources; built up considerable material assets. Was twice as dangerous as S.R.A.N.C. Banned at midnight on 8-9 December 1961.

1961 Formation of Zimbabwe African Peoples' Union (Z.A.P.U.) Aims and objects identical to both S.R.A.N.C. and N.D.P. Adopted a policy of violence and refused to accept the 1961 constitution. Received substantial financial aid from external sources. Acquired arms and explosives and sent youths "North" for para military training. Banned – September 1962 – which gave rise to the widespread disorders throughout the country.

The former executive members of Z.A.P.U. disagreed of future Nationalist Split policy. Considerable discontent over Nkomo's brand of leadership. Result – the formation of two mutually hostile organisations.

1963 Formation of Zimbabwe African National Union (Z.A.N.U.) under leadership of Ndabaningi Sithole.[1] Aims and objects as for Z.A.P.U. Membership – limited. Appealed to more educated Africans. Poor attendances at public meetings. Limited financial backing.

1963 Formation of People's Caretaker Council (P.C.C.). Nkomo elected "Life President". Aims and objects as for Z.A.P.U. A subversive organisation with access to offensive materials and "trained" men. Acts of terrorism and sabotage encouraged. Several successful boycotts implemented. N.B. – Both P.C.C. and Z.A.N.U. wasted considerable amount of their subversive potential on inter-party strife — mainly in principal urban areas. 1964 P.C.C. and Z.A.P.U. banned. State of emergency declared in Highfield Township and later Harare (African Township). Leaders of both parties, and "thugs" from the aforementioned Townships, restricted to Sengwe and Wha-Wha.

Present Situation:

1. Security situation comparatively quiet and likely to remain so while self-appointed "leaders" and "thugs" remain in restriction.
2. Main threat is from armed incursions into Rhodesia Territory from external bases by "thugs" trained in paramilitary arts. These are likely to be on "hit-and-run" basis and will no doubt involve acts of sabotage and indiscriminate terrorism. Mitigating factors are:
   (a) Tightening up of border control.
   (b) Future attitude of "Independent" African states on our borders.
   (c) Increased Communist infiltration into Africa.
   (d) Availability of arms and training facilities.[2]

The Road to the Unilateral Declaration of Independence

During the 1960s and early 1970s, it was a simple task to eliminate the enemy but, in later years, once the enemy gained a foothold, the situation altered dramatically. The insurgents changed tactics, mobilised the masses and flooded the country. Rhodesian Front intransigence grew increasingly obvious to me. In fact, Ian Smith and his government swung from: "Never in a 1,000 years would there be majority rule," to the slippery slopes of capitulation. Ian Smith and the RF were blindly certain: "We are in complete control in Rhodesia today. We the Europeans we are all powerful, we have the reins in our hands and we can pretty well do what we like."[3] They appeared oblivious and ignorant to the reality of the rapidly increasing terrorist offensive, as they sought diplomatic resolution from an imagined position of strength.[4] The RF political approach was summarised, according to Ken Flower, by P.K. van der Byl's[5] statement: "It will be over my dead body before any kaffir would be invited into this (Cabinet) room."[6]

Ian Smith, Chief Whip for the United Federal Party from 1958 onwards, supported by intransigent white farmers, including Douglas Collard "Boss" Lilford,[7] formed the right-wing Rhodesian

[1] I used to call Ndabaninigi Sithole, Maningindaba Sithole. *Maningindaba* was white Rhodesian Shona slang for "a lot of trouble".

[2] Original document handed to me by Keith Samler June 2018.

[3] Speech delivered at the Drill Hall, Salisbury, just before UDI, 11/11/1965. Michael Raeburn email (producer of video) on 14/8/2018. https://www.journeyman.tv/film/4762.

[4] Flower, K. (1987), pp. 175-178.

[5] Pieter Kenyon Fleming-Voltelyn van der Byl, Cabinet Minister at the time.

[6] Flower, K. (1987), p. 127.

Front Party, gaining power during the March 1962 elections under Winston Field.[1] The "Cowboys", as they were commonly referred to, became a small yet powerful group of white-extremist farmers, financially supporting and influencing the RF.[2]

On 13 April 1964, Field resigned as he was not prepared to support the RF's determination to declare independence from Britain. He had concluded that the consensus of memorandums from heads of ministries and others, including the CIO, on the probable consequences of taking UDI, was overwhelmingly against this step. Field was not prepared to take the responsibility as Prime Minister to declare UDI against the weight of professional advice in the memorandums.[3] Furthermore, on his departure, Field told Ian Smith that intolerable forces would be mounted against Rhodesia, and he did not believe he could go along with Ian Smith's line of thinking.[4] Ian Douglas Smith was elected Prime Minister in 1964 with the determined intention of declaring independence from Britain and maintaining white minority rule. Assistant Commissioner Mike Edden recalls: "Ian Smith called an election in May 1965, and the RF won 50 of 65 seats in Parliament, the stage was set for UDI. When Ian Smith came to office, the general expectation was that he would immediately assume independence, but he first turned his attention to gaining support in Rhodesia and toured the country, addressing scores of (white) gatherings. His theme was independence, and the need to explore peaceful avenues open to Rhodesia. He banned ZANU and the PCC-ZAPU and imprisoned Nkomo and Ndabaningi Sithole along with other leaders. The Salisbury Government put in place plans to implement UDI which included the identification and isolation of senior civil servants who were opposed to UDI,[5] the development of an effective propaganda arm in the Department of Information and political control of the Rhodesian Broadcasting Corporation."[6]

The government appointed a South African white propaganda specialist, Ivor Benson, to oversee its publicity. He was attached to the Ministry of Information (1964-1966) supported by the then Parliamentary Secretary for Information, P.K. van der Byl.[7]

Benson was considered extreme even by South African standards and opposed any form of racial integration.[8] He closed the newspaper the *African Daily News* in August 1964.[9] The Rhodesian Broadcasting Corporation (RBC) was subjected to close government control from 1964 onwards. The RBC governing board was sacked and replaced by a pro-RF board.[10] Rhodesian Television (RTV) established in 1960, with an independent governing body, was taken over directly and placed under the same board as the RBC by the end of 1964. Both news desks were headed by Harvey Ward, a pro-RF man.[11] *The Central African Examiner*,[12] some church-based newspapers, African nationalist publications and a right-wing journal, *Property and Finance*, critical of the RF's "mafia tactics" against their opposition, were also closed. The RF produced their own propaganda publica-

---

7 Boss Lilford: Unapologetically a white racist, a self-made millionaire farmer (tobacco, maize and beef), with business interests in Rhodesia and South Africa. https://prabook.com/web/douglas_collard.lilford/1718919.

1 Winston Field: A former Dominion Party MP who founded and led the Rhodesian Front political party with Ian Douglas Smith. He was the seventh Rhodesian Prime Minster.

2 Parker, J. (1972), pp. 100-101. Lilford was assaulted and shot dead at his farm near Harare on 30/11/1985.

3 Flower, K. (1987), pp. 3 and 24.

4 Smith, I. (1997), p. 61.

5 Head of the Army, Brigadier Jock Anderson, resigned in November 1964 as he refused to support UDI. See Parker, J. (1972), p. 133.

6 Mike Edden's unpublished memoirs, Chap. 10.

7 Parker, J. (1972), p. 119; Friedman, H.A. https://www.psywar.org/content/rhodesia, *passim*; Ivor Benson, https://en.wikipedia.org/wiki/Ivor_Benson *passim*.

8 Ibid. Lowry, D. (2009), pp. 94-98.

9 Parker, J. (1972), p. 124.

10 Ibid., p. 120

11 Ibid., p. 121; see also https://www.psywar.org/content/rhodproporg.

12 Claire Palley (see bibliography) who specialised in constitutional and human rights law, was a regular contributor. She married Ahrn Palley, elected as an MP for the Dominion Party in 1958 but became an Independent MP 1962-1970. He opposed UDI.

tion, *Newsfront*, which survived only a few months. The *Johannesburg Sunday Times* classified Rhodesians as "the most brainwashed national group in modern times".[1]

Benson and Ward founded The Candour League, a white right-wing organisation, with the purposes of distributing white propaganda throughout Rhodesia. Numerous cell groups were established to assist in spreading this publicity as widely as possible. They successfully penetrated into the inner depths of the country.[2] The League formed close links with pro-Rhodesian groups throughout the world such as the Liberty Lobby and the John Birch Society of the United States, *Die Herstigte Nasionale Party* (HNP)[3] and the Southern African Solidarity Congress (SASCON), an organisation enjoying support in South Africa and Rhodesia.[4]

Ian Smith disregarded the pre-UDI warnings of a gloomy political and economic outlook, widely reported by sectors that included the Farmers Market and the Rhodesian Tobacco Association. The tobacco industry provided some 40 per cent of the country's overseas earnings.[5] The Associated Chambers of Commerce of Rhodesia (ACCOR) and the Association of Rhodesian Industries (ARNI) were wholeheartedly opposed to a UDI on economic grounds and were discouraged by the government from revealing their findings.[6] Ian Smith, Ivor Benson and the Secretary for Information, P.K. van der Byl, attempted to suppress adverse information concerning UDI, promoting instead its advantages. In 1965, John Parker, Chief Sub-Editor for *The Sunday Mail*, was imprisoned and later deported for publishing the contents of the ACCOR and ARNI reports, while refusing to divulge his source. I attended school with Parker's two sons, Nigel and Neil, and have vivid recollections of that incident. In my view, they were a delightful family. As John Parker was leaving the country, Sir Roy Welensky[7] told him: "They did the best turn anyone has done for you in your life. There is no future in my country now."[8]

In order to avoid the impending illegal declaration of independence, the British Prime Minister, Harold Wilson,[9] visited Rhodesia from 25 to 30 October 1965. He handed Ian Smith a letter from the Queen, and spoke to members of the opposition parties including African nationalist leaders, Joshua Nkomo and Rev. Sithole. Businessmen and financiers and the entire Rhodesian Cabinet were spoken to. He addressed officials from the Rhodesian Farmers Market, the Tobacco Association, and the Tobacco Export Promotion Council. During the meetings Mr Wilson warned of the dire consequences, legal, constitutional and economic, of a unilateral declaration of independence. He made it clear that the British Government, "Did not believe that in the present and tragic and divided condition of Rhodesia, that majority rule can or should come today, or tomorrow. A period of time is needed, time to remove the fears and suspicions between race and race, time to show that the Constitution of Rhodesia with whatever amendments may later be made, can be worked, and is going to be worked, and that the rule of law, equally with the maintenance of essential human rights, will be paramount. And the time required cannot be measured by clock or calendar, but only by achievement. The Rhodesian Broadcasting Commission did not allow Mr Wilson the opportunity to speak to the Rhodesian public."[10]

After his departure and on 31 October, Mr Smith, "expressed appreciation of Mr Wilson's integrity, adding that he had never been misled by the British Prime Minister."[11] Interestingly, to

---

[1] Windrich, E. (1979), pp. 523-254; Gibbs, P., Phillips, H. & Russell, N. (2009), pp. 314-315.

[2] Parker, J. (1972), pp. 122-123; Horne, G. (2001), p. 103-105.

[3] *Die Herstigte Nasionale Partie* (reconstituted National Party) was formed as a right-wing splinter group of the now-defunct National Party in 1969.

[4] Henrik Ellert email 26/2/2018. Ellert, H. and Anderson, D. (2020), p. 188.

[5] Parker, J. (1972), p. 134.

[6] Ibid., p. 135.

[7] Former Federal Prime Minister who returned to Rhodesia in 1964. He opposed UDI.

[8] Barton, F. (1979), Chap. 9, p. 228.

[9] Harold Wilson, British Prime Minister 1964-1970 and 1974-1976.

[10] http://web.stanford.edu/group/tomzgroup/pmwiki/uploads/1804-1965-12-KS-a-RRW.pdf, pp. 2-3; British Parliamentary Hansard records: HC Deb 1/11/1965 vol 718 cc 630-639.

[11] Ibid, p. 3.

Hilary Squires's great astonishment, Ian Smith told him that, at a personal level, he and Harold Wilson got on very well.[1] Regardless of all warnings and premonitions, it appeared that Ian Smith and his government had prematurely decided on declaring UDI some months before the declaration. Snr. Asst. Comm. Ted Sheriff notes: "In 1965 with the rank of Chief Supt., I was the Commissioner's Staff Officer (Planning) reporting directly to him. One evening late in October the Commissioner called me to his house and told me that UDI was to be declared in the next two weeks and I was to make the necessary plans of action. I was later advised that the declaration was delayed for a further week."[2]

In 1964, prior to the announcement of UDI, the Director General of the CIO, Ken Flower, informed Prime Minister Ian Smith that, "The case for UDI was unsustainable, and the same prognosis, that it would fail. On the basis of reports, we collated from military, economic and other sources, which were still overwhelmingly against UDI, we advised that the best course of action was to do nothing because Rhodesia already enjoyed self-government and that would be damaged irretrievably if change was forced through UDI."[3] Edgar Whitehead stated in Parliament that, "Once that legality is gone, to begin with you have no Constitution at all. The government of the day may wish to preserve the Constitution but that does not help, it is gone. One of the bases was unquestionably the appeal to the Privy Council.[4] Once there has been a unilateral declaration of independence you cannot go on having the appeal to the Privy Council and the basis of the constitution has departed. The moment that legality has gone it becomes more or less a free for all and the strongest wins. At the moment our legality is a tremendous protection and it gives us the time in which to solve our internal problems for ourselves without external interference."[5] Edgar Whitehead believed that, "it is essential that every year more Africans enter into our Civil Service on merit to be trained, in the ways that a civil servant should be trained, serving any Government we may happen to have; and having a clean, decent and thorough administration, that can be done at this stage. There should be absolute choice on merit, regardless of race, with regard to Southern Rhodesia, but I think we can afford to give a bit of preference to our own local people over people from outside our borders when it comes to filling posts. The steady influence of work in harness in the Civil Service, in the other services, the local government services, the Railways and others, working together day by day under discipline produces a cadre of administrators whom you can wean away from being politicians. I believe these are the lines we should now be working on. "[6]

Ignoring all warnings of dire consequences, at the 11th hour on the 11th day of the 11th month 1965, Ian Smith and 11 of his Rhodesian Front Cabinet Ministers signed the Unilateral Declaration of Independence (UDI). The timing coincided with Armistice Day which ended World War One, a ghastly war in which some 10 million soldiers and 8 million civilians were killed. Snr. Asst. Comm. Ted Sheriff recalls the end of the First World War: "My father, like many other young men, placed no value on the 'medals' awarded. What were medals worth compared to broken lives? The wearing of 'poppy flowers' on November 11th was however a sacred event. Men, women and children proudly wore the famous 'poppy' and when the church bells rang out at 11 a.m. on the eleventh day of the eleventh month of each year the whole nation came to a halt. Buses, trams, lorries, horses and carts stopped wherever they were when the clock chimed. People stood still for the two minute silence. It is impossible for the people of today to imagine the feeling of the nation. Even the cessation of the Second World War never reached that of bygone days."[7] Like most Rhodesians, I did not question either the unilateral declaration or the timing of the event but, with the passage of

[1] Hilary Squires's memoirs, transcript, 3:2.
[2] Snr. Asst. Comm. Ted Sheriff: Unpublished memoirs and oral interview 16/12/2017; Gibbs, P., Phillips, H. and Russell, N. (2009), p. 314.
[3] Flower, K. (1987), pp. 28-29 & 283-285.
[4] Formal body of advisers to the Sovereign of the UK.
[5] Rhodesian Legislative Assembly records 25/8/1964, pp. 1214-1215.
[6] ditto, p. 1220.
[7] Ted Sheriff letter to Padbury, 4/4/2020.

time, I find myself deeply questioning both the timing and UDI. Smith's declaration also coincided with P.K. van der Byl's birthday in 1923.[1] Certainly there was no national pressing emergency demanding the declaration at that precise moment. No foreign governments were signatories to the illegal declaration. Ken Flower, reporting on the Cabinet meeting on 1 November 1965 stated: "It was reported the Government of South Africa were very concerned at the possibility of there being a declaration of independence without the agreement of the British government. They had made their position clear."[2] The South African Prime Minister, Hendrik Verwoerd, expressed his opinion to Sir Roy Welensky for the attention of the then Prime Minister, Winston Field's consideration, that the Rhodesians would not win against the British even if South Africa supported them.[3] Pik Botha clarified the matter: "Ian Smith declared independence unilaterally and in isolation."[4] Portuguese and South African policy was one of non-intervention in either British or Southern Rhodesian affairs.[5] In September 1965, Southern Rhodesia's Accredited Diplomatic Representative, John Gaunt, asked Verwoerd to make a public statement that South Africa stood alongside Southern Rhodesia. Verwoerd refused saying: "I would not make such a statement because in many respects it would be wrong and wrong tactics."[6] Ken Flower stated: "Rhodesia's friends in Pretoria and Lisbon, while not likely to withdraw support, would probably not favour a UDI."[7] Smith assumed that South Africa's policy of non-interference would logically translate into acceptance of the new state.[8] Certainly the British Government was unaware of any collusion between Rhodesia and its closest sea neighbours, Mozambique under Portuguese administration and South Africa.[9] Neither Portugal nor South Africa formally recognised the new state.[10]

By declaring Independence, the RF and white Rhodesians had voted to "go it alone", thereby isolating themselves politically, economically, socially and militarily from the rest of the world, losing the right to "demand" economic or political support when required. Thus, the doors for revolution were flung wide open.

Cecil Rhodes as far back as 1889 realised the occupation and development of Rhodesia would only be possible with British imperial protection: specifically, military and economic support. He expended considerable effort to secure this, in what was known as the "Imperial Factor".[11] By ignoring Rhodes's stance, with the stroke of a pen, Ian Smith severed relationships with Britain. He miscalculated, as Ken Flower put it: "massive support in the UK"[12] which was not to be. Conversely, the African nationalists appealed to and gained political and economic support from the world. In effect, Ian Smith's UDI played right into their hands. Harold Wilson clarified the matter in Parliament on 11 November 1965: "I repeat that the British Government condemn the purported declaration of independence by the former Government of Southern Rhodesia as an illegal act and ineffective in law. It is an act of rebellion against the authority of the British Government and against the Constitution as by law established, and actions taken to give effect to it will be treasonable. The Governor, in pursuance of the authority vested in him by Her Majesty the Queen, has informed the Prime Minister and other Ministers of the Southern Rhodesian Government that they cease to hold office. They are now private persons and can exercise no legal authority in Southern Rhodesia. The British Government wish to make it clear that it is the duty of all British subjects in Southern

---

1 Deputy Minister of Information, Immigration and Tourism. He was present but did not sign the UDI declaration.

2 Minutes of Meeting of Rhodesian Cabinet, Item 1, 1/11/1965. Top Secret report Z533 (PM). Original copy located in Flower, K. (1987), pp. 286-291.

3 de Meneses & McNamara (2018), p. 42.

4 Papenfus, T. (2010), p. 285.

5 Ibid., Chap. 1.

6 Ibid.

7 Ibid.

8 de Meneses & McNamara (2018), p. 46.

9 Prime Minister Harold Wilson addressing Parliament on 11/11/1965.

10 de Meneses & McNamara (2018), p. 43.

11 Cary, R. (1970), p. 35; Smith, I. (2008), Loc 264.

12 Flower, K. (1987), p. 284.

Rhodesia, including all citizens of Southern Rhodesia, to remain loyal to the Queen and to the law of the land and to recognise the continuing authority and responsibility for Southern Rhodesia of the Government of the United Kingdom."[1]

Dr Don Milligan comments: "The Rhodesians were the rebel forces. They tirelessly failed to recognise UDI for what it was, an act of rebellion against the colonial power — in this regard Nkomo and Mugabe were never the rebels and traitors. Many Rhodesians obviously found this hard to grasp because most of them think racially — i.e. they continue to be outraged that London would aid the blacks against the rebellious whites."[2]

I recall, as a 14-year-old, on 11 November 1965, our whole school was sent home to listen to the announcement of UDI made by Ian Smith over the radio. At its conclusion, we celebrated. As a consequence, Rhodesia, my home and country, was plunged into isolation, fomenting economic difficulties and a racial war. At the time, however, I believed that anyone opposing the RF and its ideologies was a traitor and deserved their comeuppance.

Despite Smith's assurance that "all is well" in the country, on 20 November 1965, Ken Flower points out that Smith was "anxious to re-open negotiations (eight days after UDI – the 'nine-day-wonder'), rescind UDI and revert to constitutional government".[3]

Within 20 months of taking office, as noted by Mike Edden: "Good old Smithy had a larger following than any of his predecessors, and was known throughout the world, having defied Britain, the Commonwealth, the UN, in fact the world, by his Unilateral Declaration of Independence on 11 November 1965."[4]

Ian Smith Considers Political Solutions

As early as 1972, Ian Smith was acutely aware that African majority rule was inevitable. Robin Harvey, a member of the Special Branch at the time recalls: "In 1972, I do not recall the exact date, I received a telephone call from a colleague Peter Albert Moores, that we were to meet in the office of the Director General (D.G.) (Ken Flower) at 2.00 p.m. On arrival also present was the D.G. (Internal) Derrick Robinson. Ken Flower had been asked by the PM to attend a meeting at his offices at 14.30 and to bring with him 'who he liked'. In the discussions, Ken Flower briefed Ian Smith and Jack Gaylard, Secretary to the PM's Cabinet, on the prevailing deteriorating political and military situation in the country, and potential for further deterioration. Ian Smith concluded the meeting stating that, 'If the whites want a place in this country, then we must reach an accommodation with the nationalists and get an internal settlement.' Ian Smith asked Ken Flower to launch a team of dedicated CIO/SB men to establish and maintain contact with African Nationalists, and Zambia, with a view to bringing all parties together for a political settlement. Ken Flower's team included Derrick Robinson, Peter Moores and Robin Harvey (Special Branch Officers). Every evening at 6 p.m. there was a meeting at Derrick Robinson's office with the members of the team to discuss the day's events and Derrick Robinson phoned Jack Gaylard to update him on events."[5]

During August/September 1972, Special Branch officers, Supt. Peter Tomlinson and D/S/O Winston Hart (stationed at SB Bindura), carried out a six-week patrol along the north-eastern border with Mozambique. After extensive investigations and interrogations of captured insurgents, they confirmed that ZANLA had established bases in Mozambique some 8 kilometres from the Rhodesian border. They had penetrated the Gomo, Masoso, Musengezi and Rusambo areas, subverted locals and planted arms caches. Tomlinson submitted his assessment of ZANLA's invasion into Rhodesia to SBHQ Salisbury where it was received with some scepticism by elements of the hierarchy.

On 25 October 1972, Supt. Brian Chalk was instructed by the Officer Commanding Special Branch to develop and maintain contact with Bishop Muzorewa and members of the African National Council's (ANC) Central Committee. The purpose was to conduct secret talks in order to

---

[1] British Parliamentary Hansard records: HC Deb 11/11/1965 vol 720 cc 349-364.

[2] Dr Don Milligan email 24/7/2017.

[3] Flower, K. (1987), p. 59.

[4] Mike Edden's unpublished memoirs, Chap. 10.

[5] Robin Harvey email 31/10/2018.

address the political impasse that had arisen between the ANC and the government, and to create an environment for dialogue between Bishop Muzorewa and Ian Smith, with the aim of reaching a settlement with the British Government. He held secret meetings across the country with Bishop Muzorewa and his ANC Central Committee, and other national and British dignitaries, always reporting back to the Officer Commanding Special Branch, the Deputy Director CIO and the Secretary to the Rhodesian Cabinet, Jack Gaylard. He orchestrated numerous meetings for Bishop Muzorewa including:

- Lance Smith (Minister for Internal Affairs) on 26 October 1972.
- Two senior diplomats from the Rhodesian Department at the UK Foreign and Commonwealth Office, Phillip Mansfield and Robin Byatt, on 4 January 1973.
- Jack Gaylard and the Attorney General on 25 January 1973.

These efforts culminated with a meeting between Bishop Muzorewa and Ian Smith on 17 July 1973. Of interest, between 22 and 25 June 1973, Sir Denis Greenhill led a high-level delegation to meet with Ian Smith, Bishop Muzorewa and other leading Rhodesian political dignitaries. However, on 29 June, Ian Smith told the Rhodesian Parliament that any settlement with Britain remained remote. Despite warnings from Special Branch, Ian Smith remained intransigent and would not negotiate the 1971 Constitution.[1]

On 27 November 1972, after extensive Special Branch investigations across the country, Supt. Chalk submitted a secret report to SBHQ. He referred to his previous report under reference XYS 2990/6, dated 25 September 1972. Both reports detailed the growing threat of subversion and active terrorism in the north and north-east of the country, and recommended immediate escalation and deployment of SB, CID and Uniform Branch teams to investigate these incursions. He recommended that Int.Aff. and other government departments intensify their activities in order to restore a degree of normality in the affected areas. Without such action, he warned, a large-scale offensive by ZANLA was imminent and likely to include the laying of landmines and attacks on homesteads. On 2 December 1972, insurgents attacked Altena farm in the north-east of the country. I have little doubt that this report, and many similar ones, made their way to the Prime Minister's offices.[2]

On 4 December 1972, Ian Smith said in a radio interview, consisting of a panel of six selected journalists: "…the (security) position is far more serious than it appears on the surface, and if the man in the street could have access to the security information which I and my colleagues in Government have, then I think he would be a lot more worried than he is today."[3] Why wasn't the public given the details of this serious situation affecting their very lives was my question? His "happiest Africans in the world" to me was an enormous contradiction. The RF's aggressive propaganda campaign, enabled by astute censorship, kept the unsuspecting white and moderate African public uninformed. To my regret, we were blinded to the obvious and merely fought on.[4] The government realised majority rule was inevitable but it was to be a further seven years before they finally relinquished power. A hefty price was paid for these protracted negotiations. As the government continued to lose control of the country to the insurgents, the opportunity for a negotiated settlement for a peaceful co-existence between blacks and whites was squandered and the "Breadbasket of Africa", as Rhodesia was known, would disappear from the annals of history. A nation was to be torn apart. The country faced insurmountable problems requiring immediate resolution.

During 1974, in Gatooma, the Department of Conservation and Extension (CONEX) called for a meeting to discuss the construction of a dam on the Umfuli River, to provide irrigation for Golden Valley and Chakari farms in the Gatooma area. A prominent farmer in the Chakari area, Gatooma, who served on the council of the Rhodesian National Farmers Union, C.G. Tracey, and P.K. van der Byl addressed the gathering of mainly farmers and interested persons. Hans Hansen, a farmer,

---

1 Oral interview with Brian Chalk, 19/11/2018 and his unpublished memoirs.

2 Ibid. Brian Chalk remained in this position until he left the BSAP in July 1973.

3 BBC Monitoring Service, 6/12/1972; Flower, K. (1987), p. 135.

4 Smith, I. (2008), Loc 6702.

was present and states: "We were told that black majority rule was unavoidable. The problem in Government eyes was how to implement the changes. So, in the interim the police and military had to keep law and order. We were advised to take whatever steps we thought necessary to make provision for the inevitable hand over to black majority rule. So, we put our farm on the market and lived in Salisbury, Greenwood Park, for two years before moving to Kariba."[1]

On 13 February 1976, Lord Robens conveyed a message to the British Prime Minister, James Callaghan, from Ian Smith with whom he had met in Salisbury. It was revealed that Smith had been holding negotiations with Joshua Nkomo, as he realised that he was unable to resist indefinitely the effects of the rising African nationalism campaign and the associated terrorist threat. He would, therefore, be compelled to compromise with the Africans, even if it meant severing links with the right-wing elements of his Rhodesian Front political party.

Callaghan sent Sir Denis Greenhill (the former head of the diplomatic service) on a secret mission to meet with Smith in order to assess the situation. Greenhill confirmed Lord Roben's information adding that the Chiefs of Staff in Rhodesia were confident that such a compromise would positively affect the political environment and enable the Security Forces to handle the impending guerrilla threat. Greenhill's findings were assessed and then presented to Callaghan by the Foreign & Commonwealth Office on 28 February 1976. They assessed that Smith did not grasp the gravity or serious consequences of his deteriorating security situation, how deeply his position was being undermined and that he was stalling for time. At this juncture, Callaghan met the Queen at a social event and informed her of the recent developments in Rhodesia. He stated that he was not sure whether to follow the matter up or let it simmer for the time being. The Queen did not comment but sent a letter by the hand of her private secretary, Sir Martin Charteris, the following afternoon. She advised that any initiative taken could prove ineffective but felt it was at least worth the effort. She sent him her best wishes in dealing with the "intractable" problem. Consequently, Callaghan sent a message to Smith and addressed the British Parliament on 22 March 1976 as follows: "In the view of Her Majesty's Government, the spread of guerrilla activity meant that if he (Ian Smith) was willing to give a public commitment to majority rule and to hold elections on this basis within the next eighteen months to two years, Her Majesty's Government would be willing to play a constructive part in negotiations between him and the African leaders in order to prevent chaos and loss of life, and to reach a settlement satisfactory to both Europeans (whites) and Africans. As part of the settlement, Britain would be ready to contribute towards compensation for those adversely affected, and to give financial aid for development and African education. We would also recommend that sanctions be lifted by the United Nations."[2] Mr Callaghan warned that: "As things are, Mr Smith is leading his country on the path of death and destruction. Even at this late stage, I ask the European population of Rhodesia to believe that there is an alternative path. It is still just possible for Mr Smith to follow it. If not, I hope that other leaders will emerge who recognise the realities of the hour and that the time is here when the legitimate aspirations of the African people can be met and reconciled with the desires of the European population. Only in this way can there be hope for a peaceful future for Rhodesia."[3] At this stage, negotiations between Ian Smith and Joshua Nkomo had collapsed. No announcement was made by Mr Smith.

Racial Inequality

In 1975, the Rhodesian Parliament commissioned Sir Vincent Quenet[4] to investigate racial practices in Rhodesia and "advise Government of those cases or aspects of discrimination which are no

[1] Confirmed by Hans Hansen and his brother Ulrich (joint owners of their farm in Gatooma) who attended the meeting, although Ulrich does not recall P.K. van der Byl being there. Email and discussion 20/7/2016. Hans and his wife Diana miraculously survived the Viscount disaster, 3/9/78.

[2] Callaghan, J. (1987), pp. 378-382; British Parliament Hansard: HC Deb 22/3/1976 vol 980; Smith, I.D. (1997), pp. 191-193.

[3] British Parliament Hansard: HC Deb 22/3/1976 vol 980.

[4] Rhodesia: *Report of the Commission of Inquiry into Racial Discrimination* (Sessional Papers, Cmd. R.R. 6, 1976).

longer considered desirable and necessary". The report focused on "economic (land, labour, and education as it affected employment opportunities); political (franchise and the Declaration of Rights); and social (land and housing policies, and social arrangements). The Land Tenure Act was identified as the main cause of friction between races".[1] Despite the government's acknowledgement that racial inequality existed, only a few of Quenet's recommendations were enacted when the report by the Commission of Inquiry into Racial Discrimination was tabled at Parliament in June 1976. There was no racial equality and the government did little to address the matter. As I saw it, here was a further lost opportunity to remove the political obstacles employed by ZANLA and ZIPRA propaganda. The commission noted the inequality of the rank structure in the BSAP yet stated: "Although, ideally, all ranks should from the outset be open to European and African alike, it was thought that such a step would, at present, be too drastic a change."[2]

Interestingly, as early as June 1976, P.K. van der Byl asked the South African Government not to issue Rhodesians, who had not completed military commitments, with residence or work permits. South Africa refused to comply.[3] Many black and white men volunteered to serve in the Rhodesian SF but mostly whites were conscripted. However, on 17 September 1978, it was announced that Africans were to be conscripted for military service on the same basis as whites. While some Africans were forced by insurgents to cross into Mozambique and Zambia for training, there were many volunteers.

On 5 July 1978, the Executive Council announced the establishment of a committee to report on the removal of racial discrimination. The Transitional Government had accepted in principle the abolition of discrimination, except in areas detrimental to national interests. The committee comprised Mr Chikerema (UANC), Mr Magaramombe (ZUPO), Mr Mandaza (ZANU Sithole), Mr Cronjé, Mr Hayman and Mr Irvine of the RF. On 8 August 1978, a communique, proposing the removal of racial discrimination in certain areas, was issued by the Executive Council. However, matters including the Land Tenure Act, rules governing the operations of schools, housing and hospital segregation remained in contention.

The questions I repeatedly asked myself was what prevented Ian Smith continuing the road to majority rule from the outset of his premiership? What prohibited him integrating the rank structures of the BSAP, Army, Air Force, SAS and Int.Aff. of the country? What disallowed him reforming the land tenure, education, hospitals, swimming-pools and the other fabrics necessary for the harmonious functioning of a normal society? I personally witnessed little formal advancement towards equality in the armed forces. Initiating these racial integrations, I felt, would have removed the incumbent political obstacles and gained the country international recognition, but sadly they failed to materialise. The considerable effort and expense of the war would have been better utilised on integrating the country's citizens. On the issue of land, Ian Smith argued that the TTLs were reserved for the Africans, ostensively protecting them from European occupation and enterprise.[4] This was true except for mining: "No person, other than an indigenous native, shall enter or be in any reserve or other tribal area without the permission in writing of the Secretary for Internal Affairs, the appropriate provincial district commissioner or the district commissioner of the district concerned. The above provisions shall not apply to any person who is bona fide engaged in the exercise of his rights under the Mines and Minerals Act, 38/61, in such reserve or area." I knew of no Europeans wishing to settle in the TTLs surrounded by Africans and no essential services, such as electricity, piped water, water-borne sewage, adequate housing, tarred roads and private land ownership, along with barren soil. Missionaries were to prove the exception.

However, it eventually became clear to me that the RF's political strategy of white minority rule, aided and abetted by moderate blacks, would bring about chaos, bloodshed and mayhem. In the Makoni/Manyika TTLs, the more insurgents we killed, the more it seemed they were replaced, hence

[1] Baker, D., p. 243.
[2] Ibid., p. 249.
[3] *The Daily News*, Durban, 10 June 1976.
[4] Smith, I. (1997), p. 92; Palley, C. (1966), pp. 414, 631-634.

nullifying, in my mind, the axiom "kills win wars". I was also of the opinion that the SF had settled into a "daily routine of war", a deadlock to be broken only by a revolutionary, unconventional approach. However, the governmental hierarchy was unwilling to shift their approach and outlook. In the light of this intransigence, I began to realise the very existence of not only the whites and moderate Africans was at stake but the country's entire infrastructure. SF strategies and tactics had successfully evolved to kill, while the people were abandoned and ignored. The war had become a way of life, a unique, almost pleasant, lifestyle.

Command and Control

At Cabinet level, Ian Smith, the Commander in Chief, headed the Security Council. This assembly included the Ministers of Defence; Justice, Law and Order; Finance; Information, Immigration and Tourism; Internal Affairs and his Deputy; the Commissioner of Police; the Commanders of the Army, Air Force and Guard Force (when it was formed) and the Director General of the CIO attended, affording them equal status with civilian Ministers and direct access to Ian Smith, who maintained control of the war. Command authority was never vested in his Com.Ops. Commander, Lt. Gen. Walls, who was not promoted to a full general, therefore he held no superiority over his counterparts in Com.Ops. (police, army, air force and CIO). His position was little more than that of a chairman with decisions made by negotiations and discussions. Lt. Gen. Walls had no direct authority and could not enforce compliance. He repeatedly asked Ian Smith to clarify his position but this request was not ever met.[1] Possibly, by my reckoning, Ian Smith did not trust Lt. Gen. Walls. Conceivably, Smith's reluctance was related to his pre-UDI days when he replaced top personnel whom he did not trust or thought would not support him. "Ian Smith never relinquished his control over the counterinsurgency campaign, and refused to give a free reign to the 'supremo' (Walls). He (Smith) therefore should have provided more leadership in developing an overall strategy."[2] Smith undertook responsibility for success or failure. In my opinion, in many spheres of life, failure can be laid at the feet of the overall commander. It is my opinion that Ian Smith provided a one-dimensional political aim and strategy, i.e. "the RF will win the war no matter the odds", making military victory virtually unattainable. I am also of the opinion that Smith considered himself the only man capable of leading the country to victory (see Hubris Syndrome in the conclusion). He appointed Roger Hawkins as Minister of Combined Operations (1977-1979), when he was replaced by Hilary Squires.

As the war progressed, I became increasingly confused. Very little of everyday life made sense. During 1977 alone, the following events serve to epitomise the ever-changing government policies. On 12 January 1977, Ken Flower briefed Ian Smith that the war could not be won militarily and required a political solution. The following day, Flower put the facts before the Cabinet giving them the "bleakest picture they've ever had". Two days later, the War Council was advised by Flower "that the OCC assessment of the military situation was that the country was losing so much ground militarily, that even with general mobilisation, matters could not be prolonged…it was stressed that action was required very soon, as the security forces would be unable to hold the position indefinitely".[3]

David Owen Initiative

In April 1977, the British and American Governments agreed to co-operate on a joint peace proposal for the Rhodesian crisis, known as the Anglo-American Proposals (AAP).[4] On 10 April, The Rt. Hon. Dr David Owen, MP, and his team met with Joshua Nkomo. These meetings took place in London. Two days later, Owen met with Samora Machel in Maputo, Mozambique. David Owen later met with John Vorster, the then South African Prime Minister, Pik Botha (Minister for

---

[1] Cilliers, J. (2003), pp. 68-69; Hoffman, B., Taw, J. & Arnold, D. (1991), pp. 16-18; Flower, K. (1987), pp. 114, 217, 277; Smith, I. (2008), Loc 9167; Smith, I. (1997), p. 333.

[2] Hoffman, B., Taw, J. & Arnold, D. (1991), pp. 16-18.

[3] Flower, K. (1987), pp. 175-177.

[4] The Anglo-American Proposals (AAP) formed the basis of the Lancaster House Agreement (LHA), leading to the end of the war.

Foreign Affairs) and Brand Fourie (Secretary of Foreign Affairs) in Cape Town on 13 April. Of interest was John Vorster's adamance that Ian Smith was keen to accept majority rule within two years and, should Smith not deliver on this deadline, the South Africans would ensure it was achieved. Vorster was of the opinion only Ian Smith could change the heart of Rhodesians towards acceptance of majority rule. Botha, on the other hand, noted the desire of South Africa "to wash their hands of the (Rhodesian) affair".[1] Interestingly, Ian Smith was demanding a two-year transition period during the failed Geneva talks of October/November 1976 but did not initiate proceedings leading towards his alleged goals.[2]

On the same day, 13 April at 2.30 p.m., David Owen met with Ian Smith, David Smith and P.K. van der Byl at the British Embassy in Cape Town. This was Owen's first meeting with Ian Smith.[3] Records show, that it was an amicable meeting, with discussions centring on the Anglo-American Proposals and the movement towards a new constitution and majority rule. Owen opened the talks with a detailed analysis of the Rhodesian situation. Ian Smith replied that he was grateful for the presentation to which much thought had clearly been given. A great deal was accomplished during the almost four-hour discussion. However, it is David Smith's statement I find shocking. Outlining government policy, David Smith stressed the damage being done to the prospects of Rhodesia by sanctions. He stated: "Compared with their neighbours they had a highly sophisticated economy with a developed money and financial market. It was essential to retain white people to manage the economy and its institutions. This required the government to persuade people to be prepared even to send their sons to get killed."[4] An alarming statement when considering Ian Smith knew in September 1976 that Vorster and his South African Government were under considerable international pressure to sever support of Rhodesia: "The final coup de grace came at that Pretoria meeting in September 1976. We knew that was the end, the final betrayal, and all we were trying to do was make the best of the disaster gradually unfolding us."[5] At a Cabinet meeting on 21 September, one minister stated, "Could we not get all the women and children safely out of the country, and then the men would make a stand and defy Vorster and his gang?"[6] The game was over, Rhodesians were kept in the dark, the war raged on and men, women and children died. Before the Owen/Smith meeting started, Owen had confirmed that he intended visiting Rhodesia. Ian Smith had a problem as Owen described: "His (Smith's) problem now, he explained, was that his people were expecting him to be angry with me and to persuade me to come to Rhodesia. I said I had no objection if he wanted to make that case when the meeting started and I would listen and then concede gracefully. This is exactly what we did. So realistically did he perform that even my Private Secretary thought that Smith had been pretty bloody to me and was amazed when I told him that we prearranged the whole thing."[7]

The meeting ended amicably with both parties discussing how to address the press.[8]

Ian Smith's Last Throw of the Dice

On 18 July 1977, Ian Smith announced his proposed "internal settlement" to the country, stating Rhodesians refusing to accept pending changes, were "out of touch" and advocating a course of action that would lead to "disaster".[9] On 20 July, Com.Ops. despatched their top secret document

[1] Confidential record of a discussion between the Foreign and Commonwealth Secretary and the Prime Minister of South Africa in the State House, Cape Town, 13/4/1977 at 9 a.m.

[2] Smith, I. (1997), p. 216.

[3] Owen, D. (1992), p. 303; David Owen email 16/5/2019.

[4] Confidential record of a discussion between the Foreign and Commonwealth Secretary and Mr Ian Smith at the British Embassy, Cape Town, South Africa, 13/4/1977. Owen's team included Sir David Scott, J.A.N. Graham, P.R.A. Mansfield & E.A. Fergusson. The meeting commenced at 2.30 p.m. and ended at 5.15 p.m..

[5] Smith, I. (1997), p. 236.

[6] Ibid., p. 209.

[7] Owen, D. (1992), p. 303; oral interview 19/3/18; Confidential record of a discussion between the Foreign and Commonwealth Secretary and Mr Ian Smith at the British Embassy, Cape Town, South Africa, 13/4/1977.

[8] Ibid.

[9] Mitchell, N. (2016), p. 315.

to the Prime Minister demanding he reach a political settlement or face military capitulation. It was no longer treasonable to negotiate with African nationals but, in the interim, we were now fighting and dying for the inevitability of majority rule.[1] The political outlook was bleak and continued to spiral downwards and out of control.

On 8 July 1978, the Rhodesian Broadcasting Corporation (RBC) found itself with a replaced board of governors, comprising five white and four Africans. However, the white members were RF Government sympathisers, ensuring the RBC continued as its mouthpiece. This obvious ploy frustrated two of the four African board members, Mr Sansole and Rev. Manyoba. Both men summarily tendered their resignations.

There was widespread criticism of the government when MPs, astonishingly, awarded themselves a 15 per cent salary increase, effective from June 1978, despite the fact most whites in private employment had been subject to a wage-freeze and economic hardship for a considerable period.[2] This matter incensed me.

On 13 July 1978, the Attorney General's office revealed the shocking news to our beleaguered nation that high-ranking Rhodesian officials had been participating in a multimillion-dollar scheme to divert vast sums from a secret arms-buying resource into private Swiss bank accounts, thereby misappropriating monies earmarked for the defence budget. Strict censorship of this disclosure prevented names and details of the alleged embezzlement being made public. However, two South African weekly newspapers, *The Sunday Times* and *The Sunday Express*, published stories on 16 July 1978, showing that the defendants included Mr Rodney Simmonds, a former RF MP, District Commissioner and businessman. Two civil servants, Timothy Pittard, Head of the Department of Customs and General Adviser, and Norman Bruce-Brand, Under Secretary in the Rhodesian Ministry of Defence, the chief finance officer in the Ministry of Defence, were also indicted. Edward Muller, a South African citizen and Managing Director of Rennies (Rhodesia) Ltd., a customs-clearing and forwarding-agent company, was also said to be involved in this Rhodesian trade-off. Rhodesian President, John Wrathall, too, was implicated. His death on 31 August 1978, roughly one month after the news broke, was rumoured to be suicide but officially pronounced as a heart attack.[3] Snr. Asst. Comm. Ted Sheriff recalled: "I was always curious of the circumstances surrounding Wrathall's death. As I drove home at around 5.30 p.m. on 31 August 1978 we greeted each other. Wrathall looked well. I was surprised to hear of his death." As these men were being called on to continue the procurement of military hardware urgently required for the continuing hostilities in the country, the conclusion to the matter was a mere fine with the injunction "to return the stolen cash".[4] The secrecy surrounding this incident further eroded my trust in the government. Despite the desperate attempt by Ian Smith and his officials to suppress this scandal, sufficient information circulated openly enough for the European law-enforcement agencies to seize 500 much needed MAGs destined for Rhodesia.[5]

Interestingly, on 4 September 1979, CIO's Acting Director, External Affairs, John Muir, confirmed that the CIO Director, Administration, Claude Greathead, had been convicted on 40 counts of theft, nine counts of fraud and 23 counts of illegally exporting foreign currency in contravention of the Rhodesian Exchange Control Act. All these transactions involved fraudulent and improper use of government funds. He was sentenced to five years' imprisonment, half of which was suspended for five years, provided he returned the stolen monies, a total of R$58,431. He was further sentenced to a fine of R$6,913 in respect of the 23 counts under the Exchange Control Act.[6]

1 Smith, I. (1997), p. 62.
2 British Confidential documents: Rhodesia Department Monthly Summary No 7, July 1978.
3 Ellert, H. and Anderson, D. (2020), p. 82.
4 *The New York Times*, 23 July 1978, p. 7; Ellert, H. & Anderson, D. (2020), pp. 81-82; British Confidential documents: Rhodesia Department Monthly Summary No 7, July 1978.
5 Moorcraft, P., McLaughlin, P. (2008), p. 92.
6 Unpublished memoirs of Brian Chalk, former CIO operative, and telephone call 28/11/2018.

To compound the country's woes, the economy continued to deteriorate with a R$937.3 million budget alongside a record R$262.8 million deficit announced by the Co-Ministers of Finance in the budget speech on 20 July 1978. A 6 per cent rise in public expenditure was forecast which was to be met by a compulsory 12.5 per cent National Defence Levy. This entailed taxing all Rhodesians an extra R$100 income tax per year, excluding most of the non-white population. The remainder of the deficit would likely be raised by soliciting funds from Rhodesia's neighbour, South Africa. A negative growth-rate and deterioration of the economy was expected.[1] It was estimated the war was costing the country a staggering one million Rhodesian dollars a day. In 1977 the rate of the Rhodesian dollar was R$1= USA$1.50.

Internal Special Branch Operations

Internally, Special Branch was also active in the field of international politics. D/S/O Lawrie Mabin provides insight to some of these operations: "We did quite a bit of work keeping certain individuals under observations. One evening Pat (pseudonym) and I were briefed that there was a highly ranked British political figure staying at the Jameson Hotel. We were to locate ourselves in our vehicle around the hotel and wait for instructions. An informant in the hotel was to advise when the subject left his room. In due course we were alerted and moved in to the hotel. Pat had a key for the room provided by the informant. I was a novice at this type of work and quite honestly 'shitting myself'. Pat worked quickly and efficiently that night. He got in to the brief case and took photos of all the documents. I do recall that the documents included notes for a meeting that was to take place the following day with who I cannot recall. I was very relieved when we made it to our vehicle outside the hotel. We had our own dark room and the photos were developed that same night and delivered to the awaiting recipient. Five members of the Special Branch were permanently based at the main Post Office in Kingsway. There were certain addressees that were targeted but other than that they just looked for suspicious mail – and it was opened the old-fashioned way of steaming. If there was nothing of interest the mail would be closed up again and sent on its way. Obviously, there must have been co-operation between members of the Post Office and ourselves, but awareness of what we were doing was kept to an absolute minimum. I did time at Salisbury Airport which I enjoyed a lot, especially having an ID which gained me access to any part of the airport that I wished. We kept a close tab on all in-coming and outgoing passengers. We had special keys and equipment that could open almost all types of locks and we searched baggage of certain people without their knowledge. In particular, people of political interest, and it was not contraband that we were after. One member of SB was enrolled permanently as a student at the University of Rhodesia."[2]

Military Coup

Totally disenchanted with the "internal settlement", the Rhodesian military commanders, including Ken Flower, continued to hammer away at the Executive Council, African nationalist leaders and Ian Smith. In a combined show of unity, they addressed a joint session of the Executive Council, the Ministerial Council and the National JOC (Nat.JOC) on 3 August 1978. Ken Flower stated that, in their professional assessment, all four leaders (Bishop Muzorewa, Ndabaningi Sithole, Chief Chirau and Ian Smith) had lost widespread public support by engaging in a disproportionate amount of time in-fighting, while ZANU and ZIPRA continued to rally and gain support. Flower comments: "The scene is more sombre. It's pretty desperate and needs desperate remedies…The security situation has never been so desperate…Over 6000 terrorists within Rhodesia with plus or minus 30,000 lined up against us, and their numbers probably growing to about 40,000 before the end of the year-with more support and sympathy internally and externally than they have ever had. Meantime our white security forces diminish in number and effectiveness."[3] Walls stated: "Time was of the essence and unless something positive and effective was done by Government within the next

[1] British Confidential documents: Rhodesia Department Monthly Summary No 7, July 1978.

[2] D/S/O Lawrie Mabin email and oral interview 2016.

[3] Flower, K. (1987), pp. 207-208.

two to three weeks, then it was the view of the Security Chiefs that some political solution other than that now being pursued would have to be found."[1]

Minutes of the Executive Council meeting on 22 August 1978 stated insurgents, their commanders and large segments of the population in rural areas needed political motivation which was lacking to support the Transitional Government. Hundreds, if not thousands, of blacks were leaving the country as recruits for the Patriotic Front.[2] By all appearances, Walls, fully informed by Flower and completely up to date regarding the international and national political situation, was deeply concerned for the well-being of his soldiers. He did not wish his men killed while contesting a dying cause, with this attitude reflected in many of his decisions at that time, including the attack on Mapai.[3] The Commander in Chief summed up the dire situation facing the country on 3 August 1978: "That night I was more depressed than I could previously recall. But clearly it was something I must keep to myself, because the last thing we wanted was any damage to the wonderful morale and fighting spirit of our Rhodesians."[4] Bereft of the truth and believing a lie, the Security Forces fought on. Men, women and children continued to die unnecessarily. The entire country was virtually an operational area.

At the same time, at a Nat.JOC meeting, Lt. Gen. Walls had rather bluntly broached the possibility of some sort of political action by the military commanders. He was, in effect, rebuffed. Nevertheless, a subcommittee under the direction of Brig. Maclean was convened to consider Lt. Gen. Walls's proposal. However, the committee maintained that no action was possible within the present constitution.[5]

At a Nat.JOC meeting on 29 August 1978, the coup was again broached by Don Yardley, Secretary for the Interior, generally regarded as extreme right-wing. In attendance were Lt. Gen. Peter Walls; BSAP Commissioner Peter Allum; General John Hickman, Army Commander; Air Vice Marshal Frank Mussell Air Force Commander; Air Vice Marshall Michael (Mick) McLaren, Deputy Commander Com.Ops. and Ken Flower, Director General CIO. No minutes were taken, the secretariat having been dismissed. "Yardley questioned what should be done if the present ceasefire policy failed and if the attempt to reach an accommodation with Joshua Nkomo was not successful. Yardley said that in those circumstances it seemed to him that the only viable course was to return to legality by calling in the British Government and thus ending UDI. In the course of the discussion that ensued, there was general agreement that this was probably the only course open to them. A number of reservations however were expressed. General Hickman expressed doubt on the grounds that the British, in applying the Anglo-American Proposals, (AAP), would apply also their proposals for disbanding the greater proportion of the existing army. Allum (Commissioner of Police) who had recollected that the AAP involved his own dismissal, had made the point that he would be unwilling to engage in any unconstitutional action. Air Vice Marshall McClaren had also expressed some doubts about the proposition. Flower said that he had felt it incumbent on himself to point out some of the difficulties: it was not just a matter of calling in the British Government. Lt. General Walls had held his peace, presumably happy to leave the running to others."[6] The Nat.JOC deputed Ken Flower to approach the British Government through his contacts. He did so on 29 August when he was invited to dine with the British Deputy Under Secretary, Foreign and Commonwealth Office, John Graham, in Salisbury. Graham immediately contacted Lord Owen: "The Nat.JOC would no doubt return to this subject at their next meeting on Tuesday 5 September, now that it was on their agenda, and members were aware that each of them was approaching the question from a similar position."[7] The reason that a coup was being considered was made clear in a personal

---

1 Ibid.
2 Flower, K. (1987), pp. 207-208; Smith, I. (1997), p. 260.
3 See Chap. 21.
4 Smith, I. (1997), p. 260.
5 Top Secret and personal telegram, 30/8/78. Ref.: Mirimba Tel No. 424 of 25/8/1978 (British Archives).
6 Ibid.
7 Top Secret telegram 30/8/78. Ref.: Mirimba Tel No 424 of 25/8/1978 (British Archives).

telegram from the Foreign and Commonwealth Office to the Secretary of State in Washington on 5 September 1978: "It is because they (Nat.Joc) despair of influencing Ian Smith within the relationship established by the 1969 Constitution, that they are prepared to consider a coup d'etat. In terms of the 1969 Constitution they are discussing treason. It is not a soft option for them, but goes against all their instincts and training, quite apart from personal risk."

In a letter to Prime Minister Callaghan[1] and his memorandum to the British Cabinet on 5 September 1978,[2] David Owen outlined Nat.JOC's discussions regarding the renunciation of UDI and the serious national, regional and international consequences of such action. He advised against this route, saying that Nat.JOC's first responsibility was to pressurise Ian Smith to negotiate, so as to come to a serious agreement with Joshua Nkomo and Robert Mugabe. David Owen concluded his memorandum to the Cabinet on 5 September 1978 by asking his colleagues for approval:

> (a) to continue to try to bring about a negotiated settlement on the basis of the AAP as elaborated in discussion between all the parties over the last year, and in particular to endorse, if it can be negotiated, the Transitional Constitution in annexes A and B;
> (b) to continue to make it clear that a unilateral renunciation of UDI changes nothing, unless it is clearly acknowledged that the first priority is a negotiated ceasefire and a settlement between all the parties;
> (c) to treat a unilateral renunciation of UDI which is not based on the acknowledgement, and on acceptance of the AAP as a basis for negotiation, as merely the transfer of power from one illegal regime to another illegal regime, and to demand negotiations and convene a conference between the new regime and all the other parties;
> (d) to welcome a unilateral renunciation of UDI only if it were firmly based on acceptance of the broad principles of the AAP and agreement to negotiate a ceasefire. In such circumstances:
>
> - to act immediately calling an Emergency Meeting of the Security Council, circulate the draft UN Resolution attached to annex C for consultation with the Front Line and Patriotic Front, and immediately to publish the draft Order-in-Council attached to Annex B;
> - to recall Parliament immediately or, if an election was in progress, to discuss our action with all political parties in Britain;
> - to offer to contribute urgently to any UN peacekeeping force at least one and possibly two battalions to add credibility to the force and demonstrate our own commitment to our proposals;
> - to put in place a Resident Commissioner only when the Security Council and Parliament have endorsed our action when there was a reasonable prospect of a genuine ceasefire or at least the clear assurance that Mozambique and Zambia, the host nations of ZANU and ZAPU respectively, would clamp down on any continued fighting.[3]

In my subsequent interview with Lord Owen, he stated: "One thing in particular, I think that Ian Smith was very tough on letting anybody really know about the true military situation, and I think that's what was leading to this incipient revolt – that Walls and Flower knew the truth, which I knew, that ZANU was winning this war, and that they were very soon going to be faced by Mugabe, and I think they understood that a proper involvement of all the leaders might just stave that off."[4]

Nat.JOC's discussions about a coup and return to legitimacy with Britain were curtailed when ZIPRA shot down the first civilian Viscount aircraft *Hunyani* on 3 September 1978. This incident is discussed in detail in Part 2.

---

[1] Top Secret document. Ref.: PM/78/84, dated 1/9/1978.

[2] Secret memorandum to British Cabinet CP (78) 89 on 5/9/1978.

[3] Ibid.

[4] Oral interview with Lord Owen at his residence, 19/3/2018.

White Rhodesians Face the Truth

Rhodesians were beginning to sense their ominous political situation. On 29 August 1978, official figures released showed that 1,342 whites left Rhodesia in July with only 231 entering, a net loss of 1,111 individuals.[1] The net loss of 1,245 whites in August 1978 was expected to accelerate after the Viscount incident. Despite the alleged harassment of Rhodesian Customs officials at points of departure, the rate of white emigration had risen to 60 a day.[2] When I initiated the official Sub.JOC Rusape SB duty roster on 16 November 1976, there were two rotating officers, four white D/S/Os, four African staff, three white field reservists and two bases at Rusape and Inyanga. On my departure at the end of April 1978, there were a total of 13 bases including the *mujibha* farm, staffed by the two rotating SB officers, 22 white police staff, 20 white field reservists and 10 African staff members. These figures remained relatively static until the end of the war.

Officially, 11,241 whites fled Rhodesia with their meagre R$1,500 allowance, prior to having their assets thoroughly scrutinised: 1,490 left in September 1978 alone. Unofficially, scores left on "holiday" as the holiday allowance "generously" allowed R$500 per individual. For the record, many senior government officials also lost hope. On 14 November 1978, *The New York Times* reported: "At least a dozen former Government officials and high-ranking civil servants, some of whom had been outspoken in their professions of resistance to any change in white-led Rhodesia left the country. Reginald Cowper, a former Defence Minister in Mr Smith's Government, was one of these. He left quietly a short time ago for South Africa."[3] Prior to his resignation as Minister of Defence on 14 February 1977, Reginald Cowper had addressed the Selous Scouts. Keith Samler recalled "being at Inkomo Barracks when the Minister of Defence, Reginald Cowper, visited to give the troops a 'pep talk'. As far as I can remember it was held in the WO's and Sgt's mess. The mess was packed with all ranks, Officers et. al. I really don't recall exactly what he said word for word but the salient point he made was that he was proud to be in the company of men who were prepared to die for their country. There was a deathly, (pardon the pun), silence. When he concluded his talk, he was finished as any sort of justifiable human being let alone a cabinet minister. Everybody was totally unimpressed!"[4] Immigration Minister, Wickus de Kock, the man whose job it was to convince people to move to Rhodesia, himself emigrated in 1977.[5] He moved his herd of pedigree cattle to South Africa. P.K. van der Byl was making his future plans by relocating his cattle to South Africa during 1978-79.[6] Former Minister of Agriculture, James Angus Graham, 7th Duke of Montrose, a UDI signatory, emigrated to South Africa in 1979. In an *Illustrated Life Rhodesia* article of the mid-70s, Graham suggested his family would remain in Rhodesia for future generations.[7]

A former member of the Information Section in the Ministry of Foreign Affairs, Mark Oxley, commented: "The Rhodesian Government, a party controlled by the white commercial farming sector, had no coherent information strategy, so mixed messages were being put out every day. In the absence of a central information strategy every Ministry or Department involved with the war felt free to put out information or give private press briefings which ranged from downright lies to what could only be described as the imaginings of people far removed from reality. There were the official Department of Information press releases, press conferences and facilitated trips under the control of the redoubtable Dusty Miller; there was an Information Section in the Ministry of Foreign Affairs (of which I was part), where I think we did some useful work in putting out Fact Papers which were facts shaded with propaganda. We also gave confidential press briefings where we dropped a couple of major clangers. Comops was a world of its own. SB/CIO kept very much to

1 British Confidential documents: Rhodesia Department Monthly Summary No 8, August 1978.
2 British Confidential documents: Rhodesia Department Monthly Summary No 9, September 1978.
3 Cowper resigned from the RF in February 1977 and joined the Rhodesian Action Party, an ultra-right-wing party that was crushed in a General Election on 31/8/1977.
4 Keith Samler email 29/8/2018.
5 Brownell, J. (2010), p. 123.
6 Informant worked as a customs-clearing agent at Beit Bridge and wished to remain anonymous.
7 https://en.wikipedia.org/wiki/James_Graham,_7th_Duke_of_Montrose.

itself but was a very valuable source of discreet information to the international press corps in Rhodesia; the trouble is they told nobody else. PK van der Byl had his own outlet through Lin Mehmel and Col. Vernon Gillespie, who remained a serving CIA officer the entire time. The trouble is that you start to believe your own propaganda."[1]

Global Threats

At a meeting with David Owen on 1 June 1978, held at the USA State Department, Cy Vance, the Secretary of State, advised that 50 tons of Soviet material, thought to be artillery, had arrived in Lusaka for ZIPRA.[2] When the new Zimbabwe Rhodesia Constitution came into effect in June 1979, few Rhodesians realised, as D. Martin put it "how close Rhodesia had been to becoming the focal point of an internationalised war in Southern Africa which would have certainly brought the South Africans, Cubans and Russians into the conflict and forced the Western powers to decide which side they supported".[3]

On 2 May 2019, I asked Lord Owen if he was aware that on 15 May 1978 James Callaghan (Britain's PM) offered Kenneth Kaunda's Zambian Government £15 million to entice them away from inviting Cuba to launch a full-scale attack to bring the Rhodesian conflict to an end.[4] The following was his complete reply which I include to demonstrate there was no simple answer to Rhodesia's predicament. There were regional, African continent and global considerations and implications involved in all decisions and actions. Lord Owen replied:

> There is no question of doubt that we were paying money to the Zambian Government in ways declared and undeclared to keep them as Commonwealth members and for them not to align themselves with the Soviet Union or with Cuba, who at the time had troops on the ground in Angola.
>
> On 11 May 1978, 4,000 troops invaded Zaire from Angola and took possession of the town of Kolwezi. The Belgians were the former colonial power and Henré Simonet, the Belgian Foreign Minister, was someone I was in constant touch with during the crisis. The troops were predominantly from the Congo but had been trained by the Cubans in Angola. The Angolans, whether they wished to curb the insurgence or not – and opinion was mixed on this question – did not have the power or the capacity to stop the insurgence going across the very long border. It was clear to both us, France and Belgium, that an international rescue operation was essential. President Giscard d'Estaing was thought by the Belgians to be muscling in, where they should be the leading power, for the purpose of displaying French power in Africa generally. There was looting, and many rapes by the insurgent forces were reported. The Government of Zaire demanded help and it was clear that an intervention on humanitarian grounds was justified and called for. The Belgian and French troops were flown down in big American C-F transport planes to Zaire and the Rh.AF flew down to Zambia planes charged with ferrying in extra supplies if they were needed. The Danish Government held the EC Presidency at the time and had arranged a meeting of Foreign Ministers in the format of a "Schloss Gymnich" to be held in Hesselo. It was very inconvenient for me but I flew to Denmark expecting Henré Simonet to be present and wanting to try and settle differences over Kolwezi between him and the French Foreign Minister, Louis de Guiringaud. Unfortunately Henré Simonet deliberately stayed away. I later gathered his non-attendance reflected considerable differences of approach within the Belgian Cabinet. Eventually the tensions eased between Paris and Brussels and the intervention of French and Belgian troops restored law and order.

---

1 Mark Oxley email 24/7/2020. Ellert, H. and Anderson, D. (2020), p. 73.

2 British Confidential documents: Recorded at the meeting held at the USA State Department 1 June 1978.

3 Martin, D. (1981), p. 305; *The New York Times,* 3/3/1978, section A, p. 2.

4 *The Aberdeen Press and Journal* 16/5/1976.

During this period Callaghan spoke to Kenneth Kaunda on a number of occasions to assure him that we would not allow the same thing to happen to Zambia. Whether or not we increased our financial support at this time I cannot remember but it is very likely and you will have to search the government files. There may have been loose talk in Lusaka, even by Kenneth Kaunda himself who was notoriously emotional, about inviting Cuba in to as you say "launch a full scale attack to bring the Rhodesian conflict to an end" but there is no way that Cuba was in any position at that time to undertake such military action against Rhodesia. They would certainly have offered some political support and some small military support to help Kenneth Kaunda defend Zambia from Rhodesian forces who quite frequently launched attacks on Zambian territory. But that is all they were capable of doing. What Kenneth Kaunda often tried to do was to threaten to call in Russian forces. Later that month a NATO Heads of Government meeting was scheduled for end of May/beginning of June in Washington. Giscard d'Estaing had by then persuaded President Carter to get far more involved in Shaba province in Zaire and was suggesting a Pan African force and an active Western role. At a meeting between Cyrus Vance, de Guiringaud, myself and Hans Dietriech Genscher in the State Department it became clear to me that Cy was uncomfortable with this development but could not detach himself from Carter's position. I expressed deep scepticism about such a Pan African force and afterwards discussed the situation with Callaghan who had arrived for the NATO meeting. I hoped Callaghan would counsel caution in the afternoon session of the Heads of Government. Tindemans, the Belgian President was held back from supporting the French line because Simonet, sitting next to him, was opposed and the two men represented the split in the Belgian Cabinet. Jim Callaghan made a very effective intervention in the debate in which it soon became clear to both Helmut Schmidt and Jimmy Carter that his experience of Africa was deep seated, and went back to his period as shadow Colonial Secretary in the 1950s. He said of course the Soviet Union are causing problems for us in Africa and that they will exploit every difficulty we faced but there were limits to what we could do to solve African problems and that we should be careful about this intervention and exacerbating the situation and making Africa an East/West issue. He was immediately supported by the Prime Ministers of Norway and the Dutch and Danish Prime Ministers and President Carter saw that the Giscard d'Estaing-Zbig Brzezinski line would not carry universal support. The Danish Foreign Minister and myself were completely in accord and I encouraged him with other smaller countries to sponsor an amendment to the final communiqué which was aimed at softening the tough passage about Cuban involvement and East/West confrontation. Callaghan gave a press conference and used the phrase "latter-day Christopher Columbuses" which we discussed beforehand. This made the headlines, and upset Zbig Brzezinski who came into a meeting in the White House between the Carter and Callaghan families waving the UPI tapes but Carter defused the debate by siding with Jim Callaghan.

I give all this history to you because it is important. Callaghan would never have given money to Kenneth Kaunda to stop Cuba launching a full scale attack to bring the Rhodesian conflict to an end because he knew they were not capable of doing such a thing. What he was totally committed to was to buttressing his long standing friend, Kenneth Kuanda, against attacks from Rhodesia and confining Cuba's involvement in Africa as far as possible to Angola. The moment to do that came in the middle of September 1978 when Ian Smith did attack Lusaka with troops and humiliated President Kaunda. On 22 September having had earlier a telephone conversation with a very distressed Kenneth Kaunda, Callaghan flew to Kano in Nigeria to meet him and I travelled with him. At that meeting we gave extra financial support to Kenneth Kaunda and he did not carry out his threat to become involved with the Soviet Union.

As part of that strategy and the more considered UK-American approach to Africa I flew to Moscow on 9 October and had discussions with President Brezhnev and Foreign Minister Gromyko. There were always voices in America and elsewhere for a more dramatic approach to Soviet involvement in Africa. Nowhere was it better illustrated than over the Ogaden when there were those who wished to support the Somali invasion of Ethiopian territory. Vance, myself, Genscher, and de Guiringaud were adamant that we would not support Brzezinski in his demand that we forget the African Union's commitment to no changes in the territorial map of Africa. When, as it was inevitable, the Ethiopians stopped the Somalian adventurism with the aid of Cuban forces – who had come in at the invitation of the Ethiopian government – we were able to say to the Soviet Union we did not support the Somalian invasion and we are not prepared to support the Ethiopians, having reclaimed the Ogaden, to now advance across the international boundary into Somalia. It is also why we gave great attention to achieving a negotiated settlement in South West Africa later to be called Nambia based on a UN resolution. History has shown that this patient, careful but principled approach did block Cuban adventurism in Africa, did lead to a successful Lancaster House conference eventually in December 1979 and eventually to Namibian independence and the peaceful end of apartheid with the release of Nelson Mandela from prison.

Again I give you all this history to caution against the simplicities in your first question.[1]

There was no simple solution to the Rhodesian dilemma!

1 Lord Owen email 23/5/2019.

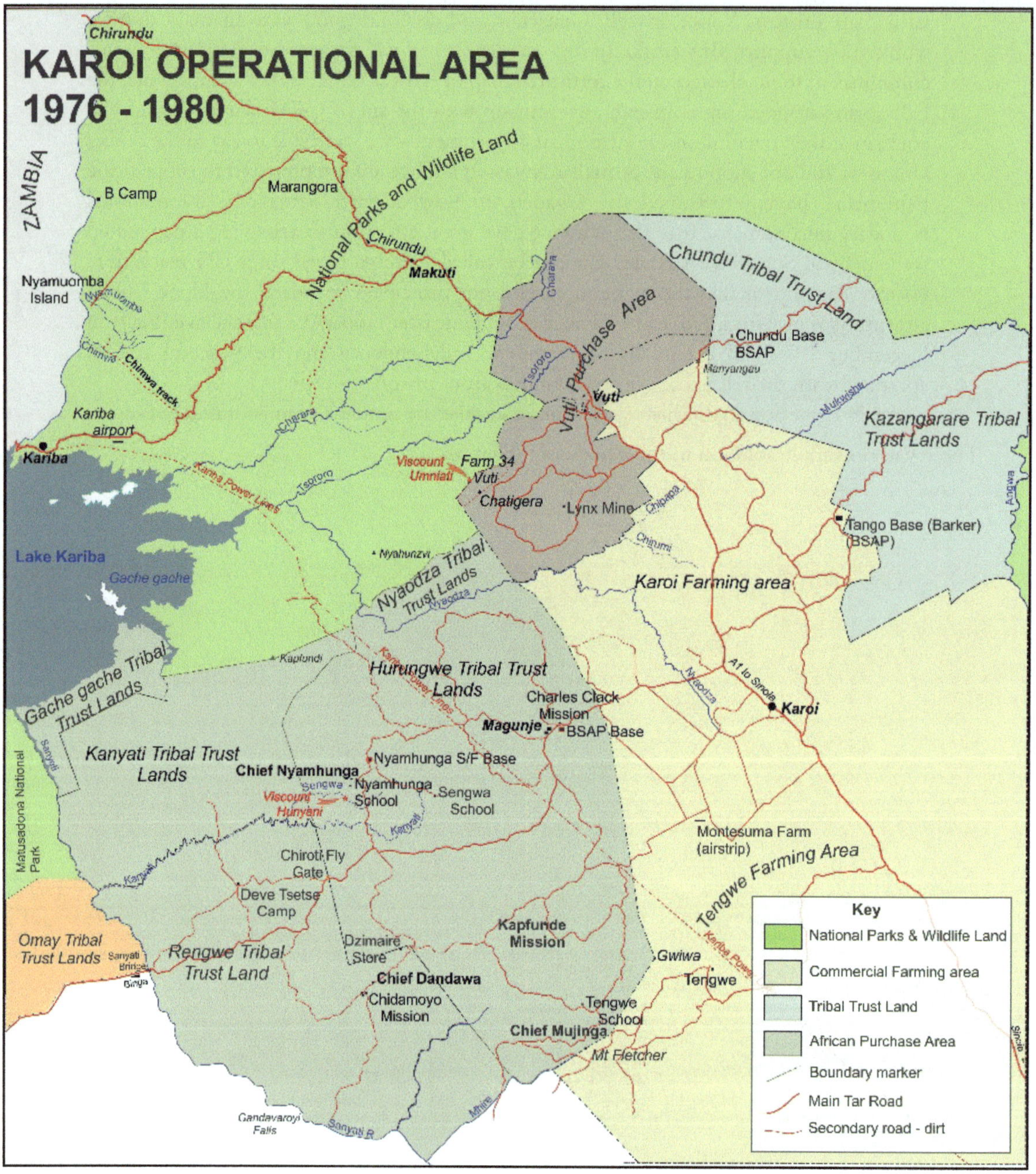
KAROI OPERATIONAL AREA
1976 - 1980
Chirundu
ZAMBIA
B Camp
Marangora
National Parks and Wildlife Land
Chirundu
Makuti
Nyamuomba Island
Chimwa track
Kariba airport
Kariba
Lake Kariba
Gache gache
Kariba Power Lines
Tsororo
Charara
Viscount Umniati
Farm 34 Vuti
Chatigera
Lynx Mine
Vuti Purchase Area
Vuti
Chundu Tribal Trust Land
Chundu Base BSAP
Kazangarare Tribal Trust Lands
Tango Base (Barker) (BSAP)
Nyaodza Tribal Trust Lands
Karoi Farming area
A1 to Sinoia
Karoi
Gache gache Tribal Trust Lands
Hurungwe Tribal Trust Lands
Charles Clack Mission
Magunje
BSAP Base
Kanyati Tribal Trust Lands
Chief Nyamhunga
Nyamhunga S/F Base
Nyamhunga School
Sengwa School
Viscount Hunyani
Matusadona National Park
Chiroti Fly Gate
Deve Tsetse Camp
Montesuma Farm (airstrip)
Tengwe Farming Area
Omay Tribal Trust Lands
Rengwe Tribal Trust Land
Dzimaire Store
Chief Dandawa
Chidamoyo Mission
Kapfunde Mission
Gwiwa
Tengwe
Tengwe School
Chief Mujinga
Mt Fletcher
Sanyati R
Key
National Parks & Wildlife Land
Commercial Farming area
Tribal Trust Land
African Purchase Area
Boundary marker
Main Tar Road
Secondary road - dirt

PART 2

BATTLE FOR HURUNGWE

If you want to know the theory and methods of revolution,
you must take part in revolution.
All genuine knowledge originates in direct experience.
Mao Zedong

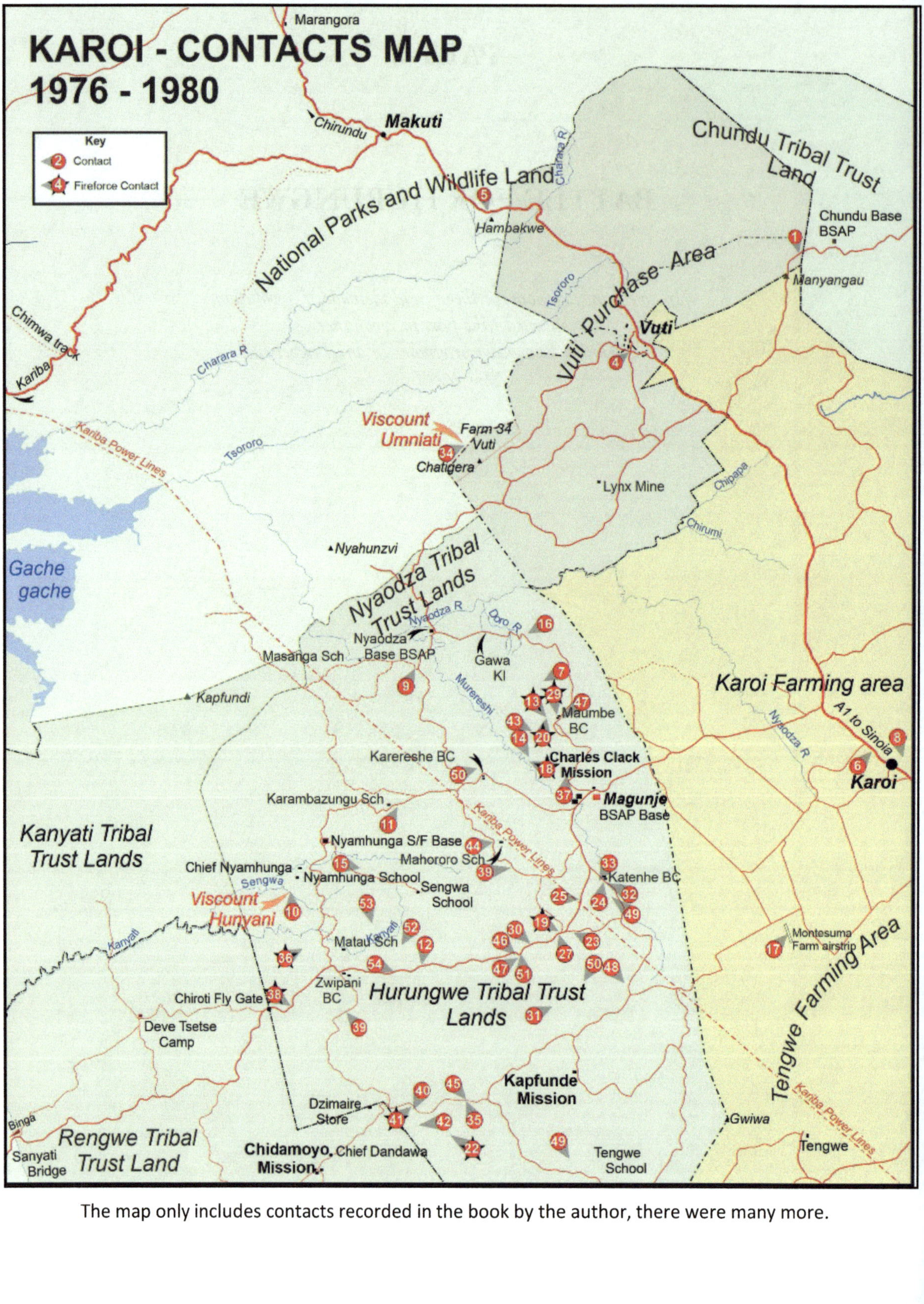

The map only includes contacts recorded in the book by the author, there were many more.

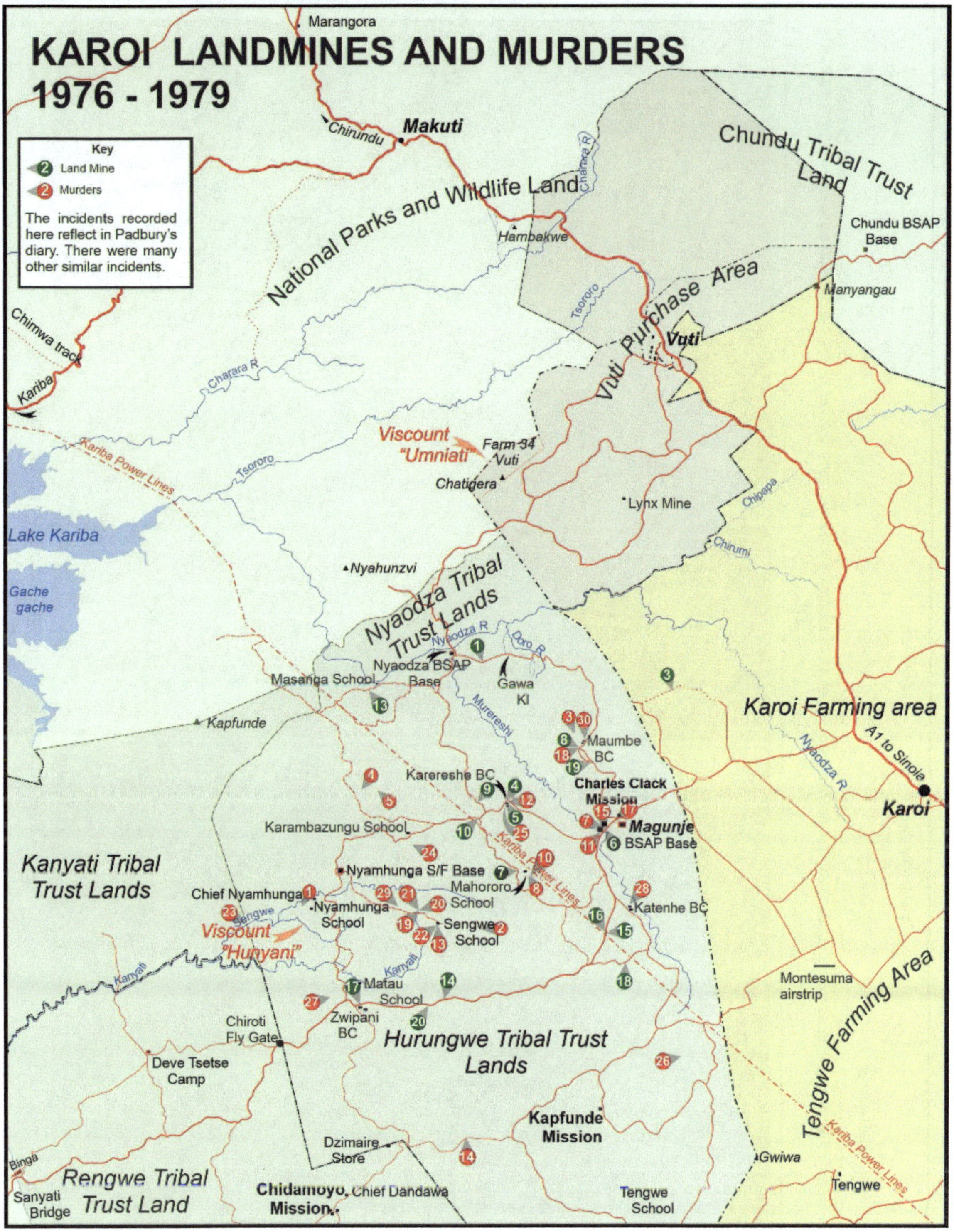

The map only includes includes incidents recorded by the author and does not include the 36 landmines recovered by the RAR as a result of information from the locals.

OP HURRICANE
Salisbury Central Armoury - Ballistics Incidents Map - 1977

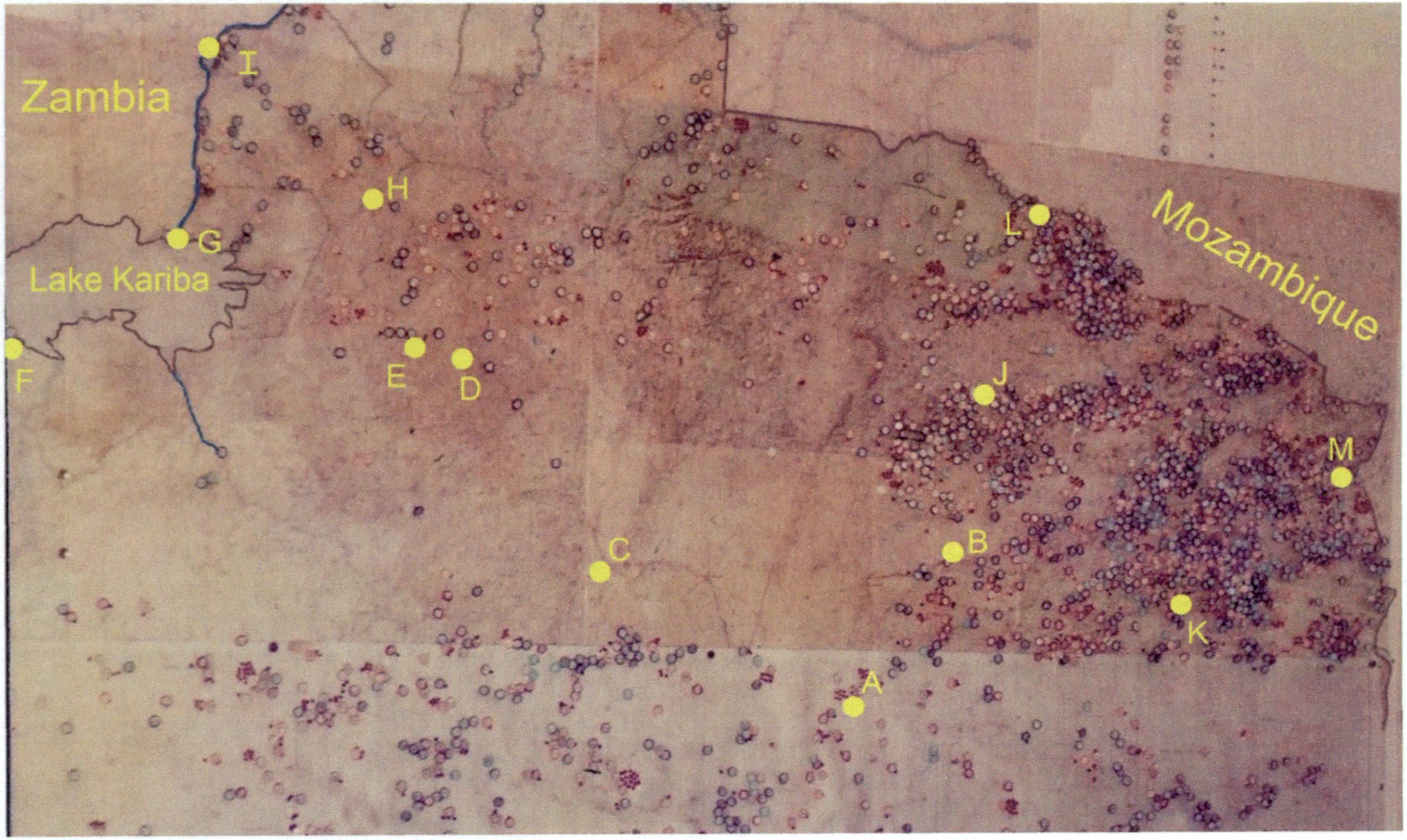

KEY

Incidents include white farm attacks, black and white civilian murders, civilian and Security Force ambushes, landmines and contacts with Security Forces.

Map provided by ballistics expert Paul de Mattos.

A - Salisbury
B - Bindura
C - Sinoia
D - Karoi
E - Magunje
F - Bumi
G - Kariba
H - Makuti
I - Chirundu
J - Mt. Darwin
K - Mtoko
L - Mukumburra
M - Nyamapanda

9 ~ HURUNGWE EARLY DAYS

Progress is impossible without change,
and those who cannot change their minds cannot change anything.
George Bernard Shaw

Mujibhas to Security Force Auxiliaries

In the government's scramble to defend their new political dispensation, gain military ascendancy and international recognition, permission was finally given to mobilise the masses. This decision reversed the Rhodesian Front's adamant opposition to the arming and advancement of Africans. Dennis Anderson pointed out:

> There was an increasing realisation that the security forces could no longer cope with the growing insurgency threat throughout the country. To say that we were overstretched and grasping at straws was an understatement as the insurgents had achieved what they had set out to do, to stretch our resources to the limit. Shortly after the March 3rd, 1978 Internal Agreement, a meeting was held at PGHQ at which Provincial commanders and JOC Officers attended convened by the Commissioner P.K. Allum. He stated there was an immediate need to recruit at least 1000 men to be known as Security Force Auxiliaries (SFAs).
>
> I was accused of being negative when I asked where the support elements for the exercise were to be found, as from my experience, if sufficient manpower (including experienced Special Branch representatives, military personnel and logistics), could not be deployed then the exercise was a nonstarter. It was more than just deploying a few men into a TTL to place boots on the ground. However, "god" had spoken so the various *mujibha* farms became training centres for SFAs.
>
> The potential to recruit and train locals "en masse" for deployment into the operational areas in order to gain political support for internal Political parties was suddenly required and envisaged, and the idea of the SFAs was conceived. This overturned the previously held view of the RF when the Minister of Defence, Lance Smith and Hostes Nicolle his Secretary, when addressing the Security Council in 1969 stated, "only over our dead bodies will we agree to firearms being passed to Africans".[1] Hostes Nicolle was an advocate of apartheid whose actions epitomised the RF's intentions to "keep the native in his place".[2]

It became evident SF were visitors in TTLs, operating on a search-and-destroy, uplift-and-regroup basis: locating and attacking insurgents then abandoning the people to resident ZANLA sections who governed them. Military deployments into the TTLs were always on a temporary basis, after which they left the area abandoning both the locals and any progress which may have been achieved. The insurgents knew this. They were kept informed of military and Fire Force deployments by their intelligence networks which gave them freedom to act by laying landmines, ambushes or simply disappearing undercover. On this basis alone, the SF could hardly expect co-operation from a population who were simply pawns in a society suffering during a revolutionary struggle. The only option, I believed, to stem the tide militarily, was through the SFAs. It was not possible, from my perspective, for the SF to create a permanent presence on the ground but the SFAs could more than adequately do so.

1 Flower, K. (1987), p. 113.
2 Ibid., p. 40; Dennis Anderson email 28/12/2019.

The *mujibha* system gave way to a Special Branch vision of introducing Security Force Auxiliaries, later known as *Pfumo reVanhu* ("Spear of the People"). Operation Favour was launched with SB officer, C/Supt. Michael McGuinness ("Mr Mac")[1] in command. Financial support was provided by the South African Directorate of Military Intelligence and the Sultanate of Oman.[2] The strategy behind SFAs was for SB to recruit Africans from their own TTLs through the mechanisms of the participating African political parties. Thereafter, they would be trained, armed and later deployed into their home areas to defend their people, permanently occupy the ground and attack insurgents. It was believed that SFAs would stabilise the war by significantly increasing the number of "boots on the ground" and pave the way for African politicians to accrue support and votes for their various political parties. In principle, we were developing our own, permanently deployed and armed *mujibha* cells. In my opinion, SFAs were a progressive step forward from the *mujibha* farm we established in the Rusape district. Members of SB were attached to the various African political parties to handle the intelligence, political aspects and deployments. For the system to work, there needed to be a connection and flow of information between the three agencies: political, military and the local population. There was no room for autonomy, the common denominator in all three being intelligence. Hence the necessity for seasoned, mature Special Branch leadership to coordinate the political, military (SFAs) and the people. Sadly, in my estimation, such was in short supply.

Generally, ZANLA and ZIPRA did not deploy into their home areas, as during the war, *vatengesi* would inevitably be beaten and often killed. Rule was established by the "barrel of a gun", which was easier to impose in the absence of family, relatives and friends. Rule by the "barrel of a gun" is a sure sign of intent of regime change as opposed to attending to the GNA of the people. SFAs deployed in "foreign" TTLs could behave in a similar manner because there were fewer restraints. Deploying them into homeground gave us a distinct advantage as they connected to their family and friends, gaining immediate access to intelligence and remaining to permanently protect them. This also appeased spirit mediums who might, in the event of intra-communal violence, convey the dissatisfaction of ancestral spirits to murder and violence with dire consequences for the perpetrators.

One significant problem facing SF, in particular SB, was the understanding of a shifting political spectrum. Many of our former nationalist enemies were now our friends. We were joining them, they were not joining us. White rule was coming to an end and African majority rule was fast becoming a reality. Naturally, previously held prejudices do not dissipate overnight. A paradigm shift in mindset was called for. The prejudiced needed to be liberated from their perceptions and therein lay the challenge. Up to this point, the SF had been directed by a political agenda, that of the Rhodesian Front and supported by its legislation. This stance clearly identified ZANLA, ZIPRA and their supporters as the enemy, hence a call for their defeat. Dramatically, this standpoint changed, with SF required to embrace Africans and, collectively, defeat the enemy. What was in doubt was whether years of well-orchestrated white colonial and Rhodesian Front propaganda could be dispensed with instantaneously. Whites expected to lead simply because they were white. A rigid and racial hierarchy prevailed, as opposed to lateral leadership, in which uniting with the locals and combining skills for a common goal was called for.

Clear tactics on how to penetrate and occupy the ground needed to be developed. Traditional command-and-control systems adapted to facilitate a true people's army. This called for a major digression in the existing military approach which found it difficult to deviate from their ingrained, fundamental approach to defeating the enemy: "kills win wars". Previous traditional military tactics prevailed, despite the Security Forces inability to stem the overwhelming flood of insurgents from Mozambique and Zambia into Rhodesia. An entirely different approach to the war was required. Thinking, strategies and tactics had to change. The SF were strangers in the operational areas: the TTLs. The principal requirement called for was, in fact, the SF becoming one with the people. The

---

[1] C/Supt. Michael John Peter McGuiness, OC Special Branch Selous, Scouts and OC SB Op. Favour. Affectionately known as "Mr Mac".

[2] Ellert, H. & Anderson, D. (2020), p. 330.

danger was that the SFAs would be considered an extension of the military strategy of "kills win wars". Certainly, kills were set to increase but this would not win the war.

Politicisation of the SFAs in training and in the field was essential as it would keep them motivated, providing a purpose and cause to persevere for, particularly in the face of adversity and even death. Equally important was the political education of the training staff responsible for the education of these new recruits. It was essential to share a common vision. The political message carried into the field, and conduct of the military, had to identify with and impart the coming political dispensation. The struggle was not limited to winning the armed battles but rather winning the support of the people. That in turn would lead to winning the battles and ultimately the war. ZANLA and ZIPRA were winning the war simply because they, at the outset, had gained the support of the people.

It was obvious to me that the military had a clearly defined role: "Defeat the enemy." That, after all, was their area of expertise. They were not trained or equipped to live among the people and remain to defend them. Troops would come and go in pursuit of specific aims and objectives. They were not to be confused with the SFAs whose role it was to dwell among their own people, occupy the ground, defend them and, where and when possible, eliminate the enemy. Simultaneously, a conducive environment needed to be created in which politicians could address the people, impart a shared vision and attend to African grievances and aspirations. The challenge was to integrate the two disciplines, to defeat the enemy and live among the people. The question was, would they? I did not envision these two elements combining successfully. It seemed to me the deployment of SFAs was a crisis-driven political decision to resolve an ever-deepening tragedy. This strategy was primarily to achieve a maximum military presence on the ground to influence voting in the forthcoming elections. The future thereafter was uncertain: I was not optimistic!

Karoi, 1978

I was offered the opportunity to command the SFA operations of Karoi for Hurungwe TTL which Geoff Price said was probably one of the most hostile areas in the country. Zimbabwe People's Revolutionary Army (ZIPRA) insurgents occupied Hurungwe. It was also the graveyard of the civilian aircraft Viscount *Hunyani* shot down by ZIPRA on 3 September 1978. Of the 56 passengers and crew, 38 were killed on impact. Ten survivors were murdered by ZIPRA with eight escaping. A *mujibha* farm was situated at Karoi but with no Special Branch personnel specifically assigned to the unit. The *mujibha* farm at Sinoia was in similar dire circumstances. Hurungwe had been placed under a type of "martial licence" in September 1978.

It was obvious to me this posting was to be a significant challenge as I now had the opportunity to implement the knowledge and experience I had gained from involvement with the *mujibha* system. As Commander of the SFAs, I would also be facing ZIPRA insurgents for the first time. My understanding of them was that they were more aggressive and active than ZANLA. This presented a unique opportunity to develop and implement strategies and tactics to mobilise the people and conduct the operation in the manner I saw fit. Success would require consolidating the years of acumen I had gained in my active service in the war. I also viewed my new posting as an opportunity to serve Rhodesia as the country's leaders negotiated the path to majority rule. At the same time, however, my position called on me to abandon allegiances to the ruling white minority and military/intelligence forces, which, as I saw matters, were opposed to much-needed progressive change in strategies and tactics required for victory in the war. My personal mindset was shifting rapidly. It was to be a lonely and difficult journey into uncharted territory but refreshing and exciting. Dennis Anderson made the comment: "John Padbury was the right man for Hurungwe as he had vast experience with the *mujibha* concept and had been involved with the inauguration of the SFAs in Op Hurricane area."[1]

I considered myself well qualified for the task in Hurungwe having pioneered the successful *mujibha* system at Rusape and been involved in many Security Forces deployments using various

1 Dennis Anderson email 26/12/2015.

strategies. Significantly, I had been involved in directing the Fire Force into contact areas using informers and understood the difficulties of this unique procedure, requiring meticulous planning to ensure success. However, it needs to be noted that my deployments were not without blemish and enormous disappointments. Notwithstanding, as in any major war, further opportunities were always present. In my view, gaining the upper hand in the war rested on gaining the support of the local population. This was my outlook for Hurungwe.

Situation in Hurungwe TTL

I had identified 12 phases as essential to our achieving victory in Hurungwe. Each phase is laid out below and provides an indication of the thinking, the period, the process and the implementation of our strategies. This was a well-planned but drawn-out process. I introduce each phase as ***SFA Strategies Phase 1*** and so on.

SFA Strategies Phase 1: Gather historical and current political and military intelligence for the operational area

On 18 September 1978, I travelled to Karoi and lodged at the Twin Rivers Motel. My intention was to spend time personally observing the local scene, while at the same time, announcing my arrival. It was not my desire to plough headlong into the operation. Rather, I chose to first observe, witness and acquaint myself with the "key players" in the police and military forces in Karoi and Hurungwe. I also needed to be acquainted with the background affairs of Hurungwe, together with the current operations of both the SF and, as much as possible, ZIPRA before formulating any specific plans and strategies.

Karoi fell under Sub.JOC Sinoia which in turn was under the jurisdiction of JOC Hurricane, the operational command centre for the entire Lomagundi police district. Sub.JOC Sinoia was staffed by two Territorial Force (TF) officers: Col. Darrell Van Zyl rotated duties with Maj. Musson. The rest of the staff were Supt. Nigel Seaward (CID/SB), District Commissioner Stan Fynes-Clinton and Dis.Pol., C/Supt. Tim Allen or Supt. Bob Bedingham.[1] Dis.Pol. Minor (Bob Bedingham's official title) was the designated BSAP Uniform JOC Officer at Sub.JOC Sinoia, although he shared the responsibility with Tim Allen, the uniform branch OC Lomagundi District (Dis.Pol.). Bedingham's duties included the control and deployment of the PRAW and PATU, co-ordination of COIN training, management of sitreps, visits to BSAP stations and posts over and above normal monthly Dis.Pol. visits, and meetings with the farmers, which helped stabilise the community. Bob attended daily meetings at the Sub.JOC where events throughout the operational area were discussed. These discussions included landmine incidents, contacts, farm attacks, murders perpetrated by ZANLA and ZIPRA insurgents, assessment of intelligence and deployment of SF. "Frozen areas" for the Selous Scouts and SFAs were carefully monitored and mapped as were deployments and locstats of all the SF in an intricate web of radio communications which were monitored around the clock. There was close direct liaison between Sub.JOC Sinoia and JOC Hurricane.[2]

D/S/O Mike Reeler was the Special Branch officer controlling the SB Karoi area, including Hurungwe TTL. His role included the co-ordination of intelligence gathered from operational areas, liaison with various SF military personnel to arrange deployments, and attend to various insurgent incidents. He was involved in the *mujibha* farm, situated nearby Karoi. It was a low-key operation due to time and operational constraints. Reeler, while simultaneously engaged in operational duties and under limited time restrictions, was overseeing the group to the best of his abilities. Notwithstanding his enthusiasm, the SFAs required a dedicated, experienced SB leader to ensure a greater measure of competence at all levels of the operation. I took over the Karoi *mujibhas* as they progressed to an official SFA operation during 1978. Grey Mutemasango from the UANC was already active in the area and assisted moving approximately 12 *mujibhas* to the Sinoia farm which

[1] Insp. Bob Bedingham was promoted to Supt. on 1/8/1977 and transferred to Lomagundi District Headquarters based at Sinoia.

[2] Bob Bedingham email 3/4/2016.

was to be our first training facility. Grey was a veteran insurgent externally trained in Algeria in the early 1960s. He was captured when he led FROLIZI[1] forces into Rhodesia in the 1970s and released in terms of the 3 March 1978 Agreement on 13 April 1978. Special Branch orchestrated the release of one hundred detainees of whom 42 went to Muzorewa, 29 to Sithole and the remainder were held in reserve by SB for training and political-orientation duties at the training camps. Grey was placed in overall command of the UANC team.

Mike Reeler explained: "While there was no Sub.JOC at Karoi, we came under the jurisdiction of Sub.JOC Sinoia, and we had an 'informal JOC'. We held regular meetings attended by the local army Commander, DC, Member i/c, Special Branch and Ground coverage details, and the Police Reserve who also manned the radio. When army were resident in the area, they provided 24-hour coverage with their radio signals branch. Additionally, Agric.Alert[2] provided 24-hour radio service for the farmers. These meetings were normally at 8 a.m. – 9 a.m. Maps of the operational areas were also displayed."[3] I did not attend these meetings and will explain later.

The SFAs in Karoi were an autonomous Special Branch operation, reporting directly to C/Supt. "Mac" McGuinness, Special Branch Bindura, via Supt. Geoff Price, my immediate superior officer. McGuinness's office provided the funding and logistical support, training facilities and staffing, weapons, clothing and other vital necessities for the group. Training staff were recruited through "Mr Mac's" well-established network which reached former SAS, RLI and police members. There were plenty of quality men available. There was no need to headhunt individuals.

As the operation progressed, Special Forces assisted with logistics. Politically, we had immediate access to Bishop Muzorewa through the UANC network. The SFAs were not an SAS operation[4] or any other specific military organisation. I had several members of various branches from the SF working under my command. These included the RLI, Support Unit, Police Reserve and former SAS members. Locally, we linked to SB Karoi commanded by Mike Reeler and the Sub.JOC at Sinoia for matters such as PRAW, deployments, demarcation of "frozen areas" and Fire Force deployments. I also had a direct link to Com.Ops. through my brother, Capt. David Padbury,[5] the Com.Ops. Intelligence Officer. When we were operational, David evaluated our strategies and tactics and reported this information to Brigadier (later General) Barnard.

Background to Hurungwe TTL

The district of Hurungwe is situated in Mashonaland West Province, to the extreme north-west of Zimbabwe. It was renowned for hunting expeditions and the control of the scourge of tsetse flies. Hurungwe was of insignificant importance in the mind of the government, until after World War Two when commercial farms were made available to white servicemen who had fought for Britain. These farmers transformed the district into a primarily tobacco-growing area. This resettlement was augmented by chiefdoms being relocated from the Zambezi Valley as a result of the construction of Kariba Dam when 57,00 Tongas were displaced. Additional chiefdoms from Gwelo and Lomagundi were, for various reasons, including land acquisition for commercial white farmers, also moved there. The result of these relocations was that Hurungwe became the gathering place of various ethnic African groups brought together due to colonial administration.

Unfortunately, most information held in archives concerns the removal of groups under specific traditional leaders relocated to Hurungwe. Information regarding those who were already in

---

1 FROLIZI: Front for the Liberation of Zimbabwe. The President was James Chikerema. It was a Zambian-based militant nationalist organisation that fought against the government of Rhodesia from its founding in October 1971 until 1973, when the Organisation of African Unity's Liberation Committee moved in favour of the other two principal Zimbabwean liberation movements. Website: https://en.wikipedia.org/wiki/Front_for_the_Liberation_of_Zimbabwe, Accessed 15/3/2017.

2 Radio system specifically for communications with farmers.

3 Mike Reeler: Oral discussion, Cape Town, December 2015.

4 Confirmed by Garth Barrett email 24/11/2015; SAS Regimental Sgt. Maj. Piet Allen telephone discussion 3/12/2016.

5 Capt. Padbury: Com.Ops. Intelligence Officer, 1977 to early 1979 and then SAS Intelligence Officer.

Hurungwe before the forced removals is scanty. Early African settlers were sparse and included Chief Nematombo and his headman in the Nyangawe area and Chief Dendera in the Magunje area. ZIPRA insurgents murdered Chief Dendera on 1 June 1979 on allegations of "selling out" and refusing to protect insurgents who came to operate in his area.[1] Chief Mujinga and his headman, Chimusimbe, and Chief Kazangarare, were also early settlers. Hurungwe is generally a region of the Korekore people, though the Karanga and other ethnic groups also constitute a sizeable proportion of the local population.[2]

Until 1944, on creation of Hurungwe as a separate district, it was a district of Lomagundi. Rutherford in his work *Working on the Margins*, points out that, until after World War Two and the mooting of the colonial administration for this becoming an ex-soldier's resettlement scheme, the district was of no commercial or economic value in the minds of government. When Hurungwe did become a separate district in 1944, there were 10 white farmers and about 19,000 Africans. Some 8,000 people occupied unassigned land.[3] These resettlements caused numerous disputes among locals and the colonial administration, which affected the locals' response to ZIPRA insurgents during the war. For example, Chief Chanetsa was removed from his home in Umbowe, in Makonde district, as a result of white commercial farmland expansion.[4] After a second move, for the same reason, he was finally settled in Hurungwe at Chanetsa Kraal. His demotion came when the DC from Mwami (Miami), who was remembered as *Nyamambishi* (uncooked/raw meat), told him to prepare to move to Sanyati after the rainy season. This is said to have infuriated Chanetsa who, outraged, fired his old muzzle-loading gun at the government representative, narrowly missing him. The DC retaliated by demoting him from chief to headman.[5] As Chanetsa lived near Magunje, which became the HQ for the SF and SFAs, he did not oppose government forces but became notorious for cattle rustling from white commercial farmers. Cattle rustling was a strategy of striking a blow at the economy of the country.[6]

A second illustration of the growing local resentment to whites in general is Joseph Mudzimu. He and his people were relocated from the Zambezi Valley floor to facilitate the Lake Kariba scheme. His dislike of the colonial system was triggered when his tribe were forced to move from Gova in the Zambezi Valley, their home since the mid-16th century, to pave the way for the construction of this dam.[7] Gova comprised a Korekore group of Shona subsistence farmers living along the banks of the lower Zambezi River. Crop agriculture was undertaken along the river as seasonal flood waters receded. Farmers did not need cattle to plough but rather utilised the traditional labourer's hoe to till the damp soil and plant maize, beans, peas and other traditional crops. Wild game was hunted free of game laws. When the people under the headship of Mudzimu arrived in Hurungwe, they were confronted by a drastic change of circumstances as the former resources available to them were no longer obtainable. Game-hunting laws imposed by the authority of the "colonial master" were particularly damaging to these rural inhabitants. Mr Simakani, later to become a ZIPRA insurgent, recalled that his father told him that in Hurungwe they were barred from hunting as they had previously done in Gova. It was pointed out to the family that the area "beyond the fence" was a game reserve. An individual or group unlawfully crossing the boundary was considered a poacher and, if found guilty, would be severely punished.[8]

Hatred for whites increased as their alternative to game-hunting, namely farming, was not lucrative. To compound the locals' frustrations, draught animals such as cattle easily succumbed to diseases spread by tsetse fly. This meant that until 1980 there were few heads of cattle in the district. Another primary hurdle was the absence of major rivers for irrigation and gardening, as was the case

1 Dr Chakawa, J. (2015), p. 187; Karoi Murder Map 3.
2 Dr Chakawa, J. (2015), p. lii.
3 Rutherford, B. (2000), p. 18.
4 Dr Chakawa, J. (2015), p. lv.
5 Chanetsa regained his chieftainship in 2016, Dr J. Chakawa WhatsApp discussion 20/1/2019.
6 Ibid., p. lvii; Ranger, T. (1985), Chap. 5, p. 180.
7 Dr. Chakawa, J. (2015), p. lxviii; Beach, D. (1980), pp. 72, 260, maps 6, 7 and 8.
8 Ibid. Dr. Chakawa, J., *passim.*

in Gova. Simakani revealed that it seemed to his people they had been abandoned to starve. Worse still, they had been cut off from relatives living across the Zambezi River. In early 1960, each family was compelled by the government to retain only four cattle. The remainder were sold for not more than one pound each. One affected resident, Mr Jera, was furious at these impositions and restrictions yet powerless to react as "the white men were too strong".[1] His hatred for whites intensified with the coinciding of blacks being forced to dig contour ridges, a highly labour-intensive task. Mr Jera and family were poorly educated on the benefits of these ridges. As a result, their assumption was that the move was intended to merely make their lives more difficult. Their loathing was also directed against the local agricultural demonstrator, Mr Bwanya, whose duty it was to enforce these unpopular pieces of legislation.[2]

Mudzimu was particularly arrogant towards the white district commissioner on his demotion from chief to headman. Although he acknowledged his error in accepting bride wealth for his already married daughter, his punishment by the DC was more than he could bear.[3] He became a loyal and avid supporter of ZIPRA and was later appointed one of their judges. He was also involved in a Fire Force contact on 7 December 1978. Such were the complexities of the people residing in Hurungwe. Understandably, these and a host of other forms of discrimination, resulted in dissatisfaction with the colonial administration.

The following is a copy of an introductory report I submitted to SB and the UANC on my interpretation of the circumstances in Hurungwe. It was also my intention to present the strategies I used to deploy the people's army. My report was submitted on 15 February 1979. I have introduced it at this junction, in order to clarify the situation we faced in Hurungwe:

> All aspects of life are based on a cell system, the body is made up of cells, plants are made of cells, trees are made of cells, politics is based on cells, communism is based on cells and the present terrorism affecting Rhodesia is based on a cell system.
>
> Communism and Socialism have been two words greatly feared by the Europeans (whites) of Rhodesia but very few have studied, in any detail, their ideologies and correlated them to the situation we find ourselves in, in the country, today.
>
> I feel it important that we should first understand that the majority African population is based on a social (Socialism) structure which was traditionally based around the chiefs. Terrorists have successfully broken down the tribal system.
>
> When I talk about African Socialism, I refer to a system of communal co-existence that involves communal ploughing, reaping of crops, and so on. A society that shared their lives, taking care of each other and involved in all aspects of life together. For example, traditionally when an African community gets together and harvests crops, the family owning the crop brews beer for the neighbours who come together to assist in the work of harvesting as a communal activity and obligation. This is just one example of the form of African Socialism I am referring to.
>
> Our European community has attempted unsuccessfully to break the African away from his social ways by introducing foreign religions and massive labour recruitment to support the expansion of cash crop agriculture and other capitalist enterprises. We drew the African away from his traditional ways in his rural settings (TTL) and introduced him to working for cash wages on white owned farms and in corporate mining ventures. We totally disrupted his family and way of life as the young men were drawn into centres where they could find labour and thus money to survive and pay the taxes demanded by the Government. When in urban areas, Africans employed as servants could not legally reside with their family members who were invariably left behind in the TTLs.
>
> African workers rarely had leave to go home to their family, even when bereaved they were often unable to attend the very important traditional burial ceremonies because their

1 Ibid., pp. lxviii - lxix.

2 Ibid., p. lxix; Ranger, T. (1985), Chap. 5, pp. 190-191.

3 Dr Chakawa, J. (2015), *passim*.

employers chose not to believe that a death had occurred! On the other hand, Christmas and Public holidays were regular occasions when urban workers were able to return home and the exuberant celebrations and family happiness over these periods was testament to the suffering felt by such separation.

African spiritual beliefs were and still are very difficult for Europeans to comprehend. But exist they do and are a very strong influence in the lives of African peoples regardless of what whites like to believe. The European made the mistake of ignoring and disregarding these beliefs (what a man does not understand he is automatically against).

We introduced taxation to the African thus ensuring that he would turn to wage labour as a source of revenue to support his family and to pay Government taxes. This question of taxation is a very delicate one but what he looks at is the amount of tax he pays (bearing in mind his minimal wages), and what he is getting back in turn – relative to his salary. Give an African 50c at a store in a remote part of the TTL and he thinks he can buy the world with it. The point I make is that he earns such minimal salaries that he believes that with the amount given, knowing that the entire population around is contributing the same amount, he expects a lot more should be done for him than he is actually being provided with. He does not understand the great expenses in dipping, paying school teachers, providing books, clinics, grading roads, etc., primarily because his salary is so low. In short, the European achieved the following:

1. Breakdown of the tribal system bearing strongly in mind that the Chief's perception was that the District Commissioner considers himself above the Chiefs – the big white *Ishe* (chief).
2. Introduction, or at least the attempt to introduce, a democratic (Capitalistic) society which was totally foreign to African Socialism.
3. Removal of family life by introducing taxation and forcing the African to find labour.
4. Community life and standards in the TTLs was not seen to greatly improve as the African expected when he paid what he considered a vast sum of money in the form of taxation.
5. The subsequent attempt at the breakdown of African Socialism. However, the bonds of African Socialism became far greater because of the greater inter family dependence with the lack of men (now employed away from home) to cater for family needs.

In other words, the bonds of African Socialism are greater now than they ever have been, and it is evident that they will never be broken.

The study of early Rhodesian History books and particularly EAH Alderson's book on the activities of the Mounted Infantry (1896)[1] during the Mashona rebellion will emphasise our attempts to break down the tribal powers of the chiefs in the Mashonaland areas. Many chiefs were murdered, some surrendered to the authorities to be dealt with by their captor's law, but the young men refused to follow suit and were never defeated. The seeds of revolution were sewn in these early days when we started our attempts to break down the tribal system. It is important to remember that although the chiefs surrendered, their men did not, and the revolutionary war had only just begun.

Having established himself in the country the Europeans commenced the exploitation of minerals and the agricultural possibilities of a potentially wealthy land. I do not intend going into this subject in great detail but the Europeans, primarily concerned with their own wellbeing, never established a thorough-ongoing understanding of the people over whom they ruled.

With the arrival of terrorism in the country the terrorists exploited our following obvious weaknesses:

[1] Alderson, E.A.H. (1971), *passim.*

1. White exploitation of the Africans generally.
2. African taxation.
3. Lack of effective and total intelligence system at grass roots level.
4. The land question (not spoken about by me but obvious!).
5. Loss of contact with the people which is the most important aspect.

The terrorists effectively achieved the following:

1. Support of the people (whether voluntarily or through the barrel of a gun).
2. Cessation of taxes.
3. Further breakdown of the tribal system which they replaced with the *mujibha* system. They did not break down African Socialism as it stood in the TTLs but merely superimposed their own externally indoctrinated form of Socialism and used the *mujibha* set up to assist them in inaugurating it.
4. Breakdown of civil administration including dipping, schools, churches, and so on.

You may well note that I have emphasised to some degree the *mujibha* networks already. It is my experience that very well-established networks run hand in hand with both ZANLA and ZIPRA terrorists based within Rhodesia. My report on *mujibhas* (XYS 9000/1 dd the 25/8/78) should be read in conjunction with this report which was based on the ZANLA *mujibha* networks. Criticism was levelled that *mujibha* networks do not exist within ZIPRA terrorist networks but having worked with this organisation now it is quite evident that *mujibha* networks do exist. For example, in Hurungwe TTL I have found that *mujibhas* operating with ZIPRA have received local training and what in fact happens when a group settles at a Kraal or base is that these locally trained *mujibhas* are given the terrs weapons and wander off protecting the group. Just one example of how well entrenched these *mujibha* networks are. As I have pointed out terrorism is based on the support of the people who become the eyes and ears for the terrs. Without the people terrorists cannot exist.

Breakdown of Civil Administration

To recapture lost areas, it must be emphasised that we depend on the people whom we have already lost. Agreed, we have a fine SF fighting capability, but we have never effectively managed to control the people. We must tend to their needs, troubles, medical requirements. We must, having established even a small area of control, contradict all that the terrorist says and does. We must not slate him as dogs/killers/kaffirs etc. but merely point out his weaknesses and his evils (killings, closing of schools, taking of food and money from the people, atrocities, etc.).

Terrorists are people within themselves and the people consider them people as well. It is fatal to lose sight of this fact! It is quite easy to exploit the terrorist weakness without openly slating him directly. By considering and taking care of the people successfully we will indirectly, but efficiently, be contradicting ZIPRA propaganda. I repeat, "the army must become one with the people so that they see it as their own. Such an army will be invincible."[1]

I think it is important at this stage to point out that the military is merely an extension of politics. Without a political problem there would be no military struggle. The social and economic arrangements in Rhodesia leaves the country wide open to revolution. Progress was being made towards majority rule. This is fine. However, political reformation must be seen to come from the people. Of prime importance at this delicate stage is farm labour and mine labour which generally has to commute to and from the TTL.

---

1 Zedong, M. (1976), p. 153.

> Salaries of the labour will have to be greatly improved as will labour relations, conditions of employment i.e. farm clinics, better housing conditions and so on. In other words, the political momentum has to be seen to rise hand in hand with the military momentum created through the SFAs. Once the political momentum falls behind, the military machine will advance and if it overtakes the political machine the military machine will turn against the political. For example, if farm labour wages are not increased, and labour conditions not improved the people and our military forces, all of whom are well aware of ZIPRA propaganda on this subject, will wonder what the hell they were fighting for – and turn against the political.

In my opinion, Ian Smith tried to retain power by using the tribal system (chiefs) to his benefit. His overbearing determination to implement his political agenda ignored two critical factors. Firstly, that African nationalists had been marginalised. Secondly, that ZANLA and ZIPRA had, in the main, usurped the tribal system.

Ground Coverage Operations: Zambezi Valley

In an attempt to prevent insurgent incursions from Zambia into Rhodesia, Special Branch and Ground Coverage operations were increased in the Zambezi Valley. P/O Charlie Sutton explained his role in these operations:

> I joined the Police in 1951 and was stationed at Sipolilo in 1957 for three years where I did month long foot patrols along the Zambezi Valley floor. I was dropped off by vehicle at the base of the escarpment, collected about eight "carriers" to convey my equipment including food and set off with two or three African Constables to make contact with the locals, gather information and intelligence, investigate criminal cases and check on persons previously convicted of criminal cases. The carriers were paid for out of a Police Fund. These patrols would end at Musengezi Mission where the missionaries would radio their HQ in Salisbury who requested Police HQ to tell the Police at Sipolilo that I had reached my destination; I would be collected three days later. (See map BSAP Ground Coverage, Sipolilo area, Zambezi Valley.)
>
> In 1960 I was transferred to the original Police post at Kanyemba established in 1911, for a six-year period which included five months leave. Shortly after my arrival, Chief Supt. Bill Bailey[1] decided to relocate the Police post three miles upstream to the confluence of the Luangwa and Zambezi rivers, a point where Mozambique, Zambia and Rhodesia met at a common border. With the help of locals, I built two grass thatched rondavels, one for the African Staff and one for myself, as the first Police buildings. Fortunately, I was afforded the luxury of a gas fridge and wood stove; supplies were parachuted in. BSAP Pioneers would later build the new Police Station in 1964, I am not exactly sure of the date.
>
> As civil unrest began, patrols and work were more of a security nature. Under Bailey's instruction I started identifying "watering holes" and potential crossing points across the Zambezi. Befriending the locals was important as Kanyemba was the only reporting place. I established liaison in Mozambique with the administrator at Feira (meaning market place) and a man in the clinic who spoke English. In Zambia I liaised with the Post Office administrator and joined the local club. I purchased my own boat which was transported from Sipolilo to Chikafa Mission, then choppered to Kanyemba, and began river boat patrols, and of course fishing and game viewing.
>
> I later went to Salisbury with Bill Bailey, to Puzey and Payne to select a new Police boat which had two 200 hp outboard engines. On my return to Kanyemba and, as a result of a leg infection, I was choppered to Sinoia for treatment. When I recovered, I was choppered to Chirundu where the new boat had been delivered. After four days familiar-

[1] C/Supt. Bill Bailey became the District Commander or Dis.Pol. Lomagundi in 1964.

isation with the boat, I set off with Arizhbowa, a local fisherman who lived on the banks of the Zambezi near Kanyemba, who had excellent knowledge of the river and was brought up specifically to help. The first overnight stop was near Mana Pools where we camped on the river banks and lit fires to keep the wild animals (leopard, rhino, buffalo, elephants, etc.) away. Next day we went through Mpata gorge (meaning rough gorge); we had to get out of the boat and let it drift through the gorge tied to ropes as there were a lot of cross currents that threatened to turn the boat over. This had recently happened to a farmer who lost his boat and equipment. We spent another night on the banks before reaching Kanyemba on the third day.

Petrol was supplied from Chirundu and delivered to Kanyemba in a 44-gallon drum which we hid in the bush and decanted into jerry cans. This was used for the boat and short wheel base open back Land Rover. During the rainy season it was impossible to use the Land Rover due to the muddy conditions of the bush roads. As the security situation deteriorated, three-four army details were stationed at Kanyemba with me. One night in 1963/64, there was a knock at my door and a Chief's messenger arrived reporting that a group of four-five strangers had arrived at the kraal to ask how to cross the Zambezi. They were directed along an incorrect path which would give us time to catch up with them. Carrying my double-barrelled shot gun, accompanied by the three-four army details, we set off tracking the strangers. I knew the sounds of the bush and suddenly just knew we had caught up with them. A grenade was thrown at us which exploded, and we opened up with our firearms – I shot off both barrels! One army man was injured but the terrorists ran, and we made our way back to Kanyemba and radioed Bill Bailey at Sinoia. Bailey sent down a helicopter which located one dead insurgent and uplifted the injured army man. The terrorist was killed by a single pellet from the shot gun.

I crossed the river to Villa Zumbo, where they had a clinic for Trypanosomiasis-sleeping sickness, and related the events of our contact to the Administrator. Three days later the Administrator advised that they had arrested one of the terrorists, so I crossed the river, collected him and handed him over to the CID.

While at Kanyemba I did a patrol to find the elusive Vadoma tribe who originated from Mozambique and spoke Portuguese and a local language. I located a local Vadoma man who offered to be my guide – it took three days to climb the Charuwa hills where the Vadomas lived. Some of them hadn't seen a white person so when we arrived at the kraals, they had all run away leaving an old man behind. I sent the guide ahead and was given permission by the old man to enter the area. He explained, (through my guide/ interpreter), that the people were frightened. Drums started sounding and the locals gradually returned. We all sat down, and I was made welcome. Communicating with them was quite an amazing experience – a first for many of us there! I stayed for three nights with the Vadomas, they are nomadic, hunted, planted and reaped mealies then moved on; they did not live in a fixed location. I was told that once a Native Commissioner had tried to entice members of the tribe down the mountain by leaving cigarettes at their fishing spot, but it did not work. One or two would work on the farms and brought back food and clothes from their wages when on leave. My main reason for visiting them was to secure their support regarding the overall security situation. Some had ostrich type feet from a genetic deformity. They lived in kraals, made with grass walls and a grass roof. They were exceptionally good trackers; I managed to recruit one man who came back to Kanyemba where he stayed and helped us tracking when required.

Periodically Special Branch deployed plain-clothed African policemen into Zambia to gather intelligence regarding the growing insurgency threat. These brave men would make their way to Lusaka and then back to the Rhodesian border gathering intelligence on the way. I would collect them by boat from Feira, bring them back to base and then arrange

> for their collection by Special Branch. These early efforts prepared the way for effective counter insurgency but did not prevent insurgent incursions into Rhodesia.[1]

Nigel Seaward recalled the experience of the late Tony Robinson, a Salisbury Special Branch detective: "After the end of the rainy season in about April 1964, Tony, a very astute and capable member, and his detectives undertook an SB 'familiarisation' patrol into District areas in Lomagundi roughly north of Karoi up towards Kanyemba. To my knowledge, this was the first of this sort of District work undertaken by SB, except of course that the late Peter Begg had been transferred to the new Chirundu Border Post. Tony's patrol was in response to information being received from sources concerning the first terrorist training being undertaken in Ghana. Tony came back pretty alarmed at what he had found, the territory was wide open for infiltration. He made some very significant suggestions, which would have been very costly to implement. It seemed to the very few ex-District types at the time to have joined the plain-clothes departments, that Tony was absolutely right, and that our leaders, all of them being ex-Town Branch types, simply did not fathom what he was talking about, and all indications were that the report was downplayed, if not altogether ignored. Tony, completely dismayed, resigned and left both the Force and the country as soon as he could. Need I tell you that the area patrolled by Tony was pretty much the route of infiltration taken a few years later, resulting in Operation Cauldron."[2]

Charlie Sutton on patrol, Zambezi Valley.

African constables and "carriers" accompanying Charlie Sutton.

First BSAP station at Kanyemba, 1960.

[1] P/O Charlie Sutton, 10/11/1932 to 21/9/2018. Joined the BSAP from the UK in 1951, sailing on the *Stirling Castle*, retiring in 1972. Various oral interviews given in 2017.

[2] Nigel Seaward email 3/8/2020.

Note: Between the late 1930s and 1960s there were few roads or tracks in existance in the Zambezi Valley. Patrols of up to two months' duration were carried out on foot by the BSAP using pack mules and bearers who carried the necessary supplies. From the mid-60s onwards, because of guerilla infiltration from both Zambia and Mozambique, it became essential to cover ground more quickly. 4 x 4 patrol vehicles operating from patrol bases (i.e. Mashumbi Pools) were used during the dry season but during the wet season, when roads became impassabe, foot patrols of up to 10 days' duration were reverted to, usually by two men, carrying a long-range radio, whose main function was to detect infiltration, investigate crime and keep in touch with the locals for information purposes. The Zambezi Valley is very hot and dry (40-42 degrees C is common) and in the dry season there is little water. Population and infiltration was therefore mainly along river lines where there were occasional pools and water could be found by observing where game dug in the sand. Adjacent police areas had similar patrol regimes during these periods.

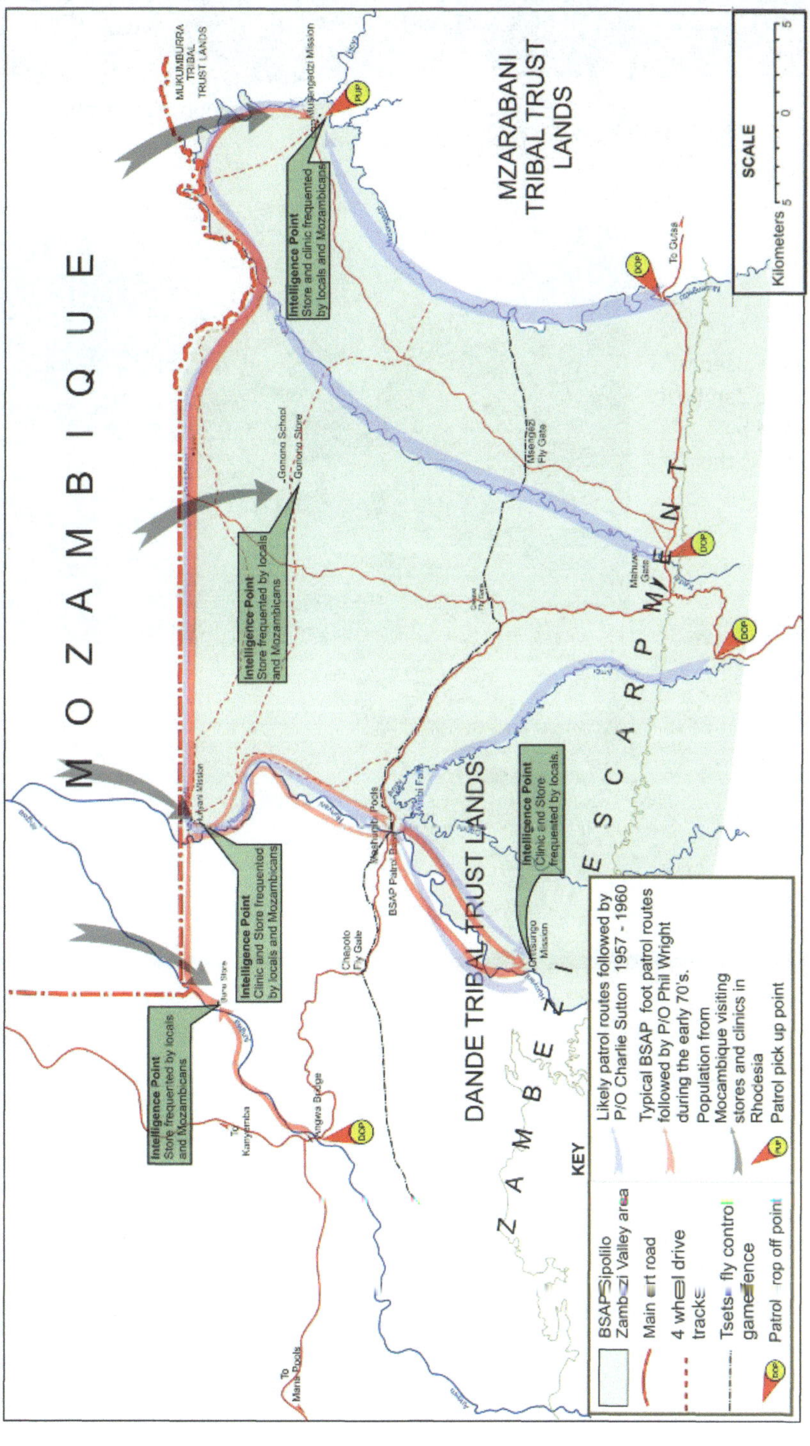

Some patrol distances

Sipolilo to Mahuwe gate (by road)	45 kms
Mashumbi Pools to Musegezi River via Hunyani Mission DOP	40 kms
Angwa Bridge to Bunu Store	16 kms
Hunyani Mission to Musengedzi Mission	65 kms
Ambi River DOP to Mashumbi Pools	35 kms
Mahuwe Gate to Mashumi Pools (by road)	37 kms
Musengezi to Mahuwe Gate (by road)	130 kms
Bunu Store to Hunyani Mission	18 kms
Kadzi DOP to Musengedzi Mission	72 kms

Outdoor kitchen.

Police pub, Kanyemba.

Traditional canoe used to fish and cross the Zambezi River. Often used by insurgents to cross the river.

Support Unit visiting Tonga villages, Zambezi Valley, 1972. Pictures provided by Barry Woan, taken by Keith Douche.

Early Counter-Insurgency Operations: Lomagundi District

Insp. Phil Wright was posted to the Ground Coverage Unit conducting intelligence operations at Karoi in 1976 and provided a background and history of insurgency and counter-insurgency operations in the Lomagundi district:

> The first overt act of terrorism happened in Rhodesia on the 4th July 1964 when Petrus Oberholser, a farmer from the Melsetter area was randomly stopped at a roadblock by ZANU terrorists of the "Crocodile Gang" and murdered. From then onwards a state of war existed in the country. Gangs of heavily armed terrorists of both ZANU and ZAPU factions began to cross Rhodesia's borders, initially from Zambia, in a quest to enter and destabilise the country. From that point, Rhodesia began to organise and structure her security forces for war.
>
> The Zimbabwe People's Revolutionary Army (ZIPRA), the armed wing of Joshua Nkomo's Ndebele Zimbabwe African People's Union (ZAPU) faction, was Russian orientated and always based in Zambia (and much later Botswana). It infiltrated its forces from Zambia all along the Zambezi River from Kazangula in the West as far as Kanyemba in the east, sometimes in company with elements of the South African ANC who wanted to transit Rhodesia into South Africa. Karoi was ethnically a Shona speaking (Korekore) area, and this invasion of Sindabele speaking armed men into the Shona area did not go down well right from the beginning. After the killing of Shona "sellouts" by ZIPRA started in mid-1977, this resentment grew and became increasingly significant. Eventually, in September 1978 this situation set the stage for the deployment of United African National Council (UANC) Muzorewa Security Force Auxiliaries (SFAs), into the area in order for them to protect the Shona people from ZIPRA's ravages.
>
> The Zimbabwe African National Liberation Army (ZANLA) on the other hand, were Shona speaking, Communist Chinese orientated and initially based in camps near Lusaka. After the murder of its Leader Herbert Chitepo in Lusaka on 18th March 1975, the ZANU leadership was arrested, and they were eventually evicted from Zambia. Thereafter they moved into and infiltrated from Mozambique. Their early infiltrations into the Karoi area were from their Nehanda Sector (Tete area), and for much of the war they saw their western boundary as the Angwa River.
>
> In the Lomagundi area, into which Karoi fell, Chief Superintendent Bill Bailey became the District Commander or "Dis.Pol. Lomagundi" in 1964. Bailey had served in the Long-Range Desert Group (LRDG) during World War II and was a far-sighted and unconventional thinker. He foresaw that a "bush war" would take place and predicted the need for local, well-trained units who could defend their own white farming communities under threat, before the army had time to mobilise and deploy in their defence. To this end, Bailey set about selecting and training small volunteer units which were initially termed VATS, or Volunteers for Advanced Training, and which were later to morph into the well-known Police Anti-Terrorist Units (PATU) used throughout the country.[1]
>
> The far sighted Bailey put these VATS to good use in these early days. In the knowledge that infiltrations would likely come from Zambia, whose President was sympathetic to the Nationalist cause, likely infiltration points, routes, water points and resupply points (farm stores, etc.) were identified and ambush positions and observation points were identified in order to counter these infiltrations and plotted on maps throughout the Lomagundi District
>
> At the same time, the BSAP had identified the problems about to befall the country and had not been tardy in recognising that good intelligence would play a crucial role in any future confrontation with Nationalist forces. Special Branch had rapidly engaged in recruiting sources and infiltrated deep inside both ZANU and ZAPU. Special Branch

[1] Flower, K. (1987), p. 123; Gibbs, P., Phillips, H. & Russell, N. (2009), Chap. 49.

offices were set up at most District Headquarters and on all BSAP district stations Ground Coverage Units came to life and began to recruit informers and collect and collate "grass roots" intelligence on activities, both criminal and political, in their areas.

Persons who had left the country for political reasons were identified as "Expats" and their kraals and immediate family identified and monitored by Ground Coverage. These reports were collated, "carded and indexed" and fed upwards in a tiered structure through District Headquarters to Special Branch Headquarters. Special Branch then, was generally well informed on what was going on in most areas of the country. Due to its northerly position in the country and the fact that it lay on the direct path of infiltrators crossing the Zambezi River making their way into the hinterland, Karoi featured early in the terrorist war.

In early April 1966 the "Armageddon Group", comprising twenty-one ZANU terrorists, crossed the Zambezi River, near Chirundu, and later divided into three 7-man groups, all of whom transited the Karoi area, destined to travel into various parts of the country. One group made a poor attempt at blowing up electricity pylons north of Sinoia. Having already been infiltrated by Special Branch whilst in Zambia, this group was cornered East of Sinoia and eliminated on 29 April 1966, in a combined BSAP and Air Force operation in which a helicopter was to score the first "helicopter kill" of the war. This action became known and celebrated by ZANU as the famous "Battle of Sinoia."

In March 1968, Game Ranger Dave Scammel discovered the tracks of a large group of terrorists in the south-eastern sector of the Mana Pools Game Reserve. It transpired a combined force of 250 ZAPU and South African ANC terrorists had crossed from Zambia, near the junction of the Chiwore and Zambezi rivers, establishing a line of base camps across the valley floor from the Zambezi to the prominent Chirambakadoma mountain. From thereon, the camps continued southwards, via the Maura River, to Mana Pools on the Angwa River,[1] leading towards the area of Shamrock Mine. This was the north-eastern corner of the Karoi area, the Angwa River forming its eastern boundary. This discovery launched Operation Cauldron on 18 March 1968, resulting in armed confrontations with terrorists in both the Karoi and Doma areas of BSAP Mangula's region. The fact that almost all 250 terrorists were accounted for by the SF, bears testimony to their preparedness and efficiency. From then on many smaller actions took place as groups of ZIPRA and ZANLA infiltrated, using the Angwa River as a route.

On the 16th July 1968, 28 ZAPU terrorists crossed the Zambezi in the area of Nyamuomba Island situated where the Zambezi exits the Kariba gorge and flows into the flat Zambezi Valley. After crossing the river they scaled the escarpment and began to follow the Chimwa River south-east along a valley to a point where their tracks were detected in the area of a track leading to the old and derelict Chimwa Mine. Three RLI troops, under command of Lt.'s Strong, Dawson and Pierce, were deployed to pursue these C/Ts. Possibly aware of being tracked, the terrorists diverted north from the Chimwa River onto one of its tributaries, the Nyadadza River which then entered the crescent-shaped and thickly wooded Griffins Gorge, where they went to ground. Lt. Strong's troop, following the tracks, soon made contact with the enemy, while the other two troops, reinforced by elements of the RAR and accompanied by newly deployed members of the South African Police, deployed as stop groups to the north and south-east of the gorge. The terrorists bomb-shelled (scattered), leaving several of their dead in the gorge. At conclusion of mopping-up operations twenty-three terrorists had been killed and four captured, accounting for almost the whole group.

Although it did not directly affect the Karoi area, I have described this action as it marked the commencement by terrorists of utilising a route to become known as the

[1] There is a Mana Pools on both the Zambezi and Angwa rivers: Phil Wright email 17/6/2017.

"Chimwa Track". Of interest is the fact that in the past the terrorists had abducted numerous tsetse "*magochas*"[1] and used them as guides and this gave them an intimate knowledge of every track and water point in this hot and desolate area.

The Chimwa track started, as described above, at the confluence of the Chimwa and Zambezi rivers just south of Nyamoumba Island. There was a well known ZIPRA transit camp at Nyamoumba Farm in Zambia bordering on the Zambezi River to the north. The Chimwa River would be followed up into the escarpment to where it met a disused prospector's track running from the old and long derelict Chimwa Mine, south-east to a point on the Kariba/Makuti Road. Infiltrating terrorists would follow the trail south east until they came to the main Kariba/Makuti road which they would cross, turning due south, and following a tributary of the Charara River until they reached the point where the Kariba power lines crossed the Charara River. Here they then followed the Kariba power lines south east until they reached the Nyaodza River. Once on the Nyaodza River they had access to the entire Urungwe Tribal Trust Lands, or they could move west around the base of Lake Kariba, cross the Sanyati river and move into the Gokwe area and beyond. It was to feature regularly in future infiltrations into the Karoi area by ZIPRA and was to become our "Ho chi min trail" and was to receive constant attention from PATU sticks and the army right up until the end of the war. As a member of PATU in the Lomagundi District I was to patrol and ambush it on several occasions.[2]

Ground Coverage Operations: Karoi District

The operations of a Ground Coverage district policeman were many and varied. Insp. Phil Wright explained:

> It is impossible for me to give a detailed description of all the activities of the Ground Coverage Unit at Karoi – too much happened, and my memory has faded. I have therefore, chosen to describe only those significant events of which I have a good recollection and which I have been able to corroborate to a reasonable degree with other colleagues who worked with me at that time.
>
> In order to do that I suppose it would be pertinent for me to begin with a broad description of my service in the BSAP leading up to my posting to Karoi. I was persuaded by my grandfather, who had joined the BSAP in 1907, to do the same. So, I joined the force in late 1970 – Squad 6/70 to be precise – and after completing depot training and the "display squad", which was huge fun, I passed out, did my Police Driving School training and was posted to Sipolilo within the Lomagundi District under Inspector Mike Harvey.
>
> After an initial introduction to investigations most of my service at Sipolilo was spent running a patrol base at Mashumbi pools, which I loved. The patrol base was shared with Kanyemba, way to the North and they usually had a Patrol Officer based there at the same time. Mashumbi pools covered large tracts of the Dande TTL between the base of the escarpment and the Mozambique border to the north, and from Mashumbi on the Hunyani River to Msengezi in the east. It was here that I started to learn the "bushwar" ropes and roles and responsibilities of Ground Coverage duties. Sipolilo had already seen many terrorist incursions and so we deployed African Constables in plain clothes along the border to mingle with the locals (few that there were) and pick up intelligence. This was my first insight into how good our African Police really were. Time was to show that there were many brave men of huge stature and intelligence among them – many the equal

[1] *Magocha* (those who roast): *Magocha* were hired by the Government Tsetse Fly Control to hunt and kill animals in areas affected by trypanosomiasis. Supplied with guns and ammunition, they were rewarded by the number of animals slaughtered. They roasted game meat in the bush when hunting and supplied meat to villages. They were excellent trackers and guides familiar with the area and terrain.

[2] Phil Wright emails 23/2/2016, 25/2/2016 and 9/3/2016.

of almost any white policemen, and they would have excelled at higher ranks but for the prejudiced rank structure that kept them subordinate to us because of the colour of their skin.

Dis.Pol. Lomagundi (often humorously referred to as Disprin), was at the time Chief Superintendent Ray Stenner – a fine officer and great district commander. However, in his wisdom Disprin decided that I was still too full of nonsense and that I should go to a real bush station, so I was duly despatched to Kanyemba under S/O Colin John. This was paradise on earth for me – apart from copious drinking on "liaison" visits to the Portuguese army and police at Villa Zumbo just down the Zambezi from us, I got to do more patrolling in one of the greatest game parks in the world. We had the luxury of helicopters and boats to drop us off and pick us up – how nice. We would be dropped off with one African Police Reserve (APR) tracker and a long range SSB radio and 7 days rations and would patrol the river lines and previously known infiltration routes looking for spoor. It was tough – the Zambezi Valley is not a cool place and in summer water is very scarce – and then there were those tsetse and Mopani flies![1] Oh yes, and let us not forget the Buffalo Beans![2] I became a most seasoned hiker – a skill I still have and use to this day – except I now hike with my wife and not an APR tracker.

After a year and a half at Kanyemba, "Disprin" again in his wisdom, decided that it was now time to teach Phil Wright some real police work and so he sent me to Mangula. The Member in Charge was Inspector John Gray, an ex-British Policeman, probably the best policeman I have ever worked with. He taught me investigation skills which have remained with me throughout a lifetime of police investigative work. Possessed of a Bachelor of Law (LLB), he had a superb ability to meld legal theory with practical police investigation and he had a brilliant ability to lecture and teach his African Police the skills of investigation in a way that they fully understood. African police promotions were frequent at Mangula, but alas they would be whisked away to other stations to lead.

It was here that I joined PATU and began to spend time on lengthy bush patrols in the Lomagundi district as a member of a Police anti-terrorist unit. My first encounter with terrorists took place here in early 1974 when we walked within a few meters of a gang of FROLIZI terrorists after they had burnt and ransacked a farmhouse in the Mangula farming area – but fortunately, a capture later told us, they did not open fire because there was at least five of us!

By mid-1974 Operation Hurricane was well on its way after the attacks on Altena and Whistlefield farms in the Centenary area in December of 1972. Realising that I preferred the operational life rather than the dockets and wanted action, I applied for and was accepted into the blackboots or Support Unit – the para-military wing of the BSAP – where I served as a Troop Commander until cupid put an arrow through my ticker and I got married. It was then, in August 1976, that I was transferred to Karoi – back to my old stamping grounds of the Lomagundi District.

I arrived at Karoi as a married Section Officer. The Member in Charge at the time was C/Insp. Tony "Pullthrough" Wilson, ex Gwanda with Insp. John Trueman as his 2 i/c. About a year after my arrival Tony Wilson was transferred and replaced by C/Insp. Mike Farrell and I, at the tender age of 25 years old, was promoted to Inspector.

It was logical, I suppose, that my background in the Support Unit on operations made me an obvious candidate to take over the Karoi Ground Coverage Unit from Dave Stanton-Humphries who was being transferred.[3]

---

1 A very small gnat-like stingless bee species native to Africa.

2 A trailing or climbing herb with annual stems growing from a perennial rootstock. The fruits and parts of the flower are densely covered in highly irritant hairs which cause a severe burning rash at the slightest touch. https://www.zimbabweflora.co.zw/index.php

3 Phil Wright emails 23/2/2016, 25/2/2016 and 9/3/2016.

One of the enormous benefits of belonging to the BSAP was that members gained considerable training, guidance and practical experience under the watchful eye of mature senior colleagues throughout the ranks. This equipped members to execute their duties to the high standards and traditions of the police force. Consequently, in general terms that is, operational areas contained dedicated men who adjusted well to operational investigations, duties and combat.

Phil continues sharing his insight into Ground Coverage operations in Hurungwe:

> The Ground Coverage Unit at Karoi was well established and had been so for some years due to the history of the area. It consisted of a regular police element comprising a Section Officer in charge, a senior GC Sergeant and some 10 African Constables. In addition to that, there were about 30 European Police Reservists (PRs) chosen from the fringe farms along borders of the Kazangarare Tribal Trust Lands to the East and Hurungwe to the West, headed up by a local farmer. These farmers had working relationships with the locals in the TTL's whom they employed and helped from time to time. Some labourers from these areas who worked on the farms were recruited as informants and were a brilliant source of high-grade information which, until the murdering of "sellouts" started, flowed in all the time.
>
> Karoi had two main Ground Coverage bases – one at Magunje in the vast Hurungwe Tribal Trust Lands to the west of the Karoi/Kariba Road, the other at Chundu in the northern section of the Kazangarare TTL east of the main road and not far from the top of the Zambezi Valley escarpment. Other small fortified bases were put in as the war progressed but I cannot recall their exact localities or their names. They were manned by regular Patrol Officers of the Karoi uniform branch and later by National Service Patrol Officers, all of whom did a fine job. They provided a police function in these areas but their primary responsibility was Ground Coverage and the feeding back of information obtained, both of a criminal and security nature.
>
> Shortly after my taking command of the Unit, and apace with the developments of the war, a Special Branch representative was sent to Karoi in the form of D/S/O Mike Reeler. He was assisted during his time by various other SB and CID representatives from time to time. (Ben Pretorius,[1] Doug Stanyon, Lawrie Mabin come to mind.) For operational purposes our intelligence gathered went through Mike Reeler. Much later, Army Intelligence (RIC) also deployed a permanent presence at Karoi.
>
> **Karoi Operations Intensify**
>
> This then, was the Ground Coverage Unit I took over shortly after my arrival at Karoi in August 1976. Upon my arrival the Karoi area was relatively quiet and I was able to get to know the area, and plan and assimilate the information which was available. The brief respite was shattered and the war intensified on 17 December 1976 when a truck returning Banket and Karoi PATU sticks from an operation in the Chundu area was ambushed at dusk on the edge of the farming area in the vicinity of Manyangau Hill on the farm owned by Mr Dave Chadwick. I was called out and immediately rushed, with other members, to their assistance. On arrival we found that Mike Nielson had been killed and George Ormerod and Alf Smith had been wounded, all from Karoi. Paul Crouch from Banket had been badly wounded and was to die with his head in my lap in the back of a Land Rover a few kilometres from Karoi.[2]
>
> It was here, that for the first time I encountered the Karoi Casualty Clearing Station, a volunteer first-aid facility staffed and run by Myra Kennedy, wife of the Karoi postmaster, George Kennedy. Karoi had no hospital, although Dr Chris Lewis was the resident medical practitioner. In the early stages of the war George Kennedy and his highly

---

[1] D/Insp. Ben Pretorius joined March 1966 and served until November 1979. He died on 30/10/2015.

[2] Karoi Contacts Map Incident 1.

qualified State Registered Nurse (SRN) wife, Myra, had foreseen the need for a facility in the area where victims of casualties could be stabilised and treated prior to being transferred to Salisbury either by air or road.

To this end a premises was provided by the Posts and Telecommunications Corporation (PTC), behind the telephone exchange, an ambulance obtained, and the essential sterilising and other equipment provided by local branches of Lions and Round Table. Myra and George set about recruiting volunteers. There were several SRNs resident in the area all of whom rallied to the cause, as did other volunteers including my wife, Sue, and other police wives. This facility was to prove a godsend and saved lives on many occasions, some of which are described below.

By 1977 the Karoi area was growing increasingly hostile and was becoming a cauldron of terrorist activity with daily vehicle ambushes, contacts, landmine detonations and farm attacks. On some occasions, 5 – 6 incidents per day. By mid-1977 terrorist murders of civilians in the TTL's had begun with a vengeance as ZIPRA tried to silence the flow of information reaching us. Our general "goodwill information" and intelligence from the locals ceased as it did in all areas of the country under such conditions. From then on it became a game of specific informers and sources, and it was through the GC bases and Police Reservists, with their sources of long standing, that much of our good intelligence was obtained.

Due to the increasing infiltration of ZAPU in Hurungwe we came to realise, as a matter of urgency, the need to secure and maintain a flow of reliable and substantial real time intelligence or the Hurungwe would be lost. To that end, with the aid of an extremely brave and resourceful undercover agent, we set up and controlled our own ZIPRA cell in the Magunje area. It was not long before other supporters of the ZIPRA cause (and there were a few, even though the area was essentially Shona territory!), got in touch with him and they started to get organised. From then on we received a stream of high quality information that we could work with. A ZIPRA contact man was identified operating from the Makuti Hotel. A "pipe line" of contact men was identified leading down through the central Hurungwe, past Chidamoyo Mission and into the Rengwe TTL.

With the situation developing all the time it was opportune to involve the *Skuzapo* (Selous Scouts) who deployed a ZIPRA pseudo callsign into the area, led by Corporal Obert Mabaleka. They initiated numerous successful SF engagements with terrorists in the Hurungwe and Rengwe TTLs. By that time ZANLA units were infiltrating the southern part of the Hurungwe and Rengwe area from the north-east and by use of highly skilful pseudo operations, Corporal Obert was able to set them off against each other with immensely satisfying results! For his superb efforts in this area Cpl. Obert was awarded a Bronze Cross on 18th April 1978.

Obert and his men, over a period, followed the pipeline from the Rengwe into the Piri Wiri TTL, continuing to the Sanyati/Umfuli rivers until they entered the Umfuli, Magondi and Zowa Tribal Trust Lands on the boundary of the Hartley and Selous areas, exploiting the situation as they went and gathering valuable intelligence on ZIPRA's contact men and *mujibhas*. However, in war there is always tragedy and these successes ended when, on 2 October 1978 Corporal Obert and his callsign, following up on information of a presence in the Selous farming region, entered an area under JOC Grapple which had, erroneously, been excluded from an "area freezing order"[1] by a security forces Operations Officer. Their presence was reported within this agricultural region and a BSAP PATU stick from Selous, reacting to the report of a terrorist presence, made contact with Cpl. Obert's callsign, and Obert, his 2 i/c Lance Corporal Murase and two other members of

[1] Declared a no-go area.

> his callsign were killed. Consequently, the lives of four remarkably brave men were brought to a tragic end.[1]

Wright continues:

> In 1978, the following incident occurred, once again illustrating the bravery of our African police. A renegade terrorist had broken away from his group, fully armed with his AK-47 and had become a nuisance in the southern Hurungwe, opposite the Tengwe farming area. He robbed numerous buses, trucks and stores and raped women.
>
> He became a menace and Tengwe PATU sticks spent hours searching for him but to no avail. I discussed the matter with my African policemen and an African Police Reservist – whom I will refer to as "007", volunteered to make a search, assisted by his compadre "008", to rectify the situation. "007" and "008" were duly deployed, each armed with nothing but .38 Webley revolvers and I forgot about them for the present time. About a week later, at home one Saturday evening, I received a phone call. A voice on the other end, that of 007 said, "*Ishe* – I have sorted the problem. You must come now!" I did as I was bid and immediately travelled to Tengwe. On arrival I was met by "007" and "008". They presented me with a bullet-riddled corpse and an AK-47. The story was that they had diligently frequented the beer drinks in the area. While at one beer drink party, they received information of the presence of the renegade some kilometres away. They went there and drank beer for most of the day before the renegade arrived, complete with AK. They befriended him and plied him with alcohol. When he was suitably inebriated, they grabbed him and a fight took place in which one of them shot the C/T with a pistol. Wounded, he still fought on with one of them holding onto his AK, the other around his neck. Eventually he broke free and tried to escape, leaving his AK in the hands of 007 who promptly used it on automatic, killing the renegade instantly.[2]
>
> Several other such incidents in the Karoi area are deeply etched in my mind, disturbing me to this day.
>
> The first of these was on 7 April 1978 I was in the Vuti east area, once again in two Land Rovers, the second one driven by SB reservist Kam Kalweit. I decided to come back through the Vuti township to "show the flag" and see if all was quiet. I turned off the main Makuti Road onto the Vuti School Road and was idling down the hill when a running man caught my eye in the school grounds. He was frantically waving me down so I deviated into the school grounds. The man turned out to be a teacher who breathlessly told me that two Ndebele speaking C/T's had just robbed the school of all its petty cash (feel the love of the Shona for ZIPRA). He gave me a brief explanation that they were both wearing blue overalls and the fact that they were both carrying hand grenades. They had apparently walked off down the hill in the direction of DD Beremauro store, situated at an intersection, which was about one kilometre down the road. We immediately drove off suspecting that their next target was the store. As I approached the store I could see that the doors were open and there was no sign of anyone around. I swept onto the forecourt of the store like an Information Room Bee Car arriving at an RLI fight at Le Coq D'or[3] and came to a screeching halt outside the doors in a cloud of dust. Spectacular, but with the benefit of hindsight, a somewhat foolish approach. I looked into the store and – lo and behold – there were two men in blue denim fitting the description of our two robbers not more than 5 metres away from me. I still have a mental snapshot of a fist clutching the lever mechanism of an F1 grenade and a set of huge eyeballs and a

---

[1] This incident was picked up by the UANC intelligence men and confirmed by D/P/O Clive Boddy on 18/10/1978. Karoi Contacts Map Incident 2, not logged on map.

[2] Karoi Contacts Map Incident 3, not logged on map.

[3] Salisbury police were often called to sort out fights involving SF, normally the RLI, at Le Coq D'or, a local night club. "B-Cars" was the name given to the rapid-response police vehicles.

gaping mouth staring at me. What now, flashed through my mind. My Land Rover was pretty standard for the time – no doors and bloody seatbelts which were done up according to standing orders! I remember, in slow motion, one gook throwing something green and heavy at me which hit me in the chest, rolled onto the passenger's floor and out of the door on the already empty left hand side of the vehicle. (My GC Sergeant had already ejected as we came to a halt!) I remember all this whilst trying to release my seatbelt and cock my Uzi at the same time. (Funny what goes through one's mind at a time like that?) I thought the gook had chucked a grenade at me and I was about to join the queue at the pearly gates. I remember thinking that if I'm going, then this brother is coming with me. By this time, one of the individuals was taking long strides to escape and turned left as he ran out the door. I opened fire, left handed, with my Uzi as he ran down the *stoep* (verandah) of the store. I remember clouds of whitewash coming off the wall of the store as the rounds thudded behind him, eventually felling him as he reached the end of the stoep, where he fell over and lay still on his back.

The second C/T turned right at the door and made a rapid departure with an even bigger wheel spin, throwing as he went, a grenade over his head which detonated just in front of my vehicle but fortunately did no real damage. I remember seeing him skipping nimbly down the road amidst geysers of dust thrown up by my three compadres shooting at him. He escaped – shit shots – all of them!

I remember hearing a shout of "lookout *Ishe*" and turned in time to see C/T number one, still lying on his back, pulling the pin out of a grenade in his hand which he then held next to his head. Needless to say no one ran forward to counsel him over his obvious decision to take his own life – we all ducked until after the bang. It was only after the dust had settled that I discovered that what I had thought was a grenade hitting me in the chest was in fact a bag of money, in a green Nedbank[1] plastic bag. I hurried home to change my underpants.[2]

In mid-1978 when we were just south of Nyaodza River, a fully loaded African bus, detonated a landmine. My GC Sergeant and I accompanied by a Patrol Officer from Magunje and his African Constable were Land Rover borne on investigations and talking to locals in the area east of Gawa Kraal, close by the Nyaodza River.

The bus, travelling from Magunje, passed us and minutes later we heard a large explosion some 3km further down the road. We rushed to the scene, which was awful. There were at least ten to fifteen people injured and there were bodies and body parts everywhere. The driver, sitting at the right front corner, had taken the full force of the blast as the mine detonated under him. We carried limited first aid equipment in the vehicle and I remember an intense feeling of hopelessness as I tried to help a grey haired *madala*[3] whose legs had been blown off. I tried to staunch the flow of blood with the limited field dressings available and injected him with Sosegon to help his agony. I remember digging in his arms for a vein to get a drip into but he had already gone into shock and his veins had dilated. I remember the screams of the other injured people, there was very little we could do for them except work with what we had, and call by radio for assistance. Eventually all other available units in the area came to help but there were no casevac helicopters available, so we took loads of people through by vehicle to our valiant little Casualty Clearing Station in Karoi where Doctor Chris Lewis and Myra Kennedy and her little band of angels did what they could for the injured. A figure of five – six people killed and 20 injured lurks somewhere in my mind. There, but for the grace of God could we have gone as we were heading in the same direction as the bus which passed us and hit the mine. I remember thinking "how brave ZIPRA were".[4]

1 A national Rhodesian bank.

2 Karoi Contacts Map Incident 4.

3 *Madala*: Respectful Shona name for elderly.

It was after this incident that it became obvious to me that we needed a permanent police base in the far north of Hurungwe, somewhere along the Nyaodza River, where infiltrating C/Ts first came into contact with Hurungwe population. I located a suitable spot, and did a little "civil engineering" by borrowing a bulldozer from the African Development fund. Accompanied by a District Officer, we proceeded northwards from Magunje, anxious all the way mind you, to a road junction on the Doro Loop Road, just east of the Murereshi Bridge, where the road goes north to the game fence, after crossing the nearby Nyaodza River. This road south was a very active part of the ZIPRA's infiltration route from the "Chimwa track" to the north. There we bulldozed a triangular defensive position, complete with corner bunkers, and from then it was equipped with a radio and staffed by an African Police Reserve section. Our APR were great guys and only too happy to get involved against the Ndebele speaking ZIPRA "invaders"! Named, as far as I remember, "Nyaodza Base", it was used as a forward post by my Ground Coverage operators, both regular and Police Reserve as well as Internal Affairs (Int.Aff.) personnel. Later on, as the war heated up, it was attacked several times and, as far as I know, was eventually abandoned because of mines and numerous vehicle ambushes.

On returning to Karoi with the bulldozer, we stopped off at Magunje and, to the overwhelming relief of the Ground Coverage Operators stationed there, we bulldozed berms[1] around its perimeter fencing, complete with corner bunkers.

Tuesday 11 July 1978 is another day I will never forget. It was the last day of the Rhodes and Founders long weekend and people were streaming home after their break. Once again, I was out on the ground with a GC Unit in the Vuti African Purchase area. I do not remember the time exactly but it must have been mid-afternoon when I heard radio chatter which indicated that the Kariba to Karoi convoy had been ambushed just south of Makuti. Convoys were formed when civilian traffic was mustered at advertised predetermined times, dates and locations. All drivers were comprehensively briefed by the convoy commanders regarding procedures to be adopted in the event of a breakdown or an ambush. The vanguard and rearguard vehicles were normally modified BSAP pick-up trucks fitted with Browning M-2 50-calibre machine guns and protective shields. They were driven and crewed predominantly by specially trained police reservists who were armed and equipped accordingly. Int.Aff. and other military vehicles and personnel would be utilised as and when circumstances dictated. The convoys were often preceded by PRAW aircraft which would overfly the intended routes as extra security precautions.

We, being two Land Rovers, reacted immediately and started to move in that direction. It took us some 20 – 30 minutes to reach the scene which was about 12km from Makuti in an area where the road wound its way through mountainous terrain. When we arrived the shooting had stopped and the C/Ts appeared to have already left the scene. The grass on both sides of the road was alight and there were several police escort vehicles and one or two disabled civilian vehicles spaced out along the road. An Express Motorways Bus appeared to have collected the brunt of the ambush. It was positioned on the wrong side of the road relative to its southerly direction of travel, and it was hard up against the wall of the cutting on an acute left hand bend. A Police Reservist on an escort vehicle told me that the C/T's firing position was up on the ridge immediately above the bus. They had carefully chosen the site to enable them to fire a volley of gunfire straight down the road as the convoy came up the hill towards them. He told me that there were bodies in the bus.

I boarded the bus. The driver was slumped over his steering wheel and had stopped a well-aimed burst to his chest through the front windscreen that killed him. Three or four

---

[4] Karoi Landmine Map 1.

[1] Artificial embankment built for defence of the base.

> seats back behind the driver lay the body of a little girl with tousled blonde hair slumped over on her seat with her teddy bear on her lap. She had been shot through the head. I removed her body from the bus and to this day the sight of her little body and painted finger nails still haunts me. I remember breaking down as I put her body in the back of my Land Rover. We removed the body of the driver. I remember thinking how futile it all was — what a waste of a little life. The Police Reservist told me that many other people had been wounded and had been taken back to Makuti. He also told me that an heroic pilot of a small unarmed red Cessna had arrived overhead and proceeded to fly perilously low down the road straight at the terrorist position on numerous occasions in order to draw their fire away from the vehicles on the road below them. According to the reservist he had drawn extensive fire and had undoubtedly saved many lives.
>
> My interpretation of the scene as far as the bus was concerned was that the driver was a hero. The bus, apart from an escort vehicle, was first in line in the convoy and was travelling quite slowly up a gradient. The terrorists must have opened fire in good time to enable them to score numerous hits on the vehicle in which they knew there were a lot of closely grouped people. That meant that the driver, probably hit in the opening bursts, crossed onto the right hand side of the road bringing his bus to a halt against a culvert directly underneath the terrorist firing location, essentially removing it from the line of fire from above and saving many lives. To my knowledge the (late) driver, Samuel Gondo, never received any recognition for his actions despite my putting in a report. Four people died that day. The driver, Samuel Gondo, 17 year old Deborah De Bres, Margaret Turk (early 20's) and little Sally Muggleton (5 years old). Another sixteen people were injured and taken to Makuti airstrip where they were casevaced by PRAW and a Rhodesia Air Force Dakota. The little red Cessna turned out to be none other than Cliff Wilcox[1], a PRAW pilot from Karoi, another hero of that awful day.[2]

Sally's mother and brother were both on the bus. Her mother was severely injured and could not attend the funeral. While escorting the convoy on 7 July 1978, PRAW pilot Jim Barker identified a "live" ZIPRA terrorist camp relatively close to the ambush site. Barker collected the border control officer from Kariba and flew him over the "live" camp, and pinpointed the location. He shared his belief that the convoy would be attacked over the holiday weekend. As there were no SF available to react to the intelligence, it was agreed to provide armoured cars as additional support for the convoy between the Elephants Walk Motel and Makuti for the duration of the weekend. Unfortunately, this did not happen and the armoured cars only arrived at the scene after the ambush.[3]

Phil Wright continues:

> On another occasion one of my GC Field Reservists from a north west border farm helped one of his sources phone in with some information. The source was resident in the area of Maumbe Business Centre, just north of Magunje. He informed us that a C/T was on his way into Karoi in a particular type of vehicle and was going to buy supplies. Realising that a formal police roadblock may well alert the driver of the vehicle we decided that an innovative solution was somehow called for. We decided to go "incognito" and I accordingly borrowed my wife's Morris 1000 – affectionately called "Richard". Mike Reeler and I, accompanied by my GC Sergeant and an SB member, squeezed into "Richard" and took off down the road to Makuti. At a point half way to the Magunje turn off we pulled over on the left of the road, stopped and opened the bonnet. The two African members hovered around the engine area, armed with concealed pistols while Reeler and I sat in the vehicle with folding butt AK-47s. After about a 10 minute wait along came the suspect vehicle with two occupants. The two African policemen leapt out

[1] Barker, J. (2007), pp. 106, 223-226.

[2] Karoi Contacts Map Incident 5. Phil Wright emails 23/2/2016, 25/2/2016 and 9/3/2016.

[3] Barker, J. (2007), pp. 223-225. Email from Jim Barker via Bill Linfield on 4/1/2020.

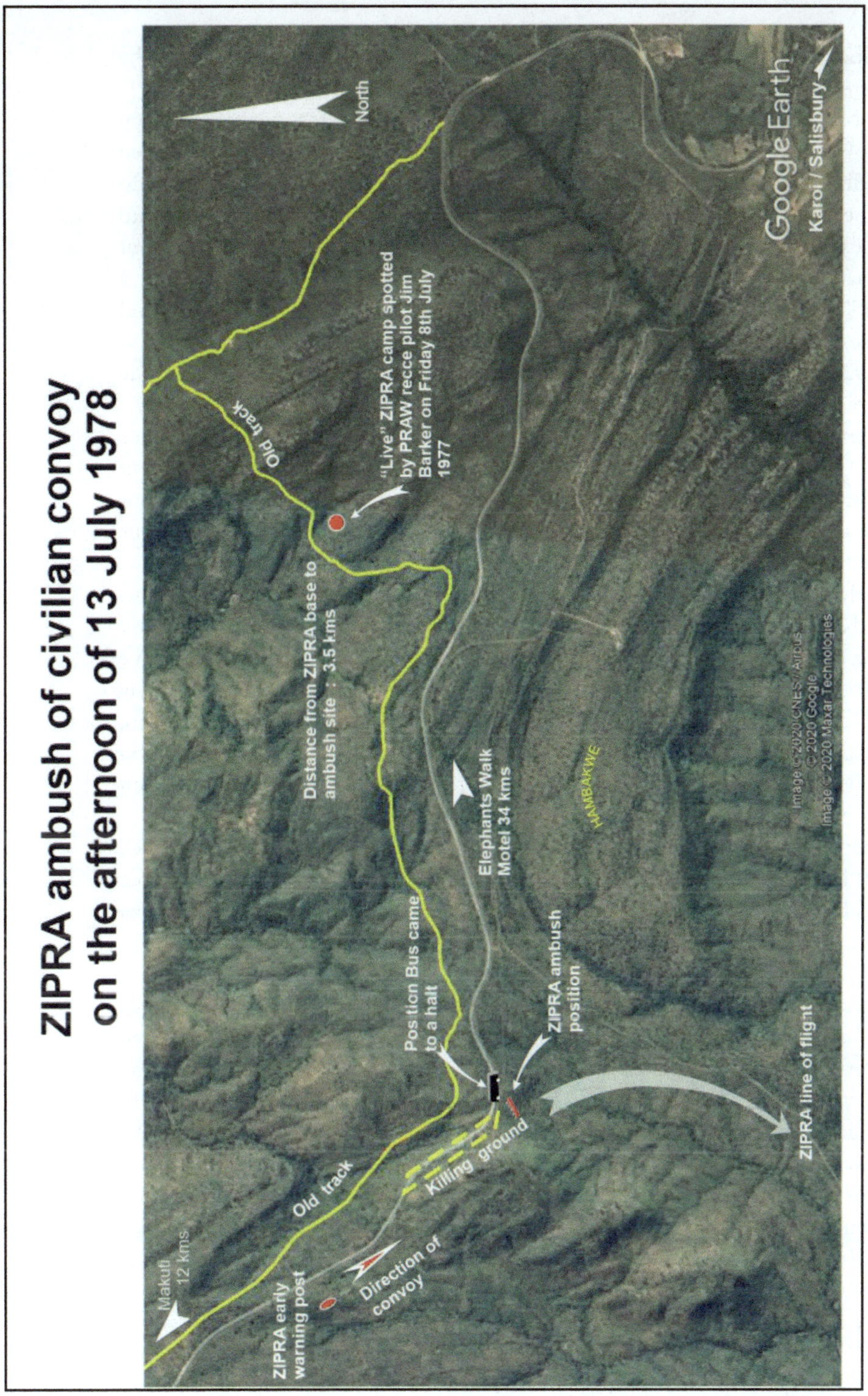

Note: Map drawn from the observations and local knowledge of Inspector Phil Wright of the Ground Coverage Unit, Karoi, who attended the scene of this incident and from information supplied by Police Reserve Air Wing pilot Jim Barker, also of Karoi.

Distances

Ambush site to Makuti	12.4 kms
Abush site to Elephants Walk	34 kms
ZIPRA camp to Ambush site	3.5 kms

Full Attribution: Google Earth and Maxar Technologies

into the road, one waving an empty petrol can, and forced the vehicle to a halt. Pistols were levelled and before the startled occupants could "blink their eyes" they were dragged out onto the road and made to lie face down. The C/T was the passenger and was carrying, as far as I recall, a Makarov pistol. They were both handcuffed and speedily transported to Karoi for interrogation. The C/T's name was David Skosana, I do not remember if that was his Chimurenga name.[1]

[1] Karoi Contacts Map Incident 6.

The story does not end there, the following day David Skosana, after interrogations by the African detectives, freely and voluntarily elected to tell us of another ZIPRA C/T – one Comrade Max, resident I think, in the Mashayamombe Kraal area, not too far from Maumbe B/C. He was apparently firmly ensconced in the kraal of his "lover". We decided to react immediately in order to prevent information of Skosana's arrest filtering back to Hurungwe. There are eyes and ears everywhere in this intelligence game; ZIPRA and ourselves had excellent intelligence networks both in Karoi and in Hurungwe, little went unnoticed. That night, the team galloped off into the sunset, deploying through a northwest border farm at about 23h00 with a guide and specific instructions where to find said "lovers" residence in the Mashayamombe Kraal area and to spoil his evening.

At around 02h00 we found the place and kicked the door down. There was Comrade Max and girlfriend happily tucked up in bed together. My GC Sergeant, who sported a large and unkempt beard, gazed at Comrade Max in his bed from the other side of his torch and AK-47 – and uttered just one word – "*Skuzapo*" (which means "excuse me" but was also the slang word used to describe the Selous Scouts) – whereupon an awful odour permeated the air in the small hut. Comrade Max had presumably heard of the Selous Scouts (not that we were purporting to be them) and creamed his jeans.

Max was duly handcuffed and took us to a place near a hedge where he produced his Yugoslavian AK-47 complete with uncapped M60 anti-personnel rifle grenade on the end of it and some chest webbing full of magazines and other soldier's accoutrements. We made good progress on the way back, suffering only one minor setback when Anthony Armstrong Allensbury Aggett (900101) – yes – the absolute original National Serviceman, who was carrying all of Max's weaponry, disappeared, falling down a huge water hole on the edge of a field. My heart missed a beat! We duly recovered the poor muddy wretch and continued back to our pick up point, reaching it at about 04h00.[1]

The informant in the above incidents was an impressive and very brave man. (And well rewarded too!) He featured in at least two other incidents which allowed the Fire Force to be successfully brought into contact with ZIPRA. The first of these was at Murodza Kraal, just west of Maumbe Business Centre on 4th November 1978 where several C/Ts were killed. (See Chapter 19.)

Another incident I recall in 1978 was the capture of a C/T in Chikangwe, the local African township situated about 2.5km from Karoi. The C/T had apparently been seen several times at a drinking venue, commonly referred to in Africa as a shebeen[2] in the township. He was apprehended by off duty policemen in plain clothes and handed over to us. After interrogation, he freely and voluntarily took us to the outskirts of the township where he handed over a brand new folding butt AKM hidden in a plastic bag under a sheet of corrugated iron. The weapon still had grease in its barrel and I don't think it had ever been fired.[3]

Sometime after the Viscount *Hunyani* incident, another interesting incident occurred on 21 November 1978. I was in my office and was monitoring radio traffic which indicated that a PRAW aircraft had been hit by ground fire whilst unloading leaflets over the Vuti area. The callsign I recognised as that of Peter Marchussen, a Mangula farmer whom I had known quite well from my days being stationed at Mangula. (Peter had run Mangula Transport and Sales (MTS) a large transport company.) His observer, who turned out to be Ian Klukow whom I also knew, stated that his pilot had been badly hit and was going to attempt a landing on the main road at Karoi as he feared that if he did not, Peter would not make it. The aircraft duly arrived overhead and commenced a

---

[1] Karoi Contacts Map Incident 7.

[2] *Shabeen*: A place where alcohol was illegally sold. The sale of liquor required a liquor licence issued under strict conditions by the government.

[3] Karoi Contacts Map Incident 8.

> landing approach in a southerly direction, touching down right outside the Twin Rivers Inn just north of the Karoi village. Ian Klukow, being a pilot himself, made a splendid landing, his groundspeed falling off rapidly as the little aircraft taxied uphill towards the Karoi Police station. The only incident was just before he brought the aircraft to a halt when one wing clipped a road sign. I remember helping to get Peter out of the aircraft and into an ambulance and I remember the ghastly wound to his chest. A bullet had come through the bottom of the aircraft and passed through the fleshy part of his chest, leaving a gaping wound. If it had not been for Ian Klukow's flying ability, the whole episode would have ended in tragedy.[1]

Lawrie Mabin recalls that Reeler and Wright were active in the Karoi area. Mabin was involved with them on occasions and remembers one incident involving a Lobels Bread van that delivered bread to the business centres in Hurungwe TTL. This delivery vehicle was robbed by ZIPRA insurgents on numerous occasions with cash from sales stolen. After a spate of robberies, Mike Reeler, Phil Wright and Lawrie Mabin collaborated to conduct their own "Trojan Horse" exercise. At five one evening, they met with the driver of the van and laid out their plan. Lawrie, Mike and Phil, fully armed, climbed into the back of the vehicle. When settled, the driver shut the doors, locking them inside. The driver was instructed to follow his usual route and if stopped by ZIPRA elements, to knock on the van's panels, alerting them of the impending robbery.

Strangely, despite driving from one venue to another until 11 p.m., they were not confronted by the insurgents. Consequently, they returned home. This particular operation was carried out two or three times without success. It was a risky act. Not only was the vehicle travelling along mined roads, but the occupants were vulnerable should events not unfold in the predicted manner. I found the fearless determination of these men in the execution of their duties, admirable.[2]

Ground Coverage Operations, Hurungwe TTL: Steve Nutt[3]

P/O Steve Nutt was the BSAP Ground Coverage detail stationed at the Magunje police base. He lived at the camp for two years from mid-1977 and his work focussed on Hurungwe. He makes the point:

> My role at Magunje/Karoi was probably both Policeman on the ground and Ground Coverage and intelligence gathering, reacting to incidents, both criminal and terrorist related and information gathering. Bear in mind there would have still been the normal criminal activities in the area and these would have varied from petty theft through to rape and murder not related to the war. All needed attention but as you can imagine very basic investigations were carried out and that was about all. Intelligence gathering was a major part of my role. I had cultivated several "contacts" and would visit them on a regular basis hoping to get the odd bit of information. At the time I am sure that I thought my contacts were truly reliable and the source of great importance. In hindsight, I think we were only ever told about issues that were not at all relevant. We may have received the odd bit of reliable information (like that regarding the Rhodesian Artillery contact), but I think most of the contacts just tried to keep us happy. The local people were pretty much stuck between a rock and a hard place. They had two groups of "foreigners" trying to interfere with their homeland. I don't think they liked either of us, but the terrs were more in their faces and were much more likely to hurt or kill them. The police and army, on the other hand were an inconvenience but not as violent.
>
> One memorable incident involved Ground Coverage and how our perception and the real situation out in the field sometimes differed. I had cultivated a contact in the form of Jackson (pseudonym), who lived near a store in "the middle of nowhere". It was actually

1 Phil Wright emails 23/2/2016, 25/2/2016 and 9/3/2016; Barker, J. (2007), p. 233-235.

2 Lawrie Mabin oral interview 2016.

3 Steve Nutt various email discussions and WhatsApp discussions 2/10/2016.

near Maririmba Business Centre which consisted of one store. Anyway, I would visit this guy on a regular basis, have a chat and ask the normal questions – never got anything (information) of any consequence but he was a nice guy and I thought he liked me. Unfortunately, the day came when he was murdered.[1] I attended the incident and that was the end of that. Sometime later we captured one of the gooks. I walked into the debrief with the gook and he told me that he knew me. Obviously surprised we asked how, and he said that he had often seen me when I visited Jackson, in fact on more than three occasions. There was a roundabout of bananas directly in front of the store and this group of about seven would watch me when I was at the store. They must have been two or three meters from me. Quite shocking as they could have quite easily sorted me out with little difficulty. Unfortunately, in hindsight this tells me that I actually had no idea at all of the real situation of the war and our standing.

One of the more unhappy times during the war involved a local farmer and his son. I was asked to take a Dutch Reformed minister to a farm in the bottom end of Tengwe. We did this at about 10.00 p.m. at night and it was to tell the parents that their son, Frans Jacobus Nel, an SAS soldier, had been killed in action.[2] The parents were devastated, and it was just a terrible experience to sit through their grief for some hours.

There were not too many landmine incidents in Hurungwe that I recall, probably about 20, fortunately I never actually detonated one. I was once travelling behind a Police mine proof Land Rover that detonated a "double" landmine. The Patrol Officer received minor injuries; Phil Wright had passed over the landmine 10 minutes earlier![3]

During 1978, a landmine was lifted on the dirt road near Laughing Hills farm.[4]

Steve Nutt continues:

My vehicle was ambushed on a couple of occasions and I had some lucky escapes. On one occasion I was the lead vehicle in a two vehicle convoy travelling north on the road. My Sergeant and I were fully seat belted in, and stationary, having stopped my vehicle at a road junction to wait for the escort Land Rover to catch up. No sooner had I stopped than the ambush began and chaos reigned; the gooks opened fire on us from 15-20 metres away. We were sitting ducks but the Sergeant and I managed to get out of the dreaded seat belts and scrambled to the ground on the driver's side of the vehicle. We shot wildly in the direction from which we were being ambushed. Fortunately, our support vehicle came around the corner on the road behind us and provided the necessary firepower and the enemy took flight.

The Sergeant escaped unharmed and I received minor shrapnel in my face, neck and chest with a bullet slightly lodged in my shoulder. There were probably about 15-20 bullet holes in the vehicle. The gook section were either really bad shots, or simply surprised that we had stopped right next to them and were just sitting on the side of the road, not planning the ambush at all.[5]

Hurungwe and surrounding areas were very active indeed and from 1977 things got progressively worse. Regarding Police matters I had to deal with all of the murders committed by ZIPRA. I can honestly say I attended hundreds of murder scenes, at a guess more than 300, mostly black locals within the TTL and adjacent farming areas, but I also attended several white murder scenes, mostly local farmers but also servicemen and one

---

1 Karoi Murder Map 2.

2 Nel, Frans Jacobus Trooper, C Sqn. SAS, KIA 23/11/1977. Killed on Operation Dingo at Chimoio in a combined SAS, RLI and Rh.AF attack on Venduzi Camp in Manica Province, Mozambique. Farmer from Tengwe.

3 Phil Wright email 30/3/17; Steve Nutt email 15/10/2016; Karoi Landmine Map 2, not logged on map.

4 Karoi Landmine Map 3.

5 Karoi Contacts Map Incident 9.

local businessman. I think we must have become numbed at seeing dead bodies because it was almost every day and often different incidents.

I am fairly confident that almost all terrorist related murders/assaults were reported. Local people, mostly relatives, would arrive at the Magunje Police Camp, where I lived, on a regular basis to make reports. To be honest I do not think that the locals were afraid to make these reports, possibly ZIPRA terrs were not at all concerned and told the family to make reports. At some stage during the war I would go to more than a couple each day. In most cases the victims would have been shot but there was the occasional bayonet wound. In every situation we were obliged to put together a Sudden Death Docket (SDD), that familiar little booklet. As you can imagine the dockets became more and more generic as the cause of death was the same. We always used to consider the "sellout" issue as relevant. As far as I was concerned it was always ZIPRA that carried out the murders in Hurungwe. ZIPRA were predominantly Ndebele and the first question we always asked was "What language did they speak?" – it was always Ndebele.[1]

[1] Steve Nutt confirms that he does not recall attending any incidents where SFAs shot and killed alleged contact men at the stores. Emails 12/07/2016 and 6/4/2017.

10 ~ ZIPRA MISSILE ATTACK ON A CIVILIAN AIRCRAFT

Politicians are a lot like diapers. They should be changed frequently, and for the same reason.
Mark Twain

ZIPRA Strela Section Strikes.

On the political front, it was clear that the "internal settlement" was failing. However, David Owen initiated secret talks with Joshua Nkomo on 12 May 1978 in his ongoing efforts to bring about a negotiated, peaceful settlement and an end to hostilities. David Owen envisioned Nkomo returning to Rhodesia as a presidential figurehead and Mugabe returning possibly as the Prime Minister. This was followed by three months of intriguing covert and overt political and intelligence operations involving diplomats from Britain, America, the Front Line States and Rhodesia. CIO and SB members, including Ken Flower, Derrick Robinson and Robin Harvey, continued their work to bring Nkomo and Smith together for talks. Owen advised Nkomo he would need to act decisively and immediately return to Rhodesia once an agreement was reached with Smith. His efforts were rewarded when Ian Smith accompanied by Jack Gaylard and Nkomo accompanied by Josiah Chinamano finally held a secret meeting at the State House, Lusaka, on 14 August 1978. Nigerian Foreign Minister, General Joseph Garba, also attended. Robin Harvey, who had accompanied Ken Flower or Derrick Robinson on numerous visits to Joshua Nkomo, accompanied the Rhodesian delegation and recalls: "I saw a draft 'document of Agreement' agreed to by Ian Smith and Joshua Nkomo both of whom had copies. Ian Smith's parting words were along the lines, 'This is a fair agreement I will recommend it to my Cabinet'."[1]

However, while Nkomo agreed to the process in principle he was indecisive, pressed for a subsequent meeting and ignored Owen's advice. This indecisiveness would contribute to Nkomo's downfall.[2] The success of Nkomo's return would depend on significant rapid political changes. This was unlikely to happen. Perhaps Nkomo was wary of being seen as Smith's puppet?[3] In a British Cabinet discussion on 7 September 1978, it was pointed out that: "It was unlikely that Mr Smith was genuinely ready to accept Mr Nkomo as Chairman of the Transitional Council and it was probable that he was trying to split Mr Mugabe from Mr Nkomo."[4] As Mugabe was uninvited, he rejected the process. Julius Nyerere, President of Tanzania, supported Mugabe in this matter. On 1 September 1978, Nkomo publicly announced the meeting had taken place but within 48 hours tragedy would interrupt the process.[5]

---

1 Robin Harvey email 2/10/2019;

2 In my view, if Nkomo had returned to Rhodesia as planned and his forces amalgamated with the Rhodesian SF, insurgent activity on the western border with Zambia would have been significantly reduced. The joint army could have focussed on tackling ZANLA, reducing Mugabe's military strength and forcing him to a more favourable settlement. Nkomo's trust in Mugabe would be betrayed when, in 1983, Mugabe massacred some 20,000 Ndebele in an ethnic-cleansing operation known as *Gukurahundi.* I remind participants in this massacre: *Pasi Pamera Ziso* (see prologue).

3 de Meneses & McNamara (2018), Kindle Location 5040-49.

4 Memorandum by the Foreign and Commonwealth Secretary (CP(78) 89) on Rhodesia.

5 Lord Owen oral interview 19/3/2018. Various Secret British papers entitled Rhodesia. British Confidential Documents: Rhodesia Department, Monthly Summary No. 9, September 1978, pp. 1-2; Flower, K. (1987), pp. 209-210; Smith, I. (1997), Chap. 18; Robin Harvey email 2/10/2019; Adelphi Papers, *Africa* Vol. 1, International Institute of Strategic Studies, London: Rutledge (2006), p. 266.

Matters of Moment

Once again, I wish to draw attention to some relevant prevailing facts I was unaware of at the times of their occurrences.

While on external operations over Mozambique on 14 April 1974, Flt. Lt. Chris Weinmann and Leading Aircraftsman Pat Durrett, flying a propellor-driven Aermacchi Trojan, were shot down by a Strela missile.[1] Six days later another Trojan flown by Flt. Lt. Willy Wilson and his technician Fl. Sgt. Roger Andrews were shot down by a Strela missile while searching for the first missing Trojan.[2] Thereafter, the Rhodesian Air Force researched and modified their aircraft. Petter-Bowyer comments: "All anti-Strela modifications were very successful and many Strela missiles were wasted against our slow aircraft."[3] He continues: "When all the Strela protection work was completed, Archie[4] and I paid a visit to Air Rhodesia's top managers to suggest to them that their Viscount airliners should be protected along the lines of our Dakotas. We were told that Air Rhodesia's engineers and upper management were fully aware of what had been done to protect Dakotas and they agreed a similar style of engineering could be employed to shroud Viscount exhaust pipes. The matter of repainting the Viscounts presented no special problem. However, despite a very cordial meeting, both Archie and I sensed that there was no real interest because Air Rhodesia's managers seemed unable to accept that Strela would ever be a threat to civilian airliners."[5]

Robin Hood initiated talks with the Rhodesian Air Force in 1976 that led to Air Rhodesia pilots flying Dakotas for 3 Squadron. Initially, they transported supplies and in 1977 progressed to flights for Fire Force deploying paratroopers into combat. Between 12 to 15 of the approximately 32 Air Rhodesia pilots flew for the Air Force.[6] Air Force Dakotas were modified to deter Strela missile attacks.

In April 1978, an SAA flight and an Air Rhodesia Viscount were unsuccessfully attacked in separate incidents with Strela missiles at Victoria Falls Airport.[7] Civilian aircraft were under threat. Rumours started circulating in Air Rhodesia circles that Strela surface-to-air missiles were being used by insurgents within Rhodesia against civilian aircraft. Consequently, the President of the Air Rhodesia Pilots Association, Capt. Robin Hood, held various meetings with both the Air Rhodesia Board and pilots, addressing concerns regarding aviation safety procedures and the threat to civilian aircraft. These concerns were specifically raised during a consultation held at the Jameson Hotel in April 1978. Air Rhodesia staff, which included Chief Executive Mervyn Ewett, Chief Pilot John Heap, Operations Manager Tony Beck and Senior Technician John Plowman assured pilots following consultations with the Air Force and their independent investigations, that a Strela missile would be ineffective against Viscounts. However, they were vulnerable up to 1,500 feet above ground level on take-off and below 800 feet on final approach. Robin Hood queried the accuracy of these calculations. He mentioned a Portuguese Air Force Dakota being struck by a Strela missile over northern Mozambique air space at 9,000 feet. Hood also raised the incident of a Rh.AF Hunter, flying in the Oman, being struck down by a Strela missile. He disbelieved the safety margins and felt the Viscounts were vulnerable to attack at higher altitudes than those presented. Capt. Hood's opinion was ignored and no further safety measures were recommended other than climbing to 1,500 feet as rapidly as possible after take-off. Both Capt. Robin Hood and Capt. Roy Downes a pilot and the airline's safety officer believed the factual threat was not revealed, in order to allay both aircrew and public fears, but held no evidence to substantiate this. Air Rhodesia flights were conducted over war zones during the hostilities.[8] Pilots were aware of the internal Strela threat but

---

1 Petter-Bowyer, P. (2005), pp. 226-230; Pringle, I. (2017), Chap. 5; Geldenhuys, P. (2007), p. 226, Air Strike Log Entry 133.

2 Ibid.

3 Petter-Bowyer, P. (2005), p. 234.

4 Flt. Lt. Archie Ramsbottom. Technical officer appointed to investigate counter-Strela measures.

5 Petter-Bowyer, P. (2005), p. 234.

6 Robin Hood email 23/4/2018 and oral interviews 20/2/2019 and 8/5/2019.

7 Pringle, I. (2017), Chap. 5; Petter-Bowyer, P. (2005), p. 330.

thought Kariba safe.[1] Their concerns were not unfounded.

Capt. David Padbury remembers: "I recall several informal discussions at Com.Ops. over the issue of the responsiveness of Air Rhodesia and the Strella threat. These were with Wing Commander D.A.G. Jones, Air Vice Marshal McClaren and Group Captain Petter Boyer. In these discussions there was a common denominator…they were perturbed that Air Rhodesia officials were ignoring warnings from the Rhodesian Air Force about the missile threat to their planes. In one discussion Petter-Boyer, PB as he was affectionally known, commented on a meeting that he had had with Air Rhodesia, his reaction was verging on anger and disdain as they would just not listen. PB stated that Air Rhodesia and the Rhodesian Government were more concerned with public morale and image than they were with the safety of the clientele of Air Rhodesia…the National Air Carrier at the time."[2] On 1 September 1967, Air Rhodesia became a parastatal or quasi-government corporation with its own chairman and board under the Minister of Transport's portfolio.[3] Flying standards were no less rigid than those stipulated by the International Civil Aviation Organisation (ICAO). However, due to UDI, Air Rhodesia was no longer a member of ICAO.[4] To the best of my knowledge, Com.Ops. had no authority over Air Rhodesia.[5]

Viscount *Hunyani* Attack

Petter-Bowyer makes the point: "Sadly, Air Rhodesia had done nothing to protect their Viscount airliners against Strela, despite Air Force warnings."[6] On Sunday, 3 September 1978 at 5 p.m., Flight RH 825, Viscount *Hunyani*, took off from runway 09, Kariba Airport, on a routine overland flight destined for Salisbury, carrying 52 passengers and four aircrew. Hans and Diana Hansen[7] were the last to board and sat in the rear port seats. At approximately 5.10 p.m., a covert ZIPRA Strela Section (ZSS), operating in Hurungwe, launched a Strela surface-to-air missile, striking the inner right-wing engine, causing a chain-reaction explosion to the outer engine. Hans Hansen comments: "Captain John Hood, the pilot, turned sharply to the right." Probably realising the extent of damage to the aircraft, he decided to execute an emergency wheels-up belly landing. He chose a roughly cultivated cotton field approximately 400-500m long near the remote area of Chief Nyamhunga in Hurungwe TTL. Chief Nyamhunga was from the Gova area and was forced to move as Kariba Dam was being constructed. He was relocated to an area between the Badza and Tengwe rivers before being moved again to the Nyamhunga area where he settled permanently. He resented being moved but was murdered by ZIPRA in 1978.[8] There was no intelligence suggesting that the ZSS was operating in Hurungwe either before or at the time of the Viscount being shot down.[9]

Phil Wright who attended the scene observed: "The crash area consisted of an approximately 400-500 metre long grass covered redundant cotton/maize field sloping gently on both sides towards a donga (a narrow steep-sided ravine formed by water erosion), which divided it at right angles. The aircraft approached the crash site from a northwesterly direction and clipped the top of some tall trees next to a road (track) on its approach. Branches and a piece of flap or undercarriage was torn off by these trees and lay in the grass some thirty metres into the cotton field. The aircraft appeared to have quite gently bellied down into the cotton field before it slammed into a donga which may have been covered by grass and invisible to the pilot at the time. One propeller stopped

---

8 Robin Hood oral interviews 23/4/2018, 27/4/2018, 20/2/2019 and 8/5/2019; Roy Downes various discussions and telephone call 21/11/2019.

1 Ibid.

2 Capt. D. Padbury various oral interviews 2018 and email 19/6/2020; Barker, J. (2007), p. 241.

3 Ian Pringle WhatsApp discussion 21/2/2019.

4 HC Deb 13/2/1979 vol 962 cc 964-969. Speech by Ted Rowlands in answer to a question by Norman Tebbit.

5 Confirmed by Capt. D. Padbury; Roy Downes telephone call 25/5/19 & Robin Hood telephone call 29/5/2019.

6 Petter-Bowyer, P. (2005), p. 330.

7 The Hansens survived the ordeal and currently live in Cornwall, England. They have given numerous oral interviews during 2016-2017. They confirmed that runway 09 was used for the take-off.

8 Karoi Murder Map 1; Dr J. Chakawa WhatsApp discussion 5/12/2016.

9 Confirmed by Mike Reeler, Phil Wright and Steve Nutt.

right there, embedded in the wall of the donga. From there the aircraft appeared to have cartwheeled and broken up – the tail section lying nearby and the centre section, which appeared to have completely burnt out, a little further away followed by part of the nose at the extreme southern end of the field."[1]

Miraculously, 18 passengers survived, five of whom, Dr McLaren, Sharon Cole and her four-year-old daughter, Tracey, and Robert and Shannon Hargreaves, a honeymoon couple, left the wreckage in search of help and water. The remainder gathered together under the cover of trees some 30 metres from the destroyed fuselage. Hans Hansen continues: "After about 30 minutes, at sunset, 6 p.m., we made our way towards the wreckage with Tony Hill[2] to find some clothing as ours was badly burned. We turned to make our way back to the ten survivors when a group of insurgents appeared walking towards us and opened fire from a distance of approximately 70m. We fell to the ground and the insurgents deviated towards the ten survivors and, after a brief political speech, shot and killed them."[3] Six insurgents armed with AK-47s were involved in the shootings. On hearing the shots, the McLaren party decided not to return to the crash site and walked away in search of help.

The insurgents departed after approximately 30 minutes (6.30 p.m.) and the Hansens, having lost contact with Tony Hill, sought cover in the tail-fin of the aircraft. Unfortunately, the hollow frame echoed with every move they made and was too noisy, so they crawled to a nearby ditch. Unbeknown to them, Hill was also hiding close by. By 7.30 p.m., darkness had set in and, by that time, the fires caused by the crash had extinguished. Suddenly, a section of insurgents arrived at the site accompanied by a group of locals. They ransacked the site, passing close by the Hansens, then left at approximately 11 p.m. when all was quiet. Roughly at midnight, an insurgent section arrived at the crash area, walking so close to the Hansens that they could see their boots. One insurgent almost urinated on them. This section left the area at about 1 a.m. with no further visits throughout the remainder of the long, cold, nerve-racking darkness. There was no moon that evening, causing poor visibility. The Hansens confirm there were at least three separate visits by insurgents but cannot say whether they were the same section(s) or not.[4]

Meanwhile, Phil Wright was experiencing a chaotic day and explains: "Jimmy Gardener, my GC NSPO from Chundu Base had been ambushed in the Vuti African Purchase Area (APA)[5] that same afternoon, and although not badly hurt, was flayed with bullet shrapnel down his back and was very shocked. I took him to my home where my wife, who worked 'as and when required' at the Casualty Clearing Station, cooked him a hot meal and was assisting in the removal of sand and bullet shrapnel from his back. It must have been about 18h30 that day that I was informed that an Air Rhodesia Viscount on a scheduled flight from Kariba to Salisbury was missing very shortly after take-off and could have come down in our (Karoi) area. The GC bases had already been notified and an air search by Air Force and PRAW aircraft was beginning. I remember waiting on standby at the Police station until late that night for information."[6]

Soon after the downing of the Viscount, Lt. Col. Garth Barrett, the last Officer Commanding the Rhodesian SAS, was alerted that the aircraft was missing and put together an SAS rescue team, including medics, trackers and a signaller.[7] Barrett had correctly deduced that the Viscount had been brought down by a missile, advising General "Bert" Barnard, Senior Army Commander in

1 Phil Wright email 18/8/2019. Confirmed by Lt. Col. Garth Barrett email 13/10/2015 who led a team of SAS men into the scene and Mike Reeler who attended the scene.

2 Tony Hill died in Harare in 2016.

3 Dr J. Chakawa confirms ZIPRA were responsible for shooting the survivors. Field research and oral interviews 15/04/2016.

4 ZIPRA and civilians looted bags, wristwatches and whatever they could lay their hands on before the arrival of Rhodesian soldiers. Field research and oral interviews Dr J. Chakawa 15/4/2016.

5 Land set aside for purchase by Africans in terms of the Land Apportionment Act 1930.

6 Phil Wright email 9/3/2016.

7 Signaller: Communications expert. Barrett commanded the Rhodesian SAS from May 1978 - May 1980 when it was disbanded.

Com.Ops. under Lt. Gen. Peter Walls, accordingly. Barrett's group included Darrell Watt, a tracker and Phil Cripps. He requested a Dakota uplift from New Sarum to Kariba with parachute jump instructors (PJIs), which included Charlie Buchan a former member of the SAS. Once assembled, the group travelled to Kariba Airport for deployment. Barrett continues:

> Briefings for the morning search were held at Kariba and while there were aircraft searching during the night, nothing of value was located. It was decided to launch our Dakota with the SAS Team and PJI's at first light so that when the aircraft was in the general search area the light would be good enough for us to see effectively. Our SAS remit from Com.Ops. was to help locate the missing Viscount and "locate and medical assist" any survivors.
>
> The Dak searched the area and at about 0830 I saw the remains of the Viscount, we circled the area to ascertain a drop zone for the parachutists. I saw a number of people about 75m from the remains of the Viscount, but no movement was detected. As the Pathfinder, I jumped first and carried the Altimeter which could read the ground pressure to give the aircraft commander the reading on the ground. Once the last parachutes were in the air I went with Phil Cripps to the site where I had observed the people lying under the tree, they were all dead – shot at close range as there were powder burns visible on their clothing and skin. An older gentleman still had a bunch of bank notes, clearly visible, sticking out of the top pocket of his shirt. As the senior officer at the site, I inspected the clothing of the deceased females and concluded that those wearing dresses and skirts had not been raped as their panties were in place.[1] I knew, from my numerous dealings with the press that this was one of the questions that would be asked as they invariably tried to sensationalise events. When Watt arrived, he had bruised his heel on his parachute landing, I sent him and his team on a wide 360-degree search for tracks and I went on a search of the area to ascertain what had happened, and to see if there were any other survivors. As we searched the area the Hansens appeared, they had miraculously survived the crash and avoided detection by ZIPRA sections throughout the night. One more survivor, Tony Hill, emerged, the three survivors explained the events of the night and were later choppered to Kariba.[2]

Once medically examined, the Hansens returned home and, shortly after settling in, were visited by two plain-clothed gentlemen, suggesting they moderate their discussions regarding their most recent traumatic experiences and observations. It seemed the request was directed towards respecting the grief of the deceased and their families.[3]

Reeler and Wright set off from Karoi for the Viscount crash site early on the morning of 4 September 1978. That same morning, Steven Nutt was also travelling to the crash site and en route met up with the McLaren party. He reported his find to the JOC. A G-Car, piloted by Flt. Lt. Ian Harvey, was despatched to uplift the survivors to Karoi. On arrival, they were treated for their injuries by Sue Wright, Myra Kennedy, Shirley Poultney and other members of the Casualty Clearing Station. Sue Wright remembers, among other things, the group were deeply shocked and traumatised. Sharon Cole had sustained a serious shoulder wound which Dr McLaren had packed with mud and bandaged to stem the bleeding. He had also fashioned them shoes from grass and tree bark as theirs had been lost in the crash. After their initial treatment at Karoi, the survivors were flown to the Andrew Fleming Hospital in Salisbury.[4] Steve Nutt visited the site on a further two occasions to assist in the collection of evidence.

After a journey of about 40 kilometres, Reeler and Wright arrived at the scene. Wright recalls:

---

[1] Barker, J. (2007), p. 230, confirms the girls were not raped.
[2] Garth Barrett email 13/11/2015. Karoi Contacts Map Incident 10.
[3] Various oral interviews with the Hansens 2016-2017.
[4] Sue Wright email 9/3/2016.

> Even though I was by then a hardened policeman and well experienced in the ways of war, it became a shocking blur, and something I have tried to erase from my mind. I remember the all pervading stench of aviation fuel and blackened, scorched earth and metal. Much of the metal that remained was still hot and smoking. There were rivers of molten aluminium and dozens of chunks and shards of metal. The contents of luggage and suitcases lay everywhere. I saw blackened and charred bodies, bits and pieces of charred remains and I remember a severed foot in a black shoe. Mike Farrell (M/I/C Karoi) had arrived with PATU sticks and a lot of APR's and was busy trying to remove charred bodies from the wreckage and assemble them in orderly rows. I remember learning from him that there were 10 bodies of people who had survived and been shot in the south western side of the crash site and that CID (Sinoia) were attending to this aspect. I did not visit this area for fear of disturbing CT tracks, evidence etc.
>
> I remember monitoring radio chatter which indicated that there appeared to be suitcases/clothing in some of the surrounding kraals. We proceeded to visit some of the very nearby kraals in the hopes of getting some information as to what had transpired but the kraals were all deserted, as was to be expected and we could not do much more due to SAS follow up troops being in the area. Later that evening Mike Reeler and I returned to Karoi and the war continued.[1]

Barrett continues:

> Within a couple of hours a vehicle arrived with I believe PATU on board, and additional military personnel continued to arrive; by mid-afternoon the whole area was secure. Watt had located spoor but the responsibility for the follow up would then be under local area operational control. I relinquished control to the BSAP/PATU and the SAS team and I were uplifted by helicopter back to Kariba as I had completed my remit from Com.Ops.
>
> At Kariba I briefed all the military, police and any members of the "civil powers" that needed to be briefed. That evening, there was a Press briefing at 1 Indep Company HQ at the Kariba Heights barracks. I gave a briefing on my findings and observations at the site. After this briefing, I was specifically asked if any of the female members of the survivors had been raped. I repeated my statement on this subject, which I had covered in my earlier briefing, that no one had been raped! Unfortunately, the South African magazine *SCOPE*, claimed that the female survivors were raped and sad to see other "story" tellers have kept this lie alive with graphic detail, they should be ashamed of themselves.[2]

Supt. Bob Bedingham provides his account of matters: "On 4 September 1978, accompanied by some nurses, I was flown by helicopter to the crash site of Viscount *Hunyani* in Hurungwe TTL. My role was to gain an overview of the scene, assist where I could and report back to Dis.Pol. and Sub.JOC Sinoia. I met some of the survivors at the scene, observed the 10 survivors who had been shot and carried out an appraisal of the crash site before returning to Sinoia. There was a considerable military presence in Hurungwe immediately and over the next few weeks. I do not recall any contact with insurgents that linked them to the murder of the 'survivors' at the *Hunyani* crash site, or the actual ZIPRA section that shot down the Viscount. I recall discussions at our meetings where we suggested Viscounts carry weapons packed in a manner that would survive the impact of a crash that would enable survivors to protect themselves."[3] Air hostesses were subsequently trained to use the GM16, a 9mm machine gun, and two were stored in the back of the aircraft.[4]

A considerable number of troops were deployed into the area, including C Company 1RAR under the command of Col. Lionel Dyck. There were several contacts but no evidence that either the

1 Phil Wright email 9/3/2016.
2 Garth Barrett email 13/11/2015.
3 Bob Bedingham email 3/4/2016.
4 Pringle, I. (2017), p. 124.

ZIPRA Strela Section or the ZIPRA section who murdered the survivors were contacted or eliminated.[1] During a BBC interview, Joshua Nkomo announced with a chuckle on 5 September 1978 that his ZIPRA had shot down the Viscount but denied his men had killed the survivors. Subsequent ballistic evidence and research confirmed categorically that a ZIPRA section was indeed responsible for the murder of the 10 survivors. David Owen recalls: "I was in my garden in Wiltshire relaxing thinking things may be getting better and then this took place. Then Joshua Nkomo came on the 1 o'clock news with his famous chuckle. I thought to myself you idiot you have killed off your chances of going anywhere now."[2]

[1] Confirmed by Mike Reeler, Steve Nutt and Bob Bedingham. Confirmed by Col. Lionel Dyck, Commander of C Company 1RAR who deployed to Hurungwe in the hunt for the ZIPRA Strela Section various WhatsApp discussions including 29/09/2016.

[2] Lord Owen oral interview 19/3/2018.

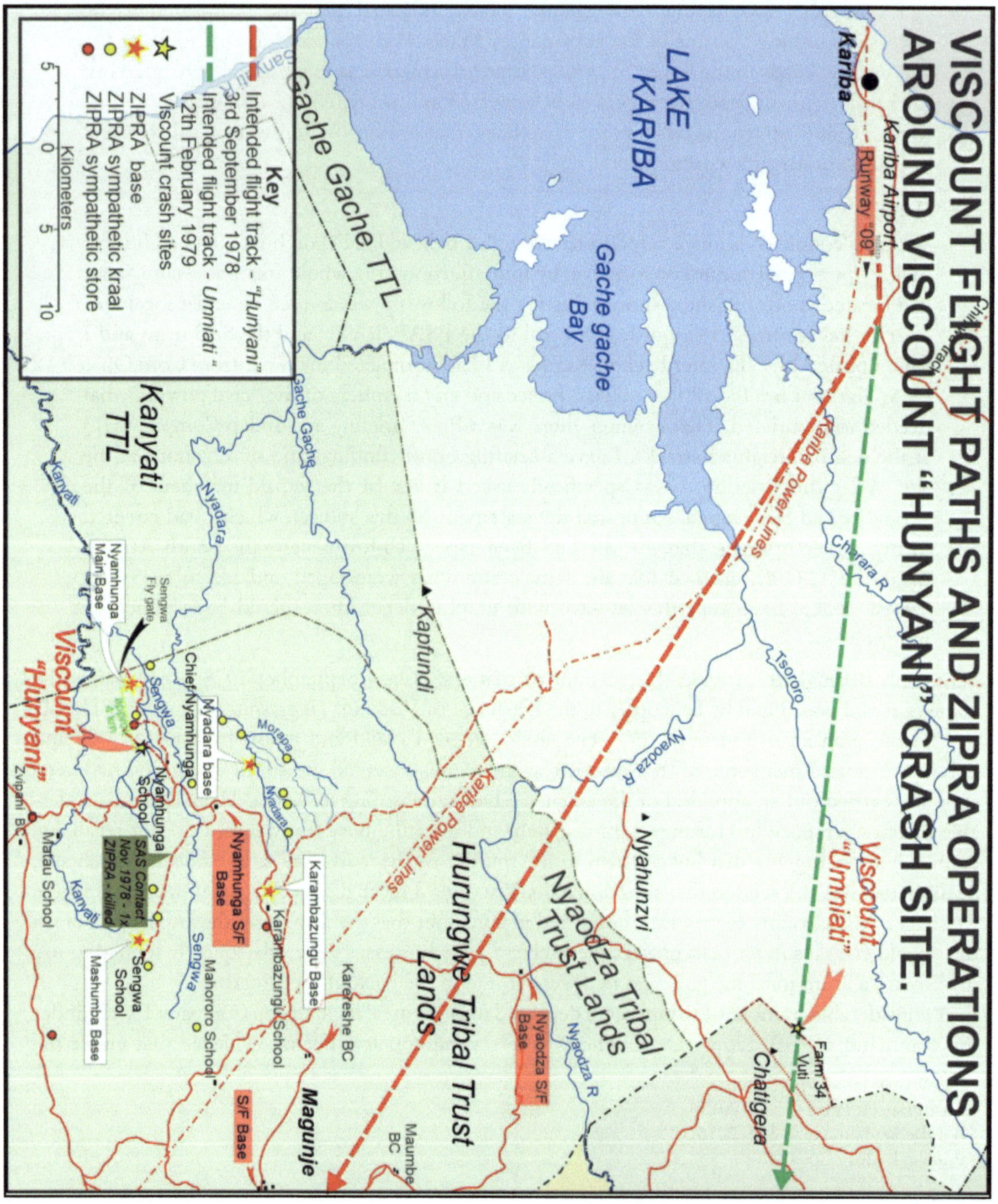

The BSAP forensic ballistics team were called to establish the cause of the incident. Extensive examinations were carried out by Supt. Donald Hollingworth and his team which included Paul de Mattos who recalls: "I located a piece of foreign metal (shrapnel) in the inner exhaust Cowling which helped Hollingworth draw his conclusions."[1] Hollingworth concluded that Viscount *Hunyani* was brought down by a Soviet Strela heat-seeking surface-to-air missile.

The Minister for Transport and Power, Bill Irvine, announced these findings in Parliament on 7 September 1978. Conservative MP, Rear Admiral Morgan Giles, announced in the House of Commons on 7 November 1978: "I was in Salisbury only two or three weeks ago and I saw the ballistic laboratory in which has been collected a fantastic armoury of Soviet weapons, including submachine guns, automatic machine guns, landmines and missiles. There are pieces of missile that were removed from the airliner that was shot down. They were put under a forensic microscope and compared with a captured Sam 7 missile. The grooves are identical and manufacture was probably by the same machine. That is proof, possibly, of how the airliner was shot down."[2]

Capt. Roy Downes, the airline's safety officer, attended the scene with members of the Department of Civil Aviation. He returned to the scene on 26 September 1978 and concluded from initial police forensic examinations and his onsite investigations that Viscount *Hunyani* had been struck by a Strela surface-to-air missile.[3] Subsequently, Roy Downes calculated Viscount *Hunyani*'s flight-path was within range of a Strela surface-to-air heat-seeking missile: "At a height of about 800 AGL (above ground level) the aircraft would have turned out right for Salisbury with an initial climbing rate of about 1500 feet/minute. 13nm from the point of turn the aircraft passed almost directly over a spot height of 3201 feet at an altitude of about 9500 feet AMSL (above mean sea level)/6000 feet AGL well within the range of the SAM7."[4]

1 Paul de Mattos email 15/6/2015.

2 British Parliamentary Hansard records: HC Deb 7/11/1978 vol 957 cc 694-921.

3 Ibid.

4 Roy Downes email 9/11/2019.

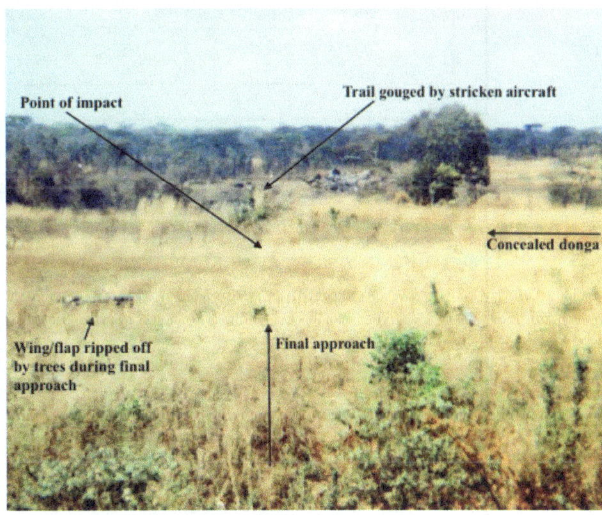

Overview of Viscount *Hunyani*'s crash site. Photo by Phil Wright.

The point of impact on the edge of the donga. Photo by Phil Wright.

View of the crash site looking towards *Hunyani*'s final descent. D/S/O Reeler examines the evidence. Photo by Phil Wright.

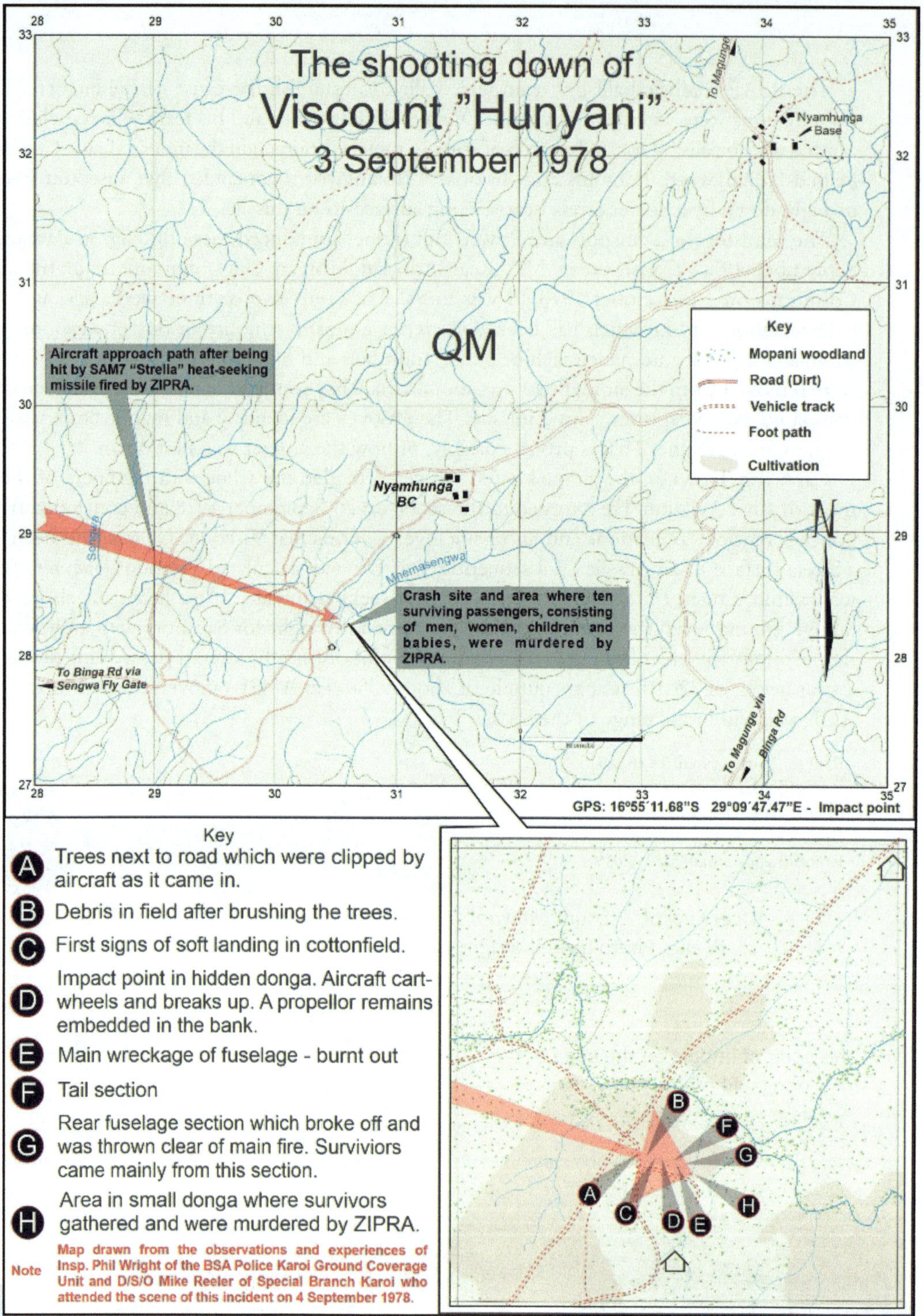

Insp. Phil Wright examines the imbedded propellor whilst standing on the donga. Photo by Phil Wright.

D/S/O Reeler examines the rear-section fuselage. Photo by Phil Wright.

International Response to the Viscount *Hunyani* Attack

The BBC News covered the tragedy on several news broadcasts including the 1 p.m. and 6 p.m. bulletins on 5 September 1978. They followed up the story on 6 September 1978 during the 6 p.m. and 10 p.m. programmes and, subsequently, the following day during the 7 a.m. and 6 p.m. transmissions. Several British newspapers also covered the incident. *The Times* of London carried a statement from Edward Rowlands, the British Foreign Secretary: "The Foreign Office expresses its shock at the incident but says it has no independent evidence of what has happened or who was responsible. Yet again there has been a horrible and tragic incident in Rhodesia involving innocent civilians. We deplore the whole incident which, once more, underlines the need to bring this disastrous war to an end by negotiation and achieve independence and majority rule for Zimbabwe."

The British Parliament was in recess from 1 September to 23 October 1978 as noted by Ronald Bell on 13 February 1979: "Last September a similar incident occurred. A civil airliner was shot down in almost exactly the same position—again by Russian missiles—with the loss of 48 civilian lives. That happened in the middle of the Summer Recess. In consequence, it was not raised in Parliament and no reference to it is to be found in Hansard."[1]

The British and Foreign Commonwealth Office (FCO) released a statement on the BBC relating to the attack at 12 noon and 6 p.m. on 5 September 1978. David Owen addressed the Royal Commonwealth Society the following day, stating: "The seriousness of the present situation is apparent to everyone – with another horrible and tragic incident near Kariba to add to the many others which have shocked and numbed us all – over 3,000 dead this year: no end to the hostilities in sight: enormous dislocations to the fabric of Rhodesia, and two other Commonwealth countries, Zambia and Botswana, and similar problems facing Mozambique. Too many innocent lives of all races have been lost, senselessly and often brutally murdered. We need to see a new spirit, a spirit of reconciliation. It would be preferable to have a temporary ceasefire while negotiations continue. If this is not possible then at the very least I would urge that nothing would do more good to establish the right spirit for negotiation and reconciliation than for clear-cut orders to go out from the leaders on all sides responsible for the fighting: clear-cut orders that they will not tolerate incidents involving the loss of life of innocent civilians and that, if there are such incidents, those responsible will be brought to account. It is time to bind up the wounds, not to create fresh ones. The basis for a settlement is now there if only all the parties could put aside past suspicions and fears and accept the opportunity. We have taken years to reach this stage: the seeds are planted. Yet, if the months pass, all could be destroyed."[2] Tragically, the war raged on.

The British Air Line Pilots Association (BALPA) wrote to the British Government shortly after the tragedy stating, "the British Government should help with technical aid and should help to try to get an international inquiry into the disaster". Norman Tebbitt, MP at the time, now Lord Tebbitt, also wrote to Prime Minister Callaghan and the Minister of State, Foreign and Commonwealth Affairs, Ted Rowlands, in support of BALPA.[3] Tebbitt, prior to his election to the Commons, was an airline pilot and continued to be a member of BALPA, hence his deep concerns of the attack.[4]

The International Federation of Airline Pilots Association (IFALPA) attempted to prevent further attacks on civilian aircraft protected by the Montreal Convention (convention for the suppression of unlawful acts against civil aviation). IFALPA wrote: "To President Kaunda of Zambia to whom Mr Nkomo and his ZIPRA element owe sanctuary, advising them of IFALPA's views on attacks on civilian aircraft and requesting assurances that positive measures should be taken to protect this vital transport medium. The IFALPA President offered to send a Deputy President and another Principal Officer for appropriate discussions. No reply was received."[5] Zambia was not a member of IFALPA at the time.

1 British Parliamentary Hansard records: HC Deb 13/2/1979 vol 962 cc 971-973.

2 Secretary of State's Speech to the Royal Commonwealth Society, Wednesday, 6/9/1978.

3 British Parliamentary Hansard records: HC Deb 13/2/1979 vol 962 cc 964-969. The previous disaster being the attack on Viscount *Hunyani*.

4 Ibid.; Lord Tebbit email 10/7/2018.

5 Report by I.M. Evans, IFALPA Director (Rhodesia).

This matter was raised in the Australian Parliament on 14 September 1978 by David Thomson and addressed by Andrew Peacock, Australian Minister of Foreign Affairs: "The Government has been closely following recent developments in Rhodesia. It has noted the harder statements now being made by both sides and is very concerned at the increasing deterioration of the situation in Rhodesia. Honourable members will be aware that recently there has been a series of tragic, grievous incidents involving innocent civilians, both black and white, as a result of the continuing conflict. That can only underline the urgent need to bring an end to that conflict by the negotiation of a settlement which takes adequate account of the legitimate political aspirations of black Rhodesians to participate fully in the political processes of their country."[1] Perhaps not in the manner we Rhodesians would have preferred but the matter was, nevertheless, addressed.

At a memorial service for the deceased on 8 September 1978, the Anglican Dean for the Salisbury Cathedral, The Very Reverend John da Costa slated the Viscount attack in an emotionally charged sermon entitled "The Silence is Deafening". The emphasis of his sermon was on the failure of world governments to condemn the deliberate shooting down of a civilian airliner and the subsequent slaughter of innocent survivors. I found da Costa's attack on Christians unsettling. He stated: "Who else (is to blame)? The churches? Oh yes, I fear so. For too long, too many people have been allowed to call themselves 'believers' when they have been nothing of the kind. Belief must bring about action. If you believe in God, you must do something about it."

I hasten to add that I was not a committed Christian at the time but I was acquainted with many professing believers. They were derided as "Bible punchers" and suffered other derogatory terms. I recall one such Support Unit member lying in his tent reading his Bible before deployment. I am convinced many sincere Christians were distraught, deeply hurt and praying unceasingly for the survivors and families alike. Their quandary was the extremes of advice by Church leadership: Bishop Lamont's call to support the terrorists and Dean da Costa's call to condemn them. What was the role and action Christians were called to? Then of course there was the government who were fighting in "defence of Christianity".

However, shortly after the incident the South African anti-apartheid activist and a leading world-renowned clergyman, Bishop Desmond Tutu, General Secretary of the South African Council of Churches, spoke out boldly from Johannesburg: "No condemnation could be strong enough for such a heartless act of slaying defenceless and helpless people. My heartfelt sympathy goes out to their relatives and friends."[2]

Intelligence Background to Nyamhunga Area

In order to gain a fuller understanding of how efficiently ZIPRA penetrated Hurungwe, read Chapter 13. I have not brought the content of this chapter forward as it was intertwined with intelligence relevant at the time it came to hand. Unfortunately, as I perceived matters, the crashed Viscount *Hunyani* could not have landed in a more inappropriate location. As our intelligence networks began to penetrate Hurungwe, the Nyamhunga area provided essential information, helping break ZIPRA's operational strategies. Nyamhunga was one of the command HQs for ZIPRA with at least five resident sections within a 12 kilometre radius of the downed aircraft. Insurgents were capable of walking considerable distances at speed so the resident sections were quite capable of reaching the crash site in a relatively short period of time. As Nyamhunga was on one of ZIPRA's infiltrations routes, on occasions as many as 250 ZIPRA were known to be in the area at one time or another, as they transited to central Rhodesia.

The Hansens maintain, while huddled together under the cover of night, the location of the crashed Viscount was visited at least on three occasions by insurgents but they cannot state with certainty whether these arrivals were by one-and-the-same or different groups, nor do they have any idea of the number of insurgents arriving. It would seem to me, however, the probability was more than one section visited the crash site over and above the section who murdered the survivors. These

1 Australian House of Representatives 14/9/1978, Hansard p. 1000.

2 Downes, R. (2017), Chap. 18.

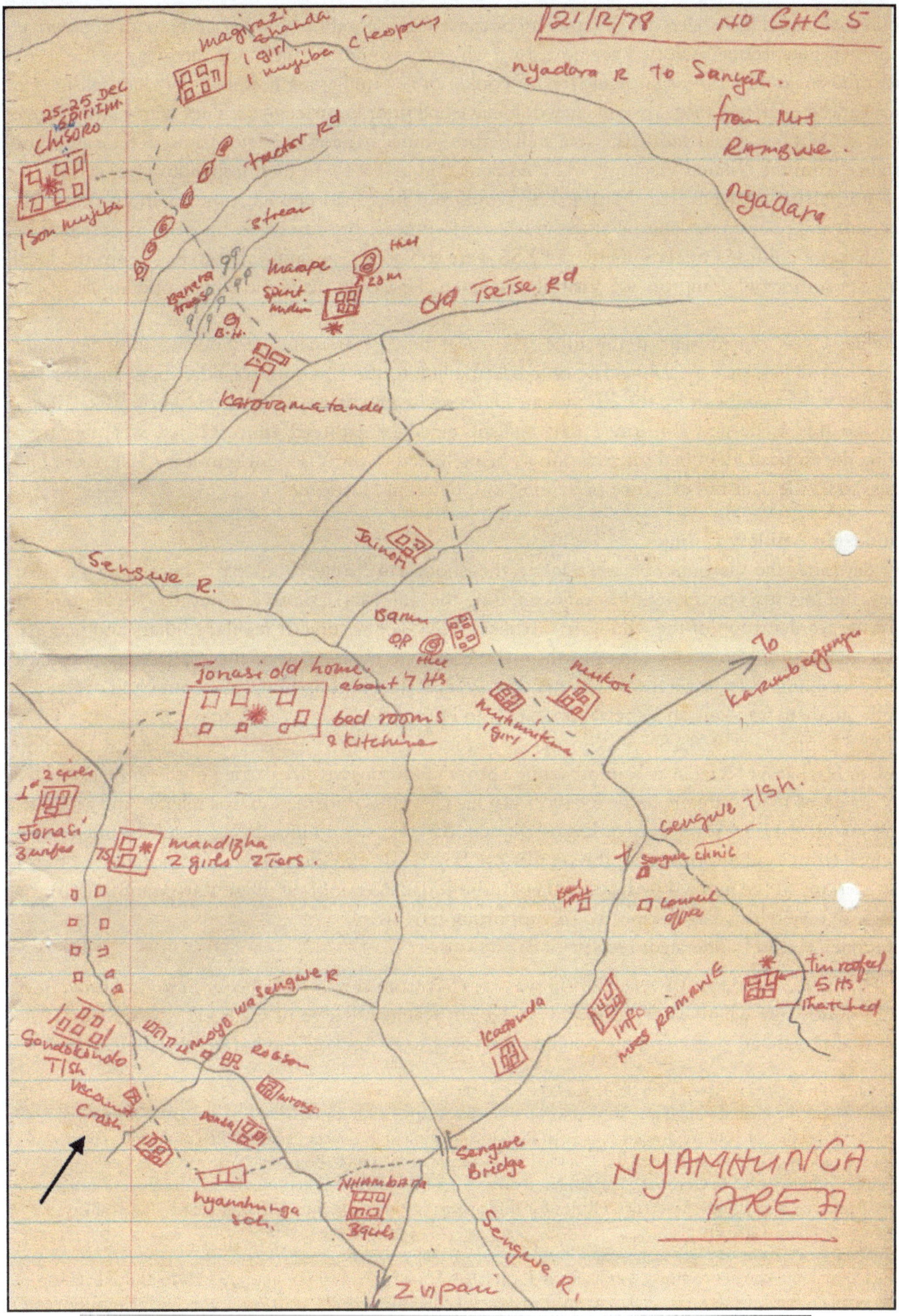

Original Sketch 21/12/1978.
ZIPRA activity around the Viscount *Hunyani* crash site.

excursions would have been out of curiosity or cause for celebration at being party to an impressive, from their perspective, victory. I see no reason why they wouldn't have made their way to the scene under the cover of darkness knowing the SF could not respond at night, unless they had callsigns in the area which ZIPRA more than likely would have had prior knowledge of. They were safe to move about at night but would vacate the area well before sunrise to allow sufficient time to relocate some distance from the ill-fated Viscount, to avoid detection by the SF in their impending follow-up.

I am personally persuaded that the ZSS would not have had enough time to shoot down the Viscount and 30 minutes later be at the crash site to murder the survivors. Subsequent research by Dr Chakawa confirms operations by the ZSS were top secret, isolating themselves from the local population to avoid compromise. Visiting the crash site would place the covert operations of the ZSS at risk.

While I was not present at the time, I have gathered statements, conducted interviews and researched all evidence available. The only ballistic link to the Viscount tragedy I have managed to establish was an ambush by the Rhodesian Defence Regiment on 27 October 1978. Mike Reeler attended this scene and confirmed that ballistic evidence gathered from ZIPRA weapons fired during the ambush identified one weapon as being linked to the Viscount murders.[1] I have not had access to all the ballistics evidence pertaining to Operation Hurricane.

Rhodesian Artillery Contact

Five days after the Viscount *Hunyani* tragedy, the Rhodesian Artillery took part in probably the most successful infantry operation in Hurungwe during the war. Maj. Eric Evans[2] recalls: "In September 1978 the regular troop of the Rhodesian Artillery (RA) – consisting of regular soldiers and national servicemen – was deployed to the North of the Karoi area as a result of the ZIPRA missile attack on the Viscount *Hunyani* on the 3rd September 1978. Half the troop under the command of 2nd Lt. Frank Moxham was sent on a special operation to Hurungwe."[3]

On 8 September 1978,[4] Steve Nutt passed on intelligence of the presence of a ZIPRA section close to Nyakarura Kraal near Karambazungu Store in Hurungwe. We carried out lengthy extensive investigations to identify the battle location.[5] In his view, this information was reliable and accurate, consequently passing it on to Maj. Evans for action.[6] Evans continues: "As a result of intelligence received from local informants in the area by the BSAP GC operator, Steve Nutt, I deployed two 4 men sections of the unit led by Bombardier Andre Johan Alers (AJ) and Sgt. Ray Beamish (RB)[7] by vehicle to observe a village suspected of supporting terrorists."[8]

Gunner Martin Lunderstedt recalls:

> Early in September 1978 our troop was recalled from the bush to go back to Salisbury. I'm not sure where we were, could have been Katanga Range near Gwelo. All we were told it was top secret and all would be revealed to us back at the barracks! I remember

[1] See Chap 11. Ballistics expert Paul de Mattos confirms this.
[2] Born 1946 in the United Kingdom. Moved with family to Northern Rhodesia (Zambia) in 1959. Educated to secondary level in that country. Joined Northern Rhodesia Regiment as officer cadet in 1964 and sent to the Royal Military Academy, Sandhurst, in the UK, 1964 to1966. Commissioned into the British Army (Royal Artillery) in September 1966. Served in Germany, England and Singapore. Resigned 1972 and moved to Rhodesia (Zimbabwe) where he served with Rhodesian African Rifles for three years before being transferred to Rhodesian Artillery.
[3] Eric Evans email 24/6/2016.
[4] Date confirmed from Ray Beamish's citation submitted by Maj. Evans.
[5] Kraal locstat and contact confirmed as likely by Dr J. Chakawa on a field trip on the 12/7/2016 and WhatsApp discussions on the same day. Dr Chakawa's information was that five ZIPRA were killed. It is likely the informants underplayed the actual numbers to save face. Phil Wright states: "It may well be the contact site, I recall going under the power line which is about 2-3 clicks east of this loc. back towards Magunje. The trees look sparse which is consistent with my memory and the ground slopes towards a stream." Emails 6/10/2016 and 11/12/2019. Site also confirmed as likely by Martin Lunderstedt email 1/11/2016 and Steve Nutt WhatsApp discussion 16/1/2020.
[6] Steve Nutt emails 16/6/2016 and 12/07/2016.
[7] Beamish R. (728094), Sgt. 1st Field Regt. Rh.Art. KIA 20/7/1979.
[8] Eric Evans email 25/6/2016.

being shepherded into our conference room near the gun hanger by a Territorial Force (TF) SGM Mc something or other. He was always there and had folded his business to serve indefinitely in the TF's. We were told about the Viscount shooting down and about the subsequent slayings of the survivors! We were told we were confined to barracks and would leave to Urungwe District the next morning! We were also told to take no prisoners as they didn't care about the survivors and as we were all filled with a white hot rage, we all agreed! We then left early the next morning to Karoi, with half the troop! The other half went in the Selous Scout bus to hunt down terrorists in some TTL and would join us later! Our camp site was near Elephants' Walk Hotel, the other side of Karoi, on the way to Makuti! We were about +- 3km's from the Hotel and used to go on liberty evening there! We were introduced to a Major Johnson (?) from IRR who was the OC of the camp there. He told us how glad he was that we were there and mentioned that his men hadn't seen any gooks and if any gooks were killed, he would personally buy us a crate of beer per gook.

Our two sticks consisted of AJ Alers (AJ), BA (name withheld), Paddy Power (PP, deceased) and Steve Luker. Our stick was Ray Beamish (RB), MC, M (both names withheld) and myself, Martin Lunderstedt (ML). Travelling down the dust road in two Mercedes Troop Carrier 4.5s between 1-2 p.m., close to the deployment locstat, we overtook three-four *mujibhas* riding bicycles in the same direction. A short while later AJ and RB told us to debus at speed hidden by a cloud of dust that followed us. We did and tumbled into the bush at the side of the road. Maybe about a minute later the cyclists came past, following the trucks and then we heard them whistling! AJ and RB decided to change frequency on our A76 radios, so they could talk to each other so as not to disrupt the normal flow of air traffic. We could see a village about a km away on top of a ridge. A long traditionally ploughed (by *badza*[1]) field stretched ahead from our position next to the road for 150m to a small ridge filled with trees and rocks, which lay between us and the village. This ridge was an ideal OP to observe the kraal as a vlei with slow gradient swept up towards the village giving an uninterrupted view. AJ's stick went on ahead and we covered them until they reached the tree line and then they would cover us as we proceeded to join them! We then got ready to proceed across the ploughed field.

Suddenly AJ's voice came over the radio and told RB to get across immediately as there was a group of gooks in the vlei on the other side of the ridge walking towards them. We sprinted across the +- 150 metres to where they were waiting observing the gooks. AJ and RB decided to ambush them right there and then and to cut them down as they came up into the trees where we were waiting. PP put on a rifle grenade to initiate the contact and we got into position. I was on the extreme left with BA the other MAG gunner on right point with the other riflemen in between us, with the two stick leaders in the middle. As we went over the ridge to initiate the contact, there were nine gooks walking along relaxed, with a group of around six nannies[2] in white clothes and head-scarves singing "Chimurenga" songs[3] to them as they moved.

PP fired the rifle grenade into the tree next to the gooks and the ambush started. It was the perfect ambush, they were in the open and we were behind trees and rocks and they had nowhere to run! All the FNs opened up and BA's MAG-gun. Somehow I couldn't pull my MAG's trigger immediately and after about two seconds I started shooting as well. I remembered bodies falling and screaming and shouting and leaves falling all around me as they shot back. There were three-four bodies from the initial burst and someone threw a grenade at us and we all dived down. I heard a soft bang, but as our ears were numbed

[1] Ploughed by hand with a *badza* (hoe).

[2] Nanny: An African woman employed to look after children. Its usage spread to embrace all African women. It was not considered a derogatory expression at the time.

[3] Traditional ZANLA and ZIPRA war songs.

> by the noise, and I thought "shit that's nothing". RB shouted "There by the tree" and we all said "Where?" He said, "Watch my dust", there was dust everywhere and eventually we saw him and blasted him to pieces. There was a guy running to my right about 80 metres and against all training, I shot across my friends towards him. No one listened to me as I shouted, "He's getting away". My bullets travelled towards him like little spouts of dust and then went through him. He threw his arms up and flopped down. As I watched, amazed, he got up and started to try to run again. Another member of the stick saw him and also shot him. He didn't rise again.[1]

Maj. Evans noted in AJ's Military Forces Commendation (Operational):

> The half sections then moved into the assault across open ground under accurate enemy fire. At one stage a member of Bombardier Aler's section was hit by shrapnel from the terrorist position. While turning to check this man Bombardier received two enemy bullets through the radio on his back.
>
> Undeterred by this, he ascertained that the man was not seriously wounded, assisted him back into the assault line and continued to advance. When RB's section was pinned down by enemy fire, Bombardier Alers directed effective covering fire into the terrorist position to enable the assault line to keep moving.[2]

Lunderstedt adds to the events:

> There was still plenty of action happening and as the shooting slowed down, we moved through and basically finished off the survivors. There was one guy lying at the end groaning terribly and PP told me to kill him. I couldn't do it and Steve shot him but he continued groaning and in anger, I emptied about twenty five rounds of a belt into his chest. I am not proud of what I did and always feel deep regret for what I did. AJ had a 9mm pistol and was shooting this one body and kept telling us to watch how this guy couldn't stop bouncing up and down with his bullets. The nannies were in a cattle kraal screaming and crying at us and shouting *Mambo mambo* and I remembered someone saying let's "slag" them and I remembered RB saying, no way, there will be no murder of civilians. We picked up nine bodies and their weapons, which included a PKM and the rest of them were AKM's, also one Makarov pistol. While searching (looting) the bodies I burnt my arm against the barrel of my MAG trying to remove a watch from an arm. With respect to goods found on the bodies, there was just over Rhod $24 which we split between 8 of us and myriad small items but nothing to link this group with the Viscount massacre!
>
> RB suddenly remembered that we had changed our frequency on our radios and changed it back to the normal frequency. All of a sudden we heard lots of voices on the radio everywhere saying "What's happening? Who's shooting? Etc", until RB said over the radio "Contact, contact, grid ref no X, eight Charlie Tango's killed, repeat, eight Charlie tango's KIA, no casualties on Sierra Foxtrot members!" There was absolute silence from everyone else as this was the most terrorists killed in a single contact in this Region till that date. We then found another body a bit further away in the reeds and then got back on the radio to report, "Negative, not eight, but nine Charlie Tango's!" We were then told to guard the bodies until we were fetched, presumably that evening!
>
> We were watching the village and the guys decided to go visit that village with the AKM's and basically go mad. M and myself stayed behind on a small rising to the West of the contact guarding the bodies and then we watched the guys do an extended line towards the village. We could see the villagers start running and then a minute later our guys entered the village to absolute silence. Then they opened up and razed the village to

[1] Martin Lunderstedt email 20/03/2016 and WhatsApp discussion 18/12/2019.

[2] Maj. Evans email 24/6/2016.

> the ground. I remember a lot of shooting and then I saw this pure white smoke rise from a few huts and realised that WP (white phosphorous) Grenades were being used to destroy the village! Someone shot at us two and the bullet ricocheted between us, and then suddenly it wasn't funny anymore. That was the last time we were shot at.
>
> In the nine bodies we found that one was a Political Commissar who had a Red Star Medal from Russia, a Regional Commander, a Sectional Commander and then six foot-troops. Their boots were boned and polished to this amazing "mirror finish" and I thought they were very brave soldiers, they didn't surrender to us and fought back to the end, and to this day I respect them. I know that they were gooks and had done some rough things in their lives but I regarded them as very brave soldiers and they died bravely![1]

The two sections gathered the nine bodies and weapons and advised HQ of their involvement in a successful contact. Weapons recovered were AKMs, a PKM machine gun on tripods and a Makarov pistol.

Lunderstedt continues:

> Eventually a truck turned up, took all the weapons and left five bodies with us to guard for the night. They said there wasn't enough space for us and they would be back tomorrow. That probably was the most frightening night of my life. We were on guard each for 1½ hours and I remember M waking me up and saying "someone's out there". We fired a few shots and got told to shut up and let the others sleep. Then it was my turn on guard. There was definitely someone there and I tried to wake the guys up and they told me that it was my imagination, so I just opened up anyway. The next morning, one of the bodies was gone, another had his brains eaten away by dogs from a village nearby and then the trucks returned and we were loaded up and taken back to the Karoi Police Station. The bodies were dropped off at the Police Station and then we went to the Club. There was a huge party going on and we went into an immense reception organised by the local farmers. They were celebrating the contact and when they found out it was us we were absolute heroes and I'm sure a few would have gladly given their daughters to us too.
>
> When we were eventually allowed to leave, with many crates of beers given by the farmers to us, we then went back to our base. The OC greeted us very coldly and strangely and also never bought us the beers that he promised at the beginning of our stint with him! Later on that trip we had a party at the Elephants' Walk Motel and gave them some souvenirs from the contact for their pub.[2]

Steve Nutt recalls: "I was called to the contact and drove there accompanied by my usual support Land Rover, arriving after dark, approximately 8 p.m. We collected all the weapons and four bodies which was all we could manage, so I advised that I would return in the morning. The RA section remained guarding the rest of the bodies and awaited pick up which was arranged for the following morning. It was a long nervous night for them! The bodies and weapons were conveyed back to Magunje and I set off early the following morning (9/9/78) accompanied by Phil Wright, and collected the remaining bodies, I noted that the contact site was just under a kilometre long in open land. It must have been a text book ambush because literally the troops, who I considered very well trained and brave, must have chased the gooks all the way as they tried to escape. There were by now more Police and army details involved and I took more of an observer role. We delivered all the bodies and weapons, including those from Magunje, to Karoi Police Station. I was keen to establish if this group had been involved in any way with the Viscount *Hunyani* tragedy, but there was no evidence found to connect them. Certainly, I do not recall any property being found on them that would have connected them, which was disappointing."[3]

[1] Martin Lunderstedt email 20/3/2016 and WhatsApp 18/12/2019. Maj. Evans puts the figure as eight killed.
[2] Martin Lunderstedt email 20/3/2016 and WhatsApp discussion 18/12/2019.
[3] Steve Nutt emails 16/6/2016 and 12/7/2016, and various WhatsApp discussions.

Evans concludes the matter: "I arranged for the troops to be uplifted on the morning of the 9/9/78, accompanied by the GC details. The men were taken to the 'mini JOC'[1] which had been temporarily established at the Police Station at Karoi where they were debriefed before returning to our base camp north of Karoi where I carried out an extensive internal debrief. To my knowledge no items like small alcohol bottles, clothes, rings or luggage from the Viscount were found on the terrorists. I spoke to the 'Mini JOC' at Karoi and was advised that there was no evidence to link the group to the Viscount tragedy. I later recommended Alers and Beamish for the Military Forces Commendation (Operational) and submitted their citation for consideration. This was approved, and the awards were presented on 25 May 1979."[2]

In the meantime, 2nd Lt. Frank Moxham had been given the task of attending to the problem concerning the bus service into Hurungwe. He recalls:

> Terrorists had been robbing the buses so we were tasked to dress up as locals, with blackened faces and arms, and were to travel in the Matambanadzo Bus, driven by one of my men, in the hope of "being robbed" so that we could engage the terrorists. On 8 September 1978 we deployed in the bus, which was equipped with Holland-Hale Organs[3] "managed" by a civilian, on the normal route in the hope of luring terrorists to rob us. Unfortunately, the operation was compromised when a local approached the bus provoking the rather "trigger happy" civilian to activate the "Organs". I was on the other side of the bus and did not witness the incident or see the civilian fleeing uninjured!
>
> As we were compromised I was instructed to take my men back to our Unit which was based north of Karoi and arrived mid-afternoon between 3 and 4 p.m. to the news of the successful contact. I recall Sgt Ray Beamish and Sgt AJ Alers had successfully ambushed and killed eight-nine terrorists. Major Evans had already debriefed the "contact section". At no time was I led to believe that the terrorists were part of the ZIPRA section that were involved or connected to the shooting down of Viscount *Hunyani* or the subsequent massacre of the survivors, much to my and my men's disappointment.[4]

Martin Lunderstedt mentioned another incident which needs clarification. He recalls: "Ten days after the successful contact we saw a group of gooks enter a village from about 2kms away from our OP position. When we got to the village they were gone, but they had been carrying a long pipe (Strela?). They hid it in the village but we never found it. On 12th February the 2nd Viscount was shot down and to this day, I think about it and was that the Strela we saw, and if we'd found it, maybe all those deaths wouldn't have happened."[5] I reminded Martin that the "tube" could have been any weapon including a 60mm and 82mm mortar tube, RPG-2 or RPG-7. Indeed, one would need to clarify if the "tube" was in fact a weapon. Martin was relieved to hear this.

I wish to emphasise by repeating an earlier statement. I was not operational in Hurungwe at the time of this contact. From the wide-ranging interviews I conducted and the statements I've personally obtained, there appears to be no evidence suggesting this ZIPRA section was connected to the Viscount *Hunyani* incident. No property from the crash site, the aircraft itself, or personal items from those killed, were found on the killed insurgents which could link them to the incident.[6] In my opinion, it is likely several sections visited the location, possibly ransacking it. Only ballistic

---

[1] "Mini JOC" (command centre) established as a result of the Strela missile attack on Viscount *Hunyani* to co-ordinate operations and was discontinued at the completion of operations. The main Sub.JOC was based at Sinoia.

[2] Eric Evans email 24/6/2016. Karoi Contacts Map Incident 11.

[3] Holland-Hale Organ. This resembled a section of girder with 1.5" holes spaced along it. Each hole was a chamber that was loaded with rocket powder and a pound or so of chopped metal bar. Each of the chambers was electrically fired, usually in a salvo. http://www.arrse.co.uk/community/threads/ridiculous-military-weapons.140903/page-15

[4] Frank Moxham emails 24/5/2016, 11/12/2019 and WhatsApp discussion 11/12/2019.

[5] Martin Lunderstedt email 20/3/2016.

[6] These included Mike Reeler (SB), Steve Nutt (GC), Maj. Evans, Frank Moxham, Martin Lunderstedt, A.J. Alers and Steve Luker (WhatsApp discussion 11/12/2019), all of the Rhodesian Artillery.

evidence could identify the actual weapons used in the murder of those surviving the initial shooting down and subsequent crashing of the Viscount. Any other conclusions would, in my view, be speculative. Not one of the individuals, either survivor or SF personnel I interviewed could recall any ballistic evidence that linked the killed ZIPRA's weapons to the Viscount murder scene. Furthermore, there appears to be no evidence connecting the killed insurgents to the ZIPRA Strela Section (ZSS) that shot down Viscount *Hunyani*.[1]

[1] These included Mike Reeler (SB) & Phil Wright (GC) (WhatsApp discussion 15/1/2020); Steve Nutt (WhatsApp discussion 16/1/2020); Maj. Evans, Frank Moxham, Martin Lunderstedt & A.J. Alers, all of the Rh.Art.

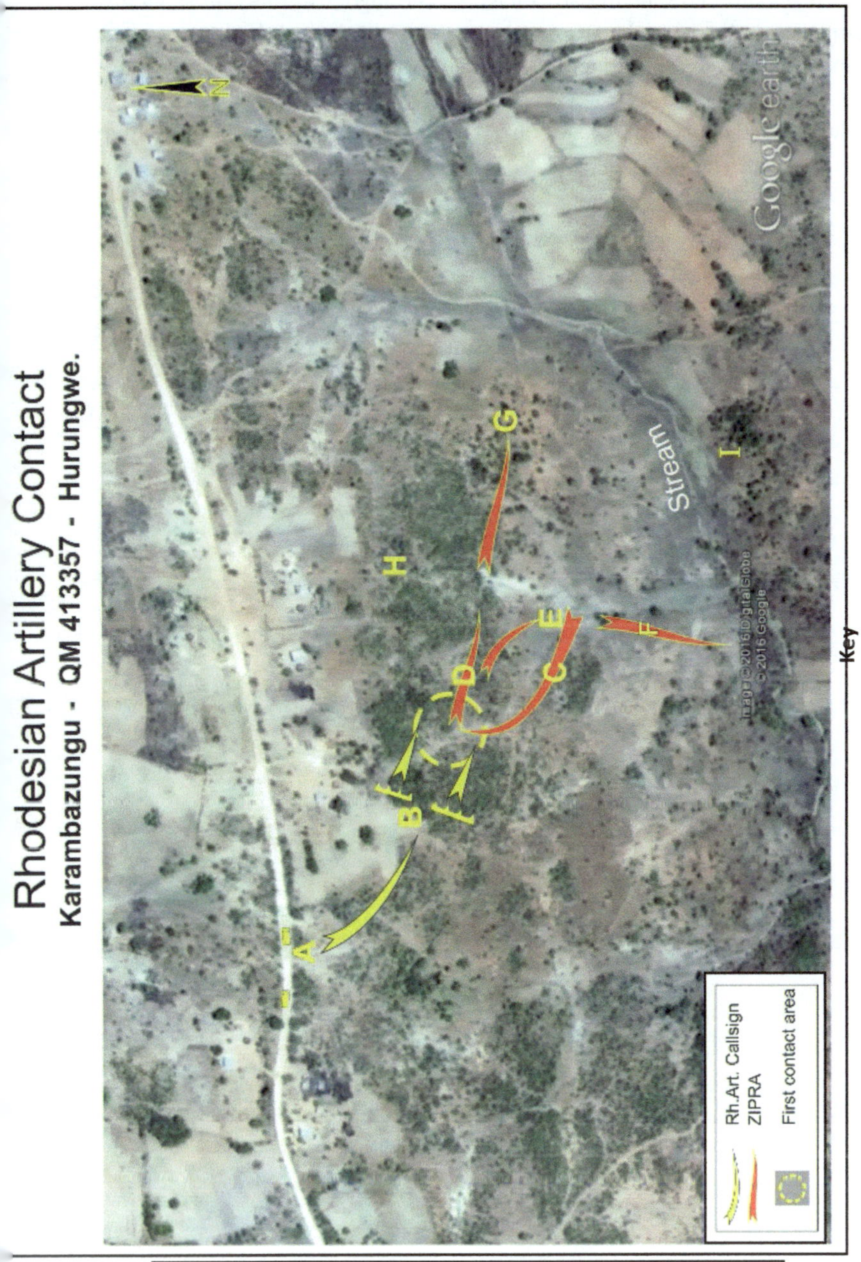

Full attribution to *Google Earth* and *Maxar Technologies*

Key

A Position where two sticks of Rh.Art. were dropped off by military vehicles.
B Position of Rh. Art. sweep line when ambush initiated.
C Direction ZIPRA , accompanied by African females, were moving at start of contact. Several ZIPRA killed here in opening burst of fire.
D Direction of flight of ZIPRA and running contact. Two ZIPRA bodies found here.
E Position of one dead ZIPRA.
F One ZIPRA shot repeadedly and eventually died in reeds here.
G Cattle kraal area where one dead ZIPRA found.
H Area where Rh.Art. callsigns spent the night.
I Village on other side of the stream destroyed after contact.

Map drawn from indications of Martin Lunderstedt, and confirmed by research of Dr Chakawa.

Assessment of the Rhodesian Artillery Contact

There can be no doubt that the Rhodesian Artillery ambush was a successful contact. Maj. Evans correctly evaluated the precise intelligence provided by Steve Nutt and deployed sufficient men, two sections in total, to act on it. The section leaders observed every basic counter-insurgency tactic, debussing at speed under the cover of dust at the correct locstat, covering each other as they crossed the ploughed field, immediately assessing the lay of the land and deploying correctly while using topography to their advantage. Their rapid identification of the approaching enemy demonstrated their alertness and their decision to ambush was pivotal. The section held their discipline and attacked on orders as ZIPRA entered the ambush zone. Although the ZIPRA section retaliated bravely, they were mismatched by an enemy taking advantage of the higher terrain, subsequently surprising and trapping them in open fields, and aggressively pursuing them until the last man fell. Unfortunately, the injured insurgents were subsequently killed. Important intelligence could have been gleaned from them.

Combined Operations released details of this contact on 10 September 1978. It was reported in *The Canberra Times* (Australia) the same day.

11 ~ SETTING THE FOUNDATIONS

Never interrupt your enemy when he is making a mistake.
Napoleon Bonaparte

Overview of the Situation in Hurungwe TTL

D/S/O Mike Reeler worked closely with Insp. Phil Wright who was in charge of Ground Coverage operations. Wright and his men spent a considerable amount of time in Hurungwe. Steve Nutt, a resident of the Magunje police base in Hurungwe and operating throughout the TTL, was included among Wright's men on the ground. A colleague from Rusape, D/P/O Clive Boddy, was working with the Selous Scouts and I met his immediate superior, D/S/O Tom Thomas, the SB detail attached to Selous Scouts operations in the area.[1] In overall command of Special Branch Selous Scouts Internal Operations was Supt. Keith Samler.[2] As time progressed, we worked well together passing on and confirming intelligence. This was important in the initial stages of our development as it helped us gain credibility.

Phil Wright makes the point: "I met John Padbury for the first time in 1978 when I was in charge of the Ground Coverage Unit. Although technically I was under command and on the establishment of the BSAP Member in Charge Uniform Branch, I worked closely and under direction of the Special Branch office at Karoi. John had been sent to Karoi by Special Branch to take command of the Security Force Auxiliaries or SFAs as they came to be known, and although I did not work closely with him as our job descriptions differed widely, he was, by virtue of his position, a member of the intelligence 'inner circle' at the station."[3]

On 17 June 1978, in a secret Special Branch report referenced XYS 7285 and XYS 9000/5/5, Supt. Seaward commented on Special Branch operations and activity in the Lomagundi district which included the Hurungwe TTL: "At this time, considerable Special Branch effort is directed at the war, and the situation is aggravated by the need to devote more attention to the internal nationalism and inter-faction problem. There is scant time left to explore new areas, to devise new techniques and to mount special operations. Special Branch manpower and resources are presently being stretched to the limit in standard reaction to the terrorist. This modus operandi has hardly altered since Operation Cauldron days. We produce good assessments of what the terrorist has done, and the history is well recorded. This expends our energy. We appear to lack the initiative and resourcefulness which develops new concepts and techniques. We can barely cope with today's level of activities, and will be utterly swamped when the terrorist doubles and quadruples his activity. The threat of classical war looms, yet we persist in stereotyped fashion." Seaward had been transferred to the Lomagundi district in view of his knowledge of ZIPRA activities gained from operations against ZIPRA in Matabeleland. He envisioned a looming conflict between ZIPRA and ZANLA and felt this matter was ripe for exploitation. At a JOC Hurricane meeting in April/May 1978, accompanied by all three Sub.JOC Sinoia members, Seaward was called upon to make a report covering the Lomagundi district. He recalls: "The focus of my report was to show the ZIPRA tactics as experienced in Matabeleland, to highlight the difference as hitherto experienced in dealing with ZANLA. At the end of my briefing, the JOC Commander ordered that my briefing be ignored, and the record be deleted entirely from the minutes. I recall some reference to 'Floppies being Floppies'."[4]

---

1 Pittaway, J. (2015), pp. 340 and 377-380.

2 Keith Samler joined the Selous Scouts unit in May 1978 as a D/Insp. In July he was promoted to Supt. and became Mr Mac's designated 2 i/c with the title "OC Special Branch Selous Scouts Internal Operations". He kept this title until April 1979 when transferred to JOC Hurricane. Email 27/12/2016.

3 Confirmed by Mike Reeler.

The situation in Hurungwe was serious. By 1978, ZIPRA had occupied and liberated it. This resulted in the typical pattern of a breakdown of civil administration, law and order, cessation of school attendance, non-compliance with government agricultural laws and regulations such as contouring of hills, cattle dipping and destruction of dips. In addition, poor attendance at Internal Affairs and SF meetings, closure of clinics and non-payment of taxes accompanied the imposition of a ZIPRA style of military law.

On 23 September 1978, the Rhodesian Government declared Hurungwe to be under martial law.[1] This followed a heated debate shortly after the attack on Viscount *Hunyani*. Ian Smith was concerned that the war was not being fought aggressively enough. Presumably, with the backing of his caucus, he decided on imposing martial law in the country on 9 September 1978.[2] This decision was made by the white Ministers, ignoring the African Co-Ministers of the Executive Council, two or three of them being abroad at the time. Minister Hawkins, who later called for support from Minister Squires, had introduced the decision to Nat.JOC on the same day. Squires and Hawkins called the PM for support. Lt. Gen. Walls, supported by all 12 Nat.JOC officials, vigorously opposed the idea in a heated discussion concerning the imposition of martial law. They were satisfied the Emergency Powers Legislation provided sufficient legal authority for tough action but insisted it was better to plan for a political settlement. Ken Flower noted Lt. Gen. Walls's thoughts on the matter: "If you really want martial law in the true sense of the phrase we will take over from the President and Government, and rule as a Military Junta."[3]

Ian Smith, seemingly not wishing to relinquish political power, overrode Walls and settled for a lesser "martial licence". Ken Flower summarises the situation: "In essence, then, Smith and his fellow politicians had lost the initiative and were offering it to the military. It was to the Commanders' credit that they realised their limitations in a losing situation and would not become politically involved."[4] They were aware of the dire international repercussions of such a move. The commanders knew there was no military solution to the war. They continued to press the politicians to pursue a political solution, as they had done since at least July 1977. The powers of this "military licence" were summed up in a government paper headed *Martial Law, What It Means To The People*, issued by the Ministry of Information, Immigration and Tourism in December 1978: "In martial law areas, the security forces can make their own laws to help them to find and kill terrorists. They will not have to follow the ordinary laws, because that can take too much time. In martial law areas security forces could arrest and detain people, confiscate or destroy property such as huts and cattle and make people work for them. They could also hold their own court with the power to sentence people to jail and death. Cases where sentences of death were passed would be looked at by higher authorities."

When the masses failed to comply with established civil administrative procedures, ignored the rule of law, when co-operation with the people waned or ceased, experience taught me these factors indicated that the people had identified with "the cause" and purpose propagated by the insurgents. This lack of co-operation may have been voluntary or the consequence of intimidation. The fact remained, we faced a distancing between ourselves and the people. At that stage of the war, the enemy had won the political battle for the hearts and minds of the masses by identifying and expounding legitimate grievances and aspirations. There was, in my view, clear evidence these issues had not been addressed in full by Smith's Government. Their strategy was to simply impose increased military force without addressing the opinions and grievances of the people. This explained the increasingly heavy-handed control of the African population by the white ruled government. Subsequently, the insurgents' promises of a better future watered the thirsty seeds of revolution.

Our understanding of the "enemy and his ways" was growing. At this stage we knew they had

---

[4] *Floppies*: Rhodesian slang for insurgents. Nigel Seaward email 31/7/2020.

[1] Rhodesian Government Notices No 733A and 760B of 1978.

[2] Flower, K. (1987), pp. 210-212; British Confidential documents: Rhodesia Department Monthly Summary No 9, September 1978.

[3] Flower, K. (1987), pp. 210-212.

[4] Ibid.

established close ties with the masses, gained their support and, through political propaganda, made them intolerant of their legitimate grievances remaining unattended to. They had well-established intelligence networks and were ruthless to opposition. Public transport virtually ceased as the minimal routes available to bus operators were controlled by ZIPRA who mined roads and, when necessary, lifted them according to their strategic needs. Security Forces patrols and vehicles were ambushed at will and white farms frequently but generally ineffectually attacked. Farm attacks were often the consequence of labour relations issues. Stock theft, instigated by ZIPRA, was a regular occurrence. In fact, Chifamba Village became known as "The Butchery"; the place where cattle stolen from white farmers were slaughtered and distributed among the people.[1] They considered Hurungwe a liberated area under their martial law. Granted, it was important to understand the enemy but also primarily focus on our now altered approach to the war, adapting from reacting to acting: a lesson I learned from our failures in the Makoni.

Colleagues led me to believe that ZIPRA were more aggressive soldiers than ZANLA. When engaged in open warfare they would seldom retreat. Rather they would make tactical withdrawals when expedient, whereas ZANLA adopted a hit-and-run approach. It was common knowledge that ZIPRA's Soviet Union influences inclined them more towards conventional warfare as opposed to the Maoist principles of politicising the people in order to gain their approval, acceptance and support, thereafter creating incidents in which the SF were forced to react. Both ZANLA and ZIPRA attacked only when advantageous, employing the methods I refer to above.

Security Force Auxiliaries Operations

Security Force Auxiliaries fell under the operational command of Special Forces. Maj. Graham Des Fountain, posted to Special Forces explains:

> In 1978 I was in Special Forces (SpF) under command of Brigadier Heppenstall, reporting directly to Major (Maj.) Tom Douglas who was GSO 2 Ops Special Forces; I was a Captain at the time. I served in the unit until shortly after I was promoted to Major in 1980. Brigadier Heppenstall was in overall command and Maj. Tom Douglas (in charge of the ZANU Wing which was included within the UANC) and Maj. Harry Harvey (in charge of ZAPU Wing, which also was included within the UANC), were both the operational staff OC's. Our main function was oversight of the SFA Operations throughout the country, including the prescribing of (freezing) areas, assimilation and distribution of intelligence and administration and logistics, the training of ex-insurgent forces and new recruited locals from the areas under SpF control. SpF had direct control of all SFA Operational areas.
>
> In terms of the 3rd March 1978 Internal Agreement, I assisted in the release from Chikurubi Prison of Grey Mutemasango and Happy Marere, both externally trained ex-insurgents. Grey and Happy were well trained, highly motivated senior military men. They had operated together against Rhodesian Security forces prior to their capture and incarceration at Chikurubi Prison. Grey was the senior man and both men had joined the UANC led by Bishop Muzorewa and were dedicated to the success of the Internal Agreement. I had a very good relationship with Happy and we got on well together, I thought he was an exceptional person. Happy was the UANC official I had most dealings with and spent long periods in close action with him in the various operations and camps throughout the country.
>
> At the outset of our operations, I worked closely with Grey and Happy as they recruited local Africans and ex-insurgents for training at the SpF Camp at Domboshawa run by my father, Major Dennis F. Des Fountain. All Special Force SFA areas were controlled by ex-insurgent military leadership, drawing its force off former captured or surrendered ZANU insurgents and local recruits. SpF then provided close co-operation

[1] Dr Chakawa, J. (2015), pp. 204-205.

and intelligence directed from SF Operative presences, through the SF operations room to the SF operatives seconded to that camp and area.

The only exception to our standard Special Forces Operational procedures was Hurungwe TTL which was a unique autonomous Special Branch operation under the command of the Special Branch operator, John Padbury based at Karoi. Padbury took command of the Karoi SFAs in September 1978. His immediate superior was Supt. Geoff Price, the Special Branch Officer responsible for liaison between the UANC and SpF. I knew Geoff Price and liaised with him regularly. Grey Mutemasango was in charge of the UANC military and political wings in the Karoi area and Happy often assisted him in the control, liaison and operational direction. Happy was transferred permanently to Karoi on the 10/11/1978, although he was an integral part of the discipline and control of the SFA operatives and camps. Special Forces, through the channel of Major Douglas, provided the logistics, including arms and ammunition for Hurungwe SFAs. Part of our function was to provide Territorial Army soldiers as well as former Regular Forces Security Force Operatives from the SAS and RLI to assist John Padbury with the training programme at Karoi.[1]

A Clean Slate

In the preliminary weeks at Karoi, I spent some time contemplating the enormity of the task at hand and evaluating the overall situation. Essentially, I was starting from scratch and would have to organise every aspect of the operation. I decided the only way to operate was to start completely afresh, to have an open mind to the task ahead. My personal vision had to be clear and focused, able to sustain us through both good and bad times, as well as give a reason to fight and possibly die for.

I kept reminding myself that our focus should be on the well-being of the people. Once that focus shifted, the battle would be lost. Take care of the people and they take care of you became my catchphrase. In military terms, I had identified that the people were the Vital Assets. Vital Assets are those assets, if captured, damaged or controlled by the enemy, would result in or significantly contribute to national defeat. The ground on which the Vital Assets are situated is known as the Vital Ground. The Ground of Tactical Importance is the best tactical ground on which to fight the battle to defend the Vital Assets and the Vital Ground which, if overrun by the enemy, would render our position untenable.[2] The people in Hurungwe, Chikangwe (the local African township) and the UANC office were the Vital Assets occupying the Vital Ground which was the Ground of Tactical Importance. This is how I understood matters.

While the Karoi SB and GC officers assured me they were receiving good intelligence, my decision was to isolate our operation from them and establish our own political networks through which intelligence would flow. This would give us the opportunity to confirm our intelligence with them. More importantly, we would be viewed as part of the Interim Government forces and not of the old colonial Rhodesian establishment, a major propaganda tool ZIPRA could use against us, and one that could turn the tide in our favour if handled correctly. In any event, our operation was forward thinking and controversial which demanded the freedom to gradually evolve without the restraints and demands of conformity and compliance to standard SF operational procedures. This revolutionary way of thinking suited me. My priority was to organise staff. I contacted Geoff Price who arranged the transfer of my Police Reserve team from Rusape to Karoi, including Todd (pseudonym), Sandy Irvine and George Hutchison, and they started rotating their call-ups to overlap duties at Karoi. George had been previously stationed at BSAP Karoi for some four years and his contacts in the area would prove invaluable. Sandy would only arrive at the end of January 1979. These men had worked well with me for four years in the Rusape district. Collectively they understood the *mujibha* system. We also trusted each other having shared some difficult experiences.

[1] Graham Des Fountain email 24/1/2018. Confirmed by Brigadier Heppenstall, CO Special Forces oral interview on 15/5/2019.

[2] Cilliers, J. (2003), p. 250.

They were extremely efficient, reliable and trustworthy men. Their main area of responsibility would be organising and managing our administration, finances (which I never touched), property leases, sourcing equipment for the farm and the men, arranging PRAW flights and so on. They accompanied me on all operational patrols/travels throughout Hurungwe. I called them Admin.

With Admin. in place I was free to build the SFA organisation and infrastructure, develop the intelligence networks and plan the penetration of Hurungwe. While the overall command, accountability and responsibility of the SFAs was mine, I believed in lateral leadership. Colleagues were selected based on their character, skill and commitment, then released to "get on with the job". They participated in the decision-making process relevant to their demarcated area of responsibility. I made it my business to utilise their gifts and talents for "the cause" and vision for the benefit of the team and the people. Decisions were made after joint discussions which gave the men the opportunity to express themselves. Consequently, we did not need to function with police or military ranks.

I grew to know Grey Mutemasango well, together with the overall political and military structure of the UANC. He was a wise, astute man. We immediately formed a good relationship. He was popular, well established in the local area and active in recruiting locals from Hurungwe for training. Grey was committed, progressive and self-motivated: an ideal man to have alongside. The UANC had previously been politically active in Hurungwe but, since the arrival of ZIPRA insurgents, their party had been savagely attacked, members killed, beaten into submission or had voluntarily sided with ZIPRA. As our operations developed, ZIPRA's attacks on the UANC members intensified, many paying the ultimate price for freedom of choice. However, the UANC lay dormant: an underground resistance movement and a veritable sleeping giant!

Grey's intelligence work was in its embryonic stages as he had focused on recruiting and was achieving positive results. Maj. Des Fountain comments: "All SFAs in the Karoi operation were local African males recruited from Hurungwe, they were not former terrorists."[1]

The success of our operation depended on recruiting locals from Hurungwe, this will become clear as we progress. Geoff Price and I opted to start our operations at the farm at Sinoia. We arranged for Sgts. Manenji and Madzinga (pseudonyms) from the Support Unit to be based there as training instructors. They would act as interpreters when needed by the white staff and also explain to them the customs, traditions and history of the Africans. I felt it important for the white staff to fully integrate with the men, so that they became one. Price and I interviewed training instructors and our first white instructor was Walter (pseudonym), a former territorial SAS soldier.

Being a policeman, I had a common bond with Sgts. Manenji and Madzinga. My policy towards staff I was unfamiliar with was to trust implicitly. I allowed them complete freedom in the execution of their duties. However, I would breach no incompetence, laziness, deviation from laid down and agreed on procedures. Should these digressions or any other matters come to my attention, I would summarily remove the inept individual. We were at war in which lives were at stake, consequently solidarity, commitment, dedication and high standards of our staff in all areas was paramount. As I saw matters, there was no compromise.

I introduced Manenji and Madzinga to the remainder of the team as ex-terrorist instructors. Comrades was the title I used for them. I was satisfied that the recruits would receive good training with the present team and supervision of Grey. Notwithstanding, I still required "eyes and ears" in the farm, therefore I established an intelligence cell with Manenji and Madzinga. They would alert me to any deviations from our plans, political agitators and dissidents, as well as gleaning valuable intelligence from the men in training and new recruits. I debriefed each cell member on an individual basis and they were not aware of each other's involvement. This was a low-profile operation.

I arranged for the relocation of David and Mike from the *mujibha* farm at Rusape to Karoi. They were the first *mujibhas* captured in the Makoni TTL. Both were excellent RPD gunners and my intention was to introduce them as ZANLA combatants. These men were loyal, well-trained and

1 Graham Des Fountain email 24/1/2018.

able leaders. They were both known by Todd, Sandy Irvine and George Hutchison: an asset and advantage. It was also my aim for them to join the camp intelligence network. An interesting feature of our time at Rusape was that we had all become comrades, in keeping with Maoist strategies. David and Mike would be my escort details when travelling in the operational area, with two RPD gunners at my side, what more could one ask for? I felt safe!

By 27 September 1978, we had recruited 58 men from Hurungwe, all of whom had commenced training. These figures are confirmed by a top secret report submitted by Supt. "Mac" McGuinness, accurately outlining the dire situation in the country as well as indicating that the SFAs offered the only solution to the continuing war and political instability.[1]

[1] Report provided by Dennis Anderson.

Strategising at Twin Rivers Motel. Note Mao Zedung's Little Red Book.

Early travels to the Karoi district.

Mao Tsetung's little red book, author's war bible. Mao Tsetung is also known, and referred to in this book, as Mao Zedong.

TOP SECRET

The Director General
CENTRAL INTELLIGENCE ORGANISATION.
THE COMMISSIONER OF POLICE.
The Officer Commanding
SPECIAL BRANCH.
27th September 1978.

OPERATION FAVOUR: MATTERS OF MOMENT

While liaison with office bearers of the ZANU remain good, discipline within the ranks of its armed followers still leaves much to be desired, and, it is suggested that the armed groups now engaged in the field be deployed to remote areas where a far more strict control can be exercised over their activities.

On the UANC scene, every assistance has been forthcoming from Party representatives and in the main they have proved more than willing to toe the Government line and discipline their recruits/armed personnel whenever they are required to do so. It is therefore the considered opinion of the author that more emphasis should be placed on the training and political re-orientation of UANC recruits and, to this end an anti-Communist line is being preached and the use of Communist clichés banned.

In recent weeks, much has been said about the 'Op Favour' scene which has been afforded particularly bad and misleading Press, one wonders why releases are made to the news media which indicate a degree of lawlessness which does not exist in those areas controlled by UANC supporters. Then one can take a second look at the scene and realise that little or nothing has been done by the Army to assist the UANC and that all the heavy weapons distributed to date have gone to ZANU, and, that the Army have failed to supply a single liaison officer to work with the UANC.

The author remains firm in the conviction that tribesmen can be recruited and trained to defend their own home areas without undue risk to the overall security of the country and provide valuable bayonets where Army are unable to operate either through lack of man-power or inability to come to grips with the guerrilla. It is, to the mind of the author, fictitious to believe that the rural African can be expected to support democracy unless he is given some means of defending himself against armed aggression.

Any suggestion that the 'Op Favour' scene may be or should be discarded would at this stage of the game be complete madness, for, if the tribes-people are not 'brought on sides' with the transitional Government, and, as previously stated, given the opportunity to defend themselves, then they will follow the Patriotic Front like a flock of sheep and all will be lost. The author is at a loss to understand why the whole concept of 'Op Favour' has been so unpopular in certain circles but now believes that its unpopularity stems from the fact that those persons who do not like the concept of arming Africans are the same people who firmly believe that majority rule will never come to pass and that the realities of life are nothing more than a bad dream. Or, do they still believe that we can win the war without the good will and assistance of the majority.

To return to the facts of the matter, the following is the present state of ZANU as at this date[1]:-

SABI NORTH	102	Operational
COPPER QUEEN	120	Operational
MARANDA	99	Operational
MPHEONGS	119	Operational
ENKLEDOORN	140	Under Instruction

In respect of the above, liaison officers both Army and Police have been appointed to each group but the calibre of men provided by the Army leaves much to be desired.

We now look at the UANC scene and let me assure addressees that this is an entirely different kettle of fish to the ZANU scheme:-

MSANA	124	Operational (Baldwin)	
	80	Under Field Instruction	
	43	Awaiting deploy to Bushu	
	18	Ex RUNDI now field training	
WILTSHIRE	12	Operational (Bird)	
	10	Under Field Instruction	
	36	Trained and waiting deploy	
URUNGWE	58	Trained and waiting deploy (Padbury)	
ZWIMBA	42	Trained and waiting deploy	
	48	Awaiting training	
MTOKO	67	Undergoing training.	Pass out 10/10
CHIWESHE	45	Undergoing training.	Pass out 10/10
CHIWESHE	29	Awaiting training	
	30	Medics	Pass out 10/10
CHESA	80	Ex Malawi/Salisbury	Pass out 3/10
MONDORO	170	Undergoing training	
SIPOLILO	60	Undergoing training	

As will be noted, the UANC volunteers are from diverse areas and given the necessary staff 'Favour' training, establishments could be opened in every Province and the number of trainees quadrupled. However, our immediate problem is not one of further training establishments, but the allocation of manpower to command and control in the field. What earthly use can it serve if one trains a man to use his weapon in a proficient manner, indoctrinates him in so called democracy and then turns him loose in the field without further guidance or backup. One is tempted to pose the question … What other armed force can deploy '100' men on a permanent basis at the expense of a two or three-man backup team?

The issue before us appears crystal clear, we either have sufficient men to stave-off our enemies or we lose any chance of participation in any future Government. We have only one means of gaining the necessary manpower and that is by the recruitment of tribesmen who are anti Mugabe/Nkomo. Time is of the essence and so it is not possible to induct trainees into a recognised force where preparation and training will far exceed the present period of one month.

[1] A note in the margin of ZANU's figures states: "Gangsters, layabouts, unemployed youth criminal elements, deception/misrepresentation. No connection with T.T.L.s." This was an accurate assessment of ZANU's SFA.

```
The final and essential ingredient which MUST be added if we are to
control the trained personnel in the field is mature policemen, who,
with tact can ensure that law and order are maintained in these so-called
'free zones'.
Bindura
27th September 1978.
```

After one of my visits to the farm on 16 October 1978, I recorded the following synopsis of developments. Present on the farm were 60 SFAs divided into six ten-man sections, some of whom were part of the original *mujibha* farm operated by SB Karoi. The remainder were locals from Hurungwe TTL, recruited by the UANC and headed by Grey. Each unit had a section leader whose responsibilities included the morale, discipline, training and administration of his section. Tawangwa had been appointed as the overall commander. He was an imposing figure and appeared ideal for the position. He had dealt admirably with one case of ill-discipline much to the satisfaction of the forces, Grey and myself.

The farm itself was a typical external-type base camp comprising a headquarters surrounded by the six suitably positioned sections. Each section lived in camouflage bunkers. Everyone's kit and equipment were conveniently packed with sections able to be mobile at a moment's notice. The farm was situated on a river, ensuring a constant supply of water. However, acquiring meat and fresh vegetables presented a problem as there were no deep-freezer facilities available. I tasked Admin. to source these items and they soon arrived.

As many sections as possible were equipped with radios, providing contact between them. These matters provided good training and preparation for field operations, although I knew that communications in the field were going to prove extremely difficult.

Morale and discipline within the farm were of a high standard. However, on the warfare front, matters were not all that encouraging. I was given a demonstration of each section's capabilities with fire-with-movement using live rounds. Although I found the standard poor and was unimpressed, I was confident of improvement.

An obstacle course was prepared traversing the nearby river. This type of a bush-training farm was what I had envisaged for some time. In my mind, it was ideal as it presented the harsh realities of life the SFAs would be living under in the war zones. The men were not pampered. No roofs kept them from being rained on. The farm contained no flushing toilets or "long drops". Equally, there were no luxuries such as cold beers or cool drinks. The men lived the realities of the everyday soldier, living and sleeping under the stars. Being daily prepared for the unforgiving certainties of war was the order of the day. The literal war zones beckoned constantly. In all truth, in our preparedness, we had created a war atmosphere within an actual war zone. The only exception was the acquiring of deep freezers and fridges which kept our provisions fresh.

One of the main ongoing and understandable complaints from the training staff was the lack of weapons and ammunition from the beginning of our training operation. Weapons and ammunition were in high demand throughout the country, a situation complicated by diminishing funds and a shortage of supply. I assured the staff everything possible was being done to secure arms and ammunition, and in time they arrived.

A major pitfall of SF intelligence agents and, in my view, a vast number of our soldiers, was a failure to understand the important role the *mujibhas* undertook in ZIPRA intelligence networks. They performed a key function in acquiring information essential to ZIPRA's cause. This deficiency on our part was further exacerbated by a lack of comprehending African culture, particularly in the home areas of the TTLs. While the SF were superior militarily in individual battles, they were generally ignorant of and unable to grasp ZIPRA strategies and tactics. This was difficult to deal with on a national basis but, on our farm, I resolved to allow the process of integration and understanding of African customs to take its natural course. As with other white training staff, living with the SFAs was beneficial as it provided the opportunity to adjust and adapt to African culture, as their acceptance of different values took root. One of our white training instructors was a South African, raised under the apartheid regime, giving me cause for concern that he might not adjust to our methodology. Time would tell!

In time, Grey agreed it was important for him to carry out regular visits to the farm in order to politicise the training staff and recruits, and keep abreast of developments. This would allow him the opportunity to update the men on the situation in the field, developments in Chikangwe and keep them focused on the vision. These regular visits would inform the forces of intelligence matters emanating from Hurungwe and prove essential in keeping them up to date with the situation at their homes, and authenticate their association with the UANC. The military should never usurp the political. It was exciting, challenging and invigorating watching the movement develop and gain momentum. I would also make regular visits to the farm and focused on building a good relationship with Grey. This was not difficult as we soon gained mutual respect and trust. We both worked hard, long hours and were committed to our common cause and vision.

Walter advised that he needed to extend the training programme. Grey and I agreed as we wanted to ensure that the men were well trained and capable of defending themselves and the people. The military success of our first deployment and occupation of Hurungwe was pivotal to our overall triumph as defeat or retreat was not an option. At this stage, I relied on Walter's interpretation of "well trained". With the training team in place at Sinoia, we focused on establishing and developing the political aspects of our operations. We had much to accomplish before we deployed our forces.

Developing the Political Component

SFA Strategies Phase 2: Establish and develop the political landscape in order to connect with the people

There are three elements that need to be addressed if a counter-revolution, or indeed a revolution, is to be successful, namely political, military and the local population. The political is the primary component and precedes the other two factors. Once the people understand, support and trust the politicians, their philosophy and vision, even if only in general terms, they begin to volunteer critical information regarding their lives and the lives and activities of the enemy. Having prepared the ground politically, the military can then be deployed to serve and defend the people while the politicians attend to their grievances. In some respects, the approach I am advocating, extends beyond mere logic and understanding. Fundamentally it is a matter of intimately connecting the political, military and the people to form one entity. The mistake I made in Makoni was approaching the people in search of intelligence relating to the insurgents. By contrast, in Hurungwe, we would approach the people through the political party with the intention of addressing their grievances and then remain to defend them. The by-product of the process would be the elimination of the enemy. Ken Flower correctly states: "A war of counter insurgency is 20% military and 80% political, which implies that greater force is needed against politicians to settle a dispute, than against terrorists in the field, or government will shelve its responsibilities and the military ignore theirs."[1]

Sadly, the life circumstances of the masses seldom, if ever, improves a great deal following political or military intervention. They remain pawns in the process of a transition of power and change.

In my view, politicians are called on to motivate the military with their vision for peace, prosperity, freedom and victory. This stimulates the soldier and SF to fight and possibly die for the political vision. When the people do not support this political vision, inevitably the military option will increasingly lose momentum, resulting in the battle switching from a political cause to soldiers simply fighting a seemingly pointless and unachievable war. Every conceivable form of military action becomes justifiable, necessary and for the "cause of good" as the soldier no longer fights for the political cause but simply goes through the motions of war, often only for comradeship, survival and the thought that "this is what soldiers do". War becomes a lifestyle. Once political aspirations

[1] Flower, K. (1987), pp. 279-280.

capitulate or become unachievable, the military dimension becomes at odds with the political and vice versa.

As we thought about penetrating Hurungwe, Grey and I decided to formulate our political vision which we regularly shared with the UANC political and military wings, training staff, SFAs and the people: "Mobilise, liberate and protect the people of Hurungwe from the ZIPRA oppressors by developing a people's army to occupy and possess the land and eliminate the enemy; to support and establish shared government headed by Bishop Muzorewa, leading to majority rule and to address the grievances, needs and aspirations of the people in the process."

For our political strategy to succeed, we had to identify and attend to the people's needs. In so doing, we would build trust and acceptance as our promises materialised. The first step was to come to an understanding of what the people's immediate requirements were. We were uncertain how ZIPRA operated or what their strategies and tactics were. We had no idea what their overall plan was. However, a key factor to our advantage was that Hurungwe was a Shona region and the invading force, ZIPRA, were principally Ndebele or at least Ndebele-speaking. Zimbabwe was not, nor is, one united nation. Many tribes and dialects reside in the country, but the essential tribal differences are the Shona and Matabele. This division was core to our planning and success. It was clear to us that the Shona had become infuriated by the Matabele (ZIPRA) excesses, particularly their murder campaign against "sellouts". The outsider Ndebele force violently oppressed any form of opposition. They raped and abused women and pillaged the people.

Another major problem was transportation which had virtually ceased due to ZIPRA's landmine campaign. Buses had been the main source of public transport to and from the TTLs although some wealthier storekeepers and teachers owned vehicles. Missionaries had vehicles, but most mission operations had been closed.

Oral news followed the flow of movement between the TTLs and townships in astonishing detail, accuracy and speed. Sometimes written letters were delivered by hand or post. The people were connected despite great distances and remoteness. Consequently, a well-established flow of information was in place between Hurungwe and Chikangwe when I arrived. All that was required of us was to use it to our advantage. I also reasoned that resolving the transport problem would go a long way to gaining momentum with our political agenda.

The groundwork was laid. At the farm we had men in training under the watchful tutoring of able, competent and experienced instructors. A good farm intelligence network was in place. We had the beginnings of a political network developing in Chikangwe.

In addition to the above, we had decent relations with the local SB, GC and Selous Scouts. I was fortunate to be assisted by willing helpers in all areas, including administration. The UANC political and military teams were developing well. They were pleasant company and good friends. At my disposal were truly highly capable, dedicated and committed men. Securing a successful team and operations included frivolous moments along with pleasant social interactions.

Initially, much of my time at Karoi was spent in planning and liaising as I had a great deal of detail and information to absorb, together with coming to terms with the enormous responsibility laid on me. It was imperative to establish the right foundations for future operations. In many ways it was a step-by-step process that I knew would gradually gain momentum. Consequently, I was not pressured to implement plans and strategies hastily.

Political Change Required

Accurate intelligence depicting events on a day-to-day basis at Chikangwe and in Hurungwe was soon forthcoming, far exceeding my expectations. However, the political matters at hand were high on my priority list. Even with an Interim Government in place, attending to the needs (GNA) of the people would be difficult to achieve without immediate and significant political reformation. On the war front, the military and air force continued to win isolated and intermittent armed conflicts but, politically, we had failed to win the battle for the hearts and minds of the people and, in fact, were losing the war. Our defeat was sweeping over the horizon. ZANLA and ZIPRA fought an astute strategic political and military battle, occupying the land and ruling the local population. I found it interesting that while we Rhodesians were engaging in a war, determined to gain the upper hand and win, many foreign governments and the international community at large were preparing the way forward following our defeat.

Here is a summary of my 16 October 1978 diary entry:

> As I saw it, political motivation would continue to be a problem in the field particularly with regard to the future intentions of our forces (SFAs) in relation to what is presently referred to as white imperialism. The immediate political motivation was to eradicate the marauding ZIPRA forces from Hurungwe; we believed that the masses would support our forces in the traditional Shona/Ndebele struggle.
>
> Once we gained a foothold within Hurungwe, the forces would in time be required to produce an African political advancement agenda. This required in depth consideration by the politicians. For the immediate future, it was enough for our political and military wings to explain that Bishop Abel Muzorewa and the Interim Government were moving towards resolving the envisaged political problems. For example, the forces, by nature of their operations, would encounter migrant farm labourers having contact with ZIPRA. ZIPRA would have drawn attention to the exploitation of African labour by white imperialist farming methods resulting in the disproportionate distribution of wealth and land. In return the labourer, albeit grateful for the employment and the meagre financial return, would have been awakened to the validity of ZIPRA's revolutionary struggle in Rhodesia.
>
> We believed our forces would be readily accepted in their home areas but the prevailing political impasse, including distribution of land, equality in business and labour salaries, and other glaring discrepancies, would in time also need to be addressed. There was no point looking at the problem as it arose in say three months' time when it would be a stumbling block to progress.
>
> I suggested that white farmers needed to be made aware of the gulf between their standard of living and that of the labourer in his employ as a matter of urgency. The poor quality of life and working conditions of the labourer called for dramatic improvement. If this was achieved we, the Special Branch and UANC, would be able to win their approval, mobilise many with the view to winning their political affiliations. I envisaged military training for farm labourers equipping them to defend the farms. Simultaneous progressive political advancement addressing their grievances had to be in place giving the farm labourer a cause to fight and maybe die for. My outlook was considered too far-sighted at the time but I felt an urgency to provide a solution to the country's woes. Transformation in all areas of life called for implementation. This included giving credit to the UANC for their progressive strides towards African majority rule when progress was made.
>
> In similar fashion, our forces would have contact with both migrant and permanent mine labourers, domestic servants and, in fact, the wide spectrum of the African community, where the dynamics I've outlined above would be certain to arise. The solution to these problems were political, needing to be addressed constructively by the politicians for our forces to have a political and military objective which, I felt, had always been lacking in our war.

With regard to the land-reform issue, a Karoi farmer, Jim Barker, writing of the situation in the year 2000 commented: "There was no one, I believe in the farming community that did not recognise the need for land reform."[1] Another case of "too little, too late".

In time, I reached the conclusion that I had no intention of fighting to sustain the existing

1 Barker, J. (2007) p. 332.

white-dominated regime in the country. I was eager for and anticipated political intervention, coupled with a visible transformation in the affairs of the African which in turn, I believed, would help create, develop and support military action in the field. The danger I saw was that the SF were still fighting to maintain white privilege and moderate African status, particularly that of the white farmers. The military was there to defend the people and bring about a political vision which, for ultimate long-term success, demanded governmental change by the removal of ingrained obstacles: in short, the removal of colonialism. Unfortunately, attitudes and prejudices are not changed by legislation. My duties and responsibilities were to make the SB hierarchy and politicians aware of the situation in the operational areas and to continue with the current war effort. Copies of my diaries were sent to the SBHQ and our links to Bishop Muzorewa, through Grey, helped with the process.

Raising the Flag: UANC Office

SFA Strategies Phase 3: Raise the UANC flag in order to create a permanent visible presence

My approach at the time focused on the importance of gaining political-party (UANC) momentum and acceptance by the local African population in Chikangwe. Here was a typical African settlement, separate from the main Karoi town in which whites had residence. Therefore, our primary task became to develop a strong political presence and networks in Chikangwe and impart our political vision to bring about unity. The strength of our political approach would determine the flow of intelligence and the accuracy of the information would corroborate the level of support of the African population. Volunteered intelligence exhibited trust, calling for confidentiality and action. Invariably, in rural counter-revolution, people who disclosed information regarding the activities and presence of insurgents were placing their lives at stake. There are "eyes and ears" everywhere, thus increasing the risk for those passing on intelligence. Increasingly, the situation arose where not even family members could be trusted.

Grey had proven to be an excellent leader and there were clear indications we were gaining local support. One of these gauges was the increasing momentum of the collection and dissemination of quality intelligence. Grey had the uncanny ability of gathering reliable and accurate information, as he was well known and trusted in Chikangwe Township.

Conversely, ZIPRA, I was certain, had well-developed, substantial intelligence-gathering networks in place, making it a straightforward process of their piecing together various sources of information and from where "leaks" emanated. For example, if information was acquired leading to a successful contact at a kraal, the ZIPRA intelligence network would have known who had the potential of informing on them. Most certainly the "hammer would fall" on residents absent at the time. Grey established the pattern of sending informants, whom I called "resistance workers", back home to protect them from being compromised. These resistance workers I identified as men and women operating behind enemy lines resisting the occupation of their homelands by ZIPRA. This required bravery and a high level of trust. We could not afford to lose the people's trust and knew they would watch us carefully to ensure we kept our word. There was a natural migration of people from Hurungwe to Karoi for work, daily provisions, health matters, family visits and so on. Once this pattern was disrupted by a lengthy or permanent visit to Karoi, with no explanation, the ZIPRA intelligence networks would be immediately alerted. Any military action within that person's kraal area would have far-reaching, violent consequences, possibly even their death.

Furthermore, when vital information was conveyed, as far as possible, military action was called for, ensuring the trust and confidence of the informant. At times, we would delay intervention on gathered intelligence in order to establish a pattern of insurgents' activities and attack timeously when least expected. In military operations, correct timing is a crucial component of victory. Ultimately, the relaying of information is based on a relationship. It is founded on a common cause with a desired mutually beneficial outcome, thus the necessity for robust, concise political direction and impetus.

Political Cells

In Chikangwe, we developed small independent clandestine political cells based initially on family and friends known to support the UANC. This created a safe environment for political discussions. Each cell linked independently and directly to Grey and his team, who held regular formal and informal meetings to propagate political vision and monitor growth. This positioned each cell to independently reach out to their immediate community, in order to source, identify and recruit sympathetic persons and introduce them to the UANC political vision for Chikangwe, Hurungwe and the country as a whole. Interestingly, each new member automatically reached out to the known "resistance sympathisers" he was aware of, and a new cell was born. This was an informal procedure, developing naturally and progressively, ably headed by a competent Grey and his team. Grey's primary role was, figuratively speaking, to ignite the flame, with the people "carrying the torch". A key factor was the spreading of a political vision to gain the confidence and support of the people and to assure them that our forces had the capability to uphold this vision. As this was progressively and rapidly achieved, intelligence began to flow. The local population knew they were dealing with life-and-death matters, and were capable of establishing their unique strategies while maintaining security.

The reason these cells were initially clandestine is that the people of Chikangwe had family ties to kraal dwellers in Hurungwe. If ZIPRA, through their intelligence networks, identified UANC supporters, they would summarily carry out violent reprisals on defenceless family and/or relatives. This was to change once we were militarily active in Hurungwe but great care needed to be taken to protect the local population in the early days.

Soon after inauguration, our political network produced worthwhile and accurate intelligence. During our operations, volumes of information were received and recorded separately to avoid repetition and relieve boredom to the reader. However, I will pen interesting specific information and intelligence that we acted on. A significant amount of effort and work goes into the collection, processing and dissemination of intelligence before an effective deployment can take place.

On Wednesday, 18 October 1978, Grey enlightened me on events and information originating from the UANC network, supplying us with a clear picture of ZIPRA's operations. He established that two *mujibhas* and two insurgents had visited the Chikangwe Beerhall at 8 p.m. on 17 October 1978, discussing plans to bomb the white residential area of Karoi. Grey felt the individuals would make regular visits to the venue, so the following two nights we carried out covert operations in the township, focusing on the beer hall. We arranged for two Support Unit callsigns to be on immediate standby at the police station, with Grey and his network briefed to carry on as normal by visiting the beer hall and their contacts during the evenings. However, it transpired we had missed the opportunity because the insurgents did not return, as there was no sign of ZIPRA or their *mujibhas*. In our review of the situation, Grey and I agreed that ZIPRA were brazen in coming to Chikangwe and obviously confident that their own intelligence network was functioning efficiently and effectively. At least we were better informed and could now plan accordingly. Grey and I decided that in similar future circumstances we would react to information at hand and liaise directly with the resident SF.

Grey had also identified three ZIPRA contact men, Paul Chitemerere, Nepia Matamba and Kennias Kahocha, residing in the Karereshi area of Hurungwe. Interestingly, residing in the same area, was Mr Hove, another ZIPRA contact man and the owner of a green Zephyr 6, who had transported a total of 50 landmines in his vehicle from Kariba to Makuti and on to Karereshi.[1] Hove had been trained in the art of laying landmines and it was one of these explosives which blasted an SF vehicle in the area approximately a fortnight earlier. I confirmed that an SF vehicle had indeed been blown up in that area two weeks previously, with no one sustaining serious injuries.[2] While the locals were used to transport ZIPRA armaments, there was no evidence suggesting they were aware of the location of arms caches. This was a closely guarded secret only ZIPRA insurgents were aware

1 Karoi Landmine Map 4.
2 Karoi Landmine Map 5.

of. In the same area, between Wenera Kraal and Mapuranga Kraal, Grey established that there was an arms cache and a 12.7mm HMG near Kapare Hill. I felt ZIPRA were confident in using local transport to ferry their equipment, demonstrating the extent of their intelligence networks and local support in Hurungwe, as well as their contempt for the SF. It also revealed ZIPRA's strategy to train and use locals to support their efforts in mass mobilisation.

In the Zwimba and Zowa TTLs (near Sinoia and out of our area), Grey learned of Selous Scouts callsigns operating prior to the arrival of ZANLA. Each time a genuine ZANLA section attempted to enter the area, the locals reported them to the Selous Scouts thinking ZANLA were in fact Selous Scouts. Interestingly, Zwimba TTL was the home of James Chikerema, one of the fathers of the Second *Chimurenga*, who was now a part of the UANC leadership in terms of the March 3rd Agreement. Future President Robert Mugabe, Chikerema's nephew, was also from Zwimba. With such good connections to the people it was no surprise to me that the web of our intelligence gathering was so efficient. Grey advised us that some members of a Selous Scouts callsign were accidentally killed by Security Forces. D/P/O Clive Boddy (SB Scouts) confirmed this incident and that Cpl. Obert was one of those killed.[1] Grey also informed me that the ZIPRA Strela Section which had shot down Viscount *Hunyani* had crossed the Sanyati with their missile. Grey also notified me that a ZIPRA section had recently ambushed an army vehicle and then murdered a former African policeman, Jaison, near the Urengovera Gate. SB Karoi confirmed this incident.[2]

In addition, Grey reported to me that on Thursday, 12 October 1978, five UANC youths were allegedly enticed by Beauty, a schoolgirl from Matsika Kraal and a ZIPRA supporter, into the bushes around Magunje area on the pretext that there was a group of ZANLA insurgents wanting to meet them. However, the group was met by a ZIPRA section who murdered three of them and wounded the remaining two. Beauty subsequently fled to live with her father, a bus driver at Kariba Airport. This information was passed on to SB Kariba for their follow-up.

The murders were reported to the Magunje police base who in turn phoned Mike Reeler at Special Branch Karoi, informing him of the incident. The informant, Chido (pseudonym), phoned Grey in Salisbury to advise him of the circumstances surrounding the murders. He also told him that the road was "bad", meaning it had been mined, but Grey neither understood the terminology of the message nor passed it on to me: a miscommunication speedily resolved. Henceforth the term "bad road" would become permanently etched in our minds. Chido requested the ZIPRA insurgents to remove the mines, allowing them to recover the bodies. The four landmines were duly uplifted. On Monday, 16 October, Chido visited Karoi Police Station and reported the incident to Phil Wright. Wright also confirmed he was unsure if the four landmines had been re-laid in the road. A Pookie was despatched on Tuesday, 17 October, to check the road to Magunje. Four landmines were lifted, two of which were double mines. A positive victory in my opinion![3] It interested me that ZIPRA followed ZANLA's preferred landmine pattern, that is create an incident, mine the road, if suitable, convenient and carries minimum risk, wait to ambush the reacting vehicle when it struck the mine. The difficulty with ambushing a vehicle was, that unless the SF were lured into a specific incident within a planned time frame, it became risky to remain in ambush for fear of compromise. It was difficult to predict when an SF vehicle would travel the mined road. This, of course, revealed our counter-strategy to remain unpredictable. We were never stereotyped, we varied our approach routes and delayed responding where and when possible. It came to our attention that a further two UANC youths had been murdered, bringing the number of murders by ZIPRA to five.[4] Once the two injured youths recovered, they passed on valuable intelligence to us.

ZIPRA had targeted the SF when laying the landmines, expecting them to respond to the UANC murders, but removed them when requested by the locals. They then re-laid the mines targeting the

[1] See Chap. 9.
[2] Karoi Murder Map 6, not logged on map.
[3] Karoi Landmine Map 6.
[4] Karoi Murder Map 7.

SF, anticipating a reaction to the information they knew had been passed to the police regarding the murders. This sequence of events supported my early convictions that ZIPRA considered Hurungwe a liberated area under their control and governance. Chido had proved a most trustworthy comrade.

ZIPRA were aware of aspects of our strategies and we knew parts of theirs. My growing conviction was that the key to gaining the upper hand was in understanding the people, as they were caught squarely in the middle. Both ZIPRA and our networks relied heavily on their support. Only a viable, implemented political solution would win the battle. For the first time in Hurungwe, I was witnessing dialogue between ZIPRA, the people and our networks. Chido spoke freely of his association with ZIPRA who were well connected to the people. Protracted interrogations were now a thing of the past. The local population were freely volunteering crucial information to us. I found a significant difference between listening to the people speaking openly as opposed to demanding they talk to us. The people needed to authenticate and trust our strategies, encouraging a flow of information into the system with confidence, knowing it was safe to do so. A reliable and accurate flow of information was critical to setting the stage for the permanent deployment of our forces.

Early Assessment of Intelligence

My early assessment of our intelligence operation was in some cases confirmed by SB Karoi and the Selous Scouts. I believed it important to secure this confirmation, as it would establish trust between the various intelligence operators and the SF in general. We were identifying *mujibhas*, *chimbwidos*, ZIPRA contact men and businessmen supporting them, enabling us to build an accurate political and military intelligence picture of Hurungwe. This was vital for the deployment of our men for when the right time arrived, the ground, figuratively "ploughed", would be receptive for the seed of the people's army.

On reflection, I began to draw some early conclusions. Firstly, ZIPRA were training locals in the art of guerrilla warfare, including weapons training and the laying of landmines. Secondly, they appeared to have a large supply of weaponry hoarded in Hurungwe and surrounding areas, confirming the general intelligence that they were preparing for a conventional attack on Rhodesia. Thirdly, their intelligence networks were well established and, at that stage of the war, they possibly knew more of our intentions and operations than we of theirs. Finally, ZIPRA were not random sections drifting aimlessly around Hurungwe with no overall strategy and objective. On the contrary, they had a goal and were painstakingly and methodically working towards it. However, they had weaknesses which we were soon to expose. A ZIPRA insurgent later confirmed my suspicions: "The purpose of caching weapons throughout the rural areas in our operational theatre was to make them readily available to our local supporters who had been trained in their use. These internal recruits laid mines and increasingly some of them became efficient with the use of weapons and carried out ambushes."[1]

All told, we had excellent intelligence arising from our political cells operating in Chikangwe Township. The UANC was traditionally an enemy of the state and would have attracted the attention of the local SB. Now we were a part of the state but our operations would still attract SB's attention, who would be keen to monitor our progress and developments. I was content with this arrangement as it produced meaningful checks and balances. Grey and I continually tightened and improved our security procedures, agreeing that we would solely oversee all military and intelligence matters. In turn, and where necessary, I would liaise with the Special Branch details, including Special Branch liaison officers attached to the Selous Scouts.

It was evident to me that Grey, through his networks, had the capacity to obtain intelligence from a wide field and we decided it was vital to concentrate and focus on the task at hand: Hurungwe. Our immediate aim was to establish a political presence in Hurungwe paving the way for the arrival of our forces. Any intelligence received from areas further afield would be passed to the relevant SF

1 Sibanda E. (2005), p.166.

in that area. We had a large enough mission on our hands in Hurungwe, let alone becoming entangled with matters beyond our remit. This decision proved beneficial in the events which lay ahead.

Communication with the Enemy

It needs to be borne in mind, once the procedures for receiving intelligence are established, one simultaneously creates the process for circulating information and propaganda. In our context, we were receiving information from remote regions of Hurungwe. We had intentionally positioned ourselves to filter information and propaganda to outlying areas without setting foot in the TTL. Furthermore, ZIPRA, through their intelligence networks, would be monitoring our movements, an intriguing situation to my mind. As a result, our political message was propagated to these remote areas by word of mouth, relaying a clear, consistent, achievable and definitive message, namely: "The people's army is coming to liberate the people and occupy and possess the land." There is a vast difference to flooding the area with troops and that of occupying and possessing the land which will become clear later. Hence I decided on this message. Our approach was that straightforward.

The lifting of landmines conveyed a significant message to the enemy. In essence it was this: "Our intelligence networks are robust, effective, efficient and productive and we have penetrated your intelligence networks." Our infiltration revealed ZIPRA did not have absolute support of the locals and that the will of the people was, even if only in small measure, opposed to them. Control of the people is synonymous with safety in guerrilla warfare and the procurement of safety holds no bounds. In warfare, as in many areas of life, the unknown strikes fear in the heart of an individual or even a group because the enemies' strategies and tactics are unknown. I wanted ZIPRA to be constantly pondering when, where, how and indeed, what will our strengths be on attack? Their focus would necessarily shift from maintaining a position, holding ground and attacking when the SF were vulnerable, to that of constant defence. Marginal gains in guerrilla warfare are significant. ZIPRA reprisals would need to increase as they ruthlessly endeavoured to maintain their psychological hold over the locals. Our negating the effects of landmines was also a moral victory over ZIPRA. Transporting landmines from Zambia, while crossing the Zambezi River or Lake Kariba, was a long and arduous process. In addition, remote arid countryside and rugged terrain en route needed to be negotiated. To have the landmines lifted at the conclusion of this energy-sapping exercise was demoralising for the enemy to say the least. Significantly, the people would be aware of our success!

My transition from Rusape to Karoi called for a reappraisal of my approach to the war. At the outset, I was astonished that locals would freely provide information of activities and locations of ZIPRA and actually expect military intervention to eliminate the invading insurgents. This was a far cry from the conventional method of interrogating locals, generally *mujibhas*, redirecting their political focus and then deploying OPs to seek out insurgents. Our revised approach gained us the support of the local population, allowing us to create a political and military presence in the immediate region, while gleaning voluntary intelligence directly from them. I was unaware how quickly the tide would turn. However, I did know it was important to be creative in our approach to the war, embrace change, resist accepted norms and to persevere resolutely. I found myself stimulated by the challenge that lay ahead as I felt we were gaining impetus.

Covert to Overt

On 26 October 1978, Grey and I agreed it was opportune to establish our UANC office in Chikangwe Township and raise the UANC flag. The office would be a visible expression of a shared political vision. It also made a bold statement that the UANC was a legitimate African party represented and supported by the people. Our premises would be a physical symbol of political change in government which now recognised and identified with African political parties, as opposed to banning them, consequently forcing them to become underground movements. My major concern in opening our office was that the men serving at the premises would create a target for ZIPRA and their supporters, thereby threatening their welfare if not their lives. However, the pendulum was rapidly swinging in our favour, making it vital to maintain the pace of those anxious for change and freedom. There could be no doubting Grey and his team had gained considerable support in Chikangwe which was promising and progressive. The office would increase the tempo. I felt that gaining the support of the local population would help the UANC build a protective network, surrounding the people from, and alerting them to, threats from ZIPRA and their *mujibhas*. Moving from a covert operation to an overt office would always entail risk, requiring that we proceed with caution. Precautions were introduced to protect those stationed at the office, UANC supporters and "resistance workers".

There was a wealth of information pouring into the township which we wanted to capitalise on. It was our intention to exploit this intelligence as well as bolster the informal flow of information back to Hurungwe, allowing us, in a literal sense, to "speak" to the enemy. The office would be an emblem, a focal gathering point for UANC staff, intelligence networks and the people: a symbol displaying to both urban and rural residents that our work was authentic and trustworthy. UANC supporters and "resistance workers" could safely visit and report to the office. Our responsibility would be to attend to their needs and act on the information they supplied. It would also present a rallying point for refugees as they arrived in Chikangwe, enabling us to assist in their resettling. Refugees had both resided with and fled from the enemy, making them an excellent source of historical and immediate intelligence. It was vital to protect them. These Africans did not vacate their traditional homes because they were happy. In short, they were afraid of ZIPRA's violence and reprisals, and were anxious to return to their homes once circumstances permitted. An additional benefit to the location of our UANC office was that it would serve as an ideal venue for recruits for the people's army to present themselves. An interesting phenomenon that unfolded in Hurungwe was that recruits volunteered, they did not need to be cajoled, conscripted or press-ganged into active service.

As matters progressed, I tasked Admin. to open the UANC office as soon as possible. A short while later, on 2 November 1978, they found an office in Chikangwe which was immediately available. The necessary paperwork was duly dealt with and signed, with occupation set for Monday, 6 November 1978. In fact, the office was officially opened on Thursday, 9 November 1978. The response of locals was favourable and encouraging. A telephone line was installed the day after opening: Karoi 419. Later in the day, the furniture arrived. The UANC office was equipped and fully functional. From conception to inauguration it had taken Admin. 11 days to find the premises, 14 days to the official opening and 15 days to have the telephone installed. I considered this a notable achievement. As I saw matters, the UANC had gained immediate credibility as, following our announcement of intent to open an office, we had promptly done so. Our commitment was sure to gain the people's trust and confidence. In an evolving movement, action has to follow agreed decisions, as this denotes progress, prevents stagnation, builds trust and demands migration from traditionally accepted norms. A further immediate, peripheral benefit was that ZIPRA would also be aware of our progress. Opening the office was significant as it was a physical manifestation of a growing political network that represented the general support and will of the local population. The people were witnessing the progress they sought and identified with it. Our prevailing philosophy was, this is your office, a key element in its establishment. It would bring together the people in Chikangwe Township, Hurungwe and the people's army once deployed into Hurungwe. The UANC office would be considered the centre of our political and military activities and, therefore, our intelligence-gathering operations. It was important that the people identified with the UANC and not the traditional authorities: BSAP/SB/GC, Internal Affairs and so on, those seen to enforce colonial government. I wanted the UANC to be recognised as a fully fledged political party and not subject to, or seeking permission from, the traditional Rhodesian hierarchy to gain legitimacy for existence. An aspect of traditional Special Branch modus operandi (MO) was to gather information about people who opposed the Rhodesian Front Government. Up to this point, the African people had been denied political representation except for the traditional tribal system.

Conversely, the UANC were now working with and for the local population. We were positioning ourselves to protect them in Hurungwe, eliminate our common enemy, ZIPRA, and address their aspirations in the process. A significant mindset change was required for both the African and existing governmental structures. My contention was there had to be change so that the political message was justified and warranted support from both the people and their army. No change would imply we were still fighting for the "old regime" which played into the hands of ZIPRA. In other words, the UANC was united with the local population.

Events continued to unfold rapidly making it a most exciting time. Grey placed Tapedza and Madison (pseudonyms) in the office to manage the political matters while Katima (pseudonym) oversaw the intelligence-gathering operation. I considered them capable, astute, committed and forward-thinking men. I had great admiration for Katima who had lost a limb in an engagement with the SF and had returned home under the March 3rd Agreement. Despite his situation, there was always a happy smile on his face and he actively worked alongside his comrades, wherever that took him. He was a breath of fresh air and an excellent intelligence operative.

It did not take ZIPRA long to react to the opening of our UANC office, confirming that they had an active intelligence network in Chikangwe. Four days later we received information confirming six ZIPRA were living in the Chishumba Church Hall at Zvarare, in the Magunje area. They were conducting door-to-door searches for two UANC Chikangwe officials, Tapedza and Madison. Fortunately, they were both resident in Karoi. We were now aware of the ZIPRA threat and alerted our staff to be vigilant and constantly exercising safety precautions. Notwithstanding, Jefter Mambiravana, an ex-UANC official from the Magunje area, was murdered by ZIPRA on 13 November 1978.[1] There were no prisoners in this life-and-death struggle.

One of my concerns in establishing the Chikangwe UANC office was the risk of repositioning the cells from a covert to an overt operation. However, with the growing involvement of the locals they were able to surround themselves with supporters and they developed a protective network of "eyes and ears", alerting them to ZIPRA activity. I found it interesting that information flowed between Chikangwe and Hurungwe for both ZIPRA's and our intelligence networks, highlighting the developing struggle for supremacy in political and military matters.

Hereafter, the UANC office was the centre of our web: our HQ. It linked the rural population and Chikangwe's urban residents. Intelligence flowed to and fro through the office imparting our political vision and gathering information regarding ZIPRA's operations. This allowed us to spread our intelligence networks throughout Hurungwe and Chikangwe. The office empowered us to attack ZIPRA employing traditional military resources, including Fire Force, ensuring our intelligence was accurate for successful operations. This process would prepare the way for the successful deployment of our forces. Swords were drawn: certainly mine was!

1 Karoi Murder Map 15.

12 ~ FOLLOWING MOMENTUM

If you are not prepared to give up everything, you have already lost.
"Act Of Valour" film

SFA Strategies Phase 4: Train the People's Army

Although we had not deployed our forces into Hurungwe at the time of establishing the UANC office, I had a premonition of victory. We were progressing through a radical transition of strategies from "kills win wars" to facilitating the people. The former approach was reminiscent of the struggle we had in Makoni, requiring violent, incessant laborious tasks as well as placing demands on the people, in order to achieve our sole objective of eliminating the enemy. On the other hand, we were now intimately involved with the people, listening to their grievances, needs and aspirations (GNA) and attending to their legitimate requests which included training their young men to defend them. This process was relevant to the political, military and the people, and success required a cohesion between the three. We made no demands of the people but moved in harmony with them to achieve our common objectives. This approach is summed up in the Shona slogan "*Povo yaramba*" (The people have spoken). We were gearing up for war and began using ZANLA's slogan "*Pamberi ne hondo*" (Forward with the war).

Grey and I were unhappy that the training farm was based at Sinoia, some 112 kilometres from Karoi. He suggested it would be politically expedient to have the men closer to their home area at Karoi. It would also make the people aware that politically the UANC were implementing their vision. I felt it would make it easier to administer the camp from Karoi and be more involved in the political and intelligence-gathering aspects of the men's training. It would also complete the link between the UANC office, Chikangwe and the people in Hurungwe, drawing them together.

In the light of our concerns, Todd from Admin. was tasked to find a suitable location for our training venue and, after a short search, located Chabwino (Shona: it is all right) farm, approximately 15 kilometres from Karoi. It was some 10 kilometres, as the crow flies, from the Mukwichi TTL where ZIPRA were operational. A small tract of state land lay between Chabwino and Mukwichi, situating the fenced and gated farm in a military active area, requiring 24-hours' security. We made several visits to Chabwino, including one on 20 October 1978, when we decided the location was suitable for our entire operation. The farmhouse was raised above the general surroundings, reducing the chance of a ZIPRA attack. There was good ground for all aspects of our training requirements. With the necessary documentation signed, Admin. organised for some remedial work to be carried out by locally based contractors. The works included the electrics, plumbing and repairs to the borehole pump.

On Friday, 27 October 1978, I visited Chabwino farm to check the progress of the maintenance operations. All the electrical and plumbing problems were being rectified and we anticipated moving the men from Sinoia by the end of the following week, 4 November 1978. This was good news as the growing momentum in Chikangwe would gain a substantial boost when the people learned that their army was in the area, being trained for action and their defence.

While at the farm I happened to meet a local and influential farmer (name withheld) who told me the reaction of local farmers to establishing our UANC base was favourable, provided it eliminated stock theft and farm attacks. It struck me that these farmers would need to be politically reorientated in line with my thoughts expressed earlier. I decided it would be prudent to have a meeting with the farmers to build understanding and trust with them. I asked Admin. to arrange a meeting with the local member in charge, district commissioner and co-ordinating committees from the Tengwe and Karoi farming areas. The date was set for Tuesday, 31 October 1978.

I took the senior training staff to introduce them to Chabwino farm on 1 November 1978, as I felt it important to keep them informed of our intentions and allow them to feel part of the team. They were happy with the farm and, in particular, that it could be satisfactorily defended, but they were dissatisfied with the training grounds.

A vast amount of work was required to clear the farm's surrounds. To me this was no difficulty as the new recruits could be tasked to undertake the necessary manual labour while undergoing basic training. Walter was also concerned that the training programme would fall behind schedule. However, Admin. and I were managing all the work required to prepare Chabwino for the move. There would be little disruption to the men's training programme as all they had to do was move and carry on. Naturally, the move would take us further from the nightlife of Salisbury which would no doubt upset at least one of the staff, but we were closer to the operational theatre. I saw no disadvantages to the move other than hard work in the initial stages which would be summarily resolved. Admin. worked hard to prepare Chabwino for the men.

Our political plan was to spread the news that the people's army was established. This news would filter to the people in Karoi and then on to ZIPRA further afield. We would gain their additional trust when they realised we were men of our word and coming to their defence.

By 9 November 1978, with the remedial work completed, we had successfully settled into Chabwino, marking a cornerstone event. Grey and I decided we would, in time, resettle Hurungwe refugees at Chabwino which would stem the flow of exiles into Chikangwe and Salisbury. Refugees occupying Chabwino would be privy to intelligence from the immediate area, as well as Chikangwe and Hurungwe, which would filter through our network. We proposed introducing a social commune system where we provided the finance, with the refugees farming the land to provide crops for their own consumption. This would maintain the independence of the migrants while, at the same time, their dependence on us as we would be supporting them financially, thereby securing their loyalty and trust. Without doubt, a mutually beneficial situation.

Field Intelligence Training

In the meantime, we continued to use the Sinoia farm for training. It was important to maintain contact with the training staff and recruits at the farm, ensuring our vision was inscribed on their hearts with no deviations. A growing priority was the necessity for me to train the men in aspects of intelligence work which would prove lifesaving in the operational areas when they were deployed. Through these regular visits I sustained a relationship with the farm intelligence-gathering team, keeping myself up to date with developments and ensuring that there were no deviations from our policies. It was not long before Manenji gathered intelligence from two new recruits confirming field information from Grey. This was reassuring and emphasised the significance and necessity of the farm intelligence-gathering networks.

Todd organised denim clothing and shoes for all the men as well as some basic maintenance tools. I took the opportunity to deliver the goods and conduct intelligence-gathering training. Morale at the farm was high, with two sections giving a competent fire-with-movement demonstration using live rounds. Both sections were unsupervised and carried out their tasks to an excellent standard. Good progress, I reflected. Earlier in the day, one section had shot a wild pig and its one piglet with four shots which was good shooting. The farm was in perfect order with deep freezers and gas cylinders, organised by Todd, suitably bunkered, as was the ammunition for protection. Seeing the ammunition bunkered in the bush, accessible to all the men was a far cry from the strict procedures in place at BSAP stations. While at the farm and with all staff in attendance, I had a meeting with the commander and section commanders. I was anxious for them to start thinking about their security in the field. I regarded the matter of deploying men into the war zone a serious business for, literally, I was dealing with matters of life and death. Solid, well-informed intelligence networks in the field were an essential ingredient to success, forming the dividing line between life and death. Ultimately, this was Grey's and my responsibility. Throughout the war I had not suffered the loss of one man through negligence and poor intelligence. My outlook was not about to change. Grey and I had full agreement on this. Death in war is inevitable. However, negligence when dealing with intelligence and strategy was unacceptable to us. Success depended on mutual trust and teamwork.

Section leaders and their deputies were instructed to familiarise themselves with the handwriting and signatures of other section leaders and commanders, to avoid complications or compromise in the field when sections were communicating with each other. This would reduce the risk of ZIPRA breaching our security by writing false letters to our men, enticing them to their ambush points. It was important for my men to realise that the UANC political wing was hard at work establishing networks in Hurungwe and in the Chikangwe Township, for intelligence flows through the political system. The men needed to understand there was a flow of intelligence drifting through the farm, the field and the UANC, including our office. They were warned that not all their family and friends were necessarily UANC supporters. Some still supported ZIPRA and much care would have to be taken when deployed, learning who to trust, as the situation continued to deteriorate in Hurungwe.

There was always the danger, once in the field fully armed, some men would assume that they were a law unto themselves, resulting in abuse of the people and, indeed, atrocities. It was important for them to know we had strong political networks, passing intelligence through to us, and that these networks would grow in strength and confidence following their deployment. In other words, we would be monitoring their actions through the political networks. This would give the people confidence and access to the political to pass information on what the SFAs were doing. We wished to emphasise that little would escape our attention. Equally important, the men needed to know they were not alone in the field, that there was a resistance movement in place which would support them once deployed. Grey agreed on the importance of this matter and would alert the field networks to identify and distinguish between ZIPRA and UANC supporters. When sections were finally deployed, they would be issued notebooks to record details of incidents, including the following information:

1. Section number.
2. Date, time and place of incident.
3. Type of operation — ambush, surprise attack by ZIPRA, base-camp attack and ground assault supported by Fire Force.
4. Enemy strengths in the incidents and, in general, in the area.
5. Enemy casualties — killed, injured, captured.
6. Section casualties — killed, injured, captured.
7. Arms and ammunition used — for resupply purposes.
8. Arms caches located.
9. A note of monies spent to be logged in the rear of the books.
10. Additional general relevant information.

Certain additional items such as weapons' numbers, comrades' names, UANC contact men and *mujibhas* would not be noted for security reasons in the initial stages. I touched on the problem of regrouping after an attack, but this tactic would need to be discussed in greater detail once we were able to assess the situation on the ground before and during deployments. Politicising the people to gain their support was vital in these early stages and would prepare the ground for our first deployments. Casualties would be airlifted if possible or evacuated by our networks. Each section would have a trained medic, responsible for treating our own casualties and the people when we deployed. Clinics had been closed in Hurungwe making for a desperate need for medical treatment. Our own medics would need to offer treatment until we gained sufficient momentum to reopen clinics. This process would help the men gain the support of the people.

Right at the outset, I made it clear that the men would be well trained. It was normal SFA policy to train the men for four weeks before deployment. This procedure had disastrous effects in the farms and field operations I had visited prior to taking on the challenge for the liberation of Hurungwe. Poor training resulted in a lack of discipline, and reduced confidence and ability, resulting in ineffective military operations leading to casualties. In my view, training that was too brief led to disarray. This was by no means the fault of the SFAs but was a command failure brought about by political agendas. I was confident that our well-trained army would quickly gain the support and confidence of the people, provided there was a high standard of discipline and that they did not abuse or take advantage of the people, particularly sexually. The key to success was becoming one with the people, supporting them, defending them and sharing a common political vision. Consequently, it was equally important for Grey and his team to prepare the people politically for the arrival of their army. Success depended on the political, the military and the people uniting.

It soon came to my attention that voluntarily extending our training programme was not well received by the formal military establishment and Com.Ops. They were determined to have our men deployed according to their schedule and agenda. I was determined to have my men well trained. A stand-off was developing. Our standard of training continued to improve, as did the men's morale: the positive atmosphere at the farm continued. Grey's regular visits to politicise the men were having the desired influence. My intelligence network within the farm was satisfied with developments, with no negative murmurings taking hold. It was clear to me that these military volunteers were keen to defend their people and, despite their knowing that they were facing a formidable, well-entrenched enemy, were unafraid and confident of the people's support. Mass mobilisation of the people in Hurungwe was the key to success. "*Pamberi nepovo, pamberi nehondo*" (Forward with the people, forward with the war).

I was in no doubt that the people would support their own military once they knew it was deployed permanently, was trustworthy and had a clear political vision. It was my contention, at this stage of the war, Ian Smith and the RF had failed to produce a clear political strategy which would have enabled the military to be more effective. Consequently, we at the UANC, took the initiative. We accepted that some of the locals would continue to support ZIPRA for varying reasons. This, we foresaw, would be inevitable, but our planning included developing a strategy to overcome this obstacle as best we could as events unfolded.

We experienced difficulties in collecting and obtaining certain equipment ordered for the farm. These items included water-purifying tablets, two 4.5 vehicles, one 2.5 vehicle, MAGs to support vehicle patrols and wristwatches for certain section leaders. Walter continually complained of not having the wherewithal to supervise the farm's affairs, particularly weapons and ammunition. I assured him these matters required patience and suggested he make do with what we had and that I would approach Admin. to tackle the problem. They promptly did so. I found it monotonous listening to Walter's complaints about shortages. In time, we gave him the nickname "Wherewithal" as he never had enough of anything. Success would bring support, not only from the people in Hurungwe but from the political leadership and military which supported us logistically. I was confident the difficulties we were facing with kit and equipment would be resolved once our success was recognised. Interestingly, people clamber to be associated with a successful operation, be it military, political, business, sporting or otherwise.

"Suicide Squads": Mudzimu Area

On 26 October 1978, we received intelligence of ZIPRA operating a "suicide squad" commanded by Doctor and Friday. Their primary task was to eliminate opposition to ZIPRA, especially among UANC-orientated support. Allegedly, Headman, Mr Joseph Mudzimu and Kraalhead, Mr Kapesa, had been elected as court judges, on behalf of ZIPRA, to put on trial suspected "sellouts". ZIPRA executed those found guilty. We found these developments perturbing, as it took the due judicial process into the hands of prejudice, where domestic, tribal, rural and nationalist agendas tended to rule, rather than the implementation of fair and impartial justice. Rural people are prone to petty family disputes. In many instances, these were of long standing with criminal suspicions often twisted to portray political and military betrayal, resulting frequently in the death of the innocent. Intelligence networks which fed information to the "judges", included *mujibhas* with insufficient expertise requisite for such intricate affairs. Notwithstanding, they were considered credible informers and prosecutors, and unfortunately remain so to this day. This was the first mention of the ZIPRA "suicide squad" in the Mudzimu area where it seemed ZIPRA enjoyed avid support. My concern was for the locals exposed to ZIPRA's excesses and that it would increase once events turned against them.

On 11 November 1978, the "suicide squad" led by Doctor and Friday, both Cuban-trained, confirmed by the local SB, held a meeting in a backroom of Nepia Matamba's store. Six locals from Karoi, including Kasaba, attended the meeting but our informant, also invited, did not attend. The "suicide squad" then moved south-east from the Mahororo area and was now operating in the area of the Maumbe and Murereshi rivers near a small dam. It is alleged the kraals of this area, approximately 3 kilometres from Magunje BC, were to be searched for *vatengesi*. The focus of the search was apparently the Chimyembere kraals. This "suicide squad" was of grave concern to us, requiring that we address the matter as soon as possible. Our information was authenticated by Special Branch which was reassuring, as it confirmed our intelligence-gathering process was sound. It reinforced my thoughts that the only way to defend the people was by creating a people's army which would remain permanently on the ground to defend them. Grey's network of support was growing rapidly in Chikangwe Township, as was the refugee problem. Locals from Hurungwe were pouring into Chikangwe to escape the oppression and violence perpetrated by ZIPRA. The actions of the "suicide squad" compounded the problem. Unfortunately, and inevitably, this violence would increase as we progressed, making it clear that once we entered Hurungwe militarily, in order to protect the people, we would have to increase momentum and expand our operations as rapidly as possible, while maintaining high standards of training. This was a formidable task, sure to place much pressure on the training staff. Kraalheads Nduna and Kapesa were working with ZIPRA and were aware of their bases and arms caches in the area. In fact, Nduna's car was being used by ZIPRA to assist them in carrying out their raids. This again gave a clear indication of ZIPRA's nonchalance and the reality of their controlling Hurungwe. However, in our view, a major surprise awaited them. Nduna was captured by an SF patrol on 10 November 1978, but was shot and killed while attempting to escape.[1]

Rhodesian Defence Regiment Contact

One incident of note occurred on 27 October 1978, which Mike Reeler attended. He recalled:

> The incident I well remember, who the hell wouldn't, but one might say for all the wrong reasons though! Returning from a resupply run, or some such like, the particular RDR[2] call-sign, who numbered around a half dozen or so, were en route back to their base at the Sanyati River Bridge on the Binga Road. Travelling in an old clapped out Bedford RL troop carrier, they came under "small arms" fire from somewhere at the roadside. The driver seemingly instinctively braked upon hearing the commotion following which he changed his mind and proceeded to accelerate, in order to get the heck out of it!
>
> The Bren gun gunner, having "risen", quite literally, to the occasion, jumped up in the rear of the vehicle and started to put down some serious "return fire". Unfortunately for him, the stop/start motion of the truck caused the "poor bugger" to be unceremoniously dumped out of the rear, the tail board flap either missing or had been deliberately left hanging open. Mercifully the only injuries (lacerations and bruises) arising from the encounter were those to our "man" who found himself lying in the middle of the road, while watching his "comrades" disappear in a cloud of dust, which must have been little consolation, I'm sure. Fortunately for him the "gooks", seem not to have stuck around,

[1] Karoi Murder Map 14.

[2] Rhodesian Defence Regiment (RDR) comprised mainly mixed-race soldiers, classified by race as "Coloureds".

this quite possibly due to his initial instant response. He too having beaten a hasty retreat back to the business centre, initially on foot and thereafter hitching a ride, of all things. It was only here that he was eventually re-united with his call-sign, they, having taken some considerable time in regaining their composure before back-tracking in search of him. There were no casualties on either side.[1]

Mike Reeler attended the scene, collected spent cartridge cases from the ambush position and sent them to Salisbury for forensic ballistics analysis. Ballistics expert Paul de Mattos analysed the two reports: "The ballistic reports established that three of the AKs involved in the ambush were linked to the Nyamhunga Police Base attack on the 6 August 1978, one of which was also linked to the murder of the survivors at the Viscount *Hunyani* scene on the 3 September 1978. There is no evidence of any weapon/s being captured or insurgents killed. It would seem unusual to find only one FCC from a PKM GP Machine Gun, but it could either have been fired from different locations only one of which was found or had a 'jam' that was not cleared."[2]

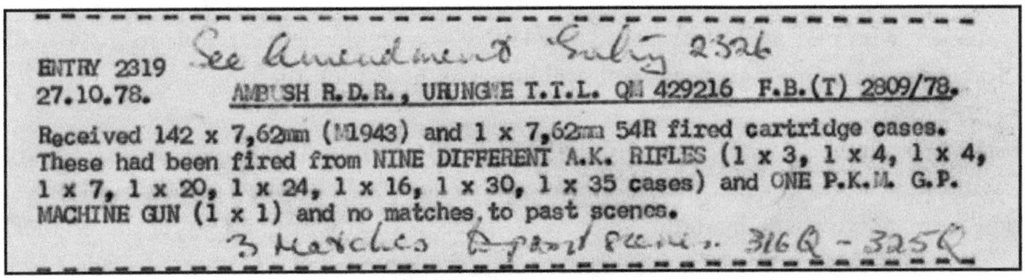
ENTRY 2319 2326
27.10.78. AMBUSH R.D.R., URUNGWE T.T.L. QM 429216 F.B.(T) 2809/78.

Received 142 x 7,62mm (M1943) and 1 x 7,62mm 54R fired cartridge cases. These had been fired from NINE DIFFERENT A.K. RIFLES (1 x 3, 1 x 4, 1 x 4, 1 x 7, 1 x 20, 1 x 24, 1 x 16, 1 x 30, 1 x 35 cases) and ONE P.K.M. G.P. MACHINE GUN (1 x 1) and no matches to past scencs.
316Q – 325Q

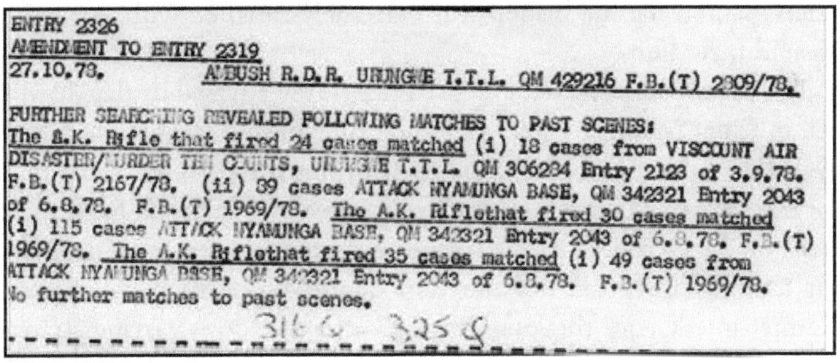
ENTRY 2326
AMENDMENT TO ENTRY 2319
27.10.78. AMBUSH R.D.R. URUNGWE T.T.L. QM 429216 F.B.(T) 2809/78.

FURTHER SEARCHING REVEALED FOLLOWING MATCHES TO PAST SCENES: The A.K. Rifle that fired 24 cases matched (i) 18 cases from VISCOUNT AIR DISASTER/MURDER TEN COUNTS, URUNGWE T.T.L. QM 306284 Entry 2123 of 3.9.78. F.B.(T) 2167/78. (ii) 39 cases ATTACK NYAMUNGA BASE, QM 342321 Entry 2043 of 6.8.78. F.B.(T) 1969/78. The A.K. Riflethat fired 30 cases matched (i) 115 cases ATTACK NYAMUNGA BASE, QM 342321 Entry 2043 of 6.8.78. F.B.(T) 1969/78. The A.K. Riflethat fired 35 cases matched (i) 49 cases from ATTACK NYAMUNGA BASE, QM 342321 Entry 2043 of 6.8.78. F.B.(T) 1969/78. No further matches to past scenes.
316Q – 325Q

Rhodesian Defence Regiment contact ballistics report and amendments.

Flowing with Intelligence Requires Change

On 26 October, Katima, of our UANC team, reported a landmine on Mahororo Road, with traffic diverted by three locals from the main road via Mahororo BC and Mahororo School, which is a link road.[3] ZIPRA had murdered three unidentified locals and left the bodies behind Petro Nechombo's house, with instructions they be left there.[4] At Kapiri Hill, Makumbirofa[5] was murdered and Silas Kakwere had been murdered at Mahororo.[6] Both murders were carried out by ZIPRA whose campaign continued unabated. Abandonment of bodies was in violation of the spiritual traditions of the people. However, while anathema to African custom, it allowed us the opportunity to expose ZIPRA and capitalise politically on the issue.

A senior UANC party official, Steven Parirenyatwa, arrived at our offices for a visit on 29 October 1978. He expressed his pleasure with our progress and developments. I voiced my concerns regarding Grey's travelling around the country on UANC intelligence and political matters. Parirenyatwa agreed that Grey should dedicate his time to our Karoi operations. Once we deployed the

1 Mike Reeler email 25/1/2019. Karoi Contacts Map Incident 12.
2 Paul de Mattos email 25/1/2019.
3 Karoi Landmine Map 7.
4 Karoi Murder Map 8.
5 Karoi Murder Map 9, not logged on map.
6 Karoi Murder Map 10.

people's army, our workload would increase exponentially and there would be no time to travel around the country.

On Sunday, 29 October 1978, Grey and I met with Geoff Price to discuss our progress and developments. Foremost on our minds was the lack of a political redirection towards African labourers, in particular the farming sector. There seemed to be a resistance to bring about political change, or at least putting mechanisms in place for transformation to become a much-needed reality. Irrespective of the evolution of a military solution, the resolution of the African workers' grievances was going to be of paramount importance in solving the country's woes and we felt that the sooner a solution to the problem was undertaken, the greater political impact our forces would have in the field. It seemed to me the SF were deployed solely to protect the persons and properties of the white population, particularly the farming community. A classic example occurred in the Tengwe area following stock theft from white farmers. When pursuing the criminals, livestock-theft teams were entering Hurungwe and uplifting two to three cattle from random locals as a form of reprisal. These reprisals needed to cease. Constructive terror retaliations against ZIPRA were acceptable but revenge on the masses, who may well be opposed to ZIPRA, was totally unacceptable to my way of thinking. Our forces would gain a significant political impact when stock-theft reprisals came to an end.

Transformation was required to safeguard political progress, which in turn would ensure military advancement. Without political change, the war continued to be a drain on the country's resources, both material and human. However, a guiding light in the process of attempting to alter the political landscape was our association with Bishop Abel Muzorewa through our UANC party officials. Grey often assured me the bishop was extremely satisfied with our work. The opportunity would soon arise to meet him.

During the meeting with Geoff Price, Grey advised us that 13 young adults from a UANC youth cell in Chief Mujinga's area, including the youth chairman, had fled from ZIPRA to Karoi as they wished to undergo military training with our forces. The young men were accommodated in Karoi for the weekend after which intelligence would be gleaned from them by Grey and myself. Two days later, on 31 October 1978, a further nine young men from the same youth cell arrived at our base for training. Grey did not hurry to debrief these men which was a change from my traditional counter-intelligence thinking. I was learning to adopt varying strategies to information gathering, as we had now secured the co-operation of the people. Without the willingness of the people, sourcing immediate intelligence and pinpointing insurgents' locations, proved a laborious, time-consuming and hit-and-miss affair. Hence our dependence on OPs for the location of insurgent sections, including the presence of their supporters. However, our intelligence strategy was undergoing a fundamental change as we had won the co-operation of the people and access to their detailed intelligence, including those of the *mujibhas* and contact men. ZIPRA's activities, and how they reacted and integrated with other groups in the area, was now within our grasp, representing a substantial change from traditional SF operations. In my opinion, counter-insurgency, mass mobilisation and, indeed, guerrilla warfare calls for patience and calculated timing. I needed to rearrange my thinking from concentrating on finding and killing insurgents to becoming one with the people. This required a paradigm shift. Grey was gently guiding me along this path of transformation.

On my return to Karoi on Monday, 30 October 1978, I collected explosives from Special Forces which were required for our training. The next day, I visited SB Sinoia's *mujibha* farm at Sinoia and immediately noticed the relative inactivity at the base. Ten *mujibhas* were present but there was little to suggest they were gainfully employed. This lack of urgency was possibly due to there being no dedicated SB officer on site who understood the *mujibha* concept. In my thinking, this was further confirmation, at a national level, of a failure to appreciate and implement the *mujibha* system. As I saw matters, local SB staff were too preoccupied to devote time, energy and other essential resources to manage these farms. I found this immensely frustrating. An enormous sum of money, to say nothing of human capital, was being squandered. In my view, with a little dedication, understanding and commitment, a well-managed *mujibha* system could have altered the course of the war to the benefit of the entire country.

Keeping the Community Informed

Murmurings had been circulating among the local farming community about our operations and affiliation to the UANC. The meeting Todd had organised at the Karoi Club with the farmers' co-ordinating committee from Tengwe and Karoi agricultural areas for Tuesday, 31 October 1978, was well attended and, as it transpired, a critically well-timed gathering. Public speculation was rampant. Gossip was circulating that our operation was based on Marxist principles, with some referring to us as the Kremlin. As a result, it became essential that we set the record straight and explain the concept behind the SFAs. I was not swayed by public opinion, as the voice of the uninformed rarely wins wars. We invited the local police member in charge and district commissioner. I was encouraged that both attended.

To begin with, I gave an overview of the current situation in Hurungwe impressing that clearly ZIPRA considered it a liberated zone which they governed. In fact, I stressed, the reality was they were correct in their assumption. I pointed out the difficulties presented by the SF being stretched beyond their limits and unable to cope with the increasing threat and presence of both ZANLA and ZIPRA forces operating in Rhodesia. The scales were weighed, in my opinion, heavily against the SF. In addition, there was a growing external military threat being posed by ZANLA and ZIPRA that needed to be addressed which the SF were unable to effectively counter on an ongoing basis. Periodic SF attacks on insurgent bases in Mozambique and Zambia would not necessarily stem the influx of insurgents armed with increasingly sophisticated military hardware across the vast, poorly protected Rhodesian borders. I also highlighted the fact that the SF were limited to search-and-destroy, uplift-and-regroup attacks on the enemy and did not have the manpower to sustain a permanent presence in the operational areas. In my estimation, this was the greatest weakness of the SF, with ZIPRA capitalising on this deficiency by creating a permanent governing presence, namely martial law. ZIPRA disrupted civil order by preventing dipping, prohibiting attendance at schools, closing healthcare clinics, controlling road links by the planting of landmines, attacks on farms and the SF, and other such disturbances. In summary, as I saw matters unfolding, the SF were increasingly losing the battle.

There can be no doubt, I imparted a bleak picture but I knew the farmers, and those in attendance, would appreciate my honesty. It occurred to me they were possibly as well informed as the SF about the truth of the situation in Hurungwe. In my view, the moment had arrived to face the reality that the SF were losing the war! The stage had been set to impart our UANC vision and strategy which I shared with them.

Our strategy was a unique concept of recruiting, training and arming local men to deploy into their home areas in Hurungwe, to occupy and possess the land and, in conjunction with the SF, defeat the enemy. This training would be carried out under the strict supervision of Special Branch, employing skilled and highly qualified military instructors. Intelligence, co-ordination of deployments, liaison with the military, co-ordination of military operations against ZIPRA, including Fire Force deployments, and general administration of the entire operation, would all fall under the umbrella of Special Branch. I further explained that the role of the Interim Government, in terms of the March 3rd Agreement, was to steer the country towards a democratically elected majority-ruled government which would protect the grievances, needs and aspirations of black and white Rhodesian citizens alike.

It was my conviction that the UANC was the only moderate political option available to the country at that moment. We were poised to implement the much-needed and called for transformation required to bring stability to our war-torn country. Questions were raised at the meeting as to the changes envisaged by the UANC. I was not in a position to address these queries and explained that this was a political matter and needed to be addressed by Bishop Muzorewa. I went on to emphasise our first objective was to establish a permanent military presence in Hurungwe, paving the way for a return to civil order and administration. In turn, this would pioneer the way for free-and-fair elections, making possible African political advancement. The farmers asked at what junction Bishop Muzorewa would be addressing them. I explained that this would be part of the due process and I would keep them informed. In fact, some five months later, on 10 February 1979, Bishop Muzorewa addressed the farmers at a public meeting.

This proved a watershed assembly, taking place in an amicable and co-operative atmosphere. There was an openness and acceptance of our plans, with the farmers giving us their full support at its conclusion. Interestingly, the district commissioner accepted the scheme and offered as much assistance as he could muster. Todd's arranging of refreshments at the meeting's end added to the goodwill generated by the discussions.

SFAs weapons training.

Stripping and assembling weapons.

Obstacle course.

Instruction on river crossings.

River crossing.

Base camp layout.

Camouflage bunker.

Behind the bunker.

Munitions bunker. A far cry from traditional BSAP standards!

Martin instructing SFAs during training.

Recruits addressed by the UANC political wing.

Recruits on parade.

Bishop Muzorewa inspects the men during a pass-out parade.

Bishop Muzorewa on parade with his men.

On parade.

Ready for war.

Recruits on their way to Bindura for training.

The author inspecting works on Chabwino farm's borehole pump. Engineer is at rear left.

13 ~ BREAKING ZIPRA'S INTERNAL STRATEGY

Understand your enemy but ensure you are constantly proactive as opposed to being reactive in your strategy, aims and objectives.
John Padbury

SFA Strategies Phase 5: Understand the enemy

I was amazed at the accuracy of the information flowing freely through the UANC as well as our increased momentum. However, what was lacking was an understanding of ZIPRA's strategies and tactics which would reveal the mind of the enemy. With the quality of intelligence at our disposal, I did not think it would be long before this vital information reached us. On 30 October 1978, Grey advised our team that an additional three roads had been mined. These landmines were placed on the roads between Magunje BC and Doro Dip, Karereshi and Masanga, and Karereshi via Nyamhunga to Sengwe.[1] This information was passed on to SB at Karoi for action as well as to Selous Scouts. Grey had also established that Kennias, living in the Nyamhunga area, was a ZIPRA contact man and had been given access to arms and landmines. A further two contact men from Nyamhunga, Manyukunyuku and Headman Paratema, were also identified.

To me, the most important issue at hand was that our intelligence was preventing SF casualties, provided they acted with immediacy, consequently nullifying the enemy's strategic planning and attacks. Our aim was to reverse their anticipated victory into defeat. In this instance, ZIPRA had not created an incident in which to lure the SF, rather they had strategically mined the roads and informed "their citizens" in order to prevent them from detonating the mines. However, their intentions had been exposed. Mistrust of the people would inevitably deepen as would their awareness of the changing political and military environment challenging them. As a result of these triumphs, our momentum increased.

The question requiring an answer was why these particular roads were mined. I was of the opinion ZIPRA would not simply mine roads at random. There was, I sensed, a clear strategy behind their campaign. It did not take long for us to unfold their stratagem.

ZIPRA Penetration of the Nyamhunga Area: Graveyard of Viscount *Hunyani*

Research carried out by Dr Chakawa confirmed the following information regarding early ZIPRA activity in Hurungwe:

> Hurungwe fell under ZIPRA's Northern Front operational area which had three regions. The first was "Northern Front 1" which covered Livingstone (Zambia) under Divisional Commander Chipa Dube Nyamupingidza who also commanded "Northern Front 2" that covered the Siyavonga area. "Northern Front 3" was under the overall command of Rodwell Moyo who was injured in a battle at Mana Pools and evacuated to Russia for treatment. Northern Front 3 was divided into 4 zones: Zone 1 covered Nyamhunga and Nematombo areas, Zone 2 covered Vuti East and West, Zone 3 under the command of Jonasi Donga covered Mhangura (Mangula), Kachuta and Kazangarare. Zone 4 covered Sanyati area. Zones 1 and 2 fell under Divisional Commanders Mbedzi (who was mainly in charge of supplies) and Soft Magarasadza. Mbedzi carried out early reconnaissance into Zones 1 and 2 visiting the Chiefs including Nyamhunga and Mudzimu, paving the way for ZIPRA deployments. Magarasadza then deployed Sectorial and Detachment Commanders into the area which included Detachment Commanders China,[2] to the Doro

[1] Karoi Landmine Map 8-10.

region, Tolbert to Nyamhunga region, and Hugh to Mudzimu region. Orders from Lusaka and intelligence from the field flowed through the command structure.

ZIPRA forces were first seen in 1973/4 moving in small groups of six men mobilising villagers and recruiting youths. By 1973/4 there were no bases in the Nyamhunga area. The small ZIPRA forces groups migrated from village to village collecting both male and female youths and escorted them to Zambia for training. Some other ZIPRA groups remained in the country mobilising villagers and their families to support them by giving them food and information. By 1975 some ZIPRA troops infiltrated Rhodesia from Zambia heavily armed this time. Masanga, Nyadara and Mahororo bases were put up. It was not easy to tell how many ZIPRA forces were in Nyamhunga area. Popularly known cadre were Van Der Byl, Mandebvu, Mponda. The locals in Nyamhunga area used to prepare food for ZIPRA, supply their forces with information concerning the Rhodesian soldiers and supply them with some clothes and shoes at times of need. *Mujibhas* were to carry out security patrols and disseminate information. They also nursed the wounded ZIPRA and *mujibhas*.[1]

At this point, I would like to direct the reader's attention to 6 December 1978, a date on which we gained considerable insight into ZIPRA strategies and tactics, subsequently providing us the information I had been waiting for. It is into this intelligence picture that the stricken Viscount *Hunyani* crashed after being shot down (3 September 1978). Also recorded here is the level of detailed intelligence we were assimilating at that time. This information was brought to my attention by Happy and referred to the Nyamhunga area, which had previously been identified as controlled by ZIPRA. My diary entry on that day reads as follows:

During July 1978, ZIPRA commenced infiltration into Nyamhunga having moved from the Nyaodza and Karereshi areas. Five ZIPRA sections moved into Nyamhunga which is an isolated remote mountainous region on the western side of Hurungwe, surrounded by numerous mountains and tributaries which flow into the Sengwe River as it meandered through the valleys, joining the Kanyati River and then on to Lake Kariba. To the west is the even more remote Rengwe Communal Land and to the north is the uninhabited Zambezi National Parks and wild life land which is in the Charara Safari area.

They commenced mobilising the young boys, setting up a *mujibha* intelligence network and some of the boys began to receive military training. These young boys showed open support to ZIPRA, although some were forced to join which caused friction among the *mujibhas*. This was interesting as the locals would know each other intimately and would be aware of the reasons why they were involved with ZIPRA, whether voluntarily or involuntarily, as well as their individual motivations and agendas. There was not necessarily one common agenda to join ZIPRA which set some of the boys at variance with each other, hence the friction. It was quite a difficult situation for these young men to join forces with an invading foreign tribe or remain faithful to their own tribe, knowing the people of Hurungwe would be targeted by ZIPRA aggression if they did not support them. Brothers would turn against brothers and families against families. One *mujibha* had recently been severely beaten for misappropriating funds. There were other reasons why the young men joined, such as adventure, power, control, purpose, intrigue, dominance over women resulting in sexual favours and an escape from dire circumstances. All this attached itself to a well-propagated political agenda. Each ZIPRA section operated in designated areas (see map p.216):

One section at Karambazungu (QM3935).

Two sections at Nyadara, near the Nyadara River (QM3134).

One section at Mashumba (QM4127).

2 "China" was a fairly well-used name by insurgents.

1 Dr J. Chakawa email 7/6/2016, WhatsApp discussion 8/11/2019.

One section at the Main Base area (QM2627).

Our informant had only been to the Karambazungu area on one occasion when he went to look for cattle and it had been raining. He went to Makudzachamba Kraal and was met by a five-man ZIPRA section who were patrolling the area and was believed to be a resident section. It is presumed that kraal dwellers were feeding ZIPRA as there were three girls present who had fetched water for them. Makudzachamba, a Government Tsetse Control worker, was called to a meeting by the five ZIPRA. However, when he did not turn up, they murdered his wife after taking her child from her lap.[1]

Two ZIPRA sections operated at Nyadara near the Nyadara River and in the area of Kraalhead Karovamatanda, where two kraals supported them.

Firstly, Chimsoro Makwiramiti (QM295343), who apparently claimed to be a *mhondoro* (spirit medium), but this, in fact, was not believed by many people in this area. This was a common phenomenon in Hurungwe where people claimed to have supernatural powers. While there were, indeed, genuine spirit mediums (as we were to find out), there were a lot of false ones. It seems they claimed these powers to enshrine themselves with some sort of protection. One of Chimsoro's children and the son of Shanda were both *mujibhas* but no girls had been seen in this area. It had been heard that the "boys" (ZIPRA) frequented the villages of Baradzanwa (QM329366) which is a long line of kraals near the Nyadara River. Kraalhead Sindoni Baradzanwa's houses were destroyed by Security Forces on the 3/12/78, although I could find no record of this. Near Bota Kraal (QM358370) and in the area of QM361378, Marufu Zvaraya was murdered three months ago because he was a UANC official.[2]

At Murota Kraal (QM375365), the son of Karenga was also killed at the same time because he was identified as belonging to the UANC[3]. It was apparent that the "boys" visited Chamunorwa Kraal (QM312371), Matenga Kraal (QM339370), Bota Kraal, but not much was known about these kraals at the time.

Secondly, there was a section near Kraalhead Muzira (QM288328), a village owner, who supported ZIPRA but, again, not much was known about him at the time.

There was one ZIPRA section operating in Mashumba (QM4127) and quite a few kraals supported ZIPRA in this area.

Kraalhead Wasakara (QM465315) was a supporter but not much was known about him other than by rumours that ZIPRA stayed there. When our source came out of Hurungwe on the 5/12/78, ZIPRA footprints were seen coming from this area and the source was of the opinion that the group was still resident there.

Kraalhead Mtinha (QM406288) was also supporting ZIPRA. There were two girls in this area which ZIPRA seemed to go for (sic), (names withheld). When ZIPRA were at Mtinha Kraal they generally go for food and assistance from Chirebvu Kraal. The *mujibhas* in this area were Clemence Matunhu who had a crippled left leg,[4] Raphael Sibanda who is an Ndebele, and the son of Enos who lives at Bvungo Kraal, just next to the Mashumba School (QM432283).

A local village owner, Matunhu (QM386290), who was actively involved with ZIPRA and the *mujibhas* in his supporting network, came from Kraalhead Mtinha above. Apparently there are no girls in these villages. Matunhu Village is close to a range of hills which divides the main base area from the Mashuma area in general.

Another local village owner, Sibanda (QM386290), an Ndebele driver, first met ZIPRA at his employer, Mr Bumhira's store at Karereshi BC (QM487384). Sibanda was a very active ZIPRA supporter and, once again, there were no girls at Sibanda's Kraal and

[1] Karoi Murder Map 24

[2] Karoi Murder Map 4.

[3] Karoi Murder Map 5.

[4] Confirmed by Dr J. Chakawa field trip and research 29/4/2016.

the *mujibhas* operating here also come from Kraalhead Mtinha. Sibanda's Kraal was about quarter of a kilometre from Masuku Kraal. Recently (during November 1978),[1] Raphael Sibanda was walking with a ZIPRA man named Van Der Byl when they were ambushed by the SF at (QM373295). Van Der Byl was shot and killed and his body was still lying in the bush rotting: Raphael made good his escape. No body or weapon was recovered, and it is likely that the SF did not realise they had killed Van Der Byl. Mr Bumira was subsequently killed by ZIPRA as he was thought to be a *mutengesi*.[2] (Important: I will refer to this section in some detail when discussing the SAS contact in chapter 14.)

Masuku, who is believed to be the "big fish" in the area, is an apostolic,[3] an Ndebele man who owns a village (QM386290) next to Sibanda's. He uses the same *mujibhas* from Mtinha's kraal. There was a girl of 12 years who had not been sexually abused by ZIPRA. Masuku was responsible for the deaths of two women, Mrs Mamoyo and Mrs Bokoro. Mrs Bokoro's husband was killed because he was a retired policeman and a successful farmer[4] and, when she returned to collect property, she was murdered. At the time she was pregnant and apparently suffered a very slow death: many bullets were used to kill her.[5] Mrs Mamoyo was suspected of being a "sellout" and killed.[6] It appears that there was an outbreak of measles in the area at the time and Masuku is now in Belingwe — he will be found.

Kraalhead Bvungo (QM431282) had been killed as he was a tribal land authority and was trying cases with the chief.[7] The son of Enos is a forced *mujibha* who was beaten to assist ZIPRA. The ZIPRA forces assaulted Kraalhead Kapamara (QM409268) after he had reprimanded them for abusing a certain female. In an adjacent kraal there was a young girl being abused by ZIPRA.

The largest ZIPRA section was resident at the Main Base area which was situated between the kraals of Kraalhead Mafuamara (QM285278), which spread westward towards the tsetse fly gate right on the boundary of Hurungwe and Rengwe at (QM257270). This really was a remote area, sheltered by high mountains. The abandoned kraals were nestled in the valleys between the Sengwe and Kanyati rivers, an ideal area to politicise and train the people. Kraalhead Mafuamara was heavily involved with ZIPRA and Tichaona Seremwe,[8] of Kadownda Kraal (QM325315), was the main *mujibha* in the area. A khaki uniform was found in the fly gate keeper's hut which was the first hut from the fly gate. He was missing and presumed killed because of his association with the Government.[9] This was highly probable as there was an open space next to his hut which led to the vacant base huts, which in turn were very close to the newly built huts belonging to Mandiya. ZIPRA would not want a potential informer living among them!

ZIPRA had managed to obtain help and assistance from several stores including, Nhari Store (QM290278), owned by Gideon Nhari; Karambazungu Store (QM410359), owned by Simeon Muteya; Chivakanenyama Store (QM475227), where Simeon Muteya, Kambe, Temba Madende and Kawanza were all assisting ZIPRA from the store and, finally, at Zvipani BC (QM352210) on the Binga Road where Kawanza and Gora were assisting ZIPRA.

---

1 The "recently" referred to a period during November 1978 as the report was documented on the 6/12/1978.

2 Karoi Murder Map 25. Confirmed by Dr J. Chakawa's field trip and research 29/4/2016: "Businessman Bumhira was killed by ZIPRA for phoning to Magunje to call Fire Force — helicopters arrived."

3 Apostolics: A Christian sect.

4 Karoi Murder Map 19. Confirmed by Dr J. Chakawa's field trip and research 29/4/2016: "Bhokoro was a retired policeman."

5 Karoi Murder Map 20.

6 Karoi Murder Map 21.

7 Karoi Murder Map 22.

8 Confirmed still alive and resident at Kariba on 5/5/2016 by Dr J. Chakawa's research email 5/5/2016.

9 Karoi Murder Map 23.

The intelligence was accurate and emphasised very little was going on in Hurungwe that did not, and would not, pass the scrutiny of the people. The murders of so-called collaborators and the death of Van Der Byl in an SF ambush was particularly important as it confirmed that, when the people's army was deployed, any untoward behaviour or actions would quickly be reported. This was reassuring and would empower us to "keep an eye" on the army through the people. Information spread rapidly through the "bush telegraph" around the rural areas and back and forth through townships. Generally speaking, the Security Forces, in particular white soldiers, did not understand this method of communication either, making them strangers in a "foreign land". However, district policemen (Ground Coverage, Special Branch and CID) operating on the ground were familiar with this process. Nevertheless, I was under no allusion that this flow of information was also accessed by ZIPRA's intelligence networks who would be aware of our plans and movements. This was important in certain instances, such as the arrival of Fire Force. ZIPRA would be made aware that their enemy was "back in town", and would make the necessary adjustments to their plans and strategies.

We received further detailed intelligence from two separate sources on 21 and 23 December 1978 concerning ZIPRA's activities in the Nyamhunga area involving a party of 15 insurgents. This intelligence identified ZIPRA activity and their supporting kraals in the vicinity of the Viscount *Hunyani* crash site. This is a summary of my diary entry: "It was reported that ZIPRA had been resident in the Nyamhunga area for about a year. The commanders were Leonard and George and the comrades were Siphon, Above, Patrick, Masuku and Ndiweni. They lived among a number of young females[1] from the surrounding area, including the Sengwe School area. The terrs spend their days occasionally at Mandizha's kraal where their clothes are washed and food cooked. They also stay at Marape's home who is purported to be a spirit medium. The terrs intended spending Christmas holidays (25-26 December) at Chimsoro's place who is also alleged to be a spirit medium. Three 44-gallon drums were being prepared at Chimsoro's place. There was no beer drink there last year. It is confirmed that a party of 15 terrs is already at Chimsoro's place. This intelligence has been confirmed by SB sources and FF has been advised. FF deployed on this intelligence on 26 December. Unfortunately, no contact was made with the enemy. The three 44-gallon drums of beer were located and two *mujibhas* picked up." (See Nyamhunga Original Sketch 21/12/1978, Viscount *Hunyani* crash site, pp.216 & 221.) This information was also passed onto other appropriate military authorities for their deployments.

ZIPRA's Internal Strategies and Tactics: Hurungwe

The strategies used by ZIPRA in Hurungwe differed to those of ZANLA in a number of ways. They established and used regular bush and kraal bases. Sections tended to move into kraal areas and overpower their inhabitants. They were well organised and had efficient *mujibha* intelligence networks while operating purposefully, and not aimlessly. Local businessmen provided material support. There was a measure of support from the youth and *chimbwidos* provided their "physical" needs. However, their parents were often forced to capitulate to ZIPRA and, understandably, husbands and fathers did not appreciate their wives and daughters being abused. But they were helpless! This latter aspect was much to our advantage as we found this a pattern throughout Hurungwe. ZIPRA's strategy of taking over kraals and commandeering wives from husbands and daughters from families was immoral, violating cultural and traditional African ethics. Nevertheless, a good number of the girls were willing sexual partners.

The locals were instructed by ZIPRA to patrol from sunrise to 10 a.m. and be on the lookout for evidence or signs of an SF presence, including OPs, foot patrols and vehicle movements. Thereafter, they were at liberty to carry out their own normal activities, namely ploughing, reaping, caring for livestock and collecting water, together with normal day-to-day household chores. These tasks were conducted until 3 p.m., after which patrols resumed until sunset. Local kraals were randomly

---

1 Fourteen of the girls' names withheld.

selected by contact men and *mujibhas* to feed visiting sections. Generally, breakfast was from 5 a.m. to 7 a.m., lunch 11 a.m. to 1 p.m. and supper any time after sunset. Insurgents tended to stay in the same area where they ate supper but did not have breakfast at the same kraal. This level of intelligence was an essential asset to the Security Forces deploying into the area. It would help them scrutinise kraals from OPs at specific times for local activity that fitted the detailed available intelligence and helped identify patterns of behaviour which were not traditional.

Their main vulnerability was being Matabele operating in a Shona territory. In fact, they were considered more of an occupying force and not necessarily regarded as a liberating army. Additionally, their sexual relationships made them static in their occupation of an area and, therefore, predictable and vulnerable. They also considered Hurungwe liberated and did not restrict their movements, especially in the more remote regions.

We learned that ZIPRA's strategy behind the laying of landmines was to deter and restrict SF vehicle deployments and patrols. It was their expectation that SF vehicles travelling on these roads would detonate the landmines resulting in casualties which would delay deployments. The mined roads protected their specific military operations and areas. They ambushed SF and civilian vehicles from advantageous positions that ensured easy withdrawal. Farmsteads and farm labour were attacked at will. Their emphasis in the proliferation of weaponry, arms caches and the training and empowering of locals for partisan activity suggested an overall conventional Soviet military-style strategy. The people were being prepared for such an attack. They had the momentum in the battle, carrying out their plans unhindered. In my view, they were taking the initiative while the SF were merely reacting to their operations.

ZIPRA demanded the support of the people. They had established martial law to subjugate and control them and, therefore, felt the right to murder dissenters and act as they wished. It appeared to me that they regarded the people in similar fashion to the Security Forces. Both sides demanded and coerced support, expecting the people to oblige. The main difference between the two approaches was ZIPRA's violent methodology and abuse of women. They were occupying the land, not possessing it and, in my view, this was the most important factor in our favour.

Our challenge was how to turn the tide and force the enemy to react to our actions. I believed we had the capacity and ability, but our planning and strategies needed to be thoroughly thought through and executed. It was my assessment that we should act swiftly and conclusively on our intelligence. We would attack marauding ZIPRA insurgents at every opportunity with available Security Forces resources before they were alerted to our operations. This would continue until our people's army was ready to deploy. I anticipated that this strategy would increase our support from the locals once we had occupied Hurungwe.

We increasingly became aware of ZIPRA's strategies, tactics and actions but our emphasis needed to be on our own mission, objectives, plans and actions. I felt it prudent to be aware of ZIPRA's activities but they were not our focus: the people were our focus. I did not want to be lured into reacting to the enemy's actions as had been the case in the Makoni. This required a complex balance of visible political advancement legitimising military intervention. We, the people's army, would be fighting with and alongside the people, and attending to their grievances, needs and aspirations were our priorities. It was my conviction that this approach would be the key to our success. As the war escalated, further groundbreaking developments occurred as our unique operation unfolded.

The People's Army

I feel it would be helpful to explain my understanding and usage of the expression "the people's army", a term coined by Mao Zedong. Ian Smith's Government adopted the term Security Force Auxiliaries but I did not want a similar association. It was essential for the people in Hurungwe to understand that it was their army being trained and equipped to protect them, address their GNA and, in the process, remove the oppressive alien force, ZIPRA.

This was the political message that the UANC, under Grey's direction, transmitted into Hurungwe. It was important for the people and their army to be united as, in my view, such an army is invincible.[1] The problem I had experienced and observed with SB and intelligence operations in the country was that the focus of attention was on the terrorist and his activities. Too much attention was directed towards identifying them from documentation and captures, knowing which detachment they operated under, including who they related to in the field. The sole aim was their elimination. While this was an important dimension of the operational intelligence jigsaw, it reiterated the "kills-win-wars" policy while failing to address the major subject, namely the people and their circumstances. I had experienced that outlook in the Makoni. We regarded the people as a further aspect of the threat. We identified them with the enemy. Granted, this was true in the case of ZANLA in Makoni but not of ZIPRA in Hurungwe, who failed to command the support of most of the people. In both cases, the key was the people. In my view, elimination of the insurgents was a secondary matter. The primary focus was identification with and becoming one with the people. In fact, without this change in approach, the people simply saw the SF and the SFAs as a force upholding the present regime and their retention of power. In my opinion, they were correct. The political commissars of ZANLA and ZIPRA were actively politicising the masses, informing them of the changes they were proposing to institute, albeit changes which were unlikely to materialise. If I may repeat myself, in these circumstances, the peasant remains the peasant. The point being the GNA of the *povo* (the people) had been neglected by the RF Government and were not being met or attended to by the Interim Government controlled by Smith's party. As I understood matters, transformation could only be brought about by the collapse of RF influence. A straightforward matter in my view!

The emphasis should have been in identifying with the people, becoming one with them, establishing their army to protect them permanently and to bring about the necessary changes which would attend to their GNA. On implementation of this course of action, the task of eliminating the enemy falls logically into place. The war is won by winning the people. Regretfully, this straightforward solution did not occur and, in my opinion, to the economic, military and social detriment of the country.

It was my contention that our UANC political vision for Hurungwe was precise. In due course, Bishop Muzorewa and senior members of the UANC often commented that our vision and operational work in Hurungwe needed to be emulated across the country. The morale in Chikangwe was rising as Grey and his team continued their sterling efforts. This momentum was strengthened when Grey announced that a further nine volunteer recruits from Hurungwe had arrived for training, bringing the total trainees to 22. Word was spreading but I knew ZIPRA would also be gathering information about our movements and strategies. My strategy was to supply them information which we wanted them to know, thus pitting two opposing intelligence organisations against each other in similar fashion to a game of chess. However, it remained critical we stay alert, united and continued political momentum, laying the foundation for our future deployment.

I collected Manenji on 31 October 1978 and brought him to Karoi to interview the 22 recruits in waiting. Grey and I had decided that the recruits and people from Hurungwe should know we had a selection procedure and were not simply admitting any individual wandering in for training. We felt it important to maintain discipline, a high selection standard and convey to aspirant recruits the privilege of joining the people's army. Experience taught us the recruits respected our approach. They knew they had gained selection following a screening process. They had not been found wanting and, in fact, had won the approval of a selection board, making for a high sense of self-esteem among the volunteers. All 22 recruits satisfied the entry standards and immediately commenced training, increasing the pressure on the training staff. Manenji was an astute, capable leader. He was not easily flustered and remained a cool, calm and collected man at the helm. I enjoyed his company and felt relaxed in his presence. He seldom complained and smiled constantly.

---

[1] Zedong, M. (1976), p. 153.

Manenji was a valuable and competent Support Unit sergeant.

The two *mujibhas* we trained at the Rusape *mujibha* farm, David and Mike, finally arrived at the beginning of November 1978. When I left Rusape, and in particular the *mujibha* farm, they requested to follow me to my new appointment. I promised to consider the matter but was uncertain of the likelihood of it coming about. Initially, while posted at Salisbury, it was not possible but, once I moved to Karoi, I arranged for their transfers. David and Mike were excellent RPD gunners, totally trustworthy and had been on several deployments with Support Unit in the Makoni. I introduced them to the men at Chabwino as former ZANLA insurgents. Their duties were to assist with training, instruction of men in operational strategies and farm protection. Additionally, they would join my now complete farm intelligence team, making them my "eyes and ears" at the farm. They would also double as my support team when travelling through Hurungwe TTL. Most importantly, they were close friends and very good soldiers.

Some six weeks after my arrival at Karoi, I was in the fortunate position of being surrounded by a highly knowledgeable team. We had excellent Admin. and training staff, coupled with a thorough and skilled intelligence network operating in the training farm. Under Grey's direction, the UANC were establishing intricate political network cells with the people in Chikangwe and Hurungwe, all in preparation of developing an accomplished and capable army. Consequently, the people were volunteering useful intelligence and helping us gain an understanding of ZIPRA operations in and about Hurungwe.

All told, we were satisfied with our progress and accomplishments. Periodically, we socialised at the Twin Rivers Motel where we enjoyed tasty meals and cold beers in the company of close friends. My approach to the war had changed. I had become one with the people, sharing the mutual objective of destroying a common enemy. I found myself living a cardinal principle of tracking: "Know the mind of the hunted." In the unfolding strategy for Hurungwe this meant I, and my team, had to live, sleep, eat and dream the vision of the people. An essential ingredient to this operation was the loyalty and partnership of the entire team, particularly Grey and his recruits at the farm. There would be no success without them.

Lynette and our son, Robin, continued to live in Salisbury. I phoned her every night but she needed to walk to a nearby telephone booth to receive the call. I rarely saw her. She made periodic visits to Karoi while I made occasional trips to Salisbury. During my eight-month deployment to Karoi I took only six days' vacational leave. I must point out, that this did not overly concern me as I was firmly engrossed in the war. My opinion was that to win the war one needed to make the necessary sacrifices which included the pleasures of family life, and the possibility of losing one's own life.

As our momentum increased, it became progressively vital to have Admin. close at hand. All aspects of their work were increasing and structures needed to be in place and running smoothly before the men were deployed. Paying all the staff, trainees and recruits was, in itself, a mammoth undertaking which would be a major challenge in the operational area. These men also accompanied me on field trips.

On 1 November 1978, Todd stood down from his position, having rendered excellent service. This vacancy made it urgent for me to have Sandy Irvine transferred from Rusape to Karoi to join Admin. Sandy was not only a very good friend but an outstanding and efficient administrative assistant. I had missed his company as, indeed, I missed and enjoyed the company of all the men previously based with me. I contacted Geoff Price regarding Sandy's relocation, to which came the characteristic reply: "Leave it with me." Sandy joined the team on 29 January 1979.[1]

On the intelligence-gathering side, Grey advised he had established that ZIPRA intended attacking the Kazangarara police base in the near future. The information he had obtained included a plan of the attack. I passed the material on to the Karoi Police Station who alerted the police base. During the same day, a Fire Force action 7 kilometres north of the base located a landmine, one

1 Sandy's last call-up at Rusape was 15/11/1978-12/12/1978. Confirmed by original Sub.JOC Rusape duty roster.

RPG-7 launcher and an AK-47. This find could well have tied in with the planned base attack, particularly the landmine. However, despite our information, an attack on the base never materialised. Until the occurrence of this particular incident, I had not experienced the receipt of intelligence pre-empting our enemy's plans. This was an extremely positive development. In addition, I felt it reflected the efficiency of Grey's intelligence-gathering networks as the information we had received was beyond our immediate area of operation.

As always, I believed it essential that information obtained was immediately followed up. To my disappointment, I later learned that the information we passed to the SF at Karoi on 30 October 1978 regarding three landmines had not been investigated. While I understood these operations involved pressure on existing resources, especially on our overworked Pookie and escort, it was vital that immediate intelligence was acted on. I laboured the point among my men that quick reprisals would increase the confidence and trust of the informant and the people, lift SF morale and strike a blow to ZIPRA. Therefore, I resolved that in our future deployments we would deal with landmines by our own methods should the Pookie and backup not be available. Subsequently, the engineers lifted the landmines.

Overview, November 1978

On 2 November 1978, I diarised a summary of our activities at Karoi as follows:

> Intelligence work in Chikangwe and within Hurungwe TTL was going extremely well and we anticipated dominating the urban intelligence scene in the not too distant future. It was now obvious that once the people's army moved into Hurungwe there would be a flood of recruits. My main concern was preempting this, so I made it known that we were going to need more AK rifles and ammunition to train the men. It would be possible to train the men with FNs and G3s, but we would need AKs for their deployments. We already had an additional twenty-two men who had recently commenced training and a considerable escalation in these numbers was anticipated.
>
> The question of deployments continued to raise its head from Com.Ops. as pressure was applied to me to provide a deployment date for the men. I made it known that, while understanding that the hierarchy wanted the men deployed to prevent further deterioration of the situation in Hurungwe, and to start to muster support for the Interim Government, I had no intention of deploying men until I considered them well trained. This would ensure that they would have the confidence and skill to take care of themselves against a well trained and equipped army, at the least to stand their ground, and, where possible, eliminate them in battle. I had no intention of sending poorly trained men into the field as that would without a doubt lead to unnecessary death. Further, a well-trained army would be able to protect and defend the people.
>
> The people had to have confidence in and trust their army before they would become one with them. Becoming "one with" meant embracing, becoming a part of, supporting materially and with information, quite a risk in any setting especially a rural one. Therefore, the men had to be well trained, simple really, and I would resist the authorities until the men were trained.
>
> Additionally, Lt. Gen. Walls had recently stated publicly that the SFAs were an extension of the security forces. I envisaged two problems from this statement: Firstly, the SFAs would expect equality such as the same wages and privileges as the SFs, this would include rest and recreation (R & R), Forces Request on the Radio, a preview of the Forces Show and so on. Secondly, the word Security Forces in the TTLs was a bad one and all we needed was to be aligned to them, particularly in the early days, and our mission would be made even more difficult. To be quite blunt about it the SFs had failed militarily internally in any case, and we did not want to be aligned, publicly, to them. Success was not possible without significant Political change which was not happening. Whether we

> liked it or not all Africans are party orientated and fighting political motivation comes from the party. As our people's army understood it, the Interim Government was only temporary pending elections to establish a ruling party to govern the country. We were, by establishing private armies accelerating civil war in Rhodesia, it seemed obvious that the Government and the European public must back a horse before the race begins (i.e. a party) because you can't place your bets when the race has started. This would involve a total commitment to change which did not happen. Our message to the people in Hurungwe was that the SFs were an extension of the people's army that is the only way we saw it could work.

This approach did cause some difficulties!

At a Special Forces meeting in Salisbury on 4 November 1978, chaired by Col. McVey, I gave a briefing of the intelligence behind our operation and summarised developments. Our training requirements were discussed and I explained the reason for the delays in our deployments, reiterating that I was not prepared to deploy our men until I was satisfied that they had received sufficient training. Col. McVey accepted my approach to the difficult situation in Hurungwe where we were facing a well-established formidable enemy.

Listening to other operators who also addressed the meeting, I was of the opinion that, in a majority of cases, they were dealing with trained men who had not been deployed into their home TTLs. I did not open the matter up for discussion as I had already covered the point of control of the masses by the people's army in both my *mujibha* report and my Hurungwe TTL reports. Success would not be achieved by deploying "foreign" SFAs into a TTL to control the masses, the insurgents had already done this. Our only counter to the rapidly deteriorating situation in Rhodesia was to develop a genuine peoples' army. I could see that this was not about to happen on a national basis!

Back at Karoi, Admin. informed me that the UANC's expenses were increasing. This was entirely understandable given their workload, travel costs, funding the intelligence networks and escalating refugee expenses. We also discovered that the member of parliament, Mr Francis Zindoga, had been attempting to contact one of our agents in the field requesting he proceed to Salisbury urgently. "Our man" had been deployed by Grey on a specific intelligence mission which we did not want disrupted. Consequently, we sent a message to Bishop Muzorewa requesting queries relating to Hurungwe be channeled to Grey for efficiency's sake and the prevention of disrupting our operation. Following our request, no further peripheral communications were experienced.

During the evening of 4 November 1978, Grey advised us that in the Mujinga area there had been a meeting between ZANLA and ZIPRA which almost ended in a fight between the two factions. This was more likely to have involved a Selous Scouts pseudo-ZANLA callsign. The information was passed on to the Selous Scouts. In fact, Security Forces engaged ZIPRA at Murodza Kraal. This was not as a result of intelligence from our offices.[1]

As mentioned, the UANC office opened on Thursday, 9 November 1978. In our view, a momentous occasion. The people were witnessing progress which they identified with. Effectively, they owned the office which, in my outlook, provided the key to its success. In establishing the UANC, the words of Mao Zedong rang frequently in my mind: "To link oneself with the masses, one must act in accordance with the needs and wishes of the masses. All work done for the masses must start from their needs and not from the imposed desire of any individual, NGO or Government Organisation, however well-intentioned. It often happens that objectively the masses need a certain change, but subjectively they are not yet conscious of the need, not yet willing or determined to make the change. In such cases, we should wait patiently. We should not make the change until, through our work, most of the masses have become conscious of the need and are willing and determined to carry it out. Otherwise we shall isolate ourselves from the masses. Unless they are conscious and willing, any kind of work that requires their participation will turn out to be a mere formality and will fail ... There are two principles here: one is the actual needs of the masses rather

1 Karoi Contacts Map Incident 13.

than what we fancy they need, and the other is the wishes of the masses, who must make up their own minds instead of our making up their minds for them."[1]

Our intelligence-gathering networks were making significant progress. True, the process was incomplete but increased momentum would follow on the deployment of our trained recruits into operational areas. Their many and varied tasks would include the collection, processing and dissemination of information gleaned from the locals. Simultaneously, the locals would be positioned to observe the actions of our men and supply us feedback through the UANC political networks. I will discuss this matter in greater detail in a later chapter.

[1] Zedong, M. (1976), pp. 124-125.

14 ~ PREPARING THE WAY: FIRST STRIKES

Revolution achieved by consensus eliminates the need
for violent oppression of the people.
John Padbury

SFA Strategies Phase 6: Strike the enemy

Understanding ZIPRA Strategies

The masses are the key to survival and victory in a people's revolution and there is a need for their unequivocal support. Once ZIPRA penetrated Hurungwe they first politicised the people, gradually bringing them under their administration as they established martial law. Prevailing civil law and order was progressively and forcibly removed along with governmental structures and associations thereof. It is my conviction there can be no deviation from this strategy as it would expose a failure in the insurgents' political-indoctrination agenda, namely: "Everything of the Government is evil, we are good, our actions justified, those of the white Government condemned." Their very lives were totally dependent on the support of the people as they could not withdraw from the battle-ground, the Vital Ground, as that would be seen as defeat. The masses are both one's friend and foe. Therefore, total control of the people was essential for ZIPRA's survival, and elimination of opposition obligatory. "Sellouts" were considered sub-human, merely *vatengesi*. They were viewed as white colonial government supporters, consequently justifying their elimination as a matter of course, with no emotional attachment to their murders. The resistance movement was aware of the life-and-death risks yet continued to oppose ZIPRA.

Our military aim in Hurungwe was the establishment of a permanent presence in the area. In the process, and leading up to our first deployments, we would utilise the intelligence supplied to our office in directing SF operations to eliminate ZIPRA groups and, in so doing, increase our integrity and further gain the people's trust in our cause. Once our men were deployed, we continued to use this strategy in areas we had yet to occupy. This phased strategy was necessary as it was clear we could not occupy and possess the whole of Hurungwe in a day, but we could occupy and possess the land one kraal at a time. With the growing momentum of incoming intelligence, our ability to strike ZIPRA with the full might of the SF increased. Furthermore, it was our strategy to release into Hurungwe the reality that the people's army was in training and soon to be mobilised. Since our intelligence networks encompassed the entire Hurungwe region, our aim and objective was to strike ZIPRA at various locations, subsequently creating fear and uncertainty as well as destroying their perceived sole occupancy of the region. This would undermine their authority and their control of the people and destabilise their rule over what they considered liberated areas. ZIPRA would be aware of the political changes brought about by the March 3rd Agreement. The changing political environment accompanied by our rising popularity would bring about a degree of uncertainty into their midst.

Through the mechanisms I have mentioned above, the political wing of the UANC, essentially through the Chikangwe office, began to propagate the fact that ZIPRA would soon face a backlash from the people they were abusing, as their allegiance was transferred to their very own people's army supported by the SF. Increasingly, the people would support the political party of their choice. This outcome would lead to an escalation in ZIPRA violence, atrocities and the continued imposition of martial law, which I believed, would work to our advantage as the people became antagonistic towards them. Naturally, ZIPRA's own intelligence networks would be aware of some young men leaving their home kraals to undergo training with us which would further weaken their operations. Needless to say, I was pleased with our progress.

Behind Enemy Lines

In order to give the reader an understanding of the intelligence strategies we used at Karoi, I will illustrate by way of the story of Davidson (pseudonym), a loyal UANC member. Essentially, an intelligence officer's task is the skilful management of the intelligence cycle, namely the collection, the collation, the interpretation, the processing and the dissemination of a continuous flow of information from the war zone with an all-enquiring, creative mind. Timeous distribution of this information is critical for the successful exploitation of a given situation, failing which, it becomes outdated and ineffective for gaining advantage in a hostile environment. Intelligence amassed over a lengthy period, commonly referred to as "historical intelligence", can be of use in establishing patterns and deciphering strategies and tactics, as well as applying insights gained from past experiences. It goes without saying that an effective intelligence officer requires specialised attributes, including an astute mind, a sound and retentive memory, and the ability to apply relevant information for specific deployments. These factors underline the need and importance for experience and diligence in a war environment.

Grey's knowledge and understanding of terrorist intelligence operations was outstanding and extremely valuable to us. On Thursday, 9 November 1978, at 9 a.m., he brought Davidson into our offices for a meeting. This was an unusually early hour for such a conference. It transpired Davidson had information which was to substantially expose ZIPRA operations in the southern area of Hurungwe. A wealthy and prominent member of the community, had been threatened with violence by ZIPRA *mujibhas*. I was surprised that Davidson reported this information to us as he had no prior dealings with our operation. However, it indicated to me that he had the confidence and trust in our growing momentum to confront ZIPRA and their intelligence networks. The realisation came to me that the victim had been a former ZIPRA supporter, hence the threat. I could not establish whether his support was voluntary or involuntary but, without our UANC backing, his family would have been in dire straits.

Davidson informed Grey of two ZIPRA bush-bases near Zvarayi School and Mashayamvura Kraal. Both had good OP positions with ideal camouflage nearby. Their permanent command HQ was near Chifamba Village where local *mujibhas* were receiving training. At times, there were as many as 150 ZIPRA insurgents in the area. This information was confirmed by the local Special Branch.

Under the supervision of Davidson, 50 men volunteered to join the ranks of the people's army. They were eagerly awaiting the go-ahead to commence training. In the Mujinga area, ZIPRA were poorly established, as the people generally opposed them, favouring the UANC. This fact would be underlined by the many recruits zealous to join us for training. With freedom of movement in and out of the TTL, ZIPRA were unable to stem their undertakings.

Davidson had dedicated himself to the UANC and was enthusiastic for further training in our establishment. He was keen to deploy in order to protect his people. Grey and I assessed his information, established its reliability and I passed it on to the Selous Scouts for follow-up in due course. As a result of this, I began to sense a general disquiet among the people in Hurungwe, sensing an awakening among the masses.

Later in the day Grey, Davidson and I held a meeting to discuss the situation and strategy for operations into southern Hurungwe. Our decision was for Davidson to return home the following day to collect his wife and child under the pretext he was taking his child to Salisbury for medical treatment, requiring them to be absent for two weeks. This would allow us some two weeks for military intervention prior to Davidson and family returning home. During that period, the UANC would provide for his wife and child.

Davidson returned safely to Karoi on 10 November leaving us free to deploy. Our two-week window had begun, the unanswered question was on strategy. We decided to deploy Davidson to his home area. I briefed the Selous Scouts and they deployed with Davidson on Monday, 13 November 1978. The mission was to clandestinely move into an OP position in order to ascertain whether ZIPRA were present in the area. We instructed Davidson not to visit his village to make enquiries regarding them, as this would directly connect him with the SF should there be action against ZIPRA. Davidson would serve as the callsign's "eyes and ears" and could readily interpret developments in the field of operation. Unfortunately, the callsign was com-promised en route to the area, forcing a withdrawal. However, Davidson, to our relief, was not compromised, consequently on Tuesday, 14 November 1978, we sent him home by bus to conduct additional intelligence gathering.

I admired men like Davidson who risked their lives for what they believed was right. He, and many others, were undercover agents operating a resistance movement in occupied enemy territory. We took countless precautions to conceal their presence and identity, developing elaborate systems and methods of contact through our intelligence networks, to communicate with our men in the field and at Chikangwe. They risked their lives in a lonely, hostile environment where trust was virtually non-existent. It is worth noting that electricity was unavailable in the rural areas. Other than candles and torches darkness prevailed, making the masses vulnerable to enemy onslaught.

Since ZIPRA had introduced the *mujibha* intelligence networks headed by contact men, the people no longer trusted one another. This mistrust included entire family members, not excluding wives, husbands, brothers, sisters or close relatives. In brief, no individual was beyond suspicion. The population at large guarded their conversations for fear of reprisals. Seemingly, only those supporting the liberators had freedom of speech, but this was guarded and could be swayed, betrayed or simply misunderstood. Tethered dogs served as "night alarms" but they could not prevent intruders mercilessly assaulting defenceless residents constantly facing the threat of beatings or murder at the hands of ZIPRA. Affiliations of support for the Rhodesian Government, whether actual or suspected, or simply the product of unfounded, unconfirmed rumours, malicious scandal or jealous neighbours, further entrapped terrified residents continuously. Nevertheless, while seemingly alone, vulnerable and isolated, a resistance movement was gathering momentum with, unfortunately, the inevitable casualties.

On 28 November 1978, Davidson returned to our offices confirming the return of a ZIPRA section to his area. During his debriefing the following day, he revealed that ZIPRA were believed to be at the Chifamba base in the area of Kraalhead Gasura. They were mainly fed at the base and Chifamba himself was a leading contact man. Davidson informed us that some 100 ZIPRA were estimated to be in the area.

A hill situated on the eastern side of Chifamba Kraal was thought to be a ZIPRA base. Water was available from the shallow-flowing Nyaruchekwa River. Since water was essential for survival, this level of intelligence was vital for our troops carrying out reconnaissance and OPs. The Chifamba Kraal comprised three circular houses where there were two girls. Takawira commanded the ZIPRA section and it appeared both he and his second in command slept with the girls. It was likely Headman Gasura was also harbouring ZIPRA. In the past he had brewed beer for these men, subsequently providing a social dimension to their activities. Most of the young girls from the local vicinity congregated to cook meals for ZIPRA and this activity occurred around 7 a.m. The girls travelled about freely, were readily identified, and therefore not difficult to uplift. Against this background, it was decided to deploy Davidson with an army callsign on 28 November 1978. The group were deployed to an OP position overlooking Chifamba base the following day. However, we did not confront ZIPRA in these operations. At least the callsign was not compromised.

On 11 December 1978, Davidson returned to his home. As planned, he remained uncompromised. Days later, on his return to Karoi, he advised us of rumours emanating from certain labourers employed by the surrounding white farmers who wanted to volunteer for training at our UANC base. We requested he return to the area and ascertain the truth regarding the rumours and, should they prove accurate, recruit the men wherever possible.

Even though we did not directly engage the enemy from Davidson's efforts, we did in the process gather extensive knowledge of ZIPRA's intelligence networks in this area, proving beneficial when our men were finally deployed. We had detailed information of ZIPRA sympathisers and conversely those who would support our forces in the inevitable hostilities. The gathering of intelligence was frustrating, painstaking and tedious, yet invaluable and essential as we prepared for our men's deployment, their advancement and their occupation of the land: our ultimate long-term goal. Additionally, the people were made conscious of our pending arrival.

My altered outlook and approach to the war represented a paradigm shift in my thinking. Previously, I had judged military success on enemy kills achieved, an essential ingredient in the maintenance of SF morale. However, I noticed the confidence of the white population soared following the announcement of enemy fatalities by the radio and television media, and the newspapers. I considered these broadcasts to be subtle and psychologically manipulating, thereby supposedly ensuring a boost in the white population's morale once informed of the success of their SF. In my view, the reasoning that our kill-rate was superior to the enemy's was insidious and premeditated in misleading the country's citizens. It was my perception, that this misinformation concealed the truth that we were rapidly losing the war. Insurgent kills were "pooled" to bolster statistics when SF personnel or civilians were killed. This showed a high ratio of insurgents' deaths when compared to those of the SF and white civilians. This skewed presentation continued propagating the "kills-win-wars" approach which, in my mind, was thoroughly misguided. As I reviewed matters, it seemed to me my core function at Makoni was to provide intelligence leading to the elimination of the enemy. I was employed to kill! The higher the fatalities, the greater the demand and expectations from my commanding officers and myself. If the truth be known, I succumbed to the notion of the greater the enemy death-toll, the greater my service to Rhodesia. This outlook led me to an increased desire to account for more enemy deaths. I had become depersonalised, desensitised and isolated from society. Added to this, I became distanced from Lynette and our son, Robin, and intolerant of those uninvolved in the war effort. I was obsessed with the war and worked seven days a week. There were no weekends in this war!

I believed failure to be wholly absorbed in the war could have fatal consequences. There can be no letting down of one's guard. A single mistake or misjudgement could have led to my own, or men under my command, unwarranted death. I was employed as a professional intelligence officer and my business at hand was to kill the enemy. My belief was that war was a tough man's world and in large measure revelled in the comradeship of like-minded men driven to outwitting the enemy at the potential of losing one's own life. The world of war, I thought, was an enviable lifestyle.

Battle For Chikangwe: Urban Counter-Terrorism Operations

It was soon clear to me that ZIPRA had well-established information networks in Chikangwe and Karoi. This intelligence included tracking our Security Forces and Fire Force movements. It became important we adopted the most efficient strategies in countering the enemy. Grey's networks revealed that, on the evening of Thursday, 2 November 1978, three insurgents came into Chikangwe and stayed in room 451, a dwelling owned by Kakamba, a ZIPRA cell leader in the township. Kakamba's unit comprised Zendende, of room 600; Kenneth, of room 317, and a tenant, Phillimon. Phil Wright confirmed he was aware that ZIPRA had visited Chikangwe on 2 November 1978. Grey believed there were more ZIPRA sympathisers in Chikangwe, therefore we did not interfere with the cell. This enabled us to clandestinely monitor their activities, without compromising our own intelligence operations.[1] When the opportunity presented itself, especially in the rural areas, we could strike ZIPRA.

Later we learned of another alleged ZIPRA intelligence cell in Karoi. Those involved included Lovemore, a BP employee in Karoi; Enoch, a construction worker resident at No. 995, Karoi

1 On 22/12/1978, we confirmed that five ZIPRA insurgents were present in the town, two armed with revolvers and three with AK-47s. At 1.30 a.m. on 23/12/1978, the network located the five-man ZIPRA section which unfortunately evaded us.

Township; Nicholas, a driver with Hurungwe Distributors; Patrick, a watch repairer at Jacob's Store; Chibondo, head chef at Karoi Hotel; Makoni, a clerk at Swift Transport; Muzengeza, a kiosk worker at Chibuku Beerhall in Chikangwe; David, a radio repair technician in Chikangwe and Govera, an employee at a bicycle repair shop in Chikangwe. In addition, we established that Tinapis, head waiter at Karoi Hotel, was a part of ZIPRA's network. We subsequently established that Patrick and Tinapis facilitated eight ZIPRA on 20 November 1978.

As matters progressed, Grey was confident the ZIPRA cells would "turn" and assist us once the people understood our vision and witnessed the UANC increasingly gain political and military superiority. We did not react immediately to this intelligence but decided to allow the cells to remain intact for two reasons. Firstly, we knew who comprised the ZIPRA network and could use this information to our benefit, conveying selected intelligence to ZIPRA. Secondly, should we remove them, they would merely be substituted by a replacement cell, forcing us to establish the newcomers' identities, requiring the expenditure of valuable time, a commodity we lacked as delays could well cost lives. Furthermore, ZIPRA would not know the extent of our intelligence if their intelligence cells remained in tact. I was concerned for the safety of my men. Grey did not view matters as I did. He felt they were not under threat. However, it would soon be revealed to me that I needed to reconsider my approach to the security and safety of my team at Karoi.

Now that the UANC office in Chikangwe was well known and the training farm at Chabwino operational, we were constantly occupied as our momentum increased. Geoff Price had foreseen this progress, hence we arranged to meet at the Twin Rivers Motel on 10 November 1978. On his arrival, he was followed into my room by Joseph (Joe) Nyandoro, a high-ranking UANC official, and another African. Introductions followed. "This is Happy Marere," announced Geoff. Happy moved towards me. He was possibly ten years my senior, roughly my height, of slim build, intense and, in my instant appraisal, an astute man. He was fashionably dressed in denim jeans, khaki shirt and a denim jacket. Short hair complemented a cropped beard to complete his appearance. We shook hands, making direct eye contact: two individuals baring their souls. Neither of us flinched.

Geoff smiled, adding: "Happy is externally trained and will be working with you." After a few pleasantries, Geoff enquired after our political and military progress and, following my brief update, he and Joe left, leaving Happy and I together. I later learned that on leaving, Joe had said to Geoff: "They'll be all right."

Happy and I sat for a brief while gazing at each other. It was to be a defining moment for both of us. After a short silence, I gave him a more detailed update of our progress but gained the impression he had been briefed on our situation in Hurungwe. Happy listened intently and, after about an hour, we parted company. I found myself deep in thought. I reflected on the need to continue establishing trust among the members of the team being assembled at Karoi, especially between Happy and myself. It intrigued me how the UANC were placing men in the positions most suited to their individuality. They were well trained and completely aware of their roles within the party. We seldom experienced conflict, as each man was dedicated and committed to our one vision. It was obvious to all that Grey held the most senior position within the UANC, an important feature of the team in my estimation. I was in deep thought as Happy and I parted company.

After a few hours, Happy was fully involved gathering intelligence from the UANC office. Two youths arrived with a report of their relatives being burned alive in their kraals in the Karereshi area on 8 November 1978. They further notified us of ZIPRA disallowing the bodies to be buried: a disturbing practice on the part of the enemy.[1] Our team instructed the youths to return home and pinpoint the precise location of the insurgents and, if possible, penetrate their intelligence network. Once again, I was amazed at the team's understanding of revolutionary strategies and tactics. I found commendable the willingness of the people to risk their lives while serving in their resistance movements. Excitement mounted as, yet again, our momentum increased. Chikangwe and Chabwino were now fully operational, with well-trained men occupying key positions. The sole

[1] Karoi Murder Map 12.

remaining requirement was a strike at the enemy, which would provide the ultimate confirmation of our operational intelligence accuracy.

Kariba Break

Earlier on, we received information of the whereabouts of Beauty whom we were searching for and decided to use the information as an excuse to take the team on a weekend getaway to Lake Kariba in order to locate her. Unfortunately, our excursion was unsuccessful but, on leaving, we informed Ben Pretorius, the local Kariba SB officer, of her details. He assured us he would be on the lookout for her. Notwithstanding our failed venture, we spent an extremely pleasant weekend and a refreshing break at Lake Kariba, a breathtaking and unique "Mediterranean" haven in central Africa. Lavish hotels with swimming-pools, casinos, bars, restaurants and lake-facing rooms dot the banks of this "inland sea". During the still of dusk, visitors are immersed in the sounds of Africa while surrounded by plush flora and fauna. As gentle lake-water waves lap the shores, an aura of peace and tranquility prevail. Despite the horrors and brutality of war, Lake Kariba offered a haven from the harsh realities of bloodshed: a sanctuary for weary soldiers and an embattled nation. On Sunday, 12 November, with renewed zeal and vigour, we returned to Karoi.

On my return, I learned that Happy was settling into his new environment, providing accurate and well-documented intelligence, confirming our insights of ZIPRA's extensive intelligence networks. I was equally impressed with his various presentations, underlining his vast experience and worth to our organisation. The combination of Grey's, Happy's and Katima's knowledge and experience of revolutionary principles, with that of my familiarity with SB/SF activities, proved a decided asset to our internal operations. Many of our recruits were formerly in close association with ZIPRA, either as *mujibhas* or acquaintances, consequently gaining insight into their strategies and tactics. In addition, they were associated with the people who supported ZIPRA in their home areas. It is worth noting two of our men, Tapedza and Madison, had considerable local political involvement which united a formidable political, intelligence, military and operational team. Ours was not a pyramid-shaped, authoritarian or rank-structured organisation. Rather it was a laterally arranged team, with each member functioning in their area of expertise, allowing for mutual respect. In time, additional well-equipped and experienced UANC and Security Forces men would join our team.

Understanding the development and process of our operations was a remarkable experience. It is one thing drifting through life as opposed to gaining wisdom and understanding of the "bigger picture" while immersed in the matter at hand. Fortunately, at this stage of my career, I was open-minded and uniquely positioned to experience developments first-hand as they unfolded.

The acquisition of weapons and ammunition were an ongoing difficulty but, fortunately, during a prearranged meeting at Sinoia with Geoff on 14 November 1978, he gave us vital arms and ammunition. While travelling to collect them, I called in at Chabwino. This stop-off contented our formerly disgruntled Walter, satisfying his continued wherewithal complaints.

Our internal intelligence network was functioning satisfactorily with Manenji receiving intelligence from recruits identifying locally trained *mujibhas* operating with ZIPRA sections in their areas. This intelligence was vital for our men following their deployment as they would readily identify those in support or opposition to us.

My meeting with Geoff at Sinoia was brief as usual. He was a no-nonsense man and did not suffer fools lightly. Trivialities were unimportant to him and he allowed me to simply get on with the job. We updated each other on our spheres of operations and he supplied me with a good number of AK-47s, promising me 2,000 rounds of ammunition for collection the following day. I delivered the armaments to Chabwino, and the following day collected and delivered the additional munitions. The recruits and training staff were jubilant. I did not want training thwarted and was determined to provide the staff with as much assistance as possible in order to accelerate momentum and deploy men into the field. Com.Ops. was pressuring me to deploy the men into the operational area, but I remained resolute that they would only be deployed when adequately prepared. Success hinged on good training. I relied on Walter's interpretation of "well trained". Field radios 971007 and 971087 were despatched by Admin. to Salisbury for repair via Geoff Price's office. We also traded six SKSs for six AK-47s. George Hutchison and I collected a further six AK-47s and additional equipment when visiting Salisbury on 20 November 1978, while collecting funding for the operation.

Our progress continued. Volumes of detailed intelligence flowed constantly into Chikangwe. The interesting aspect of this information was that several operations were developing simultaneously. As the intelligence swept into the office, it became important to document and focus on each strand as an individual operation. Each thread required specific planning, strategy and timing, leading ultimately to the deployment of Security Forces. Each battle plan was individual and unique. No "blueprint" was or is provided for this type of warfare. In fact, it was my conviction that routine and stereotyped patterns led to casualties, if not deaths. Happy was satisfied that the northern Hurungwe locals were UANC-orientated. He was convinced of their opposition towards ZIPRA and of the people's support for our forces. What we lacked at this stage of developments was a successful military operation to confirm the intelligence we had gathered and, in so doing, gain credence. One difficulty we faced regarding our intelligence was our reliance on the SF to react timeously. This matter came to a head when Grey and Happy expressed their concern that the landmine in the Karereshi area, first reported on 13 October 1978, had not been lifted. They correctly believed that, should intelligence from the field not be promptly acted on, the UANC would lose credibility among the people. Unfortunately, there was little we could do in this instance, but I had plans for the future when we deployed our men.

During a briefing visit on 9 November 1978, Supt. Anderson suggested we take over the failing *mujibha* farm at Sinoia. I declined. I informed him it was clear that my *mujibha* report, XYS 90000/1, of 25 August 1978, had either not been widely circulated or not read. It was my conviction, I continued, that there was a general lack of understanding, training, strategy and direction by Special Branch. He agreed, promising to look into it: an unenviable task, given the ominous circumstances facing the country.

On the same day, we received information that ZIPRA had murdered one of their known supporters, Adam Bunda.[1]

Bishop Abel Muzorewa Meets the Men: Our First Pass-Out Parade

In the build up to our first pass-out parade at Chabwino on Friday, 17 November 1978, Grey and Happy suggested we invite Bishop Abel Muzorewa to attend. They had approached the bishop through their channels, with him expressing a willingness to attend. During a private conversation with Geoff Price, he confirmed that Muzorewa was free, willing and able to attend. His presence at our parade would provide a significant boost to the morale of our men, connect our forces to the UANC leadership and identify them with the UANC party's political vision. I duly informed the training staff and men of the bishop's pending visit to our parade. In my view, it was important to inform the training camp of his visit as it was our first pass-out parade. A concerted effort in the build-up for the actual parade was required to ensure the event was significant and successful.

Our UANC office staff passed on this news to the people. It was important they observed us fulfilling our promise that their army was preparing to deploy. By implementing our word they would learn to trust us. It was also our desire that this news would filter through to ZIPRA in Hurungwe through the UANC networks and the people.

Grey, Happy and I laboured to ensure that the bishop's visit would be a success. It was necessary for the men to understand the mechanics of the war they were about to enter. Firstly, the war was political. According to Zedong: "Politics is war without bloodshed while war is politics with bloodshed."[2] Secondly, as Zedong states: "The Party commands the gun, and the gun must never be allowed to command the Party."[3] I felt it important the military did not see itself independent of

[1] Karoi Murder Map 13.
[2] Zedong, M. (1976), pp. 58-59.
[3] Ibid., p. 102.

the political. Counter-revolutionary (and revolutionary) military action without the political objective of serving and uniting all the people is a dictatorship seeking to impose its own will. Such an army isolates itself from the people, has no meaningful cause or purpose, and faces inevitable defeat. Victories in sporadic skirmishes, coupled with scattered acts of individual heroism divorced from a political vision that includes the majority of the people, become increasingly senseless political and military operations of an occupying force detached from the masses. This outlook perpetuates racial and supremacist attitudes strategically shackling political and military progress.

White Rhodesians may have coexisted with moderate, conservative, like-minded and "acceptable" Africans but they failed to allow their advancement. Furthermore, the refusal to include the majority of citizens as a component of future development, in my opinion, stifled progress. Consequently, Muzorewa's visit was of paramount importance to us, together with the unveiling and presentation of our diverse strategy. Regardless of the obstacles, our parade called for a profound impact on both the people's army we were training, as well as the people themselves.

The bishop's presence allied himself and the UANC to the military (SFAs), allowing the men to witness the cohesion between the political and the military, both serving and defending the people. The military was not above the political but strategically placed to overcome the obstacles that stood in the way of the political. The main obstacles we faced in Hurungwe were firstly, a confused white community misguided and misled by an intransigent Rhodesian Front agenda which had agreed internationally to progress towards majority rule, demanding extended deadlines, yet failing to achieve meaningful political change. Secondly, the marauding occupying ZIPRA forces who were imposing their agenda on the people. Removal of these obstacles would defeat ZIPRA's legitimate political objectives and complement our military action. This was not to be!

On 16 November 1978, Geoff Price contacted me to confirm Bishop Muzorewa's attendance at the parade. I assured him all was in order. Grey had visited the farm days before, paying attention to every detail of the arrangements, including security precautions. Understandably, the men were eagerly anticipating the bishop's visit, having laboured long and hard at the preparations and determined to ensure a successful day.

The day after my discussion with Geoff, we met the bishop on an isolated dirt road near Chabwino. As was the UANC tradition, Happy officially handed the bishop "his weapon", an AK-47, for ceremonial purposes, identifying the political with the military. We escorted him to the farm where the men eagerly awaited commencement of the parade: a significant occasion. Following a political address, the bishop, as is the custom at such events, inspected the people's army. He was a spectator to various activities and military drills, after which he toured the farm. All went precisely to plan. The bishop and his team were suitably impressed. That was my first meeting with Bishop Muzorewa and the success of the day paved the way for personal and direct communications with him.

Strike 1: Selous Scouts

On 16 November 1978, we began working on intelligence which led to our first battle with ZIPRA. It required three days to establish their whereabouts and deploy forces into the area.

Grey and Happy reported the abduction and murder of one of their supporters. Mufaro (pseudonym) informed them that the deceased had been abducted from his kraal and shot dead near Magunje Business Centre by ZIPRA on 7 November 1978.[1] Mufaro returned to his home roughly a month later to meet Wilson, a ZIPRA *mujibha* sent to buy cigarettes for a ZIPRA section. The two were not confronted by ZIPRA while making their way to Wilson's home. Wilson still retained the cigarettes, indicating he was about to meet the insurgents.

On the afternoon of Tuesday, 14 November 1978, while searching for his cattle, Mufaro met two insurgents, Silos and Christopher, both of whom were carrying AK-47s. He made no conversation with the two but recognised them as members of an 18-man ZIPRA section that he had met in the

---

1 Karoi Murder Map 11.

same area 10 days before. This encounter highlighted the value of the *mujibha* system for, while the young men were carrying out their normal duties in the field, they were the "eyes and ears" of the force they supported. Furthermore, they had a natural ability to track and accurately identify footprints belonging to residents of the area, SF or ZIPRA, and a thorough understanding of their home environment.

Mufaro identified Makai, Jamus and Anesu (pseudonym), of the Magunje area, as key men in ZIPRA's intelligence network. Makai was a leading contact man. Jamus provided ZIPRA with beer at his home on a previous occasion while Anesu, an ex-UANC official, was required to provide teenage girls for their sexual pleasures. These ZIPRA sections were definitely members of ZAPU as those letters were inscribed on their belts emphasising the link and flow between the political and the military. On previous occasions, they had drunk beer at Jamus's home, yet another contact man. Mufaro had no doubt that they remained based in the hills close by the Magunje area and were still in the vicinity. Consequently, we sent him home to confirm the information and contact his close friend. We were confident he would pass intelligence on to us.

After intense investigations, the following day Mufaro relayed through his friend, Vimbo (pseudonym), information identifying ZIPRA operations in the Magunje Business Centre area where some 60 insurgents were operating in roughly seven-man sections. This confirmed the intelligence we received on 15 November 1978. Vimbo, a member of the ZIPRA intelligence network, confirmed they slept in the kraals where females lived, thus continuing their now familiar pattern. Generally, around 10 a.m., after their *mujibhas* had cleared the area, they moved into the nearby river lines, seeking protection from the SF. The general area of their operations fell within the Maumbe, Murereshi and Kajere rivers, and the road from Charles Clack Mission to Maumbe, at approximately QM528398.

In the region of Kraalhead Jotam Makayi, Wireless's kraal was identified as supporting ZIPRA, along with the residents of Chandiwira, Manyembere and Murovashangu. Kasvinga, from Kraalhead Zindoga, was also a ZIPRA informant. Vimbo assisted us in drawing a map of the area, helping us pinpoint its locstat, QM528398.

Happy produced a sketch of the area and, as this intelligence was confirmed by two sources from the local SB offices, I decided to deploy the SF. (See Strike 1: Selous Scouts. Murereshi (1) Original Sketch.) The Support Unit were unable to react on the day but D/S/O Thomas from the Selous Scouts had available men to deploy. I took Vimbo to the their base and briefed Thomas. I handed him the sketch and left the matter with him. The general plan was for Vimbo to lead the callsign into the contact area on 17 November 1978, and identify the kraals involved. I will explain the significance of these sketches later in my dealings with the SAS.

On the morning of 18 November 1978, the day after the bishop's visit, the Selous Scouts callsign engaged a ZIPRA section at QM528398 which we named the "Murereshi (1)" contact. In the ensuing battle in the kraal area, one ZIPRA insurgent was killed, one AKM and one RPG-7 launcher with its projectiles were recovered. During the battle, two arms caches which were inside two separate kraals were detonated, causing the destruction of the kraals belonging to Wireless. I spent much of the day examining the body, searching for intelligence and organising the ballistics and intelligence relating to the contact.[1] While this was our first strike against ZIPRA, disturbing repercussions followed.

On 23 November 1978, Grey and Happy confirmed the killings of Vimbo, a local from Zindoga Kraal, and Ramio Makayi. They were murdered by ZIPRA on 21 November 1978, their bodies being abandoned in Magunje Township.[2] It was alleged that Wilson, a resident from the Chiyanganya Kraal line, near the Murereshi River had informed ZIPRA that the three deceased were "sellouts". These deaths highlighted for me the willingness of many people prepared to pay the ultimate price for their beliefs and it confirmed ZIPRA had returned to the area. Naturally, we were disturbed by

---

1 Karoi Contacts Map Incident 14.

2 Karoi Murder Map 17.

the murders but remained determined to monitor the situation and strike again. Patience and timing are key elements in war. In my view, revenge is counterproductive. After a short while, we did indeed mount a successful counter-attack. This event reinforced my commitment to deploy the people's army in order to protect the masses. We also established that in the Kebvunde area Headman Mapepa's Kraal had been burned down by ZIPRA. Our informant was tasked to return to the area in order to gather further information regarding ZIPRA's operations.

There were two key aspects to our operations. The first to attack ZIPRA at the most opportune moment and second, equally important, deploying the people's army to defend the people. These two elements needed to coincide with the pace determined by the people. The people were prepared to pass on intelligence regarding ZIPRA's locations and movements but suffered severe consequences for doing so. ZIPRA carried out reprisals on alleged, and often confirmed, "sellouts", in their efforts to maintain control and their enforced imposition of martial law. It is crucial to understand ZIPRA correctly identified that contact with the SF could come about by one of two methods: either OPs or information supplied by the people. Their intelligence networks (the *mujibha* system) were in place to counter OPs and to be their "eyes and ears" among the people. ZIPRA understood that the people were the key, consequently when compromised, the source of their exposure could only have been the people, hence their rule by fear and martial law. ZIPRA judges in the Mudzimu area, and the "suicide squad", were part of their mechanisms of enforcing martial law. This pattern would continue until our forces deployed and removed the threat. In the meantime,

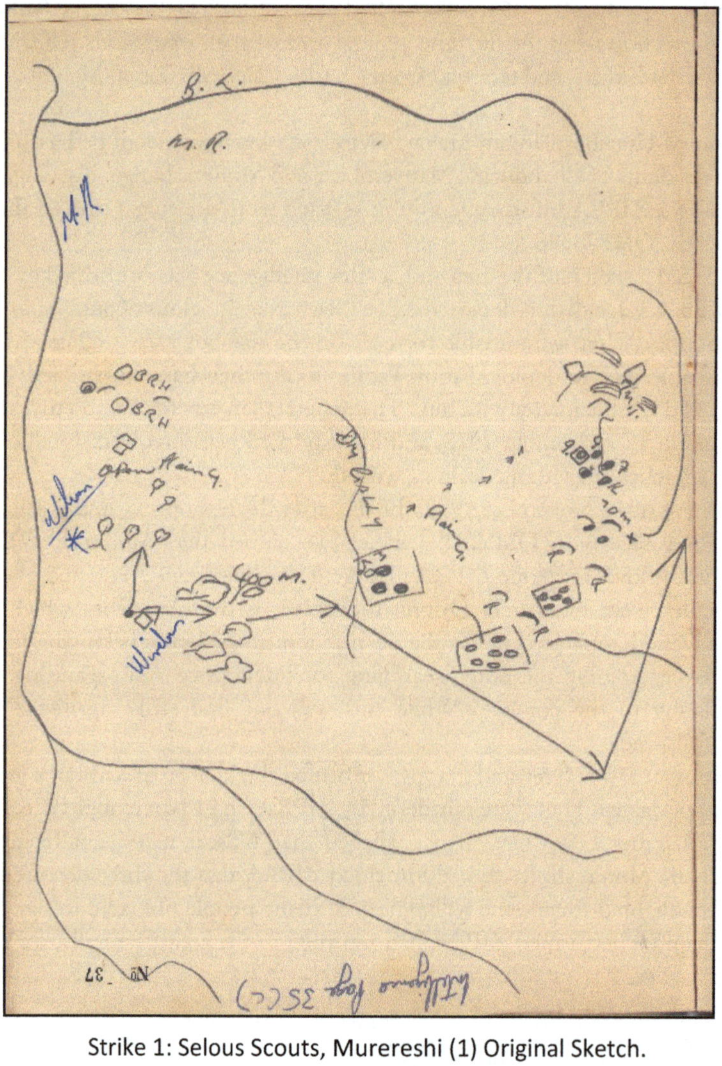

Strike 1: Selous Scouts, Murereshi (1) Original Sketch.

the people continued to live in fear without protection and support. The anomaly intrigued me. Our Law and Order (Maintenance) Act made provision for dealing with collaborators by passing appropriate sentences, including capital punishment. ZIPRA, in their area of control and governance, established a complementary judicial structure dealing with SF collaborators, where sentences for the guilty varied from corporal punishment, physical abuse to death. Kephas Matamba was accused of being a "sellout" and murdered by ZIPRA at Maumbe on 22 November 1978.[1]

After the Selous Scouts strike, intelligence continued to flow into our offices from areas further afield in which ZIPRA committed carnage. On Sunday, 19 November 1978, in the Mukwichi area, an agent reported that a tractor driver, Farayi, had been in contact with two insurgents informing them that there were no SF in the area. The next day Faryai, accompanied by the two insurgents, was led to a grinding mill where they met Veremu. Veremu was accused of pinpointing landmine locations to the SF and was beaten to death.[2] Faryai was also assaulted and then warned not to use the road leading from Masau to Kapiri Mountain as it was mined. This confirmed information we received on 14 November 1978 that the road between Kapiri School and Masau had been mined.[3] Our agent was on the same bus as a young girl who had been abducted and sexually abused by three insurgents and was fleeing to Umtali. On the way to Karoi, the agent had spoken to a local farm owner at the farm store where he used to purchase fertiliser. The farmer was also on his way to Karoi. I mention this meeting to exemplify the "eyes-and-ears" connection between the white farmers and the people.

Strike 2: SAS Contact

This contact is subject to considerable controversy. Therefore, I intend to meticulously filter through the facts in order to rectify the records, as well as matters pertaining to it. The reader will, in the course of the following pages, appreciate my scrupulous attention to detail, my careful collection and correlation of the facts relating to the incident, and my own and the team's deciphering, processing and dissemination of intelligence gathered immediately prior to, during and after the contact, concluding with the consequences of this particular deployment. I am aware of four published books in which the details of the contact are in conflict with the facts. My attention to detail was applicable to all our intelligence operations.

(1) *Intelligence build-up*

On Monday, 13 November 1978, Happy arrived at the office with intelligence identifying ZIPRA activity in the Doro area of Hurungwe. Mrs Gasura, of Nyamupfukudza Kraal, was near Manguwe's Kraal when assaulted by a ZIPRA section on Saturday, 11 November 1978. Henry Nyamupfukudza, a leading ZIPRA contact man and his son, Bhinya,[4] both from the Doro area, were aware of the incident. Both father and son were staunch ZIPRA supporters. Bhinya had travelled to Karoi on Friday, 10 November 1978, to purchase supplies for ZIPRA. This was our first intelligence gathered concerning Henry Nyamupfukudza and Bhinya. In time, more information regarding their activities in the Doro area would come to light. At that particular moment, there was insufficient intelligence to justify the deployment of Security Forces, thus matters were left in abeyance.

On Tuesday, 21 November 1978, Grey and Happy provided information to the office gathered from Bravo 70 (pseudonym now deceased). Bravo 70 notified our UANC office that two females, Dorcas, along with Robson Madyavanhu's wife, Fiona, had been detained by *mujibhas* and sentenced to execution on 2 December 1978, should their husbands fail to return to their homes by that date.

Bravo 70's intelligence of the ZIPRA section was specific: they were resident in the Doro area. China was their commander, while Tall Man was the second in command. We believed that China

[1] Karoi Murder Map 18.

[2] Karoi Murder Map 16, not logged on map.

[3] Karoi Landmine Map 11-12, respectively, not logged on map.

[4] Confirmed by Dr J. Chakawa's field research 15/4/2016. Henry Nyamupfukudza is now deceased and was father to Bhinya who survived the war.

was a part of the ZIPRA High Command for Hurungwe but later established that he was a detachment commander. The cadre included Dzapiringana, George and Michael. China slept at the home of Jim with a girl.[1] Tall Man slept at Marangu's dwelling and often travelled to Lynx Mine, Vuti APA.[2] Dzapiringana slept at Lucas's (alias Joburg's) home.[3] Chenai was Joburg's wife,[4] with their house situated alongside a borehole. George slept at Chipisai's home,[5] while Michael, in turn, slept at Masibanda's (a female Ndebele) house.[6] Masibanda, wife of Bazil Nyamupfukudza, was the mother of two teenage daughters. Unfortunately, the names of the girls were not known. Both girls had recently visited Karoi to collect supplies for the insurgents (See Strike 2: SAS Contact Original Sketch p.294).

Some remaining insurgents slept at Soraidema's[7] house whose son, Clever,[8] transported supplies in a scotch cart for ZIPRA from Justin Matamba's store at Maumbe BC. Napier Matamba was Justin's father. A teenage girl, Fadziso (pseudonym),[9] was in love with a ZIPRA comrade and they lived in the home of a local family. A further two young girls, Rosie (pseudonym) and Danai (pseudonym), lived with members of ZIPRA at Thomas Manguwe's home.[10] Two ZIPRA lived with the girls including Anopa (pseudonym),[11] at Mangwende's Kraal,[12] while Chamai (pseudonym) also housed ZIPRA. Each morning the ZIPRA section would rendezvous at the houses of Harvey Chiweshe[13] and Dhongijena.[14]

Other local men involved in the ZIPRA intelligence network were Charles Mavunga, Pedro Raphael, Jivas Masaiti and Joe Masaiti. The leading ZIPRA contact man was Henry Nyamupfukudza and the main *mujibhas* in this area were Bhinya, Gift Nyamupfukudza, Tapedzwa, brother of Chipesai, Rawson and Nelson Makiyi.[15] Benjamin, Gibson Madyavanhu, Dzawanda and Martin issued ZAPU political cards, obtained from Zambia, to the people. All four were *mujibhas*. Some of the people accepted these cards willingly, while others reluctantly carried them in order to authenticate party loyalty.

To the south of Doro River, Canan Mapikilela was the foremost contact man who had knowledge of arms caches, base camps, ZIPRA movements and general intelligence involving them and their supporters in the area. The headman of this region was Madyavanhu (QM552502). He was also involved with the ZIPRA intelligence network. China travelled to Karoi sporadically, usually to obtain clothing from Pedro. Our informant also identified two locals in Karoi connected with ZIPRA in the Doro area. A young man named Nathan worked at Mrs Merriman's (pseudonym) home as a gardener, and an older man, Mackenzie Nyamupfukudza, also worked there.

Later the same day we clandestinely arrested Nathan and Mackenzie Nyamupfukudza and Pedro, thereby isolating them from the public eye. We did not wish the ZIPRA intelligence network to have an inkling of our operations.

---

1 See Strike 2: SAS Contact Original Sketch (A).

2 Lynx Mine (QM6164): State land in the Vuti APA. There was a large African compound at the mine.

3 Confirmed by Dr J. Chakawa's field research 15/4/2016; Strike 2: SAS Contact Original Sketch (C).

4 Ibid. Dr J. Chakawa's research revealed that Chenai was Joburg's daughter and his son, Emmanual, became a ZIPRA insurgent.

5 Confirmed by Dr J. Chakawa.

6 Strike 2: SAS Contact Original Sketch (B).

7 Dr J. Chakawa interviewed Wellington Soraidema and his brother, Bhinya.

8 Confirmed by Dr J. Chakawa, Clever is now deceased.

9 Dr J. Chakawa confirmed Fadziso is now deceased.

10 Strike 2: SAS Contact Original Sketch (F).

11 Dr J. Chakawa confirmed Anopa is now deceased. Temba from Mangwende Kraal joined ZIPRA.

12 Confirmed by Dr J. Chakawa; Strike 2: SAS Contact Original Sketch (G).

13 Confirmed by Dr J. Chakawa; Strike 2: SAS Contact Original Sketch (D).

14 Confirmed by Dr J. Chakawa; Strike 2: SAS Contact Original Sketch (E).

15 Confirmed by Dr J. Chakawa. Gift joined ZIPRA. He is now dead. Tapedzwa joined *Pfumo reVanhu*. Rawson (Kambonje) was thoroughly beaten by soldiers during the war. On his death, his memorial service was held on 29/4/2016.

We felt the time had arrived for us to act on the information we had at hand. Consequently, on Wednesday, 22 November 1978, we spent the day analysing the intelligence, and planning our options and strategies to eliminate China and his group. Grey's and Happy's assessments of the intelligence was accurate and detailed. They prepared a sketch of the target area with Bravo 70's help. (See Strike 2: SAS Contact Original Sketch.) Once the sketches were drawn, I would convert the information onto a survey map, define the area in question and establish locstats. Having pinpointed the target areas, the sketches, survey maps and locstats were then presented to the relevant SF to aid their strategic planning for deployments. I found the procedure fascinating and was always amazed how accurately tribal folk knew their areas, and how precise the sketches and locstats were. These detailed sketches included the following:

1. Kraal layout.
2. Identification of occupants resident in each kraal, in particular those actively supporting ZIPRA.
3. Identification of ZIPRA (names and numbers) known to occupy the kraals, including the specific kraals they slept in and with whom.
4. Identification of important features used by ZIPRA, such as rivers, forests and kopjes used as their lookouts (OPs).
5. General intelligence, such as known bush-bases, arms caches and rendezvous locations.

This process gave the SF a clear interpretation of intelligence which they used to strategise and plan their attacks. The use of sketches was vital when mounting airborne attacks with Fire Force. Routes could be carefully planned based on features the informant could readily identify and recognise from the air. It was astonishing how quickly informants adapted to flying and directing helicopters into battle zones. I was also learning how to deal with a population who wanted our help to remove the invading ZIPRA, freely volunteering information about events at their homes in Hurungwe. Grey and Happy were learning to adjust their interpretation of intelligence to suit SF operations, especially when working with Fire Force. This was all new to them. In fact, we were all learning and adapting to this unconventional counter-revolutionary and mass-mobilisation process.

The presentation of intelligence in this manner helped convince the SF, in particular FF, of its authenticity and helped formulate strategy for deployments. It was important to always present intelligence in a positive, confident and detailed manner. Naturally, it had to work as success proved reliability, built reputation, created enthusiasm and inspired positive response. It was an extremely successful strategy, although we did encounter failures which were called "lemons".

Selecting the right military unit to deploy on reliable intelligence was one of the most important decisions an intelligence officer could make. Receiving accurate information on the enemy's whereabouts, plans and strategies was essential but how, when and with whom to respond were possibly the most critical of decisions. Bravo 70 was willing to direct forces into the area, provided we guaranteed his and his immediate family's safety. Fortunately, our preparation included being able to house refugees at Chabwino. Our preference was to use the Fire Force, but we decided to finalise the intelligence and deployment options the following morning. We knew we were still operating in a safe period of time and calculated that the group would remain on site until at least 2 December 1978. ZIPRA were more static than ZANLA which was to our advantage, not only on this attack, but also for our future strategic planning and operations.

From this informant, we established a great deal of precise intelligence:

1. Foremost, identifying Henry Nyamupfukudza as a ZIPRA contact man and the young Bhinya as an involved *mujibha*, was confirmed by two sources on two separate occasions. Maintaining my diaries was an extremely beneficial CID/SB practice and was paying dividends. Forty years later, in the course of writing this book, they are still proving helpful.
2. From the information supplied to us, it was clear that China's group had remained in the Doro area for some time, making them a "resident section". China and his men had established relationships with the people, particularly the women with whom they slept. This pattern of residency was confirmed throughout Hurungwe. It was not uncommon for ZIPRA to take

possession of another man's wife while young unattached teenage girls were either volunteered or forced into relationships. These abuses would work in our favour when we deployed our forces. Their lust for sexual activity was a significant weakness, leaving ZIPRA men vulnerable to attack and often despised by the locals, especially resentful husbands, fathers and, indeed, many of the women themselves.

3. The group slept in particular kraals or established areas and had fallen into the old trap of creating a pattern of behaviour which is fatal in warfare as routine makes one vulnerable to the enemy.
4. While it was not uncommon for ZIPRA to sleep with their women in specific kraals at night, some members of the section would sleep outdoors in defined areas in order to keep guard.
5. There was a strong, well-established network of contact men and *mujibhas* in the area.
6. ZIPRA had established rendezvous points at which to assemble after attacks or when gathering in the mornings and evenings.
7. ZIPRA trusted their intelligence network and the people in the Doro area. They had lapsed into a routine of behaviour which led us to believe that they considered Hurungwe a liberated area under their governance: martial law. On the other hand, we had gained considerable momentum. Strategically, we could attack our enemy with precision.
8. Politically, we could now target the people using the tribal differences and social issues surrounding the violation of their marital and parental rights.
9. Strategically, our greatest advantage was that ZIPRA considered this area liberated. They were completely unaware that we had penetrated their intelligence network and the level of information we were receiving.

It was our intention to strike with maximum force when and where we found ZIPRA in the build-up to the deployment of our forces. I considered this an ideal opportunity to eliminate the unsuspecting ZIPRA command element in the Doro area whom, I believed, had lapsed into complacency. We would be given this one opportunity to attack our unsuspecting enemy, therefore failure was not an option! I was aware that, once China and his section became alerted to our strategies and tactics, our war would become more difficult as they adjusted strategies and tactics accordingly.

(2) *SAS officer's assessment: Hurungwe*

I was at the Twin Rivers Motel on the evening of Wednesday, 22 November 1978, when George Hutchison and Walter met me for a drink. We chanced upon several SAS men, led by Lt. Darrell Watt. They had attended an officer's assessment training exercise in Hurungwe for approximately 10 days and were returning home to the SAS HQ in Salisbury.[1] Mike Reeler recalled briefing Watt prior to his deployment. After the briefing Watt placed a TR 28 radio in his office for Reeler to update him with any relevant intelligence to act upon. Darrell Watt led the deployment. His unit included officers being assessed: Lt. Andre Scheepers,[2] Capt. Johannes "Joe" du Ploy,[3] Lt. Richard "Rich" Stannard, and Troopers Eugene Pomeroy and Robert "Rob" Slingsby.[4] There were two other soldiers in the team who wish to remain anonymous. For the sake of this work, they will be named Fred and Stan. The men operated in two four-man sections.

Lt. Rich Stannard attended the selection course and recalls the following: "I had left the SAS to join the Selous Scouts, so on my return to the SAS I was required to complete the SAS Officer's Assessment course in Hurungwe in November 1978 led by Lt. Darrell Watt. We soon learned that the area was 'flooded' with ZIPRA and it was clearly a liberated area. They were aggressive soldiers, well trained and disciplined, we had three contacts in the first three days. The first one was a fleeting contact while sweeping in extended line, there were no kills or injuries. Then we collected an old

1 Confirmed by Eugene Pomeroy email 15/11/2017.
2 Scheepers was involved in Operation Neutron on 13/2/1979.
3 Capt. Johannes du Ploy: He was also involved in Operation Neutron on 13/2/1979 and KIA on 6/9/1979 during Operation Uric (5/9/1979-7/9/1979), the assault on Mapai.
4 Robert Slingsby: KIA 11/4/1979.

man for interrogations but got nothing out of him. Shortly after releasing him we were attacked with mortars, RPG7s, RPD or RPKs and AKs, again there were no confirmed kills or injuries. Obviously, the old man went and told the gooks where we were indicating how many gooks were actually in the area, the strength of their intelligence network and the control of the people they had. We then ambushed a lone gook walking with a young *mujibha*, he was carrying a Getto box that was booming out the song 'Staying Alive' by the Bee Gees. Scheepers shot and killed him, the *mujibha* ran away and Watt decided to leave the body, I do not recall what happened to the weapon. I recall that the deceased had a very nice leather jacket but unfortunately it was holed, full of blood and was of no use to me. After the contact Watt sent me down the road to sweep and ensure there were no further gooks following as the deceased may have been a 'lead man' for the rest of his section."[1]

Stan recalled: "During the first part of the operation we were doing an ambush when a lone terr walked confidently along a path 25-30m away from my ambush position. I don't recall if anyone was with him. I was standing next to a rock and did not have my weapon, an RPD, it was leaning against a nearby tree. I froze and hoped he did not see me. The terr walked straight past me into an ambush laid by Scheepers who shot him with a weapon that had a silencer. The body was left in the bush, we booby trapped it by putting a hand grenade underneath it."[2]

Rich Stannard was recalled to Salisbury as he was required to attend another SAS selection course at Matopos, which he passed. Immediately after the SAS selection course, successful candidates were required to attend a three-week paratrooper's course, in this instance from Monday, 4 December to Friday, 22 December 1978 at Tempe, Bloemfontein, 44 Parachute Brigade. Stannard was not required to attend the paratrooper's course as he had previously achieved his "wings".[3]

On 6 December 1978, I received and recorded the following intelligence in my diaries, demonstrating the accuracy of my journals and the depth of my research for this book: "Recently,[4] Raphael Sibanda was walking with a ZIPRA man named Van Der Byl when they were ambushed by Security Forces at QM373295. Van Der Byl was shot and killed and his body was still lying in the bush rotting. Raphael made good his escape. No body or weapon was recovered and it is likely that the Security Forces did not realise that they had killed Van Der Byl."

Mike Reeler recalled: "During the debrief of Watt after his team had deployed into the Nyamhunga area, Watt mentioned they had shot and killed one lone terr walking down a path and left the body in the field. I asked Watt where the weapon was as it was required for a ballistics check and Watt gave me quite a rebuff: 'What did you expect me to do, carry the thing out with me?' He explained that he had blown up the barrel of the weapon with Cordtex. Of course, I expected the weapon to be kept for evidence and to be informed about the deceased terrorist. I explained the importance of legal investigation procedures, as well as essential evidence that could be procured from the body, and ballistic evidence that could be gleaned from the weapon."[5] Watt confirmed: "The body was left behind, we were just going about our ways like we did external ops. Did not want chopper attraction."[6] Garth Barrett clarified procedures: "Your comment that Cordtex was used to destroy the weapon does not make sense and sounds like BS to me. Cordtex is only issued for 'demolition' work of a specific nature and it also requires the issuing of detonators, which would not happen on an internal deployment for routine internal Ops. Standard Operating Procedures for all JOC.'s and Sub.JOC's were that all 'bodies, documents, weapons and any evidence' was handed over to BSAP/SB. This applies to SAS personnel deployed internally. SAS would be deployed internally under a Main JOC., but could be under a Sub.JOC. The only exception would be if the callsign was

1 Rich Stannard various telephone call interviews June 2016 and emails June and August 2016.

2 Stan telephone interview 9/12/2017, Karoi Contacts Map Incident 15.

3 Dates of the paratrooper course confirmed by SAS officer, 2nd Lt. John Borrowdale's course photograph. Borrowdale confirms he attended the selection course with Rich Stannard. The paratrooper course was traditionally held immediately after the selection course. These dates are significant as they helped Rich Stannard confirm that the SAS deployment in Hurungwe was in November 1978. Emails 8/11/2016 and 9/11/2016.

4 The "recently" referring to a period during November 1978, as the report was documented on the 6/12/1978.

5 Mike Reeler WhatsApp discussion 28/6/2016 and oral interview.

6 Darrell Watt email 27/8/2016.

on a 'hot' follow up after a contact. However, the contact time/date and location would be logged in immediately for BSAP/SB follow up via the JOC or Sub.JOC. The callsign would not leave weapons in the contact area unless follow up SFs were very close."[1]

Dr Chakawa carried out independent research during August 2016 and made the following comment: "Confirmed Van Der Byl was a ZIPRA Cadre in the Nyamhunga area who was remembered for atrocities carried out in the general Nyhamunga area. Van Der Byl was carrying a beat box when he was shot dead. Van Der Byl wore a leather jacket, he was walking with Raphael Sibanda and body left there. Sibanda, whose home is near Masuku Kraal, ran away with Van Der Byl's weapon. Sibanda survived the war and now lives in Mrewha. The issue of Van Der Byl is one that I expended much energy on. Sibanda was not just a simple *mujibha.* He was being trained to become a locally trained guerrilla. It was therefore possible that he used his skill to take the weapon. There was also a shoot-out as he evaded with the weapon. Being a local man, that he went with the weapon is not in doubt. Further, that Van Der Byl was suffering from an advanced STD[2] which made him unable to walk at the same pace with other guerrillas is also known. There was no evidence to connect him to the murders of the survivors of the Viscount attack on 3/9/78 except his reputation for being ruthless. His remains have been taken to Magunje District Heroes acre. While he was not popular, the general area where he operated has been named after him. To ease your analysis, treat Sibanda as a trained guerrilla."[3]

I am satisfied that Van Der Byl, a comrade and not a commander, was shot by the SAS callsign. Had Watt conducted the correct procedures, SB would have been able to carry out the necessary investigations, identify the deceased and verify the facts. By not doing so, he blatantly disregarded the internal legal aspects of post-contact procedure.

(3) ***SAS deployed***

While conversing with the SAS in the bar, I mentioned that I had information worth deploying on. They were excited at the prospects and we arranged to meet at our "safe house" in the morning, as a pub was no place to discuss military intelligence. On page 41 of my diary on 22 November 1978 I wrote: "Day spent planning operations as outlined on page 42 and SAS reacting to this intelligence." The same day we decided to move out of the Twin Rivers Motel. There was too much suspicion among local patrons regarding our activities and, by law, Africans were not permitted into the motel as patrons. Furthermore, we kept suffering from diarrhoea. George found a vacant CONEX[4] house and asked one of his contacts if we could use it for a couple of days. This was agreed and another of his friends from the Posts and Telecommunications Corporation arranged for the installation of a telephone. The number was Karoi 372. A stir was caused when it was discovered we had moved into the property permanently. Our occupation problem was resolved by the inimitable Geoff Price and his hierarchy. The property became our "safe house".[5]

Watt, with some of his men, arrived at the "safe house" on the morning of 23 November 1978. Grey, Happy and I discussed all the information we had regarding China, commander of the Doro region and thought to be a member of the Zipra High Command in Hurungwe. In fact we later established that China was a detachment commander. We discussed the intelligence regarding the insurgents we had identified in China's section. I showed the SAS the sketches and maps of the eight-square-kilometre Doro target area, emphasising our certainty that the group was still resident in the region. I was convinced China and his group could be eliminated and made it clear that China was the target. Watt considered the intelligence accurate and worth deploying on. Stan recalled: "I don't recall who gave the briefing, but I specifically recall being told we were going after elements

---

[1] Garth Barrett email 5/2/2016.

[2] STD: Sexually transmitted disease.

[3] Confirmed by Dr J. Chakawa on 29/4/2016 during a field trip and research, and various WhatsApp discussions 29/4/2016 and email 19/8/2016.

[4] Conservation and Extension: A government department.

[5] Confirmed by George Hutchison during various Skype discussions July/August 2018.

of the ZIPRA High Command for the area."[1] I found this an interesting situation. The SAS team fell under the command and control of the local Sub.JOC at Sinoia. However, I was the Special Branch officer providing the intelligence and making all the necessary arrangements: I was in command of the deployment!

Subsequently, the plan was set. Bravo 70 would lead the callsign overnight through the white farmlands bordering Hurungwe to the target area, at approximately QM515516, a walk of some 15 kilometres. Our sketches would identify where ZIPRA members slept in the kraals, their usual morning rendezvous locations and their general operational area. I outlined the resources available to Watt which included the Fire Force based at Karoi Country Club. Their helicopters were positioned on the cricket field while the men stayed, conveniently, in the country club buildings. I suggested our planning and execution of the operation incorporate the Fire Force to give valuable air support. I was convinced this would assist in the complete elimination of China and his unit. Watt, by contrast, was confident of their ability to deal with the matter without air support. When on official deployments, the SAS had access to arms, ammunition and equipment of their choice. This was the first and only occasion I worked with the SAS throughout the war. I was eager to witness their effectiveness.

Once our planning was concluded, the FF were advised of the impending action and were provided with the locstats, as were the Sub.JOC at Sinoia, thereby ensuring no other forces were present in the area. This was standard procedure to prevent the SF from engaging each other. Such unfortunate occurrences were referred to as blue-on-blue. JOCs and Sub.JOCs were kept well informed of all Security Forces deployments within an area. This information was also passed on to the ground forces in order to prevent such incidents. One could not merely randomly wander in and around the operational area. Inevitably, however, there were casualties from blue-on-blue incidents but every precaution was taken to prevent them.

The SAS were cleared to deploy. I assured Bravo 70 that I would attend the scene the following morning. In addition, I assured him that we would care for his family by removing them from Hurungwe until our forces occupied his area. As the Special Branch representative, I was required to attend the scene in order to collect dead bodies, carry out investigations and immediate interrogations. There were no SFAs deployed in the field at this time as they were still finalising their training.

The SAS team deployed on the afternoon of Thursday, 23 November 1978. Of the original team, only Rich Stannard did not deploy for reasons I've mentioned. In view of the large area to be covered and the significance of the battle ahead, I was surprised Watt did not wish to include Walter in the deployment. Stan recalled: "We were given an old African male informer who led us into the contact area. Always wondered why he led us in and what happened to him, I did not think he had much chance of survival for informing on the ZIPRA section. During the walk in I remember walking up a dry riverbed behind a kraal with dogs barking – not excessively – and the moon playing through the trees."[2]

Bravo 70 led the SAS through the white farming area. They walked through the night, arriving in the target area before first light. The men positioned themselves on a nearby hill. Watt sent Scheepers forward to recce the kraals to establish whether ZIPRA were present. Scheepers spotted a weapon in a kraal hut, reported back to Watt which resulted in the team's assuming suitable ambush positions. Pomeroy made the comment: "We were deployed into ambush positions around some kraals and came across some *mujibhas*. Joe du Ploy told me to guard them and not allow them to escape as it would compromise the operation and they were needed for intelligence purposes. When the ambush was sprung,[3] I noticed that there was a terrorist in a kraal in front of me. I kept shouting, 'He's in here, he's in here' to our men trying to get their attention and then decided to throw a phosphorous grenade onto the roof. The grenade bounced off the roof onto a nearby kraal

[1] Telephone discussion with Stan 9/12/2017.

[2] Telephone discussion with Stan on 9/12/2017. During an oral discussion on 11/11/2017, Stan expressed his pleasure of knowing that Bravo 70 had survived the war and returned to his home.

[3] The ambush was compromised when a terrorist came out of a kraal to urinate.

roof, exploded and set it alight; I recognised the kraal from a picture shown to me by John Padbury. The terrorist ran out of the kraal followed by a burst of fire from our men – he escaped only to be shot by the other callsign some distance away."[1] Two insurgents were killed in the initial battle. Three civilians were also killed in the crossfire.[2] Stan recalled: "I was a stop group in the contact which was sprung at first light, but we were not involved in the shooting."[3]

The SAS carried two radio sets: one was a very high frequency (VHF) and the other was a high frequency (HF). VHF sets produce radio waves travelling in a straight line. At ground level the radio waves are obstructed by physical obstacles such as mountains, kopjes and forested areas, hence the radios are used mainly for short-range, line-of-sight (LOS) communications. While these instruments required relay stations in LOS to continue the message transmissions, they were perfect for communications with aircraft. They were ideal for the FF as they were in direct LOS. HF radios, however, produce waves which curve as they are subject to refraction or twisting by the ionosphere and are perfect for long-range communications.

After the battle, Watt instructed Slingsby, the radio operator, to arrange for the FF at Karoi to uplift them. Watt sat down to brew tea. As Slingsby set up the HF aerial, an insurgent opened fire on him with an RPD from a nearby hill. Pomeroy says of the incident: "When the contact was over, Slingsby was busy putting up the aerial for the radio when a terrorist opened up on him with an RPD from a nearby kopje. The bullets were spraying all around him and he knelt down almost trying to hide behind his radio. How he was not killed I will never know. He kept trying to give me distance and location of the terrorist but I could not see where he was positioned, every time I moved forward to see what was going on, the *mujibha* prisoners began to move away as if they might make a run for it, but I was at a loss as to where the shooting was coming from. I think it was Fred who made his way behind the terrorist who was so focused on trying to kill Slingsby that he did not see Fred. As I remember, Fred eliminated the terrorist. From memory I recall that we killed 2-3 terrorists. We rounded up some civilians for the Special Branch and I remember Du Plooy talking about keeping a particular African female whom he said had been sleeping with the terrorists. I got the impression that this was a settled resident group."[4] Fred confirmed that he shot the RPD gunner.[5]

The SAS leadership had overlooked our information that ZIPRA positioned some men to guard those in the kraals and took to high-ground rendezvous positions after contacts with the SF. In my view, this oversight could have proven fatal. Scheepers later noted how aggressive the insurgents were that the SAS had encountered. He considered it dangerous operating in an area liberated by ZIPRA which was teeming with insurgents and *mujibhas*.[6] That could well have been the case, but it needs to be borne in mind that SB and GC units travelled and patrolled throughout the Hurungwe daily in one or two mine-proofed Land Rovers: two men in each vehicle armed solely with FNs! There was little or no back-up.

Miraculously Slingsby survived, regained his composure, set up the radio and contacted SAS HQ in Salisbury, giving them a situation report (sitrep) and locstat. He then called for the SB representative to attend the scene and requested uplift by the FF. SAS HQ relayed their request to the FF at Karoi. The SAS gathered the bodies and weapons, and awaited their arrival.[7]

During this period, while at Karoi, I was advised that the SAS had successfully killed three insurgents and requested that I attend the scene. This was standard procedure as it gave SB the opportunity to search the bodies for documents and evidence in attempting to identify them and gather intelligence relating to their operations. The weapons would be sent for ballistics examination and the locals spoken to in order to gather additional information. Locals suspected of involvement would be taken back to base for further debriefing. I collected Happy and drove to the FF at the

1 Eugene Pomeroy email 15/11/2017.
2 Confirmed by Dr J. Chakawa oral interviews and research 15/4/2016.
3 Telephone discussion 9/12/2017.
4 Eugene Pomeroy email 15/11/2017.
5 WhatsApp discussion November 2017.
6 Wessels, H. (2018), p. 83.
7 Karoi Contacts Map Incident 16.

Karoi Country Club where two G-Cars had been allocated for the uplift. The G-Cars' crews were Flt. Lt. Mike Gardner[1] with technician/gunner, Sgt. Phil Archenoul, and Flt. Lt. Kerry Fynn[2] with technician/gunner, Sgt. Robin Buckle.

(4) *Rhodesian Air Force uplift*

Flt. Lt. Mike Gardner recalled the incident:

> On Wednesday 22 November 1978, I was deployed to Karoi with my Tech/Gunner Sergeant Phil Archenoul[3] where we based at the Karoi Country Club. The cricket field was where we positioned our aircraft for take-off and landing. As I recall we slept in the buildings at the Club; generally, we slept in this type of accommodation or tents which was cost effective.[4] One of our "watering holes" was the pub at Twin Rivers Motel.
>
> On the morning of Friday, 24 November 1978, we were called by the SAS callsign who had made contact with a terrorist group and required the bodies and themselves uplifted and returned to Karoi. I remember the incident well as this was my first tour of duty and it was the first time that I would be working with the SAS. The contact area was approximately 36 kilometres (as the crow flies) North West of Karoi. We located the SAS callsign and landed. I was required to uplift five men which was unusual as we usually worked with 4 man callsigns in the Fire Force; the accepted "lift" capacity for our G-Cars was six men, made up of one pilot, one technician/ gunner and a four man callsign. For me this was a significant issue and the second reason why I recall the incident well. I do not recall if all the men were members of the SAS, but I do recall that there were five men who required to be uplifted. After a discussion, I wanted to leave one of the SAS men behind as this was one of my first operations and I did not want to go against laid down procedures and regulations. I recall the SAS soldier who would have had to remain behind was Joe du Ploy; he is the only person I remember in the callsign as generally the men were just faces that "jumped" into the helicopters, were moved to their destination, and disembarked. However, I looked at Joe and felt that I could not leave him behind so told him to "climb aboard"; with some difficulty I managed to take off and return to Karoi. The G-Car flown by, I believe Kerry Fynn, carried the terrorist bodies and weapons back to Karoi; I do not recall how many terrorists' bodies or weapons there were.[5]

Phil Archenoul recalled the SAS uplift: "The nearby club cottage was occupied by a lady, who it coincidentally turned out, I had a connection with. On questioning her about an SAS stable belt and beret on the mantelpiece above her fireplace, she told me that it had belonged to her son, Lance Corporal Steve Donnelly of C Squadron SAS. Ironically, I had brought his body home from an external raid in Mozambique called Op. Snoopy,[6] (a sort of Viscount retaliation raid), a month earlier on 21 September 1978, with my pilot Alistair Thorogood. It was one of the more touching moments that has stayed with me to this day. On the morning of Friday, 24 November 1978, as normal procedure, at first light I carried out the usual preflight inspection on our helicopter ensuring it was

[1] Mike Gardner: Achieved his "wings" at Thornhill on 29/6/1978. He moved to 7 Squadron where Dave Rowe was the course instructor. Initial training for conversion from fixed-winged aircraft to helicopters lasted, on average, 110 hours. Thereafter, a final handling test (FHT) was spread over a period of approximately 20 hours and was performed in the operational areas under the supervision of the senior instructor. Gardner's last flight with Rowe was on 13/1/1978. His FHT was on 14/11/1978 with Sqn. Ldr. E. Lunt. He was then deployed to FAF 5 at Mtoko on 15/11/1978 and then on to FAF 8 at Grand Reef until 22/11/1978 when he was relocated to Karoi until 28/11/1978.

[2] Flt. Lt. Kerry John Fynn, a pilot with 7 Sqn. Rh.AF., KIA on 3/1/1979.

[3] Sgt. Phil Archenoul: Helicopter technician/gunner with 7 Sqn. Rh.AF. qualified on the Alouette 2 and Alouette 3 helicopters at the end of February 1978.

[4] Confirmed by Phil Archenoul flight log book and email 17/6/2015.

[5] Mike Gardner various emails, including one on 8/1/2018.

[6] SAS Trooper Stephen Michael Donnelly was accidentally killed by a golf bomb while on Operation Snoopy, an external raid into Mozambique 19/9/1978-24/9/1978; Geldenhuys, P. (2007), p 226, Air Strike Log Entry 868.

ready for the day's action. We were called by an SAS callsign that had had a successful contact with a terrorist group and required the resulting dead bodies and themselves to be uplifted and returned to Karoi. Two G-Cars were allocated for the uplift, I recall Rob Buckle was the Tech/gunner in the second chopper, I am not sure who the Pilot was. We flew directly to the SAS callsign and landed. I recall there were five men to uplift which created quite a problem for Mike Gardner; this was one of Mike's first tours of duty and he was careful to ensure he followed procedures and regulations. Initially, Mike thought to leave one of the SAS men behind, we did not usually get the names of the troops unless we knew them personally. However, after a discussion between us, we broke protocol and Mike decided to take the fifth passenger and was able to lift-off and ferry them all back to Karoi safely. Rob Buckle's G-Car carried the terrorist bodies and weapons back to Karoi; my thoughts are that there were three bodies. When I wrote up my logbook, which was required standard procedure, I recorded the name of the Pilot, Mike Gardner, the type of trooping duty and the number of men we lifted out of the contact area as five, as this was quite a memorable day, particularly for Mike."[1]

Sgt. Robin Buckle confirmed: "On 24 November 1978 I was based at the Karoi Country Club, my pilot was Flt. Lt. Kerry Fynn. We were called to uplift a SAS callsign who had killed three or four terrorists – I do not recall the exact number. Two G-Cars were allocated for the uplift; I recall Flt. Lt. Mike Gardner was the pilot of the other chopper and Phil Archenoul was his Tech/gunner. Mike is a personal friend of mine and we have often reminisced about this particular incident through the years as this was both Mike's and Kerry's first operational tour; they had trained together. We flew directly to the SAS callsign and were supposed to uplift the SAS men, but Mike dropped in ahead of us and collected them; we collected the three or four dead terrorists. During one of the trips we uplifted some civilians and carried them to Karoi."[2]

(5) ***Special Branch to the contact area***

It was exhilarating flying into a scene knowing that we had provided excellent, accurate intelligence. I had high expectations that China had been killed, which was our aim. The descent to the scene was difficult as there was no clearly demarcated landing zone for the pilot. He was forced to manoeuvre the helicopter vertically in order to avoid the numerous trees in the area. This would complicate take-off with a fully loaded helicopter as there was no place to gain forward momentum to assist with the lift-off. Mark McLean explained: "Helicopters derive lift not only from the rotation of the blades. Bonus lift comes when in a stationary hover from a 'ground cushion', and also from horizontal speed, 'translational lift'. But these bonuses cannot exist at the same time. Start moving and the helicopter 'falls off' the ground cushion before the translational lift bites in. At maximum take-off power the engine cannot produce any more power and if the helicopter is heavily loaded and unable to climb vertically the pilot must utilise his bonus lift to get going. Pilots need horizontal space to transition from the hover and gain enough speed so that the total lift from rotor thrust and increasing translational lift can drag the airframe into a climb which will clear the tree line."[3]

The pilot landed the helicopter close to the SAS men and the three dead insurgents. We discussed the contact and I took custody of the weapons: two AK-47s and one RPD, and the three bodies. I searched the bodies for documents and some type of useful evidence but found none. No documents were handed to me by any of the SAS soldiers. I found no evidence linking the deceased ZIPRA to the Strela section. No Strela launcher or missiles were recovered. Happy and I set about our tasks. We carried out a search of the kraals and general area and talked to the remaining locals from the kraal. It is important to remember that intelligence was freely and accurately given by the informant and his family. We established that there were eight ZIPRA insurgents in the kraal complex at the time of the contact. The SAS had killed three lower-ranking cadre, identified as Sam, Davie and Vhera. China, positioned between the contact kraal and Nyamupfukudza Hill, made good his escape with the remainder of his men. Joshua Chakawa confirmed that three civilians were killed in the action:

1 Phil Archenoul email 17/6/2015.
2 Sgt. Robin Buckle email 18/7/2015.
3 Mark McLean email 13/12/2020.

Chimheno Thomas, his wife and his sister, Theresa Kashiri. In time the bodies, recovered weapons, Bravo 70 and his immediate family were uplifted back to Karoi as I had promised. Flt. Lt. Gardner flew five members of the SAS callsign and Happy and I returned in the other chopper. As far as I recall, the remaining two SAS soldiers were with us. On arrival at Karoi, I organised for the refugees to be conveyed to the farm while I took custody of the bodies. I arranged the usual ballistics reports for the weapons and the sitrep to Sub.JOC Sinoia which were our normal procedures. As I mentioned previously, the SAS had clear command and control procedures. They were attached under the command of the Sub.JOC and, in this instance, Special Branch, namely me, was responsible for the deployment. The SAS were tasked to carry out a specific mission which was the limit of their responsibility. Thereafter, SB were responsible for the reporting procedures and intelligence follow-ups. This was not the responsibility or the role of the SAS.

Happy and I were later joined by Grey and together we carried out further investigations regarding the three deceased insurgents. However, we gleaned no worthwhile intelligence. I informed Geoff Price of the results of the contact, ensuring he would be the first to announce the success of the operation, giving him a political advantage. Likewise, he kept me informed of all events appertaining to our work, thus maintaining a friendly relationship. Grey and Happy were elated with our progress and informed Bishop Muzorewa, keeping him abreast of recent events. On the same day on page 43 of my diary, I noted: "As a result of deployment of SAS to intelligence as outlined on page 42, SAS made contact with 8 terrs and killed 3 terrs — 2 AKs and 1 RPD recovered. Map ref 515516."

Grey and Happy took the opportunity to update me with intelligence they had received the previous night. Flushed with success, we felt it was time to plan our next significant operation in Hurungwe. Their informant was in touch with a group of 20 ZIPRA, commanded by Philip Ncube. They had taken up residence in the Birimahwe Hill area, close by St Boniface's Mission and Katenhe School. I admired Happy's ability to focus on the SAS mission and then, when the time was right, deal with a fresh supply of intelligence. Our informant had a letter from the ZIPRA commander and the sum of R$8 to buy supplies and return to the group in the company of another contact man, name withheld, by Wednesday, 29 November 1978. We sent the informant on his way assuring him we would react to his information, guard his identity and protect him in future deployments. We made the crucial decision to deploy our forces on this information and immediately began working on strategy and timing. I asked Sub.JOC Sinoia to proscribe the area for us. The plan was set and timing was important.

During the remainder of the day, we displayed the three corpses from the SAS contact at Chabwino. Grey and Happy used the opportunity to motivate and politicise the men whose morale had rocketed. I organised a *braaivleis* (barbeque) and beers for the men. The frivolities, singing and laughter progressed well into the night. We took delight in teasing Cecil, one of the trainees who spoke with a lisp, requesting he recite: "See Cecil swing on the see-saw" and suchlike difficult pronouncing sentences for him to articulate. Needless to say, his whispery pronunciations added to the merriment as the evening rolled on. Despite the euphoria and festivities, the men were keen to enter the battle and were looking forward to deploy into Hurungwe and engage with ZIPRA. I told them that their deployment was not too far off and instructed the training staff to prepare the men for battle.

This SAS deployment demonstrated the reliability of our UANC office's intelligence-gathering mechanism. It also provided Grey and Happy the opportunity to employ my method of presenting thorough, detailed intelligence. This allowed the SF favourable circumstances to conduct operations with precision. However, it concerned me that the major targets (China, Tall Man and the bulk of his section) had managed to escape. Notwithstanding, I consoled myself that, even though the SAS had failed to eliminate China and the command element of his section, we had provided accurate and trustworthy intelligence.

In order to corroborate the SAS contact, I asked Dr Chakawa to visit the scene of the battle. He travelled to the Doro region on 15 April 2016. He was not told of the involvement of the SAS prior to his departure but was merely given the details of some locals to assist him in locating the battle site. No details of the contact, or of the ZIPRA section involved, were provided, neither were details of the number of ZIPRA and civilians killed. The evidence found by Dr Chakawa has been included in footnotes and this additional information was established from his research and visit to the battle site: "The *mujibha*, Bhinya, was, at the time of writing, still alive and assisted with my research. Two helicopters were confirmed to have landed at the battle area. ZIPRA guerrillas still remembered are China, resident detachment commander of the general area and is still alive; Napoleon, his deputy; and cadres Godfrey, Tarirai, Sam, Desire, Susuman, Vhera, Davie, Double Chess, White. China and White returned to the area after the war. The battle occurred around 4 a.m. November 1978. Chimheno Thomas, his wife and sister Theresa Kashiri were killed in the battle. The ZIPRA men killed were Sam, Davie and Vhera. Bravo 70 brought the soldiers to attack. He ran away from the area as ZIPRA wanted to kill him. Most ZIPRA were not directly in the huts attacked or in the nearby hill where they used to hide, but were in the general area. China was between the contact home and the hill when the attack occurred and escaped with the rest of his men. Edson Chimheno's huts were burnt during the battle. ZIPRA used to camp at the nearby hill. Home attacked had men and girls in it. One day, China and one other guerrilla almost shot each other over a girl. Chimheno had a son Francis who was a soldier. ZIPRA did not kill him for that. Mentioned was a female *mujibha* called Giredhesi. Kunze her brother was in the army. He died during the war."

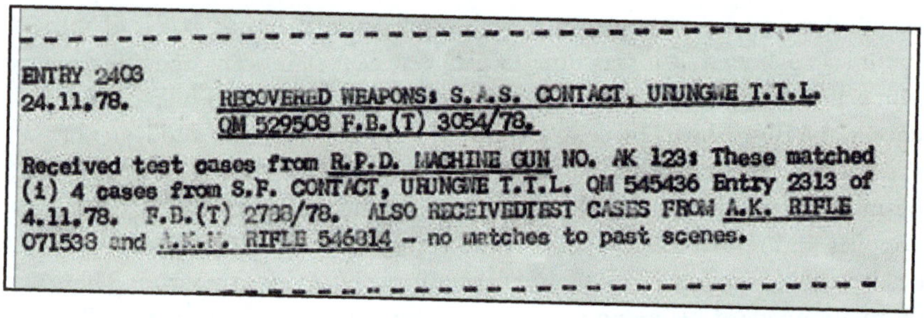

ENTRY 2403
24.11.78. RECOVERED WEAPONS: S.A.S. CONTACT, URUNGWE T.T.L.
QM 529508 F.B.(T) 3054/78.

Received test cases from R.P.D. MACHINE GUN NO. AK 123: These matched (i) 4 cases from S.F. CONTACT, URUNGWE T.T.L. QM 545436 Entry 2313 of 4.11.78. F.B.(T) 2798/78. ALSO RECEIVEDTEST CASES FROM A.K. RIFLE 071538 and A.K.M. RIFLE 546814 - no matches to past scenes.

SAS contact ballistics report.

Air Lt. Mike Gardner and the author discuss the SAS uplift.

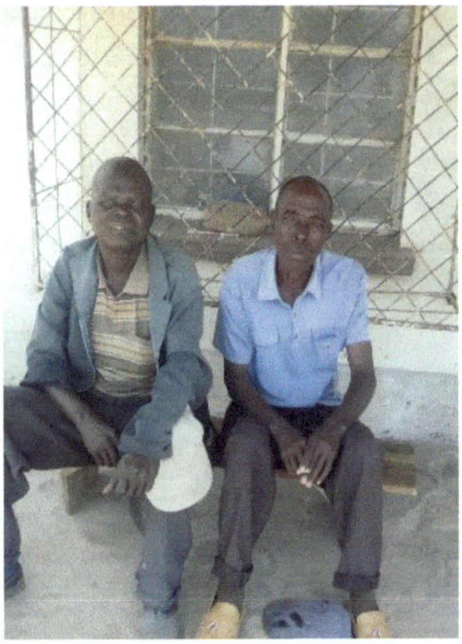

Two former ZIPRA *mujibhas*.

№ 41

4. [redacted] 3 days ago Headman Mapepas' [illegible] learned [illegible], and sent back home to find out what is going on. Should be many boys ready for training & recruiting going to commence.

22/11/78

Day spent planning operations as outlined on page 54 and SAS reacting to this intelligence.

Intelligence gathered that [redacted] lovers and local SB agent name. To be interrogated by me on the 23/11/78.

23/11/78.

The Motel is no longer suitable for meeting as we have all got the 'shits' from the food. There is too much suspicion surrounding our movements and an alternative place/house is to be found.

27/11/78

Cover house located and we have moved into it (phone 37?). Intelligence from Grey & Happy has advised that [redacted] were killed by [illegible] on the 2/11/78. It appears that they were not compromised by the operation as outlined on page 57 but were fingered by WILSON [redacted] who resides at [redacted] family [redacted] line near the Mapepa's store opposite the [redacted] Terrs are obviously back in this area now.

We have decided to re-settle refugees from the TTL on the vacant European farming lands surrounding our farm at Chabwino. This will serve the following purpose:-

1) The refugee problem in an already deteriorating situation in Salisbury.

2) Our farm will be surrounded by our own people and our immediate intelligence & security will be catered for.

3) The people will farm on a social commune system which will maintain their dependence and loyalty to us.

Original diary entry noting that the SAS was reacting to our intelligence.

Author with two elderly refugees at Chabwino farm. Refugee on left was 100 years old at the time.

SAS CONTACT
ORIGINAL SKETCH

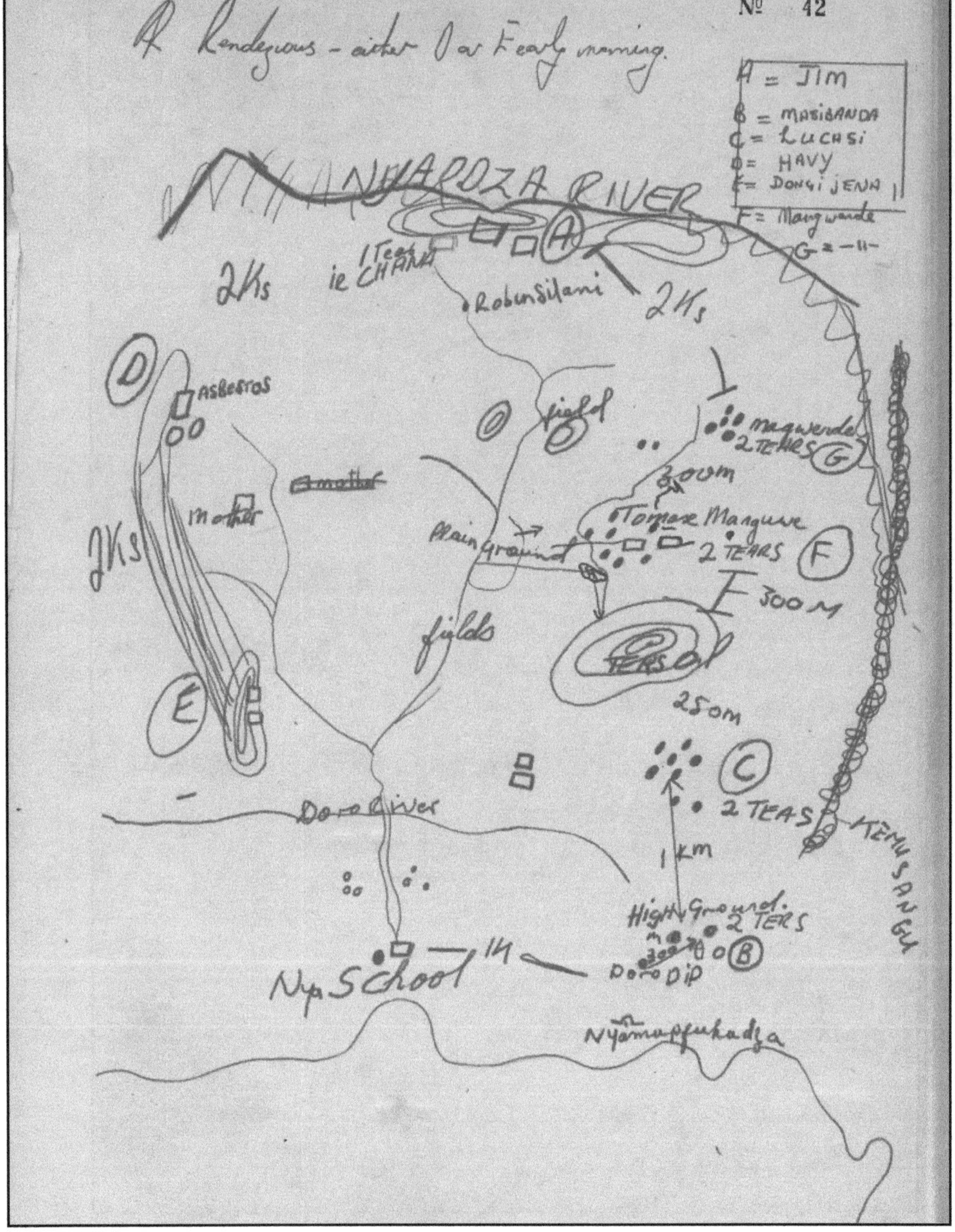

Key

Persons

A	Jim's Kraal (1 resident terr ie China)
B	Masibanda's Kraal (2 resident terrs)
C	Lucas's Kraal (2 resident terrs)
D	Harvey's Kraal
E	Dhongijena's Kraal
F	Manguwe's Kraal (2 resident terrs)
G	Mangwende's Kraal (2 resident terrs)
H	Terrs observation post (OP)
I	Nyamupfukdza School
D & E	Terrs early moring rendevous locations

Key

Distances

A - B = 4 kms
D - G = 2kms
A - D = 2 kms
A - G = 2 kms
G - F = 300 m
F - H = 300 m
C - H = 250 m
C - B = 1 km
B - I = 1 km
D - E = 2 km

Areas of ZIPRA residency = $8km^2$

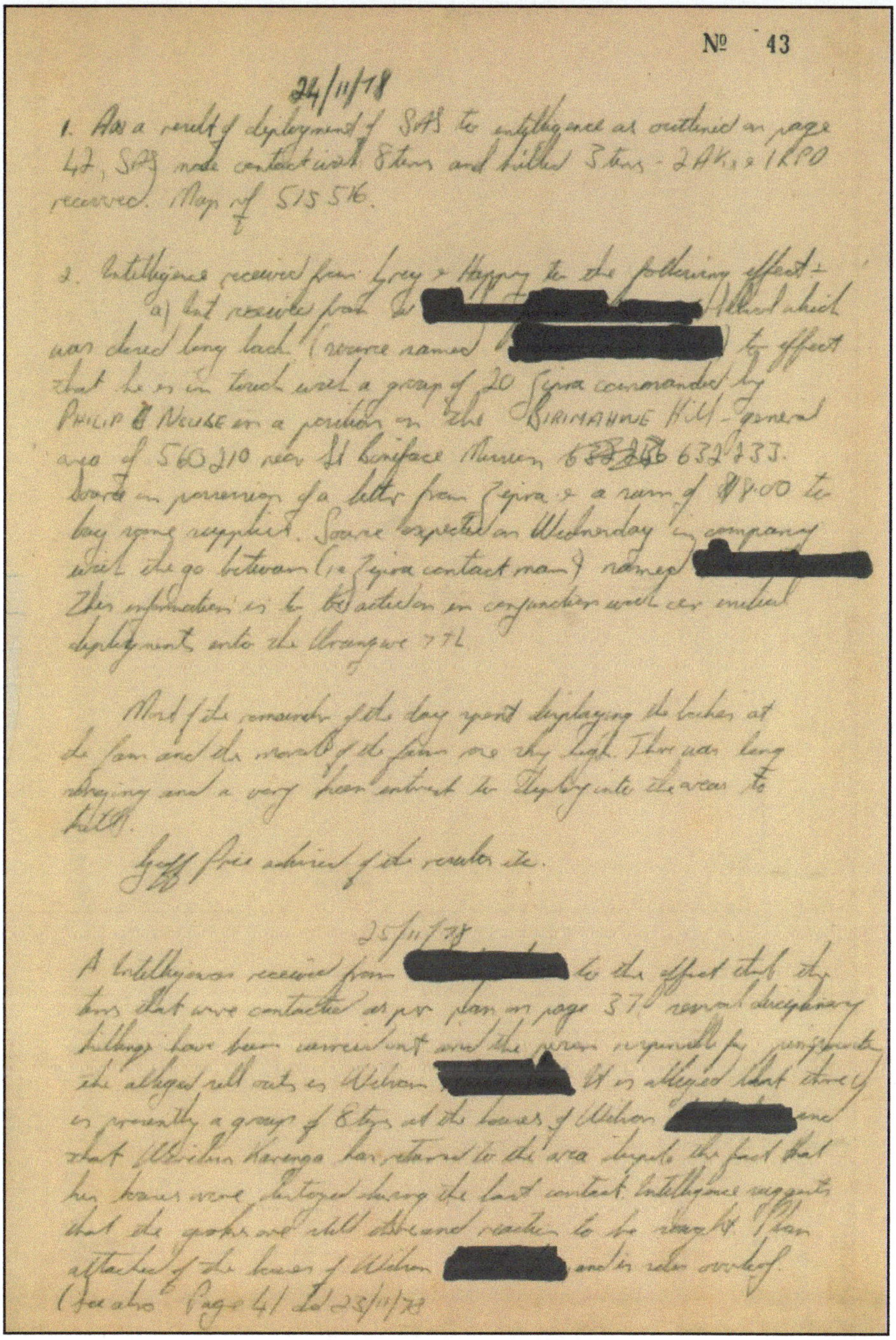
№ 43

24/11/78

1. As a result of deployment of SAS to intelligence as outlined on page 42, SAS made contact with 8 ters and killed 3 ters - 2 AKs & 1 RPD recovered. Map ref 515516.

2. Intelligence received from Grey & Happy to the following effect:-

a) that received from [redacted] which was closed long back (source named [redacted]) to effect that he is in touch with a group of 20 Zipra commanded by PHILIP & NCUBE on a position in the SIRINAHWE Hill - general area of 560210 near St Boniface Mission ~~633236~~ 632233. Source in possession of a letter from Zipra & a sum of $8.00 to buy some supplies. Source expected on Wednesday in company with the go between (i.e. Zipra contact man) named [redacted]. This information is to be actioned in conjunction with our initial deployments onto the Urungwe TTL.

Most of the remainder of the day spent deploying the bushes at the farm and the rounds of the farm one day high. There was long [illegible] and a very keen interest to deploy into the areas to kill.

Geoff Price advised of the results etc.

25/11/78

A Intelligence received from [redacted] to the effect that the ters that were contacted as per plan on page 37 several disciplinary killings have been carried out and the person responsible for [illegible] the alleged sell outs is Wilson [redacted]. It is alleged that there is presently a group of 8 ters at the kraals of Wilson [redacted] and that Wilson Kavenga has returned to the area despite the fact that his kraals were destroyed during the last contact. Intelligence suggests that the group are still there and ready to be [illegible]. Plan attached of the kraals of Wilson [redacted] and is also overleaf. (See also Page 41 dd 23/11/78)

Diary entry announcing the result of the SAS contact.

Southern side of the ZIPRA OP and base near to the SAS contact.

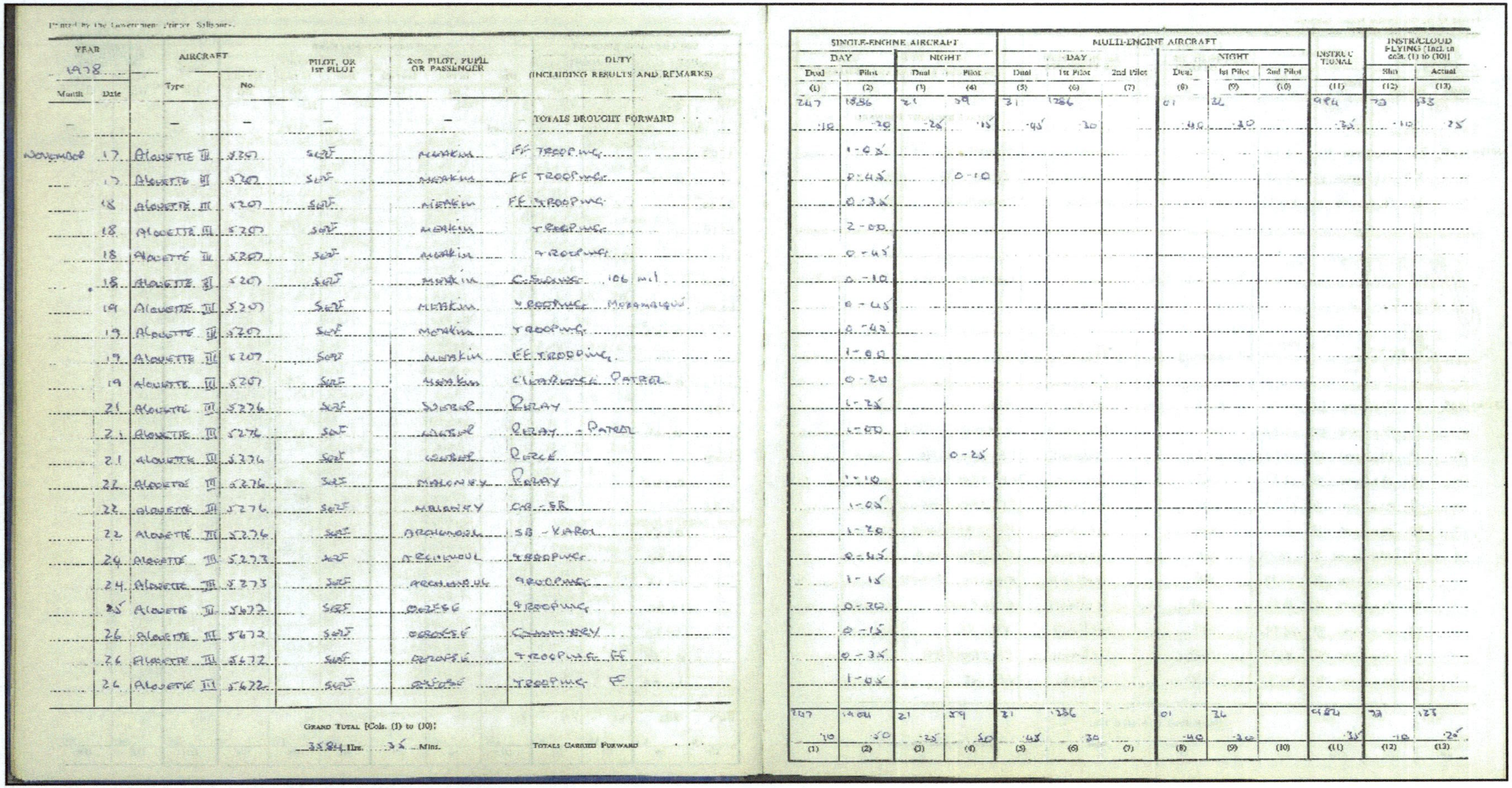

Printed by the Government Printer, Salisbury.

YEAR 1978 Month	Date	AIRCRAFT Type	No.	PILOT, OR 1st PILOT	2nd PILOT, PUPIL OR PASSENGER	DUTY (INCLUDING RESULTS AND REMARKS)
—	—	—	—	—	—	TOTALS BROUGHT FORWARD
November	17	Alouette III	5207	Self	Meakin	FF Trooping
	17	Alouette III	5207	Self	Meakin	FF Trooping
	18	Alouette III	5207	Self	Meakin	FF Trooping
	18	Alouette III	5207	Self	Meakin	Trooping
	18	Alouette III	5207	Self	Meakin	Trooping
	18	Alouette III	5207	Self	Meakin	C. Sloane 106 mil
	19	Alouette III	5207	Self	Meakin	Trooping Mozambique
	19	Alouette III	5207	Self	Meakin	Trooping
	19	Alouette III	5207	Self	Meakin	FF Trooping
	19	Alouette III	5207	Self	Meakin	Clearance Patrol
	21	Alouette III	5276	Self	[illegible]	Relay
	21	Alouette III	5276	Self	[illegible]	Relay - Patrol
	21	Alouette III	5276	Self	[illegible]	Recce
	22	Alouette III	5276	Self	Maloney	Relay
	22	Alouette III	5276	Self	Maloney	CAS - SR
	22	Alouette III	5276	Self	Archenoul	SB - Kiarol
	24	Alouette III	5273	Self	[illegible]	Trooping
	24	Alouette III	5273	Self	Archenoul	Trooping
	25	Alouette III	5672	Self	[illegible]	Trooping
	26	Alouette III	5672	Self	[illegible]	[illegible]
	26	Alouette III	5672	Self	[illegible]	Trooping FF
	26	Alouette III	5672	Self	[illegible]	Trooping FF

GRAND TOTAL [Cols. (1) to (10)]: 3584 Hrs. 35 Mins. TOTALS CARRIED FORWARD

	SINGLE-ENGINE AIRCRAFT DAY Dual (1)	Pilot (2)	NIGHT Dual (3)	Pilot (4)	MULTI-ENGINE AIRCRAFT DAY Dual (5)	1st Pilot (6)	2nd Pilot (7)	NIGHT Dual (8)	1st Pilot (9)	2nd Pilot (10)	INSTRUCTIONAL (11)	INSTR/CLOUD FLYING [Incl. in cols. (1) to (10)] Sim (12)	Actual (13)
Totals brought forward	247 .10	1886 .20	21 .25	59 .15	31 .45	1286 .30		01 .40	32 .20		484 .35	73 .10	133 .25
17		1-05											
17		0-45		0-10									
18		0-35											
18		2-00											
18		0-45											
18		0-10											
19		0-45											
19		0-45											
19		1-00											
19		0-20											
21		1-35											
21		1-00											
21				0-25									
22		1-10											
22		1-05											
22		1-20											
24		0-45											
24		1-15											
25		0-30											
26		0-15											
26		0-35											
26		1-05											
Totals carried forward	247 .10	1904 .50	21 .25	59 .50	31 .45	1286 .30		01 .40	32 .20		484 .35	73 .10	133 .25

Mike Gardner’s log book showing the SAS contact uplift, 24/11/1978.

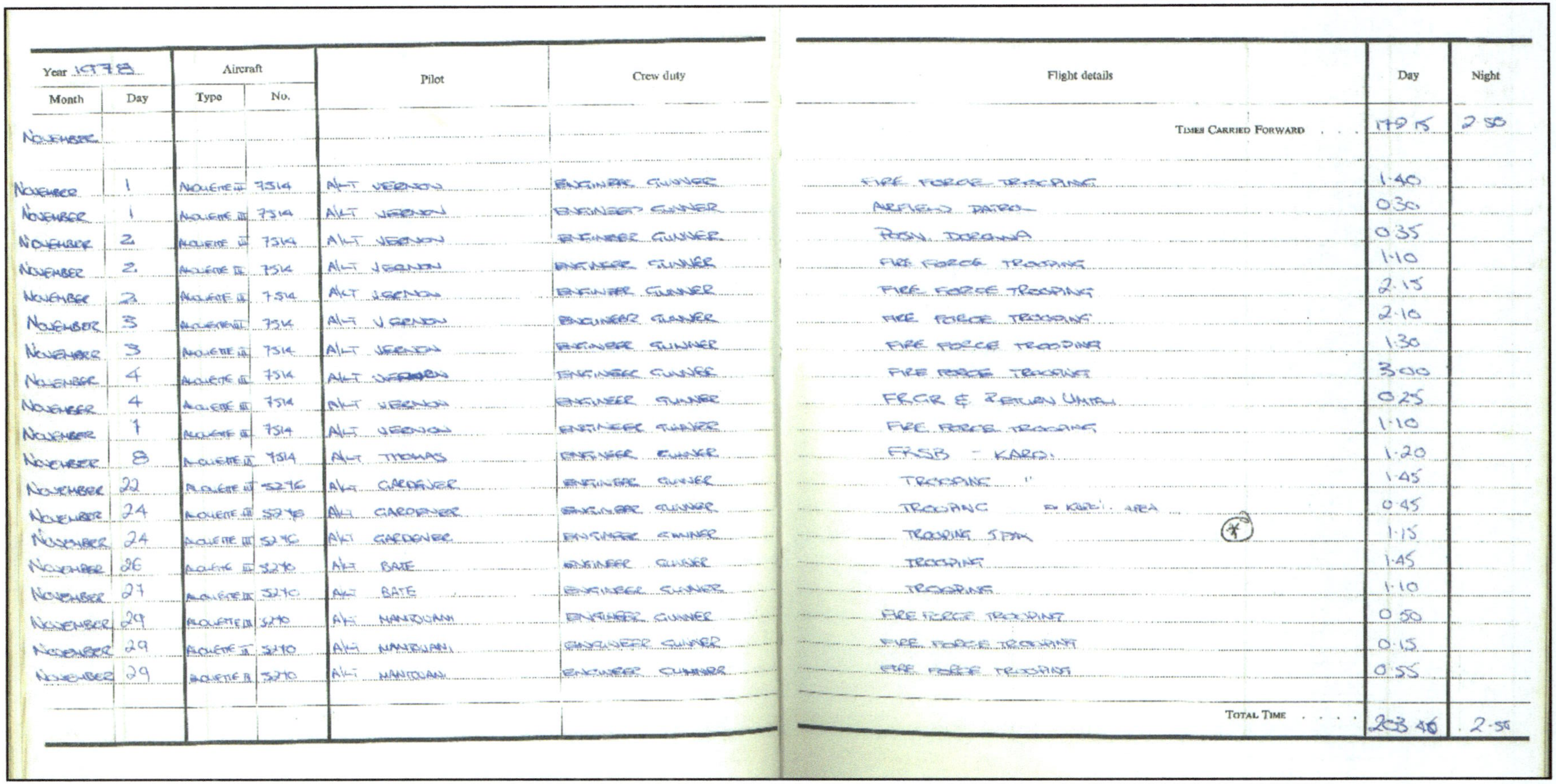

Year 1978 Month	Day	Aircraft Type	No.	Pilot	Crew duty	Flight details	Day	Night
NOVEMBER						TIMES CARRIED FORWARD . . .	179 15	2 50
NOVEMBER	1	ALOUETTE III	7514	A/LT VERNON	ENGINEER GUNNER	FIRE FORCE TROOPING	1.40	
NOVEMBER	1	ALOUETTE III	7514	A/LT VERNON	ENGINEER GUNNER	AIRFIELD PATROL	0.30	
NOVEMBER	2	ALOUETTE III	7514	A/LT VERNON	ENGINEER GUNNER	POSN. DORAWA	0.35	
NOVEMBER	2	ALOUETTE III	7514	A/LT VERNON	ENGINEER GUNNER	FIRE FORCE TROOPING	1.10	
NOVEMBER	2	ALOUETTE III	7514	A/LT VERNON	ENGINEER GUNNER	FIRE FORCE TROOPING	2.15	
NOVEMBER	3	ALOUETTE III	7514	A/LT V. VERNON	ENGINEER GUNNER	FIRE FORCE TROOPING	2.10	
NOVEMBER	3	ALOUETTE III	7514	A/LT VERNON	ENGINEER GUNNER	FIRE FORCE TROOPING	1.30	
NOVEMBER	4	ALOUETTE III	7514	A/LT VERNON	ENGINEER GUNNER	FIRE FORCE TROOPING	3.00	
NOVEMBER	4	ALOUETTE III	7514	A/LT VERNON	ENGINEER GUNNER	FRCR & RETURN UMTALI	0.25	
NOVEMBER	7	ALOUETTE III	7514	A/LT VERNON	ENGINEER GUNNER	FIRE FORCE TROOPING	1.10	
NOVEMBER	8	ALOUETTE III	7514	A/LT THOMAS	ENGINEER GUNNER	FRSB - KAROI	1.20	
NOVEMBER	22	ALOUETTE III	5276	A/LT GARDENER	ENGINEER GUNNER	TROOPING "	1.45	
NOVEMBER	24	ALOUETTE III	5276	A/LT GARDENER	ENGINEER GUNNER	TROOPING KAROI AREA	0.45	
NOVEMBER	24	ALOUETTE III	5276	A/LT GARDENER	ENGINEER GUNNER	TROOPING 5 PAX (*)	1.15	
NOVEMBER	26	ALOUETTE III	5270	A/LT BATE	ENGINEER GUNNER	TROOPING	1.45	
NOVEMBER	27	ALOUETTE III	5270	A/LT BATE	ENGINEER GUNNER	TROOPING	1.10	
NOVEMBER	29	ALOUETTE III	5270	A/LT MANJOUAN	ENGINEER GUNNER	FIRE FORCE TROOPING	0.50	
NOVEMBER	29	ALOUETTE III	5270	A/LT MANJOUAN	ENGINEER GUNNER	FIRE FORCE TROOPING	0.15	
NOVEMBER	29	ALOUETTE III	5270	A/LT MANJOUAN	ENGINEER GUNNER	FIRE FORCE TROOPING	0.55	
						TOTAL TIME	203 40	2.50

Sgt. Phil Archenoul's log book and flying log sheet showing the SAS contact uplift, 24/11/1978. Note: 5 pax confirming the uplift of five SAS soldiers. Photo by Phil Archenoul.

1A

NO 8 SQUADRON
RHODESIAN AIR FORCE
PERSONAL FLYING LOG SHEET

DATE: ____________

	AIRCRAFT					DAY		NIGHT		INSTRUMENT	
DATE	TYPE	NO	CAPT	CREW/PAX	DUTY	DUAL	SOLO	DUAL	SOLO	SIM	ACT
8.11.78		7514	THOMAS		TROOPING UMALI AREA	5.25					
27.11.78		5270	BATE		TROOPING - KAROI AREA	1.00					
22.11.78		5276	GARDNER		FRSB - KAROI, ROUTINGS.	1.20					
24.11.78		5273	"		TROOPING KAROI "	.45					
(*) —		—	"		" 5 PAX	(*) 1.15		(*)			
29/11/78		5270	MANTOVANI		TROOPING KAROI	80					
"		"	"		"	15					
"		"	"		" CASEVAC	55					
"		"	"		"	55					
30.11.78		"			"	1.00					
"					"	45					
"					"	35					
1.12.78					"	55					
"					"	20					
"					TROOPING CASEVAC	25					
"					+ TROOPING	30					
"					CASEVAC	20					
"					TROOPING	1.00					
"					"	15					
2.12.78		"	"		"	55					
"		"	"		"	1.05					
"		"	"		"	15					
"		"	"		"	15					

Kraal destroyed during the SAS contact, it was not repaired.

Grave for Chimheno Thomas and his wife killed in the SAS contact.

(6) *Did the SAS eliminate the ZIPRA Strela Section?*

The outcome of the SAS contact needs to be clarified, as much controversy surrounds the subject. The question that needs answering is whether the SAS eliminated five members of the Strela gang who shot down Viscount *Hunyani* or, for that matter, any Viscount. In summary, I reiterate that the primary task of eliminating China and Tall Man was not achieved, as they were not killed in the contact. China was a resident ZIPRA detachment commander operating in the Doro region of Hurungwe. I was continually mindful of the Viscount disaster and keen to eliminate the group responsible for the aircraft's destruction, and the subsequent loss of life. However, in this SAS contact, there was no evidence linking China's section with the Viscount *Hunyani* massacre of 3 September 1978. No documentation, weaponry or evidence of any nature was found to associate them with the incident. Certainly, the captured weapons did not connect ballistically to the murders. In addition, there was no diary or documentation relating them to the Strela section that attacked Viscount *Hunyani*. No Strela launchers or missiles were recovered. The ballistics report linked the RPD to a contact with the SF on 4 November 1978 at Murodza Kraal, nearby what we subsequently learned was the operational area for a ZIPRA section close to the Maumbe BC. The ballistics report also identified the SAS contact locstat as QM529508. There were no further SAS deployments into Hurungwe while I was in command of the SFAs.

Mike Gardner commented: "I do not recall being told the terrorist group that the SAS contacted was related to the Strela group that shot down the first Air Rhodesia Viscount, *Hunyani*, on Sunday the 3 September 1978. I feel that had that been the case and this information was made common knowledge, there would have been quite a celebration and the news would have been broadcast across the nation."[1]

John Redfern, Director of Military Intelligence (1976-1980), commented: "I do not recall ever seeing any report, or hearing that the ZIPRA Strela section responsible for the two Viscount tragedies had been contacted or eliminated. Certainly it was not mentioned at Comops, nor at intelligence meetings in CIO. Had it been announced, I'm sure I would have remembered such a significant report. In view of public concern after the shooting down of the two Air Rhodesia

[1] Confirmed by Phil Archenoul email 17/6/2015; Robin Buckle; Eugene Pomeroy email 15/11/2017; Fred WhatsApp discussion 29/11/2017; Stan oral discussions 11/11/17 and 9/12/17, and various discussions with Mike Reeler and Phil Wright.

Viscounts, and the desire for retribution, had the ZIPRA Strela section been eliminated, I believe the authorities would have been eager to announce their elimination to boost the morale of the white population and possibly demoralise ZAPU/ZIPRA. I have mentioned this to the author of *Viscount Down*, Keith Nell."[1] The Military Intelligence Directorate was: "Primarily responsible for strategic military intelligence and counter-intelligence. We received and processed information from a number of sources, including intercepted military radio communications, aerial photography and reconnaissance, situation and contact reports from military units such as the SAS, Selous Scouts, Rhodesian Intelligence Corps (RIC), liaison with other military forces and Special Branch. Meetings were held in the Director General's office at the start of most work days, and lasted about 30 minutes. Heads of branches 1 (Special Branch), 2 (CIO External) and 3 (Military Intelligence) generally attended, as well as the Deputy Director General of CIO. Intelligence reports based mainly on radio intercepts (COMINT) were sent to Comops, Army and Air Force HQ and specialist units (SAS and Selous Scouts) on a daily basis, or more frequently if considered an operational priority. As I recall, periodic military intelligence reports (INTREPS) were distributed to Director General CIO, Commander Comops, Commanders of the Army and Air Force; laterally to OC Special Branch (Branch 1 of CIO) and Director Air Intelligence; internally to brigade commanders, and COs of SAS, Selous Scouts, and RIC. Comops would re-distribute INTREPS to JOC commanders. The shooting down of the two Viscounts on the 3rd September 1978 and 12th February 1979 were significant landmarks in the war. Our intelligence confirmed that the two Viscounts had been shot down by ZIPRA terrorists using a Soviet-made Strela 2 surface-to-air infra red missile."[2]

Rich Stannard recalled: "On my return from the SAS selection course I met up with Watt. I was jealous because he said that he had a good contact. We were very competitive with regard to contacts, kills and operations. He never mentioned that he had killed the ZIPRA Strela Section. He never mentioned it in the Officers Mess or on our various 'piss-ups', it would have been a morale booster at the time. Darrell and I are best of friends and in our many years together he never mentioned killing the Strela section. It only came up when the saga around the book *Viscount Down* began. Andre Scheepers I associated with occasionally, he never mentioned it."[3]

Commanding Officer of the SAS, Garth Barrett, clarified the matter: "The subsequent claims that have materialised over the last couple of years and particularly recently by Andre Scheepers, Darrell Watt and Keith Nell (author of *Viscount Down*) are incorrect, in which the claim is that Darrell Watt shot the 'missile gang' that shot down the Viscount. As the CO of the SAS and having been the first person on the ground at the Viscount *Hunyani* crash site, I had a very deep interest in the whole tragedy and the belief that I would ignore information that Darrell Watt, an officer in my unit, had shot the 'missile gang' is preposterous! I would have advised COMOPS immediately and it would have made headline news! When I was asked by Darrell Watt in 2010 if I recalled that he had shot the 'missile gang' I stated NO! When Keith Nell, author of *Viscount Down*, asked me in 2011 the same question I again said NO! No one else, which includes SB, CIO, BSAP or even my 2IC, IO or Sqn Cmdrs can back up their claims."[4]

Dennis Anderson recalled: "With regard to the two Viscounts shot down over Hurungwe TTL on the 3 September 1978 and 12 February 1978 I was at ComOps and at no time was there any intelligence indicating that the Strela section responsible for either or both of the action/s had been either contacted or eliminated. Had this been the case the information would have been widely circulated throughout Rhodesia to boost the rapidly deteriorating morale of the nation suffering from an ever increasing insurgency threat. When the first Viscount *Hunyani* was shot down on the 3rd September 1978, ten survivors were murdered by a Zipra section. To the best of my knowledge there was no intelligence that confirmed that this section was contacted or eliminated by Rhodesian

---

1 John Redfern email 19/1/2016.

2 John Redfern emails 17/1/2016 and 19/1/2016.

3 Rich Stannard email 17/8/2016.

4 Garth Barrett email 13/11/2015.

Security Forces. Once again, had this been the case, the information would have been immediately widely circulated throughout Rhodesia."[1]

Once Dr Chakawa had confirmed the facts of the SAS contact, I asked him to establish if China or any of his section were involved in the Strela section that shot down either of the Viscounts, and this is the conclusion of his investigations: "China was a resident ZIPRA Detachment Commander of the Doro area and Napoleon was his second in command — he had no connections to the ZIPRA Strela Section which was a top secret operation and the resident ZIPRA sections were not aware of their locations or operations. They had no connections to the Strela section or the ZIPRA section that murdered the survivors from Viscount *Hunyani.* China and White returned to visit the area after the war."[2]

Intelligence gathered in our hunt for China (1).

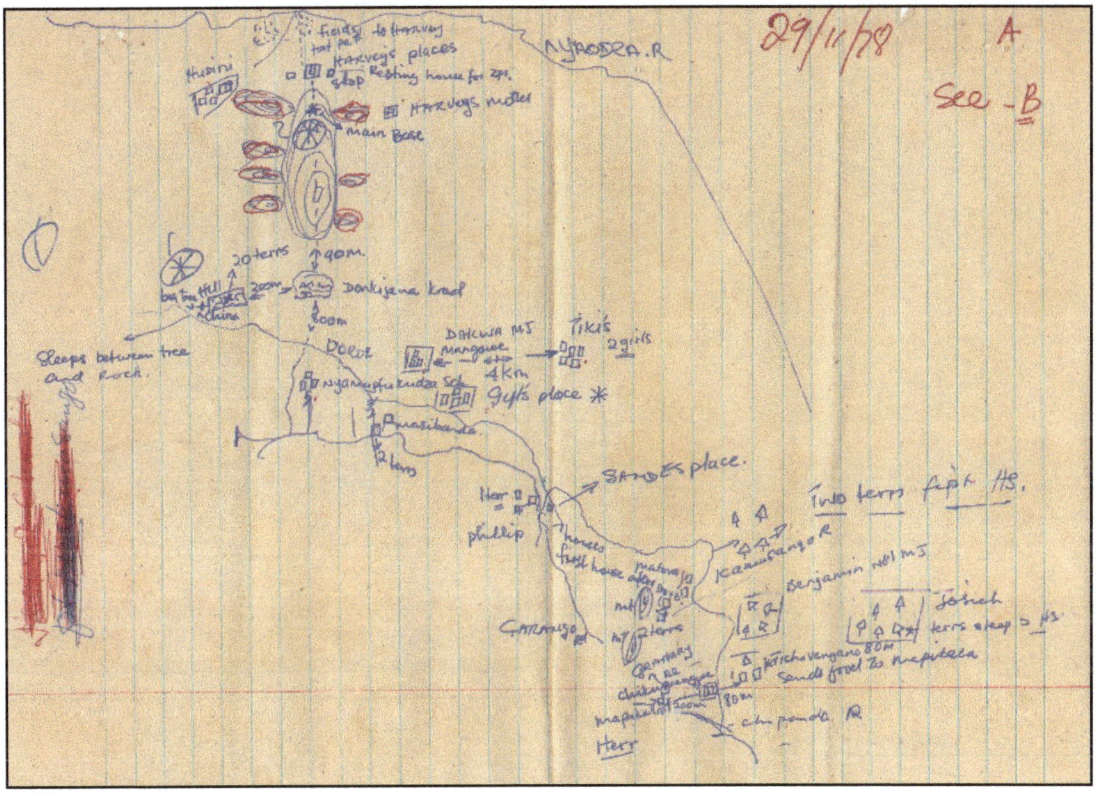

(7) *China's subsequent movements*

On 26 November 1978, we received further intelligence, confirmed by Chido, that a ZIPRA section was sleeping at the kraal of Henry Nyamupfukudza and his sons. Chido was convinced that the insurgents had remained at Dhongijena's Kraal in the Doro area despite the recent contact with SF. This confirmed information which had come to our attention five days previously on 21 November 1978.

Later, on 29 November 1978, Chido and Garai (pseudonym), confirmed that several older and well-established ZIPRA sections in Hurungwe "hated" China. Consequently, he had taken to realigning himself with fresh ZIPRA sections entering the area. Garai didn't know the cause of this dissension. In my diaries I wrote: "China is currently based in a hill feature known as Harvey Hills.

[1] Dennis Anderson email 27/1/2016.

[2] Dr J. Chakawa field research 29/4/2016.

When he is near the Doro River area, he stays with the Sunday family although he sometimes stays with the family of Dhongijena. When China is around Dhongijena's place he sleeps below the hill just to the west of Dhongijena's houses. Usually he places 20 ZIPRA on top of that hill more in fear of the old ZIPRA sections than of the SF. When China moves beyond Harvey Hill he sleeps at Hudini's houses. There are times when he crosses the Nyaodza River and when he does, he is accompanied by one of his men. Here, he sleeps at Kangama's house and this is the furthest North China goes. The other terr that accompanies him sleeps at Anderson's house where there is a girl,

Below: Hunting China (2); Right: Hunting China (3)

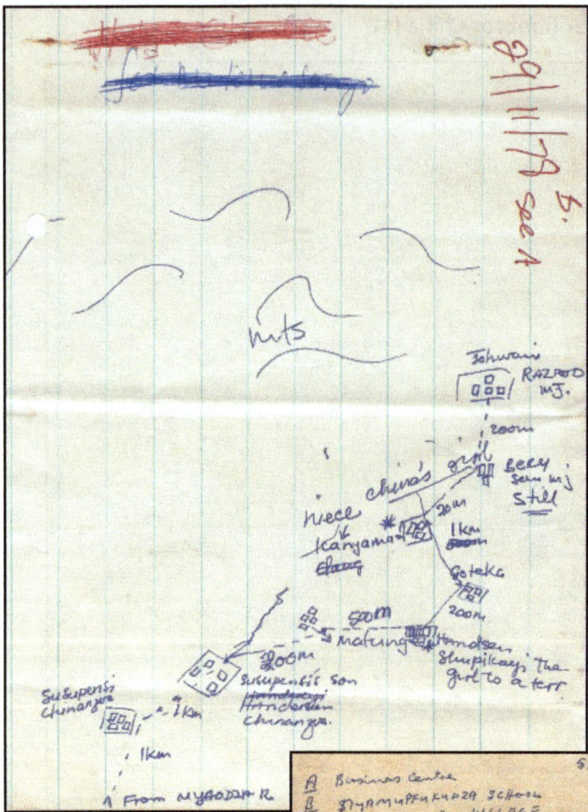

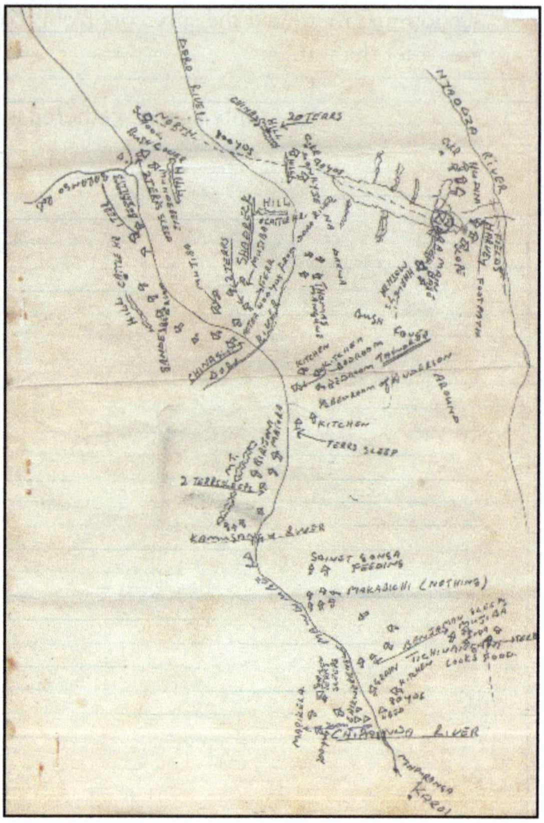

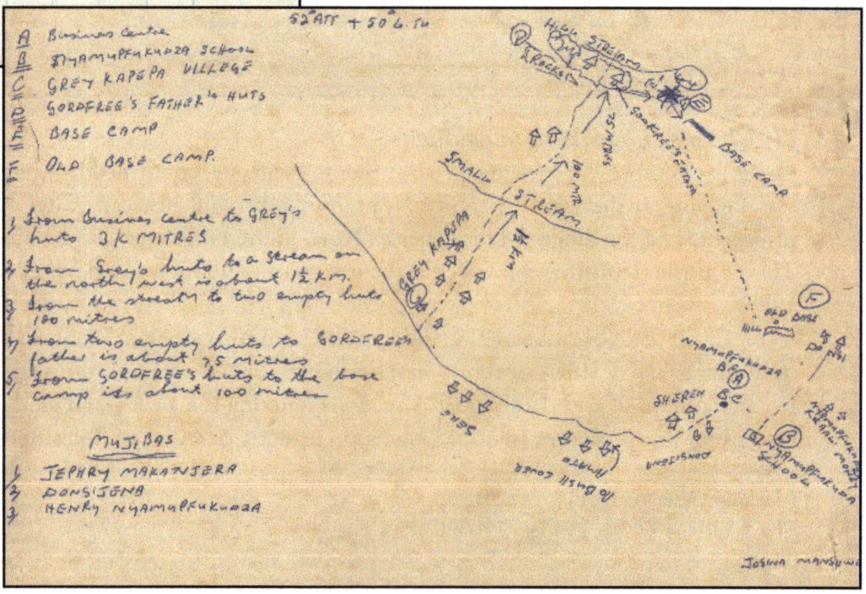

Hunting China (4)

but her name is not known. There are two ruthless *mujibhas* named Benjamin and Gift who live near Dakwa's place. Garai is prepared to indicate the base areas and where the terrs are. After any action the terrs generally converge at Harvey's place where they also meet for breakfast and *Mahewu* — non-intoxicating beer. The two girls that usually converge at Masibanda's place are Aneni and Mayita (pseudonyms), they are normally collected for nights out and then they come back in the morning. The informant is to be deployed with the army on indications on 30/11/78 to locate China — hopefully." China had several girlfriends whom he lived with in the villages.

Once again, this was immediate and accurate intelligence that needed to be acted on with precision. Happy produced sketches, illustrating the intelligence. (See Hunting China (1)-(3) Original Sketches). I presented all the intelligence to the Selous Scouts who were eager to act on it. Our informant was prepared to deploy into the field therefore I introduced Garai to the Selous Scouts. The plan was for them to move clandestinely into an OP position where Garai would interpret events on the ground. As our plans unfolded, I grew more optimistic of finally achieving our objective of eliminating China and Tall Man.

However, on 4 December 1978, on Garai's return to Karoi following the deployment, he informed us that the Selous Scouts callsign was compromised from the first night of deployment while attempting to uplift a *mujibha*. To my dismay, yet another frustration in our attempts to eliminate China and Tall Man. It annoyed and disappointed me when callsigns deviated from agreed-on strategies and tactics meticulously researched, developed and planned. The execution of these deployments was out of our hands, with deviations difficult to accept and tolerate.

(8) ***ZIPRA's response to the SAS attack***

I would like to explain that once the attack on China was concluded, the surprise elements of our intelligence operations were exposed. China had been alerted and obviously changed strategies and tactics. This would make it increasingly difficult to locate and eliminate both him and his section, hence my emphasis on the first attack requiring maximum force and utilising all available resources. The failure to eliminate China in that first strike complicated our search to find him again. This is clarified in my following detailed diary entry describing how China and his section made every effort to avoid detection. This was war, the enemy do not sit around waiting to be shot!

ZIPRA were now aware that their intelligence network had been penetrated and immediately established that Bravo 70 had provided the "leak". Forthwith, they adjusted their security arrangements but, fortunately, Garai gathered further intelligence from his relatives, relaying it to us on his return on 4 December 1978. The following is a summary of Garai's information taken from my diaries:

> Godfrey had been installed as the leading *mujibha* in the Doro area and on Thursday, 28 November 1978 he collected Rosy and Mudiwa (pseudonyms). Mudiwa was commandeered because her husband Peter Manguwe was alleged to be a government official. While travelling to Godfrey's house they met three ZIPRA carting kitbags near the homes of Seke. At Godfrey's house were some 44 ZIPRA, including China. The men were given supper, after which they journeyed to their new base camp near Godfrey's house with Mudiwa. Rosy remained at the houses.
>
> Before sunrise, the whole group, including the girls, returned to Godfrey's house where the water for their bathing had been prepared. After they had washed, Mudiwa and the girls were despatched to the base camp, followed by Rosy and the terrs. Rosy told the terrs that she wanted her young sister to return home with her but China refused her request. Later on Mudiwa and Rosy were released to go home where they stayed until 1/12/78.
>
> While at Godfrey's bush base, a load of war material arrived requiring some two days to transport from the previous base at Dhongijena to Godfrey's home as only the

insurgents were engaged in the transfer.[1] Terrs had resided at Dhongijena base for 3 months but decided to relocate as Bravo 70 was now considered to be the sellout.

The weapons transported included RPG7's, DP's, rifle grenades and general ZIPRA armaments. While the Dhongijena base was operational, one man was directed to the base to replenish ZIPRA section's ammunition when running low. It appeared this pattern was to continue. In time, we established that by 5 December 1978 China along with Desire and Dixon, had taken a lot of their supporters from Doro region to Zambia for training. This group included Godfrey and the girls from the Nyamupfukudza area. China did not expect to return to the area until the end of December 1978. In his view, the accompanying girls travelled too slowly. A section of 8 ZIPRA had remained in the same area. Their intelligence network included Henry Nyamupfukudza, his son Bhinya, and *mujibhas* Jonga Andreke, Ago Mutasa, Jeffrey Makanjera, Amato, Rawson and Dhongijena. Tonderayi (pseudonym) and Amato also remained to feed the ZIPRA whose previous eating patterns continued as before with breakfast at 7.00 a.m. at the base. During the afternoons the girls prepared food in the kraals but ZIPRA consumed their meals in the immediate area of the kraals in groups of two and three. At night, however, they ate together at the same kraal. ZIPRA changed their patrolling strategy and moved in couples or units of three, while the rest of the section remained at the bush base, which they considered secure as it was surrounded by dense overgrowth. Prior to December 1978, ZIPRA would sleep in the kraals but as most of the girls from the area had been relocated to Zambia by China, they tended to sleep in the bush base. One insurgent lived at Grey Kapepa's house with a girl. Some were thought to sleep at Amato's house as he had been elevated to a leading *mujibha.* But none stayed or slept at Seke's house. No ZIPRA slept at Godfrey's home as the bush base was too close by. Before sunrise, they awoke and walked from the bush base to Godfrey's house where they washed using water provided by one of the girls. Once washed and fed, recce patrols were sent out as late as 8 a.m. in twos or threes. The remainder of the section stayed in Godfrey base which was well concealed in thick bush cover. Previously ZIPRA had started patrolling between 7 and 8 a.m., the extra hour was to allow their *mujibhas* time to clear the area. Friday, 1 December 1978, was the first day ZIPRA started to move around looking for Garai. (See Hunting China (4) Original Sketch.)

Our intelligence at that time indicated ZIPRA were still at the bush-base, as the thick overgrowth provided good camouflage against airborne attacks. Lush vegetation found along river lines offered cover in the event of ground-force attacks. The river also supplied drinking water. Kopjes, caves and mountains were ideal hideouts. We had struck a blow and disrupted their operations, requiring them to adjust their strategies and tactics immediately. However, ZIPRA were by no means in disarray. Their intelligence network continued to function intact. Our networks were also efficient but growing exponentially. In my thinking, we were well placed as we had them second-guessing and totally unaware as to when, how or where we would launch an assault. The enemy knew full-well we could and would do so. We still held the crucial element of surprise. As was my original intention, the enemy were now reacting to our operations and not vice versa.

Following the SAS deployment, ZIPRA moved their main base area, relocated their considerable arms cache and moved the people they considered vulnerable to Zambia for further training. As opposed to patrolling with a full section, they changed to two- or three-man patrols, spending more time at their base, as they considered it safer. They no longer felt secure in the kraal environment. This pattern meant only a few insurgents slept in the kraals at night. However, they did not abandon the area but simply upgraded their security arrangements. Naturally, they could not vacate the area as that would be deemed defeat, or at least a retreat, thus losing their position as the occupying force.

---

[1] ZIPRA were meticulous about the locality of their arms caches. While civilians assisted transporting the weaponry, generally only the ZIPRA insurgents physically concealed the arms. There were rare exceptions.

It was clear to me that the section remained static, which correlated with our increasing understanding of ZIPRA strategies and tactics.

Although our information indicated that China had taken recruits to Zambia, I felt it was still worthwhile attacking the remnants of his section. This would afford us the opportunity of locating the arms cache despite the difficulties and complexities of the hunt. While locals frequently assisted in transporting armaments, as a rule, only ZIPRA insurgents were involved in concealing them. Theirs was a top secret mission, understandably, considering the vast distances and obstacles they needed to overcome when hauling the armaments across the Zambezi River or Kariba Dam, depending on the route they followed. Once across the border, the weaponry was lugged overland to its final destination in Hurungwe, a considerable distance and achievement. The arms were concealed in well-thought-out camouflaged locations which were difficult to find. In addition, armaments were generally divided up and cached in various locations, including kraals and their surrounds. When we secured ZIPRA captures, they were normally handed over to the Selous Scouts for immediate intelligence gathering and deployments, further diminishing our ability to locate arms caches. We were never officially informed of Selous Scouts operational successes, or failures, rather we depended heavily on our own intelligence networks for this information. However, to our credit, we were up to date with ZIPRA's changing strategies and tactics, a reflection of the excellent UANC intelligence networks.

As a result of SAS and Selous Scouts deployments, I remained adamant that the only solution to the ZIPRA threat and, indeed, the ZANLA menace throughout the country, was to deploy the people's army. Reflection on the experiences gained would help in future attacks.

On 5 February 1979, we received intelligence that in the Maumbe area a section of ZIPRA were residing with Kraalhead Mashaya, whose kraal was situated between Chivere and Matundahuruwa kraals. This section had been seen on that day. We intercepted a letter between Napoleon, whom we had identified as a ZIPRA commander in the Doro area, and China. However, we had confirmation of the latter still being in Zambia. Our last information regarding China was received on 7 March 1979, in which we learned he had returned to Hurungwe with 40 newly trained ZIPRA insurgents. They had brought with them "a big gun on wheels" which we assessed as a 75mm recoilless rifle. We assumed China would join up with the other two overall detachment commanders, namely Napoleon and Moses. At the time, there was a definite build-up of ZIPRA in northern Hurungwe. To my understanding, China was never again engaged by the SF and, with his former comrade, White, returned to visit the area after the war.[1]

Strike 3: Wire Strike

On Saturday, 25 November 1978, Katima reported to us that the ZIPRA section's first engagement with the Selous Scouts, Murereshi (1) contact, on 18 November 1978, had resulted in several disciplinary reprisal killings allegedly directed by Wilson. Wireless Karenga had returned to the area even though his houses had been razed during the initial contact. This intelligence was significant and verified in two separate ways. Firstly, it was independent confirmation that two kraals had been burned in the initial contact. Secondly, it confirmed the three reprisal deaths including Vimbo, killed by ZIPRA on 21 November 1978. It was also fresh and relevant intelligence as it confirmed ZIPRA were still resident in the area. We drew sketches of the target area and these confirmed the original sketches from the initial contact on 18 November 1978. (See Strike 3: Wire Strike Original Sketches.)

It was my assessment ZIPRA had correctly calculated our general Security Forces modus operandi. Traditionally, we were known to attack then withdraw from the area, leaving the people vulnerable to ZIPRA reprisals and their return to continue occupation of the land. As I have previously mentioned, ZIPRA had no withdrawal policy. Their occupation of the land was ongoing: to withdraw would imply defeat. Their approach was to control and dominate the people. With this in mind, we decided to attack again but with the different strategy of using the Fire Force for the

[1] Dr J. Chakawa field trip 29/4/2016.

deployment which would surprise ZIPRA and, in my view, was worth the risk. Our intelligence was positive and inspired confidence. The FF had relocated from Karoi Country Club to an airfield at Montesuma farm, just outside Karoi, on 25 November 1978.[1] I approached the Fire Force with the relevant intelligence, including the sketches and locstats, informing them of the informant's willingness to identify the base camp area. We had enough detail to show them the plan of the kraals we intended attacking and the approximate locstats. After our briefing, the FF was eager to proceed with the operation.

Fire Force Operational Instructions

Accurate and detailed intelligence, confidently presented, was essential in convincing the FF to deploy. Maj. Nigel Henson commented:

> In 1978 the number of Fire Forces were reduced in number and increased in size which resulted in Fire Forces serving more than one Joint Operational Centre (JOCs). The Fire Force was positioned by Combined Operations (Com.Ops.) who considered existing and potential internal and external intelligence and deployments. Fire Force was deployed to a JOC and requests for Fire Force deployments from callsigns in the field were sent via the Sub.JOC (if there was one) or directly to the JOC where the request was assessed and, if supported, the request for deployment was made to the Fire Force for deployment. The planning range for deployment of the Fire Force was approximately 50 nautical miles from base. The senior pilot and the FF commander were the real decision makers, they were generally very circumspect in the way they dealt with requests, particularly if they were some distance away, for the situation on the ground would always have changed by the time the FF arrived. Com.Ops. and most JOCs and Sub.JOCs were content to leave the deployment decision to the FF commander and his pilots, who on occasions diverted to sightings with more potential – such was the flexibility of the FF.
>
> Once the JOC had been informed of the FF call out, standby or pre-positioning, all Sub.JOCs were briefed accordingly. On receipt of this information Sub.JOCs passed it on to whatever troops they considered necessary but particularly Selous Scouts. Generally, the Fire Force was positioned to favour the Selous Scouts who would also receive priority for deployments. Any request for the FF contained the following essential information:
>
> (a) Location of terrorists or incident; over 80 per cent of all FF deployments were information driven, they were not incident driven.
> (b) Details of the sighting.
> (c) Number of terrorists involved.
> (d) Callsign and location of requesting station.
> (e) VHF channel.
> (f) Any other relevant information. This could include:
> - Dress and description of terrorists.
> - Weaponry of terrorists.
> - Direction of movement, speed and formation of terrorists.
> - Most likely escape route.
> - Location and callsigns of other troops in the area.
> - Best direction of approach of the Fire Force.
>
> The Fire Force initiated any follow-up but once a follow-up was in progress the JOCs or Sub-JOCs would arrange for troops to take over as soon as possible.
>
> The first Fire Force tour in Hurungwe came about by accident…we were on Fire Force duty at Grand reef in the early part of November 1978, and at the same time carrying out FIBUA training (Fighting in built up areas) up in the Vumba, as the assault team that

[1] Confirmed by technician/gunner, Sgt. Mark Jackson's log book; Karoi Contacts Map Incident 17.

> would attack an ex Federal Army barracks that housed ZIPRA, on the edge of Mulungushi dam to the east of Lusaka. On 23 November we moved to Inkomo barracks north of Salisbury and there had various briefings given by Selous Scouts, who were already in the target area carrying out OP duty. On 24 November we moved up to Karoi with 3 Cdo. and various RLI HQ elements and stood by to be uplifted or parachuted into the target. On the 25th, the Selous Scouts reported from the target that it was heavily fortified, so it was decided that air effort only should be used on this target, to avoid heavy SF casualties. As a result of this, we and 3 Cdo. were formed into a 'strike force' with Support Cdo. acting in the fire force role and 3 Cdo. in reserve. We were deployed to Hurungwe (Montesuma farm in the Tengwe block if memory serves me correctly) and so began operations.[1]

Subsequently, all was in place. The Fire Force Commander organised for a Lynx to arrive at first light the following morning which would fly my informant, a Fire Force member and myself to pinpoint the kraals we were planning to attack. Our task was not complete. I returned to the "safe house" and re-examined the intelligence, sketches and map references, to ensure that we would be deploying onto the correct locstat. I also checked with Grey and Happy whether additional intelligence had arrived supporting the deployment. There was none. Both Grey and Happy were confident that the attack would be successful: we were prepared to take the risk.

Air Lt. Christopher "Chris" Tucker[2] continues:

> On 26 November 1978 I was the Lynx Pilot (Cessna 337) based at Kariba. The Lynx was bought from France as a military version of the Cessna 337 known as the Cessna 02 which had a 6g wing (6 x gravity – 6 times its weight). However the version that arrived only had a +3g wing which technically was not a strike wing and made it useless for military purposes; we were lucky not to rip the wings off in our strikes. The military version would also have had self sealing fuel tanks but ours didn't. When testing the Rhodesian Lynxes, a Denel Aviation Test Pilot found that about one-third of the Lynx's lift was generated by the area over the cockpit where the guns were mounted, this further increased the stall speed significantly and probably was a factor in the loss of at least two Lynxes. We were either brave, stupid or just ignorant!
>
> I had been called out on the evening of 25 December 1978 to a Fire Force Deployment in the Karoi area. Not long after first light I landed at Montesuma farm air strip and was briefed to do a recce of a terrorist base camp approximately 33 Ks west of Karoi with three packs on board, the FF Commander, John Padbury the SB Officer and an informant; the Fire Force Officer sat in the front seat next to me and Padbury sat in the rear right seat. The recce was of a base camp which was alleged to be occupied by eight insurgents.
>
> I taxied to the end of the grassed runway, turned 180 degrees, held the foot brake, and faced the rural farm strip; the Fire Force camp was at the middle right side of the strip and cut grass surrounded the entire edges. Final cock pit checks, no stray animals on the strip, I powered up to 2850 RPM maximum power as it was a short run way, released the brakes and rolled forward with the flaps at 1 notch. At 85 knots I pulled back the control column and eased the Lynx into the freedom of flight, set the gears up and at 400ft. retracted the flaps, setting course for the base camp area cruising at 2400rpm with 24-inch manifold pressure, 140 knots and at a height of about 1200ft.

---

1 Nigel Henson email 3/1/2016 and 22/8/16; Nigel Lamb email 27/1/2016, although he was not sure about the figure of 80%.

2 Chris Tucker received his "wings" and commission (Air Sub. Lt.) in November 1976 and was a pilot with 4 Sqn. Rh.AF., flying Lynx aircraft (Cessna C-337s) until March 1979. During his service he flew a total of 1858 hours and received the Military Forces Commendation (Operational), and the Rhodesia General Services Medal.

Generally, we flew at 2000ft to avoid small arms fire which could not reach us or 50ft as our speed was too fast for ZIPRA to locate and pinpoint our position; recces were carried out between 1000ft and 1500ft depending on visibility on the day.

The plan was to do one flight over the base camp with a slightly left orbit so the informant, sitting behind me on the left-hand side of the plane, could look through the elongated bubble window which was designed and ideal for observations, and identify the base camp and surrounding area. We hoped that if insurgents were in the base camp the flight might alert them, but they would relax as we flew straight over their position paying them no attention. I had used this method before with some success. Padbury had provided us with an accurate sketch and locstat of the base camp and surrounding area.

As we approached the target area, I powered back to 120 knots to give more time for the recce, the informant indicated the base camp and target area, accurately confirming Padbury's sketch and locstat. All went according to plan and we headed back to the Montesuma airstrip. Both the Fire Force detail and I could confirm the location of the base camp which was important as we would both be involved in the full Fire Force attack. The FF commander would have to pin point the target on the first approach to maintain the element of surprise.

On approaching Montesuma airstrip, landing into sun, the FF Officer shouted "wires"; I saw them and instinctively reacted by applying power and pushing the control column forward which stopped the aircraft stalling and we were able to fly away.

I did hit the wires but had enough height, we were about 30ft above the ground, power and speed to successfully complete a missed approach and land. Only on landing did I realise that we had broken the power lines, fortunately they were not the main 330V Kariba power lines but the commercial lines which the farms fed off. The Lynx was armed with 2 x 37mm SNEB rocket pods (18 rockets per pod) able to fire single or triple rockets and 2 x 303 browning dorsal fuselage mounted; it was also capable of carrying a further 2 fran tan (napalm) bombs. Had we crashed we most certainly would have not survived; apart from dented pride, we survived to fight another day. After the recce, having survived the wire strike, I flew in support of the Fire Force deployment.[1]

[1] Chris Tucker oral interview 10/4/2015 and emails 25/4/2015 and 3/10/2015.

Dr Chakawa, Phil Wright and the author examine the maps.

Chris Tucker and the author discuss the "wire strike", April 2015.

Strike 3: Wire Strike Original Sketches.

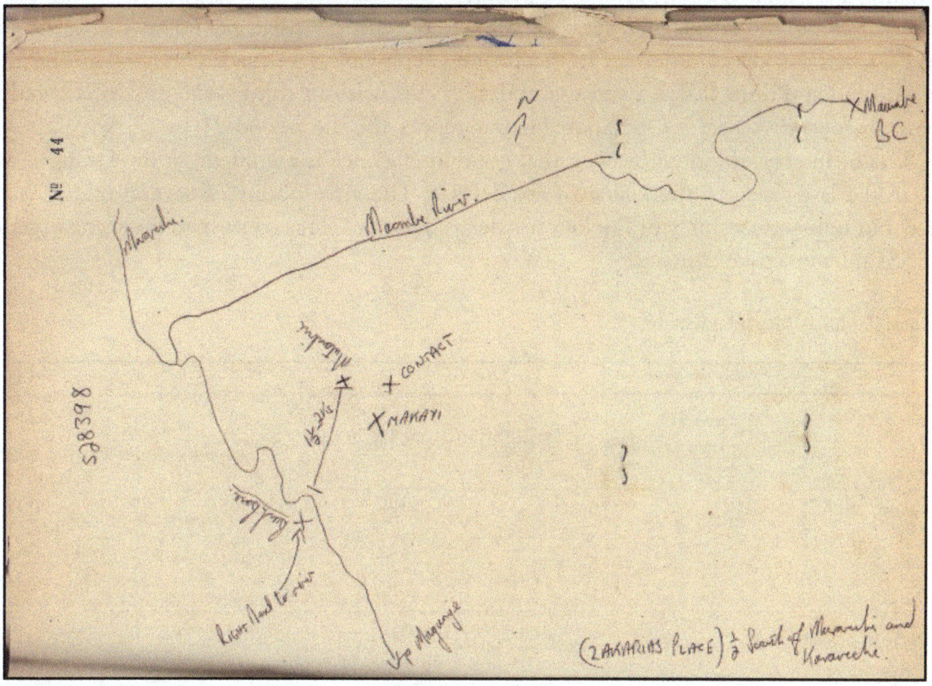

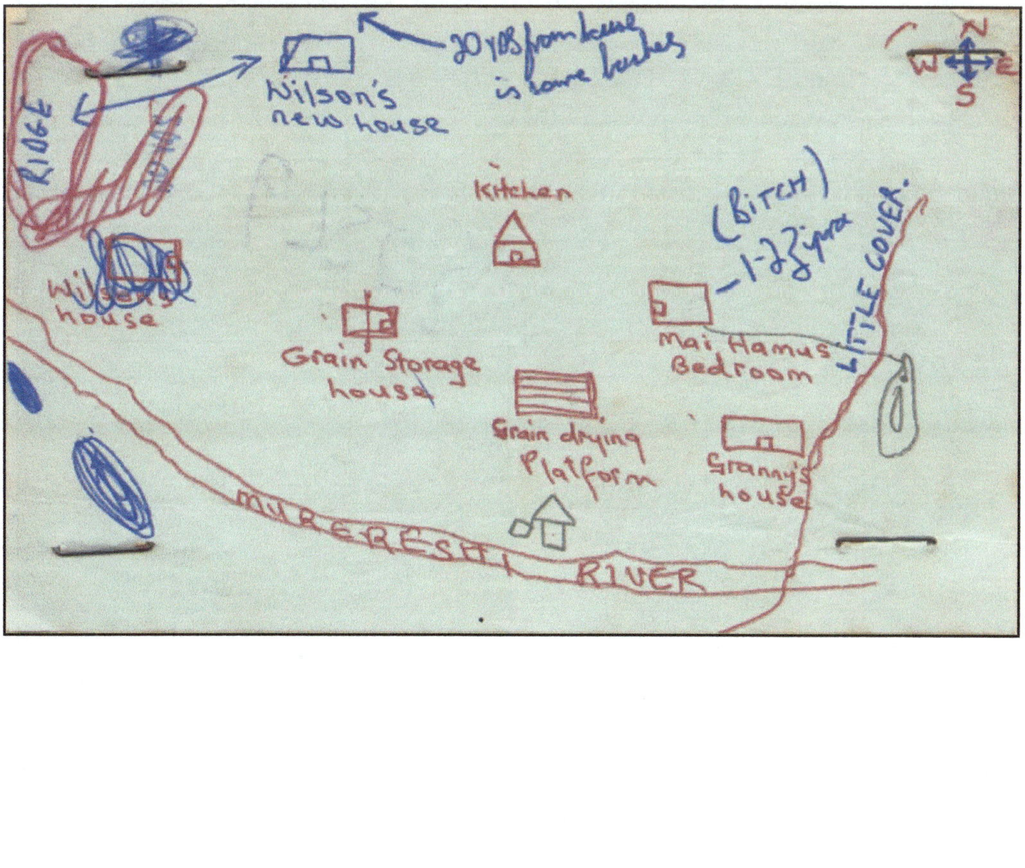

Once the aerial indications were successfully completed and the base camp identified, the full Fire Force was deployed. They made contact with three insurgents, all of whom were killed. One RPD and two AK-47s, though badly damaged, were recovered. Unfortunately, several locals were killed in the crossfire. The attack was executed as planned, the sketches were accurate, as was the map reference: a credit to the intelligence network. Most importantly, we had gained the confidence of the Fire Force. Chris Tucker comments: "In the ensuing deployment we made contact with the ZIPRA section. All said and done it was a successful day."[1] This was our third strike on ZIPRA and there was more to follow! A Secret Operation Favour report for the period 21 to 27 November 1978 stated: "It is of interest to note however, that good intelligence is coming in in the Urungwe which has led, in the last week, to the killing of six ZIPRA. The area locality of several mines has been indicated, but non-serviceability of Pookies has delayed lifting." This confirmed the six insurgent kills in the SAS and wire strike contacts.

1 Ibid. Karoi Contacts Map Incident 18.

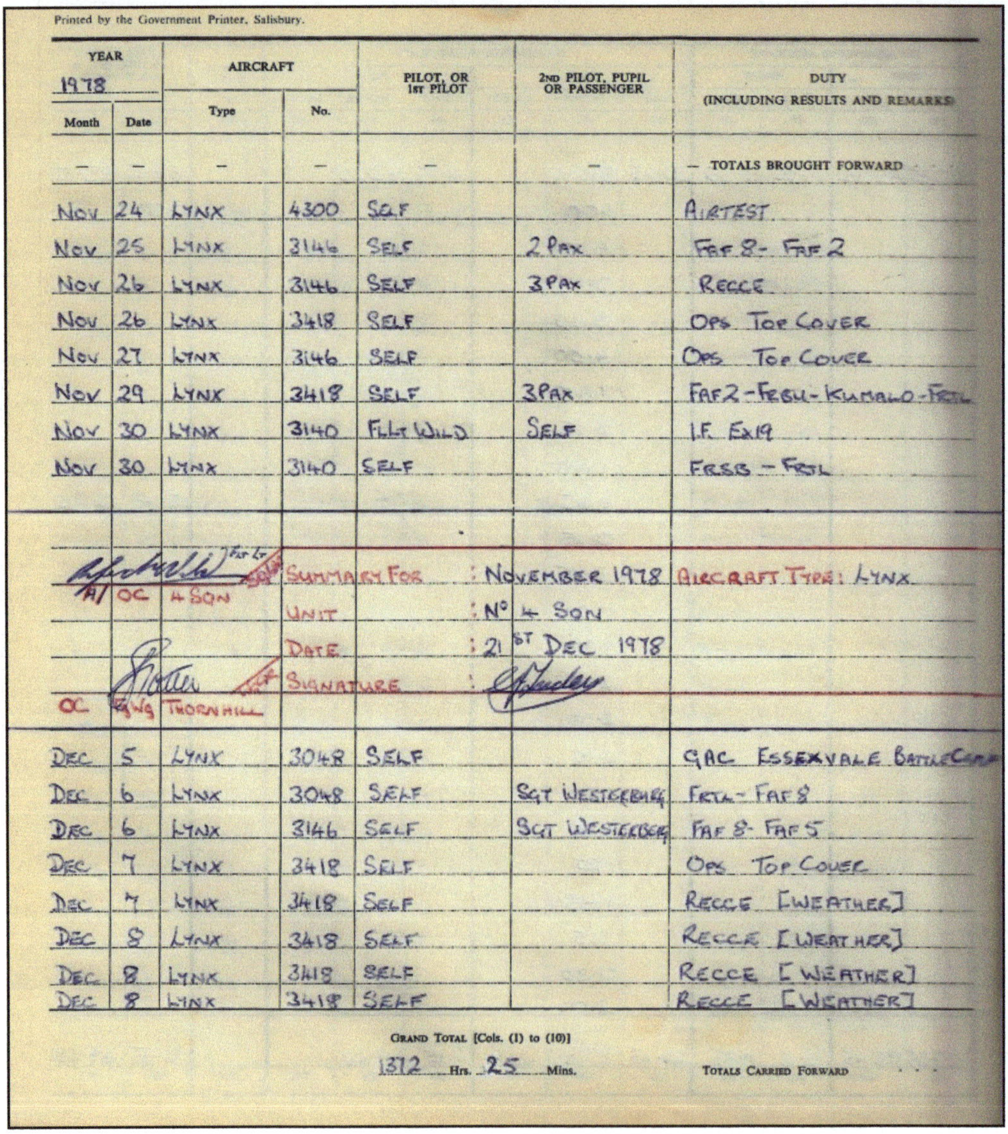

Printed by the Government Printer, Salisbury.

YEAR 1978 Month	Date	AIRCRAFT Type	No.	PILOT, OR 1ST PILOT	2ND PILOT, PUPIL OR PASSENGER	DUTY (INCLUDING RESULTS AND REMARKS)
—	—	—	—	—	—	— TOTALS BROUGHT FORWARD
Nov	24	LYNX	4300	SELF		AIRTEST
Nov	25	LYNX	3146	SELF	2 PAX	FAF 8 - FAF 2
Nov	26	LYNX	3146	SELF	3 PAX	RECCE
Nov	26	LYNX	3418	SELF		OPS TOP COVER
Nov	27	LYNX	3146	SELF		OPS TOP COVER
Nov	29	LYNX	3418	SELF	3PAX	FAF 2 - FBSU - KUMALO - FBTL
Nov	30	LYNX	3140	FLT WILD	SELF	I.F. EX 19
Nov	30	LYNX	3140	SELF		FBSB - FBTL
A/OC		4 SQN	SUMMARY FOR		: NOVEMBER 1978	AIRCRAFT TYPE: LYNX
			UNIT		: No 4 SQN	
			DATE		: 21ST DEC 1978	
			SIGNATURE		:	
OC	Wg	THORNHILL				
DEC	5	LYNX	3048	SELF		GAC ESSEXVALE BATTLE CAMP
DEC	6	LYNX	3048	SELF	SGT WESTERBERG	FBTL - FAF 8
DEC	6	LYNX	3146	SELF	SGT WESTERBERG	FAF 8 - FAF 5
DEC	7	LYNX	3418	SELF		OPS TOP COVER
DEC	7	LYNX	3418	SELF		RECCE [WEATHER]
DEC	8	LYNX	3418	SELF		RECCE [WEATHER]
DEC	8	LYNX	3418	SELF		RECCE [WEATHER]
DEC	8	LYNX	3418	SELF		RECCE [WEATHER]

GRAND TOTAL [Cols. (1) to (10)]

1312 Hrs. 25 Mins. TOTALS CARRIED FORWARD

Air Lt. Chris Tucker's log book for 26/11/1978. Note 3 pax onboard.

Regarding the documentation recovered from the body of a deceased insurgent, we confirmed that the three dead insurgents were responsible for the reprisal murders including Vimbo, carried out on 21 November 1978, after the Selous Scouts contact on 18 November 1978, when they killed one insurgent. They intended eliminating two more alleged sellouts, including a man by the name of Danger. Our timeous attack proved lifesaving.

I enjoyed the thrill of flying and, when the opportunity arose to fly in the Lynx, I was delighted. The rear seat was narrow and the space confined, as I was crammed behind the weapons positioned immediately above my head. Once seated, I could see out of the window on my right. I always enjoyed observing the operational theatre from the air as it put matters into perspective and made it easier to orientate myself to the maps. Chris had a good understanding of the procedures required to "talk" the informant into the area, identifying features he could recognise. The flight and identification of the base camp and target area proceeded well. Chris was a professional, pragmatic and competent pilot. Once the indications were complete, we turned for home. On approaching Montesuma airfield, I suddenly heard the FF detail shout, "Wires!" We lunged forward, the engine pitch increased but we continued the flight. I looked out the window and saw a power line "whipping" through the air and realised we had struck it. To my, and all the occupants' relief, we landed shortly afterwards. Amazingly, we all remained calm throughout the incident, including the informant who had limited flying experience. To put the episode succinctly, Chris's aviation skills saved our lives.[1] The men back at camp enjoyed the wire strike story and the success of the contact as the deceased insurgents were known to some of the recruits. Morale was once again high and the men were enthusiastic to deploy.

As an aside, during the war, at least eight wire strikes were recorded: (One Canberra; two Dakotas and five helicopters), resulting in 12 deaths (six air force and six military personnel).[2] Mike Reeler recalls another Fire Force deployment in the Hurungwe TTL on the same day (26 November 1978): "Trooper Anthony John Millar, 2 Cdo, 1st Bn, RLI, was killed in a Fire Force deployment in the Hurungwe TTL in a 'blue-on-blue' incident. He was hit by fire from the K-Car. I remember being at the base when his body was recovered. The medic, actually I think he was a qualified doctor, did the preliminaries. As this was being done, his personal kit was gathered and neatly packed by his buddies. Understandably the mood there was really somber, the guys returning from the deployment sitting around in small groups, with very little being said and then in quiet tones, each one seemingly dealing with the grief in his own way. Sadly he had three days to go before his demobilisation following which he was due to start university."[3]

Strike 4: RLI Ground Force/Fire Force Attack

As a result of this success, the RLI were willing to act on our intelligence. I discussed the ongoing debrief of Chido and informed them that we had sufficient information to identify another ZIPRA base camp. Once again, we were convinced that they were a static group operating in this area. The RLI Intelligence Officer, contacted me during the same evening, requesting we attack the Maumbe base the following morning. Naturally, I agreed. However, to my dismay, the Lynx was not available. I immediately contacted Dis.Pol. at Sinoia, requesting assistance from the Police Reserve Air Wing for three passengers to fly on a recce. After some negotiating and wrangling, Dis.Pol. arranged an aircraft for us to proceed with our hastily planned sortie. Happy, Chido and I spent a good part of the night reviewing the intelligence until we were satisfied all was in place.

During the early hours of the morning of 27 November 1978, the PRAW aircraft arrived at Montesuma airfield. The FF Commander, informant and I were soon airborne. Utilising the same strategy of the Lynx pilot the previous day, the informant successfully identified the Maumbe base. We did not consider the flight over the base would arouse ZIPRA's suspicion, as we were flying in a civilian aircraft.

---

1 Karoi Contacts Map Incident 17 shows the position of the wire strike at Montesuma airfield.

2 Petter-Bowyer, P. (2005), p. 365 (confirms four of the helicopter wire strikes).

3 Mike Reeler WhatsApp discussion 1/4/2020.

The Fire Force did not deploy on the intelligence immediately due to other priorities. Our attack was held in abeyance. Later, on 2 December 1978, we received further intelligence that a ZIPRA section was at the Maumbe base. As usual, the FF were enthusiastic to deploy but decided on a change of tactics. Their plan was to walk the informant into the target area, set up an OP under the cover of darkness and then direct the FF in at first light. The RLI men executed the walk-in perfectly and, at first light on 3 December 1978, the FF deployed. In the ensuing battle, they had a contact with four insurgents: three were killed and one was injured but managed to escape. Another successful FF operation![1]

Observations and Assessments of First Four Strikes

The reader needs to bear in mind that ZIPRA considered Hurungwe a liberated area and had developed and settled into routines and patterns, subsequently making themselves vulnerable. In my estimation, this was the ideal scenario in which to strike the enemy before they became aware of our tactics. I recognised that "kills did not win wars", but our attacks and their deaths forced the enemy to move frequently, remain vigilant and, in time, erode their confidence in the people and their established intelligence networks. They would be forced to carry out harsh reprisals in order to maintain their firm grip on the people which I believed would create the environment for the deployment of our men. Success in these early battles was paramount.

I believed that once intelligence was confirmed, maximum available force should be applied to strike decisively, utilising all available resources to eliminate the enemy. We had the added advantage of the growing support of people prepared to risk their lives and identify where ZIPRA sections were actually resident. Their willingness provided us with a significant advantage over the enemy which we needed to exploit and utilise to the maximum before ZIPRA changed their strategies. Thorough planning and preparation was of the essence. In addition, assessing the terrain, considering the intelligence provided and deploying the optimum number of SF with a unique battle plan for each attack was vital. It was also important to maintain momentum and attack at every available opportunity, once again preparing the way for the deployment of our men.

Strike 1: Selous Scouts. The Selous Scouts contact was disappointing. I was not aware of how many men deployed, but with the quality of intelligence provided and the number of ZIPRA in the area (up to 60 in sections of seven), I was hoping to strike a major blow which would damage their morale and eliminate a good number of them. When one strikes the enemy, one is potentially exposing one's intelligence networks. ZIPRA immediately responded by murdering three of our resistance operators.

Strike 2: SAS Contact. I considered this the most disappointing contact given the accuracy of the intelligence provided and the intended target, a resident detachment commander, whom we believed, at the time, was part of the ZIPRA High Command. The SAS had insufficient troops to cover the target area and the additional available resources were not utilised, let alone considered. The Fire Force was available. Reinforcements from the local area or SAS HQ could have been requested. Walter could have provided extra manpower but did not join the deployment. The main target, China, and the remainder of the section were present but escaped. They were not tracked down. Warnings of ZIPRA taking to high-ground rendezvous points were ignored which could have proven disastrous. Lower-end cadre were eliminated but, regrettably, the commanders escaped. What should have been given more consideration was the option of OPs with a combined FF action: the terrain was ideal. The FF would have dramatically increased the ground coverage. In my view, this was a missed opportunity as ZIPRA changed strategies. China left the country and, to my understanding, the SF never engaged with him again.

Strike 3: Wire Strike. A successful engagement. The strategy of using the informant to indicate the base by air prior to the FF deployment worked well. His indications were accurate and the FF deployment precise. Three out of three insurgents were eliminated: a strike well executed by the RLI.

[1] Karoi Contacts Map Incident 20.

Strike 4: RLI Ground Force/Fire Force Attack. Patiently waiting for the right time to strike paid off as did our changes in strategies and tactics. The FF Commander used the intelligence, resources and terrain to his advantage, deploying ground forces overnight led in by the informant. Prepositioning his forces gave the FF Commander the ability to pinpoint the target area and then use the FF's increased capability, flexibility, manoeuvrability and capacity to cover the ground to his advantage. With the helicopters providing "airborne eyes", the chances of success were greatly increased as three out of four insurgents were eliminated. This was the strategy I had in mind for the SAS but it was overlooked.

15 ~ HURUNGWE STRATEGY

The only way to prevent ossification of the mind is to accept nothing as fixed, to realise that the circumstances of war are ever changing, and that consequently, organisation, administration, strategy, and tactics must change also ... Adherence to dogmas has destroyed more armies and lost more battles and lives than any other cause in war.
Maj. Gen. J.F.C. Fuller

SFA Strategies Phase 7: Prepare the people

Military Intervention by Consensus
In my experience and study of counter-revolutionary warfare, the following points are apparent. Firstly, revolutionary military deployments must be preceded, and accompanied, by a political effort which both prepares the people and gains their approval, thereby ensuring their support. Secondly, the people's army and the people are one. This army is trained and armed to defend the masses and be totally dependent on a mutual symbiotic relationship for their defence and preservation. Thirdly, without the people's approval and mutual consent, military force is required which diminishes co-operation, isolates the people from their army, leading to a determination to rule by the "barrel of a gun", instilling fear into the people and martial law.

I realised that once our forces deployed, it would be essential for the UANC to maintain close ties with the people. The actions of our men would be "seen" through the "eyes and ears" of the people who would keep us informed of all events and activities in Hurungwe. Our forces would be accountable to both the people and ourselves. The UANC continued to work on this objective.

The men had received over eight weeks of training and I could no longer resist Com.Ops. demands to deploy. A considerable amount of work had taken place to reach this stage and it was important to keep the momentum flowing and, at the same time, move at the pace of the people. A fine balance was called for. The political message was being circulated by the UANC networks among the people of Hurungwe, preparing them for the arrival of our army to fulfil our vision. It was critical for the people to know that this was their army and they, the people, were the focus of attention. In my view, therein lay our solution.

We had struck ZIPRA in north-east Hurungwe in the Doro region and the central Maumbe, Magunje and Murereshi areas. They had adjusted their strategies, carried out reprisals and were still resident in the areas. Intelligence continued to flow through the UANC office as did the flow of voluntary recruits, indicating the people's desire to remove the ZIPRA insurgents. This would force ZIPRA to apply harsher methods of control and we needed to be well placed to combat this anarchy. Our first troops trained at Chabwino had officially passed out and were prepared for deployment.

We had received acceptance by the spirit mediums. Their approval was a significant benefit to our efforts.[1] It needs to be remembered that the Matabele invasion, and subsequent harassment of the Shona tribe, was historically deeply rooted and well known among the Shona ancestors. Mediums would consult the ancestors for advice. Clearly the UANC had their approval, hence our acceptance. The people were ready, the stage was set. Timing, intelligence and strategy needed to be brought together in the form of deploying the people's army.

Zedong summed up our position: "If we try to go on the offensive when the masses are not yet awakened, that would be adventurism. If we insisted on leading the masses to do anything against

[1] Ranger, T. (1985), Chap. 5.

their will, we would certainly fail. If we did not advance when the masses demand advance, that would be right opportunism."[1]

A personal entry in my diary related to the above quote reads as follows: "Before I go into the plan used to penetrate Hurungwe TTL, I would like to mention once again that the entire concept of counter-revolution depends on the people. We must move at the pace of the people. The primary military task is to remove the terrorist threat by defending the people. Thereafter, the people must be politicised by regular meetings and we then move at their pace. They will tell us (as I have found out) where the terrs are, who the *mujibhas* are and feed us with all the intelligence required. They will ask us for medical assistance which must be provided. At a later stage, they will ask for schools to be reopened which we must facilitate. Grading of roads and all other administrative requests will then be called for and, as and when they are called for, they must be provided. We must move at the pace of the people. By doing this, we are psychologically eating away at the cancer of terrorism and, with the establishment of a people's army, catering for the people. There is little the terr can achieve other than accelerate atrocities and killings which is exactly what we want…these will occur in the areas we do not occupy, and later occupation is in fact made easier, believe it or not."

SFA Strategies Phase 8: Define military strategies and deployments

SFAs Deployment Strategies

In the discussion of the strategies implemented in Hurungwe, it is important to understand this was a deliberate approach emanating from a strategic appreciation. This included analysis of my knowledge, training and practical experience gained throughout my CID and SB career. Mao Zedong's *Little Red Book* was a reference I frequently consulted to gain a revolutionary perspective. My approach stood in stark contrast to the RF Government which, in my view, had no political or military strategies of any substance whatsoever. I had no intention of putting a haphazard operation on the ground, hoping it would work. In my estimation, Rhodesia was facing ruin. I believed workable strategies called for primarily the influence of the political over the military, together with meeting the needs and aspirations of the people for the long-term well-being of the nation. In order to be successful, these strategies needed to embrace cultural and racial differences. The following explanation of our strategies should be read in conjunction with my drawings marked "SFAs Deployment Strategies Original Sketch", p.318.

Development in any form of organisation or institution requires a series of incremental advancements which I shall refer to as cells. The principle is that, in order to gain ground, a small area needs to be penetrated and held successfully. This would be the first and most important cell, and maximum effort would be required to penetrate and hold the ground. Failure was not an option as the whole operation hinged on the success of the first cell. Great care would be needed to make the initial deployment a success.

Grey, Happy and I concluded that the most convenient area to occupy would have to be relatively close to the white farming area, providing us ready access to our field of operation. (Marked "European Farming Areas" on the original sketch.) Travel for our commanders when meeting the men would be safer and, if necessary, we could walk during initial deployment phases. While on the subject of command, we decided Grey and Happy should "front" our operations and oversee the initial visits into Hurungwe. Our view was that they would be more visible to the people, subsequently gaining increased credibility for the UANC. The people would see the UANC people's army clearly distinguishable from the Security Forces. I envisaged a time when I and the white staff would frequent Hurungwe. That would be when our forces were accepted, we whites had the approval of spirit mediums and the people were ready.

A great deal of political activity would be required before deploying and establishing our first cell. Grey's and Happy's considerable experience gained as insurgents prior to their return to Rhodesia was extremely beneficial in the training and preparation of our men for their operations. The men

[1] Zedong, M. (1976), p.126.

would have good intelligence, identifying key people belonging to the ZIPRA intelligence networks and their supporters. They would also know who supported the UANC which was vital, as this first deployment presupposed a direct clash with ZIPRA. This would be a battle to hold the ground and rapidly gain the support of the people. As can be expected, a great deal was at stake.

Once deployed, each section would need to rapidly establish themselves, securing not only their own protection but also the people's, in case ZIPRA launched an attack. This would involve identifying and establishing safe bush-bases, sleeping-and-feeding strategies, and guard systems which we trained them to have in place, even when their own *mujibha* system was established. When you know someone is trying to kill you, survival becomes paramount!

Initially, sections would be self-sufficient but would need to rapidly create local support structures and initiate and execute day-and-night patrol strategies for their own protection and that of the people. This would call for the establishment of their own *mujibha* intelligence networks which would connect them to their families and the people, and help identify ZIPRA movements. At the same time, the traditional way of life was not to be interfered with. Efforts would need to be directed to involvement with the community and the commencement of political activities in a concerted endeavour to mobilise them. This mobilisation of the masses would initially take the form of one-on-one discussions, progressing to kraal meetings with the aim of holding mass rallies attended by significantly high-ranking UANC officials, including Bishop Muzorewa. The UANC's hard work was about to be rewarded as the establishment of reliable political intelligence networks would now work to our benefit, as we would deploy and monitor our forces through the "eyes and ears" of the masses. Our actions and progress would be observed by the people: we would need to cement expectations. The presence of the people's army would be the fulfilment of a UANC political statement that would filter through Hurungwe.

However, it does need to be noted that it would have been naïve to imagine Hurungwe was a "free-for-all" where ZIPRA, the SF or, indeed, our SFAs could operate with impunity. Information relating to the actions of all three forces would be brought to our attention by SB, GC or our own intelligence networks. The people's voice would be heard, increasingly, as we penetrated deeper into Hurungwe. I remind the reader that the military is an extension of the political. Where the military rules, one seldom wins the hearts and minds of the masses. That was the position our Security Forces were in. Our aim was to reverse this state of affairs and force ZIPRA into a situation of being the undesirable element.

Our intention was for the people to regard us as committed, determined and relentless. They needed to view our every action as geared towards their own benefit. As the men settled into the first cell, procedures for communications, regular command-and-control visits and the replenishment of vital supplies would be established. Reports from the sections would be closely monitored and verified by the UANC intelligence networks, ensuring field intelligence from the sections and the masses continued to flow through the party. Difficulties and discrepancies would be addressed immediately, consequently ensuring, in the words of Zedong yet again: "The Party commands the gun — the gun must never be allowed to command the Party."[1] Naturally, the local Special Branch and Ground Coverage remained operational, although restricted from entering our demarcated areas, they would keep us informed of matters from their perspective.

I do need to emphasise that the people's army was not a covert operation. We were a visible force, suitably armed and prepared for confrontation with the enemy and inextricably connected to the people. In my view, there was no other alternative as we were in this together. Increasingly, we would depend on the intelligence of our networks to identify the whereabouts of ZIPRA sections, their intentions and movements. ZIPRA would be unaccustomed to this threat. As I perceived matters, we would wrest the initiative from them, progressively increasing our areas of operation and control, and subsequently forcing them to react to us as we became one with the people. In the words of Zedong: "The revolutionary war is a war of the masses; it can be waged only by mobilising the masses and relying on them."[2]

[1] Zedong, M. (1976), p. 102.

The people's function was to provide essential intelligence on ZIPRA operations, ensuring our men remained alert to attacks planned by them. These tasks would include foot patrols to identify landmines laid by ZIPRA in their campaign to control and contain Security Forces movements and protect their operational base areas. I stress the point that our operations were overt and only possible with the co-operation and involvement of the people. ZIPRA's only response could be hit-and-run attacks from areas outside of our occupation and control. We intended reversing the current situation to where we would be permanently resident and dwell among the people in Hurungwe, and ZIPRA isolated from the masses. We would be proactive, whilst ZIPRA would be reactive.

---

[2] Zedong, M. (1976), p. 88.

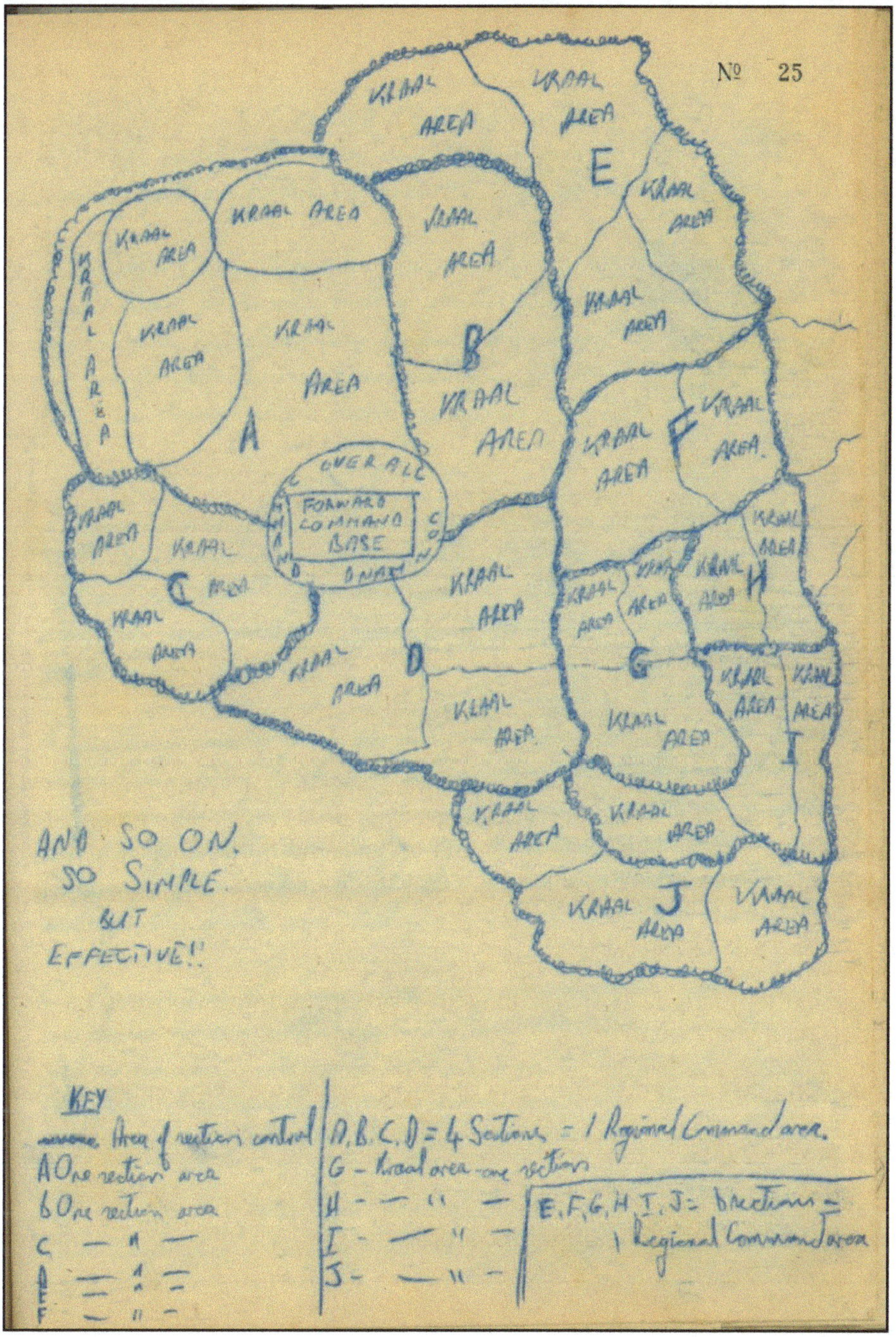

SFA Deployment Strategy

Original Sketch

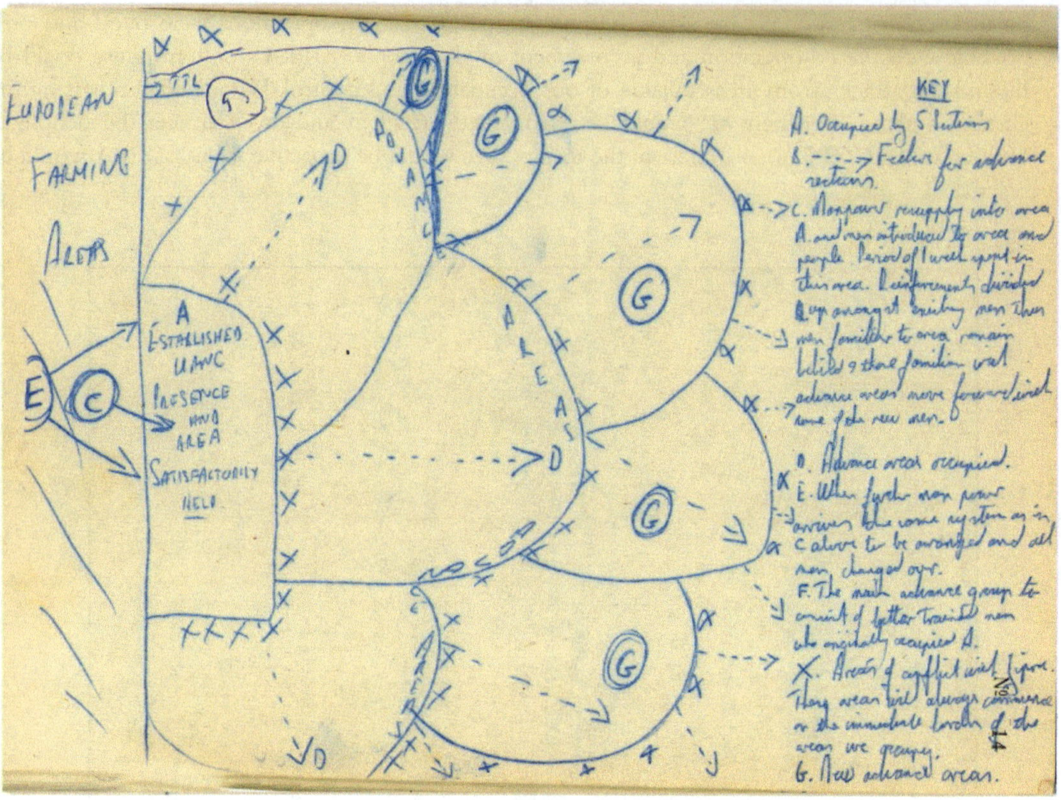

Key

A Occupied by 5 sections.

B ·············> Feelers for advanced sections.

C Manpower resupply into area "A" and men introduced to the area and people. Period of 1 week spent in this area. Reinforcements divided up amongst existing men then men familiar to area remain behind and those familiar with advance areas move forward with some of the new men.

D Advance areas occupied.

E When further manpower arrives the same system as in "C" above to be arranged and all men changed over.

F The main advance group to consist of better trained men who originally occupied "A".

G New advance areas.

X Areas of conflict with ZIPRA. These areas will always commence on the immediate borders of the area we occupy.

Establishing Order and Acceptance: Cell Number One

As per my thinking, cell "A" represented the first cell comprising three sections, each containing 10 men. Each section would have a section leader, deputy section leader, logistics officer, political commissar, signals man and a medic. The remaining four men would be cadre. In view of the mountainous terrain and remoteness of Hurungwe, communications in the field would be problematic for our VHF A63 radios. Pre-empting the problem, Sub.JOC Sinoia would be asked to provide a PRAW aircraft to contact the men on a daily basis. This was an important function, entailing pinpointing the men's position on a map which was vital during the early stages of deployment. Each section was required to remain in a demarcated area proscribed by Sub.JOC Sinoia, in order to prevent blue-on-blue incidents with the SF and other SFAs sections. Precise communications between sections was therefore essential. Medics would treat their own section's ailments and injuries as well as the people's until such time as we reopened the clinics.

Cell boundaries were to be selected honouring the traditional tribal system based on areas controlled by headman and kraalheads. In other words, we would not violate existing boundaries but use them to define the areas we wanted to penetrate. In order to facilitate this, and when necessary, we were prepared to define a larger area encompassing the traditional kraal structure that we intended to occupy.

Each cell area we proposed occupying would be demarcated by Sub.JOC Sinoia at least a week before deployment. Therefore, the area and its environs would be restricted to SFAs operations only, ensuring no other SF or government agencies such as Int.Aff. operated or entered these areas. In Hurungwe, the areas were well controlled by Sub.JOC Sinoia and we were confident that our men would be safe and not mistaken by friendly forces. The SF had an orderly, systematic approach to their deployments in designated areas. SFAs were dressed and armed like ZIPRA. It would be difficult to distinguish between the two forces: there was always that risk.

The primary responsibilities of each cell would be to protect, defend and politicise their people. Holding and defending the ground and attacking ZIPRA when the opportunity arose would effectively force them out of the area. In reality, I did not expect much resistance from ZIPRA once they experienced the rapidly turning tide of support towards the UANC and the people's army. It needs to be remembered that the political wing of the UANC had performed excellent work in politicising, preparing and mobilising the people. Each section would receive good local information and support from an expectant mass of people. In addition, the people's army comprised men being deployed to their own kraals which was an immense benefit. Provided there was political change that addressed the GNA of the people, success was certain.

On the original sketch, "X" on the border areas of the first cell "A", would mark the conflict areas with ZIPRA. No doubt they would launch attacks into cell "A" as often as possible from the neighbouring kraals in order to disrupt our plans and operations. Hence our decision to initially deploy three sections, a total of 30 men, into a relatively small area. ZIPRA were likely to carry out disciplinary killings within our areas in order to disorientate the masses. Likewise, attacks on white farms might occur to discredit our operations and prove ZIPRA were still fully operational.

The people would carefully watch our men's response to ZIPRA's actions. They would also observe their attitude towards ZIPRA collaborators, particularly those enmeshed in their intelligence networks. They had experienced disciplinary beatings, tortures and killings by ZIPRA which, unfortunate as it may seem, was to our benefit. To respond in a similar manner would immediately isolate us from the people, subsequently continuing their life of fear. They would withdraw their support and fail to recognise that we were their army. In the words of Zedong: "Without a people's army, the people have nothing."[1] In metaphorical terms, ZIPRA would be the "fish out of water" while we "swam with the people".

---

[1] Zedong, M. (1976), p. 99.

Cell Number Two

Once the first cell was established, stabilised and functioning, with the residents co-operating, the kraals beyond their immediate perimeter would be proscribed and become our focus of attention. Our men would commence sorties to establish links, politicise and mobilise the people, preparing the way for the arrival of new sections into advance cells "D". (See "B" on the original sketch.) It was imperative that our men realised that the kraals we did not occupy might oppose us and continue to harbour, sustain, assist and, more specifically, supply ZIPRA with intelligence pertaining to our whereabouts, habits, modus operandi and relevant operational matters. Whether this support was voluntary or obtained under duress was irrelevant. The fact remained that it would become available.

As our efforts gained momentum, we anticipated a demand for our men placing pressure on the training farm and its facilities. Securing recruits was the least of our difficulties as many willing volunteers constantly approached us to join our forces. However, training and equipping larger numbers would be demanding. Once reinforcements had been trained and were ready for deployment, the masses in the next demarcated area would be notified a week before their pending arrival, paving the way for the advance section. These advance areas would be considerably larger than the first cell. This would necessitate the advance areas "D" being divided into cells and section(s) designated to each cell depending on their size, terrain and logistics. Each cell comprised a manageable number of available section(s).

The new section(s) would be stationed in the first cell "A" for a week, thereby gaining first-hand operational experience, while establishing relationships with the locals. (See "C" on the original sketch.) Later, these reinforcements would be divided among the first deployed sections. I felt it important to adopt an "evolutionary" tactic to placing the men in their section(s). The men from kraals in cell "A" would be retained, while those who lived in the forthcoming cells "D" would advance. The new men joining the established cell "A" would ensure that they knew the people and vice versa. This strategy would prevent ZIPRA from launching pseudo-Selous Scout-type operations against us. In other words, "pretending" to be a part of the people's army while intending to engage and eliminate our men. In our overt deployments, we would always be visible. This would help the people identify our men and expose "sellouts", another reason for our operations being overt. There had to be a flow, a presence, a oneness with the masses as we became the occupying force. As Mao Zedong says: "Our point of departure is to serve the people whole-heartedly and never for a moment divorce ourselves from the masses, to proceed in all cases from the interests of the people and not from one's self-interest or from the interests of a small group, and to identify our responsibility to the people with our responsibility to the leading organs of the Party."[1]

This continuous interchange of men in sections in the early stages would be beneficial as they would learn from each other and be thrust into new operations as we progressed. The battle-hardened men from the first deployment "A" would be able to provide ongoing training for the newcomers entering the war zone. In my estimation, it was the most effective method of gaining insight into our operations: "If you want to know the theory and methods of revolution, you must take part in revolution. All genuine knowledge originates in direct experience."[2]

We made a point of scrutinising those in key leadership positions, although we anticipated some initial problems once the men were deployed. Those deposed would be replaced by others who aspired to leadership. It was our stated policy that the deposition of a leader would be thoughtfully handled by the commander in the field and the party's leadership structures.

Having familiarised themselves with the terrain and the people, and the resolution of leadership discrepancies, the advance sections would be moved to the forward areas "D" assisted by our men whose homes were in the new locations. The people would quickly accept them. Holding sections left in cell "A" would continue to mobilise and defend the masses. Gradually, life would return to

---

[1] Zedong, M. (1976) pp. 170-171.

[2] Zedong, M. (1976), p. 209.

normality. Political progress would be evidenced as we began to attend to the people's needs. This process would keep the masses on our side.

Following the establishment and stabilisation of cell "A", the occupying number of sections would be reduced to one or two, depending on the number of available newly trained sections. The advance areas would be the battlegrounds and the maximum number of sections would be sent forward into these new cells. A considerable amount of politicising would have been carried out by the early sorties into the advanced areas "D", significantly aiding the advanced sections to settle and convert the people to our cause. Seasoned veterans from cell "A" would spearhead the advance. (See "F" on the original sketch.)

With the progress of the advance sections into cells "D", the front "X" would move once again to the extremities of the areas we occupied. The pressure would be released from the sections occupying cell "A", thereby completely liberating the area. However, cells "D" would become subject to ZIPRA attacks. As ZIPRA were removed from cells "D", they would no doubt launch hit-and-run attacks into the newly occupied areas. I did not believe, however, that these attacks would reach cell "A". I felt that ZIPRA would direct their efforts at eradicating us completely from the areas they had most recently occupied and in which they were still supported.

Once established in cells "D", the people in newly demarcated advance areas "G" would be politicised, mobilised and prepared for the arrival of the people's army. Reinforcements would be supplied into cell "A" and introduced to the sections and their operational strategies, the people and terrain. (See "E" on the original sketch.) The sections would be reorganised prior to moving into cells "D" and met by the occupying sections before being divided and establishing new sections, learning their operational strategies and being introduced to the locals and terrain. The main advance sections would then push on into cells "G".[1]

The reader will notice that in our adopting this system of placing cells, we had introduced the classical Mao cell system into our strategies: small areas effectively patrolled by the military, politicised, administered and medically treated. The front "X" would be continually extended until we had fully occupied Hurungwe. Once momentum was gained, I believed that the masses would surge into our training farms. ZIPRA's tactics would naturally become more aggressive towards the people whose support they were losing. Retaliatory murders and assaults would rise sharply and, consequently, the further we penetrated inland, the greater the safety of the people. While I personally laid out the above pattern, the entire movement had to be progressive, calculated and systematic. We would always need to learn to adjust and remain flexible, particularly with regard to operational strategies which would be unique to each section. There was enormous potential for the swift growth of our operations. By the time cells "G" had been penetrated, we would introduce a regional command structure.

Regional Command Structure

Our initial concern would be ensuring that the men had enough training and leadership abilities for the first deployment. The whole operation hinged on the success of this first phase.

Section leaders were carefully selected and given additional training in leadership skills by the training staff but, most importantly, by Grey and Happy who would be responsible for the command and control of the men in the field. Grey, Happy and I spent much time together. We enjoyed a close and open relationship and had total agreement on all aspects concerning Hurungwe, in particular, intelligence, strategies and organisational structures, ensuring we spoke as "one" to the men. We would command the operational unit until the correct moment arrived to open the forward base command, therein reducing our workload and assisting with control and communications in the field. Grey, Happy and their team spent considerable time teaching the men discipline and military ethics. It must be remembered that we were recruiting rural men, training and arming them with live munitions and later empowering them to serve as soldiers. Their newly acquired responsibility, authority and power called for discipline and self-control: new dimensions of life to formerly

[1] Maj. Rawstron's diaries 2/9/1979, p. 4, confirmed our strategies.

№ 20

the lines of the following:-

FORWARD FIELD COMMAND BASE
(Manned by military wing of the UANC – liaison SS [illegible] and assisted by a trained military officer to assist with OPs etc)

R·E·G·I·O·N·A·L C·O·M·M·A·N·D·E·R·S.

(REGIONAL COMMAND STRUCTURE TO CONSIST OF:-
a) REGIONAL COMMANDER.
b) REGIONAL POLITICAL COMMISAR.
c) REGIONAL SECURITY & INTELLIGENCE OFFICER.
d) REGIONAL LOGISTIC OFFICER.
e) REGIONAL MEDICAL OFFICER.

SECTION COMMANDERS.

SECTION COMMAND STRUCTURE TO CONSIST OF:-
a) SECTION COMMANDER
b) SECTION POLITICAL COMMISAR
c) SECTION SECURITY & INTELLIGENCE OFFICER
d) SECTION LOGISTIC OFFICER
e) SECTION MEDICAL OFFICER

P E O P L E

FORWARD FIELD COMMAND BASE [TRAINING CAMP]
Responsible for all men in the field, their discipline, training, retraining, reception of the locals recruited for training, field intelligence

untrained men. The following explanation should be read in conjunction with my original drawings entitled "Regional Command Structure".

Responsibilities of Regional Commanders

Regional commanders would be primarily responsible for politicising and mobilising their men and the people. Their additional responsibilities included:

1. Discipline of men in their own sections.
2. Discipline of men under their command. Each region should have no less than five sections with a maximum of 10 sections under his command.
3. Remain in close liaison with the forward base for instructions, and ensure feedback of all intelligence and problems from both his men and the people.
4. Responsibility for the welfare of his men, i.e. logistics, pay, health and mobilisation, etc.
5. Responsibility for the welfare of the people under his command, i.e. health, education (where possible), protection of the Church authorities and protection against ZIPRA's attempts to mobilise, control and discipline (with reprisals) the masses.
6. Co-ordination of intelligence, particularly appertaining to ZIPRA presences and co-ordination of section(s) attack: a most important aspect.
7. Their liaison with the forward base to select advance areas, ZIPRA targets and any support required, i.e. Fire Force and ground forces.

The regional commander, to a large degree, would therefore be an extension of the forward base command, with many of his duties similar to those at base level. Close co-operation between regional command and base command would be essential, as was close liaison and control essential between regional command and sections under his command.

Responsibilities of Section Commanders

1. Welfare of his men in all aspects.
2. Welfare of the people under his control which would normally be no more than five kraals. Welfare in this aspect includes their health, mobilisation, education, total protection from the enemy and any general matters arising.
3. Selection of *mujibhas* to form their intelligence networks, bearing in mind the closer the men are to the people, the greater they assist the people's needs; the greater co-operation the section is receiving, the better the intelligence networks would be. Without the support of the masses, we were lost. The people would provide the intelligence we required when they were mobilised.
4. Feedback of intelligence to regional command for combined section attacks when required.
5. Continual alertness to ZIPRA attacks especially, at night. Emphasis to be co-ordinated on both day-and-night operations.
6. Feedback of changing ZIPRA tactics to regional command.

Of all the aspects of our work, I would single out the following to be of prime importance:

1. Discipline throughout the command structure.
2. Continual mobilisation of the people and pursuance of their needs.
3. Establishment of intelligence networks which followed on during the normal course of events if (2) above is correctly implemented.
4. Elimination of ZIPRA through intelligence.
5. Correct and systematic formation of cells.
6. Advancement of reinforcements in correct and called-for (by the people) direction. To advance without the wishes of the people would be disastrous.
7. Continual propaganda aimed at ZIPRA.
8. Ever-growing recruitment and training.
9. Close co-operation and co-ordination between all command levels.
10. Commanders learned from the man-in-the-field and were to pass this knowledge on to their subordinates.

I considered section level as the grass-roots level. It was at this level that the men had daily contact with the people, where mobilisation was important and where our mistakes would be made, corrected and, more importantly, lessons learned passed on to higher command in order that the senior command would not lose touch with reality and become "armchair warriors".

Forward Field Command Base

The following explanation should be read in conjunction with my original drawings entitled "Forward Command Base".

The forward field command base at Magunje would be responsible for:

1. All men in the field.
2. Updating of weaponry when possible.
3. Logistical resupply of clothing and war material through the regional command structure.
4. Discipline in the field (when necessary action required).
5. Field intelligence, including interrogation of captures and *mujibhas* when necessary.
6. Co-ordination of all deployments in order to avoid errors.
7. Liaison with the local SB, GC and military when required.
8. Payment of men through the regional command structure.
9. Reception of recruits and their onward transfer to training farms.
10. Updating of ZIPRA tactics at training level in order to facilitate constant up-to-date training.
11. All communications, forward and rear.
12. Politicising the masses at public meetings whenever and wherever possible (UANC).
13. Receipt of ceasefire terrs when and if they come onsides.
14. Propaganda against ZIPRA.
15. Overseeing of medical treatment in the field of the people and the SFAs.
16. Overseeing the return to normalisation of the TTL, i.e. opening of the schools, clinics, grading roads and opening churches, etc. This would be done on an "as-and-when" basis, bearing in mind our priority was military strength first and normalisation later. However, the needs of the people must be facilitated in the process where possible.
17. Co-ordination of advance areas (in liaison with Security Forces), reorganisation of field callsigns and commanders when and where required, and overseeing of reinforcements, i.e. their even and satisfactory distribution among established callsigns, and election/nomination of new commanders. On this particular aspect, close liaison was kept with training farms in order to nominate aspiring commanders who showed natural leadership abilities. If these men did not progress through a natural course of events, they might become disillusioned and disciplinary problems in the field would arise. The replacement of field commanders did not present any problems. Deposed commanders would be told that they were merely being relieved to allow others necessary field experience. Deposed commanders could be released to take over another advance section at a later stage. (In reality, this did not often happen and was not a problem.)
18. Field transport in emergencies (wounded men, etc.) was a priority and local resources had to be utilised to the utmost.

Code of Conduct

An area of concern to me was discipline in the field. Our men had been recruited from Hurungwe and had experienced first-hand the extremes of ZIPRA's aggressive oppression of the people as they introduced martial law. Some of our men may have, as *mujibhas*, received minimal training from ZIPRA but they had little, if any, competent military experience. They had progressed from a rural environment through basic military training, along with the acquisition of a firearm with live ammunition: a volatile cocktail if ever there was one! Notwithstanding, since our men had specifically volunteered for training, it was evident they were aggrieved by ZIPRA's actions and the threats they posed in Hurungwe, allowing the situation to work to our advantage.

We already had in place appropriate checks and balances. These included the farm intelligence network, the UANC office intelligence networks for Chikangwe and their field operations in Hurungwe, and also the political work Grey's and Happy's team were doing with the men in the field. Keeping in touch with the people through the intelligence networks and political meetings would be vital as we progressively became one with them through open communications, and their recognising that we were the people's army.

As the masses had been subjected to extreme violence due to not supporting ZIPRA, it became imperative we avoid a similar approach. The consequence of aggressive oppression is that, once brutality is initiated, it leads to a never-ending cycle of tortures, gross human violations, with death becoming an unavoidable reality. Subsequently, dehumanising those failing to "tow the party line" is justified and legitimised as a means to an end. As areas where the masses, contact men and *mujibhas* opposed to us were penetrated, their resistance would intensify should we have tortured or killed "sellouts". I believed the only way forward was the political reorientation of the masses supported by disciplined actions and good conduct of the SFAs. In my view, there was, nor is, a substitute for integrity and ethical conduct. If we conducted ourselves correctly, success would follow. In the light of our thinking, we introduced a code of conduct for our men to follow:

1. No disciplinary killings of any nature whatsoever.
2. No raping of women.
3. No interference in traditional African way of life.
4. No taking of money from the people. Our men would be paid an adequate salary, not excessive, but adequate.
5. No assaulting of the people. This might prove to be difficult when a "sellout" (*mujibha* or contact man opposed to us) is captured, especially if we lose men in a battle or the people are killed by ZIPRA. However, training of the section(s) PCs and experience would diminish this problem if it occurred. Field intelligence from captures should be gleaned expeditiously in the field and, where possible, acted upon. Thereafter, the capture would be handed over to the party for indoctrination, reorientation, training and eventual deployment to his home area.
6. If the section is unable to glean intelligence from the capture, he is to be handed over to the party and myself for discussions and reorientation.
7. In the forward areas, after contacts at kraals and when politicising the people in preparation for the coming of the people's army, the seed of the people's army has to be merely sown for it to germinate. The people would draw their own comparisons between ZIPRA and the people's army: reputation always precedes! It was my opinion that the people knew themselves that we were right and, in their minds, were desperate for us to occupy their areas. At these meetings, known ZIPRA *mujibhas* would be collected and interviewed according to our procedures. Every time the people come into contact with ZIPRA, the seed of liberation in the true sense of the word planted by the people's army would grow fractionally.
8. The effect of returning a repoliticised, reorientated and trained *mujibha* to his home area would have a far greater psychological effect on his relatives and friends than if he were not to return at all, and be presumed dead. Once the seed of doubt and hate is sown, it can never be removed and that "corrupt seed", once sown, would germinate and grow against us.

Restoration Process

Once our men had successfully occupied an area, we could turn our attention to the restoration of normality in Hurungwe. In the long term, this would prove challenging. However, our short-term goals included the reopening of bus routes, clinics and schools. While appearing ideological and overly optimistic, I for one remained positive, committed and determined. The alternative was not worth considering.

African Political Development and Advancement

It was my outlook that progressive political development, advancement and education of the people, with increasing momentum as we penetrated Hurungwe, would keep the people informed of national political progress towards majority rule. Section PCs and UANC mass party rallies addressed by influential party members would support this process. I reiterate that these important aspects needed to coincide with our military successes: success being defined as our ability to hold the ground and defend the people. I was also of the opinion that these advancements needed to address the subject of increased wages and improved working conditions for the African farm and mine employees. They were, after all, the dominant labour forces surrounding the Hurungwe TTL at the time and, therefore, of the utmost importance. Transformation in these areas would have an immediate effect on the people, demonstrating tangible progress. Naturally, a close follow-up to matters relating to labour would be the need for an injection of capital into Hurungwe in order to sustain effective, organised and prolonged development.

White Political Education

I made a diary entry which highlights the urgency for political changes: "Continuing (or more to the point, commencement) of the education of the European's (white Rhodesian's) attitude towards the African was vital. For too long now the Europeans of this country have considered the Africans as ignorant peasants incapable of work, thought and education. They could never be further from the truth and I believe that the truth is beginning to come home, too, and hurt. Once the European is awakened to the power and capabilities of the masses, only then will our society become one. I am of the firm opinion that this political reorientation of both the masses and the European minority is of grave importance."

During a visit to Chabwino on 28 November 1978, I had an encouraging conversation with the refugees from Hurungwe who were settling down well. Some had medical problems which were treated at the farm or by the local hospital, for which they were profoundly grateful. As the number of refugees grew, it was clear our limited resources would be stretched. I decided that, in due course, we would have to work towards establishing a clinic and a school to cater for the education of the children. George Hutchison of the Admin. team was in the process of organising with a local farmer the ploughing of 75 acres on which to sow maize seed to feed our people. Our thinking was that, should the harvest prove bountiful, we could sell the leftovers for further expansion and recoup our costs. He arranged for an area of about one acre to be ploughed for a vegetable patch for the people which would be irrigated from the farm's reservoir. However, the supply of meat was problematic, therefore we planned for the acquisition of our own cattle. We thought it possible to herd the refugees' cattle from Hurungwe to Chabwino where they could take care of them. Potentially, this step would alleviate our meat shortage, but our plans would have to be agreed to by the refugees. We had no desire to unsettle them. Unfortunately, the plan did not materialise.

I spent a substantial time at Chabwino talking to the men and to the refugees. It was a most interesting experience because our work was greatly appreciated. At the *mujibha* farm in Rusape, the compromised *mujibhas* had no other choice but to remain loyal and friendly. Chabwino was different. All the men were volunteers and the refugees were grateful to live away from the ravages of war in Hurungwe. Ours was a unique environment where we were accepted, fully integrated and one with the people. I recall a conversation with one 100-year-old refugee. He had vivid recollections of the first whites arriving in his area. The old man, born in 1878, was 10 years old when the Rudd Concession was signed and 18 years old when the First *Chimurenga* began. His son, another refugee, with whom I also held conversations, was also elderly, and they were both intriguing men to talk with. I learned a great deal from them, in particular that our white-colonial history in Rhodesia was recent and still residing in the memories of a generation who would pass on their oral history for decades to come.

Reflecting on these frequent visits to the farm, I recorded in my diary the looming difficulty facing

Rhodesia, requiring considerable effort in reorientating the white population to the fast-approaching political changes. Among the many discriminatory practices found in the country were the following three which immediately sprung to mind. Firstly, African soldiers were not allowed in the Twin Rivers Motel. Secondly, farmers continued to treat their labour aggressively and thirdly, the wages of African employees, across most spheres of employment, remained minimal. Resolving these, and many other shortcomings, required the collective will of the nation but I, for one, had misgivings regarding the white population's zeal to work towards greater racial harmony. I envisaged the problems increasing in magnitude as military victory demands political, social and economic changes. Despite little being done at government level to resolve these pressing issues, I continued to report on the matters relating to our progress in Hurungwe, hoping that they would inspire change. I felt it necessary to address the problems proactively and hopefully avert serious problems in Hurungwe when we were successful.

I envisaged a solution to our ailing country as being the development of a successful people's army which I felt confident would win the war in Hurungwe. However, unless the national political obstacles were addressed and removed, we would have a strong people's army continuing to fight for the people, in direct opposition to the ruling government.

I felt it important that a united, deliberate and committed strategy was required at a national level, empowering leadership to common objectives and purposes which, in my view, were lacking in the SF. The political objectives that the SF were fighting for were collapsing. Nevertheless, at a local level, I was confident of our vision and direction for Hurungwe. I had worked out the strategy and structure for our penetration into Hurungwe. Granted, we faced a formidable, well-established enemy, yet my confidence prevailed. The only outstanding question was when should we deploy our forces?

16 ~ DARE TO STRUGGLE, DARE TO WIN

The supreme art of war is to subdue the enemy without fighting.
Sun Tzu

SFA Strategies Phase 9: Deploy, occupy, and possess the land

The People's Army Deploys

On Wednesday, 29 November 1978, Happy received intelligence advising him that 16 ZIPRA insurgents had been based on Birimahwe Hill for close on six weeks, while using the villages near the business centre to sleep in at night. They met at Love's place, a shop on the main Binga road intercepting the old Binga road. The informant, Victor (pseudonym), had met the group on several occasions, mainly when providing them with general supplies such as food and clothing. Philip Ncube commanded the group. A large part of the group was thought to be resident at Mashuma's Kraal. It was reported that five girls (names withheld) were thought to be sleeping with the insurgents. Happy brought the intelligence to me the following morning. (See First SFAs Deployment Original Sketch p.333.)

We had received the same information on 24 November 1978, and had already made the decision to use the intelligence in conjunction with the first deployment of our Security Force Auxiliaries. At the time, I had the area proscribed by Sub.JOC Sinoia and had instructed the training staff to prepare the men for deployment. Shortly thereafter, they were on standby awaiting final orders. We were fortunate that Victor's information was now confirmed by another source. For our SFAs inaugural deployment it was my preference to deploy on positive intelligence in order to attack and hopefully eliminate some insurgents in the process. After the battle, we would then occupy and hold the ground. This contrasted with SF typical search-and-destroy, uplift-and-regroup operations. It was also fortunate the Fire Force was still deployed in Karoi, therefore I arranged a meeting with them and discussed our intelligence with the Fire Force Commander. I showed them the sketches of the area and our estimated locstats. The Fire Force included one K-Car, piloted by Flt. Lt. Dick Paxton with technician/gunner, Sgt. Mark Jackson, and one K-Car, piloted by Flt. Lt. Mark McLean with technician/gunner, Sgt. Gary Carter. Air Lt. Luigi Mantovani piloted an accompanying G-Car with technician/gunner, Sgt. Phil Archenoul.

I was firmly convinced that the time had arrived to mobilise our men and begin our assault on ZIPRA. Our plan was for the informant to walk our first three sections into the target area for deployment overnight. Thereafter, under the direction of Martin, the detachment commander, armed with an RPD, the men would take up positions as "stop" lines before first light. Each section would be equipped with a radio and sufficient armaments for the day's battle. Their remaining personal equipment for permanent deployment would be transported to them after the encounter.

David and Mike, my trained *mujibhas* and seasoned soldiers from Rusape, would join the attack. They were both armed with RPDs, I was confident of their capabilities. The training staff were also to deploy, with Admin. positioned to provide transport and backup. Fire Force would deploy as soon after first light as possible and be directed into the target area by our now situated forces. Our distinct advantage was that our men were familiar with not only the area, but also with the people. Grey, Happy and I planned to attend the scene in order to address the people and the men in the field subsequent to the battle.

While it was our intended policy for white members of our team to remain unexposed in Hurungwe until our UANC forces were established and accepted, I felt it was important to monitor closely their first deployment, thereby ensuring the attack was as successful as possible. Success would signal to both the local residents and ZIPRA that the people's army had arrived, was well trained and committed to the defence of the masses, while permanently occupying the area. It was equally vital to gather immediate intelligence following the battle, as well as assess the response of the locals to the arrival of their army. Additionally, it was essential for Grey and Happy to be viewed as being in overall command. Success on this first operation was paramount. With the Fire Force and three sections deployed, we were applying maximum force to eliminate the enemy.

During the course of the day, I informed Geoff Price, Com.Ops., Sub.JOC Sinoia, the local police and SB that I was deploying our forces and requested a daily PRAW flight from Sub.JOC Sinoia, commencing 2 December 1978, in order to provide essential communications with our men in the field. I felt it imperative to maintain communications with the men, who had been instructed to ensure their radios were switched on when they heard or saw a civilian aircraft. We had installed a radio in our "safe house" for communications with the men and maintained a continuous radio watch. Although we were unable to communicate directly with them, we would overhear transmissions from relay stations and the pilot.

Later in the afternoon, Grey and Happy visited the men for a final address before their first deployment. An air of expectancy gripped the farm. The men literally could not wait to be deployed. It was a long, tense evening as our plans began to unfold. As sunset loomed on Thursday, 30 November 1978, and with the weekend approaching, we anticipated that ZIPRA would lower their guard in preparation for a relaxed few days of socialising, beer drinking and other revelries. Little did they know!

Our overnight walk-in went according to plan and was well executed. The men were in position before first light, awaiting the arrival of the FF. They had the distinct advantage in this type of operation by having an intimate, local knowledge of the area. It was their homeground in every sense. It was here that they had played, worked and socialised. They were aware of which kraals and neighbourhood dogs should be avoided, and were familiar with the safe shortcuts and paths to follow, along with suitable escape routes in the event of a compromise. They were in harmony with the sounds and smells of the TTL and had an inherent ability to detect danger, especially when the normal and mundane activities of everyday life in the kraals, and immediate surroundings, changed from normal to abnormal. Not only were they one with the environment, they would soon be one with the people and, in my opinion, invincible. They would bear witness to the teachings of Mao Zedong: "The guerrilla must move among the people as a fish swims in the sea."

Possibly the greatest advantage they enjoyed was fighting for what they truly believed in: the defence of the masses and the removal of the invading ZIPRA forces. The men were not conscripted, nor coerced into defending unachievable political ends. No, they were ready to fight for their legitimate human rights. Our resistance movement had been armed, trained and given hope. I considered it a privilege to experience this unique process.

The FF arrived on schedule at first light on 1 December 1978 and made contact with our men. Two insurgents were located in the kraals, both of whom were killed by the FF. One attempted to flee but, in apparent confusion, turned and hurled a grenade back into the hut, resulting in minor injuries to two females and three juveniles. Regrettably, the husband was seriously injured in crossfire and was attended to by Capt. Webster, the Regimental Medical Officer, 1 RLI.[1] He was evacuated to Salisbury Hospital in a helicopter at 8.55 a.m. One fortunate aspect of this contact was that the only hut destroyed was the site occupied by the deceased insurgents.[2]

Before first light Grey, Happy and I were prepared for departure. However, our radio, although tuned into the FF frequency, remained silent. Shortly after sunrise we received a radio message that the RLI FF had engaged the insurgents. We left knowing that our travelling would not compromise the operation. Admin. followed, carrying the men's kit and equipment for their long-term deployment. On arrival at the contact area, we learned that two insurgents had been killed and one *mujibha* captured.

1 A. Binda, (2014), eBook Location 9756 of 16593.

2 Karoi Contacts Map Incident 19.

The Fire Force Commander commented that our callsigns had reacted appropriately, with measured discipline. As was anticipated, he encountered minor problems but these were to be expected on our first deployment. Naturally, our shortcomings would be addressed in due course. In my opinion, the men had worked well with the Fire Force and had achieved a positive outcome with no fatalities to our forces. What more could be asked of soldiers? The men's morale was elevated and the masses were jubilantly celebrating their army's accomplishments.

Following the contact, our men gathered together the locals from the area. Their relatives were delighted at their return as a resident military unit, specifically for their protection. Once settled, I emphasised to the masses that they were to protect their newly established army and that, in turn, their army would serve as their guardians. While generally well received, one old man asked what would happen if one of our men was betrayed and killed by ZIPRA. He was concerned about the fate of the people. I responded that it was up to the people to report "sellouts" to the people's army who would address the matter accordingly. Another elderly man stood up and pleaded for the army to remain in the area and protect them. His sentiment was chorused by the remainder of the crowd, who requested the permanent presence of the people's army. Their joy knew no bounds when informed by Grey and Happy that their army was there to stay.

I emphasised that our men had not harassed the locals and would forthwith work alongside them. A little later, we established that there were only two insurgents in the kraals at the time of the contact. Gradually, details of how the ZIPRA section had resided in the area and harassed the people emerged. They were forthcoming with information, which I found encouraging. I found myself in the unique situation of receiving information from the locals regarding a resident section of insurgents immediately after the contact. This fuelled my desire to continue our approach to the war. I was satisfied with developments and arranged for the injured family to be moved to Chabwino for treatment, and to receive new clothing. As soon as the injured were treated and recovered, they would be returned to Hurungwe by the UANC, and we were determined to gain maximum propaganda from this situation. To the surprise of us all, we found the reaction of the locals to our success was far above expectations.

Following the successful deployment of the people's army, we left the men in the field, reminding them to make daily radio contact with the PRAW plane each day while they settled into their new environment. The men were well organised and eager for action: a compliment to the training staff. The UANC networks were instrumental in gathering the intelligence required for politicising the people. Admin. and the SF proved unwavering in their support. As I reflected on these aspects of our operation, I marvelled at the harmony the team had achieved. Once matters had returned to normal, Grey updated the bishop regarding our successful developments. On my return to the "safe house" in Karoi, I informed the relevant authorities of the success of our first deployment. Dis.Pol. Sinoia confirmed he would supply a PRAW aircraft at 12 noon daily to help maintain contact with our sections in the field, until we rectified our communications problems. He had been helpful, which was encouraging. Bob Bedingham recalled the procedures for despatching the Police Reserve Air Wing: "When a request was received from the field for a PRAW flight, it was scrutinised before an official request was sent to the Supt. Police Reserve and Security (PR & S) at Mashonaland Province explaining the details of the flight. Once verbal confirmation was received and the flight authorised, the PRAW pilot would be put on stand by and details of the flight explained which would include timings, airfield locations, pax (reference to number of passengers on board), and flight details. Official BSAP Reserve Air Wing Flight Authorisation – Form P.R. 28 – would be issued in quadruplicate; the original and first copy to the pilot, second copy filed at District Headquarters of issue in this case Sinoia, and the third copy remained in the book. Once the flight was completed the Flight Log (Form P.R. 21), a copy of Form P.R. 28 and the hire account were forwarded to the Staff Officer (Police Reserve) within 30 days of the flight. Payments were then made by cheque to the Pilots; flights were not paid for in cash. It was a well-managed system. Dis.Pol.'s were issued with budgets by Chief Insp. Pringle (Police Reserve Office at Police General Headquarters Salisbury) who carefully monitored them. In emergencies we would make immediate decisions but thereafter all laid down procedures and documentation followed suit. PRAW was an efficient method of visiting Police stations and Posts. On Boxing Days Tim Allen and myself would take off at first light and visit remote police posts such as Bumi, Mushumbi Pools and Kanyemba taking them 'goodie parcels' and mail."[1] (See Appendices pp.479-481 for relevant PRAW forms.)

Former PRAW pilot and Commander of the Air wing, Bill Linfield, recalled: "When on call up the PRAW operated under the directions of the Air Force and were fully briefed on all the latest developments which might effect our flying duties. The Flight standards section was also responsible for training, development and implementation of any new flying tactics. These included the use of weapons for air to ground attacks. The Flight standard Section was a designated group of PRAW pilots, mostly instructor rated, who carried out all proficiency testing, both initial and annual flight tests of all pilots in the PRAW. As the PRAW worked in close liaison with the Air Force I know that there would have been expert advice where necessary. After the Viscount *Hunyani* incident on 3 September 1978, the government paid to have PRAW aircraft painted with the anti-Strela paint, a mat grey finish. Before Viscount *Hunyani* was shot down, the war started hotting up. Indiscriminate ground to air small arms fire was being experienced by both the Air Force and the PRAW. Our tactic, generally, was to remain at tree top height which limited the Terrs ability to see us coming and passing overhead their position before they could have a chance to react."[2]

In the glow of the day's success, we were the recipients of more good news. Geoff had arranged a new Peugeot motor vehicle for Grey. He had also purchased a Jaguar XJ6 vehicle for me for our travels back and forth to Salisbury.[3] Geoff handled the vehicle transactions personally and had organised for us to collect our vehicles the following morning. Prior to owning vehicles, our practice was to hire them from Echo Car Hire: an expensive exercise. I hasten to add that the XJ6 was not an economical vehicle to drive and, adding to expenses, was the fact that, as Hurungwe became safer for travel, we began to drive it on the dirt roads. This resulted in exhaust-pipe damage which required frequent visits to the garage for repairs. The vehicle was not a personal choice but it was a luxurious motor car to travel in.

The timeous arrival of a vehicle for Grey and the Jaguar for my personal travels were most welcome. It resolved the immediate transport difficulties we had been experiencing. As our previous vehicles had been compromised, I was concerned for the safety of the UANC military and intelligence operators. The newly acquired vehicles provided immediate relief in this regard. To supplement our fleet, we had ordered a pick-up truck which, when it arrived, would solve the last of our transport deficiencies. At the same time, Geoff had organised a mine-proofed, short wheel base Land Rover for our sojourns into Hurungwe.

A bullet-proofed windscreen was fitted to the Land Rover, and the driver and passenger windows were also exchanged for bullet-proofed glass. We installed two loud speakers into the front of the Land Rover for our musical entertainment. I also arranged a stock of cigars to smoke while on our journeys. On both sides of the vehicle Sandy had inscribed: "Twinkle twinkle little rectum, you hear the bangs when you least expectum." My policy was that if you are going to die in battle, die enjoying life.

At a personal level, the build-up to the first deployment had been demanding but I was pleased the men were finally successfully deployed. I had resisted the demands for early deployments and the whole team had excelled in preparing the masses for the arrival of their army. Observing the success of the operation, especially the reception and acceptance by the masses of their army, was a privilege. This was an unique moment and my concerns for the safety of the men waned when I realised the UANC had politically gained the consent of the people: one of the keys to our successes. I held the view that, once the army and the masses united, we would be invincible. As can be expected, our celebrations knew no bounds that night.

1 Bob Bedingham email 3/4/2016. Confirmed by Snr. Asst. Comm. Ted Sheriff oral interview 5/10/2019 and C/Insp. Bill Linfield email 10/10/2019.

2 Bill Linfield emails 9/11/2019 and 10/11/2019; Gibbs, P., Phillips, H. and Russell, N. (2009), pp. 361-362.

3 Remembered by George Hutchison, Sandy Irvine and Todd.

The Morning After the Battle

A recurring danger following victory is the victor allowing his guard to drop while, simultaneously, the defeated "licked their wounds" and prepared to retaliate in order to regain the initiative. I firmly believe that, in war, victory should be followed by immediate preparations for the next battle, thereby ensuring that the enemy gains no perception of the vulnerability of the triumphant. We had continually warned the men to remain constantly alert, as one of the critical aspects of battle preparation is to be permanently ready at all levels to exploit incoming intelligence in order to enable rapid response.

True to his word, Dis.Pol. organised a PRAW aircraft which arrived in Karoi at 12 noon, Saturday, 2 December 1978. I instructed Walter to act as an airborne radio relay station (Telstar) for the first flights and report back to me. That day, we established radio communications with the three sections in the field: I felt relaxed! They were continuing to establish themselves among the masses who were still celebrating the arrival and support of the people's army. I considered it imperative to ensure we did not lose momentum, therefore I arranged for Grey and Happy to assemble the recruits waiting in the field for training. I also arranged for the remaining sections at Chabwino undergoing their final days of training to be paid and prepared for deployment, to maximise and maintain progress. This would give the existing deployed sections time to establish themselves, overcome any immediate security and logistics problems, and prepare the ground for the incoming sections.

The same day, I arranged for Grey and Happy to travel into Hurungwe to visit the men in the field. Initially, these visits would be daily and serve to keep in touch with the men, attend to their needs, politicise them and advise on strategies and tactics. This ensured that Grey and Happy were seen by the men and the people to be in command, an essential ingredient in our operation and process of promoting a new dispensation. Simultaneously, the people were also visited and politicised, ensuring they understood that they were a vital component of the people's army: in fact, one with the army. The masses and their army would not fear each other as they were one. One was not above the other but an extension or part of each other. In the early stages, this message was critical, as it would set the tone for the entire battle for Hurungwe.

In view of the overwhelming support we had received from the people on our first deployment, even at this early stage I was confident that we had ZIPRA on the run. I was of the view that if they lost the support of the masses, they would relinquish ground. In my mind, the matter was straightforward. The masses were the key and we had won their initial support. I was anxious we strike while the odds were in our favour.

To maintain this momentum, Admin. ordered more equipment from Special Forces. We emphasised that this equipment was essential in maintaining the early gains achieved by our men. My diary recorded the extensive list:

(1) 60 AK-47 rifles.
(2) 240 AK-47 magazines.
(3) 60 AK-47 webbing sets.
(4) 120 water bottles.
(5) 60 belts of webbing.
(6) 120,000 AK-47, 7.62 intermediate rounds of ammunition.
(7) 1 Heavy vehicle (an important asset). We only have one heavy vehicle. Our area is extensively mined and we will have to react to contacts and incidents, etc., not forgetting of course deploying our troops when we would need two vehicles. It is imperative for the successful continuation of our operations that an additional heavy vehicle be obtained.
(8) Anti-ambush Land Rover (similar reasons as above).
(9) 30 x 2-man shelters.
(10) 60 groundsheets.
(11) 180 blankets (3 per man).
(12) 120 khaki "T" shirts.

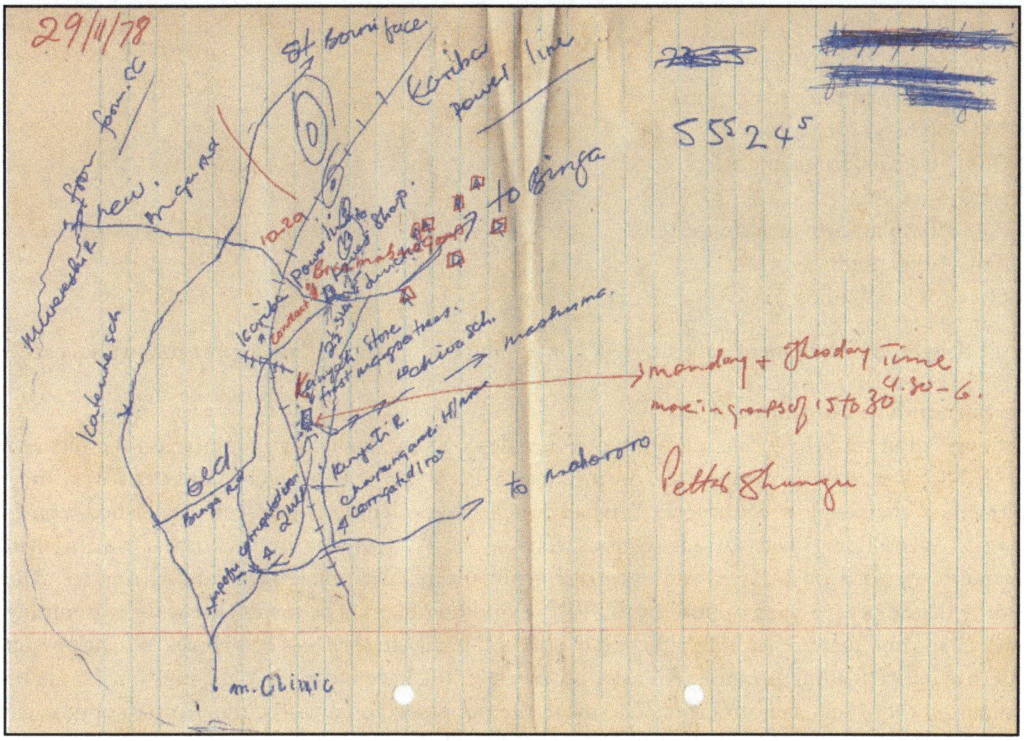

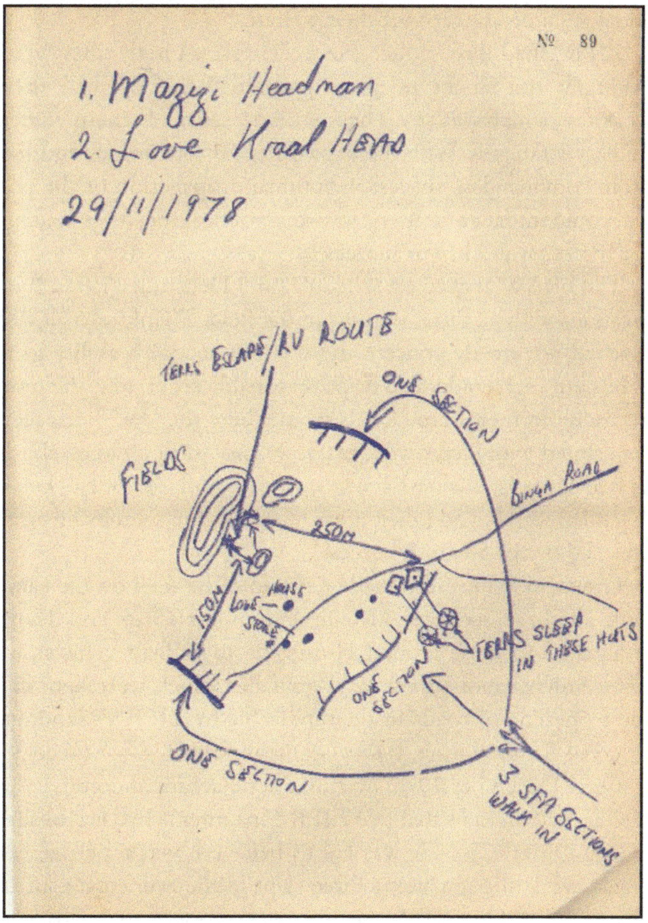

First SFAs Deployment
Original Sketch of the general area and Battle plan sketch.

(13) 120 pairs of blue shorts.
(14) 60 pairs of hockey boots.
(15) 30 x 60mm mortar bombs.
(16) 60 hand-grenades.
(17) 12 icarus parachute flares.
(18) 6 mini-flares.
(19) 30 mini-flares projectiles (red).
(20) 1,000 sandbags.
(21) 6 x A63 radios.

To my delight, the equipment soon arrived, confirming the principle that support follows success.

The Situation in Hurungwe TTL

In conversation with the locals following our first deployment, including the refugees, recruits and the UANC, it was further impressed on me that ZIPRA had a great deal to answer for in their treatment of the people in Hurungwe. We had conclusive evidence of their well-established *mujibha* networks surrounding their various sections. The *mujibha* system was similar to that which I had previously reported on prior to my departure from the regular police force and thereafter. The majority of the people were opposed to ZIPRA exploiting them. The insurgents were committing murder, rape and theft, disrupting public transport and paralysing schools and clinics in their pursuit of destroying civil administration. All told, however, ZIPRA were playing right into our hands by committing these acts and atrocities. The more the people were harassed, the greater support we would enjoy, hence it was important to emphasise our policy of peaceful coexistence with the locals, and a genuine concern for their welfare.

ZIPRA had three noticeable weaknesses. Firstly, they were principally Ndebele in a Shona area. Secondly, not all the people supported them. We had already successfully exploited their third weakness which was sex. These weaknesses made them vulnerable and helped us form political and military strategies. With the deployment of our forces and the forthcoming rainy season, I became more convinced of success. Continual propagation of the people was paramount and, to this end, we would initiate a series of low-key political meetings leading to larger gatherings. Politicisation of the masses was a key to success.

The PRAW arrived on schedule on 3 December 1978. Subsequently, we had successful communications with all three sections in the field. Thankfully, all was going according to plan. One aspect that did not overly concern me was our section's ability to remain within their demarcated areas. While our men could read maps reasonably accurately, the more significant factor was that they were returning to their home kraals from where they had been recruited. Since they were extremely well acquainted with their own areas, it was not difficult to establish natural operational boundaries, such as rivers, roads, business centres, schools and, of course, kraals. I insisted that the demarcated areas extended well beyond their areas of operation, thereby ensuring our men were not compromised or attacked by the Security Forces.

Grey and Happy also made a trip into the field on the same day and established communication with all three sections. My admiration for Grey and Happy continued to grow as they were compelled to drive around Hurungwe in civilian vehicles with no protection against landmines. Their only weapons were hand-grenades which were kept in their pockets. Our planning included the reopening of roads made impassable by ZIPRA's landmine strategies. This step, however, was reserved for the future, following the unfolding of our tactics.

On 4 December 1978, Martin, the detachment commander, returned from the field and passed intelligence on to us that five ZIPRA insurgents had established themselves in a kraal complex in his area at QM606226. He was led to believe it was a permanent base, as two insurgents slept in the kraals, while the remaining three slept in the immediate surroundings of the kraals, possibly in the nearby hills. The ZIPRA section was resident in kraals nearby our men, indicating they either disregarded our threat or they felt secure and were too comfortably settled to move. I preferred to think the latter. Martin had already established an extensive *mujibha* network and the information he was obtaining was factual and reliable.

I was pleased to see Martin and discuss our field operations. He was a likeable, committed and determined young man with a constant smile on his face, regardless of the circumstances. He was observant, astute and a capable leader. His standard headgear, a well-worn school cap, gave him the appearance of an armed schoolboy. A clear case of "don't be deceived by looks". He informed us that the masses had openly accepted our men, and the passing of intelligence between the people and their army was rapidly developing. Locals from the surrounding areas had consciously migrated to contact our sections. They were extremely pleased and grateful for the work we were doing. The favourable reaction of the people, while anticipating it to be positive, was beyond expectations. In this constructive environment, our men were living in the bush while mobilising the masses during the day. We spent time planning the attack on the ZIPRA section mentioned previously. The time had arrived for Martin to take the initiative, lead his men and attack the insurgents. He relished the opportunity. To accommodate the attack, I arranged for the three remaining sections at Chabwino to be deployed and assist with the operation. At the conclusion of the attack, they would remain in the first demarcated area under Martin's command.

Prior to Martin's deployment, we received news via our office radio, that the PRAW pilot had established communications with the callsigns in Hurungwe. This boosted his confidence in knowing that he was "connected" to us and encouragement that his sections were functioning satisfactorily in his absence. I regarded this as a good omen for what lay ahead.

Later that day, Martin and the additional three new sections were deployed into the field after a thorough briefing by Happy. Yet another jubilant day as the men celebrated their departure, keen for the planned attack on ZIPRA set for early the morning of 6 December 1978. Final details of the planning were left to Martin once in the field. What I found heartwarming was that the men had the courage, determination and confidence to carry out the attack. My sole concern was for the safety of the men. While killing several of the enemy would boost the men's morale and confidence, more important was not losing sight of our prime objective of occupying and securing Hurungwe militarily, by gaining the support of the masses. In the process of achieving this, ZIPRA would be isolated from the masses, lose their support and gradually be forced out as we occupied the land. I considered killing ZIPRA an undertaking for the SF who were effective, equipped and trained for the task. It was important not to digress from our separate functions, although at times our men would be required to engage the enemy. If we could capitalise on the intelligence gained from the field while employing maximum force of the SF, in particular the Fire Force, confidence and morale of both the people and our forces would be boosted.

As Sunday, 6 December 1978 dawned, we anxiously awaited the results of Martin's first attack on ZIPRA. At midday, as the PRAW aircraft flew over the area, we learned that the attack had gone to plan but, unfortunately, no ZIPRA were present in the kraal complex. One section was left in the area to take control and support the locals. Martin deployed the remaining two sections into their area of operation. He had secured a positive outcome.

We now had six sections deployed in the field. Sixty men were permanently operational in Hurungwe and Chabwino housed many volunteer trainees. Pressure was mounting on the training staff. It was overwhelming watching the response of the local young men signing up for the people's army. Momentum had increased since witnessing our men in action. Grey and Happy continued to screen the men with help from their office in Chikangwe. It was busy times for all. I was grateful for Admin.'s support and could not have managed without them.

A day earlier, Happy brought us information of approximately 100 ZIPRA based and supported at farm 86 in the Vuti APA, belonging to the late Mumvuri. The informant asked Tapedza at the UANC office for R$50 to give to the insurgents. He was prepared to introduce Tapedza to them at our convenience and planning. As this was not an area in which we were operating, I passed on the intelligence to the relevant authorities. Naturally, we would assist should we be called upon.

Happy had also been made aware that in the Mashumba area, our informant, Simba (pseudonym), had been visited by eight insurgents resident in a nearby base camp. He had been providing meals for the section but had subsequently fled, leaving his family behind. The camp's location was known.

With the area becoming increasingly subject to our influence (six sections deployed), the UANC's regular communications with our callsigns and, with the freedom of travel Martin was experiencing, we decided to suspend the PRAW communications flights. It was a formidable challenge. I was inclined to believe that it would strengthen the men's position as they were forced to rely on the support of the people. In my thinking, this step would further entrench Happy's and Grey's positions as commanders by their regular communications with the men. Ostensibly, it would remove me and other white operatives from the operational zone until the opportune time for our introduction.

I addressed meetings arranged by Admin. with the farmers surrounding our farm at Chabwino and the Tengwe farmers. Their reaction to our work was favourable. There were no adverse comments and I advised them that generally our deployments were successful. Our achievements emphasised our ability to hold the ground we occupied. It was not my place to discuss the political changes I envisaged necessary for future racial harmony. This required the politicians to make bold changes. The priority, I felt, was for our forces to be established militarily in support of these political changes.

In time, life settled down in Hurungwe although one could question "normality" of life during the hostilities of warfare. Our "safe house" was finally fully furnished and occupied. All told, a costly exercise, but it reduced considerably our expenses as opposed to lodging at the Twin Rivers Motel. We were fortunate to have modern electrical luxuries, including a fridge, a stove and a toaster to boot, all of which made us totally self-sufficient while housed in a very comfortable home. Most importantly, we were ideally placed to carry out our operations without disturbances. As an aside to the multiracial arrangements at our "safe house", the continued policy of racial separation at Twin Rivers Motel, run by the flamboyant Rufus Angus Snyman, made it glaringly obvious that the country's view on segregation demanded an urgent review. The integration of blacks and whites in day-to-day living was an imperative, yet vast numbers of white Rhodesians failed to comprehend the urgency of the matter. I often wondered whether they grasped the gravity of the situation in the country. Sadly, to me, it did not seem so!

Grey and Happy insisted on having our property guarded by our own *mujibhas*. This proved to be a wise decision. Other minor innovations included converting the dining room into an "operations centre" in which our maps were displayed indicating incidents, contacts, demarcated areas and the sections therein. The radio was also placed in this area with a continuous "radio watch", ensuring that the house was occupied at all times. It was an exhilarating experience living in a completely non-racial environment with a shared common purpose and vision. A large table occupied the centre of the lounge which was utilised not only for meals but also for our planning, briefing and debriefing sessions. My bedroom opened out on to the garden. It had a single bed, bedside table and light, and a cupboard: my needs were basic! Collectively, we shared similar conditions. Times of relaxation were spent sunbathing on the verandah. There were no formalities and the men were free to move in and out of the property at their liberty. We were free from pomp and ceremony. Our dwelling was not conducive to female company, hence when Lynette paid me periodic visits, we stayed at either the Twin Rivers Motel or the Karoi Hotel.

Strike 5: Mudzimu Fire Force Action

On Wednesday, 6 December 1978, a Selous Scouts callsign requested a Fire Force deployment to the southern part of Hurungwe. In the ensuing battle, four insurgents were killed, striking yet another blow to ZIPRA. I was not aware of the location of the battle.[1]

---

[1] Confirmed by my diaries. Karoi Contacts Map Incident 21, not logged on map.

During the morning of Thursday, 7 December 1978, our callsigns in the field sent two females and a store owner into Karoi to collect supplies. The three called in at our "safe house" on their way into town. I found this visit encouraging as it showed the men trusted them and were unafraid that they would betray us to either ZIPRA or their intelligence networks. During our discussions, they informed us that our men had been very well received by the people. However, the men did not trust the people to provide them with meals, consequently they purchased most of their provisions from local stores. They were conscious of instances in which ZANLA and ZIPRA insurgents had been poisoned by food provided by locals, normally from the hands of individuals acting on behalf of the SF. The local store owners welcomed the additional income. These legitimate business transactions formed part of our strategy, as we were aware of ZIPRA simply helping themselves to provisions. We made it a matter of everyday practice to pay the going rate for our acquisitions. The store owners were well-known and influential members of the TTLs: it was important to win their favour.

A further benefit resulting from this visit was that it showed our communications strategies were well placed. It was important the people knew they had free access to our high command and the political echelons of the UANC, thereby giving them the confidence to report cases of abuse, rape, murder and misdemeanours of our men in the field, should they occur. Our men also knew they would be held accountable for their actions. The flow and counterflow of intelligence was developing at an encouraging rate, with the masses and their army firmly uniting. As I have previously recorded, little went unnoticed in the TTLs.

Later in the morning, our plans for the day took an unexpected turn. Ben Pretorius from Special Branch Kariba arrested a ZIPRA *mujibha* from Hurungwe whom he had intercepted in Kariba Township. Aware of our operations, Ben sent the *mujibha* to us thinking that he would be able to assist us in locating ZIPRA insurgents. Happy and his team soon learned of his depth of knowledge of insurgent operations in the Mudzimu area. The *mujibha* was adamant that the resident section would be found at the homes of Maponga in the Nyamhondoro area, southern Hurungwe. I was convinced the intelligence was current and immediate, and contacted the Fire Force based at Montesuma airfield. To my relief, they were eager and available for deployment. A prompt decision was called for. Mudzimu was a remote area on the eastern border of Hurungwe, nearby the Rengwe Communal Lands. Whereas the *mujibha* had not been compromised, tangible intelligence needed to be established and acted on to ensure success. I reflected on the risks and decided to deploy.

We identified the target area on the map, referenced it and pinpointed surrounding features, such as business centres, roads, footpaths, rivers and hills. With this information, we produced a sketch map and transposed it onto an ordnance survey map. This would help Happy and I identify the terrain from above, ensuring the informer did not become disoriented in the air, and also bearing in mind this would be his first flight in a helicopter. Coincidently, it was also Happy's first airborne attack, providing him with a challenge. The information would help the FF pilots chart a flight-path for navigation to the battleground. It took the whole morning, up to the early part of the afternoon, to organise the intelligence before we were satisfied that our presentation was in order and accurate.

Armed with this intelligence, Happy, the informer and I drove to the Fire Force in our Jaguar, convinced in our minds that the resident ZIPRA section would be at the kraal. I was optimistic and hoped the others felt the same as, in my experience, confidence is infectious. Maj. Nigel Henson was the FF Commander, Air Lt. Nigel Lamb, flying the K-Car, was the airborne commander and Sgt. Beaver Shaw served as his technician/gunner. All were keen to deploy. Our sole difficulty was that with the informer, Happy and I occupying the chopper leading the Fire Force into the contact zone, one "stop" group would be removed from the vital first deployment. This seriously reduced the number of fighting men on the ground.

Sgt. Beaver Shaw picks up the story: "I do recall the incident and my Log Book confirmed that I was the K-Car technician/gunner for Nigel Lamb on the 7 December 1978. We were set to go. As it happened a G-Car flew overhead and was called down to our location. There was no tech in the G-Car as it was ferrying so it was decided that the Special Branch man John Padbury would operate as the tech and G-Car gunner. He was given the necessary instructions to operate as technician and shown how to operate the .303 twin Browning's mounted in the G-Car, and the Fire Force, including the Para-Dak, set off."[1] FF Bravo included one K-Car, four G-Cars and the Paradak. One G-Car was piloted by Air Lt. Mark McLean, with his technician/gunner, Sgt. George Paar.[2]

This was an entirely new and exhilarating experience for me. I found myself as the G-Car technician/gunner. However, I felt a weight of responsibility leading the Fire Force into the contact area. The informant was seated between Happy and the pilot. I sat in the gunner's seat. The outcome of our entire operation rested on the informant. He was "the man in the know". This being his first flight, he had to adjust his local geographical knowledge of the area while adapting to the role of "airborne lead scout", simultaneously directing the FF to his predicted target of a ZIPRA section. One minute he was in Kariba, later Karoi, and now he was in a helicopter leading an assault on our enemy. The thought went through my mind how far too many whites would, despite his abilities, consider this man an "ignorant local".

Once airborne, the pilot followed the predetermined flight-path and kept Happy and me up to date with the key identifiable landmarks, while we in turn, orientated the informer. We flew at treetop level to prevent the noise of the choppers alerting the ZIPRA section. I felt the pressure mounting as we flew over Kapfunde Mission. To my relief, the informant immediately identified it, signalling that he was completely orientated between air and ground. We flew on, soon identifying the Chidamoyo road. As we approached Mudzimu Business Centre, the informant quickly recognised it and excitedly began indicating to the left. The pilot immediately banked left and began heading south. The pressure mounted. Our informant kept pointing in the direction we were to follow, making minor deviations from time-to-time.

After approximately 15 minutes' flying time, he turned to Happy and excitedly pointed out some kraals straight ahead in the distance, indicating them as the target area. The ground below flashed past as the helicopter thundered on. As we approached the kraals, the informant excitedly shouted "*Apo*" (There).

A large crowd of about 300 people had gathered at the kraal complex but, as we approached them, they began walking away. According to Dr J. Chakawa: "The insurgents had gathered for a traditional beer-drinking party, nicknamed *bhavhadhe* (birthday party) in the vernacular, although in practice they were not celebrating anyone's birthday but just enjoying themselves in an area which they deemed was free from Rhodesian forces."[3]

The helicopters gained height and circled the kraals in an attempt to contain the escaping crowd. Anticipating what was to come, Happy asked whether the civilians below would be safe. I assured him that everything would be done to protect them, but casualties in war were inevitable. The K-Car Commander took over and deployed "stops" into position. They immediately came under fire and several intense skirmishes broke out. The K-Car entered the battle firing intermittent bursts from the 20mm cannon.

When the action on the ground started, I asked the pilot if I could cock the twin Brownings, preparing them for firing. He agreed but said: "Don't fire at anything unless I tell you to." I never did get to fire the weapon, much to my disappointment. In fact, I found it extremely difficult interpreting the unfolding battle on the ground and soon realised that I lacked the ability of evaluating ground warfare from the air. That flight revealed to me a skill I clearly lacked.

[1] Sgt. Beaver Shaw email 2/4/2015. This was not the first time this had occurred. On 2/10/1972, Air Lt. Barry Roberts was engaged in a battle with ZANLA when his technician/gunner, Sgt. Eric Thomson, was hit by an enemy bullet which shattered the bone of his arm. Roberts returned to the Rushinga base where there was a doctor and a Trojan aircraft on standby to fly Thomson to Andrew Fleming Hospital in Salisbury. After cleaning out the helicopter's cabin, Roberts spotted SAS Sqn. Sgt. Maj. Stan Hornby and invited him to be the technician/gunner, an opportunity obviously not to be missed. Email 6/1/2016. Maj. Nigel Henson had a similar experience when he was the K-Car gunner for Air Lt. Norman Maasdorp during a Fire Force changeover at Karoi on 21/2/1979. Unfortunately, the 20mm barrel fell off after the first round was fired: it had not been secured correctly. Confirmed by Maasdorp WhatsApp 21/11/2016 and Henson email 12/11/2016).

[2] Confirmed by Mark McLean's log book.

[3] Oral interviews and various WhatsApp discussions.

Two insurgents were killed. Two externally trained insurgents and three locally trained insurgents were captured. The remaining insurgents, dressed as women complete with plaited hair, managed to escape. While debriefing one of the captures on 12 December, we established that during the contact the section leader, Khumalo, was attempting to change into a dress while in the granary, when it caught alight and burned him to death. The local SB confirmed Khumalo's death. This brought the number of ZIPRA killed to three[1] and four civilians were killed.[2]

Kraalhead Joseph Mudzimu was present at the ZIPRA gathering when the Fire Force arrived. Dr Chakawa said of him: "He was also one of ZIPRA's greatest supporters during the liberation war. Headman Mudzimu attributed his survival during the war to the spiritual world which SFAs too had no choice but to accept. When he became headman in 1977, the war had already engulfed Hurungwe district. He was a young unmarried man when he was appointed headman. He immediately decided to give guerrillas a hand. According to him, as was also confirmed by his village heads, Zaranyika, Bandera and Nyamharepare, Mudzimu regularly travelled with guerrillas. It was his duty to take any new group of guerrillas to the spirit medium of Nyanhewe for snuff, treatment and other blessings. When ZIPRA guerrillas were attacked at Nyamhondoro battle close to Mudzimu Township, Mudzimu was there and he alleges it was miraculous that he survived. He attributes his survival to the traditional snuff which he always carried with him as well as his stick."[3]

At the conclusion of the battle, we were flown back to Montesuma airfield along with the captures, the deceased and the captured armaments. The externally trained ZIPRA insurgents were taken to the Selous Scouts for their immediate deployments and we detained the three locally trained insurgents in the police cells. We would later take the local captures to the farm for debriefing, reorientation and future deployments into Hurungwe. It was important for the people to witness the reorientation process in action as our enemy saw the folly of their ways. This would serve in our favour. The news would also filter through to ZIPRA sections in the field, invoking essentially two observations. The first being that we were learning their strategies, tactics and penetrating their intelligence networks and, secondly, we did not kill captures. This second point was significant as ZANLA and ZIPRA kept their sections intact by making them fear death at the hands of the SF once captured. It was a popular method of dealing with dissidents. Needless to say, there was much celebration that evening. I was something of a laughing stock, having served as the G-Car gunner yet without having fired a shot in the battle.

Strike 5: Observations and Assessments

Ours was a well-executed engagement. Maj. Henson, the FF Commander, took the brave decision of believing in our strategy of using the informant to guide the FF onto the target. He trusted both our intelligence and our ability to execute the lead-in. The RLI troops were remarkable. They were well disciplined, aggressive and brave. The timing was perfect as ZIPRA were holding a daylight political meeting, considering themselves safe and beyond the reach of the SF. This was a high-quality intelligence operation demonstrating the link between SB Kariba, under Ben Pretorius, and ourselves. It also exemplified the progress made by Happy and the UANC team. Here were top-quality, counter-insurgency intelligence operators who quickly and effectively adapted to changing strategies. The whole operation was a classic deployment, emphasising the significance and importance of accurate intelligence, and the skills, dedication and commitment of the pilots, the FF Commander and the troops on the ground.

While assessing the situation on the ground, I knew we had struck two important blows in two successive days on ZIPRA in Hurungwe and that they would not know where, when or how we

[1] Dr Chakawa, J. (2015), pp. clxx - clxxi, 208-209; Binda, A. (2014), pp. 318-320, eBook Location 8963-8983; Shaw, B. (2018), pp. 246-248. There were two FF deployments on 7/12/1978 but, according to Nigel Lamb's log book, there was only one contact. It is my opinion this contact ties in with Geldenhuys, P. (2014), Air Strike Log Entry 907. Karoi Contacts Map Incident 22.

[2] I did not record the number of civilian deaths and asked Dr J. Chakawa to research this. He spoke to Joseph Mudzimu who confirmed that four civilians were killed. Email 30/7/2019.

[3] Dr Chakawa, J. (2015), pp. 208-209.

would strike next. We were gaining momentum, occupying and possessing the land, and attacking when opportunities were presented.

Progress in the Field

We spent the next morning debriefing the three locally trained ZIPRA insurgents[1] who had quickly been reorientated. Their's was an interesting transition. Once addressed by the UANC political team and gaining insight into our vision, they were rapidly reorientated to embrace our MO. An item of major significance was that they soon learned we accepted and trusted them. Granted, we confiscated their weapons and they were in our custody, but that was only for the short term. They were not assaulted, tortured or killed, which is what they had expected. Yet again, I witnessed, to my continued amazement, the rapid reconciliation between soldiers once opposed to each other who now shared a common objective.

Unfortunately, the Fire Force departed Karoi on 8 December 1978. Since our arrival at Hurungwe, we had orchestrated several successful engagements with ZIPRA and enjoyed a continuous flow of intelligence. Sixty men were permanently deployed and I had no doubt that we could sustain the momentum. I made a personal entry in my diary: "I am confused by the thinking of Com.Ops., as I am sure they are themselves. We definitely have ZIPRA on the move with a potent intelligence network connected to the people. However, we have to move on and thought will have to be given to the best strategies and tactics, using local military callsigns." Com.Ops. had more serious problems than Hurungwe to contend with and I certainly was not aware of "the bigger picture" at the time.

Later in the day, Martin returned from the field to give us a complete update of developments. According to him, all was going well. He had heard about the Mudzimu contact which confirmed the efficiency of our intelligence networks. Our meeting was timeous as he could speak to the captures, glean information from them as to ZIPRA's strategies and tactics, as well as learn about their thoughts regarding our people's army. As he would be staying at Chabwino, the captures, in turn, could meet the people's detachment commander in person, a positive part of their reorientation cycle. He would also have the opportunity of meeting the recruits in training, talking to them and discussing strategies and tactics from his first-hand experience.

George Hutchison had stood down after a six-week stint, having done an excellent job with our Admin. He was dedicated, supportive and had given tirelessly of himself to our operations. More than that, he was a good friend. I would miss his company and his skill. Unfortunately, his replacement would not arrive in time for a handover, consequently there would be a gap before the next man arrived. As was my practice, I noted in my diary: "I have enough on my plate trying to keep up with the intelligence that is pouring in, the deployment of troops, managing the UANC networks and monitoring our men in the field, etc., without having to worry about the menial tasks such as local purchases, paying bills, administration and so on. I have approached Mike Reeler on the subject and he will assist where possible, but he is going on leave, so his manpower problem is in the same predicament."

Geoff Price arrived on the same day to discuss our progress and the successful FF deployment. He told me Bishop Muzorewa was grateful for our work and pleased with our successes. I also used the opportunity to unburden myself regarding our staffing difficulties. We had additional ongoing logistical snags, such as lack of radios, shortages of weapons and ammu-nition, but similar issues were being experienced throughout the operational areas. However, I was aware that staffing matters could be readily rectified. Geoff, flamboyant as ever, assured me that he would organise the personnel I required. Our conversation ended on that note. I dismissed the matter knowing that I could depend on Geoff. Having solved the problem, we moved on to the update of developments in Hurungwe and he was pleased and supportive, indicating that the UANC party was particularly enthusiastic with developments. It was another successful meeting with Geoff. I considered him an

[1] Names of the captures withheld to protect their identities.

excellent officer. He did not interfere with our operations and allowed us to continue our war effort unimpeded.

Intelligence Flows

Happy and I travelled to Chabwino on Saturday, 9 December 1978, as he wanted to continue his debrief of LK (pseudonym), seemingly the most senior of the captures from Strike 5. I also wished to spend some time with the men and "touch base" with the intelligence network. We enjoyed these regular trips to the farm as it was a brief respite from the complications of the war. Happy also arranged for the men from the UANC office in Chikangwe to visit the farm and gain maximum propaganda exposure from the success of the Mudzimu contact. This completed the flow of political and intelligence operations between Chikangwe, Chabwino, the field, the people and our office. It was an unique experience scheming, planning, operating and co-operating with the people in unity with one vision and one purpose. We were indeed "one"!

Our recruits were content, enthusiastic, positive and keen to deploy. As Happy and his team held discussions with LK, I spoke to Manenji who advised me that two men had "taken the night off" to go to Chikangwe. The culprits had been disciplined and I felt the matter was in hand. Morale of the men had increased dramatically as a result of the successful Mudzimu contact and arrival of the capture who was known to some of the men. All was well at the farm!

To date, LK had been co-operative and forthcoming with intelligence from the field. Debriefing him away from his colleagues gave us the opportunity to independently corroborate his information. We were in the unusual situation of having three sources of intelligence which should be consistent, provided the truth emerged. I had experienced this strategy in the Makoni with *mujibhas*. Once arrested and placed among recruits from their own villages, they very quickly identified with them, reorientated and volunteered intelligence. Accentuated by the fact that they could not return to their villages as ZIPRA would definitely kill them, we were in a strong position. The key, however, was to deploy our forces onto the ground where these battles had taken place in order to protect their families and relatives as soon as possible, and prevent or at least minimise ZIPRA reprisals.

Katima, from our Chikangwe office, and I debriefed Martin. He had made significant progress in the field in a short space of time which immediately spoke of the good work the UANC political wing had achieved prior to their deployment. He informed us of the following developments in the demarcated areas which our forces now occupied:

1. Our men had been accepted by the masses who were pleased that the ZIPRA threat and anarchy had been removed from their areas. ZIPRA were reported to be migrating westwards from our demarcated areas.
2. At the request of the Salvation Army, our men were accompanying them and protecting their church services in our liberated zones. ZIPRA previously prohibited Salvation Army activities.
3. A local store (name withheld), formerly destroyed by ZIPRA as the owner was a UANC official, was being rebuilt. Locals and our men were working on the project. In a short while, the store was functional.
4. Section medics had commenced basic treatments of the locals and requested resupplies.
5. Traditional life was being restored and authority returned to the tribal leaders. Previously, ZIPRA had controlled matters such as the brewing of beer and the burial of war victims.
6. The people requested that Kathene School be reopened in January 1979. The school had been closed by ZIPRA. I felt it imperative to honour this request as soon as I was convinced our men could protect the premises, teachers and children. To allow ZIPRA to close the school again would seriously hamper our progress. This was a classic example of moving at the pace of the people: responding to their requests. I started provisional proceedings with the relevant authorities to reopen the school when the opportunity presented itself.
7. Resumption of bus services in Hurungwe were requested. Again this was a sensitive issue

requiring a safe, permanent solution. ZIPRA's landmine campaign was a clear indication of their control of Hurungwe which, once wrested, would definitely cause a reaction. My thinking was that a permanent solution involving participation of the masses would have to be sought. One landmine incident would be a serious setback to our progress.

8. Callsigns were requesting UANC political meetings be held in Hurungwe. Anticipating this, we had arranged a meeting for 23 December 1978 to coincide with the influx of people from the cities to Hurungwe. The benefit of these meetings would be that the progress of the people's army in repelling ZIPRA from Hurungwe would spread to the cities.
9. Locals wanted to start cattle dipping in demarcated areas but were reluctant to pay the fees of R$1 per animal, per year. ZIPRA had successfully campaigned against all alleged government "institutional abuses". Dipping, as with other government programmes, would have to be addressed by the politicians. While we had to work with Internal Affairs, my determination was that our forces should not be identified with the "old regime".
10. Martin requested finances for each section to purchase rations from local stores. It was agreed that each section would receive R$40, in addition to the R$20 per man, per month.
11. Martin requested that I hold intelligence-gathering and dissemination courses for a man from each section. I agreed to start as soon as possible.
12. Finally, Martin was concerned that, since our men were dressed and armed like insurgents, they might be inadvertently attacked during Fire Force or Security Forces actions. I recommended the following precautions:
    - Men to ensure that they remained within demarcated areas.
    - Hats to be turned inside out to expose the day-glow on the inside.
    - Fire Force deployments to be carried out on channel 19 for radio compatibility.
    - Should the Fire Force or "friendly forces" be deployed into our men's sections, they were not to react.

Each section was provided with one smoke-grenade to use in the event of an emergency with the FF. I was satisfied with the progress in the field.

A Major Shift in Mindset: From "Kills Win Wars" to Occupying Territory

Regarding the matter of killing ZIPRA, I held the view that mobilising the people and gaining their support was our priority, to be followed by attacks on the enemy to eliminate them. I was firmly convinced that, without the backing of the masses, we were on a "hiding to nothing". Mobilisation of the masses would come hand in hand with the elimination of the enemy by our people's army. Our success would not be determined on the number of kills but on our ability to hold the ground and possess it which, as I saw matters, would inevitably result in ZIPRA kills. This was a completely different thinking and strategy to that of the traditional Security Forces approach, whose war was based on the principle of "kills win wars". It was clear that internally the SF were killing increasing numbers of insurgents yet, at the same time, they could not stem the influx of them into the country. It followed logically that the kill-rate would increase but, if the truth be known, our SF could simply not contain the onslaught. It was difficult for the SF to accept our strategies. Holding the ground indicated the growing support of the people who were turning away from ZIPRA. This confirmed that the political commissars were effective in their politicising of the people. It was important to increase the politicisation of the people which would be enhanced by the larger meetings we were planning.

Late in the afternoon of 9 December 1978, while the whole UANC team were together, we discussed the idea of opening a Kariba UANC office in liaison with Ben Pretorius, the local SB officer. We had received intelligence that ZIPRA had sent *mujibhas* to explore the area and ZIPRA themselves had visited Kariba Township. The success of the Mudzimu contact created an ideal opportunity to establish an office and we decided to send a team to Kariba the following week to survey the scene. Knowing ZIPRA and their *mujibhas* had visited the area made it clear that there was at least one ZIPRA cell operating in the township. We had also received intelligence that there was a ZIPRA base at Gache Gache, a good fishing venue frequented by tourists. ZIPRA would strike a serious blow to the tourist industry and white morale if they controlled this area. Following the visit to Kariba, we decided to establish a UANC office in the township. Much was achieved that day. Our momentum was increasing rapidly with strategies and tactics unfolding positively. Without the restriction of a hierarchy which demanded pursuance of traditional military, political and intelligence strategies and tactics, was a most liberating experience.

Defining Moments: Reorientating Captures

We had reached a defining moment in the war in securing our first captures and setting about incorporating them into our future operations. It was important to set a clear precedent with their treatment while focusing on our agenda which was integration. They had inherent fears and anticipations of being subject to traditional procedures, such as arrest and prosecution, which carried varying incarceration terms including the potential death sentence for proven murder charges. Since we believed in our cause, I felt the political reorientation of captures would not prove onerous.

As of December 1978, our men were not deployed in the Mudzimu area. Our priority with these captures was to extract immediate field intelligence in order to strike at the remaining ZIPRA insurgents. Thereafter, we would focus on detailed debriefs regarding ZIPRA operations. Finally, the captures would be integrated into the people's army. Our process was logical and chronological with integration always our aim. How we handled each step depended on how readily the captured would adopt and adapt to our way of thinking.

Our golden rules were to treat them as soldiers, not to use violence and recruit them into the people's army as soon as possible. The treatment of captures would become common knowledge within the UANC party, our men, the people and the enemy at large. This information would eventually filter through our intelligence networks into Chikangwe, on to the locals and ZIPRA in the field. In these circumstances, we were in the fortunate position of debriefing each capture independently and corroborating their intelligence.

We concluded our initial debrief of the three captures on Sunday, 10 December 1978. These sessions reinforced our previous information that resident ZIPRA sections were relatively static and operating from kraal bases. It was interesting to note that in this people's revolution, intelligence was historical, current and immediate, depending on the ZIPRA section's location at a specific time. Historically, in that the people supporting ZIPRA remained in their kraal locations, they did not move away. The insurgents may have moved to another base but the people remained static. That was a constant historical fact: they supported ZIPRA. It was also current intelligence as they were still supporting ZIPRA, unless circumstances had dramatically changed. From our perspective, the intelligence became immediate when we knew ZIPRA were at the kraal at that precise moment and the information helped pinpoint their location. We gleaned the following intelligence from our three captures regarding ZIPRA activity in the Mudzimu area:

Kawanza Kraal (QM550068).[1] Three girls were living there. The house was frequented by insurgents, one of whom was Professor.[2] The only known *mujibha* was Best Brown who was resident at Best Brown Kraal. A ZIPRA section slept there with the girls every night. Old Nyamhunga stores used by ZIPRA included Basket and Rwere stores. Private vehicles were still used on the roads, which were not believed to be mined. There were more than 15 houses in the area. A good OP position was at Nyaruchekwa. Kraalhead Kawanza owned two vehicles. One was a light-blue Peugeot pick-up vehicle and the other a white Toyota 7-ton truck which he frequently used for collecting supplies in town.

Best Brown Kraal (QM532038). Best Brown was a locally trained *mujibha* and his two brothers, Carol and George,[3] were also *mujibhas*. Both were possibly locally trained. The third brother, Micho, worked on white farms.[4] There was a banana plantation near three houses and a granary where six

---

[1] Dr Chakawa, J. (2015), p. 202.

[2] Ibid.

[3] Confirmed by Dr J. Chakawa email 11/1/2018. Carol survived the war and is still alive. George is now deceased.

insurgents lived and slept. It appeared that they enticed females from other areas to sleep with them at this base.

Chifamba (QM515023). Regis Chigara (son of Kraalhead Chigara) was the leading *mujibha*, assisted by Chamu Murenza. There were three houses at Chifamba. Alfred, the commander, slept in the granary. It was not known where the remaining four men from his section slept. Chigara Kraal was destroyed, explaining why Regis was operating at Chifamba.

Munyongani (QM475023). The *mujibha*, Chamu Murenga, operated with insurgents based there. They always slept in the four houses. One insurgent lived at Makuranje Kraal with the two girls, whom he had claimed.

Gandawa (QM438042). Two insurgents, Clever[1] and Khumalo (KIA), mainly stayed here with two girls (names withheld). There were no *mujibhas* at Gandawa. There were five houses at Gandawa Kraal. The section that stayed there was mainly static. Insurgents from other areas visited from time-to-time.

Mupomba Kraal (QM452069). This was the contact area. Here was to be found several women from other kraals, (all names withheld). Three insurgents escaped from the contact area, namely Clever, Sikalele and Isaac.[2] Some of the insurgents had hidden their ammunition in the hills near the houses of Muponda. *Mujibhas* here were LK, Nicholas Nyamande, Nebert Machedzani, Ebrai Gumi and Edmond Mugomba.

Of the bases mentioned, it is most likely that the following would have contained insurgents:

Munyongani. Best potential for a successful attack.
Best Brown.
Kawanza. Best potential for a successful attack.
Gandawa.

The intelligence elicited from these captures regarding Kawanza and Best Brown kraals was reliable and we acted on it in due course.

We also decided to phase the three captures into our forces as soon as possible, therefore we took LK to the farm, while detaining NK and EK (pseudonyms). I briefed the intelligence team at Chikangwe, accordingly. I felt it important to balance the psychological integration of captures with the recruits. The captures' "conversion" was evidenced by their releasing all their information, thereby enabling them to experience our acceptance, trust and mutual respect. While deployed with ZIPRA, they enjoyed "significance" when armed and carrying live ammunition. In our environment, they were exposed, compromised, vulnerable and in the uncertain process of becoming one of us. I was concerned that the attitude of "significant somebodies" would ferment and fester on the farm, hence our concentrated attention to realign their thinking. I believed that this was a key to integration, therefore we separated the three and allowed LK time and space to integrate before the other two were phased in individually.

We tolerated no self-styled heroes in our army. We viewed this mindset as destabilising and dangerous, leading to possible destructive results. The captures would also be trained in separate sections, ensuring they did not get the opportunity to conspire with each other. Once they started talking to their peers at Chabwino they would be further compromised. Their colleagues knew who they were and what they had been up to. There were no secrets!

As much as the captures needed to accept and trust us, our men were also called upon to reciprocate. Our captures were part of ZIPRA and may well have been directly or indirectly involved with atrocities known to our men. This was a possibility with all our men. Personally, I saw the process as a matter of focusing on the vision and moving forward in unison. The past remained the past. At hand, was the present reality of a war, requiring the full utilisation of our resources and intelligence. If we allowed ourselves to reflect morbidly on the wrongs of the past, there would be

---

[4] Confirmed by Dr J. Chakawa email 11/1/2018.
[1] Dr Chakawa, J. (2015), p. clxxi.
[2] Confirmed by Dr J. Chakawa email 11/1/2018.

no time to move on into the present. We would forever be seeking revenge or reprisals. There is no place or time for that in war: revenge blinds and, in my view, is dangerous.

The news of the captures' transformations would soon reach the ears of the people and filter through the ZIPRA networks back to their sections. ZIPRA became aware of who had been killed or captured. Consequently, locally trained cadre or captured *mujibhas* would be earmarked for suspicion, their families harassed, tortured or even murdered. Ours was a cruel war, hence the importance of expanding our operations as efficiently and as widespread as possible, without compromising our own sections' safety and security. We were engaged in a delicate process but remained confident that, with the right strategies, we would succeed.

An indication of the success of our men in the field was the arrival of a fresh batch of volunteer recruits. Their personal details are not included in order to protect their identities. Shortly after their arrival, they were put through our selection process and transported to Chabwino in order to commence training. Since I was about to go on leave, we decided to introduce NK and EK to this group and keep them in separate sections. Although unlikely, I wanted to be close at hand prior to my absence in case any difficulties arose. Grey and Happy fronted the process ensuring that they were seen as our leaders. This countered the opinions that the SFAs were simply another branch of the Security Forces.

On 10 December 1978, Special Branch Karoi confirmed our intelligence of a fairly static presence of 11 insurgents at Kawanza Kraal. We immediately began preparing our sketches and plans for military action. These were ideal situations for the Fire Force and I still considered we had a sufficient flow of reliable intelligence to keep them occupied, while continuing our momentum. I informed Sub.JOC Sinoia of our current intelligence position and requested the return of the FF. We also received intelligence that insurgents had returned to the Doro area.

SB Karoi advised us that one of their sources confirmed that the locals had accepted our men with open arms. Local reaction had been encouraging with ZIPRA stating that our men were Selous Scouts who had deserted. However, the informer mentioned that the locals believed our men were indeed the people's army, with the mobilisation of the masses continuing at a steady pace. This was positive feedback from SB, confirming our men's good work in the field. It also, importantly, confirmed that the SB intelligence networks were keeping an "eye" on our men, which was encouraging.

With the right strategies and tactics in place, a single section, tactically deployed, could give the appearance of being multiple sections to the observer, subsequently giving the impression of a greater ground coverage than was the case. ZANLA and ZIPRA had successfully used this tactic to exhaust SF resources by continually forcing us to react to their actions. By occupying and possessing the land, and defending the people, our men were able to use the identical tactic and reverse the trend ZIPRA had imposed on us. The various FF and ground-force attacks on ZIPRA, particularly in areas not yet occupied by our forces, accentuated this strategy. The combination of these attacks and our visible permanent forces occupying the ground, in my estimation, must have concerned ZIPRA. They were used to avoiding the SF in their traditional roles (Selous Scouts, OPs and patrols, etc.), but ours was a new and permanent threat which was reversing the tide. Essentially, ZIPRA were compelled to react to us. It was important to increase the momentum, keep ZIPRA on the move and work "at the pace of the people". By working alongside the people, I am referring to the progression from their acceptance of our political message, recognising the permanence of our men on the ground, as well as their ability to defend and protect them. Once the people had accepted us in new areas, we needed to be fully prepared to deploy. This was a formidable process, hence the necessity to increase momentum in training and politicisation. Fortunately, our capable team, led by Grey and Happy, were well placed to keep abreast with these increasing demands.

A further indication of our successful field operations was the request from our medics to replenish their diminished supplies. Their appeal suggested that they were treating the wounded, ill or injured among the people. This was deliberate and intentional on our part and formed a vital aspect of our work.

Grey and Happy continued their visits into the field and reported that the men were integrating well with the people. They had established their own *mujibha* intelligence networks and, most significantly, had been accepted by the spirit mediums, who were supplying them with snuff and beads for their protection. As these events unfolded, I continued to reflect on my need to improve my understanding of the African spiritual world.

I met with Dis.Pol. on 11 December 1978 and briefed him on the current situation which seemed to satisfy him. He suggested that when things were running smoothly, Int.Aff. should be reintroduced in a civil affairs role. I pointed out that their presence could well instigate problems, as they were regarded by the locals as being part of their unaddressed grievances: objections that ZIPRA had exploited. Consequently, I saw no place for Int.Aff. in their present form and this matter would require thoughtful political considerations.

A watershed event occurred on the same day. Insurgents successfully attacked and destroyed some 23 petrol, diesel and kerosene storage tanks in Salisbury. This revealed the rapid deterioration of the national security situation, and was a significant psychological and logistical blow to the Rhodesian population.

My Break from the War

At this stage of developments, I felt the need for a break from the war. I was due to take leave from 13 to 19 December 1978. I had planned to fly to Cape Town from 14 to 17 December and meet my good friend, Martin van Rensburg, who had offered me a "commission-only" sales position with his company, Watertite Guttering (Pty) Ltd. Martin was a big-hearted man, and had employed several friends and former Rhodesians into his expanding business. I had no desire to leave Rhodesia but felt it necessary to make suitable arrangements should I resign or be forced to leave the country. I did have reservations about my ability to sell, but Martin's offer provided the opportunity to scrutinise the job and its prospects.

Unfortunately, Admin. had not been replaced. I had no alternative but to use Walter from the training staff to manage the operation in my absence. This was certainly not the ideal solution to my problem, as training and intelligence techniques are two entirely different disciplines. Grey, Happy and I had decided the best areas to strike ZIPRA were on Kawanza and Best Brown bases, and we had gathered all necessary intelligence to assist the military. The Fire Force was not in the area, which was unfortunate.

On 12 December 1978, I instructed Walter to join me for the day in order to bring him up to date with events and familiarise himself with my diary and proceedings. I wanted him present at the initial briefing with 1Rhodesia Regiment as I tabled plans to attack Best Brown and Kawanza kraals.[1] LK and NK, escorted by David and Mike, accompanied Walter and me to the briefing. We presented our sketches of the target area as well as our locstats on the survey maps. We discussed routes into the target area, drop-off points and strategies and tactics, despite these being military decisions. At the conclusion of our discussion, the men from 1RR were keen to deploy. I knew David and Mike would be of great benefit in the attack as they had vast experience in this role.

Unexpectedly, the FF arrived at Karoi. I returned to the 1RR base with Walter and suggested that they delay their deployment and work in conjunction with the FF. They agreed but also suggested that they deploy their men in the meantime in order to be closer to the target area. I had to explain the *mujibha* system in detail and the probability of their men being compromised. Following this discussion, they decided against the advance deployment.

Later on, Grey brought intelligence relating to a local man sent by the resident ZIPRA section to purchase shoes for them in Karoi. Once purchased, the section, 15-16 strong, would send *mujibhas* to collect the footwear. The area was demarcated by the Selous Scouts and the information was passed to them. Shortly after, I left for Salisbury and began my leave.

From a business point of view, the trip to Cape Town was a disaster. I recall flying into Cape Town over the shanty towns surrounding the airport and the negative impact it had on me. I was

[1] Dr Chakawa, J. (2015), pp. clv-clvi.

uninspired by the poverty I observed from the air. Martin's factory was situated in the industrial area of Bellville which seemed remote and desolate. I arrived the day the factory closed down for the compulsory builders' holidays and literally learned nothing about the work. Socially, however, my stay in the Cape Town provided lighter moments of life. I was surrounded by beer-drinking friends: we drank the days away! At the conclusion of my six-day break, prior to leaving for home, I was led to believe that Martin would take care of me if and when I returned to settle.

On my return to Karoi, and much to my disappointment, I noticed that, despite our reliable intelligence, ZIPRA had not been engaged during my absence. I also learned of a conflict between Walter and Ed Robinson,[1] of the Karoi SB office, which needed my attention. Ed pointed out to me: "It was quite obvious to me that Walter did not have a lot of experience dealing with either intelligence matters or deployments. He had an arrogant disposition and tried to give the impression that he was in overall command (of the whole area) which obviously he wasn't. I made my impressions clear to him, which he did not like very much and as I recall reported me to higher authority." I did not like leaving the operational area as my absence was not conducive to maintaining progress. Furthermore, it was clear to me that my men should remain in their areas of expertise. Training officers did not necessarily make good intelligence officers and vice versa. In fact, I did not leave the area often which meant my non-attendance at home made life stressful for Lynette

On 13 December 1978, the day I left on leave, K-Car pilot, Nigel Lamb, and his technician/gunner, Beaver Shaw, flew from Salisbury to Karoi and joined the RLI Support Commando Fire Force. Maj. Henson was the K-Car Commander. They had been involved in the two previously reported Fire Force deployments (6 and 7 December 1978), before returning to Salisbury. They remained in Karoi from 13-19 December, and confirmed the difficulties with Walter and intelligence while I was on leave.

Nigel Lamb's log book tells the story: "Operating from the south of Karoi initially with good success in Hurungwe TTL but then sent on a merry-go-round with No 1 Commando RLI to Umtali & then back to Karoi by which time the int. system was in a shambles and we then had very little success."

[1] P/O Edward (Ed) Robinson: Served from 1968-1973 and then joined the Police Reserve in Ground Coverage and Special Branch until he left the country in 1979. Email 22/4/2015.

Air Lt. Nigel Lamb's log book, 6/12/1978-19/12/1978.

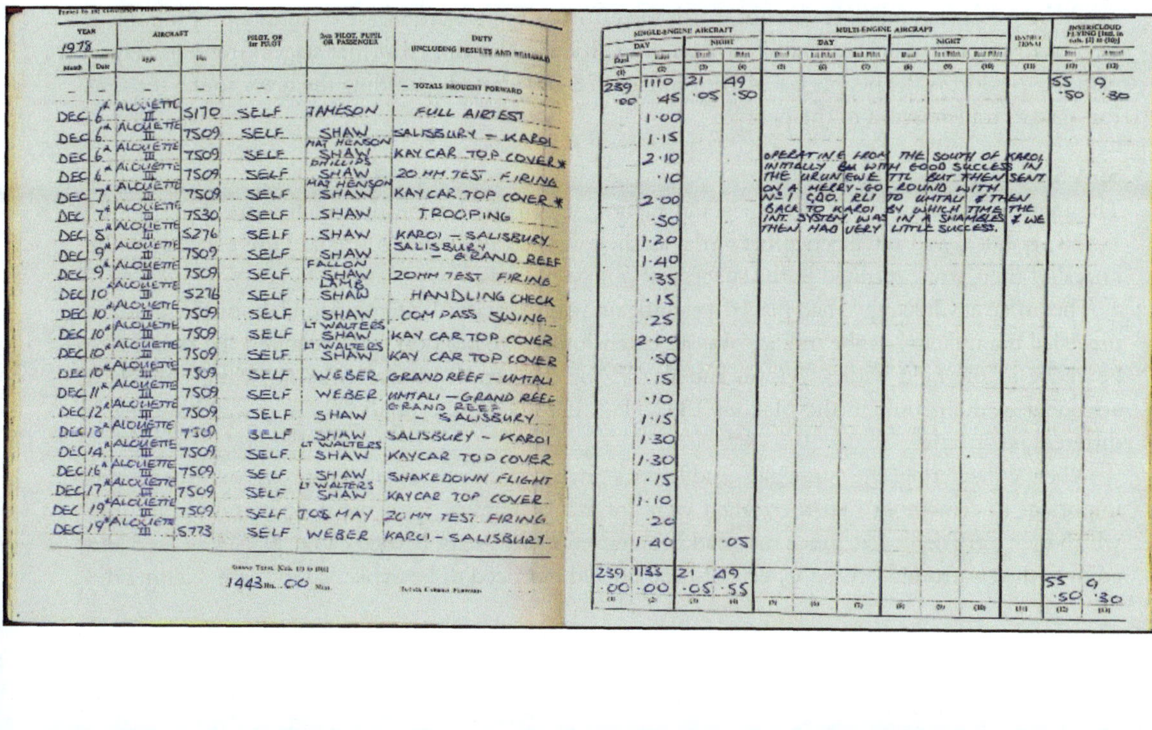

Year 1978 Month	Date	Aircraft Type	No.	Pilot, or 1st Pilot	2nd Pilot, Pupil or Passenger	Duty (including results and remarks)	Single-engine Day Dual (1)	Single-engine Day Pilot (2)	Single-engine Night Dual (3)	Single-engine Night Pilot (4)	Instrument/cloud flying (12)	(13)
–	–	–	–	–	–	– Totals brought forward	239 ·00	1110 45	21 ·05	49 ·50	55 ·50	9 ·30
DEC	6th	ALOUETTE III	5170	SELF	JAMESON	FULL AIRTEST		1·00				
DEC	6th	ALOUETTE III	7509	SELF	SHAW	SALISBURY – KAROI		1·15				
DEC	6th	ALOUETTE III	7509	SELF	MAJ HENSON SHAW	KAY CAR TOP COVER*		2·10				
DEC	6th	ALOUETTE III	7509	SELF	PHILLIPS SHAW	20 MM TEST FIRING		·10				
DEC	7th	ALOUETTE III	7509	SELF	MAJ HENSON SHAW	KAY CAR TOP COVER*		2·00				
DEC	7th	ALOUETTE III	7530	SELF	SHAW	TROOPING		·50				
DEC	8th	ALOUETTE III	5276	SELF	SHAW	KAROI – SALISBURY		1·20				
DEC	9th	ALOUETTE III	7509	SELF	SHAW	SALISBURY – GRAND REEF		1·40				
DEC	9th	ALOUETTE III	7509	SELF	FALLON SHAW	20MM TEST FIRING		·35				
DEC	10th	ALOUETTE III	5276	SELF	LAMB SHAW	HANDLING CHECK		·15				
DEC	10th	ALOUETTE III	7509	SELF	SHAW	COMPASS SWING		·25				
DEC	10th	ALOUETTE III	7509	SELF	LT WALTERS SHAW	KAY CAR TOP COVER		2·00				
DEC	10th	ALOUETTE III	7509	SELF	LT WALTERS SHAW	KAY CAR TOP COVER		·50				
DEC	10th	ALOUETTE III	7509	SELF	WEBER	GRAND REEF – UMTALI		·15				
DEC	11th	ALOUETTE III	7509	SELF	WEBER	UMTALI – GRAND REEF		·10				
DEC	12th	ALOUETTE III	7509	SELF	SHAW	GRAND REEF – SALISBURY		1·15				
DEC	13th	ALOUETTE III	7509	SELF	SHAW	SALISBURY – KAROI		1·30				
DEC	14th	ALOUETTE III	7509	SELF	LT WALTERS SHAW	KAYCAR TOP COVER		1·30				
DEC	16th	ALOUETTE III	7509	SELF	SHAW	SHAKEDOWN FLIGHT		·15				
DEC	17th	ALOUETTE III	7509	SELF	LT WALTERS SHAW	KAYCAR TOP COVER		1·10				
DEC	19th	ALOUETTE III	7509	SELF	TOS MAY	20 MM TEST FIRING		·20				
DEC	19th	ALOUETTE III	5773	SELF	WEBER	KAROI – SALISBURY		1·40		·05		
						Totals carried forward	239 ·00	1133 ·00	21 ·05	49 ·55	55 ·50	9 ·30

Grand Total [Cols. (1) to (10)] 1443 Hrs. 00 Mins.

OPERATING FROM THE SOUTH OF KAROI INITIALLY WITH GOOD SUCCESS IN THE URUNGWE TTL BUT THEN SENT ON A MERRY-GO-ROUND WITH No 1 CDO. RLI TO UMTALI & THEN BACK TO KAROI BY WHICH TIME THE INT. SYSTEM WAS IN A SHAMBLES & WE THEN HAD VERY LITTLE SUCCESS.

I visited the Selous Scouts to discuss how their deployments were unfolding. It appeared that general ZIPRA movements and activities had been in a westerly direction from where the Selous Scouts were deployed. Grey and Happy reported that all was well in the field which was good news, and the callsigns were safe, well and accepted by the people. The men continued to establish themselves with the locals and develop their intelligence networks. They were holding the ground well.

Grey and Happy had continued their regular visits in my absence. When the opportunity allowed, they held small meetings in the field to develop momentum for the forthcoming meeting later in the month. They were still waiting to hear from the UANC hierarchy who would address the event. This was a difficult task for these men as they travelled into previously occupied enemy territory to meet their own men who were dressed and armed similarly to ZIPRA insurgents. Added to their dangers was travelling on potentially landmined roads. In due course, I would be required to travel in Hurungwe to meet our forces and the people. It was interesting that ZIPRA had not responded in any way to our occupying forces. There had been no ambushes or attacks on them, no landmines on the roads in the proscribed areas, nor reprisals on the locals. We were prepared for all of the above which, we believed, would inevitably occur.

Grey had gathered intelligence from a victim assaulted by ZIPRA about their operations in the areas under Kraalheads Marumahoko, Murota and Chigamba. On 20 December 1978, Grey, Happy and I spent a good part of the day putting sketches, maps and detailed intelligence together for the Fire Force deployments to Chigamba and Murota kraals the following day. The deployments were unsuccessful.

Thereafter, Grey and Happy took a trip to visit the men in the field while I visited Chabwino to ensure that our training was on target. As momentum increased in the field, pressure was increasing at the farm. It was essential to keep the training on schedule. All seemed to be in order. I spoke to Manenji who confirmed the captures had settled down and integrated with the men. At that stage, there were no problems, although he raised concerns regarding delays in the training programme. I advised him that I would monitor the progress made and ensure that the UANC team continued with their regular visits.

In the build-up to Christmas, Grey and Happy decided to hold the first of a series of political meetings themselves in the field rather than bring a UANC dignitary to Hurungwe. They considered it a better option to increase the general momentum first and, when they were satisfied that there would be popular support, arrange a mass rally to be addressed by Bishop Muzorewa and or James Chikerema. I agreed with them as I considered it unwise at this stage to organise any event which would be poorly attended. It was not worth the effort as there were massive security precautions to be undertaken for such a rally, and we were not sufficiently equipped at that stage. Grey and Happy planned to address the people on 24 December 1978 and started spreading the news to the sections for onward transmission to the people.

SFA Strategies and Tactics

The implementation of our strategies and tactics, supported by the thorough work done by the UANC political and intelligence networks as they worked tirelessly to prepare the people for the arrival of their army, resulted in the success of our operations.

The office at Chikangwe had played a significant role in establishing this foundation. The political preceded the military, as the military was an extension of the political. This required the political to be active in the field with a "vision and heart" for the people. There were no white politicians attending to the people in the Makoni TTL. Had there been, the politicians may well have had a different perspective.

When considering the strategies and tactics involved in the deployment of our men, it is important to remember that these men were intimately familiar with the people and terrain into which they were deployed. Since they had been raised in the areas, herded cattle, played, walked and enjoyed their surrounds, these aspects of rural life did not need to be explained to them. Neither did the role of the enemy's intelligence systems need explanation, as in many cases they had been a part of it or, at the very least, knew about it. These were two advantages very much in their favour.

Once deployed under the overall command of Martin, the detachment commander, each section communicated with family, relatives and friends they knew they could trust, while fully aware that some could betray them to ZIPRA, as the war had divided families. For security reasons, the list of supporters was initially short, supported from intelligence provided by the UANC networks. They established safe bases in well-concealed areas and provided their own 24-hour protection, and purchased food from the local stores. In time, trusted *mujibhas* would be invited to the safe bases. It was an interesting reversal of roles for *mujibhas*, as they were no longer searching for SF spoor, OPs and providing intelligence about the SF to ZIPRA. They were now identifying ZIPRA *mujibhas* and supporters, and providing intelligence about them to our men. A significant reversal of roles with fatal consequences should matters go wrong.

The men wore typical insurgents' civilian clothing, mostly denim and khaki, *veldskoens* and miscellaneous hats and caps. Our emphasis was not to identify with SF camouflage clothing. They were armed with communist Eastern Bloc weapons, mainly AK-47s with one RPD per section, hand- and smoke-grenades and, as they became available, one RPG-7 and one 60mm mortar tube and shells per section. Spare magazines and grenades were carried in Russian/Eastern Bloc chest webbing. These men were a visible permanent, presence on the ground who continued to gain the support of the masses. In time, official *Pfumo reVanhu* (Spear of the People) uniforms were provided.

Moving at the "pace of the people" was important. When they were ready, that was the right time to move. Grey, Happy and their team were quite capable of commanding the men and developing the political work. Their direct link with Bishop Muzorewa and the party was very important, as that would provide a feedback mechanism of our, and the people's, progress.

Spirit Mediums and the People's Army

The spirit world played a crucial role in the acceptance and protection of the people's army in Hurungwe. Spirit mediums, in African traditions, are the owners of the land representing great ancestors who founded certain chieftainships. They are responsible for the installation of chiefs, rain making and warding off catastrophes, including locusts, droughts and diseases. Their role included responsibility for the welfare of the people and, as long as the mediums were proven and authentic, they were considered superior to the chief. Fake spirit mediums drove in motor cars, drank clear beer, and were friendly to whites. If snuff was administered to insurgents and they were killed, the spirit medium was considered fake.[1] Once accepted by the mediums, the individual became a "son of the soil" and was accepted by the whole community. The relationship between spirit mediums and the people's army was crucial. It was imperative that our commanders gained favour with the spirit mediums, therefore they were approached early on in our operations in order to receive their "blessings" and to guide and protect our people's army. This paved the way for their acceptance by the people. Once a person was given a totem, for example, *mbizi* (zebra), he "became" an *mbizi*. Spirit mediums in Hurungwe included Dande and Mhondoro. The men were given snuff and beads to wear. In time, I was accepted by the spirit mediums and given snuff and wore beads. To offend them could bring about serious consequences. I did not fully understand the spirit mediums' procedures, but I respected them. It was vitally important for our men to accept and show respect for the established traditions in Hurungwe. Failing to do so, would be viewed as emulating ZANLA and ZIPRA and, therefore, lose the trust of the people.

ZIPRA attempted to lay down the law within the TTLs. This was confirmed when one of our men confronted a female friend, Ariko (pseudonym), whom he identified as working with ZIPRA in the Kavaya Kraal area. She confirmed that she had been with ZIPRA in mid-November but also stated that they had recently returned to her kraal. A local, Gamba (pseudonym), had been given a wife by ZIPRA and additional intelligence indicated he was, understandably, frequently protecting

1 Dr J. Chakawa email 6/3/2019.

ZIPRA. On 20 December 1978, Gamba went to the home of his new wife and instructed the people to notify him of any SF activities in their vicinity. He then left with three girls from that kraal, aged 15, 7 and 5 (names withheld). Gamba was also now a store owner as ZIPRA had given him an abandoned store (locstat withheld). It was believed that the store owner had moved away. This was another instance of ZIPRA imposing martial law in their attempt to govern Hurungwe.

As our men gained ground in the field, we expected the incoming intelligence to increase, giving rise to two matters. Firstly, our intelligence activities into ZIPRA's networks had to increase and continue to inform them of what we wanted them to know. Grey and Happy would attend to this. Secondly, we needed to plan on how to react to the influx of incoming intelligence. Fire Force could not be relied on as we had no control over their deployments and the SF were likewise often not available. In any event, I felt it important for us to develop our own Combat Reconnaissance Unit (CRU) which would elevate our authenticity in the field. Not only that, we had fine soldiers capable of sterling service with the added advantage of being well acquainted with the terrain and the people in Hurungwe: a considerable asset for ground forces. This was a decided advantage as, in the event of them being compromised during sorties, there was a good chance the locals would identify with them and protect them from ZIPRA. We all agreed it was time to introduce the principles governing our own CRU, and I undertook to present these proposals to our men.

I kept Geoff Price up to date with the status of our operations as well as the increasing momentum and mounting tensions regarding training. The men were settled in the field and we were getting regular, daily radio sitreps as well as feedback from locals passing through our offices on their way to Karoi.

The need to react to fresh intelligence was illustrated by an incident occurring during the Christmas period of 1978. An army vehicle travelling along the Masanga road detonated a landmine, confirming information passed two months prior to the episode. This event clearly indicated our intelligence was not acted upon.[1] As can be expected, I was bitterly disappointed. The frustration with this type of incident was that the informer, who had taken the risk of passing on the intelligence in the first place, was "let-down" by our failure to react and lift the mine. Our inactivity could have led to the informant, together with others, doubting our ability to react to intelligence, leading to an overall lack of confidence in our ability to protect the people and vehicles in Hurungwe. This incident was a serious breach of trust. I tasked our team to assure the informer that it would not happen again. On learning that the Binga road was mined, we asked the army to remove the mine(s), which they did.[2]

Intelligence from our men in the field advised us that some *mujibhas* had been posing as ZIPRA and taking money from the people. I issued instructions that these individuals were to be captured. In time they were indeed apprehended, followed by a meeting confronting them with the allegations. During the meeting, the stolen monies were recovered and returned to those from whom it was pilfered. This recovery of cash led to a favourable reaction from the masses. The accused were subsequently brought into town, handed over to us where they were reoriented, politicised and sent for training. In my estimation, a task well performed with a galvanising effect between the UANC and the people. The relatives of the two men arrived at our office on 27 December 1978 to enquire of their whereabouts. When the sons were presented to the parents, they individually owned up to the misdemeanours. Interestingly, when the parents requested they return home, the boys refused, saying they wanted to be trained to fight for the people. One boy, suffering ill health entreated his mother to seek medicine from the spirit medium for a remedy. Once cured, he resumed his training. Happy had again proven his worth to the UANC by resolving this matter.

[1] Karoi Landmine Map 13.
[2] Karoi Landmine Map 14.

A Diary Update

On 23 December 1978, I recorded the following entry in my diary: "We have arrived at a point where our military strength in the proscribed area has gained in momentum to the stage where it has equalled the present political and civil incentives offered by both the past Smith Government and the present Interim Government. In the proscribed areas, we have achieved military stability. Large numbers are attending our meetings, our *mujibha* intelligence networks are established and SB reports confirm our acceptance in the field. There is also a definite flow of intelligence which was and remains one of our main objectives. In one incident, the masses reported to our forces that a crime had been committed, the accused arrested and money returned to the complainants. Here lies the problem. What is the correct political and civil punishment required to sort the accused out? The difficulty with handing the accused over to the police is that we would be identifying with the 'old regime'. No doubt, the accused would end up in jail, a familiar pattern. It is my opinion that petty criminals will have to be dealt with in another form with an emphasis on reorientation and re-politicising. It is not for us at our level to say what these political initiatives and incentives are, and likewise what future civil/criminal precedent is to be adopted, but it was an issue that needed attention urgently. The need now is to implement political change in order to keep abreast with our political message and military progress. I have already mentioned this aspect of the war and suggested that the problem should have been addressed some two months ago. The war which we are involved in is, at the outset, political. The political aspect comprised three categories: economic, social and tribal. All these areas need to be addressed by the politicians, urgently."

As the war continued, I felt myself gradually developing an affinity with the people. I identified with them and was in the process of understanding them better than before. I wanted to be with them and help them. The strange thing was that I was able to do precisely that. They were no longer the enemy, rather they were fellow countrymen. I found it a strange phenomenon moving into a community of people who accepted, trusted and protected us. My understanding of being one with the people became clearer. I found myself realising that it was not "them" who had to change, become civilised, more loving, caring and more human. It was I who had to change and I was, indeed, undergoing a change in mindset. The war, the people and the men in my team I served with had become my world. Naturally, this did not exclude our local establishment, the Twin Rivers Motel, where much time had been spent. However, in sober terms, ZIPRA remained the enemy and needed to be eliminated.

The Shona/Ndebele tribal factions continued to challenge our national political and military efforts. The struggle for ascendancy posed a serious threat to continued stability within the region. This division was particularly important during the struggle in Hurungwe. Despite splits among the Shona people, it was clear that there would come a time when these people would, like it or not, unite. The Shona people had a common fate: suppression by ZIPRA. Through the efforts of ZANLA, the Shona had gained a large measure of support throughout the country. The Ndebele occupied a relatively small proportion of the country and, in places where they penetrated Shona territory, they enjoyed little support. I believed the stage had been set for an uprising among the Shona people which would occur once elections were over. Essentially, we in Hurungwe were at the stage where establishing good governance was fundamentally concerned with addressing the grievances, needs and aspirations of the people. A new dispensation urgently needed to be determined and implemented because the previous white governmental structures, in my estimation, had failed. It was my view that, failure to grasp the necessity to implement political change, would quickly result in disastrous military reversals.

Late in December 1978, Geoff Price brought a team of SB operatives to Karoi for a briefing on our strategies and tactics. I gave a detailed rundown on all aspects of our operations. Henrik Ellert, an attendee at my briefing, achieved some success in the Kana Communal Lands, Midlands province. ZIPRA were again occupying Shona territory. However, by the end of 1979, ZIPRA had overrun Kana and re-established control.[1]

[1] Ellert, H. and Anderson, D. (2020), pp. 348.

17 ~ THE PEOPLE'S ARMY: FIRST CONTACTS

The object of war is specifically to preserve oneself and destroy the enemy.
Mao Zedong

On 24 December 1978, our men approached a kraal near Maziza Kraal to capture a *mujibha* working for ZIPRA. Having collected him, they withdrew to some cover for a rest, and posted sentries. During the break, a lone insurgent was observed following their tracks. A hastily arranged ambush was set up to eliminate him. As the trap was sprung, he was injured but managed to escape. Later, unconfirmed reports suggested that he had died from his injuries.[1]

Martin, the detachment commander, callsign 77A, reported that at 4 a.m. on 25 December 1978, a ZIPRA section of nine men moved into their proscribed area. They mistakenly thought our men were based at Katenhe Store. Led by a ZIPRA *mujibha*, who had previously been "accepted" by our men, they attacked the store expending 300 rounds as well as a rifle rocket-grenade. Expecting some form of reaction to the attack, they had laid two landmines in separate locations. As the insurgents made good their escape, they attempted to blow up the main Kariba to Salisbury power line but failed to cause any serious damage. At first light, Martin's callsign found tracks and began to follow the spoor of the fleeing insurgents to the location at which they had attempted to sabotage the power lines. On arrival, they found that one insurgent had blown himself up during the failed attempt. The two landmines were marked with branches as a warning and were later lifted by engineers.[2] The callsign continued to follow the spoor to the border of the proscribed area where the follow-up ended.[3]

On the same day, five insurgents attacked one of our sections holding a political meeting with the locals. Our men returned fire, killing two insurgents in the ensuing battle. There were no SFAs casualties.[4]

The men had stood their ground in their first battle. Significantly, their morale was high and they were eager for further action. I reminded them not to lose sight of the fact that our role was to occupy the ground, thereby denying ZIPRA access to the people and gradually forcing them out of Hurungwe. Conversely, this was ZIPRA's first battle with our men which was a strategic and tactical failure. ZIPRA's reputation had been that they stood their ground and fought "to the end". Up to this point, I had been concerned that ZIPRA would overwhelm our men, but that did not happen. I was proud of our men. Although on the one hand our intelligence network had been penetrated by the ZIPRA *mujibha*, our information was still accurate enough to alert us. More importantly, we had ZIPRA converting to hit-and-run operations. They no longer occupied the ground and could not remain in our territory. This represented a significant moral victory for the men.

This was a good day for us in the field. The men had learned not to trust all the locals and the significance of accurate intelligence, as this was a matter of life and death. The locals who helped in the collection of doppies and the location of the landmines were well rewarded. This incident inspired us to honour the people's requests to make their roads safe from landmines. In consultation with the people, we introduced a strategy using the existing *mujibha* systems and the locals. Roads were divided into parts (cells) and each cell allocated to a kraal area. The resident UANC *mujibha* cell with the locals were responsible for "clearing" the roads in their cell area daily. All information was

---

1 Karoi Contacts Map Incident 23.

2 Karoi Landmine Map 15-16.

3 Karoi Contacts Map Incident 24.

4 Karoi Contacts Map Incident 25.

passed to the resident SFA section who would alert us if any landmines had been located. Once fully implemented and tested, this system would pave the way for buses and civilian vehicles to resume travelling on the roads. Involving the people in the reopening of roads was an important step, as they had called for them to be reopened. Their co-operation meant we could now rely on their help.

Dealing with sections of the Roman Catholic Church during the Rhodesian War

In my view, sections of the Roman Catholic Church's media were biased and, in most instances, favoured ZANLA and ZIPRA forces. I found their stance unacceptable. *The Sunday Mail* of 24 December 1978 contained an article written by Roman Catholic bishops studying a report claiming that private armies in the rural areas had set the stage for "political intimidation on an unprecedented scale". The article said: "The seriousness of the situation created by the existence of private political armies and the serious disregard these men have for life, morality or human decency make it vital for some strong reaction to be forthcoming from the Church." It was compiled by the Catholic Commission for Justice and Peace in Rhodesia. The confidential document had been presented to the Rhodesia Catholic Bishops' Conference earlier in December 1978. A copy was made available to *The Sunday Mail.*

Gathered from field reports by the commission's members, the document contained details of murders, beatings, rapes and thefts allegedly carried out by forces loyal to both the UANC and ZANU (Sithole). The report alleged that these forces were known to be operating in the Gokwe, Mrewa, Plumtree, Wedza, Manyeni, Hurungwe, Copper Queen and Nyabira areas. The document stated that there were serious implications in the formation of private armies by the military wings of the nationalist parties. The likelihood of a full-scale civil war was substantially increased, the report maintained. It added that malnutrition was aggravated by the irregular demands on the rural Africans' food suppliers. In contrast to the report, our men fed themselves, were self-disciplined with accountability prevailing in the field. The report continued that low agricultural productivity was likely to suffer further and that the flow of refugees to the towns would increase. It concluded by urging the Church to show courage in standing up against blatant and gross injustices. To my surprise, no mention was made of ZANLA and ZIPRA atrocities. From my experiences with the Roman Catholic Church in the Makoni, I felt they had hardly any room to talk, as they openly and actively supported ZANLA and, as I perceived matters, they were legal accomplices to the enemy's atrocities.

However, as one is aware, assumptions and generalisations often lead to faulty conclusions. It so happened that the local white Roman Catholic priest, Fr Rainer Zinkann, was travelling in and out of Hurungwe under our protection. The church service at St Boniface's Mission for the Christmas celebrations was held under our guard. Attendance at the church was low but that was as expected in these turbulent times. The positive aspect to the service, in my view, was that it signalled a gradual return to normal civilian routine. I informed Geoff Price that maximum publicity must be made of the situation. In time, this happened when the BBC and international TV reporters and journalists visited Hurungwe. Further, at a local level, we were to build a sound relationship with Fr Zinkann. He had planned, in conjunction with our sections, to conduct Mass at Chisape Church on New Year's Day, 1979. We would ensure security arrangements for him and the congregation.

Operations Intensify

Manenji had for some days been expressing concerns that the discipline and training at the farm were deteriorating. This followed a previous urgent visit from a distressed Walter when he arrived at the "safe house" seeking help to resolve a matter of ill-discipline at the farm. As Todd recalls: "My recollection of the discontent amongst the men is that Walter took far too long to train up the first batch of recruits. Walter did not seem to comprehend that they did not have to be trained up to conventional military standards as long as they could shoot and were willing to engage the enemy, we didn't care less at how well or not they could dress, salute or march! It was urgent that they became operational asap. They eventually let Walter know their feelings of frustration and I believe he panicked as he was on his own at the camp. Grey was called in and calmed things down."[1] And this is what happened. This incident was no more than the men expressing their discontent with Walter's training programme and his methods. In our view, it was obvious that we needed to review the training programme and those responsible for its implementation to suit a revolutionary army.

This was the benefit of having an "in-house" intelligence network which allowed for timeous intervention. The staff were concerned that matters would quickly spiral out of control. However, discipline continued to falter and on 26 December 1978, I noted in my diary that discipline at the farm had lapsed below the expected standard and this, in my view, was as a direct result of a lack of skilled manpower. There was no doubt that we were losing momentum in training, resulting in a lack of impetus in the field. ZIPRA were on the run at that moment. It seemed to me that this was the perfect opportunity to deploy additional troops. However, regarding training, time was not on our side. The process required acceleration as we no longer had the luxury of indefinite training periods. We were going to have to be satisfied with the available weaponry, facilities and wherewithal. I discussed the matter with Geoff Price, concluding that it was time for adjustments. At that time, Walter was on leave and Geoff told me to leave the matter in his hands. Walter did not return to Karoi and was, in due course, replaced by Ian Suttill, a former SAS soldier.

By the end of December 1978, ZIPRA operations began to intensify. We received intelligence to the effect that the family of a serving SFA member was assaulted by ZIPRA and their kraals at Kebvunde were razed to the ground on 27 December 1978. The family was rescued by our network. They were destitute. We purchased clothing and other personal items and resettled them on our farm. One of the sections was tasked to investigate the matter when I met the callsign in the field the following day. The *mujibha* who allegedly led ZIPRA to the family was Tanaka (pseudonym). His whereabouts was known to us and we proceeded to find him. I tasked Manenji to debrief the family concerned and to glean as much information as possible for suitable action to be planned. This was again a demonstration of the benefit of Chabwino for refugees: a place of shelter and a fountain of intelligence.

Later in the day, on 27 December 1978, I undertook a PRAW flight into the proscribed area and liaised with all the sections. I felt it necessary to ensure there were no problems after their first contact and wanted them to know that they were not operating in isolation. Our entire operation was functional and motivated. I arranged to meet the men in the field the next day to address any matters concerning them. I decided to take some men from the reaction team with me as an escort in case we encountered ZIPRA insurgents en route. As mentioned, our men were dressed and armed in a similar fashion to ZIPRA and I did not know them all individually. For all I knew, the enemy could well have been stationed at the roadside to meet me. I also felt that, if ZIPRA received news that the leader of the SFA was entering the field, they would surely have attacked me. Despite my apprehension, I took what I considered reasonable precautions and then enjoyed the experience.

Refugees continued to pour through our office in Chikangwe and then on to Chabwino. We purchased a considerable amount of kit and equipment for them. Large numbers of men were wanting to join our forces but we had to curtail the influx momentarily as, at that stage, we had sufficient recruits. During the day, I learned that the area had been visited by JOC Hurricane. Clearly, I mused, my personal invitation had been "lost in the postal system". I was informed that the question of Int.Aff. involvement in Hurungwe had been discussed regarding the opening of schools and other civil administration issues. This was always going to be a sensitive topic. In my opinion, this was part of the bigger political picture that needed to be addressed by the politicians. The question that had to be answered in the new dispensation was, do we want to hold on to the old dispensation? Holding on to the old dispensation would effectively confirm ZIPRA's strategy that SFAs were nothing more than puppets for the SF and that there would be no political changes in the country. Whether a specific branch of the civil service was functioning well or not was not the question. We needed to be seen to be addressing the people's and the broader communities' needs,

[1] Todd email 4/10/2016.

and this required change. The old no longer fitted into the new. A nationwide change of mind was called for, failing which, in my opinion, would lead to the country's collapse. I was not about to let that happen in Hurungwe!

In the late afternoon, our "house *mujibhas*" (we had an intelligence network set up around the house and neighbourhood) detected a local man drawing plans of the property and promptly captured him. We identified him as Shohiwa (pseudonym) from the Mujinga area and detained him overnight for questioning in the morning. We discovered that he had been sent to recce our residence by a ZIPRA section but was, in fact, a somewhat reluctant *mujibha*. After discussions with the UANC team, he volunteered to join the people's army and was sent to the farm for training. The "house *mujibhas*" remained on high alert. Happy joined the reaction team and myself on our journey to meet with the men in the field.

One of our sections advised us that 10 ZIPRA were presently resident at Karova Kraal which was known to our men. We thereupon planned to deploy the newly formed Combat Reconnaissance Unit (CRU) to assist in their elimination. For some time, we had been considering developing our own independent CRU to respond to immediate intelligence. The men had been carefully selected, trained and were thoroughly prepared for this their first deployment. Our strategy was to first introduce them to the UANC *mujibhas* and supportive locals, followed by our base-camp locations, rendezvous points and the general intelligence appertaining to each relevant section. They would, in other words, be made fully aware of those who supported our cause prior to any attack, in order to make their ground patrols efficient and ensure their acceptance. The CRU had the sole function of deploying on immediate intelligence to eliminate the enemy. They were well armed with two RPDs, one RPG-7, AK-47s, hand-grenades, smoke-grenades and a radio. Essentially, they would be engaged on short-term deployments and return to Chabwino on completion of their mission.

The location of two other ZIPRA sections were also identified. During this time, one of our men in the field, Bazooka, accidentally shot himself in the left foot and was taken to hospital by the UANC network. Strange as it may seem, this proved a positive incident in that the networks had responded rapidly to the emergency, thereby reinforcing my outlook that we must be equipped to care swiftly for our own members. Helicopters and Security Forces were not always available and I considered these assets as "luxuries".

The planned meetings in the field on 28 December 1978 were successful. It was good to see the men healthy, confident and jubilant in spirit. We had been blessed with capable, skilled and competent men doing an excellent job of soldiering. I admired their professionalism under difficult conditions. We were determined men on a mission, and I felt privileged to be a part of the operation. There was a positive feel to Hurungwe now. The people in our occupied territory were happy, supportive and sending their sons for training. Recruiting was not problematic and field intelligence continued to flow. It was a surreal phenomenon being part of the people's revolution and was an incredible personal experience. To look into the eyes of our men and the people knowing that I was one with them was, frankly, indescribable. I felt safe driving along the roads knowing that the people were protecting us with their patrols. I was confident that either our men or the people would warn us if ZIPRA were in the area. As I saw matters, this was the gauge of success in a revolutionary war. The criteria was acceptance by the people, militarily occupying the ground to protect them, propagating and gradually fulfilling a political vision and, where necessary, eliminating the enemy when they failed to recognise the choice of the people. The critical junction is having the people at the core of the struggle. I kept reminding myself that kills did not represent success, neither was it the aim. The aim was to occupy and possess the land.

It was always good to return to Karoi and spend the evening at the Twin Rivers Motel. We usually met up with Ian Suttill who updated us with the developments at Chabwino. Geoff Price had sent Ian Suttill to join the training staff and was waiting for my assessment before we made other structural changes. He had settled down well and was enjoying the challenge. I visited him regularly at Chabwino to ensure that he had "found his feet", at the same time allowing him time and space to develop and implement reforms. He was surrounded by a competent team and I felt it best not to interfere. Ian was a professional soldier who understood his mission: train a revolutionary army.

On 30 December 1978, the UANC team confirmed intelligence that Munuyaradzi, a clerk at the Magunje co-operative store, was harbouring and assisting elements of a ZIPRA section. A further 16 insurgents were reported to be living at the house of Petros, where the leading *mujibhas* were reported to be James Chikaya, Siton Charanechombo and Mazoe Dobiya. This intelligence was filtered back into the field for the attention of our men for appropriate action. The deciding factor would be our response to the "fingered" *mujibhas*. If they acknowledged their involvement with ZIPRA, which was normally the case, they could be politicised, reorientated and recruited as our own *mujibhas* or for training when vacancies arose. Once they abandoned ZIPRA, they were safer being trained and armed in order that they could return to the area and protect their own families. This was the ideal scenario for them and for us. ZIPRA's heavy-handed approach to dissidents would continue to function as they lost ground, making reprisals inevitable. Just as expected was our progress in occupying the land, for it is what the people want that dictates the outcome of a revolution, provided they receive protection and support. Victory was achieved by gaining momentum with the people. In the event of a *mujibha* failing to co-operate, we would remove him from Hurungwe, place him at Chabwino where he would meet his friends and family, see the thrust of training and be subject to politicisation by the UANC team. Grey and Happy were exceptionally effective in these circumstances. Usually, the *mujibhas* would join our forces, either by returning to the field as *mujibhas* or by joining the people's army.

Martin returned from the field and arrived at the "safe house" having captured Tanaka and David (pseudonyms), which was an excellent achievement. Tanaka admitted his involvement with ZIPRA and to identifying the family of a serving SFA member to them. Happy took charge of the debrief. David, however, proved obstructive. It became evident that our men needed to carry out their own interrogations in the field and react to information gleaned. This would no doubt exponentially lead to success in penetrating ZIPRA's intelligence networks. Our men were inexperienced but receiving hands-on training in counter-intelligence operations. One learns rapidly when one's life is at stake. The more they interacted with captured ZIPRA *mujibhas*, *chimbwidos* and the people, the quicker they would learn how ZIPRA operated, and this would help them counter the enemy's intelligence networks.

The following day I returned to the field to visit the remaining callsigns I had not met the previous day. My rendezvous was for 11 a.m. but debriefing Martin delayed me and I was late arriving. Our men had moved away from the meeting place which was appropriate from a security aspect. However, I managed to meet with Tall's section and discussed in detail the deployment of the CRU. I felt alive when in the field, driving the dusty, dirt roads and passing locals who were pleased to see us. It was amazing how quickly the word spread about our presence in Hurungwe. Also, it was a unique situation as we had to put our trust in the locals that they would protect us by surveying the roads for landmines and passing on intelligence regarding ZIPRA's movements and intentions. The beauty of the changed circumstances was that we were informed, rather than wandering around aimlessly. On my return, Happy advised me that the UANC required additional accommodation in Chikangwe. Two six-room flats and one four-room flat were his requests. I tasked Admin. to approach the rural council to arrange for the accommodation. An official from the rural council had previously proved helpful and was once again obliging.

Fr Zinkann, the Roman Catholic priest, arrived quite unexpectedly at our "safe house" on 31 December 1978. He was a kind, soft-hearted man and easy to talk to. In my view, the opposite from the priests in the Makoni. Fr Zinkann brought the following matters to my attention: He was very satisfied with the work our men were doing and stated that all the people he made contact with, both in the TTL and the township, were very happy with our work. He knew of no incidents of rape, assault, murder and robbery, etc., perpetrated by our men in the field. Our men had protected him when he visited his missions and congregations. They met him before he entered the TTL, escorted him to the mission, checked the roads for landmines and protected him at the church. He was concerned that we would withdraw from the area and I assured him we would not do so. Fr Zinkann mentioned SFAs in other areas, namely Chesa and Msami, and said as far as the people were concerned, these areas were not as well organised as ours. There were, apparently, considerable problems being experienced there. He expressed his opinion that what we were doing was the solution to the problems of the war and hoped that we had plans to extend out operations to the Vuti, Kazangarara and other areas. We advised him we intended moving to these areas as soon as possible. He asked if he could visit the farm to preach and I agreed, providing that our men were willing to listen to him. I thought it would be to our benefit to have him visit the farm. We planned for our men to meet him at the TTL border on 1 January 1979 and to escort him to Chisape Mission, and then on to Magunje.

It was a most congenial meeting. Fr Zinkann certainly had a heart for all people. He was not afraid of speaking the truth or being identified with us. I considered him a likeable and brave individual. He was deeply concerned about the oppression of the people and the atrocities carried out by ZIPRA. He was not a political priest, but was deeply concerned about victims of torture and violence who needed healing, physically and spiritually. His attitude was the very antithesis of the priests in the Makoni.

18 ~ OPERATIONS INTENSIFY AS THE WEB WIDENS

If they fight, we will wipe them out completely.
This is the way things are.
Mao Zedong

There was still some delay in the delivery of weapons and equipment from Special Forces, therefore I contacted Mr Mac and advised him of our situation. He said he would investigate the matter and asked if we could meet to update him with our programme and discuss any other problems. I knew that he was, as was Geoff Price, a man of his word and that our weapons and equipment would arrive soon, which they did.

On 2 January 1979, the Combat Reconnaissance Unit received news of a ZIPRA section resident at Nylon's Kraal at QM5526. They attacked the kraal complex during the day to avoid any contact with the SF. While approaching the kraal, ZIPRA were warned that our men were approaching. Consequently, they beat a hasty retreat. Our men opened fire but secured no kills. Locally brewed African beer and ZIPRA clothing were recovered. Four girls and a *mujibha* were captured and brought to our "safe house" in Karoi. Once again, our men acted positively, taking the initiative and thereby confirming their intelligence, and engaging ZIPRA. However, it was important for the men to learn to carry out their own interrogations in the field rather than transporting the captures to Karoi, which would compromise them and waste valuable time. Protecting identities of the captures and immediate reaction to "ground intelligence" was essential to successful engagements with the enemy. Thereafter, and in the process, the masses needed to be politicised and mobilised, the primary tool being our men's treatment of the captures who were all connected to the villages. This process was naturally going to evolve and develop with experience, but it was essential to mobilise the masses of the affected area and give them the opportunity to witness what our political and military objectives were. If we humiliated, beat or harassed these people, they would not support us in the long term. Should they decide to continue to support ZIPRA, they stood the chance of being killed in a contact when our forces engaged them. The opportunity to defect required consideration, bearing in mind that we would eventually be occupying areas outside the demarcated zones, and would have to depend on the masses to protect us. It was clear that the men needed training in the area of field intelligence and Grey, Happy and I worked on this matter, as well as appropriate encouragement for work well done.

Military Operations with BSAP Support Unit

As a result of information received at the beginning of January 1979 from Daniel, one of our SFAs, we deployed him into the Piriviri Communal Lands with a Support Unit callsign in order to check out some known ZIPRA bases which were, apparently, still occupied. Strictly speaking, this was not our geographical area of responsibility but ZIPRA's operations were not bound by borders, and I saw no reason why ours should be. The area was remote. Access was both difficult and dangerous. We cleared the deployment with Sub.JOC Sinoia, and the Support Unit deployed. While sweeping through a kraal line in the early hours of the morning of 3 January 1979, they observed two African males fleeing and fired at them. One *mujibha* was injured and captured and one locally trained insurgent was killed.[1] They remained in the area and deployed to Matenga Kraal where intelligence had indicated there were two insurgents suffering from an alleged spiritual tribal infliction contracted

[1] Karoi Contacts Map Incident 26, not logged on map.

from sleeping with another man's wife. As in most cultures, married women were prohibited from sexual intercourse with other men. In traditional African culture, a violation of this principle led to a mysterious illness known in Shona as *runyoka* or *rukaho* among the Korekore in Hurungwe. It is a common fact in religion that immorality has a negative spiritual consequence. I found this matter interesting as it showed a significant shift in the spiritual aspect of the people's way of life and how it displayed their displeasure of ZIPRA's immorality in the war. At 5 a.m. on 6 January 1979, Mantle and Daniel initiated a contact with two insurgents with no casualties on either side. A minor cache of one tin of ammunition and two ZIPRA packs were recovered.[1]

Daniel and the Support Unit moved on to recce Mugumbura's Kraal where our intelligence indicated a ZIPRA presence. No contact was made with the enemy during this operation but, overall, the deployment had been a success. ZIPRA had been harassed, kept on the move and would have no idea where the SF would strike next. This was in keeping with my strategy which was not all about kills. There are many victories in a revolutionary war. Penetrating and reorientating ZIPRA's intelligence and support networks were, in my mind, a more significant victory. Deceased insurgents could be replaced as there were literally thousands of ZIPRA in Zambia waiting for deployment into Rhodesia. But an intelligence network, penetrated and exposed, resulted in a major defeat, particularly when our troops remained on the ground and consolidated the local's support. That, in my mind, is a victory. Daniel's knowledge of the area was thorough. He worked well with the Support Unit which had also performed admirably.

During the morning of 3 January 1979, Fr Zinkann, known locally as Zingani, arrived at the "safe house" with clothing for the refugees at the farm. He was supposed to be going to the farm to visit the men, but we could not make it as we had a considerable amount of work to do. We made arrangements for him to visit the following week. It was a pleasure having a Roman Catholic priest serving our people, especially since there was so much negative propaganda from the Catholic Commission for Justice and Peace directed at SFAs.

A positive development that day was the formal request by locals for the resumption of the cattle-dipping programme. ZIPRA had halted the programme. The problem was not the dipping process itself but rather who would bear the costs. ZIPRA's political strategy was to blame Int.Aff. for exorbitant fees and such worthless programmes but the locals, with no choice until our arrival, were now suffering the consequences of the non-dipping of their valuable assets. The sensitive political situation required was to distance ourselves from Int.Aff. This was a dilemma only the politicians could resolve. Rapid political changes were required to authenticate our growing military successes. Admin. collected a motorbike organised by Geoff for use at the farm, which proved invaluable. Tawengwa was able to ride it and had been deployed to locate callsigns and convey messages and manageable resupplies. Here was a perfect example of the faith placed in the intelligence supplied by the locals regarding matters of safety when travelling along the rural roads, especially the danger of landmines.

On 4 January 1979, we received information of a ZIPRA section based at James's Kraal. We deployed the CRU to investigate. It was alleged that there was an arms cache in the granary. A sweep of the kraal in the early morning was carried out without success. During the same evening, ZIPRA attacked a village occupied by the family of one of our men. Unfortunately, the kraal was outside the proscribed area and difficult to protect. Fortunately, however, no one was killed and all refugees were removed to Chabwino. Happy and I agreed that recruiting should increase and training accelerated.

That evening when I met with Ian Suttill at the farm, we discussed increasing the momentum of training. He had assessed the existing programme and agreed a shortened, efficient and professional alternative could be developed and introduced. Suttill confirmed that he would analyse the matter as I was due to travel to Bindura and then into the Msana in order to collect men being trained at Puck Rage farm who originated from the Zwimba TTL. It was an arduous journey, especially in an

[1] Karoi Contacts Map Incident 28, not logged on map.

old Puma supply truck. Unfortunately, the trainees from Zwimba were a "shower": hopeless, poorly trained and of no use to us. However, we came across 35 trainees who originated from Hurungwe TTL. They were far more aggressive and keener to deploy, therefore I arranged to uplift them. A further 26 men from Hurungwe announced that they also wanted to return and fight in their home areas, and arrangements were put in place to uplift them as soon as their training was completed. The 35 men were well received at Chabwino. Suttill would ensure they reached our required standards before their deployment. Towards the end of the day, I left for Salisbury with Clive Boddy: a long day of driving. Clive was interested in our operations and we decided to approach our respective superior officers to establish whether he could work with us, as he would be an asset to the team.

Our First Fatality

Sadly, we received news of our first casualty on 4 January 1979, when two of our men were ambushed near Chanetsa Kraal by two insurgents, one of whom was armed with a PKM, killing one of our men instantly. The deceased's weapon and webbing were removed from his body by ZIPRA. During the battle, one insurgent was injured and died near Birimahwe the following day. This marked our first field tragedy. The rest of the section returned to the scene, capturing the ZIPRA *mujibhas* involved and returning them to our farm. Doppies from the contact were recovered and handed to SB, and the body recovered.[1] Despite the loss, the men's morale remained high. My perception was that they were annoyed with ZIPRA rather than being downhearted. This was a delicate stage of our operations as we did not want reprisals on the locals, as was the norm with ZIPRA. Grey and Happy emphasised this to the men. We had to stand firm and focus on the principle that victory was in penetrating, "turning" and gaining the support of ZIPRA's intelligence networks and support bases. If the people witnessed this approach by our men, I was convinced the tide would rapidly turn in our favour. Grey and Happy also spent time talking to the people, imparting our vision for their emancipation with passionate commitment and accuracy. We were determined to overcome the setback of our first loss. Fr Zinkann kindly conducted a burial service for the deceased at the farm on 10 January 1979. His service drew widespread interest, particularly the sermon. Standard military protocol of such occasions was followed, including a 21-gun salute. Morale after the service continued to be high, particularly after Grey had given his usual wise and motivating speech. I found it a sad and difficult day emotionally. Few things are worse than witnessing the death and burial of a fellow soldier.

Back at Karoi, Fr Zinkann visited the house and requested escorts for five church services he wanted to hold in Hurungwe at various locations; St Boniface (7 January 1979), Dombo (11 January 1979), Gasva (14 January 1979), St Boniface (21 January 1979) and Mapusambe (25 January 1979). I agreed to provide the escorts. Fr Zinkann and I had established a good relationship. I found him a kind, unassuming and genuine man who never demanded agreement or participation with his religious beliefs. He was simply there to serve his people and I could identify with that.

Recruiting and training continued to gain momentum and on 7 January we undertook what I referred to as The Great Trek, reminiscent of the early South African pioneers, conveying 42 recruits to Retreat farm, Bindura, for training. Retreat farm was one of the official establishments where SFAs from around the country were sent for a one-month training period. The five-hour drive in our Puma supply truck turned out to be more of a survival exercise but, all in all, it was a pleasant journey. On arrival, the recruits were presented to the "quartermaster" and they were most efficiently kitted out. Neither the training staff at Retreat farm nor I considered four weeks' training with only 100 rounds per man enough, but that was the time frame and our munitions allocation forced us to make the best of the situation. I took the opportunity to meet with Mr Mac and updated him with events and progress in Hurungwe. I enjoyed his company. He held the belief that "everything was possible", an attitude that helped us a great deal.

[1] Karoi Contacts Map Incident 27.

The next day, in the early hours of the morning, we left for the Msana to collect the 30 trained SFAs from Hurungwe for deployment. On our arrival and while assembling the men, several others from surrounding areas volunteered to join us at Hurungwe. While it was not our recruitment policy to accept men from other areas, some of these men were enthusiastic and keen to join us, and we ended up with 26 men from Hurungwe and 10 men from other areas: one each from the Makoni, Obva, Domboshawa and Malawi, two from Shamva and four from Sipolilo. It turned out to be a good decision. On the way through Salisbury, I called in at Special Forces and managed to obtain 10,000 FN rounds, various items of clothing, kit and equipment. I met Ian Suttill who was also successfully obtaining kit and equipment for Chabwino. We managed to gather ample supplies for the training programme as well as an additional 40 AK-47s. Unquestionably, a profitable day for our stores!

Maintaining Order

While in Salisbury, I had a meeting with Geoff Price to discuss and resolve various domestic matters. Since Hurungwe SFAs were a Special Branch operation, Geoff's ruling was final and, following our discussions, we made the following decisions:

I would maintain overall command of the SFAs in Hurungwe.

The training staff were to focus on the training of men recruited by the UANC networks. Their duties were to include the complete running of the farm, i.e. discipline, training, refugees' welfare and the general farm upkeep, including the maize and vegetable garden, etc.

The training staff were to assist me with any military attacks and field discipline when and if required.

Once the men were trained, they would come under my command in all regards, i.e. deployments, pay, clothing, material resupply, radios, batteries and intelligence.

Grey, Happy and I were to be responsible for all aspects of military field intelligence and planning, including the opening of new areas and the recruiting of manpower which was to go ahead at "full steam".

A request was to be made to Special Branch Sinoia for us to utilise their *mujibha* farm as a training/holding facility in our present desperate efforts to expand.

Grey, Happy and the UANC were responsible for continual mobilisation of men undergoing training, and men in the field. They were also responsible for mobilising the masses by holding regular meetings in the field, as many and as frequently as possible.

We also planned to open a forward base in Magunje for the following reasons:

1. Forward control of callsigns in the field. At present, we were too far away to effectively control our men. Reaction to intelligence, which primarily means interrogations of captured field *mujibhas*, was far too slow. Captured *mujibhas* were to be sent to the Magunje base.
2. Resupply of ammunition, radios, batteries, clothing, etc., including pay, to be co-ordinated with far greater and easier access from Magunje.
3. Field risks were to be lessened by decreasing the travelling of our men in private vehicles. The UANC men invariably carry a hand-grenade only and were easy prey to the enemy. Geoff had sidearms earmarked for the UANC team from previous discussions. He would arrange for them to be delivered to Karoi. Geoff's portfolio included close-security protection for the UANC and he managed their training at a farm outside Salisbury.
4. Closer co-ordination of intelligence by both the UANC networks, local SB and GC at grass-roots level.
5. Radio communications between the field and base made easier, making field control, discipline and reaction to intelligence expedient.
6. Callsigns were to remain on a more constant basis in the field without having to come in and out of town.
7. Callsigns naturally to come out of the field on retraining when time permits and when required.

Additionally, we agreed that any persons recruited yet found unsuitable for continued service would be immediately discharged once Grey, Happy and I had been consulted, and the necessity for their removal confirmed. This also applied to people seconded to us for various tasks, including training. Sitreps reporting contacts and incidents to be compiled by myself and passed to Geoff Price for onward transmissions to Special Forces and Special Branch. Requirements of clothing, blankets and suchlike, required for our new recruits, to be requested well in advance from Special Forces. On completion of training, men to be issued with a complete set of uniforms, including denim clothing, a pair of new shoes, a raincoat and personal toiletries. Any queries whatsoever to be directed to me for discussion and passed on to the necessary parties after consideration.

UANC Office in Kariba

After one month of deliberations, we felt the time had arrived to open a UANC office in Kariba and on 9 January 1979, Todd organised accommodation for us all. Our journey to Kariba was memorable. It reminded me of the fishing trips we had made to Kariba and the Zambezi River with my father and brother, David. During those youthful, blissful days my chief concerns were for wild animals, the surrounding vegetation and a successful catch of fish. On this occasion, my concern was for ZIPRA. It was refreshing to get away from the war zone. On reaching our destination, we checked into the Caribbea Bay Hotel, a magnificent Mediterranean-style haven built on the edge of the lake.

The same day I had a meeting with D/Insp. John Gibson,[1] Member in Charge CID/SB Kariba and explained our plans. He was keen to help and offered to find a suitable office in the township for the UANC. More importantly, he was prepared to help co-ordinate the operation, which was appreciated. Todd left a float of R$200 with John Gibson to cover any immediate expenses. It was not possible for me to co-ordinate the Kariba office from Karoi, therefore our only alternative was to use the local SB who were able to give "hands-on" immediate assistance when and if required. In the afternoon, we had a meeting with local UANC officials which, once again, was successful. The political and intelligence set-up was in place but at a low key. Our timing seemed perfect and the Kariba officials were eager to participate.

These were the UANC terms of reference for the Kariba office. The senior official was Lenard and his deputy was Joseph. A car would be provided once positive intelligence or activity was identified. We felt that it was good to have an incentive for the men to work towards which would establish their commitment, dedication and connection to the people. Certainly, a vehicle would help but it was not essential to the activities of a grass-roots movement. It did not take long for us to provide the vehicle. Each member of the team would be paid a weekly allowance which would increase when the office was considered operational, and then additional funding for expenses would be provided. The office would be responsible for:

1. Establishing a UANC network based on the cell system in Kariba Township and bringing the operation out into the open (covert to overt).
2. Mobilising the people towards the UANC by initially private, but once established, public meetings.
3. Clearly, ZIPRA had already established an intelligence network in Kariba and this needed to be identified, penetrated and, where possible, reorientated. I warned the men that this ZIPRA cell would observe their movements and keep ZIPRA updated with events. Our men could use the cell to feed ZIPRA with what we wanted them to know, but they also had to take precautions to protect themselves.
4. To obtain intelligence from refugees, in particular *mujibhas*, who had fled the war zone in Hurungwe for various reasons. Refugees could be sent to Chabwino.
5. To recruit men, in particular, *mujibhas* for the people's army.

[1] John Gibson died on 4/11/2009 in Durban, South Africa, following surgery.

I warned the men that they would all be well known by the local SB who would be monitoring their activities. Lenard offered to accommodate some of the staff as he had a large house. Mention was made of one man (name withheld), who was widely known throughout the Kariba district. He was in contact with numerous fishermen, all of whom had Zambian connections, which was an intriguing development. They would be in a position to pass on intelligence of ZIPRA's movements and bases in Zambia as well as their Zambezi River and Lake Kariba crossing points. Grey and Happy updated the men with developments in Hurungwe, emphasising our successes and left them with our vision.

On reflection, I thought it remarkable that in one day's work, we had established an operational intelligence structure and network. It would be arrogant to claim the credit as that would overlook the one major factor: it was what the people wanted, we were moving at their pace. We were not imposing our will on them. Rather, we were developing and revealing what was dormant and latent. This was the people's success. We did, however, celebrate and Grey, Happy, Todd and I went on a boat cruise on Kariba during the late evening. I think it was the first time Grey and Happy had been on a speedboat. We spent a memorable evening together.

With time to reflect, I made the following diary entry:

> I have mentioned that recruiting is to go ahead at "full steam". The reason is that if we do not recruit the masses, ZIPRA will. It is of utmost importance to increase training momentum to keep astride with the momentum in the field. There is little doubt that our training has fallen behind completely and this matter will have the following serious effects:
>
> (a) The masses do not see a build-up of our forces and think we are going to remain small in numbers, thereby losing face in the field.
>
> (b) ZIPRA counter-intelligence will pinpoint our strategy, numbers, supporters, M.O., etc. Attacks into our area must, therefore, be expected to increase.

As matters progressed, a problem at Chabwino needed to be resolved. Volunteer recruits were arriving on an average of five per day which was significant. I was reluctant to turn them away and contacted D/Insp. Driver at Sinoia CID to see if we could use their *mujibha* farm in order to assist us house and train a limited number of recruits if necessary. In doing so, the recruits would be accepted and involved. D/Insp. Driver agreed, confirming that we would have help when needed.

While the break in Kariba was relaxing, we had to leave early as we had arranged a meeting with D/Insp. John van Rooyen (CID photographic studio) and the Psychological Operations Unit, better known as (Psyac) from Salisbury. I was prompted to initiate a propaganda-pamphlet campaign into Hurungwe to drive home to ZIPRA and their supporters that the people's army was now a strong, growing permanent force, which was gaining military ascendency as well as a growing support from the people. Todd and Happy took the Psyac team to Chabwino in order to take photographs of the men in training and simulated contact situations. I also wanted to have photographic records of all our men. Grey and I escorted John van Rooyen into the field to meet the men. Grey had previously alerted them through the networks that we would be coming to photograph them, and organised appropriate venues. It was a busy, pleasant and enjoyable day. I relished watching the men pose for their individual photographs and then assuming the most unusual, aggressive military group postures for the camera. Having photographs taken, to the rural African, was not a common occurrence during the 1960s-1970s. It was quite an event and each picture told a real or perceived story which would be remembered well into the future. I took with me a resupply of hand-grenades, sleeping bags and other items for the men. They thought that Christmas had arrived early, albeit in the context of war.

While in the field, I took the opportunity to discuss with the men their strategies and tactics. They were continuing to expand their intelligence networks and spent much time holding political meetings with the people. Their acceptance by local spirit mediums was an important progress, legitimising their role among the people and providing a margin of safety. They felt there was growing support from the people and were keen to expand their areas of operations which required more manpower. I found this an inspiring visit. Morale was high and I was particularly impressed with their security arrangements and alertness, which was noticeable. Perimeter guards and roving patrols were posted around each venue. I felt safe in their company. They had implemented their own cell systems which were functioning well. I explained that a clothing requisition had been placed to resupply all men with an additional set of denim and shoes. We were also progressing well with the recruits' training and were preparing them for deployment. Pressure was mounting in Chabwino. While John van Rooyen was with us, we took the opportunity to photograph all the men in training at Chabwino. This was all done in time for me to attend the funeral of the aforementioned SFA killed in action which was conducted by Fr Zinkann at Chabwino.

Rural Political Meetings Begin

Grey was scheduled to hold his first political meeting in Hurungwe on 11 January 1979, heralding the beginning of rural political meetings. The UANC office in Chikangwe and men in the field had been spreading the word to the masses for several days. We were excited as this would give us an accurate assessment of how events were unfolding in Hurungwe from the people's perspective. In fact, it was a challenge to ZIPRA to "try and stop us". They would be aware that the meeting was taking place and would be in a position to lay landmines in order to prevent attendance and attack our men or the masses, thereby preventing the meeting from convening. The men in the field had been left to their own initiative to make all necessary security arrangements. Sections combined to protect the venue. They cleared the roads for landmines and patrolled the surrounding area before, during and after the meeting. It took great courage for Grey and Happy to travel the roads in their civilian vehicles without an escort. I continued to admire them. They stood little chance of survival if they detonated a landmine or were ambushed. My one consolation was that they at least had the sidearms provided by Geoff Price. Geoff had supplied us with several sidearms which included .38 Smith and Wesson Specials. In that indomitable African spirit, the men pressed on. They were enjoying themselves.

ZIPRA did not respond to the rally which was attended by 800 locals. I viewed this as a major success, especially as it had taken place in an area previously occupied by ZIPRA. Grey was ecstatic when he returned, reporting that: "It was wonderful!" The people were very happy with the military intervention of our men. In fact, they were calling for reinforcements. People from outside the demarcated areas were appealing for men to be deployed into their areas. Here again, I considered this as significant progress and did all in my power to ensure we once again moved at the pace of the people, and expand the military operations. Grey made a point of travelling to Chabwino to let the recruits and training staff know how well our operations were developing. He had the ability of inspiring men and used every opportunity to do so.

Back at the UANC office in Chikangwe, recruits were pouring in from the Mujinga area. A further 20 recruits from the field had been selected by our men and were waiting to be uplifted. The UANC was also receiving recruits from Hurungwe men residing in Salisbury, Sinoia, Charter, and further afield. We experienced an increase among recruits from Hurungwe wishing to join the battle. The word of our successes was spreading. A further 20 men had already been recruited by the Kariba office which had sprung into action, a clear indication of their commitment and determination. I was confident that the Kariba office would be "worth its weight in gold". Their enthusiasm meant more pressure on the training aspect of our operations, calling for urgent attention. The number of recruits was not the problem, rather it was the slow pace of training which was problematic.

On the night of 12 January 1979, a farm adjacent to our area was attacked. A ZIPRA section had infiltrated it from the neighbouring Wasakara area which was beyond our jurisdiction. We reasoned that ZIPRA wanted to convey a psychological message that they were still fully operational and, in doing so, discredit our men in the minds of the people and the white farmers. The fact that ZIPRA moved through our area undetected indicated that our intelligence and military networks may have been infiltrated and this disturbed me. After a meeting with Grey, he travelled to the field in order to instruct the men to increase night operations. I felt there was little to be gained in being seen by the locals during the day, while not affording the people protection throughout the night: there had to be a balance. The farm attack concerned me as did the possibility that we were not affording maximum protection to our people, and leaving ourselves open to disciplinary killings within our own area.

Our intelligence indicated a build-up of ZIPRA to the west of our currently demarcated areas which worried us. I felt it was time to advance and expand our operations, and occupy the land. This needed to be done before ZIPRA could consolidate their forces and launch a concerted attack on our men, forcing them to retreat. My perception was that expansion was our best form of defence and to stagnate, in my view, was dangerous. The Selous Scouts had proscribed the area, preventing our intended expansion. Our request to remove the restriction was vetoed. Despite meeting with D/S/O Thomas, the Selous Scouts Special Branch liaison officer, who agreed to investigate "unfreezing" portions of the area, the matter remained unresolved. This intransigence was all too common in operational areas, and especially when circumstances such as ours arose. We needed to maintain our momentum, as it was essential for our continued successes. We never did receive any feedback as to the outcome, if any, of Selous Scouts deployments. We relied on our own intelligence networks to discover what transpired. As I saw matters, yet another tactical advantage was lost. I wondered what the Selous Scouts were achieving in Hurungwe other than kills in a "kills-win-wars" policy. Since this neglected the mobilisation of the masses, I saw this as a waste of time, manpower and resources.

Forward Base in Magunje Opens

As we opened our forward base in Magunje during January 1979, I requested, through Sub.JOC Sinoia, that the Int.Aff. staff be confined to a radius of a kilometre from the Magunje base camp, in order to give our men a "free hand" to carry out operations.[1] In fact, there were two issues at stake in my request. One was the likelihood of blue-on-blue incidents occurring if Int.Aff. made contact with our men, mistaking them for ZIPRA. The second issue was that ZIPRA had convinced the people that Int.Aff. was an obstacle supporting and representing the "old regime" and, as such, had to be eliminated. In order to gain control of the people and establish martial law, ZIPRA had to remove every obstacle in their way. They had revealed some genuine grievances relating to civil administration. Naturally, within the "new regime", the old obstacles would have to be dealt with as well as others, for the rural people, generally, must bear the brunt of revolutionary change. If the SFA were seen to reinstate or support Int.Aff., they would be identified with them and immediately lose credibility. We would have to work with Int.Aff. remotely, as we did with the uniformed police, Special Branch and Security Forces. It was agreed that our men could only enter, unarmed, into Magunje Township and I made it known that they would carry their identity cards and pay-books.

Time for leave and a change

I was due a few days' leave commencing 12 January 1979, and left the revolution in the hands of Todd who was up to date with developments. Suttill was overseeing Chabwino and providing admirable service under difficult conditions. I felt comfortable leaving the operation in Todd's hands. He was mature and, as we had worked together for some years, he understood my thinking. He was a thorough SB-orientated operator and identified with all the UANC staff. On arrival in Salisbury, as my leave began, I had a meeting with Maj. Tom Douglas at Special Forces HQ where I briefed him on the current situation in Hurungwe. Among other matters, we discussed our radio communications problems. Maj. Douglas said he would arrange for the installation of a radio at my "safe house" in Karoi. He never visited us in Karoi, therefore the radio would assist with communications when ordering and following-up orders for our kit and equipment. Once installed, it certainly did. I handed Maj. Douglas a list of our urgent field requirements, which he said he would organise. We also discussed the problem of the areas that had been "frozen" by the Selous Scouts which we

[1] Maj. Rawstron's diaries 2/9/1979, p. 5.

needed to be "unfrozen" for our deployments. He assured me that he would investigate the matter and report to Todd as I was going on leave for a week. Maj. Douglas was efficient and a man of his word. He was supportive and, soon after our meeting, the supplies arrived.

I then drove to meet with Geoff Price and updated him regarding the current situation in Hurungwe, in particular, our problems at Chabwino. Following our discussion, we agreed on the way forward and I left him to take the relevant action. Geoff wanted to implement the changes during my leave of absence.

A week later, on my return from leave, I observed that Geoff Price had introduced the changes we discussed. I noted much progress had been made with the training at Chabwino. This is a summary of events recorded by Todd. On 15 January, Geoff Price advised Ian Suttill that Walter would not be returning to Karoi and offered him his position. Suttill accepted the offer and officially took over the training at Chabwino. Suttill had pioneered a comprehensive 19-day training programme which was indicative of his knowledge and appreciation of the need to train a people's revolutionary army, identifying clearly that conventional military training did not suit guerrilla warfare. In doing this, he displayed knowledge of one of the major roles of the SAS, that of training and advising in "irregular warfare". This was exactly what was needed, and it was highly effective and professional. The men held him in high regard. The training was done in two phases:

Phase 1: Basic Drill and Weapons training

1. Drill relevant to the basic needs of the tasks and weapons.
2. Use of, care of, and safety procedures of relevant firearms.
3. Specialised weapons training on RPG-7s and mortars.
4. Live-firing exercises.

Phase 2: Battle Procedures and Fieldcraft

1. Patrol formations.
2. Hand signals.
3. Fire-with-movement.
4. Ambush and counter-ambush procedures.
5. Zigzagging.
6. Tracking procedures (how to protect the tracker and anticipate enemy positions, etc.).
7. Security of base camps and continual vigilance.
8. Camouflage.
9. Tracking, anti-tracking and knowledge of locals, kraals and terrain, etc.
10. Political mobilisation of the recruits and strategies to mobilise the masses.

Most of these aspects were well known to the recruits, therefore the training was focused on refining their skills and applying them to the military requirement.

Suttill assisted Todd with the deployment of 30 men he had trained. Walter made a brief appearance at Karoi on 17 January 1979 and settled some personal matters. Todd informed the assistant district commissioner (ADC) that the people had asked for the schools at Katenhe and Chinembiri to be reopened. The ADC gave the assurance that it would be addressed as soon as possible. Todd also briefed all the Int.Aff. staff at Magunje about SFA operations, as they had many unanswered questions. Specifically, Todd addressed three issues: "(a) SFAs were not Selous Scouts; (b) their only enemy was ZIPRA; (c) Int.Aff. and SFAs could not meet or operate in the same area due to recognition problems."[1]

Special Forces were notified of our urgent need to equip 150 men undergoing training, who were soon to be deployed. Intelligence continued to flow through the office with confirmed sightings of ZIPRA at Mahororo, Jocmore and Bvunzawabaya kraals. Naturally, relevant deployments were in

[1] Maj. Rawstron's diaries 2/9/1979, p. 5.

hand. The road near Zvipani BC was also landmined.[1] Unfortunately, the Selous Scouts were still operating in our target areas. As usual, Todd had produced sterling results during my absence. ZIPRA insurgents in the western region of Hurungwe were identified. Among them were Alfred, Mundoza (aka Mahomed), Makuranje, Crispen, Mandebvu, Mpostori, Takawira and Matias.

SFA Strategies Phase 10: Restore civil administration

Civil Administration Returns as Momentum Increases

With the beginning of the new school term in January 1979, Katenhe School was opened by our forces in liaison with Int.Aff. and relevant government departments. Attendance at the school was overwhelming resulting in many children, unfortunately, being turned away. This was a resounding victory for our forces, having made significant gains since their deployment a month earlier. The people had been calling for the schools to be reopened and the seemingly impossible had been achieved. Once again this confirmed the principle that, in a revolution, one must move at the pace of the people. More pointedly, ZIPRA were unable to reclaim the ground and the school remained open. Such was the success of Katenhe School that other areas called for their schools to be reopened and we followed suit. By the end of January 1979, seven schools had been reopened: a credit to the people and their army. The people also requested that rural clinics be regenerated. At that stage of the proceedings, our preparations were at an advanced stage, and they were soon functioning as normal.

The aspect of establishing civil administration in conjunction with the military effort is extremely important and significant. Essentially, what was being achieved was that the politicisation of the people had imparted a vision within them which the military were fighting for in order to remove obstacles. This would result in democratic elections for majority rule. Simultaneously, moving at the pace of the people, civil administration was being re-established, effectively introducing good governance which was acceptable to the people. The political and the military were working hand in hand for the benefit of the people. This co-operation avoided leaving a civil administrative vacuum in the wake of military success. This is frequently seen when the political strategy, to the detriment of the people, is either regime change, the support of a failing unpopular regime, or the collapse of a government through a revolutionary victory. In Hurungwe, we were not fighting to uphold the lost cause of entrenched colonialism, which I suspected was the situation in the rest of the country. Immediate and radical political changes were required across the nation in order to gain the acceptance of the people and, of course, international recognition. The RF had to relinquish power and fully support and embrace change. It seemed to me this was not to be. What was happening in Hurungwe was the implementation of a pre-emptive strategy, which was being successful and effective in its application. This was not the picture in the rest of the country where there was no obvious or tangible strategies. As I perceived matters, all that was happening was a dependency on "kills to win the war", a product of a reactionary strategy as opposed to being progressively pre-emptive, and this led to the ultimate downfall of the country. Granted, we were capable of continuing the war effort, but we would not win a protracted war with dwindling resources and a rudderless political direction.

Combined Operations had been pressurising me to come under the command of a military authority. I had considerable reservations about this move and will discuss this matter later. I could, however, see the benefit of a military presence in the areas we could not immediately occupy. It was agreed that we would continue with our own operations in our demarcated areas, with the army operating in areas we currently did not occupy or were unlikely to reach for some time. It was, however, envisaged that we would gradually come under military command and control. The UANC political and military wings would give their full assistance to both operations.

On 27 January 1979, we received reliable intelligence that 30 insurgents were currently based at Bvunzawabaya Kraal, which was passed on to the Selous Scouts and Fire Force the same day. The

[1] Karoi Landmine Map 17.

Chiroti Fly Gate area, which straddled Hurungwe and Rengwe TTLs, was evidently a well-used area by ZIPRA. I wanted to establish the layout of the area and organised for PRAW assistance to fly me on an aerial recce as a prelude to either a ground or Fire Force offensive, depending on the specific intelligence at the time. It was an area where an OP could observe transiting ZIPRA groups. This was a remote, inaccessible region on the western border of Hurungwe. There were excellent OP positions that overlooked the villages: a haven for insurgents. During the flight, we noted several fresh paths indicating the probability of feeding routes that led into base-camp areas. The flight provided an aerial perspective, not only of target areas, but Hurungwe in general, creating a clearer picture in my mind of our operational area. Once I had mapped out the target areas, which included specific kraals, base camps, OP positions, schools and BCs, we returned to base. (See Chiroti Fly Gate Original Sketch.)

Around midday the Psyac pamphlets arrived for despatch to the field and arrangements were made to have them distributed. A requisition for watches and radios was sent to Special Forces through our newly installed communications set-up. Urgently needed medical supplies, mainly for the people, were purchased locally and transported to the field.

Naturally, other Security Forces actions were also taking place. A Fire Force deployment, based on Ground Coverage intelligence, resulted in the annihilation of five insurgents. Phil Wright continues the story: "On 22 January 1979, our informant and his handler requested an urgent meeting with us near the Magunje Road within the farming area. His information was so positive relating to the presence of a ZIPRA gang at Maumbe that we called for the Fire Force from my vehicle immediately. The Fire Force, which had been operating in the area was available and within ten minutes the K-Car was overhead our position and landed beside us shortly afterwards. It was decided to uplift the informant who felt he could show the chopper jockeys where the C/T's were. He was last seen being pulled into a helicopter, with the hugest white eyes I have ever seen, and off they went in a cloud of dust. The FF K-car pilot was Nigel Lamb, his Eng./Gun. Sgt. Willem Joubert and the FF Commander was Capt. Hean RLI. A short while later the familiar da doom, da doom, da doom of the K-Car cannon could be distinctly heard, and we knew that ZIPRA were having another bad day. The interesting part of this was that the informant was returned to us, with a huge smile and even bigger eyes, about 15 minutes later, and went skipping back into the TTL, arriving home apparently before the dust had settled, the locals none the wiser for his absence. I seem to remember that five ZIPRA, the entire section, were killed. I remember the helicopter pilot telling me that our man was absolutely 'spot on' with his aerial indication, something very unusual because many people become totally disorientated when flying at low level."[1] Nigel Lamb's log book stated: "Pinned down 5 in a hut, no Lynx available to use a Fran so killed all 5 of them by firing through the roof with the 20mm."[2]

On the same day, 20 recruits arrived from Tengwe, southern Hurungwe, and were handed over to the army under the new Com.Ops. directive, as this was not our operational area. I, optimistically, was hoping that the army would adjust to this new role.

Geoff Price confirmed that Francis Zindoga would be visiting me on 29 January 1979 to discuss the future of the SFAs and the forthcoming visit to Hurungwe by the international media. We also received confirmation that Bishop Muzorewa would be holding a mass rally in Salisbury on 4 February 1979. As many UANC supporters as possible were to be bussed into Salisbury to support the bishop. The UANC team had already been advised and arrangements were well advanced to announce the event in Kariba and throughout Karoi and Hurungwe. We decided that the men should remain in the field in order to maintain our presence, although we acknowledged that this might prove difficult to enforce. Admin. were mobilised to arrange as many buses as possible and we would utilise vehicles based at Chabwino to assist if necessary. This was the first time I had been involved in such an activity and was unsure of the support we would achieve. However, Grey and

---

1 Phil Wright email 23/5/2016.

2 Karoi Contacts Map Incident 29.

Happy convincingly informed me that there would be great numbers attending. I, however, remained sceptical.

Sandy joined me on 29 January and immediately acquainted himself with the administrative requirements and, to my immense relief, promptly took charge of these matters.[1] I introduced him to the UANC officials over the next couple of days as he was to deal with their general logistical requirements as well as their pay arrangements. I also introduced him to Ian Suttill who, as the senior instructor in charge of SFA training, would need much support from Admin. Sandy was and remains a likeable friend. He was extremely efficient and, more importantly, he was well received and popular with the UANC men and Ian Suttill.

Operations in the field were going well and we were ready to open our second regional command area in the Birimahwe region. This advance section would fall under Big, the regional commander, who would respond to the people's call to occupy the area. Martin, who had been promoted to a regional commander, remained in the Kathene area, thereby implementing the regional command structure I have outlined previously. Both regional commanders had four men attached to their own sections and commanded five 10-men sections, bringing the total of permanently deployed men in the field to 110.[2] I believe it was the cell-based structure which gave the men the liberty to exercise their natural abilities in the field. They were not conscripted but volunteer resistance fighters who had been given the training, equipment, structure, liberty and support to come out into the open and express the will and desire of the people, who sought liberation from the occupying ZIPRA forces. The political was being expressed by the military, not vice versa. When the military enforces the political, that is a dictatorship. In fact, that was the stance of the Rhodesian Government at the time, hence the absolute necessity to address the people's grievances, needs and aspirations. We found ourselves in a "minefield". ZIPRA had effectively established martial law policed by their *mujibha* intelligence networks, usurping traditional morals, values and customs. Families turned against each other: parents against sons and daughters, sons and daughters against parents, families against relatives, villagers against kraalheads, headmen and chiefs. Any individual openly taking sides became the enemy of the opposition. The punishment for betraying ZIPRA was severe beatings, kraal burnings and the distinct possibility of death. From my perspective, the only solution to the country's dilemma was the people's army.

There was immediate action on 29 January from Big's section which had decided to follow up on the intelligence received from Martin. They observed 12 insurgents in the central Birimahwe region but were unable to call FF as no radio communications were available, consequently deciding on a wait-and-see approach. Unfortunately, the OP was compromised by a *mujibha* who had been captured. The callsign moved in to eliminate the insurgents, but they had fled. One ZIPRA pack containing documentation was recovered.[3] Although we did not engage with ZIPRA, our forces certainly created an impact from a psychological aspect in the field where the locals witnessed us to be the aggressors and ZIPRA fleeing. Big organised for his political commissar to mobilise the people in the kraal, announcing that our forces had arrived and were now occupying the ground.

On the same day, one of our callsigns reported a battle at Jecha Kraal where incoming intelligence had informed us that 12 insurgents were resident there. At first light, they initiated a contact by firing an RPG-7 at one of the kraals where some insurgents were sleeping. The kraal erupted in flames and four ZIPRA were killed in the inferno. Several insurgents fled from the nearby area and the section opened fire on them, but there were no further kills. In the follow-up operations, two locally trained insurgents were captured. Both were able to rapidly fire, strip and assemble an AK-47, and knew all forms of ZIPRA movements, including zigzagging and taking cover.[4] The most interesting aspect of this contact was that both captures were assisting with immediate operational intelligence, and

[1] Confirmed by original Sub.JOC Rusape duty roster; Sandy Irvine email 29/11/2016.

[2] The full list of names is held in my diaries but not included to protect the men's identities. Similarly, the names of the 20 men recruited from the Tengwe area for attachment to the RAR were also recorded in my diary.

[3] Karoi Contacts Map Incident 30.

[4] Karoi Contacts Map Incident 31.

our men had agreed for them to be armed. No retraining was required. They merely joined the section, were armed and continued in the field. This was a positive outcome as the men had clearly grasped the significance of reorientating a capture, embracing him, and then allowing the people to see this process in action. There was no doubt that the people would be greatly encouraged, particularly those still involved with ZIPRA in one way or another. This reconciliatory approach, I hoped, would encourage them to forsake ZIPRA and join the people's revolution.

Combined Operations Demand Military Takeover of Our Operation

Grey, Happy and I had a meeting on 29 January 1979 with Francis Zindoga regarding the future of the SFAs. It was my opinion that there was a complete lack of understanding of the principle of a people's army and the insistence of Com.Ops. to integrate with the Security Forces proved this. In my mind, there would be negative consequences. While it was obvious the military could assist in specific roles, as well as operate in areas not yet occupied by the people's army, I did not believe they had the capacity, understanding or the ability to work with and become one with the people and remain on the ground on a permanent basis. The major issue was permanent occupation on the ground for the duration of the conflict and not on a six-week or three-month basis. To win the war required the forces to remain permanently on the ground and not at any time abandon the people. My understanding of the situation was that this had always been the SF problem. The war was too widespread and the military did not have the capability to deploy permanently in one arena. In my view, ZANLA and ZIPRA had won the battle by extending the war beyond the capacity of our SF. The only solution was the people's army, but time would tell if my outlook was correct. Integrating the SF with the people's army would create numerous problems, for example:

1. Rank structure. How would the two organisations relate to each other in rank? It was my opinion that the army would consider themselves senior.
2. Conditions of service. In particular, benefits such as salaries, leave, medical aid, pension, sick pay and other allowances would have to be addressed as there were considerable discrepancies between the two operations.
3. Discipline. The people's army remained deployed in the operational area which was their home. Naturally, they had girlfriends, attended parties and lived a community life, in addition to being members of the people's army. The military had different and more stringent military and discipline procedures which forbade activities such as drinking and fraternising with females. They also had time off from the operational arena in order to be with their families and socialise. These varying disciplines could not coexist on a permanent basis. There would need to be a compromise with the military authorities.
4. We had spent a considerable amount of time explaining to the people that the SFAs were the people's army which was a part of the new dispensation. To suddenly introduce the SF, made a mockery of the political message we had propagated. Nothing would be seen to have changed, thereby playing right into the hands of ZIPRA propaganda. The problem was that the military did not, generally, have a good reputation among the people and was seen to support and uphold the "old regime": a matter capitalised on by ZIPRA. To negate ZIPRA's propaganda, we emphasised that the SFA were a part of the new dispensation and the military would provide support when invited to assist in specific battles and circumstances. This approach was working well and helped explain Fire Force and military actions.

While I had a great respect and admiration for the military, I felt we both had specific functions and I had concerns about the long-term problems I foresaw in integrating the two "armies". Simply put, in their current form, I could not envisage the two operating side by side. It was important to ensure that Zindoga understood our position, therefore we gave him a comprehensive briefing regarding our strategies and tactics. I gradually realised there were clearly two opposing lines of thought. Firstly, military intervention to establish, or retain, political power and, secondly, political intervention to support and defend the people aided by the military. I believed in the latter but it was becoming obvious that the former took precedence. The lack of understanding of the principles behind the people's army and the intervention of the Security Forces was extremely frustrating. Zindoga advised us that our operation in Hurungwe had been selected as a showcase for the UANC SFAs to the world press, including the BBC, primarily because our operations were successful. I was in favour of this as I believed it would strengthen our case in being the only way to succeed militarily in the Rhodesian conflict. It was also an opportunity to counter negative press about the SFAs, in particular that from the Catholic Commission for Justice and Peace. Bishop Muzorewa would be accompanying the tour party and it was planned that he would address a mass meeting of the locals.

UANC Office in Kariba Penetrates the Omay TTL

The men from the UANC office in Kariba called and asked us to attend a meeting as soon as possible, as they had positive developments to discuss. An early start saw us in Kariba at 10 a.m. on 30 January. We met up with the UANC who were making significant progress. An office had been located at Machipisa Shopping Centre, Maumbe Township, complete with a telephone (number 228) and postal address in the name of Terry Eleftheriades (P.O. Box 64, Kariba), both being commissioned. The office was presently being renovated in lieu of occupation. Politically, the townships were being awakened and the mobilisation of the people was progressing well. Inter-district and youth meetings had been held and were well attended. Youth activities appeared to be intensifying in anticipation of a future for themselves in both Hurungwe and the country. This was interesting as clearly they did not see a future for themselves in an Hurungwe oppressed by ZIPRA, and had migrated to Kariba for safety. Hence the growing number of volunteer recruits presenting themselves for enlistment. Most of the recruitment was being achieved from youth meetings. These young men were presenting themselves to fight in a war in their home area against an occupying force which was well armed, generally well trained, ruthless and aggressive. I did not believe the public at large were aware of the young men's commitment to the ideals of the UANC, the people's army and the people in their struggle for liberty. Certainly, I understood and commended their bravery.

Meetings had been held with Paramount Chief Negande and Chief Msampakaruma from the Omay, who had visited the UANC offices and were informed of the party's policies, principles, aims and objectives. This resulted in the UANC being officially invited to visit the Omay, home of the Tongas, and talk to their people who had been through difficult times: "The Tonga tribes were moved from the Zambezi River Valley between 1957-1958, to make way for the rising waters from the building of Kariba Dam. Giving up fertile land on the river banks has had major repercussions. 'If fields could be carried,' said one narrator, 'we would have carried them.' Others speak of the deep sense of loss they felt at leaving behind the shrines and graves of their ancestors. Yet despite the anger and disappointment in these accounts, they are also full of ideas for moving forward, and of positive hopes for the future. The Tonga want to tell their stories, and they wish others to understand what they have been through. They know all too well how complex the impact of resettlement is on families and communities, on their culture and their resources. Their experiences can contribute to greater awareness and understanding of the many different ways the resettled have to change and adapt to new environments."[1] In fact, the Tongas (which means chiefless and/or subject. They used to be chiefless and were then ruled by outsiders), remained disgruntled at the time of writing.[2] They are known to have been resident in the Zambezi Valley from at least the 16th century.[3]

The UANC officials were ferried across Lake Kariba and carried out meetings with three Tonga chiefs. The meeting at Chief Nebiri's Kraal was attended by six of his headmen, their families and scores of others: a total of 86. They then moved to Chief Negande's area where 16 kraalheads (two were absent) and a total of 264 people attended. Turnout was low here because the party officials

1 Thomson, E. (2005), *passim*. See Beach, D. (1980), p. 158.
2 Dr J. Chakawa WhatsApp discussion on 13/5/2016.
3 Beach, D. (1980), Chap. 1.

had arrived late. Finally, at Chief Mola's Kraal, four headmen and their families were addressed. The Tongas' grievances, needs and aspirations were identified. They were living below the subsistence level. Their staple food was grass seed as they had not been able to grow mealies. By all accounts, a pathetic, tragic situation. In view of the inaccessibility of the area, the Tongas were generally politically inactive but loosely supported the UANC. I felt they needed to be increasingly politically mobilised. There were limited medical facilities and little transport. The Tongas were ready for a revolution and could be swayed to the faction assisting them: we were determined to seize the initiative! We decided to commence a feeding programme into the Omay as soon as possible. This was a significant expedition and would pave the way for us to penetrate the area.

The Kariba office planned to extend their operations into adjacent areas, including Quarry, Crocodile farm, Banana farm, Marongora (near Makuti) on the Chirundu road and Charara, which might prove difficult due to the deteriorating security situation. A decision was also made to start a separate UANC cell at Makuti. Our first visit to Kariba regarding the UANC office occurred 20 days previously. A great deal had been achieved in a limited time. This hard evidence confirmed the significance of moving with, for and at the pace of, the people. I watched enthralled as the flame of hope ignited in their faces. We returned to Karoi in the evening as Geoff Price had summonsed me to Salisbury for a meeting with the bishop, who wanted to learn more about our Hurungwe operations.

Meeting with Bishop Abel Muzorewa

On 31 January 1979, we were on the road again. My trusty Jaguar was mobile. What could have been considered a luxury was, in fact, now a necessity. However, it was an awkward vehicle to drive on rural dirt roads as we were often required to repair or replace sections of the exhaust system. In attendance at the meeting with the bishop at his house was Francis Zindoga[1] and the OC SB, Snr. Asst. Comm. Derrick Bennison.[2] The bishop wanted to establish why our operations in Hurungwe had been so successful. I summarised our vision and then explained the strategies and tactics we used to penetrate Hurungwe, emphasising that ours was a people's revolution and success depended on materially assisting the people. I gained the impression that the bishop genuinely understood our practices and principles. Possibly it was his religious background and his heart for the people which allowed him to empathise. In fact, during the meeting, he mentioned that he wanted to increase substantially the number of UANC SFAs, concluding that he wished he had more operational teams like ours. As can be expected, I was in total agreement. Interestingly, Mike Edden confirms that Bishop Muzorewa wanted to increase the number of SFAs to 26,000 after he was elected to power in 1979 but, due to administrative problems, it was eventually agreed to increase the number to 16,000.[3]

After some discussions, he moved on to his forthcoming visit and asked if there were any issues that needed to be addressed. Indeed, there were. I was not concerned about our operations and single-mindedness achieved with the UANC political and military wings. However, I felt strongly that the white population, particularly the farming community, needed to be addressed and prepared for political changes, in order that our military campaign would be supported accordingly. It was my view that if this did not happen, the counter-revolution and mass mobilisation of the people would stagnate and justify ZIPRA's existence, despite their growing suppression of the people. We decided to hold a meeting for the whites during the bishop's forthcoming visit.

I spent the night in Salisbury. While it was good to be home, my stay was difficult since my life was the war and I was intolerant of anything distracting and interfering with my commitment and involvement in it. I found this confusing in some ways. In opposing bays were the comfort of home with seemingly more significant demands as a husband and father, alongside that of the attractions

---

1 Francis Zindoga was to become the Co-Minister of Justice, Law and Order and Co-Minister of the Public Service.

2 Snr. Asst. Comm. (4258) Derrick Bennison: He served from May 1948 to August 1980. He was stationed at SBHQ. He died on 1/3/2007 in Durban, South Africa. Henrik Ellert email 11/10/2016.

3 Mike Edden email 30/11/2016.

of the war. I found neither time nor desire to stop and contemplate the situation: the war took priority. I was unsympathetic towards those not involved in the conflict. I became angry when driving in Salisbury and seeing the city crowded with white people seemingly oblivious to the country's dire situation. The irony of those involved in the war being expected to behave in a certain "civilised" manner annoyed me further. Politically, it seemed to me, most whites were unaware that the country was collapsing under the ever-increasing military threat of ZANLA and ZIPRA.

D/Insp. John Van Rooyen and the author taking field identity photos.

A welcome break on Lake Kariba. Happy (left), Grey and the author.

Posing with the men.

Mobilised for war. Action.

The author welcoming new recruits.

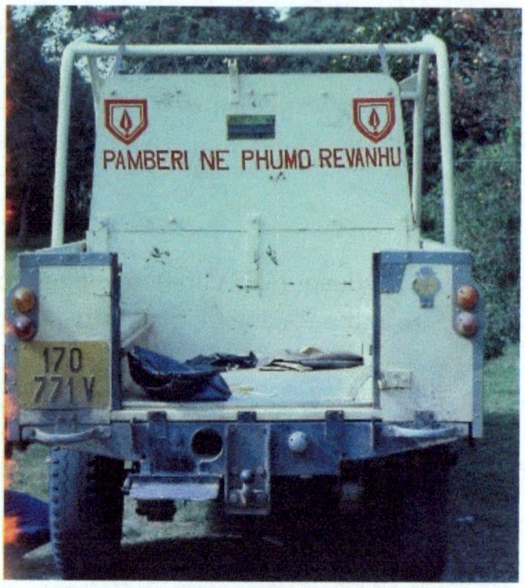

Forward with the Spear of the People.

Author, Happy and UANC official at the "safe house" with our Land Rover.

Chiroti Fly Gate Original Sketch.

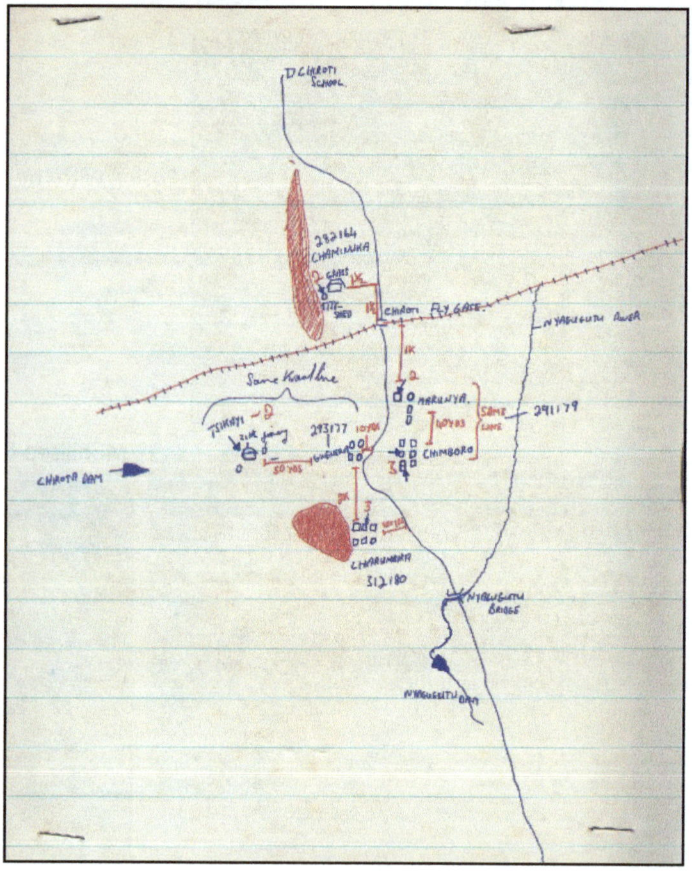

19 ~ MILITARY INTERVENTION, VISCOUNT *UMNIATI* & COMBINED OPERATIONS

However active the leading group may be,
its activity will amount to fruitless effort by a handful of people
unless combined with the activity of the masses.
Mao Zedong

SFA Strategies Phase 11: Expand politically, militarily and civically

In February 1979, Rhodesia officially moved closer to becoming a non-racial society with legislation abolishing the Land Tenure Act and prohibiting segregation and racial discrimination in public schools, hospitals, housing and public places. Many of the changes had been recommended in the Quenet report mentioned previously. A spokesman for the Transitional Government had accepted in principle the abolition of discrimination "except where its retention is necessary or desirable in the national interest". This step was the result of work carried out by a council appointed by the Executive Committee on 5 July 1978, to examine the contentious subject of racial discrimination. The committee was composed of Messrs Chikerema (UANC), Magaramombe (ZUPO), Mandaza (ZANU Sithole), and RF members Messrs Cronjé, Hayman and Irvine. The council's first proposals announced on 8 August were condemned as insufficient: the Land Tenure Act and rules governing schools, housing and hospital segregation remained unaffected.[1] Of interest, the United Federal Party, who proposed similar measures in the 1962 elections, lost to the RF who adamantly opposed reform but had displayed a complete reversal of policy, turning the clock back 17 years. As I saw matters, almost two decades wasted!

Field Strategies Defined and Developed

Back in Karoi on 1 February, we learned that Big and his men intended attacking Chidzimamoto Kraal, as he had confirmed intelligence of the presence of 11 insurgents in the area. The plan was for the men to walk in overnight and ambush the kraals in the early morning. As it transpired, no ZIPRA were found at the kraals. However, it was extremely encouraging to know that the men were actively following up on intelligence and prepared to engage ZIPRA in battle. Furthermore, ZIPRA would be aware that our intelligence networks were being informed of their movements, which would unsettle them and keep them on the run.

The cell system continued to work well in the field. Grey and Happy were proficient hands-on leaders, making regular visits to the men and giving them support, encouragement and advice. A matter requiring their attention was the masses' requests for the return of regular bus services to our liberated areas. It needs to be borne in mind that buses were their main means of public transport, with the multitudes totally dependent on their operation. Only a few cars were owned by the privileged. The daily morning cell-based checks for landmines had been working effectively for a month. We organised for the buses to recommence operating, thereby securing a major political and military breakthrough. Each bus was escorted by at least five of our trained men, should ZIPRA attempt an ambush. This security arrangement provided a further incentive for our men to ensure that the roads were clear of landmines. Self-preservation is a great motivator.

In time, further good news arrived from the Katenhe region. We were informed that attendance at Katenhe School was encouraging. ZIPRA had failed to respond to this astounding success, a

[1] British Confidential documents: Rhodesia Department Monthly Summary No 8, August 1978.

reflection of our men's excellent work. By the end of January 1979, we had liberated the following areas: Katenhe, Magunje, Kebvunde, Chidzimamoto, Kweche and Mudzimu. Our efforts had proven worthwhile, productive and of benefit to the people. I was further heartened in that we were totally self-sufficient and poised to penetrate further into Hurungwe when the RAR arrived.

RAR Deploy

Maj. Gavin Rawstron, of B Company 1RAR, deployed into the area in late January 1979 in response to Com.Ops. orders for the SFAs to integrate with the SF.[1] Although my brother, David, was an officer in the RAR, I had only worked with the regiment on Fire Force deployments which were far from personal. Maj. Rawstron was an astute officer, fluent in Shona and well informed regarding African customs and traditions. We agreed to continue our UANC operations as they were proving successful, and gradually introduce our men to the military command after the April 1979 elections.

I introduced Maj. Rawstron to our procedures, strategies and tactics which he readily understood and accepted. All that was required of him, was to simply emulate our success. At that time, we had 20 recruits from Tengwe waiting to be trained. Maj. Rawstron would open new areas in which to operate, with the UANC providing complete political and military support, and recruits for training. Despite all that was said and agreed on, I still had my reservations on various matters, including the conditions of service, the integration process and long-term commitment which was a Com.Ops. prerogative. I believed we had to make the most of the situation confronting us. However, I was aware that we had a strong UANC political and military team which would be the backbone of both our operations. Grey, Happy and I had spent many hours deliberating these issues and they were both adamant they would be able to win the support of most of the people in Hurungwe, even with the current changes. I introduced the team to Maj. Rawstron. To my delight, they were all amenable which, at this stage, was positive. The UANC political and military wings fully supported the RAR operations and co-operated with them.

Jan Meyer, a former SAS soldier, left his unit at the end of July 1978 and took on a civilian occupation for six months while waiting to be recruited by SB. After that, he joined the team which was a great boost for Ian Suttill.[2]

Occupation of the Birimahwe region was proving interesting. At 5.30 p.m. on 2 February, a callsign was ambushed by 7-10 insurgents. In the ensuing battle, the insurgents retreated, with no casualties on either side. The area was swept and doppies were collected.[3] I travelled to the field to meet with the men to both encourage and congratulate them, reaffirming our strategy of occupying the ground, which they were achieving. It was significant that they had retaliated and beaten back the ZIPRA attack. This was good for their confidence and morale as well as that of the people who would, in due course, hear the story first-hand from the men. Increasing our boundaries and deploying more men into the field was a priority which would help secure the territory we occupied and isolate any ZIPRA sections operating in close proximity, or even within, the proscribed areas that we were in the process of occupying. There was no room for two opposing forces in the same cell as one had to give way and, if I had anything to do with it, it was not going to be us!

One of our sections recovered the body of Martin Berebende, a Roman Catholic catechist from the nearby St Boniface's Mission, murdered by ZIPRA on 2 February 1979.[4] Another brutal act by ZIPRA, the effects of which would ripple through the Roman Catholic Jesuit Community at the mission, especially Berebende's mentor, Fr Zinkann and the people in Hurungwe. Doppies were recovered from the scene for further investigations. Politically, this was an opportunity for our men to show compassion, gain support and demonstrate where our allegiances lay.

Field operations were progressing well and the men continued to gain momentum. ZIPRA had no counter to our threat. There were now 110 men deployed, an additional 190 at Chabwino

1 Maj. Rawstron's diary 2/9/1979, p. 4.
2 Jan Meyer email 10/11/2016.
3 Karoi Contacts Map Incident 32.
4 Karoi Murder Map 26.

undergoing training and a further 100 training at Retreat farm, making a total of 400 men. Ian Suttill's training programme was progressing well and there was a positive atmosphere at Chabwino. He had turned matters around and we would soon feel the effects in the field as momentum gathered. He advised us that a further 60 men would shortly be available for deployment, therefore I arranged for new advance areas to be demarcated. As previously mentioned, the people were literally demanding our forces to be deployed into their areas, and we were moving at their pace. This simplified expansion and created a safer environment in which our men could operate.

The men had started establishing bases in abandoned school buildings. This made sense as it created a permanent visual presence that broadcast their expansion and occupation into the area when they raised the UANC flag. It also secured the buildings for the reopening of schools when the time was right. This permanency could possibly attract ZIPRA retaliation. We insisted that the men continued to "swim among the people" day and night. The last thing we wanted was a scenario where the men patrolled during the day and returned to base at night, a pattern of some SF operations such as Special Branch and Ground Coverage. Knowing the men were protecting their own families would keep them alert, for to abandon them would, as I saw matters, be pronouncing their death sentences. I was determined that this scenario would be avoided. Schools were another focal point of the communities' structures.

UANC Salisbury Rally

We had an early start to the day on Sunday, 4 February 1979, as buses started motoring in from Hurungwe carrying supporters for Bishop Muzorewa's rally in Salisbury. This was a well-publicised national event aimed at promoting the "internal settlement", and was the "road map" to African majority rule. We hired seven buses and made our troop carrier available for transporting people to the venue. During the morning, over 800 people, far exceeding my expectations, filtered into Karoi travelling to the rally in our hired buses, and other available transport. The experience remains etched in my mind. Happy took the opportunity to introduce me to some of the local people, as this was an ideal time to meet them at one location. They accepted me warmly. Grey, Happy and the UANC were seen to be in charge, with my simply being a part of the team. Although brief, the meeting was significant, as the people were made aware that some white men were fighting for them. Being accepted by the people, increased access to them and our men in Hurungwe. A milestone in becoming one with the people.

Supporters arrived from Katenhe, Magunje, Karoi, Chikangwe and as far afield as Kariba. Rallying so much support from a war zone was an exceptional effort by our men. I found it affirming, as I knew their presence translated into our growing support and acceptance in the field.

The role of our men was to escort the buses and vehicles from Magunje to Karoi in order to ensure they were not attacked by ZIPRA. In fact, they neither mined the roads nor ambushed the vehicles, which we found surprising. They knew there was a large exodus of people from Hurungwe travelling to the bishop's meeting in Salisbury. It was to be expected that we would meet some sort of resistance. One incident occurred near Magunje when two of our overzealous escort guards fired their weapons over the heads of a Security Forces patrol. It took some explaining to the SF patrol that our men were probably caught up in the moment, mistakenly deciding to demonstrate their authority and successful military prowess. In time, calm returned. The only other problem we had was that some of our commanders and men decided to travel with the people to Salisbury. We had instructed them to remain in the field. From a discipline perspective, I found their behaviour unacceptable but Happy explained that such a high-profile event would naturally create a desire for the "fighters" to mingle with their people. He reasoned that this practice was acceptable in a revolution and did not consider it a serious breach of discipline. I was swayed by his explanation. However, we set up roadblocks to address the men on their return from Salisbury. I felt they needed to be aware that we knew they had disobeyed our orders and that we considered it poor discipline.

I had arranged for the PRAW to fly me over Hurungwe, as I wanted to ensure the callsigns were in place during the Salisbury rally. It was important for them to know that their high command had not gone to Salisbury for the meeting and was fully functional. All the callsigns were located and all was well in the field. One callsign had received information that a ZIPRA section was in the area of Mudzimu BC. *Mujibhas* had been sent to locate the insurgents in order for an attack to be launched. I found it encouraging that the men were managing with their matters at hand, and with their own intelligence operations and battle plans.

Events the next day proved to be thought-provoking. Our operational area was overseen by callsigns functioning only within proscribed areas. These areas were permanent "no-go" zones for any other SF or government officials. The army and police callsigns could operate in any of the zones not proscribed. Selous Scouts, however, in view of the nature of their pseudo-operations, also "froze" areas and SF were not permitted into them to prevent blue-on-blue incidents. As it so happened, periodically Selous Scouts and military vehicles were required to travel through our areas to reach their various destinations. Generally, we were given prior notice of these movements and certainly enough time to inform the men in the field, as I had done in this instance. Unbeknown to us Chinhamo, the section leader of callsign 7 Bravo, was holding a political meeting at a short distance from the road. When the people saw a military convoy approaching from a distance, they asked him why SF were travelling on their roads if they, the SFAs, oversaw the operational area. This logical question left Chinhamo in a predicament. He had no choice but to act. To not do so would result in his losing face among his people, as there was a great deal at stake. Chinhamo took his loaded RPG-7, walked to the road and took up a standing firing position facing the oncoming Selous Scouts convoy. As can be expected, the Selous Scouts column was heavily armed. Fortunately, common sense prevailed at the stand-off, as the Selous Scouts knew they were in SFA territory. Undeterred and despite serious discussions with them, Chinhamo refused to allow the convoy to proceed and it was forced to return to Karoi.[1] I was soon notified of the incident and summarised it in my diary as follows: "We now sit and wait for the shit to hit the fan." It did not take long for controversy to surface. Mac phoned me and was furious about the event and, particularly, the Selous Scouts having been forced to abort their operation. However, it was my opinion that Chinhamo had taken the correct action. Had he not acted as he did, he would have lost credibility among the people. To my immense relief, no one had been killed during the stand-off, although the situation was tense and could have ended tragically.

Later I diarised: "Today is totally cancelled." However, Happy and I travelled to the field to visit the men and ensure that, when the Selous Scouts convoy passed through the area the following morning, there would be no interference again. Happy spoke to the elders at the kraal and the section, gaining their approval for the deployment of the Selous Scouts. We explained that the military was under our command and were deploying to attack ZIPRA in areas that we did not currently occupy. The Selous Scouts had a poor reputation among the locals and we simply referred to them as the Security Forces. I was hopeful that the conflict had been resolved. In this case, hope did spring eternal and the convoy passed through unopposed the following day.

I later learned of another military convoy belonging to B Coy 1RAR who were travelling along the same access roads to Hurungwe. Chinhamo repeated his earlier action forcing the convoy to turn around.[2] Fortunately, there were no injuries. One is definitely caught unawares with incidents like this. The aftermath was having to convince the military that I had control of the men in the field. In fact, I did! As far as I was concerned, our men were committed to their task. They depended on the people for their survival and could not afford to lose their trust and favour. This trust would have been breached if Chinhamo had backed down. Needless to say, the military were not particularly pleased with our actions. I was proud of Chinhamo.

On my return to the "safe house" the same afternoon, Geoff Price contacted me to advise that the bishop would be holding a rally at Katenhe on 10th February 1979. He told me that the international media, including the BBC, would be attending. There was much to organise and I briefed the UANC and Admin., accordingly.

---

1 Maj. Rawstron's diary 2/9/1979, p. 5.

2 Ibid.

George from Admin. had carried out a "hunter-gatherer" operation in Salisbury and managed to obtain a large amount of kit and equipment from Special Forces and other sources. We were becoming efficient at these "special operations".

Three days before Bishop Muzorewa's Katenhe rally on 7 February, we received disturbing intelligence that a UANC member, Hachina, had been murdered in the area of Bvunzawabaya Kraal, where some 30 insurgents had taken up residence in the kraals of Shadreck, Chapupa and Bvunzawabaya himself.[1] This confirmed previous intelligence supplied to us. Sub.JOC Sinoia confirmed that Fire Force was not available, therefore I passed on the information to the military for deployment.

The same day, Ian Suttill confirmed that 60 men were prepared and ready for deployment. We made the necessary arrangements. There was much jubilation as the men left Chabwino alongside their comrades who, with the people, waited eagerly to penetrate further into ZIPRA territory. The people's army advanced, securing greater territory, resulting in the liberation of the people and psychologically damaging ZIPRA's "stranglehold" of Hurungwe. The harsh reality of our war was that, when we were deploying relatively inexperienced men into the battleground, the greater was the likelihood that some of them would not return home alive, therefore, as can be expected, we took every precaution possible to ensure their safety. Strange setting this world of war, especially where men trusted and placed their lives in one's hands! In the brutality of war, men inextricably bonded, which made the death of a fellow soldier profoundly sorrowful. I found the safest mechanism of self preservation was withdrawal to a position of non-attachment, a zone devoid of emotions, yet strangely secure in the boundaries of friendship among those immediately involved: those who covered one's back, a place of mutual trust. Trust remains the unwritten code between soldiers on the war front. One simply does not break that trust. We now had 170 men permanently deployed, 230 under training at Chabwino, 100 under training at Retreat farm, Bindura, 50 under training with the RAR destined for Hurungwe and 50 under training with the Support Unit destined for the Mukwichi and Vuti areas.

ZIPRA Landmine Attack Fails

Local UANC officials had arranged a meeting in the field for 8 February. The previous night, ZIPRA laid a landmine to eliminate them. This was one of ZIPRA's first attempts to obstruct our movements, but it failed. Our landmine-detecting cell structure located the mine on the morning of the meeting and placed branches across the road, to prevent vehicles from detonating it. We opted to deal with the matter ourselves as the Pookie was not available. Ian Suttill decided to personally neutralise the life-threatening mine. While watching him making the necessary preparations to blow up the item, several vehicles were turned back by our men, saving the occupants from serious injuries or death. Ian was familiar with discharging these devices and, on eruption, a loud explosion followed. I watched enthralled, as this was the closest I had ever come to experiencing a landmine explosion in Hurungwe.[2]

The day before Bishop Muzorewa's rally, on 9 February, a difficult situation unfolded when one of our sections arrested a major cattle thief, who had been sought by the police since 1974. So lucrative was his trade, that he had bought a motor vehicle from the profits of his illicit enterprise. Up to this point, cattle thieves attracted the attention of the police and SF into the area with varying levels of reprisals. The people decided to hand over the cattle thief to us. We were called on to resolve the problem and decided that, since the people were involved in the capture of the cattle thief, it would be in order to place him in the custody of the BSA Police. My main political consideration was not to be identified with the "old regime" in defending the white farmer's cattle, as ZIPRA and those opposed to us would immediately turn this to their advantage. In my opinion, farmers needed to implement better stock management to prevent strays and thefts. In his memoirs, Hilary Squires agreed with me. Furthermore, he suggested that the Treasury had to ensure that

1 Karoi Murder Map 27.
2 Karoi Landmine Map 18.

compensation paid to farmers due to terrorist activity was legitimate and not for strayed or incorrectly counted cattle.[1] The preservation of life by the prevention of attacks on all civilians, however, was another matter.

[1] Ranger, T. (1985), Chap. 5, p. 180. Hilary Squires's memoirs, transcript 3:2.

Landmine located by locals.

Branches laid to pinpoint the landmine.

SFAs patrol stops vehicles until the road is safe.

A focussed Ian Suttill prepares to light the fuse to detonate the landmine.

The author sensibly stepping back from the action!

Detonation observed from a safe distance.

Ian Suttill inspects the crater for forensic evidence.

Bishop Muzorewa Mass Rally: International Press Coverage

Preparations for the bishop's rally and the accompanying international contingent were progressing well. We knew that a vast number of locals would be attending, thereby making security precautions our major concern. Happy had taken charge of the planning. He had regular meetings with the regional commanders and section leaders, and together we had put the following precautions in place:

The army was to provide a Pookie escorted by George (Admin.) with some of our men in order to clear the roads to be used for the transportation of the people, the bishop and the international press.

Fourteen sections of our men would be deployed strategically protecting the road from Magunje BC to Katenhe and the road from Katenhe to Kweche BC, as well as a 2 kilometre radius of the Katenhe area. Happy would follow the Pookie and escort vehicles once the roads were cleared. He was to make regular deviations in order to ensure all security arrangements remained in place. Sections were to be positioned on the afternoon of 9 February.

The bishop would be officially handed his "ceremonial" AK-47 at the boundary between the white farming area and Hurungwe, and then would be escorted to the rally at Katenhe.

An additional relay station was positioned for VHF radio communications in the event of problems prior to, during and after the meeting. The relay station would remain in place until completion of the event.

An eight-man gun salute (three rounds per man) would take place as the bishop assumed his official position on the grandstand.

After the meeting, we would convey the bishop to Chabwino in order to inspect the men and meet the training staff. It was politically and militarily important that the men see the bishop as their leader. Later in the afternoon, the bishop would address a meeting with the local white farmers. He would then be briefed on our progress in Hurungwe.

Happy would arrange security checks of all people attending the meeting prior to arrival of the bishop. Late arrivals were also to be checked.

At their own initiative and expense, the people had built a platform and security fence for the bishop. This demonstrated the power of the people and the importance of joint co-operation. It was also a reflection of the good work that the UANC team and people's army were doing in the field previously occupied by ZIPRA.

Tony Coom, a former Sgt. in the RLI who joined us towards the end of January 1979,[1] and a section of men would remain at the meeting place in the event of an emergency or penetration of our defences by ZIPRA.

Happy would organise the chairs, seating arrangements and order of speeches.

Refreshments, in the form of traditional beer and meat, were to be prepared early in order to ensure that the people returned to their homes before nightfall. Our men could then ensure they returned home safely. We did not want ZIPRA attacking the departing supporters.

As I saw matters, we were as prepared as we ever would be. However, ZIPRA struck the first blow when 10-15 of their men attacked one of our sections near the Katenhe BC at 1.40 a.m. Saturday, 10 February. One SFA was killed in action. A civilian, Balance Newton, was killed, and three civilians were slightly injured and casevaced to Karoi.[2] One insurgent was killed in the battle. His body was recovered from a nearby river.[3] One RPG-7 projectile and booster, two hand-grenades, three AK-47 magazines, one water-bottle belt, one SKS adapter and one M60 rifle-grenade were recovered. We attended the scene and collected the doppies for onward transmission to Special Branch.[4]

Although we had lost a man, I was impressed with the aggressive response of our men, who stood their ground and retaliated. ZIPRA could only resort to hit-and-run tactics which was our aim, and no longer held the ground. In my mind, we had secured another victory.

The remaining security arrangements continued with no further incidents. Despite the initial setback, 10,000 people attended the meeting. It was an impressive turnout and a clear indication of the will of the people. People travelled considerable distances, intent on lingering and exploiting most of the day. Families, relatives, friends and tribal authorities met and exchanged news and views. There are a great many traditional procedures involved in these rural meetings. The symbolic handing over of the "ceremonial" AK-47 to Bishop Muzorewa identified the relationship between the political and the military, acknowledging the military support and acceptance that the war was to overcome political obstacles. Seating arrangements were structured and well organised. Two of our commanders were seated on either side of Bishop Muzorewa. In traditional custom, a woman and child knelt before the bishop to present a bowl and cup for water. Spirit mediums possessed by ancestral departed spirits invoked the acceptance and direction for attending dignitaries. To the uninitiated, this could be an intimidating procedure. Various dignitaries, including the regional commanders, addressed the people in order to demonstrate their approval, acceptance and leadership of the political. Bishop Muzorewa's speech was a resounding success. The attendees were excited, optimistic and supportive. At the conclusion of the rally, they embraced the bishop and his support team. Our men mingled with the people, demonstrating the untruthfulness of the allegations of countrywide hostilities carried out by the SFA. Indeed, we found ourselves in a festive season in the middle of a war zone. I established the practice that we recorded all political meetings in order to ensure that our military objectives corresponded with the political. The recordings were played back to the UANC political and military wings, and the training staff, thereby keeping us all in unity.

After the meeting, the international press interviewed the bishop, our commanders and their men, the people and myself. Attending the rally were James MacManus (foreign correspondent of *The*

[1] Tony Coom email 23/3/2017 and various oral discussions.
[2] Karoi Murder Map 28.
[3] Confirmed by Dr J. Chakawa.
[4] Karoi Contacts Map Incident 33.

Guardian), and his cameraman, Rowley Carter. Thereafter, we took the bishop to Chabwino where he inspected the men, and Ian Suttill showed him our facilities. After lunch at the farm, Bishop Muzorewa buried our man killed in the ZIPRA raid. It was a moving ceremony. Later, we took the bishop to a local hall for a meeting with some 300 whites, which included many farmers. He outlined his political direction and the present military situation in the country, stating there were no moral or legal grounds on which Rhodesia could be denied entry into the world community after the April election. He assured the audience they had no cause to fear living under a UANC Government because: "We believe in democratic ideals and through these ideals we believe we can build a progressive nation in this part of the world".[1] He was confident that international recognition would be forthcoming, even with a 50 per cent poll at the elections. The bishop had faith that this would bring about a lifting of sanctions. He stressed it was essential that all communities united in forgetting the past and strive vigorously together in the construction of a new social order, in which each citizen would be treated humanely, regardless of race, colour or creed.[2] When questioned whether it was planned to introduce and implement a uniform minimum wage, the bishop replied: "If employers raised the worker's conditions, standards and wages themselves as was already happening in some areas, the implementation of a general standard wage would not be required."[3] Reaction by the whites to the bishop's speech was generally favourable. Once again, I diarised a previous request that a high-powered Psyac team address the tension between employer and employee regarding the labour problem in agriculture and other industries. It was my opinion that, once this was addressed and implemented, it would support our military efforts in three essential ways: First, we would remove the insurgents' ideological and psychological attack on colonialism. Second, men in the field would gain more credit as the political made advances in support of the military. Third, the international community would have to recognise the changes which would help with recognition of the "internal settlement".

My final comment on the matter was: "There is little point sitting back now and saying that it's not our problem the new Government must sort it out. It is our problem and our country and the sooner the white community adjusts to changes the better for the new Zimbabwe." To my dismay, nothing changed. It was a seemingly impossible task to convince the whites to realise that, unless the order of things changed from removing the old to embracing the new, there could be no harmony between the whites and Africans.[4] The day ended badly with notification that three of our men had deserted, much to my annoyance, with their weapons, among which was a folding-butt AK-47. Happy undertook to alert all the men in the field and the UANC offices in Chikangwe and Kariba. These were the only desertions that occurred under my command.

We were still experiencing problems with areas "frozen" by the Selous Scouts for protracted periods, which was inhibiting our expansion in Hurungwe. The success of our operations was fundamentally entrenched in moving at the pace of the people. I saw little point in military operations which would simply lead to the elimination of ZIPRA, to the detriment of occupying the ground and possessing the land. Certainly, a combination of both killing the enemy and occupying the ground was ideal but overall success depended on occupying the ground. I found it difficult convincing many of my countrymen to break from the mindset of the greater the number of kills, the greater the success. Ideally, the ground should be occupied and the expertise of the military used to strike and kill. Locating the enemy was our specialty. What we required was military might in support of our intelligence-gathering mechanisms. Fire Force was ideal for the killing role, but we had no access to the FF which seemed to arrive randomly at Karoi with no consultation or regard for immediate local intelligence. My views were known at Com.Ops., resulting in my being summonsed to a meeting with Brig. Barnard on 13 February 1979.

---

1 *The Sunday Mail* article 11/2/1979.
2 Ibid.
3 Ibid.
4 Flower, K. (1987), p 270.

ZIPRA Strela Section Strikes Again: Viscount *Umniati*

My father had been fishing on Lake Kariba on his shared houseboat with a group of friends and was due to leave on 11 February 1979 in order to celebrate his 61st birthday on the 12th. It was a rare occasion when all our family were together, as I would also be in town. While having a few drinks in the evening prior to his planned departure, his friends tried to persuade him to stay one further night and then fly home to Salisbury on the 12th. I would imagine it was a great temptation having "sundowners" on the deck of a houseboat and enjoying the African sunset while surrounded by close friends. However, he declined as he did not wish to disappoint the family. Had he stayed, he would have booked to fly home the following day. This was to prove a life-changing decision. On the fateful day of 12 February 1979, Air Rhodesia Flight RH 827, Viscount *Umniati*, lifted off from runway 09, Kariba Airport, at 5 p.m. en route overland to Salisbury and was shot down by a Soviet Strela surface-to-air missile at approximately 5.05 p.m..

The aircraft plummeted and hit the ground on the boundary between farm 34 of the Vuti African Purchase Area and the Charara Safari Area to its north, killing all 54 passengers and five crew on board. A ZIPRA Strela Section had struck again.[1] Robin Hood comments: "In November 1978 Jack Cocking, Senior Engineer Air Rhodesia, designed a cooling pipe prototype which was designed to be fitted at the rear of the tailpipe to cool and disperse the jet pipe exhaust heat. Once the Viscounts achieved 400ft above ground level the missile would be unable to acquire its heat signature. However, this was rejected by Air Rhodesia Management because it would inflict a 5% penalty on performance. In December 1978 Air Rhodesia Operations Manager, Tony Beck issued a directive that Viscounts should depart on random headings at low level for 10 miles before climbing steeply. Andre Du Plessis, Captain of Viscount *Umniati* followed these instructions. He was a former South African Air Force Pilot who flew Mustangs on the Cheetah Squadron, Korea in the early 1950's. I wrote to Tony Beck and pointed out that I considered the procedure dangerous to the extent that it would cause another disaster. The Strela teams would soon observe our tactics and simply wait at 10 miles to attack the planes as they started climbing. Most of our Pilots were taking off and 'spiralling up' over Lake Kariba to gain at least 8000ft before they set off for Salisbury."[2]

Steve Nutt also commented: "I clearly remember the second Viscount disaster. At about 5.00 p.m. in the afternoon the GC Sergeant that I worked with, and I, were driving back from Karoi to the Magunje Base camp. We had turned off from the main Karoi/Makuti Road and were travelling on the Magunje Road. Looking towards the north we saw a mass of black smoke, definitely, not a grass fire. I said to the Sergeant: 'I bet that is another Viscount' and sure enough it was. The plane must have come down almost vertically. I visited the crash site on foot in the form of a follow-up and in a sort of PATU stick, (not my normal role really), but we found no spoor or evidence of ZIPRA in the area as the plane must have been shot down from a point some distance away from the crash site. I remember thinking that the crash site was not much bigger than a tennis court. More importantly everything was burnt to cinders. There was nothing left at all, no bodies, clothing, everything was burnt. I think we may have found one or two pieces of jewellery on the whole site. The plane must have been full of fuel at the time and everything was incinerated, hence the pall of black smoke I had seen. I cannot remember if they ever identified any bodies, but I do not think so. On the second site visit I was flown in by Chopper and accompanied an Anglican priest and I think one member of the Press. The Priest was there to bless the site I guess and the photographer to witness the event."[3]

Once again, Supt. Hollingworth and his team confirmed that a Soviet Strela heat-seeking surface-to-air missile had been used in the attack. S/O (Tech.) Lance Combrinck recalls: "Supt. Hollingworth brought back a port engine from the wreckage of Viscount *Umniati* and asked me to see if I could find any 'foreign' element among the wrecked housing. I found a small piece of metal

[1] Karoi Contacts Map Incident 34.

[2] Robin Hood oral interview 20/2/2019.

[3] Steve Nutt email 16/6/2016 and various other emails, and WhatsApp discussions 2016 to 2017.

which I took to the forensic team to have a metallurgical analysis done, but they told me it was too small. I took it to Hollingworth who examined it under his 1930's comparison microscope and before long he had identified the piece of metal as part of a Strela war head. Supt. Hollingworth was a legend."[1] Later, Roy Downes calculated Viscount *Umniati*'s flight-path was within range of a Strela surface-to-air heat-seeking missile.[2] Joshua Nkomo again confirmed in an interview on 14 February 1979, that his troops had shot down Viscount *Umniati*. The continued escalation of the war had taken another dramatic turn. ZIPRA seemed capable of striking the Viscounts at will and, with that, the white population continued to lose heart. Rhodesian military external raids increased, as did SF casualties. Young men continued to face call-ups, while white emigration escalated. Official figures released on 29 August 1978, showed a net loss of 1,111 whites in the month of July 1978 alone.

Capt. David Padbury, makes an additional comment on the incident:

> On Sunday 11 of February 1979 our father had boarded a Viscount at Kariba Airport in answer to a request by Jean, my wife, in order for him to be able to celebrate his birthday on 12 February with family. He arrived home safe, and in very good time for the birthday celebrations. On the following day, Monday 12 of February the Viscount that Dad could have flown home on, the *Umniati*, took off at 17h00, and was shot down by ZIPRA at about 17h06.
>
> The day after the tragedy, Tuesday, July 13, it was announced to the world that, yet another Viscount had been shot down. This time there were no survivors. I had gone into Com.Ops. in the early hours of that morning as it soon became clear that it was going to be another long day.
>
> During the latter part of that fateful day, I was summoned by Lt. Gen. Walls to accompany him to the Prime Minister's Office to report on the emerging facts surrounding the latest Viscount shooting. Once the facts were presented, an angry Ian Smith abruptly terminated the meeting with the words; "I want blood to flow in the streets of Lusaka today". Such was the Prime Minister's fury. On the walk back through the corridors to Combined Operations Lt. Gen. Walls commented: "David, there will be blood flowing in the streets of Lusaka, but at the right time, and well planned. Now go and find me the right targets." In the early evening, in a somber atmosphere, the various targets were presented for discussion to the Senior Commanders of Combined Operations, the planning cycle had got underway. It is important to emphasise that from the Commander in Chief (the Prime Minister) down, there was a united anger and a deep desire for a just reprisal, along with an unmistakable and significant urgency to bring the perpetrators to account.

Maj. Nigel Henson recalled: "The RLI Fire Force (Support Commando) were deployed to Karoi on 13/2/79 where we remained until the end of February 1979 when it re deployed to Sinoia and shortly thereafter Mangula."[3] The FF pilots included Air Lt. Norman Maasdorp who deployed to Karoi from 13 to 27 February, Air Lt. Mike Gardner from 13 to 15 February, and then from 21 February to 6 March. On 14 February, Mike Gardner, with his technician/gunner Darryl Peacock, flew three senior Government officials: Bill Irvine and James Chikerema (Co-Ministers of Transport and Power) and Hilary Squires (Co-Minister of Defence and Combined Operations) to the crash site.[4] Air Lt. Roger Thomas and technician/gunner, Beaver Shaw, also deployed to Karoi.[5]

Additional troops deployed in the area included C Company 1RAR, under the command of Col. Lionel Dyck,[6] and Maj. Gavin Rawstron from B Company 1RAR, who had arrived to commence deployments in conjunction with our SFA. Various PATU and Police Reserve callsigns were

[1] Lance Combrinck email 7/10/2017 and WhatsApp discussion 14/1/2019.
[2] Roy Downes email 20/11/2019.
[3] Nigel Henson email 22/11/2016.
[4] Mike Gardner email 25/6/2017.
[5] Shaw, B. (2018), p. 259.
[6] Lionel Dyck WhatsApp discussion 29/9/2016.

deployed. The SAS did not deploy to Hurungwe on this occasion. Lt. Col. Garth Barrett stated: "To the best of my knowledge no members of the SAS were deployed, and I would have known."[1] While there were several contacts, there was no evidence that the ZIPRA Strela Section responsible was eliminated.[2] Supt. Bob Bedingham attended the crash site of Viscount *Umniati* on 13 February. He compiled an initial report for Sub.JOC Sinoia based on his observations and preliminary investigations. Bob stated: "At no time did we get any information that the ZIPRA Strela Section responsible for either of the missile attacks on the Viscounts had been contacted or eliminated during follow up operations. Had this occurred our Sub.JOC and indeed entire Lomagundi district and Nation would have been elated, but this was not to be."[3]

Com.Ops. was chaotic when I arrived for my meeting with Brig. Barnard in view of the Viscount incident. However, he allowed me time to provide a detailed briefing of our operations in Hurungwe, the continual flow of accurate intelligence through our networks, the unavailability of the FF and the problems we had with the lack of access to areas "frozen" by the Selous Scouts. Brig. Barnard learned first-hand from me the extent and success of our operations. He was impressed and offered to send one of his men to assess our operations. To my surprise, the Com.Ops. Intelligence Officer, Capt. David Padbury, my brother, was despatched eight days later.

After the meeting, I returned to Karoi and began piecing together intelligence in order to assist military deployments in response to the Viscount *Umniati* incident. As far as I knew, and this includes the SB and GC men at Karoi, we had no information indicating that there was a ZIPRA Strela Section (ZSS) operating in Hurungwe. The UANC networks in Chikangwe and Kariba were informed of the situation, although they were by that stage aware of the tragedy, and we spread the word to the callsigns in the field. It was highly unlikely that the ZSS was operating within our proscribed areas and it was important to ensure we did not lose focus on our aims and objectives. We were able to offer intelligence to the military for their operations outside of our areas, while at the same time ensuring we held the ground. We had to look beyond the immediate tragedy and focus on our mission. Seeking revenge was, for us, pointless and would deviate from our plans and progress in the field which in itself was a victory.

Since we had no specific information regarding the ZIPRA Strela Section, the best we could offer was intelligence regarding the location of known resident ZIPRA sections, their bases and known supporting kraals. As it happened, we received information that a resident ZIPRA section was based at Gandawa's house in the area of Chivakanenyama. We arranged for one of our men to lead an OP to Chidzimamoto Hill overlooking the target area, with the prospect of a Fire Force or ground-force attack, depending on the circumstances and situation, as well as the availability of the FF. The Bvunzawabaya scene was reviewed and we felt it worth deploying the FF into it as soon as it was available. Hondo (pseudonym), an SFA from the area, was deployed with the military to recce the following bases:

1. Chipanda Hill, with Mapikilela's kraal the target.
2. Tangesa Hill (QM 5652), with Kandengwa's kraal the target.
3. The area of the Nyaodza River to Kufazvineyi's kraal and north of the river, with Goteka's kraal line (QM 5055) as the target.
4. Gawa's kraal near the Nyaodza River (QM4854).
5. Time Nyamupfukudza's kraal (QM520518).

Immediate intelligence was received indicating a ZIPRA section was resident in the Masanga area. They slept at Chasara's house and apparently had a base camp at a nearby hill at QM370479.

We also prepared the necessary intelligence documentation for the following Fire Force possibilities: Marowa Kraal, indicated to us by one of our men with a view to undertaking an OP.

[1] Garth Barrett email 29/11/2016. Mike Gardner does not recollect any specific facts regarding uplifts of SAS callsigns after Viscount *Umniati* was shot down. Email 16/12/2016. Confirmed by Maj. Henson email 22/11/2016 and Norman Maasdorp WhatsApp discussion 29/11/2016.

[2] Confirmed by Lionel Dyck, Mike Reeler, Phil Wright, Steve Nutt, Bob Bedingham and the author.

[3] Bob Bedingham email 4/3/2016.

Mararakanda, Chirebvu and Matinha kraals were to be attacked by Fire Force deployments. This intelligence was filtered through to the military for their operations. It would be difficult to engage ZIPRA as the word regarding the second Viscount incident would have quickly spread throughout Hurungwe and ZIPRA would go to ground knowing the area would be flooded with SF. Word of the arrival of the FF would rapidly spread, confirming their suspicions. Fortunately, a positive development occurred on 15 February, when one of our callsigns captured a local *mujibha* (name and location withheld), and gathered immediate field intelligence which they forwarded on to us:

Napoleon and Moses were currently the two ZIPRA commanders in the Doro Region. This tied in with our intelligence as China was still in Zambia. The ZIPRA men frequented the following kraals:

(a) Pasipamire Kraal (QM4653), where they visited the houses of Tabros and Bisha Muneka Mubataripi where there were two girlfriends (names withheld).
(b) Rawson Kambanje at Nyamupfukudza Kraal near Doro Township (QM509509).
(c) Bandera Kraal, under Kraalhead Goteka (QM5155), where there was one widow.
(d) Makiwa's village (QM4253).
(e) Jim's kraal (QM505535),where there were three girls.
(f) Time Nyamupfukudza (QM520518) where there was one female (name withheld).

We provided SFAs to guide the military into the target areas listed for (b), (c), (e) and (f).

During the same evening, a callsign in the Mudzimu area captured a well-known ZIPRA *mujibha*, Jengwe (RC X325501[1]), who had been sent to recce our section's movements and report back to ZIPRA. While our men were interrogating Jengwe, he attempted to escape and failed to stop after warning shots were fired. He was shot and killed.[2] Our investigations confirmed that ZIPRA intended attacking our section. War is cruel with survival the foremost thought in a soldier's mind. In my view, I considered the shooting of Jengwe the correct action. We reminded the callsign that it was important to confirm with the locals that Jengwe was shot as a result of his own actions, which clearly indicated his support for ZIPRA. I felt he bore the consequences of his choices. While the shooting of Jengwe was against our general political and military objectives, the safety and security of our men were issues of paramount importance.

During all the Security Forces activities, ZIPRA remained active and murdered Mr Kadozora. The actual date of his slaughter is uncertain, but it is believed to have been around 15 February 1979, in the Nyamhunga area. Mr Kadozora was axed to death as he was believed to be linked to a serving soldier.[3]

Following information supplied by one of our men, the FF deployed onto the Bvunzawabaya base on 16 February. In the ensuing battle, two insurgents were killed. Two AK-47s and one RPG-7 launcher were recovered. One African female was injured. It was disappointing to kill only two insurgents but ZIPRA would be kept on the move.[4] Hachina was murdered at Bvunzawabaya Kraal on 7 February. Patience and timing were required to orchestrate the attack 11 days later, which was a credit to our team.

International Response to the Viscount *Umniati* Attack

On 13 February 1979, the British Minister of State, Foreign and Commonwealth Office, Mr Edward Rowlands, stated: "Fifty-nine people were killed including, according to press reports, at least two United Kingdom citizens when a Rhodesian civilian airliner crashed near Kariba yesterday. According to the news agencies, the Patriotic Front claims to have been responsible. I am sure that the whole House will deplore this senseless attack, involving further tragic loss of innocent lives in Rhodesia. The escalation of the war reinforces our determination to continue our efforts to bring an

1 RC: Registration certificate *(situpa)*, an unique identity document issued only to Africans and required by law to be carried at all times.
2 Karoi Contacts Map Incident 35.
3 Karoi Murder Map 29. Confirmed by Dr J. Chakawa during field trip and research on 29/4/2016.
4 Karoi Contacts Map Incident 36.

end to the fighting by negotiations within a framework likely to prove acceptable to the people of Rhodesia as a whole. Until that happens, we fear that the drift into uncontrolled violence and chaos will continue." He further stated: "This attack has been deplored. It is deplorable. It was a senseless attack. It has no purpose or value in promoting freedom, justice or liberty in Rhodesia."[1] Members on both sides of the British Parliament deplored the killing of 59 people in the attack.[2] The attack was condemned in Parliament on the same day. Prime Minister Callaghan stated: "There can be no sympathy for those who shoot down a civilian airliner. It is a barbaric act, the latest in a series of barbaric acts which, I regret to say, have not been confined to one side."[3]

Robin Hood commented: "Shortly before the 34th International Federation of Air Line Pilots' Associations (IFALPA) Conference in Amsterdam, Netherlands, held between 15-20 March 1979, the President of the British Air Line Pilots Association (BALPA), John Laurie, accompanied by three members of the Association, visited the Pilots Association of Rhodesia in Salisbury. Detailed discussions were held regarding the attacks on the two civilian Viscounts by ZIPRA insurgents. Thereafter John Laurie and his team flew to Moscow and met with the Russian Pilots Association (RPA). The RPA was requested to put pressure on the Kremlin to prevent further attacks by ZIPRA on civilian aircraft. No further Viscounts, nor civilian aircraft were shot down by missiles during the war."[4] In attendance at the IFALPA Conference was the Director, IFALPA (Rhodesia), Ian Evans. The two Viscount incidents were discussed in detail. With the help of the Regional Vice President of Africa, the Chairman of the Security Study Group and the Chairman of Committee B, a paper

1 British Parliamentary Hansard records: HC Deb 13/2/1979 vol 962 cc 964-969.
2 British Parliamentary Hansard records: HC Deb 14/2/1979 vol 962 cc 1111-1113.
3 *The Times*, 14/2/1979.
4 Robin Hood oral interviews 23/4/2018, 27/4/2018 and 20/2/2019.

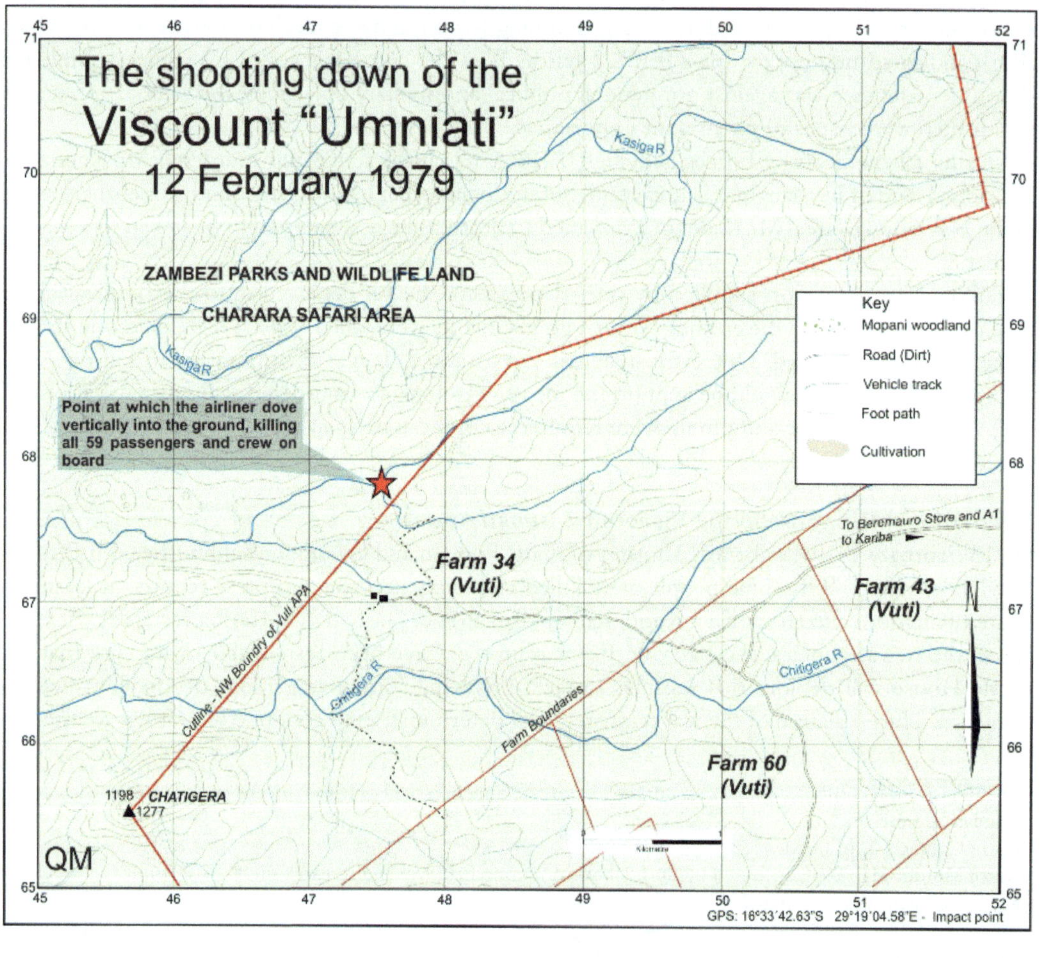

was drafted, presented and passed without dissension. This paper condemned any attack on civilian aircraft. By the time of the conference, the Viscounts had been acceptably modified to prevent further such attacks.[1] Petter Bowyer noted: "Subsequent to the second disaster, Air Rhodesia succeeded in shrouding Viscount exhaust pipes and painting the aircraft with appropriate low-radiation paint. The Air Force's modified Strela-test bed was unable to detect Viscounts flying above 2,000 feet."[2]

On 26 March 1979, in Hong Kong, Capt. D.F. Pearce, President of IFALPA condemned the missile attack against unarmed civil aircraft. He urged all nations to take resolute remedial action as a matter of urgency.[3]

---

[1] Report by Director, IFALPA (Rhodesia), Ian Evans, after the conference.

[2] Petter-Bowyer, P. (2005), p 331.

[3] *The Times*, 27/3/1979.

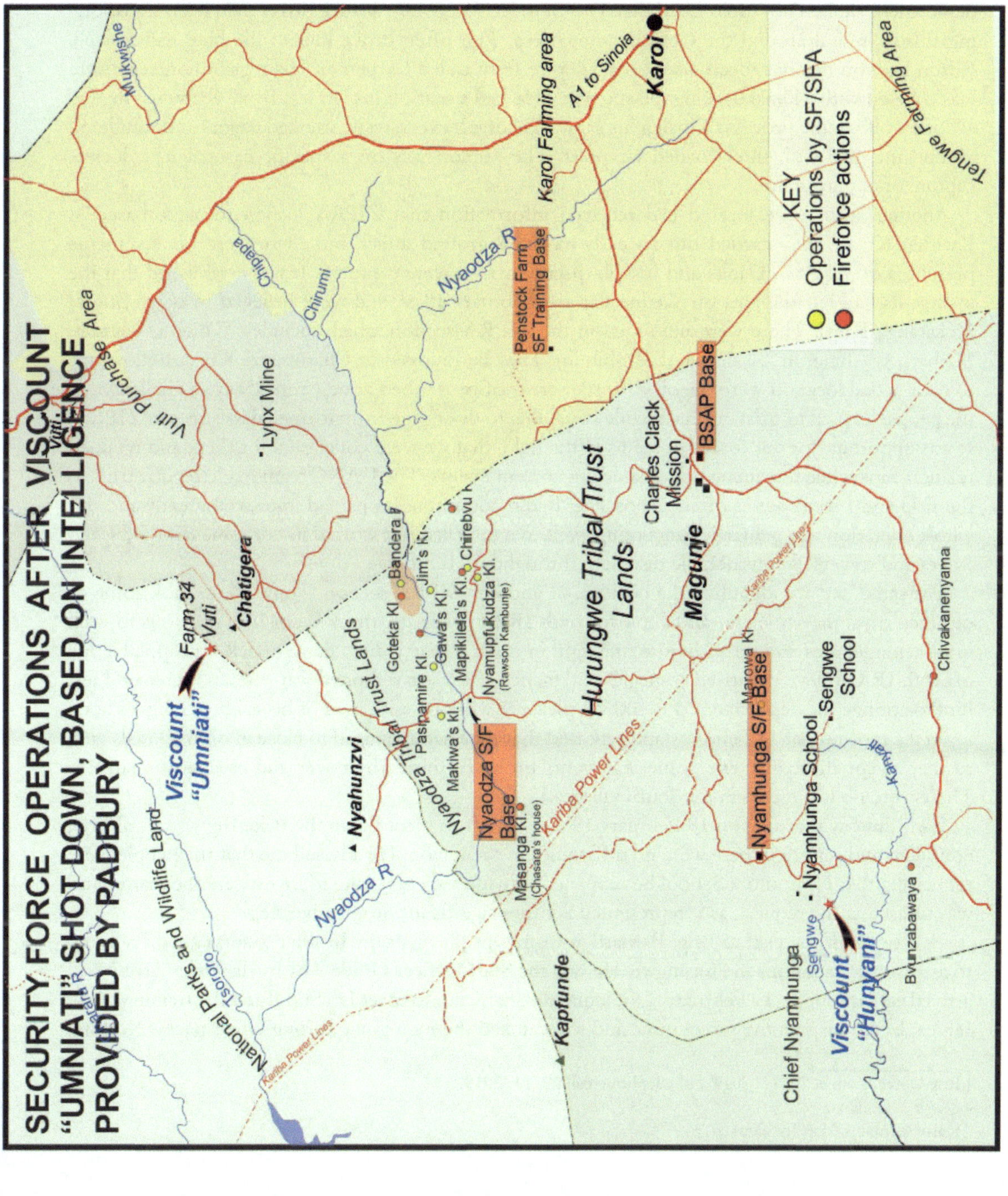

About the same time as the Viscount *Umniati* was shot down, a third attack occurred on a commercial Viscount en route from Kariba to Salisbury. Once airborne, the plane flew at low level for about 20 miles over Lake Kariba, before changing course to Salisbury. It continued at 500 feet for about 20 minutes into the flight. Flight crew heard a loud bang outside of the aircraft. The pilot climbed to cruise level. On arrival at Salisbury, engineers found some damage to the elevator tabs. Roy Downes told me: "I am aware of the incident. I understand that engineers, on inspection, found one or more of the three elevator tabs were distorted."[1] The weapon used was not identified.

Combined Operations Assess Our Operations

On 17 February, I travelled into Hurungwe to meet the men. We met with one of our sections following up on intelligence regarding the activities of a lone ZIPRA insurgent, Edson. Our men were grasping the importance of intelligence gathering and developing their assimilation and deployment skills. They established that Tito Bero (RC X28920), a truck driver, had been transporting Edson in and around the Chidzimamoto area. Tito often drove him to the beer hall as well. Edson had, on this day, been taken to a Tengwe farm called Carpenter. His registration certificate was covered with a khaki backing (plastic type). He had a scar on his left leg. By all accounts, he was a "lone wolf" in the process of losing his sanity. He drank excessively, smoked dagga[2] and wandered around the area with three loaded weapons. The section was on a specific campaign to locate, capture or eliminate him.

Another section we located had received information that ZIPRA insurgents were based at Kwirirai Kraal. They carried out an early-morning ground attack but there were no insurgents present. Two *mujibhas*, Daniel and Joseph (pseudonyms), were captured. It was established that the insurgents had left the area on Wednesday, 14 February 1979, and were believed to be staying at Makaranga Kraal. There were nine men in the ZIPRA section which included Witness, Wander, Mzibayi, Washington, Sikalela and Mtobibum. They had moved to Charumbira Kraal. Follow-ups to their actual location were ongoing. Border areas of proscribed zones were always a challenge, as the people learned to trust our men while struggling to disengage from former allegiances to ZIPRA. It was important for our forces to see us in the field, that we were concerned for them and retained relationships while remaining up to date with current events. The UANC team made regular trips to the field and I went out as often as possible. Radio communications had improved greatly and our whole operation was generally functioning well. We travelled unescorted in our mine-proofed Land Rover and traversed considerable distances throughout Hurungwe.

The same day, we identified the position of another ZIPRA section. Tony Coom took some of our men from the same area and deployed with 1RR in order to attack them. The plan was to walk into the target area and arrive before first light in order to carry out a dawn attack. I dropped Tony off with 1RR and we discussed strategies and tactics. He was a seasoned war veteran therefore I left him to arrange the deployment. I found it a pleasure working with men of his calibre. Tony radioed in on the morning of 18 February and reported that they had managed to close in on the kraals and, as they swept through them, some insurgents broke from nearby cover and escaped unharmed. There were no insurgents in the actual villages.[3]

Early Sunday morning on 18 February 1979, I set off to meet Big in the field. Big was, as always, confident and reported there were no difficulties in the region. He advised me that the people were requesting that Nyamutora School be reopened. I made a mental note to investigate the matter and was pleased at the request, as it represented another significant progressive step.

As a result of my visit to Brig. Barnard at Com.Ops., he sent my brother, Capt. David Padbury, to assess our operations in Hurungwe. He was the Staff Officer Grade 2 of Intelligence (Army) and arrived early Monday, 19 February. I took him to Chabwino to meet Ian Suttill and the training team. Ian explained his training programme and we watched the men going through their paces. Nothing

---

[1] Roy Downes email 20/11/2019 and telephone call 22/11/2019.

[2] *Dagga*: Marijuana.

[3] Karoi Contacts Map Incident 37.

special was laid on as I wanted David to see things as they were. As usual, the base was a hive of activity. Ian had the men fall in for parade and then demonstrated patrol formations and fire-with-movement. The impromptu display was impressive by any account. We then introduced David to the refugees and showed him their facilities.

I always found it humbling speaking with the refugees. People displaced by war possessed nothing more than what they carried, yet made the most of trying circumstances. Fortunately, we were able to provide for all their needs, with the generosity of people such as Fr Zinkann adding to their home comforts. David and I then went to Chikangwe to meet the UANC men. The office was lively. There was always much activity as people gathered to chat, supply information and, on occasions, share problems and difficulties with the team. Maps of Hurungwe were feature items in our offices, displaying the growing areas occupied by our forces. In brief, Chikangwe was a happy place, a genuine African communal office with traditional African music in the background.

I deployed into Hurungwe with David to meet the men, allowing him to see them in an operational role. Normally, an SB patrol would comprise two Land Rovers with two men in each vehicle. A military deployment would have two heavy-duty vehicles with support troops. The UANC travelled throughout Hurungwe unescorted in a civilian vehicle. We travelled in our short wheel base Land Rover with two RPD men in the rear. I thought it showed we trusted our men and their landmine-detecting cells' skills in the villages. The day ended on a pleasant note with Ian, Admin., David and I enjoying a relaxing evening at the Twin Rivers Motel.

The following day, 20 February 1979, one of our sources brought in intelligence resulting in an FF deployment on a ZIPRA section at Chiyanga Kraal. During the battle, one insurgent from Gatooma and three locally trained insurgents were captured. Tony Coom deployed to the battle-ground and, as a result of his initial interrogations, recovered a nearby arms cache comprising 8 hand-grenades, 11 slabs of 200gm TNT, 13 slabs of 400gm TNT, 1 Pom Z anti-personnel grenade, 2 pull switches, 10 detonators, 2 electric clips, 400 rounds and a medical pack.[1]

David and I travelled to meet with Tony. One of the captures denied he was a ZIPRA insurgent. David continues the story: "It had been an extremely busy build up to this particular Fire Force deployment, and it was very interesting to see how effective the whole system worked. It was impressive to see how quickly good intelligence could be followed up. There was an air of confidence, as well as a great determination displayed by everybody involved…from the population on the ground to the operators at all levels. I was interested to see how quickly, with the correct approach to interrogations, that a capture could be won over. In this case, there was still a lot of action on the ground. Helicopters were flying, and there was the usual excitement of the battle and ongoing follow-up operations. Sitting in the traditional manner was the capture, being watched over by a small group of the SFA soldiers and Tony Coom. John walked up to him and sat in front of him in the same manner. He started to talk to him in a pleasant manner, almost as if he was a fellow combatant. The tension in the prisoner's face and demeanour slowly dissipated. The ZIPRA prisoner denied that he was a trained soldier, but that he was rather a *mujibha* for the group. John reassured him that nothing would happen to him, and that he would be looked after. He then asked him if he would like to join the SFA team, to which he replied that he would. John's response was that they would appreciate the help, but needed to make sure that he knew a bit about weapons, so he handed the prisoner an empty AK magazine and asked him to fill it. This the prisoner did, pretty efficiently, and when he had finished, he turned the magazine upside down to look at the hole at the bottom of the magazine to see if it was full…immediately realising his mistake…and smiled! Without any further explanation, he admitted that he was indeed a fully trained ZIPRA insurgent. He was then taken away by the SFA soldiers for processing and was later incorporated into the SFA teams. On my return to Com.Ops. I submitted a full report on the success of the SFA operation at Karoi."

David returned to Salisbury later that evening. This was the first time we had operated together,

[1] Karoi Contacts Map Incident 38.

though unwittingly we had been in close proximity during a number of previous operations. The following two days were spent in the field in preparation for the next influx of men due to arrive from Retreat farm, Bindura, having completed training. I had new areas proscribed working with the local SB, RAR and Sub.JOC Sinoia. The UANC were actively programming the people and Big and Martin were consulted regarding changes that would be made to sections as the new advance sections were selected. Happy assisted the men with strategies and tactics, working out the best combinations of sections to undertake a mass move into the new areas. Occupation with visible strength and force would have a negative effect on ZIPRA as we pressed on fulfilling our visions and promises to the masses. The people were calling for more men and we were sending them!

There were exuberant celebrations when our additional 50 recruits arrived, in uniform, from Bindura on 23 February, fully kitted out and prepared for deployment. Our momentum was once again on the increase. Strategies were formulating and successes, in my estimation, would inevitably follow. Ian Suttill controlled the operation well and soon had the men seated in the vehicles ready for deployment. They were excited and eager for action. We headed off to the field and met up with the regional commanders who, with the help of Happy, reorganised the sections. From a military perspective, I found this a heart-warming sight as men were shuffled into sections, briefed by their regional commanders and concluding with instructions from their section commanders. The new resident sections were led to their respective areas while the large "occupying force" made their way to the newly proscribed areas. I could not ignore the profound sense of responsibility I shouldered as my men strove towards the battleground. As always, I greatly admired them. Happy and I returned to Karoi in a sombre yet elated mood.

While this was taking place, at 1 p.m., our callsign 72 made contact with eight insurgents at Chendamora Kraal. There were no casualties on either side although 100 doppies were recovered. A leading *mujibha* from the area (name withheld), was captured and was assisting callsign 72 with follow-up operations. It transpired that the *mujibha* had been travelling to Zambia for external training but was shot in the foot and forced to return. The ZIPRA section leader involved in that contact was Mandebvu. According to reports, this was his third contact of the week: he was not having a good time![1] We also received intelligence that a landmine had been placed on the road leading to the Maumbe advance area. Subsequently, a double landmine was lifted. It was booby-trapped with a hand-grenade set to detonate if the landmine was found. Fortunately, the engineers were alert and skilled.[2] This was a significant blow to ZIPRA, loosening their grip on the people and allowing us to assert our authority in the intelligence field in a new operational area.

Simultaneously, there was a build-up of ZIPRA in the Gache Gache area who were being pushed out of Hurungwe. I discussed the problem and the opportunity it presented with the military. I suggested that we expand our deployments into the area, as well as the Omay in order to pre-empt penetration by ZIPRA. The UANC were able to provide the manpower and political support.

[1] Karoi Contacts Map Incident 39.
[2] Landmine Log 19.

Com.Ops. visit Hurungwe. (L-R) Happy Marere, David Padbury, the author and George Hutchison at the "safe house". Photo by David Padbury.

Interrogating a captured insurgent during a Fire Force action. (L-R) Happy Marere, the insurgent, the author and Tony Coom. Photo by David Padbury.

Tony Coom and the author introduce David Padbury to some operational SFAs. Photo by David Padbury.

Tony Coom (seated left of the author) recording field reports.
Photo by David Padbury.

SFAs instructed on HMGs.
Photo by David Padbury.

A military convoy passes through our operational area.

Bishop Muzorewa rally

Happy Marere hands military authority to Bishop Muzorewa prior to a political rally.

Guard of honour for the bishop.

Traditional presentation of drinking water for the dignitaries. Martin is seated to the right of the bishop.

Water bearers officially thanked for their services. Author is to the right of the platform.

Bishop Muzorewa accepts the water. Chinhamo, who held up the Selous Scouts patrol, is seated holding an RPG-7.

A platform view of the rally. Happy Marere is front left with his back to the camera.

The people meet the bishop. The author is to the rear.

Preparing for Bishop Muzorewa's rally, Kathene School, 10/2/1979.

International media at Bishop Muzorewa's rally, Kathene School, 10/2/1979. In the foreground are Gavin Rawstron, the author and Sandy Irvine. James MacManus and Rowley Carter in attendance.

The author briefing the international press.

The international press interviewing the author.

On patrol. (L-R) Tony Coom, Jan Meyer, the author, an SFA and Sandy Irvine. Kneeling are Ian Suttill and an SFA RPD gunner.

The author briefing the press with Maj. Rawstron regarding the April 1979 elections. The tagged, shaded areas on the map indicate the areas occupied and liberated by the SFAs.

Occupation of a school base. (L-R) Sandy Irvine, Nzou, a section leader and the author. The flag reads:"'Forward with peace among the people. This is what the people want."

Lighter moments — except for Ian! (L-R) Tony Coom, Ian Suttill, the author and Sandy Irvine with a section of SFAs.

Tony Coom on operational duties. Photo from Tony Coom.

20 ~ OPERATION OMAY

Anything and everything is possible in war.
John Padbury

Background to the Omay TTL

At this stage of events, the time arrived to journey into the Omay. The Kariba office believed they could win the support of the Tongas. I felt the time was right to penetrate Omay before ZIPRA made a concerted effort to occupy it. Former P/O Gavin Cooper provides the background to police work in Omay:

(i) General duties and patrols

With the advent of July 1975, the strength of the BSA Police Kariba included Member in Charge, Inspector Paul Rens, S/O David Lemon and P/Os Ray Escott, Duncan Stewart and Gavin Cooper. There was an African Sergeant, the late John Chademanah, and various Constables whose names have been lost in the ether of time. Inspector Mike Kettle was in charge of Bumi Hills under whom, on rotation, served Gavin and three African details.

On behalf of Special Branch Kariba there were D/S/O Ken Stewart and D/S/O Ben Pretorius, with their regular African staff comprising half a dozen Sergeants and Constables all in plain clothes. They made sorties up and down the lake in the SB launch, but never ventured inland to the Omay or to the vicinity of Siakobvu. All GC reports were formulated then sent to Special Branch on a national basis. Posing as tourists fishing was high on the agenda.

From June 1975 to September 1976, I was stationed at BSAP Kariba which area extended west from the Tsetse gate some 20km east of Kariba airport on the Makuti Road, southward to the Vuti and Urungwe Tribal Trust Lands, around the edge of Lake Kariba, and west to incorporate the entire Matusadona National Park, bordering the Gokwe area as far as the Sengwa River. Therein lay the Omay Tribal Trust Land, a vast, rugged, and wild area, well populated with dangerous game and tsetse fly, that fell ostensibly under three Chiefs; Chief Negande, Chief Nebiri and Chief Msampakaruma. The terrain was ideally suited for the Rhodesian Army's Tracker Combat Training Wing in Kariba which, at that stage of the Wing's history, fell under the command of the School of Infantry in Gwelo. The unit trained potential trackers and the art of bush survival; magochas were employed to assist. During one of these exercises run by the OC of the Unit Lt. Albert Tourle BCR and Sgt. Pete Clements (both RLI), and Sgt. Andre Rabie (SAS), on the evening of 9 April 1972, Al Tourle was attacked and killed by a lioness which was subsequently killed by a National Parks game ranger, Rob Francis.[1]

As far as the Lake and Border Control was concerned, Police Kariba had a Marine Section operated by regular qualified staff with Launch Master Class 1 Licenses, enabling license holders to pilot vessels up to 60 tons. Various fast launch vessels were moored at Anchorage Marina and used for boat patrols between Kariba town, Bumi Hills and further down to a base at Paradise Island in the Sengwa Basin. The number of vessels and operating strength was augmented by privately owned launches belonging to Police Reservists seconded to the Marine Wing, in similar fashion as with the PRAW. As CTs infiltrated into Rhodesia from Zambia, crossings were made largely at night. This meant

1 Full details of this tragic story is found at https://www.africahunting.com/threads/night-of-the-lioness.14782/

marine patrols were in the main nocturnal with vessels patrolling up to the border which followed the old Zambezi River line (before it was dammed), and travelling east and west. On nights when the Kariba ferry travelled between Kariba town in the east and Mlibizi towards the western end of the lake, the night patrol would dock alongside the ferry and the BSAP contingent would board for the journey to or from Binga. From the height of the ferry with its powerful spotlights on the bow, observation for the presence of CTs using canoes and boats to cross the lake was more efficient than being in a low smaller vessel. The ferry sailed a zig-zag path, hoping for a fortuitous intercept. This random, method of patrolling, would make such subversive crossings more difficult. After the war I was introduced to a former ZIPRA commander, Dumiso Dabengwa, at a social function. He mentioned that a BSAP launch had travelled at considerable speed within about 100 feet of his canoe while on a crossing into Rhodesia from Zambia in the dark of night, between Chipoto and Van der Riet's camp.

Due south, inland of Bumi Hills at some 80km, was a BSAP base, Siakobvu, which was staffed by one Patrol Officer, 4 African regular details, and 2 African Police Reservists who were seconded to night camp guarding duties. The role of all Siakobvu staff was that of Ground Coverage, checking for and on known "expatriates" from the area known to have left for any reason, those known to have crossed over into Zambia, Witch Doctors and Nyangas, communications with all three Chiefs and their Headmen, as well as monitoring of the rather "thin on the ground" populace at large.

The monthly rotation of Patrol Officers for the Siakobvu Ground Coverage base was between me and another Patrol Officer. We had no escorts and travelled alone to liaise with the 2 GC two-man teams patrolling the various chiefs' areas. One foot patrol travelled the area to the south of the Mapongola Hills in Chief Negande's area. The other foot patrol travelled Chief Nebiri's area, skirting the unfenced Matusadona Park and east through to Chief Msampakaruma's area and close to the Sanyati high level bridge. North of the Mapongola fell under Mike Kettle and Bumi Hills Police. My Police Issue Land Rover clocked up on average some 2000km per week on the 3 roads and numerous bush tracks of this vast and sparsely populated area. PATU sticks from Karoi were regularly deployed into the Siakobvu area for purposes of conducting Observation Point (OP) duties, intersecting with spoor of CT groups and searching for the alleged presence of a wheeled "recoilless rifle" purportedly delivered into the Negande area from Zambia.

(ii) Security situation

From July 1975 onwards, in what had been a relatively quiet area for some time, after the infiltrations of Operation Cauldron, prior in 1972-73, the buildup of CTs in Zambia rose significantly, as did infiltrations. The Omay was however an area they traversed on the journey to Matabeleland, making reports of sightings and incidents of hostility sparse.

It needs to be noted, in my estimation, there was a degree of folly on the part of the Rhodesian Government, the consequences of which would be felt as the war progressed. Primarily, the fact that the government decided to move the Batonka fishing tribe, traditionally surviving from the fruits of the Zambezi River, away from the lake, forcing them to sustain themselves from crops and thereby showing scant consideration for their way of life. As can be imagined, imposing this relocation and break from tribal custom, produced resentment. Tilling the soil was not an activity the Batonka relished and government agricultural assistance was limited to the African Development Fund (ADF). No equipment or Advisers were established in the area for purposes of educating this tribe on matters agricultural. Consequently, should Ian Smith's government attempt to win the hearts and minds of these displaced people, they would be facing a formidable, if not impossible, challenge. The men folk would till the soil and their women folk would plant corn in the sand of the river beds. However, with regular summer rains came raging torrents down every riverbed, washing the corn into Lake Kariba with annual famine and hunger ensuing.

Chief Negande experienced trauma at the hands of the CTs in 1972-73, when they murdered some of his people and abducted others. This was followed by a settled period up to 1975. He was biased and harboured resentment towards the CTs for their past actions. Chief Nebiri was a pleasant but insignificant leader, an insatiable "soak"[1] with a thirst for copious quantities of South African Brewery (SAB) products. Plied with cases of beers at frequent intervals, petrol for his dilapidated Land Rover, as well as battery acid for the battery made him an interesting character.

Chief Msampakaruma's kraal was situated nearby TTLs falling under BSAP Karoi, with the Sanyati high-level river bridge in close proximity. The bridge was a well-known crossing point for CTs making their way to Matabeleland and the Midlands, owing to the deep Sanyati River gorge. Not only that but Msampakaruma Business Centre was within an easy walk of the bridge. He owned the main store. Msampakaruma spent most hot days drinking beer and lazing at his kraal. No doubt he frequently socialised with passing customers requiring various supplies for their subsistence during protracted foot travel to the south. Occasionally buses ventured through this the "Hostes Nicholle Trail" from Karoi to Dett via Siabuwa. Hostes Nicholle, having previously been the Interior Minister in the Rhodesian Government, opened up this route no doubt for colonials to engage in their time-honoured pastime of big game hunting into areas teaming with game. Siakobvu had the most picturesque old thatch type DC's Hunting Camp. This was to become the BSAP Siakobvu Police Post. Hostes Nicholle was responsible for the opening up of the Hostes Nicholle Institute for Wild Life Research situated in the Sengwa Wild Life Area near the Sengwa Gorge.

(iii) ZIPRA incidents — landmines and ambushes

During 1976, the Rhodesian military command decided to "up the ante" with Psyops[2] operations to win the hearts and minds of the Batonka people in an attempt at securing the northern border and lake frontier. This "stepped-up" approach led to "fire power" demonstrations incorporating all elements of the Rhodesian Defence forces; Police as the Senior Service, the Army and the Air Force, followed by hand-outs of food and blankets. At Chief Negande's home kraal a Hawker Hunter performed supersonic manoeuvres and Alouette helicopters, with a "fire force" demonstration, served to intimidate the Batonka population. With the notion that their welfare was at stake, a decision was made to migrate this relatively sparse population into PV Protected Villages in demarcated areas within the Omay TTL. Word of this decision, announced to the Chiefs of the area, spread rapidly to the CT cells and supporters within the Omay. In less than a week, a landmine was laid in the driveway leading down the escarpment and into the BSAP base at Siakobvu. It was detonated by a Police Bedford RM, a four-wheel drive troop/supply carrier, while travelling on a supply run. There were no casualties.

On the day Police, Army and Internal Affairs made their first pick up of Negande's kraal dwellers to take them to the newly prepared PV, I was informed of a landmine having been placed on the track into the first kraal to be collected. The informer had mentioned the identities of the ZIPRA CT supporters and significantly, the identity of the Batonka furnished with a TM46 landmine which he laid along the track the previous night. A general proximity was also provided within a few 100m of the mine. The suspected collaborator was picked up by me along with 5 other African men prior to the convoy arriving at the declared location. They were loaded into the back of the Land Rover and driven down the track in the direction of the approaching convoy vehicles.

[1] A consumer of large quantities of alcohol.
[2] Psychological Operations Unit.

Some 100m from the convoy, while approaching a bend in the road near a small kopje feature, one African Male Adult was observed placing one leg over the side of the load space of the Land Rover, while demonstrating a high state of anxiety. I stopped the vehicle and with the accompanying Sergeant, removed the now confirmed collaborator from the vehicle and questioned him regarding his obvious anxiety, and the whereabouts of a landmine. It was put to him that his actions indicated to the BSAP that a *chimbambayira* (landmine) had been placed on the track being driven along by the convoy for this relocation operation. The suspect refused to divulge any information and was clearly concerned with the prospects of being branded a "sellout". He was returned to the Land Rover and we continued driving around the kopje feature. Mid way past the kopje the suspect soiled himself and emptied his bladder in his trousers. I again stopped the vehicle and removed the suspect from the vehicle and asked him to explain the problem he was having. Again, he denied all knowledge of any pending ill. A concerted effort was made with mine prodders and other available resources, to locate freshly turned soil which might indicate the precise position he had laid the mine. After about an hour, with no discovery of a landmine, I opted to continue the journey. The convoy was commanded to proceed. The lead vehicle, a Toyota RL with double rear axle, detonated the mine as it went through the kopje. There were no casualties. The suspect was immediately arrested, along with the others identified as CT collaborators and eventually tried in the High Court. With the evidence led indicating firstly his reluctance to cooperate, and secondly his commitment not to compromise the CT structure he was collaborating with, and thirdly the fact that he had reconciled his mind to the fact that the detonation of the mine might cause severe injury, or even death, to the personnel in his presence, as well as destruction of government property, he was duly sentenced to death, the maximum penalty in law.

Shortly thereafter, a somewhat similar incident occurred on the weekend of 5 June 1976 at the Bumi Hills airstrip, when a private aircraft was damaged and destroyed overnight by an explosive device. The Safari Lodge, a popular weekend destination until then, had the number of its fly-in visitors severely curtailed in one fell swoop. D/S/O Doug Stanyon from CID Sinoia was at the Lodge on the night of the attack. He did periodical patrols into the Omay.

On one occasion the Minister of Defence, Mr PK van der Byl, flew into Siakobvu by helicopter to visit the resident GC Operative. PK periodically frequented a hunting camp in the Omay and in the recent past, had dated my cousin – a London based model at one time. In explaining his visit, PK mentioned that he was eager to glean information and opinions about the war from men at the "grass roots" level rather than from Members in Charge or Officers Commanding. PK himself was a "Sword of Honour" Sandhurst graduate. I explained that the Chipoto camp in Zambia had some 4000 CT trainees, many Rhodesian expatriates and other "hangers on" ensconced near the northern bank of Lake Kariba. He was questioned as to why the security forces had to wait for such CTs to cross the lake instead of attacking the base(s) in Zambia. PK pondered the question and a short while later the first external raids commenced.

In 1977, as political and military pressures against the country began to mount, the government built a new airstrip at Siakobvu with capacity to accommodate both light and long-haul aircraft. In due course, a copious number of earth-moving equipment, together with skilled labourers, arrived to remove vegetation and grade or bulldoze the length of the proposed airstrip.

We had very good rapport with Chiefs Negande and Nebiri and so with their people. I was never attacked or ambushed. The locals must have seen the escalation in government staff and facilities as some step up in countering terrorism and naturally the anti-establishment thinking and CT inspired counter measures began to increase. The previously unfenced Police post was now subjected to a security fence and general upgrade of defence facilities and personnel. With this development, another landmine was placed one night in the driveway to the camp. An RL delivering equipment and supplies was about to be welcomed into the camp when it struck the mine in clear view of the BSAP personnel that, on the day, included an SB D/S/O from Sinoia carrying out his monthly operational tour. There were no casualties.

To summarise the strategy the CTs appeared to implement, one could assume that they left lighter types of "ordnance", (TMH46s landmines and so on), which the locals could use to demonstrate a degree of subversion and resistance. The region was largely a "transit" zone with CTs passing through, hopefully without drawing attention to themselves. The heavier weaponry, such as "recoilless rifles", bazookas and the likes, were presumably hauled further into the centre of the country, and the more populated areas from Gokwe to Bulawayo and the ZIPRA (Joshua Nkomo) backed operating areas in the middle to southern parts of the country. ZIPRA did not want to draw attention to themselves in these "transit" areas. Their operations intensified as they entered the more populated areas such as Urungwe, closer to the Karoi area. To compliment this thought, the GC Operatives travelled thousands of kilometres using a single vehicle, often "bundu bashing" tracks through the Matusadona and there was not a single ambush incident.

The notion that we "were public friend number one" was endorsed one day when GC Operative's parents arrived at the Bumi Hills Safari Lodge for a weekend visit. Having arrived from Siakobvu to see them said GC Operative was observed by one of the more elderly African staff visiting his parent's room. Later in the evening the waiter, who hailed from Chief Nebiri's area, enquired privately of the Operative's mother: "is this man your son Ma'am?" She responded in the affirmative, whereupon he replied: "A ma'am…your son, he is a good man." A mother who had lost most other members of her family, bar her husband, to the ravages of war suddenly felt less anxious about the welfare of her youngest son, as she was to disclose some years later. I was that GC Operator.

The "transit route" from Zambia, across the lake, and on into the Rhodesian hinterland, appeared to be no different to the ZIPRA routes in from Zambia, east of the Kariba dam wall, utilising for example the "power lines" as a navigational aid to Salisbury. Few incidents were reported in the Kariba area, but intensified as CTs entered the more populated areas of the Urungwe and so on, closer to the Karoi area.

One of the factors remaining in my mind was that the Siakobvu police post was extremely vulnerable. Positioned "scenically" half way down a precipitous escarpment, with a driveway that comprised "near perfect" ambush sites at both ends of the camp, with a 160m high cliff immediately behind the camp, coupled with thatch buildings, the camp could have been destroyed with minimum planning or effort. Police Reserve camp guards armed only with Greener shot guns would have been no match in any gunfight. Moreover, radio communications were severely limited. Designated 902 Alpha, being the sub-station of Bumi Hills at 902, could not transmit directly to 902, nor Kariba 906 – there being no "line of sight" necessary for airwave radio signal. The only callsign capable of establishing transmission was Oscar Alpha 4, positioned to the north-east of Makuti. Radio signal from the Land Rover (Scouter 902A) was unobtainable by any station unless within say a 20km radius. Subsequently, I enjoyed a life of solitude with no radio schedules reporting one was "alive", other than through the kindly operators on Oscar Alpha 4, and Vera Johns's father (Vera was a Miss Rhodesia) who was a farmer in the Umvukwes area and an enthusiastic "Ham" Radio who was available pretty well all night, every night. A comfort, to say the least, knowing that there was always such a man listening out and able to relay messages for one, in the event of any trouble.

> The bush tracks and trails gave the Land Rover a thorough beating. Consequently, if one broke down, one had a long walk through dangerous country teaming with lion, buffalo, rhino, elephant and many other predators including hyena. Following constant usage, a series of broken half-shafts rendered the Land Rover unserviceable and in time, the vehicle literally split in two. The front section was connected to the rear by the prop shaft only with the road way clearly visible through the floor space. The weight of mine proofing was far too much for the suspension and with all the bounce over "rock and rut" the body just gave way, with an ever-stretching crack in the metal work in the floor of the passenger compartment. This rendered the mine proofing of no worth whatsoever. The CMED mechanic sent to Bumi to conduct repairs had little sympathy with the result and accused one of a gross disregard for Government property.[1]

The BSAP Ground Coverage and Special Branch teams were not restricted to war-related duties and still functioned as policemen, often in life-saving situations. D/S/O Doug Stanyon, when based at Siakobvu, was called to rescue a pregnant African female who had been trampled on by an elephant. After a difficult drive and treacherous walk accompanied by an African D/Sgt. and an informer, he located the patient. She had at least one compound fracture and two internal fractures of the opposite leg, and a serious injury to one arm. With the help of some locals, they made a hammock using blankets, ropes and poles cut from trees. They carried the stricken patient to a makeshift helicopter landing zone hacked out of the bush. After some difficulty, Stanyon managed to arrange for a helicopter flown by Air Lt. "Baldy" Baldwin to uplift the patient to Kariba Hospital. Mother and child survived the ordeal.[2]

Gavin Cooper, Doug Stanyon, Steve Nutt, Phil Wright and Mike Reeler were typical rural police officers operating in isolated areas, and their accounts demonstrate the wide diversity of their activities. These men were and remain the unsung heroes of the war, completing difficult tasks with the minimum of fuss and, normally, little or no support. They were familiar with their areas and were highly respected for their skills and expertise.

UANC in Kariba Penetrate the Omay TTL

By the end of the first week of February, the UANC office in Kariba was functioning successfully. I received regular reports of the work it was involved with. Lenard and Joseph were serving professionally, they were committed and self-motivated. Their exploratory expedition into the Omay on 30 January was paying dividends with some of the chiefs from the Omay crossing over to Kariba to learn more about the UANC, presumably to establish their credibility.

Between 8 and 10 February, Paramount Chief Negande and Chief Msampakaruma were entertained by our Kariba staff and accepted the UANC's policies, principles, aims and objectives. Chiefs Negande and Msampakaruma were taken on a tour of Kariba and introduced the UANC men to various important officials as "our children, who are representative of the UANC." They were also informed of the UANC's proposed visit to the Omay and their intention to provide maize for the impoverished people. Apparently, a good number of the people from the Omay were UANC supporters. The trip was agreed on and, with the help of Admin., preparations were made for a visit to the Omay by the Kariba office personnel. Loaded with maize, general food supplies and political material, the UANC men from Kariba set off to the Omay shortly afterwards. On 23 February they reported on their trip as follows:

> **(i) *Journey over Lake Kariba***
>
> Having completed all the necessary arrangements for the journey, we got into the "Chaka" (a boat) and sailed for 1.5 hours to Bumi Hills. We stayed at the BSA Police Camp waiting for transport to carry the food to the various Chiefs in the Bumi Hills area. We were given a lorry called "Heavy"[3] and left around 5 o'clock in the morning for

[1] P/O Gavin Cooper email 30/1/2020.
[2] D/S/O Doug Stanyon email 26/11/2017.

Paramount Chief of the Tonga, Chief Negande. Prior to that all the Chiefs in the area were radioed the very day we arrived. When we arrived at Chief Negande's place, we were shocked to find such a big gathering. There were over 1,700 people there. We took Chief Negande and explained the purpose of our journey. We gave the crowd all that denoted the UANC, and taught them how to vote, emphasising the importance of knowing the Hoe and Spear.

After that we distributed the food in this way; every person was given equal share irrespective of age. They were all satisfied. After that we gave them party flags, badges and voting papers. We preserved some for Chiefs Nebiri and Mola.

At Chief Nebiri's place the attendance was more than 400. We distributed some food gave them badges and everything that denoted the UANC. We also gave them voting papers.

We next moved to Chief Mola's area and also distributed food, flags and badges and voting papers. The attendance was more than 700. At all the places we went to, we made a point of explaining what the UANC stood for and making them know the symbol of the UANC, and how to vote and what to expect on voting day.

We slept at the BSA Police Camp and the following day we left for Kariba on the boat *Mbizi*.

(ii) *Comments by the officers of the UANC*

All the people in these areas of Chiefs Negande, Nebiri and Mola, need thorough political education and to teach them how to vote. This is so big a task that there must be two or three more field-workers, who shall reside in those areas for a period of one or two weeks.

Due to the shortage of staff in our area, as we two are always in the field, and not in the office, it is becoming more and more difficult for us to do the most difficult job.

(iii) *Next target*

Next week we are to visit the Kachekache and all other fishing farms, around Lake Kariba and we do not know who to leave in the office. The area is also a sensitive one and our request is for escorts by members of the SFAs. We put this request and were promised something would be done. Up till now, there have been promises after promises on this request but nothing has yet materialised.

This report provoked us to provide additional staff for the Kariba office, escorts into the more sensitive areas, a vehicle and sidearms for the men's protection. It emphasised the plight of the Tonga people. Among other matters, they were desperate for food, therefore I tasked Sandy to source and provide their staple diet of mealie-meal[1] on a regular, ongoing basis. I was keen to recce the Omay and tasked Sandy to plan an expedition there. He made rapid progress with arrangements. I was looking forward to the undertaking.

Operation Omay

The purpose of our expedition to the Omay was threefold. Firstly, to attend to the people's GNA which was primarily to alleviate starvation. Secondly, to gain their support for the UANC's vision which would pave the way to deploy their people's army and, thirdly, to pre-empt ZIPRA's occupying, ruling and oppressing the people on a permanent basis.

Sandy's search for food led him to James Chikerema, the Co-Minister of Transport and Power with Bill Irvine, the Member of Parliament for Marlborough, a Salisbury Suburb. James Chikerema was scheduled to hold political meetings in Hurungwe and was keen to help in the Omay. Chikerema approached numerous corporations for donations to feed the Tongas. He secured large monetary

---

[3] Heavy: Common nickname for a heavy-duty vehicle used to convey troops or supplies.

[1] Mealie-meal: Ground maize cooked in boiling water and mixed to a pulp, pressed into small rolls by hand and eaten with relish (cooked vegetables) and meat.

donations which purchased substantial quantities of mealie-meal on an ongoing basis. Sandy established that the Kariba Ferry could transport our two Land Rovers and food across Lake Kariba to Bumi Hills, which would be our staging base. The police heavy-duty transport vehicle was available to carry the mealie-meal into the field. He also organised a powerboat to transport the senior officials across the lake which would take less time and give us the opportunity to establish ourselves at Bumi Hills.

With our preparations complete, we were ready to penetrate the Omay. Grey, Happy and the men from the UANC teams in Chikangwe and Kariba, Sandy and I, all set off and met at the Kariba Ferry. Our expedition represented a challenge as, except for the Kariba team, the rest of us had never been to the Omay. It felt more like a safari than a military operation. For some of the men this would be their first trip on a boat, which was a challenge for them.

The two vehicles were loaded onto the Kariba Ferry along with the kit, equipment and mealie-meal. The men boarded the vessel and we departed. It would take 5-6 hours to reach Bumi Hills dependent on the weather conditions. Grey, Happy, Sandy and I travelled in the powerboat. I found it exhilarating to be on the vast expanse of Lake Kariba on a bright, sunny day, heading off into the unknown.

Around 2 p.m., we checked into the luxurious Bumi Hills Safari Lodge. Perched on a hill overlooking Lake Kariba's panoramic views of the lake and the game-rich shoreline was a serene setting for a military base camp. We collected the heavy-duty truck from CMED[1] and drove it to the quayside awaiting the ferry's arrival. Late in the afternoon, the ferry arrived and we offloaded the vehicles, kit and equipment, and stacked the mealie-meal. We were ready for an early-morning start.

After a substantial breakfast, we left the lodge with our first objective being finding Paramount Chief Negande. The dirt roads into the Omay were in a shocking condition, but a small comfort was that we were travelling along roads and not through the bush. It was important to gain Paramount Chief Negande's acceptance and approval of our operation. The Kariba office had sent him prior notice of our arrival. As we approached the chief's kraals, I noted that the people were gathering grass, bundling it and carrying the bundles on their heads to their mud huts. Glancing further afield, I noticed the women grinding grass seeds to a pulp which was then used as their staple food, as there was no maize. I had never seen such abject poverty but, to my amazement, they appeared a happy and content people.

We arrived at Paramount Chief Negande's village around midday. The elders had gathered and were seated in a circle in the centre of the village. For some strange reason, I found this an inspiring sight. It would be difficult to estimate the hours the men had patiently waited for our uncertain arrival. I found myself humbled. We took our places in the prearranged seating after the traditional ceremonial greeting. The chief introduced us and then passed around the *hari*, a large cup or pot, containing *doro*, a traditionally home brewed beer. Each of us took a mouthful and then passed the container on to the man alongside. This represented a ceremony of being accepted by the chief. To decline would be anathema in his company. Thankfully, the *doro* was palatable, making for a heart-warming formality. The UANC men gave political speeches, informing the people of our aims and objectives as well as the military purposes of the people's army. We ascertained that there were no ZIPRA or ZANLA insurgents resident in the Omay at the time. Therefore, it was important to establish ourselves politically and militarily in order to hold the area. After the meeting, the UANC handed out mealie-meal to the people, and we promised to return with further supplies. We spent some time with the people as it was important to gain their acceptance before meeting the other chiefs in the area. Later that afternoon, we returned to Bumi Hills.

We spent the next three days travelling the area meeting Chief Nebiri, Chief Mola and their people. Our travels took us to Msampakaruma and Siakobvu where we inspected the airfield which would be useful to fly in dignitaries for political meetings. The chiefs and their followers received us

---

[1] CMED: Central Mechanical Equipment Department. They supplied, repaired and maintained government vehicles.

well which was understandable as we had provided them with essential food supplies! It felt to me that we were among people at the end of the world: isolated, abandoned and desperate. Paradoxically, close by was the luxury of Bumi Hills Safari Lodge while, in the opposite direction, lay the small town of Binga.

When returning to Bumi one evening, we heard a loud bang from the front left wheel, bringing us to an abrupt halt. On inspection, we found that the front left shackle spring had snapped, making it difficult to proceed. One of the UANC men we nicknamed Nzou (elephant) stepped forward and took control. He collected some large rocks and then, with the help of two other men, lifted the vehicle, allowing us room to place rocks to rest it on. I had never seen such strength. Nzou then examined the problem and walked off into the bush, returning a short while later with strips of bark he had peeled off a tree. He bound the shackle, the three men lifted the vehicle off the supporting rocks and we continued on our way. On arrival at the CMED, the mechanic inspected the "repair job". He was impressed and said that we would have been able to finish the trip without any further problems. He continued by saying that he would be able to repair the vehicle in the morning and could loan us another vehicle with which to continue.

It was a successful expedition. Naturally, we would need to return and maintain our political work, as well as expand military operations into the area as soon as possible in order to prevent ZIPRA incursions. Our political efforts would need to continue, thereby ensuring Bishop Muzorewa retained the support of the people. The airfield at Siakobvu could prove useful for emergencies and the transportation of dignitaries. We believed it important to continue the supply of mealie-meal to the people while other solutions regarding their food shortages were sought. Sandy reported our findings directly to James Chikerema who offered to investigate the Tongas' plight. He organised regular shipments of mealie-meal for distribution by the UANC office in Kariba who also worked tirelessly to gain the people's support. The time would come for James to visit the Tongas and to secure political votes in the forthcoming elections but, in the meantime, the UANC continued with their work.

To my disappointment, we were not permitted to expand our military operations into the Omay or Gache Gache. However, we remained politically active in both areas.

Special Branch Report

On 26 February 1979, I sent the following summary of current events in Hurungwe to Special Branch in Salisbury via Geoff Price. I included our entire strategies and tactics as well as diagrams of the cell system with the intention of informing Special Branch nationally of the success of our methodology. Would this transpire? I doubted it! My report read as follows:

> The system designed as outlined previously, has worked very well and as we have gained control of areas, we have pushed ZIPRA out. The only events we have had within our area are hit-and-run attacks which have been ineffectual, and the reaction of masses has been of concern for the wellbeing of our men, very favourable. We have carried out attacks on ZIPRA operating on our border areas and the masses tend to over react to these attacks with exaggerated rumours that we killed excessive numbers of ZIPRA. We do not curb these rumours but allow them to spread.
>
> Schools have been opened, buses have commenced running, essentially civil administration is returning to the area at the pace of the people. On the aspect of landmines, the roads are checked daily by the people on a cell basis, i.e. one kraal clears a certain portion of the road, the next kraal clears an adjacent area and so on. We have picked several landmines in this manner.
>
> People from areas we do not occupy have called for us to advance, which we now have done, some have migrated to our areas for protection. Our training farm caters for refugees, both war victims and families of our men in areas we do not yet occupy. In terms of Advance areas, we have found that the areas we effectively control only require two to

three sections to control them. When we advance now, we call all available callsigns together and advance in a conventional role. Recently an area in the South of Hurungwe – a new Regional area, was taken over by deploying 100 men, some tasked on OP roles overlooking known affected areas, the rest were deployed as a show of strength to:
1. Impress the locals with our strength.
2. Impress and push out ZIPRA with our strength.
3. Give our own men the psychological advantage of mass numbers to encourage them to get stuck in. The period of occupation is only a week to 10 days at the most.

Once the area has been conquered, the Regional Command structure takes over and sections return to their respective areas, which includes the occupation of the new areas.

One aspect which we have found important is the support of local stores in the TTLs. This disrupts totally the ZIPRA food and clothing supply system and they have to depend even more on the taking of food from the locals who, with the present lack of rains and crop failure, are struggling to survive as it is. This will certainly help them side with us and we are making maximum use of this propaganda.

Control in the field has been one of our main problems and this is due primarily to the lack of radio communications. We have placed several requests for radios with Special Forces and we will continue to source them.

We are focusing on training the men on field interrogations to help them gain critical immediate intelligence from captures in the field. The men have a great advantage with the support of the people, their local knowledge, and growing knowledge and understanding of ZIPRA's strategies, tactics and identification of supporting individuals in their sections and intelligence networks.

From my experiences in the Rhodesian war, I concluded that the key factors in the counter-revolutionary intelligence work we faced were as follows:

1. Gaining the support of the locals and providing them with military support and protection so that they are confident in their permanent safety.
2. Gaining knowledge and understanding of ZIPRA's military strategies and tactics. My diaries went into detail regarding where the sections operated, where they slept at night, any nearby hills/gomos where they rested or had OPs, RV points if known and so on. This enabled us to convey to captures that we already knew about their strategies and tactics. They were simply confirming them. This was my general pattern for interrogations.
3. Gaining knowledge and identifying ZIPRA's breakdown of sections. Once this was known, when dealing with a capture, he could be placed in the relevant area and section in which he operated. Armed with this intelligence, it was easier to encourage the capture to admit his involvement by disclosing as, when and, if necessary, the odd ZIPRA name he knew or had operated with. This allowed the capture to understand that we knew who he was and awaited his confirmation.
4. Gaining knowledge of ZIPRA's intelligence networks. I took time to include these details in my diaries, i.e. who the main contact man was, the main *mujibhas* and common *mujibhas*, the girls sleeping with insurgents, stores assisting with food, clothing and general supplies and information common or unique to that section. Once again, when talking to the capture, we could initiate the discussion in the following manner: "Oh yes, Kraalhead Matamba, that is where Tavengwa is the main contact man and Matamba himself supplies you from his store." Then let the capture continue the conversation and thereby expose himself by passing on information known to us. The interview becomes a conversation between men sharing common knowledge. It was important for the capture to understand the extent of our intelligence regarding his ZIPRA comrades and himself: we knew what he knew!
5. Soliciting knowledge of previous incidents in the capture's area by way of cross-questioning was also useful: "Did you lay the landmine that blew up the SF vehicle on the road to Maumbe?",

“Were you involved in the contact with SF at Karotza Kraal when Comrade Wilson was killed?”, “Were you there when the helicopters attacked Mudzimu Kraal?” and so on.

6. The capture always watched our response to his revelations, therefore it was important not to show anger in any way.

From my perspective, this method of intelligence gathering surpassed extracting information by means of harsh interrogations as I was accustomed to in Makoni. The field intelligence officers had improved greatly in this area but we were still required to go into the field to assist on occasions, forming part of the process of the men’s development and ongoing training.

21 ~ ELECTIONS & RAR OPERATIONS

The military don't end wars. Politicians end wars.
David Padbury

Psychological Warfare

In my view, the greatest psychological victory we were achieving over ZIPRA was the permanent occupation and possession of the land that they had previously ruled and considered liberated. In this process we had:

1. Gained the support of and liberated the people ZIPRA had previously ruled, gradually and significantly eroding their areas of influence.
2. Penetrated their intelligence networks and established our own.
3. Developed the capacity to strike when we found them, killing or at the least keeping them on the move.
4. Lifted landmines and located arms caches.
5. Re-established civil administration which ZIPRA had, up to this point, successfully destroyed.

These were major psychological setbacks to ZIPRA and I wanted to take our propaganda to a more damaging level. I drafted two leaflets and sent them to Salisbury for printing. Our plan was to attack ZIPRA emotionally in order to further alienate them from the masses, thereby exposing their vulnerability. Simultaneously, the leaflets would motivate our forces, the UANC and those people supporting us, providing an example of our commitment and determination to win the war. Once printed, I arranged for a PRAW aircraft to undertake an airdrop. I also sent large quantities of leaflets to the men in the field and the UANC offices in Chikangwe and Kariba. Our leaflets contained the information which I entered in my diary at the time. (See appendix.)

Pressing On

At 4 p.m. on 1 March, a callsign had a long-range contact with eight insurgents in the Kambamuchero area with no casualties reported on either side. A ZIPRA *mujibha* compromised our men as they moved in to attack the insurgents sheltering from the rain in local kraals.[1] The following day, a callsign had uplifted a *mujibha* and, after interrogations, confirmed that insurgents were presently resident near Mazindora Kraal. The FF was available and keen to deploy. They joined us at 5.15 p.m. Unfortunately, we did not engage with the enemy.[2] However, we reasoned, at the least ZIPRA would know that we were aware of their movements, that our intelligence networks were efficiently working and that we would strike as opportunities arose.

Two days later, information was received that insurgents were sleeping in the huts at Kambamuchero Kraal. At 12 midnight, the callsign attacked the kraal, only to learn that the insurgents had left and were sleeping in a nearby kraal. The insurgents returned fire but soon fled, escaping into the night. Heavy blood spoor was located and followed up in the morning but the injured was not located. One hundred and fifty rounds of ammunition, two RPG-7 projectiles and boosters, and two Soviet FI hand-grenades were recovered.[3] This was good work as we continued to harass ZIPRA, gain the support of locals and occupy the ground.

After attending the scene, I visited the entire area and liaised with various sections. At the new advance area, Mudzimu, the men reported they were doing "very well" which was encouraging. We

[1] Karoi Contacts Map Incident 40.
[2] Karoi Contacts Map Incident 41.
[3] Karoi Contacts Map Incident 42.

handed them a UANC flag which they raised, signifying our occupation of the area. A number of locals gathered at the celebration and seemed pleased with the arrival of our forces. They were holding meetings to spread the word about the forthcoming elections scheduled for the morning of 17 April 1979, concluding on 21 April. Occupying the Mudzimu area was strategically a significant step for our forces. It was the home of the judiciary appointed by ZIPRA, and one of their strongholds. One callsign handed me a damaged SKS for repairs.

As there were no other matters to attend to in the field, we returned safely to base. There was a good aura around Hurungwe now. Travel was considerably freer and the people were friendly towards us. We were confident that the roads were not mined and felt reassured we were travelling in our own liberated area. I was pleased to be out and about among the men who, as always, remained positive and enthusiastic.

During the war, the BSA Police maintained strict control of weaponry and equipment. On 1 March, I was instructed to account for a missing pair of binoculars from Rusape. It angered me that one pair of binoculars held such value and took priority over an operational policeman facing stressful situations, including death, each day. However, I understood how strict station inspections were. Those in leadership were still held to account for every item issued and signed for. I submitted my report to Geoff Price and heard nothing further about the matter. Around the same time, I returned two AK-47s[1] and six magazines to Supt. Seaward at SB Sinoia, which were on loan to us. The UANC bearers were given a note to ensure that, if they were stopped and searched, either Supt. Seaward at Sinoia (2431), or myself at Karoi (372), could be phoned for authentication.

From the beginning of March, we began to hear several rumours concerning individuals wishing to abandon ZIPRA and join the UANC in terms of the government's ceasefire plan. In Hurungwe, ZIPRA's morale had plummeted as we continued to expand into areas they had previously occupied. Frequently, we engaged them in battles forcing them to retreat, which further lowered their spirits. Although these contacts did not necessarily result in kills, it certainly harassed them and kept them vulnerable. I was certain our strategy strained ZIPRA's relationships with the people and their intelligence networks, as they realised our growing acceptance among the people.

1 AK-47 numbers 028587 and 287248.

Presenting the UANC flag to the newly occupied Mudzimu operational area.

Sections parade the flag.

Liberating the people one cell at a time.

Pfumo reVanhu and UANC flags signifying our occupation of the Mudzimu area.

Ian Suttill, Big (regional commander) and the author at the Mudzimu flag ceremony.

Grey politicising new recruits in the field.

Sandy Irvine, Martin and the author at a political rally in Hurungwe.

The author and Sandy Irvine with a local chief at a political rally.

SFA Strategies Phase 12: Orchestrate the freedom to vote

Preparing the People for Majority Rule

By 4 March, impetus for the forthcoming elections had gathered pace. The UANC offices in Chikangwe and Kariba were working hard at distributing UANC literature and holding regular political meetings in the field, preparing the people for majority rule. They were continually building momentum for rallies to be addressed by prominent UANC party officials, including James Chikerema, a popular figure in the district based on his long-term association with the liberation movement. Additionally, he lived in nearby Zwimba TTL, his birthplace. He was well respected and considered a man of integrity. We also opened and equipped UANC offices in Makuti and Bumi Hills, creating a permanent political presence for Hurungwe and Omay TTLs, and surrounding areas. We were set to politicise the entire district. Elections were an integral part of our counter-revolution and formed the pinnacle of our military successes. Since the military is an extension of the political, it was vital, not only from the outset of our operations, but more so now that the people saw their part in the military had progressively led to participation in the political. The difficulty with revolutions is that while people's participation is vital for success, frequently they are the first to be abandoned once the political and military elite occupy positions of power and, thereafter, follow their own agendas. As I examine these matters, it seems to me the key to success is for the people to be made aware that they are the power base and, when things go askew, they have that power to bring about further change. In conjunction with the RAR we had captured much of the Hurungwe.

Our strategy was to hold small meetings throughout the established cell-based intelligence networks, spreading the word and depositing UANC voting material, while emphasising our political and military vision. We were in a strong position as the people could see our forces increasingly gaining control of Hurungwe. Civil administration was returning with schools reopening and bus services resuming. We were politically moving towards majority rule. In short, we had fulfilled our promises to the people, gained their trust and support for the UANC.

While many across the world may find it strange, we faced the daunting and vital task of teaching the people voting procedures. This was the first time that the country's African population had been given the freedom to vote, irrespective of gender, educational or financial status. They needed to be shown how to mark their vote on the relevant ballot papers and, above all, that it was safe to cast a vote in a secret ballot. Assurance of secrecy removed their fears of violent reprisals from opposing political parties and ZIPRA. In the war zone of Hurungwe, this was a daunting task and the political wing of the UANC had much to do.

As the war progressed and following a lack of response to my reports, I remained sceptical that our highly successful strategies and tactics were being emulated by other SB operations. With the efficient Admin. team, and high-quality training staff, I was fortunate to have the freedom to execute my duties which had evolved into liaising with the UANC political and military wings through Grey and Happy, and co-ordinating with the UANC offices in Chikangwe and Kariba. I was also in contact with local and Salisbury SB, military officials, including the Fire Force, regarding intelligence and deployments, and communicated frequently with Sub.JOC Sinoia. I monitored training at Chabwino, strategised and deployed trainees, and kept in contact with the men in the field to ensure all was in order. This was an active season with momentum increasing as we planned for the forthcoming elections. Early in March 1979, Ian Suttill recruited a former SAS soldier, Mike Mingay,[1] to assist him with training. Mike was another valuable asset.

I preferred leaving early morning when departing for field patrols, as this allowed me time to deal with unexpected events should they arise. While travelling on 4 March, callsign 72 contacted me and reported that they had been ambushed by five ZIPRA at 8 a.m. near Mahororo School and the Kariba power lines. We drove straight out to meet them and, on arrival, established that when the insurgents initiated the contact, the SFAs callsign deserted the battlefield, leaving behind a dead comrade. One SFA was also injured in the foot but managed to escape. The insurgents absconded

[1] L/Cpl. Mike Mingay, ex-SAS January 1976 to January 1979. He left the SFAs towards the end of 1979.

with the deceased's weapon and a mortar tube. We collected one of our senior commanders, Albert, and brought him to the contact area. Albert spoke to the men, reprimanded them and gave them all 10 strokes with a cane for deserting. My initial response was that Albert was being harsh but, as I reflected, it occurred to me that we were dealing with matters of life and death in a major war, with cowardice in the face of the enemy a serious breach of the military code of conduct. Albert paraded the men then addressed them, assuring them that we had the ability and capacity to defeat ZIPRA, and this was just a minor setback in the process. He emphasised the experience gained and that the men were to learn from it. Albert asked me to address the men which I did, emphasising that death in action was the severest teacher of lessons unlikely to be forgotten. I mentioned my hope that they would learn from this traumatic occurrence. Personally, this was a sad moment, as I felt the burden of responsibility in deploying men into the battle zone, one of whom had now been killed. I certainly did not want to lose any more men. We sang songs in honour of the deceased soldier, after which Albert organised some combat drills to help them regain their confidence. We left the men in high spirits. I was humbled by their commitment to fight and possibly die for what they believed in. We organised for the deceased to be conveyed back to Karoi and continued into Hurungwe.[1]

On the way, I located Dzingayi's section and learned that on 3 March, while sweeping through Kraalhead Sikanya's huts, near the infamous Murodza Kraal, they had received information that ZIPRA had deposited an arms cache in the vicinity. During a search of the kraal, the section recovered 235 AK-47 rounds, one TMH57 landmine and detonator, one RPG-7 projectile and three boosters, two anti-tank (SKS launched) rifle-grenades, four anti-personnel grenades, electric cables and a homemade battery pack for explosives. The section political commissar had gathered the locals and given them the usual UANC propaganda speech. The people appeared co-operative but had been concerned with what to do about the cache. To continue concealing it meant conflict with the SFAs, while conversely, to report it to the SFAs, could spell death at the hands of ZIPRA. They were relieved that their dilemma was over and they were safe under the SFAs protection.[2]

Continuing the journey, I met Martin who reported that the programming in his region, Katenhe, was going well and our leaflets were well received. I then met Big who advised that he had information on two kraals in the Kweche area where it was suspected insurgents may be residing. He was planning to attack the villages in the morning. Big was also distributing leaflets and receiving a good response. Later, we took Tonga, a section leader, to Mudzimu area as our men had information about a ZIPRA section still residing there. The plan was to leave Tonga in the general area with the sections carrying out a series of dawn ambushes on various villages and, should ZIPRA be in the vicinity, attack them. Once the military operations had been concluded, the sections would conduct political exercises to increase the support of the people. UANC literature on the elections would also be distributed. I have included Tonga's deployment to show the level of military and intelligence competence our sections were achieving.

I found it interesting to watch the sections develop their intelligence operations and launch their own attacks on ZIPRA. It was my conviction that the more we attacked and harassed them, the greater would be their instability, while our position would strengthen as we occupied the ground. As I observed matters, each ZIPRA "retreat" represented a success on our behalf. All that was required was time to "convert" the people to our way of thinking, strategies and tactics. The Mudzimu area, however, was generally militantly opposed to our forces. It would take much time and effort to win the people's confidence. We had a least established a presence in the area and gained support from some of the people.

On this trip, I realised the importance of efficient communications with the men in the field. When I returned to Karoi, I tasked Sandy to secure telephone lines to Katenhe, Maumbe and Magunje schools where the buses were now running. Sandy immediately placed the notification with the PTC. An account was opened in the name of J.P. Da Silva, P.O. Box 21, Karoi, and the required deposits paid. As the matter was a priority, the PTC was informed that we would escort their vehicles

1 Karoi Contacts Map Incident 44.
2 Karoi Contacts Map Incident 43.

into the area for their protection. They were also concerned that the lines would simply be cut down by ZIPRA, but Sandy assured them we now controlled the areas and the lines would be protected by the people and our forces. The PTC responded promptly and established the lines, thereby providing us direct communications with the men in the field.

Developments in Hurungwe affirmed our growing progress as elections loomed. Both ZANLA and ZIPRA condemned the "internal settlement" and forthcoming elections. They propagated that the Interim Government was merely a puppet of the Rhodesian Front Government who still controlled the Security Forces and, in turn, the Security Forces were puppets of the government. On the political front, this was true, hence our deliberate isolation, as far as was possible, from colonial structures and our propaganda implying that we controlled the SF. I believed that it was still possible to have successful elections in Hurungwe. The fact that ZIPRA did not support the elections would be to our benefit. We promoted the fact that they wanted to continue to occupy Hurungwe and would maintain their violent oppression of the people. They were in no position to assist them in any productive way and, indeed, their record so far affirmed this.

Generally speaking, I considered Rhodesia a country in a shambles both politically and militarily. Government efforts at securing peace would be exacerbated if they failed to include the masses in their future political planning and adopt the guidelines of mass mobilisation which we had developed in Hurungwe. Our vision was consistent and achievable: the political and military working in unity with the people. We had reached the stage where we could offer the people a choice of leadership and continue to gain and hold ground.

On 5-6 March 1979, I spent two days in Salisbury attending an Operation Hurricane meeting and obtaining more kit and equipment. I did not achieve a great deal but succeeded in leaving the base with 50 AK-47s and 10,000 rounds of ammunition. The top secret report entitled Operation Favour Briefing: 5 March 1979 (XYS 10344/1), reported under the heading (1) Area 2: Urungwe TTL, clarified our successful progress in Hurungwe: "The area continues to run smoothly, locals are pleased with SFAs and ZIPRA have stepped up anti-SFAs activities. There have been a number of contacts and kit and equipment have been recovered."

On my return to Karoi on 7 March, I learned that Tonga's section had captured Joe (pseudonym) from the Binga area, a locally trained insurgent who had been moving with three other insurgents for two months, and was based mainly in the Obva area.[1] However, he had recently been operational in the Mudzimu and Katenhe areas, Hurungwe. At Mudzimu, Blocks, known as a spiritual dancer, supported the ZIPRA section, while in the Katenhe area, Tsarange, Daffy and Gushungu kraals supported them. Joe could not remember the names of the supporting kraals in the Kweche area, but was able to identify the three insurgents with whom he soldiered. All the information regarding these insurgents were incorporated in propaganda leaflets. (See appendix.)

We arranged for the printing of the leaflets to be effected by Psyac[2] and, on their arrival, distributed them to the UANC offices in Chikangwe and Kariba, and the men in the field. These three insurgents faced a predicament. If they returned to ZIPRA, they would most likely be killed. They might still have been wary of surrendering to the SFAs, therefore they were caught in the middle of a difficult situation. They did not surrender and we did not hear of them again. I am not sure what happened to them. This was a merciless war, devoid of compassion, where the enemy either surrendered and joined our forces or were killed in battle.

Update Report: Summary and Observations

On 7 March 1979, I wrote a full and detailed report and have included it in this chapter. In reading this report, the reader can understand the detail and accuracy of intelligence that was received from the field on a continuing basis. It outlines our achievements and impact made in a relatively short period of time, and reflects the overall success from the deliberate execution of the strategy, the commitment and belief of those who applied it, the dynamic response of the people and the growing foundation for the forthcoming elections:

[1] Karoi Contacts Map Incident 45.

[2] Psyac: Psychological Operations Unit.

Special Branch (UANC)
PO Box 21
Karoi
The PSBO Salisbury & Mashonaland
JOC Lomagundi (SB Rep)
JOC Hurricane (SB Rep)
Combined Operations (Att. Capt. Padbury)
Company Commander (RAR) Hurungwe TTL
SFAs Hurungwe TTL

I wish this report to serve as an update to developments in Hurungwe TTL and the present situation in both Hurungwe and adjoining TTLs.

At present we have 330 men deployed in the field armed with both communist weapons and new G3's. Our strengths by the end of this week will be some 400 men in the field. We had an additional 110 men under the early stages of training, but these men have now been sent to the Mantle troop (Support Unit) for training and subsequent deployment into the Mukwichi TTL which, I regret to say has stagnated to some degree.[1]

I wish to point out that I believe that it is incorrect to deploy men from one TTL into another as this will merely create problems, which could well be serious, in the future. I have agreed to the concept in the Mukwichi merely in an attempt to get the ball rolling in view of the obvious stagnation of the scene there and I envisage that at a later stage these men will have to be returned to their home areas for operations.

We have therefore now reached the target figure of 400 armed men in Hurungwe TTL given to me by Special Branch Salisbury. (Author's Note: While our target was 400 men, I intended increasing the number to 500 to gain maximum control and momentum. As far as I was concerned, there was no limit to the number of men we could deploy. The people's army had to grow to succeed.) Our farm at Chabwino is now virtually empty. However, it is my intention to recruit an additional 30 men from the various parts of Hurungwe TTL which we occupy with a view to the following:

(a) Cater for casualties.
(b) Supply additional man power as and when additional weaponry becomes available.
(c) Farm Defence.
(d) Assist in retraining exercises (to be discussed later with my views on future intentions SFA).

(i) *Situation in the field*

I am satisfied that the situation in the field is going extremely well. We presently occupy the following areas which were previously dominated by ZIPRA Forces. These areas have been reclaimed satisfactorily: 151, 149Z, 149X, 149Y, 149, the Eastern portion of 148Y (by local arrangement with Army Commander) 149A, the Central and Eastern portion of 144L and the Central and Eastern portions of 144J.[2] The latter two areas will be occupied by our forces once the present Selous Scouts operations cease in these areas.

In the areas that we occupy, I would safely estimate that 80% of the locals are now mobilised to the UANC party and to our People's Army. I substantiate this figure by the following:

Tremendous flow of intelligence to the men in the field which has resulted in many contacts and the recovery of considerable war material from the contacts, including arms caches and the pin pointing of landmines laid on the roads within our area.

---

[1] I was not responsible for operations in Mukwichi but was assisting in initiating deployments.

[2] These figures represent the official national designated boundaries of proscribed or demarcated areas. Unfortunately, I did not keep the original maps.

Regular meetings are held in the field by all regional commanders and by the UANC. Attendances at the meetings are high and increase all the time. Voting procedures are presently being concentrated on and we expect a high poll from the areas we occupy.

Flow of intelligence into both the UANC Office and Special Branch Office continues at a very regular pace.

The following schools have been re-opened:

Katenhe	QM600287	Kebvunde	QM545340
Magunje	QM580362	Kweche	QM6019
Mudzimu	QM4709	Chidzimamoto	QM517225
Nyamtora	QM662185.		

The following schools have requested to be re-opened by the people and the teachers themselves and machinery is in action to have them re-opened as soon as possible:

Maumbe	QM555432	Chitimbe	QM495375
Chiva	QM506255.		

It is intended to have the following schools re-opened once our occupation is complete. We hope to have the schools open by the elections:

Chidamoya Mission	QM325030	Mahwada	QM507045
Zvarayi	QM572050	Nyarumwe	QM623105
Kapfunde School	QM586100		

Buses are presently running from Karoi to Magunje (QM585370) up to Maumbe (QM555435), from Magunje to Katenhe (QM600287). From Katenhe the buses leave the area via the Southern Pompey road. All buses are protected at all times while in our area by a minimum of 5 SFA's.[1]

It is proposed to have the bus routes extended to Kweche (QM605193) and up to Mudzimu (QM485095), also to be extended from Magunje to Karereshi BC (QM487384) as well as from Katenhe to Chidzimamoto area (QM515225). Once the army secure Zvipani area (QM352210), the bus routes will extend there as well.

We find it important to reopen the five clinics in the area. At the moment we are catering, medically, for not only our own men but the people themselves. Once we can relieve the burden from our men and place it in the hands of the correct authorities, we will lessen our own immediate medical problems. The relevant authorities are being approached in this respect.

Field discipline problems have arisen, and we have had an alleged rape case reported (which I am investigating and later handed the accused over to the police), the stopping of Security Force convoys and other minor problems. These problems are sorted out as and when they arise. I do not believe that our discipline problems are any different or more serious than any other military organisation.

One of the problems we pay particular attention to is our army's relationships with the people and of course the people's relationships with their people's army. It is important not to lose authenticity with our people and as soon as the military are seen to be in command of the people the concept of a people's army will disappear. To this end, when we have disciplinary problems, the matter will be investigated by the High Command in the field and in conjunction with the affected people, the relevant tribal structure (i.e., Chief, Headman, Kraal Head), the regional commander and soldiers concerned. Military discipline will be carried out by the High Command and any tribal damages to be sorted out by the tribal system.

Command in the field does not present too much of a problem but is

[1] Dr Chakawa, J. (2015), p. clxxv, confirms that SFA were guarding buses.

greatly hampered by the lack of radio communications. At present we have a flow of 14 radios in the field (working, bearing in mind breakdowns, etc.) which will be distributed among 400 men. In the remote areas of our command the sections require big means HF radio sets for communications as they cannot even raise nearby callsigns on the A63's (radios). It is accepted that this is a nationwide problem but the introduction of 3 big means sets would greatly increase our efficiency both from a command aspect and immediate feedback point of view (i.e., Fire Force call outs, intelligence, contacts, etc.).

(ii) *Ceasefire in Hurungwe*

This is one aspect of the war I did not envisage we would encounter in Hurungwe at the outset of our operations. However, with our success there are encouraging signs that ZIPRA are now showing interest in ceasefire plans and want to join us. To this end propaganda was prepared by this office directed specifically at the ceasefire groups interested in coming across and this is presently being prepared by P.O.U. (Psychological Operations Unit) I substantiate this ceasefire aspect by the following specific evidence:

Locally captured and trained terrorist was with a group of 3 ZIPRA (Shona) who wanted ceasefire and stood on a road on 28/2/79 from 0800 to 1300 waiting for a military vehicle to surrender to. However, no vehicle came, and the callsigns became afraid and moved away. The 3 men had on numerous occasions wanted to come across and had discussed the matter among themselves. Propaganda has been put out to get them across naming them specifically giving their descriptions as well, so if they did not come across ZIPRA will probably sort them out.

A section of ZIPRA sent our callsigns a ZIPRA hat with a note asking directions as to how they could come across on the ceasefire plan. The *mujibha* was given a note to return to the terrorists and a further reciprocating note has been received. Negotiations are still going on with this delicate matter and propaganda in this regard has also been prepared.

There are positive signs from the central and southern areas that certain ZIPRA wish to defect, and the initial indications are being exploited. (No ZIPRA insurgents defected while I was in command of the SFAs.)

(iii) *Overall situation in Hurungwe TTL*

The return of the detachment commander, China, has been recently reported and he returned with 40 new men. They brought with them a big gun on wheels which is assessed to be a 75mm recoilless. China will presumably join up with the other 2 commanders Napoleon and Moses. There is a definite buildup of terrorists in the north of Hurungwe and hence our request for the areas 151A and 148V to be proscribed to counter this build up.

The RAR have moved into the West of the TTL and with their efforts in the West, coupled with our intended moves in the South and North of the TTL it is assessed that the terrorists will move across to the north of Nyaodza TTL bordering the Vuti - probably into the Vuti. It is also assessed that the terrorists will continue their flow into what is considered safe areas, i.e., the Rengwe TTL the Gache Gache TTL (Kariba area) and the Charara Game Reserve which has always been considered a safe area. The internal pipe line presently being used by the terrorists is across the Zambezi just north of Kariba, then down to Gache Gache which is their first step. Thereafter they make their way to either Masanga QM3748 or Nyamhunga area QM 2828. Those coming to the Msanga will operate in Hurungwe TTL and those going to Nyamhunga will push on down to the

Rengwe and thence southwards to the Piriwiri and so on.

The narrowest gap in this pipe line is between the Gache Gache and the Masanga area. The Gache Gache poses an immediate threat to the Kariba fishing areas i.e. Charara, etc., and more to the point Kariba itself. There is known ZIPRA presence which is believed to be building up in Gache Gache and obviously this poses a considerable threat to the Kariba people and the tourist industry in the form of convoy attacks.

It is therefore, proposed that part of our forces occupy Gache Gache. To occupy it, it is relevant at this stage to mention that Gache Gache comprises of people from Hurungwe TTL intermingling with some Tonga fishermen. There is considerable overflow of refugees from Hurungwe to Gache Gache in attempts to avoid ZIPRA whose disciplinary killings are definitely increasing as both we and now the RAR advance. Our acceptance in Gache Gache would I believe, be immediate and would achieve the following:

(1) Securing a TTL both from a military and voting point of view.

(2) Disrupt the internal infiltration pipeline.

(3) Create a staging base for our operations to the west with a view to securing the pipeline between the Gache Gache and Hurungwe at its most narrow point.

The men in the Gache Gache will be directed by whites and their immediate reports would go back to Kariba SB. This would not be an integrated scene with the army, as time is not on our side and we require to get stuck in and secure the area.

While still on the subject of the Kariba area, I mentioned some time ago that we (the UANC) had successfully penetrated the Tonga people in Omay TTL. We have provided considerable quantities of food and general supplies and succeeded in gaining their political support. They are sold on the UANC as a Party and we still continue to supply food and welfare material.

My plan (for the Omay) as I mentioned earlier, was to create the climate for an SFAs deployment into the area which has now been done. Thereafter establish a training farm in the area and militarily mobilise the people for the following reasons:

(1) Self-protection in view of their inbred dislike for ZIPRA.

(2) Secure a considerable number of votes for the UANC.

(3) Mobilise an area which was basically unaffected by terrorists.

(4) Create an eastward push towards the Rengwe TTL in conjunction with a westwards push from Hurungwe TTL with a final military objective of squeezing into the Rengwe and securing it. This overall operation would secure quite effectively the internal pipeline and the threat from Hurungwe to the south-central areas of Rhodesia.

When this plan was devised it was an opportune moment to move because of the lack of terrorist threat. However, the terrorists have now attacked (3 terrorists only and very ineffectual) the Omay Paramount Chief. If this area is not secured rapidly, we are going to lose another area to ZIPRA and will eventually have to fight our way back.

Special Branch Kariba have advised me that the SFAs presently deployed in the southern Gokwe areas are in fact pushing the terrorists in that area northwards into the terrorist haven of the Omay TTL. The terrorist threat is going to increase there now and must be stemmed. I would emphasise at this juncture that the weapons situation in Rhodesia is fully appreciated but if an additional 300 weapons were made fully available to my organisation, I believe the Omay and with a push, the Rengwe TTL's could probably be secured. G 3's would be ideal. (Whilst we continued to be politically active in the Omay, we were not given permission to deploy militarily.)

I would like to express my views as to what I believe should be the future intentions with regard to the SFA in Hurungwe TTL.

In terms of the Com.Ops. directive it is evident that our men will come under the command of the military. Programming of our men has commenced some time ago and generally the men have accepted that they will become part and parcel of the new army. This fact has generally been accepted by most of the callsigns but one in particular is giving problems in rather a critical area. The concept of *Pfumo reVanhu* is definitely going to help. (The men would be wearing brown *Pfumo reVanhu* uniforms.)

In conjunction with Major Rawstron it has been arranged to send army callsigns of up to 5 strong to the callsigns who accept the present concept as directed by Com.Ops. It is hoped that this increase in efficiency i.e. radio communications and assistance in military experience will have a "snow balling" effect on the rest of the men in the field. (This only came into effect after the elections when Com.Ops. insisted that the RAR take over our operation.)

However, the most important aspects of this system are going to be the following points:

(1) Pay of Auxiliaries will have to be reviewed and brought up to the standards of the army.

(2) What is the permanency of the RAR structure presently in the field, i.e. how long is it anticipated that they will be in the area after the elections? If they remain, there is no problem, but if they do move out what is the command structure of auxiliaries in the field going to be?

(3) There is no R & R for auxiliaries at the present time which is contrary to the military.

I envisage auxiliaries in Hurungwe as being an ongoing exercise. I do not believe we will ever be rid of the external ZIPRA threat. Even if it is removed a permanent force is going to be required to prevent any further incursions at a later stage.

It is apparent that we are a holding/occupation force. Our training is not of the required military standard. We lack professionalism in the killing aspect, radio communications and map-reading...these are important military aspects of war. However, we have won the hearts and minds of the people and this is what guerrilla warfare is all about.

I would like to add at this point that my concept of SFAs was that they should occupy T.T.L's under a suitable command system, backed up naturally by a Special Branch representative. By occupying the T.T.L's the necessity to introduce the professional, i.e., R.L.I., R.A.R., PATU, Territorial Army, Mantle, etc., is not required. These units may then be deployed to the job they are best suited to, that is a conventional strike force in a guerrilla warfare. These units will also be required to counter the external threats and the probability of a conventional type attack launched into this country. In other words, the SFAs should be built up to a guerrilla force within the country to contain the internal threat under suitable military command. (Author's note: I considered suitable military command as having a complete understanding of the operations of a people's army, which was significantly different to traditional military counter insurgency command structures and operations.)

We in Hurungwe have now reached our establishment of some 400 men. To increase our efficiency in the field our farm at Chabwino is going to be used as a retraining farm covering the following important military downfalls:

(1) Military tactics in the killing aspect.

(2) Map reading.

(3) Radio comms and Radio Procedure.

(4) Intelligence.

A programme is presently being drawn up and these retraining courses will be held as from 21/3/79 and these courses will be at an advanced concentrated level. Two sections at a time will be retrained. Of interest in this aspect is that now we have established our cell system each section can be issued with a map appertaining to his area which he now knows, and he can be trained specifically on that map which makes the aspect of map reading a lot easier.

There is no reason why this training programme cannot be overseen by the military to satisfy themselves that the men are reaching a required standard to defend their T.T.L.'s and contain the internal threat. Indeed, their assistance would be appreciated. Integrating of army personnel who will remain with the callsigns in the field in a permanent basis could well begin at this stage depending naturally the permanency of the military in the field. This is in fact the crux of the integration as I see it, i.e., what is the permanency of the military in the field. There is little point in integrating for the sake of integrating on a temporary basis. It would be preferable to have our commanders trained up to the required standard, military speaking, and to come under overall military command system.

I would mention once again that it is difficult to explain to our men that they are earning R$20.00 a month and the military man next to him is earning quite a lot more. I need not elaborate any further on this particular aspect.

In short therefore, I foresee the future of all S.F.A.s in one of two ways:

(1) If the military are to remain permanently, a system of complete integration under the overall command of a suitable military commander assisted by a Special Branch representative. Coupled with suitable increase in salaries of the auxiliaries, R & R will naturally prevail with the military, but I do not believe the Auxiliaries will demand this as they will be in their home areas in any case. Individual cases will naturally be considered and have leave granted on an "as and when basis".

(2) If the military is not to remain on a permanent basis the appointment of a permanent suitable command structure and the retraining of men, especially regional commanders and section commanders up to the required military standards as I have mentioned earlier. Pay conditions will have to be considered here in the long-term aspect but is not an immediate problem.

All the best,

Special Constable (38820) Padbury.

We were in a strong position. Our forces had gained the people's support and were holding the ground. ZIPRA had effectively been moved out of our proscribed areas and we had forced them to react to our occupation. Militarily, this was a significant success. Their landmine campaign was ineffective as they had lost the people's support in our proscribed areas. As I understood matters, the only action they could take would be to increase violence on the people and carry out hit-and-run attacks on our forces. I felt it was critical to continue expanding our areas of operation beyond those currently proscribed. Happy and I also took time to warn our callsigns to be vigilant for their own safety as well as the people's. It was important they ensured that their intelligence networks remained secure. This necessitated continual checks for any breaches of security. They were also to ensure that no personal or domestic issues blurred or tainted the information they were receiving. It was crucial to expand their intelligence-gathering networks in the advance areas, thereby ensuring they received timeous warnings of ZIPRA's intentions, as well as preparing the ground for expansion.

At the time, we detected a developing trend of ZIPRA sections periodically revisiting kraals in the advance areas and staying overnight with their female companions. Their strategy appeared more aligned with securing female companionship than a strategic military purpose. It continued to be my observation that women remained a ZIPRA downfall!

Having received this intelligence, our strategy was to ambush the kraals at dawn and then the section's political commissar would be tasked to mobilise the people in order to gain their support. This was a difficult period for the people if they were forced to support ZIPRA. Naturally, there were those kraals determined, for one reason or another, to support the enemy. This resulted in tensions between our men and those kraals. The important issue was the people were aware that our forces and our intelligence networks knew they were still ZIPRA supporters. The people were in a tenuous situation. Those supporting ZIPRA voluntarily placed themselves under threat from our forces, and those supporting our forces were under threat from ZIPRA. The only difference being there were no limits of retribution for betrayal by ZIPRA, whereas our men were limited by the considerable influence of the UANC political wing and military command structure. Once the people realised they were one with the people's army, the flow of intelligence protected them. They had the assurance we would not be imposing or enforcing any form of martial law declared by the Rhodesian Government on 23 September 1978 and, of course, by ZIPRA.

This was a critical time as we prepared for the coming elections. It was important to focus on our plans and intentions as well as being aware of ZIPRA's movements. We were forced to strike a balance between taking the initiative, maintaining momentum and retaining our vision. Victory was essentially secured by becoming one with the people and not simply focussing on the enemy. Consequently, we spent much time in the field, motivating the callsigns politically and militarily, who in turn continued the pattern. While ZIPRA were virtually inactive in the proscribed areas, it was vital our men did not become complacent. A great danger lurks following a victory, in that euphoria brings about a relaxing of one's guard rather than a heightening of vigilance and remaining alert. No two battles are the same, therefore watchfulness and preparedness, and a regular reappraisal of strategies, needs to be uppermost in the soldier's thoughts, as opposed to a feeling of invincibility once the enemy has suffered a loss. I believe one of the keys to our success was the support of the people, while the solution to our UANC war effort was a complex combination of politics, military might, determination and commitment.

Motivating our forces politically ensured that, in turn, they continued mobilising the people to support them and vote appropriately. Grey, Happy and the UANC team held regular meetings in Hurungwe with growing support and attendances. They were building momentum for high-ranking UANC officials to mobilise the masses, culminating in a visit from James Chikerema nearer election time. Mr Chikerema availed himself to speak at rallies in Chabwino, Chikangwe, Hurungwe, Kariba and the Omay. Although a formidable logistical task awaited, the UANC could competently organise such events. Large rural rallies were a communal and social event which attracted locals from Hurungwe and its surrounds. Many walked considerable distances to attend, making refreshments and home-brewed beer essential elements to the planning. Traditionally, such meetings could continue well into the weekend but, to ensure the people's safety, we organised and timed our events to allow them to return home by mid-afternoon, thereby minimising the risk of attack from the enemy.

While the various teams focused on the rallies, Happy and I gave our attention to deployments and assisting the men in the field. The RAR were integrating well with the UANC, SFAs and the people in western Hurungwe, creating a settled community. Around mid-March, I received a message that SB had intelligence of a build-up of ZIPRA in Zambia who were thought to be planning a conventional warfare attack into Rhodesia. We were asked to return all our RPG-7 launchers and projectiles, mortars and RPDs to cover this eventuality. My thoughts were that, if ZIPRA launched a conventional attack, we may well end up as one of the first in line to face the enemy. Consequently, I ignored the message and carried on as usual. I felt little was to be gained by placing ourselves at risk and being defenceless. SB's instruction was raised once or twice more but I ignored it. To my relief, the conventional attack did not take place.

On Saturday, 17 March, two noteworthy events occurred which I will detail below. One of the sections in the Birimahwe region advised us that at 9 a.m., near Chidzimamoto School, three insurgents attempted to attack their base camp but were compromised by our *mujibha* network. Our callsign opened fire on the insurgents who promptly fled. In the morning, the callsign located and tracked the insurgents. They were sighted again and were engaged but made a hasty retreat with no casualties. A single pack was recovered.[1] During the course of the day, one section in the Katenhe region was warned by the *mujibha* network that ZIPRA were planning to attack their base near Maumbe BC. The section laid an ambush and, as expected, at 10 p.m., insurgents approached the base firing 47 rounds before being repelled. The doppies were collected in the morning for onward transmission for ballistics checks.[2] On 18 March, a Birimahwe section received intelligence leading them to a small arms cache comprising one pack, 200 rounds of ammunition, one AK-47 magazine and miscellaneous clothing.[3] Another section operating in southern Hurungwe recovered one anti-tank grenade.[4] Operations and deployments continued with reliable information flowing into the sections.

These exposures of ZIPRA's previous intelligence networks confirmed the growing support and trust of the locals in our men. I admired the work they were doing in the field as well as the support of the masses. While these recently recovered arms caches were not significantly large, by directing our men to them, the people placed their trust and lives in our men's hands, highlighting the responsibility thrust upon us. However, ZIPRA would retaliate with increased violence against the locals, making it imperative that we continued protecting them. In more ways than one, the battle lines were more clearly drawn than when we first entered the war, thereby narrowing the fine margins between life and death.

On the same day, we deployed 35 reinforcements into the field. One section was deployed to the Chitiki area, totalling four sections in the Chidamoyo advance areas under the command of Douglas, the detachment commander. One section was deployed to Mahwada, totalling four sections with two additional recruits under the command of Muchadura. Finally, one section with three additional men was deployed to Zvarayi, making a total of four sections under the command of Mandebvu.[5] Our strategy was to leave one section in the Mudzimu area, and the remaining Mudzimu sections, combined with the Chidamoyo sections, to advance en masse into the Chitiki area in a conventional military role. On 19 March, from the Katenhe region in the area of Renchos Kraal, we received intelligence that ZIPRA had dug a hole in the centre of the hut and placed a drum in it which concealed an arms cache. The hut was near a plantation close by Tapfuma's kraal. A young girl (name withheld) knew the whereabouts of the drum as she frequently slept with the insurgents. Once the cache was recovered, the section used the discovery as an opportunity to politicise the people.[6]

The time had arrived for a weekend getaway to Kariba in order to "liaise" with the local SB and visit the UANC office. Sandy, Happy and I drove there on 19 March. Another weekend at Kariba was a welcome break. It was encouraging to observe the enthusiasm, commitment and resourcefulness of the UANC in Kariba. The short respite passed too soon.

We continued to filter trained men into the field and by the latter part of March 1979, in good time for the elections, 500 men were permanently deployed. A significant portion of Hurungwe was now occupied which appeased the people who continued to call for our forces to advance into their areas. This was a formidable task to manage. Paying the salaries of the men in the field was an onerous undertaking, let alone replenishing their weapons, ammunition, kits, medical supplies and additional equipment as and when required.

Our team comprised an interesting combination of former regular members of the BSA Police, Support Unit, SAS, RLI and ex-*mujibhas* working alongside the UANC political and military wings, and the SFAs. Remarkably, battle-hardened men trained to hate and kill each other now fought together.

---

[1] Karoi Contacts Map Incident 46.
[2] Karoi Contacts Map Incident 47.
[3] Karoi Contacts Map Incident 48.
[4] Karoi Contacts Map Incident 49.
[5] Mandebvu, not to be confused with the ZIPRA insurgent of the same name.
[6] Karoi Contacts Map Incident 50.

We held no ranks and were continually adapting and adjusting to an ever-changing environment. I found the dynamics between these various working parties fascinating. There was no conflict amongst the men, including the UANC party and SFAs, which was a great asset, making management of the operation enjoyable. In my estimation, this co-operation gave credence to the potential for successes in similar operations. Our focus shifted to the country's historic forthcoming elections being held in the middle of a war zone. The UANC political wing worked relentlessly in Chikangwe and the field.

During these activities, Geoff Price called for a budget which Admin. masterfully produced, providing yet another vital component to the overall enterprise. Although we worked to a tight budget, entertainment was included. (See appendix.)

Operations continued. In the early hours of the morning of 20 March in Maumbe, approximately eight insurgents killed a local UANC man.[1] They tied a hand-grenade to the Maumbe Store door, blowing it open, thereafter looting the store before making good their escape. When our men arrived at the scene, they secured the store and surrounds before contacting me. In the morning, our men located tracks which headed in a northerly direction, but were eventually lost. Happy and I met with the men to discuss deployments which might assist in locating the enemy. It was important to remind our men and people that ZIPRA were on the run. They could only strike randomly and the fact that they had murdered a UANC member clearly indicated that they only believed in the rule of the gun and had lost the battle for the hearts and minds of the people: a struggle we were winning! We assured the people that our callsigns would step up their night patrols and we reminded them that, in this war, they were our "eyes and ears" and must remain vigilant and alert. The death of the UANC official was tragic but the outcome was positive and reinforced the success of our operations. The next couple of weeks we continued our preparations for the forthcoming elections, another busy period for us all, as there was much to do to ensure that the men and the people were well prepared and aware of the event.

Float-Plane Safari

At the beginning of April 1979, Sandy and I felt the need for a short holiday and decided to incorporate a break in Kariba with some work. Sandy suggested flying by the Kariba float-plane which was quicker, safer and, to our delight, yet another adventure. We subsequently agreed on the plan and with his usual efficiency, Sandy organised the flight through the Sub.JOC Sinoia offices. Sandy was a competent pilot, holding a valid private pilot's licence. In addition, he had flown with the PRAW on several occasions to Salisbury, arranged our own PRAW flights and was well versed with organisational procedures. The float-plane belonged to Peter Anderson, a member of the BSA Police Reserve Air Wing, Lomagundi district. Peter Anderson continues:

> As the only float-plane in the area, I was pretty much a lone unit with all of my work based around the Zambezi River system or Lake Kariba. It was a magnificent scenic area to fly in and I knew I was quite privileged. Some of the flights logged in my log book included:
>
> December 21st, 1976, I flew the Police Commissioner from Kariba to Paradise Island and returned to Kariba.
>
> September 4th, 1978, three hours search for missing Viscount *Hunyani.*
>
> February 12th, 1979 three-hour search for missing Viscount *Umniati.*
>
> May 1979, I did five days of army supply drops to the lower Zambezi; on supply dropping I could fit 8 parachute boxes and the despatcher.
>
> I would probably have been one of the first in the air for the Viscount searches. We covered the power line area north of Kariba all the time hoping to locate any survivors before the terrorists and give them some form of aerial protection before rescuers/ground forces arrived. One thing I remember vividly was having unbelievably tired eyes from constantly trying to find wreckage in the bush. Owing to the high probability of a terrorist attack, accompanied by an observer, we flew with the pilot door off and a Browning 303 machine gun fitted, our standard operational procedures. I also carried a folding butt AK, an Uzi 9 mm, and a couple of hand grenades.
>
> As with all PRAW duties, flights were requisitioned by the BSAP Member in Charge or,

[1] Karoi Murder Map 30.

> in my case, on occasions, by the Senior Officer in charge Marine Division Kariba; most of the time by telephone and the official Requisition paper work followed on a weekly basis. I forwarded the official documentation to BSA Police HQ and payment for flights was made monthly based on hours flown, so no cash was involved. All our work was done through these Police channels and followed strict procedures.[1]

I arranged for Lynette and Robin, our son, two years old at the time, to drive to Karoi on Saturday, 31 March for the weekend, and then join us for the flight. Lynette was looking forward to the escapade. We spent the weekend at the Twin Rivers Motel at which there was a swimming-pool for Robin to indulge in. Strange as it may seem, I always found such occasions awkward. It was difficult to be present as a husband and father when my mind was so focused on the war. I found it extremely difficult being separated from my men and the war effort with the result that tensions arose between Lynette, Robin and I. As is so often the case, these situations are dealt with superficially at the time and only with the benefit of hindsight did I come to realise the strain the war placed on not only my family but, indeed, general social relationships. At the time, however, the stress seemed a prerequisite to daily life in Rhodesia.

Manenji drove us to the Karoi Dam early on Monday morning, 2 April 1979, where the float-plane had landed. Here we met the pilot, Peter Anderson. He was relaxed, confident and amicable while familiarising us with his plane: a six-seater 1969 Cessna 185. On 17 March 1978, Peter had fitted and tested a full Robertson Short Take Off and Landing (STOL) kit with Wiplane floats.

It transpired Peter was a comical character. He had conducted the world's first aerial streak with a float-plane at Kariba with two nude nurses, one on each float, on New Year's Day, 1978, while flying over the beachfront hotels. Spectators to this event included Lt. Gen. Walls and the Director of Civil Aviation, Wing Commander Maurice Barber. Peter's eyes widened as we produced our kit for the flight. Sandy and I both had AK-47s, our webbing (carrying three AK-47 magazines and one or two hand-grenades), and a suitcase each. Lynette had her fair share of gear including a suitcase for herself and Robin, as well as a pram. After a brief silence, Peter commented: "You have too much kit!" Sandy and I did not particularly want to leave our weapons and webbing behind in case we were confronted by the enemy, either during the flight or once we landed at Kariba. Likewise, Lynette considered her luggage essential, therefore I suggested that we leave our webbing behind. After some discussion and debate, Peter changed his view, saying: "We will take the lot!" The newly fitted Robertson STOL kit and Wiplane floats gave him the confidence to make the decision.

We should have been relieved but, knowing we were overloaded, dampened our spirits somewhat. We made a half-hearted attempt on insisting that we could leave some kit behind, but Peter was confident that we could take it all. We packed all the equipment into the rear two seats. Sandy, Lynette and Robin in the middle seats with myself in the front seat alongside the pilot. As we all buckled up and Peter started the engine, he attempted to reassure us that normally, at 2850rpm, with a speed of 45mph, he required 225 metres of waterway for lift-off. When overloaded, he needed 450 metres. My heart sank as we were more than overloaded. However, as the Karoi Dam was approximately 1 kilometre in length, we had a margin of safety.

In total confidence, Peter taxied the Cessna to the end of the lake, turned it to face the dam wall, powered up the engine to gain maximum power for take-off before beginning the aircraft's surge along the aquatic runway. At approximately 400 metres, while increasing speed, Peter attempted to ease the aircraft from the water with the floats grappling to separate from it. It took a while but eventually we began to "ski", achieving the required 45mph. What should have been exhilarating, was rapidly becoming a nightmare as I fixed my sights on the fast-approaching dam wall which I was convinced would soon terminate our lives, and a deathly silence prevailed. No one spoke, even Robin sensed the tension.

In what appeared to me to be the final moment prior to impact, Peter calmly pulled back the control

---

[1] Police Reservist Peter Anderson email 25/1/2016. Confirmed by Snr. Asst. Comm. Ted Sheriff oral interview 5/10/2019 and C/Insp. Bill Linfield email 10/10/2019.

column, added a notch of flap and coaxed the Cessna over the awaiting dam wall, clearing it by only some metres. He smiled at his nervous passengers and confidently continued to gain height. Once clear of what appeared to us to be immediate danger, we relaxed and began to chat while Peter set course for Kariba, flying at treetop level in order to avoid ZIPRA ground fire or a Strela surface-to-air missile attack. The flight lasted some 40 minutes and, as we approached the dam, Peter gently pulled on the control column promptly gaining height to provide us with a picturesque view of Lake Kariba, the dam wall and the hotels on the lake's shores.

Shortly after our spectacular sightseeing flight, we landed on the open waters of Lake Kariba, taxied into the Caribbea Bay Harbour and pulled into the floating jetty. After thanking Peter for a roller-coaster experience, we made our way ashore and checked into the hotel. It felt to us as if we had landed in paradise. The hotel and surrounds were beautiful and seemed a world apart from the war zone in Hurungwe.

After depositing our luggage in our rooms, Sandy and I collected the prearranged hired vehicle and drove to the UANC office in Kariba to deal with the business end of the trip before returning to Caribbea Bay, where we intended to relax for the remainder of our break. We appreciated the wonderful facilities at Caribbea Bay, our Rhodesian "Mediterranean paradise", situated at the edge of the lake. We relished the sunshine, the stunning views of the lake from the hotel, the luxurious rooms, together with scrumptious dining and lazing about the swimming-pool. We were immersed in a beautiful, peaceful bliss. It was a most refreshing, relaxing time but, far too soon, we were returning to Karoi in a hired car: a somewhat less enthralling experience than the float-plane. Lynette and Robin returned to our home in Salisbury and, before we knew it, Sandy and I plunged back into the war.

Build-Up to Elections: Political Rallies

With elections fast approaching, we had 500 SFAs in the field, i.e. 500 men recruited, trained and permanently deployed. The RAR had an additional 200 men deployed. We had a well-structured political capability through the offices in Chikangwe, Kariba, Bumi and Makuti which penetrated the surrounding townships into Hurungwe and beyond. There was an abundance of intelligence flowing through our networks which reflected the considerable support of the locals in Hurungwe. The Bumi office penetrated the Omay where we had extensive support, despite our lack of military intervention in the area.

Thirteen schools had been reopened under the watchful eye of our men and the RAR. Buses and vehicular traffic were flowing safely through Hurungwe under the protection of our men and our *mujibha* networks. In addition, rural clinics were reopening and landmines were regularly pinpointed and lifted. It is worthwhile pointing out that we had no incidents of vehicles detonating landmines. Our men had intermittent contacts with ZIPRA who had essentially been purged from the proscribed areas and could only muster their ineffective hit-and-run attacks on the locals and our sections. The further we penetrated into Hurungwe, the less frequent were the ZIPRA attacks.

As can be expected in a warring and hostile environment, we had issues of ill-discipline in the field and these were dealt with swiftly and firmly. I wish to stress, however, I considered the discipline of the men to be of a high standard, bearing in mind that they were permanently deployed with no periods of rest and recreation. In fact, the "field" was their home and there were bound to be indiscretions committed. The men were performing a remarkable undertaking among their own people, not only protecting them from ZIPRA, but also thwarting the enemy's attacks. They continued to have my admiration.

The UANC military-wing leadership had grown and developed along with the phenomenal expansion of the people's army. They were firmly in control and at no time, from the inception of our operations, were there indications of threats or an attempted mutiny.[1] I wish to point out that this was the level of discipline from the inauguration of the people's army. It is important to bear in mind there

[1] Confirmed by Maj. Graham Des Fountain email 24/1/2018; Brig. Heppenstall, OC Special Forces 15/5/2019 oral interview. Also George Hutchison who was at Karoi from the outset of our operations, various Skype discussions July/August 2018.

was no rank structure in our military operations. We were not a pyramid-structured organisation but functioned laterally in our areas of natural skills, abilities and expertise. We were an army of men united in a common cause, motivated by the right political vision and determined to defeat a marauding enemy.

Back at Karoi, the pressure was mounting to ensure that the political and military wings of the UANC, and all our men, were prepared for the forthcoming elections. The principal objective was to secure a large poll turnout while ensuring the people's safety. At the same time, we had to leave sufficient sections in the field for not only the daily protection of the people but also while they travelled to and from polling stations. Additionally, we had to implement security measures around the polling areas on the voting day itself. We anticipated long queues of voters which would cause considerable delays.

The UANC political wing's efforts paid off when James Chikerema arrived to hold rallies in our operational areas. On Saturday, 7 April 1979, in Kariba, he held our first large rally in that area.

On the morning of the rally, we toured Kariba, visiting the usual tourist locations. James Chikerema later signed the photographs we took of the events. After the successful rally in Kariba, we flew James to the Siakobvu airfield in the Omay for rallies organised by the Kariba office and the chiefs of that area. James organised maize and other supplies for the people which we ferried over to the Omay. This step proved efficient politicking as the masses were able to meet the man who was attending to their needs. Maize and other essential items were provided on a regular basis by Chikerema and the UANC office. Even in the remoteness of the Omay, the meetings were extremely well attended. I considered it appropriate that James Chikerema witnessed the poverty of his people and the good work he, and his men in the UANC, were doing in alleviating their plight. We spent a fruitful few days in the Omay. There was little time to spare as we had to return to Karoi in order to attend rallies scheduled for him in Chikangwe, Chabwino and Hurungwe.

On Saturday, 14 April, in keeping with the UANC political and military traditions, I met Chikerama just outside the operational area and handed him an AK-47 which identified him with the military cause, thereby symbolising overall political authority. He addressed a well-attended meeting at Chikangwe at which he had overwhelming support. The proceedings, including the mobilisation of the masses and security, were arranged by the UANC political and military wings, with all going to plan. Later, we took him to Chabwino and introduced him to the training staff. The men were excited to meet him. After all, he was one of the "fathers" of the Second *Chimurenga* and here he was, large as life, addressing our men in Karoi. He then addressed meetings at Tengwe and Karoi for the white farming community, where he stressed the need to achieve a high turnout of voters at the election: 85 per cent of the 2.8 million voters was the target. He said: "The March 3rd Agreement had brought an end to UDI and ushered in a democratic constitution under which, for the first time the African majority were given their democratic rights under universal franchise. The elected government emanating from the election would mobilise the masses throughout the country to confront murderous terrorists."[1] This was his theme throughout his tour and emphasised the need to reverse UDI and return Rhodesia to a legal constitutional status. The following day, he addressed the masses at Magunje, a meeting organised solely by the UANC political and military wings. Once again, this included the mobilisation of the masses, coupled with the necessary security arrangements and landmine clearance of the roads. The meeting was also well attended. Chikerema made the comment: "When you see a fire threatening to engulf your home what do you do? Are you not supposed to start your own fire so that the two fires quench each other without destroying your houses and your food? Terrorists have started a fire and SFAs are out in full force to stop that fire from destroying law-abiding citizens like you. In order to stop terrorists, we have armed our local boys who are also our own children."[2]

The final meeting was held at Katenhe, which again was well attended and successful. At the Katenhe and Magunje meetings, we employed strict procedures. The local UANC political leaders took turns in addressing the masses, followed by the regional commanders and section leaders from

1 *The Sunday Mail* 15/4/1979.

2 Dr Chakawa, J. (2015), p. 215.

that area. They had their say as we felt it important to communicate the political message, reinforced by the military, ensuring that the people saw unity between the two. The senior UANC political dignitary was always the last to speak. I never addressed these gatherings, it was not my place to do so. ZIPRA did not attempt any attacks during this period, thereby demonstrating the success of our operations and a credit to those involved. I considered the meetings a triumph and remained convinced that the elections would be a success. By "success", I mean well attended by the masses, safe and secure, with the UANC achieving a victory.

These meetings also served the purpose of motivating the men in the field, ensuring they understood the political message was from the hierarchy and that there was political unity and support for the work they were doing. When the political goals are clearly defined and achievable, the military are inspired to fight on.

Election Time: Hurungwe TTL

After the wonderful African float-plane safari, and a flurry of political meetings, it was time to focus again on arrangements for the elections. Meetings with the police and SB, the army and Int.Aff., culminated in my issuing the following instructions to our men in our operational areas:

> The election period is to extend from the morning of the 17/4/79 to the afternoon of the 21/4/79. Polling booths will be positioned at the following locations and under the respective command of the undermentioned:
>
> A. Magunje — static booth for entire period (17-21/4/79).
> Todd and Sgt. Magombo, Booth is to be positioned at Magunje School.
> People from Karereshi, Kebvunde, and Magunje areas to vote here. Any overflow of people unable to vote at the static booth at Maumbe to vote at Magunje i.e. the people of Maumbe and Chishumba areas may vote at Magunje after the 17/4/79. However, every effort must be made to have the latter two areas voted at the Maumbe Mobile.
>
> B.(1) Maumbe mobile — two days at Maumbe (17-18/4/79).
> Sandy Irvine and Moses. Booth is to be positioned at Maumbe School.
> People from the Maumbe area to vote here and people from Chishumba. People from Doro area presently under the command of RAR will also vote at the Maumbe Mobile as will the RAR callsigns in closer liaison between the company commander and liaison officer.
>
> B.(2) Katenhe Mobile three days at Katenhe (19-21/4/79).
> Booth at Katenhe school.
> The Maumbe Mobile staffed by the same personnel will move to the Katenhe School and people from the Katenhe and surrounding area will vote here.
>
> C. Chidzimamoto area three days (19-21/4/79).
> Polling booth to be established at Chiva School. People from the Chidzimamoto area including Bhirimahwe area to vote here.
>
> D.(1) Kapfunde Mission three days (17-19/4/79).
> George Hutchison and Manenji. Polling booth at the mission. People from the area surrounding the mission to vote here.
>
> D.(2) Kweche BC. On 20/4/79 the polling booth will move from Kapfunde Mission to the Kweche BC and people from Kweche area will vote here. The liaison officers will move with the booths.
>
> E. Kavaya School area. Static booth (17-21/4/79).
> Mike Mingay and Jameson. Polling booth at Kavaya School.
> People from the Mujinga and Kavaya area to vote here.
>
> F. Chimusimbe BC. Static booth 17-21/4/79.
> Jono Smith and Spencer. Booth in the BC.
> People from the area around Chimusimbe to vote here.
>
> G. Mudzimu Area /Chidamoyo area – to be confirmed.
> Ian Suttill and Lucky. It is hoped that the booth will spend 2 days at Chidamoyo and 3 days at Mudzimu. Should this fail the liaison officer will have to arrange for the people

and SFA from Chidamoyo to vote at the Mudzimu booth. This booth will be positioned at the store west of Mudzimu School.

General

Base camps situated in the middle of polling areas such as Mahwada, Zvarayi will have to, in liaison with the respective liaison officers, mobilise the people to vote at the nearest polling booth. Likewise, the liaison officer will ensure that the sections in middle areas vote at the most convenient areas.

Food, cooking utensils and R$200.00 (for the purchase of relish and meat) will be given to each liaison officer. Once the people arrive at the polling booths it is essential that they remain until they cast their votes. It is suggested that when people come to vote the entire family is brought along to avoid excuses that they have to return to their families. As many blankets as available will also be provided for the exercise. Under no circumstances will the people be allowed to leave the booth areas until the they have voted. (Many locals would be walking long distances and required to stay at the polling stations for some time, possibly overnight. The allowance of R$200 was for the liaison officers to purchase meat, relish and refreshments for the people. This was in essence a celebration and we felt that it was our traditional responsibility to provide for the people.)

The duties of liaison officers at polling booths were clearly set out so that everyone knew what was expected of them:

Duties of liaison officers

1. Liaison between polling staff, Security Forces protecting the booths and callsigns in the field.
2. Assurance of the removal of all UANC flags, badges and political identifications of individual soldiers to the party. Party banners and posters presently used in the campaign may be left up, but personal kit must show no affiliation to the party.
3. Headquarters base camps need not be abandoned at this stage. However, when the press arrives in the area it may be required that specific, if not all HQs, close to polling booths are vacated for the day to avoid any undue international criticism.
4. It is essential that all sections remain out in the field to:
   a. mobilise people to vote;
   b. protect voters and their villages in the absence of the people;
   c. avoid confrontation with the Security Forces protecting the polling booths.

   It is obvious that we need as many men in the field as possible and only minimal men should remain at the HQ over the election period.
5. Assurance that all callsigns are uniformed by election day.
6. Liaison between the Security Forces protecting the polling booths and callsigns when callsigns coming in to vote. Sections to vote one section (or 2 as seen fit) at a time. Weapons to be left outside the polling booth area and section to leave the area immediately after they have voted. No sections to loiter around the polling booth area, they are to remain in the bush.
7. If the “Pookie” is not available normal sections and kraal cell system are to check roads daily for landmines and possible ambushes.
8. Sections are not to be seen to be herding people to the booths and if this is necessary sections to remain out of the sight of the booth while the people are sent forward to vote.
9. Close liaison between sections and detachment commanders and liaison officers to ensure that as many kraals are visited, and the people sent to vote.
10. Each liaison officer to select, in conjunction with the detachment commanders, 4 women to search African female voters i.e. 4 African females per polling booth. Females to be paid R$1.50 per day per person.
11. All sections coming in to vote to be given priority over the people to avoid them hanging

around. If press around care to be taken if possible that no sections are seen voting as the men may well sing or chant political slogans as they come out. This is to be avoided.

12. On the arrival of the polling booths and the UANC military wing, the local detachment commander to be introduced to the staff concerned to identify themselves, their uniforms and weapons, to avoid any possible confusion. A full briefing of the current situation in the area to be given by the local detachment commander.

The necessary arrangements and procedures were well in place. Shortly before the election period, we received information that one of our deserters had taken refuge in Chikangwe. Following a search, we located him in a crowded area of the township. As can be expected, he attempted to abscond and did not respond to our calls to halt, neither were we in a position to shoot him and, therefore, we gave chase. In a flash, my rugby-playing prowess returned and I caught up with the deserter and crashed-tackled him, landing awkwardly in a culvert. Unfortunately, I damaged my left knee, forcing me to receive treatment at the Andrew Fleming Hospital, in Salisbury. The doctors diagnosed that I had torn the cartilage and decided to operate immediately. The hospitalisation forced me out of action for several days and, I unfortunately missed the elections. However, there were two positive results to note. Firstly, I had managed to subdue the deserter. We subsequently collected his weapon and returned him to Chabwino. Secondly, our plans for the elections were in place and we had a reliable team to manage all eventualities.

This temporary respite from the war forced me to reflect on my life. As I pondered, five matters became obvious to me:

First, it was clear to me that Mugabe and Nkomo would not participate in any government except one of their own making, hence the war would continue. My thinking was, why should they participate in a shared government when their military victory was close at hand?

Second, I truly believed the only way to win the civil war was to use the system we had developed in Hurungwe, which had proven successful. Despite the success of our operations, I did not believe this achievement was understood or shared elsewhere in the country. It was obvious we were an isolated example and the remainder of Rhodesia was in a downward spiral.

Third, the Com.Ops. directive to hand over our operation to the RAR was inevitably materialising. While I enjoyed a good relationship with the military in our area who were doing a good job, I could not see the two methods of operation working together. There were benefits to amalgamation but they were greatly overshadowed by negative implications. The RAR's strength was in their conventional role, particularly their ability to strike and kill the enemy on specific intelligence. I believed that the military had specialised fields of operations, such as the Fire Force, Support Unit, PATU, RLI, Selous Scouts and Grey's Scouts. The people's army was another specialised operation. This was a people's war with a people's army and a very complex relationship between the political, the masses and the people's army. In my opinion, we had masterminded and implemented the only successful way to win this internal battle. I felt strongly that, if one is going to fight, then fight in a way that will be successful, where there is a believable and achievable political vision which attended to the GNA of the masses, whose support and trust should, under no circumstances, be broken. Otherwise, why is one fighting and facing death?

Fourth, the major question I had regarding the army was how long they would stay in the area after they had achieved their objective of free-and-fair elections. To leave at the conclusion of elections would, in my thinking, be abandoning the people.

Finally, I saw no logic in Com.Ops. demanding that we relinquish our operation in favour of the RAR. With no clear military understanding and thinking, it seemed to me, from this point forward, we would be deceiving the people who were, yet again, the "pawns in a game". I found these musings difficult to reconcile while recuperating.

22 ~ FINAL DAYS

If my soldiers were to begin to think,
not one of them would remain in the army.
Frederick the Great

Bishop Muzorewa Calls for More SFAs

The election in Hurungwe was a resounding success. All went according to plan and the men and staff carried out their duties exceptionally well. Sixty-five percent of the Hurungwe population turned out for the elections which the UANC won unanimously, winning all six seats in the Mashonaland West district.[1] Nationally, the UANC won 51 of the 72 Common Roll seats with the RF winning all of the 20 White Roll seats. Joseph Gumede became the first African President and Bishop Muzorewa was elected as the Prime Minister. It was interesting that there was minimal retaliation by ZIPRA during the election period in areas controlled by our men.[2] Maj. Rawstron recalls that ZIPRA were active in the area under his control during the elections.[3] On 22 April 1979, Lord St Oswald, a Conservative MP visiting the country, saw the victims of three incidents. Firstly, the deaths of four passengers killed when a bus returning from voting detonated a landmine. A further 41 passengers were injured, 15 seriously. Secondly, he saw two women who had been bayonetted as they prepared to leave their kraal to vote. Thirdly, an African male and female assaulted by five insurgents as they made their way to vote. Lord St Oswald condemned the violence carried out by insurgents.[4]

Nationally, 6,000 UANC and 2,000 Sithole SFAs were deployed at the time of the elections.[5] Following the election, Bishop Muzorewa proposed increasing the UANC forces to 26,000 men. Mike Edden was one of the team to visit the bishop to discuss the matter. Bishop Muzorewa realised the potential and necessity to drastically increase his military capability in order to support his political vision. The bishop was an African and, as such, had a clear concept of the African solution for the war. However, Edden did not consider SB had the capacity to administer and manage this increase in armed personnel. Edden approached the Commander of the Army, Brigadier Sandy Maclean, a former commander of the RAR. While proud of the RAR's record, Maclean, according to Edden: "Was adamant he wouldn't touch the SFAs with a barge pole." Consequently, Edden presented the problem to Nat.JOC, detailing the logistics and the inability of Special Branch to cope with the recruiting, training, equipping and deployments of the men to their respective operational areas. He further stressed that any weakening of SB's ability to provide intelligence would have a negative effect on the war and, more to the point, few in SB were trained as drill or musketry instructors. (Obviously I strongly disagree with Edden's perspective.) Nat.JOC agreed and the "job" was ironically handed over to Sandy Maclean. SB would be relieved of its role in the administration, as this was detrimental to their specialist role of intelligence gathering in the field. Maclean promoted Col. Dave Heppenstall to the rank of brigadier and handed him the task.[6]

Interestingly, in 1973, the OCC and JPS had considered forming an African militia that would enable the rural population to defend themselves against terrorist attacks. This idea was unpopular with both the politicians and the military, who did not want to arm the African population, and the

[1] http://www.rhodesia.nl/elect1.htm.
[2] Confirmed by Sandy Irvine and Mike Mingay oral interviews 19/4/2019.
[3] Gavin Rawstron WhatsApp discussion 19/4/2019.
[4] *The Sunday Mail* 22/4/1979.
[5] Mike Edden's unpublished memoirs, Chap. 26.
[6] Ibid pp. 350-352. Confirmed by Brig. Heppenstall oral interviews 14/5/2019 and 15/5/2019.

army refused to take them seriously as a legitimate fighting force.[1] After years of resistance, Ian Smith finally realised the necessity and benefit of the SFA on 4 September 1979. Ken Flower noted: "We officials in the War Council have had to listen to insistent demands for 'Militia-types', more 'Security Force Auxiliaries' and the rest, with Ian Smith for the first time strident in his demands. Yet, how many years ago was it that I was advocating just that – a 'Home Guard', or what the Bishop now calls 'The Presence of Men-with-Guns in the Tribal Areas' – advocating to deaf ears and against the bitter opposition of Ian Smith's Ministers who swore 'only over our dead bodies would we agree to munts[2] being armed'."[3]

In October 1979, Prime Minister Muzorewa, in London for the Lancaster House talks, instructed the SFA to immediately be increased to 26,000 men. However, it soon became apparent that the administration could not successfully monitor this number. A maximum of 16,000 was set by Nat.JOC, the highest figure ever achieved.[4]

As I reflected on these matters and re-examined my reports, I become intensely annoyed. I can only speak for our operations in Hurungwe which I knew were capable and poised to expand rapidly and orderly, yet at this vital junction of the war, denied the opportunity to do so. Clearly, in my view, there was a lack of understanding of the link between the political, the people, the people's army and intelligence aspects. I regarded these components as a single entity, yet many in leadership structures did not share my views. I envisaged control of the people by the military machinery as a retrogressive step, unless the military could adjust their operations to fit in with the people's army operations. This implementation would include permanent deployment in the same operational area. While hopeful, I was deeply aware nothing would come of the suggestion.

Bishop Muzorewa was an African leader who knew the potential of arming his people but was prevented from doing so by a military regime that would not break from traditional thinking, and was not prepared to relinquish control. This, even though their wholly African enemy had proven themselves a more-than-equal adversary, running amok in Zimbabwe Rhodesia. Mike Edden makes the point: "During the second half of 1979 considerable successes were achieved on operations, 66 terrorists were killed and another 93 captured. SFA losses during the same period were 98 killed in action or vehicle accidents, a further 100 were wounded or injured. There can be no shadow of doubt that the SFA had proved that they were an essential backup to the security forces and provided a link between the Government and the people in many of the areas in which the SFA were deployed. The situation would have been far worse in the country without them and they proved to be a thorn in the side of the Terrorists."[5] Unfortunately, although successful, SFAs were still seen as an extension of the Security Forces "kills-win-wars" strategy.

As I perceived matters at this stage of the war, the Security Forces were incapable of moving from the "kills-win-wars" mentality and continued to misunderstand that the people were the key to success. SFAs, in fact, were structured to support the SF and the existing government while vital, radical political changes were not considered necessary. The most fundamental principles of counter-revolution and mass mobilisation, which I had the experience of successfully implementing, in my view, were unfulfilled. The white population, and may I add, segments of the conservative African populace, were misled and deceived by a false psychological rhetoric of "the one who kills the most wins". To my way of thinking, the strategy adopted by the SF blinded them to the inevitability of defeat. I further considered Ian Smith's approach a suicidal denial of the unavoidable. Historical racial prejudices considered the African incapable of providing a military solution to the country's well-being. White politicians continued to assume that they could outmanoeuvre their African counterparts.

---

1 Mike Edden's unpublished memoirs, p. 347.

2 Derogatory term for Africans.

3 Flower, K. (1987), p. 231.

4 Mike Edden's unpublished memoirs, p. 354.

5 Ibid p. 347.

James Chikerema rallies in the Hurungwe and Kariba.

The author handing military authority to the political, represented by James Chikerema, for his rallies.

Solidarity.

Meeting the local officials.

Speaking to the people observed by the author.

Meetings gather momentum.

The author recording the meeting.

James Chikerema, Sandy Irvine and an UANC official overlooking the Kariba Dam wall.

James Chikerema addressing a rally at Kariba.

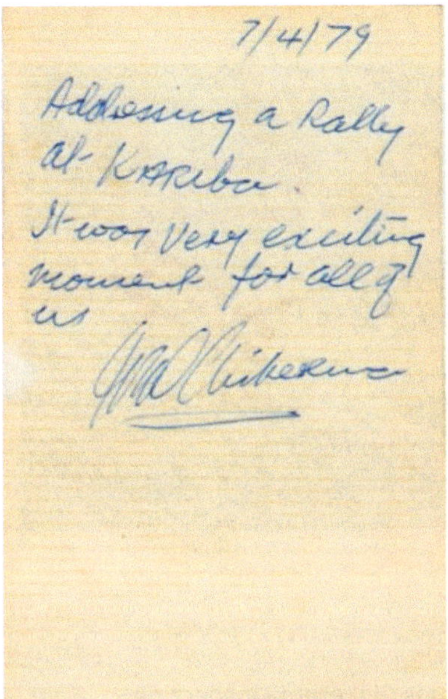

James Chikerema signed his photographs.

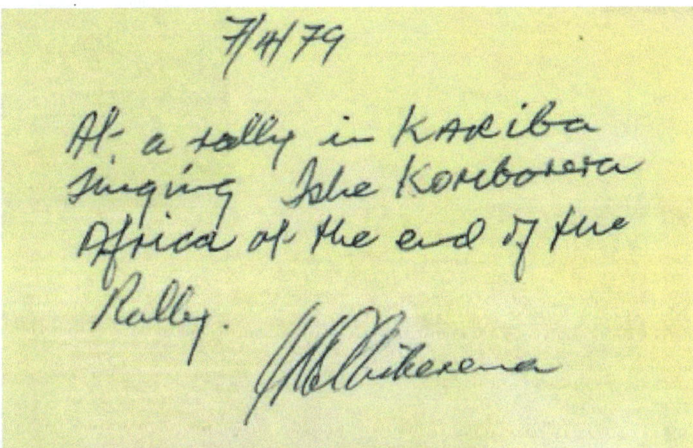

Singing *Ishe Komberera* (God bless Africa). L-R Chikerema, Lenard, Joseph.

James Chikerema rallies in the Omayi

Sandy Irvine loading the Kariba ferry for the Omay expedition. Maize bags front left and right. Photo by Sandy Irvine.

The Kariba ferry.

James Chikerema inspecting African policemen at Siakobvu police camp. Changing times!

Operation Omay. (L-R) Lenard, the author, James Chikerema, a UANC official and Sandy Irvine.

James Chikerema accepts the *hari*, signifying acceptance by the people.

The author enjoying the *hari* with Chief Nebiri.

James Chikerema in discussions with Tonga Chief Nebiri and his elders observed by the author.

The author, Manenji, a UANC official, Chief Nebiri, James Chikerema and Lenard. Note Lenard's .38 special revolver.

On the back of a truck driving to a meeting in the Omay. No fear of landmines or ambush! Lenard and James Chikerema seated next to Sandy Irvine (just out of the picture).

Maize-crop failure, in the Omay.

James Chikerema and the author contemplate the future at Siakobvu airfield.

The author, recovering from knee surgery, discusses Hurungwe operations with Capt. Padbury (carrying his operational diary).

Peter Anderson's float-plane.
Photo by Peter Anderson.

Time to Leave

Com.Ops. now demanded that our operation should be taken over by the military. We had 500 men trained and deployed permanently in the field, an effective administration, competent support structures, a strong training structure at Chabwino led by Ian Suttill, who had commenced retraining the men, and a strong combat-reconnaissance unit. Politically and militarily, in conjunction with the RAR, we had regained control of most of Hurungwe with only the western area remaining under ZIPRA control. Our men had successfully held the ground, protecting the people, continuing to develop intelligence networks and expanding their areas of operation and control. As a result of the people's vigilance, landmines and arms caches were pinpointed and lifted. When located, ZIPRA were attacked. Retaliations against ZIPRA did not necessarily yield kills but certainly harassed, demoralised and kept them at bay, with their influence and support continually on the wane.

The UANC political and military leaderships were loyal, faithful, trustworthy and completely committed to their cause and not to that of the "old regime". They were fighting for their own survival. Politically, the UANC were well established which resulted in a continuous flow of intelligence throughout our operational areas, including Hurungwe, Kariba, the Omay and bordering areas.

There was an endless flow of recruits desiring to join *Pfumo reVanhu* and, in my estimation, presented a virtual limitless number to the size of army we could train and deploy. Likewise, there was little except Com.Ops. opposing our expansion into adjoining TTLs. We had been denied the opportunity of extending our military operations into the Omay and other critical areas.

In conjunction with the RAR, we had achieved a major victory in Hurungwe. What was now required was a radical shift in political thinking, leading to rapid and significant political changes. SFAs numbers needed to increase meaningfully in order to support the newly elected Muzorewa Government. Bishop Muzorewa had personally told me that he wanted to exponentially increase the numbers of SFAs but was prevented from doing so. I found this news distressing, as our operations and approach to the war had proven that victory was achievable. Sadly, this did not occur. Ian Smith and his regime lurked in the background, retaining power and influence, while ZANLA and ZIPRA vowed to continue hostilities. To the dismay of scores of Rhodesian citizens, the international community, the British Government included, did not recognise the newly elected government, in spite of Lord Owen's efforts. Zimbabwe Rhodesia's only hope was the recently elected British Conservative Government, led by Margaret Thatcher. However, the Conservative manifesto for the elections held on the 3 May 1979 was clear: "The Conservative Party will aim to achieve a lasting settlement to the Rhodesia problem based on the democratic wishes of the people of that country. If the Six Principles, which all British Governments have supported for the last fifteen years, are fully satisfied following the present Rhodesian Election, the next government will have the duty to return Rhodesia to a state of legality, move to lift sanctions, and do its utmost to ensure that the new independent state gains international recognition."[1] This was yet another "not to be". In short, the war intensified as Mugabe and Nkomo methodically continued the bloodshed en route to victory.

Despite our undeniable political and military successes, Com.Ops. demanded that I hand over my operation to the country's military leadership. Faced with no alternative, I reluctantly did so. Despite their assurances to the contrary, I had reservations, in particular regarding their length of stay in Hurungwe. In time, I would be proven right. In my view, Com.Ops. were in a state of crisis management as they tried to maintain a semblance of peace in a rapidly deteriorating situation throughout the country. They steadfastly ignored the significance of our operations and were incapable of adopting the alternative approach to military strategies and tactics. The fact that Ian Smith and the RF were determined to maintain control exemplified the futility of the war effort and plummeted the country into capitulation.

I had walked with, worked with, fought with and, in time, became one with the people. I had observed the war from their perspective. I had witnessed young men volunteer willingly to face

---

1 Located at https://www.margaretthatcher.org/document/110858.

death in order to protect their own lives, those of their families and friends and, indeed, their land. Such was their commitment to our cause. I had seen unarmed men and women who were prepared to infiltrate and operate "behind enemy lines" in a resistance movement which grew daily in intensity, strength and resolve. I had witnessed men from the UANC risk their lives driving civilian vehicles while unarmed and unescorted into areas traditionally held by ZIPRA prior to our occupation of Hurungwe. Why? Because they had been invaded by ZIPRA who were murdering those opposed to their political and military agenda, destroying administration, destabilising the entire area, including road travel, clinics, education and plundering families of household resources, and prostituting their wives and daughters. In Hurungwe, the UANC was achieving their political vision through the military wing of the Special Force Auxiliaries, which offered and achieved for the people peace, stability, protection and a promise backed up by action for eventual majority rule. At no time did I feel under threat from the 500 armed men in the field. In fact, I felt safe with them, knowing they had the support and complete co-operation of the people. The experience of such mutual trust and general security in a war zone, knowing the people were one's "eyes and ears" was deeply etched in my mind.

We had proven beyond doubt that our counter-revolution and mass-mobilisation strategies functioned. We had demonstrated it was possible to integrate with armed Africans and gain the support of the people by employing the correct political agenda, despite the opposition of the RF Government and many SF personnel. I had also seen first-hand the dedication, commitment and expertise of the SF, fighting relentlessly for an unachievable political agenda. This irony was not lost on me as I contemplated my future in the country I loved.

From the commencement of our first *mujibha* farm, I was convinced that we were on a pathway to success. The SFAs provided a sound strategy for winning the war but, sadly, in my opinion, our efforts had become pointless. In addition, my personal life lay in tatters. I faced a bleak future with no immediate career prospects. I felt abandoned by my own country's political and military leadership, coupled with the growing realisation that I could no longer consider "Rhodesia" home.

As I reflected on the "the seasons in my life", I felt that I had reached the end of this chapter in my life. The door had shut. My agreement to continue serving in the BSAP Special Branch Reserve, with Geoff Price, had already been extended by two months and our visas for residence in South Africa had arrived. Living there was not my first choice. I considered their apartheid laws archaic but at least I had work available, providing the opportunity of earning a salary. The Rhodesian Front policies had succeeded in indoctrinating me against the British, therefore, for the time being, the United Kingdom was not an option for repatriation. Additionally, in my state of mind at the time, this was a "bridge too far". My only consolation was that my men were officially under the wing of the Com.Ops. directives. Notwithstanding, I did not trust their leadership for the long term, as I felt their approach to the country's political future was crisis-driven. It was my view that they discussed ideas but failed in the implementation of their many lofty ideals. In fact, I was firmly convinced that Com.Ops. was directionless. As I considered Zimbabwe Rhodesia's long-term prospects, in my view, there was no distinct political vision, and Ian Smith and his fellow politicians had failed abysmally. I believed defeat was "knocking at the door". I despised the politicians who had failed their citizens and led the country to defeat and many of her people into exile.

With our operations now in the hands of the RAR, I recorded my final diary entry:

SUBJECT: SECURITY FORCE AUXILIARIES 1/5/79

This report is compiled from experiences gained in the field, interrogations of captured terrorists, ideas gleaned from externally trained and indoctrinated terrorists (in Russia, Cuba, Libya, Tanzania, etc.) who have now returned to this country and who have been released from detention in terms of the March 3rd Agreement, and ideas gleaned from operational SB Police Reserve personnel.

This report should be read in conjunction with my reports dated the 14/3/79 on the same subject, and my report headed SFAs Hurungwe TTL which I regret was not dated

> but was circulated to addressees during the latter part of February 1979. The latter report is of particular interest with regards to this report.
>
> I find it debatable as to whether these reports play any significance in policy decisions whatsoever and, in fact, whether or not the contents are understood and digested. Certainly, with regards to my latter previously mentioned report, there are important policy decisions that we are still awaiting decisions on.

I closed my diary abruptly. This was the end! Our operations had been a complete success and I foresaw the victory slipping away. Maj. Graham Des Fountain continues: "Hurungwe SFA operation, often referred to as the 'Cinderella Operations Area', was our most successful area, largely due to the tight control of the UANC force by the in-house command and control, monitored and directed by John Padbury and the Rhodesian staff under his control, in close liaison with Grey, Happy and the UANC team. This success was based on close liaison of its UANC military forces with the local Hurungwe citizenry. There was a good flow of intelligence to and fro throughout the area and as a result great military successes were achieved. This area differed from all the other SpF areas because of its complete localised infrastructure."[1]

Dennis Anderson commented: "I visited John Padbury on the 9th November 1978 and on other occasions. On this visit the Officer Commanding Ground Coverage, Ch.Supt. Jamie Whitelaw accompanied me. The Hurungwe was the most successful SFA operation and probably the only area where civil administration was returned to normal; schools and clinics were reopened, dipping restarted and roads kept clear of mines for bus and general vehicle transport."[2]

RAR in Hurungwe TTL

When Maj. Gavin Rawstron from B Company 1RAR arrived in Hurungwe on 27 January 1979, we were fully operational. The RAR officially began the process of assuming command of our operations after the April elections. Up to this point, as a combined operation, it was successful, as we had developed a good working relationship. As I saw matters, this would be a difficult transition and, while I could envisage the benefits, I felt there were pitfalls which I have previously mentioned. I was concerned about the integration of the army with the SFAs. Our forces and the people had been politicised with the understanding that the SFAs were in charge of military operations in Hurungwe. As Maj. Rawstron commented: "The local population would not accept any member of the SF in uniform, be they Army, Police, Intaf or Guard Force. The reason for this was due to previous experiences by them of considerable SF harassment, beatings and in some cases, alleged murder. The result of this was that all SF credibility had been lost. The SFA's themselves did not accept SF as they regarded themselves as the only representatives of the people and their sole 'liberators'."[3] Long-term success of Com.Ops. insistence that the RAR take command of our SFAs depended on detailed specific "marry-up drills and procedures". Marry-up drills and procedures is specific military terminology and activity to ensure cohesion and co-operation between the forces concerned in order to ensure a successful operation. In my view, the RAR was integrating with the SFA. The SFA were not becoming RAR soldiers. I felt a two-tier system would not function adequately. The role of the military was to assist with the training and equipping of the SFA to operate in their specific (SFAs) function. We had our own effective modus operandi and code of conduct which challenged traditional military thinking. The full force of the political was interwoven in all aspects of our operations, including conduct and discipline, which contradicted conventional military thinking. In my opinion, the military had failed. Their only hope, in my view, was to become one with the SFA. A three-phase approach was required:

---

1 Graham Des Fountain email 24/1/2018. Confirmed by Brig. Heppenstall, CO Special Forces oral interview 15/5/2019.

2 Former BSAP Insp. Will Keys email 28/7/2018.

3 Secret Handover/Takeover report: Pfumo re Vanhu, dd. 2/9/1979, pp. 2-3.

First, induction of the RAR (military) to the SFA in order to become one with them and, thereby, one with the people.

Second, introduction of white personnel to the SFA in order that they could integrate with the people's army, and understand the African and his ways, as well as being accepted by the SFA and the people.

Third, SFA schooled and integrated into the military. This final stage was essential for the greater benefit of the nation as a whole. It would enable the SFA to understand and accept that they were a necessary and vital part of the bigger picture in the defence of the nation as a whole in the new political dispensation, and alleviate the likelihood of the political militia running amok.

The UANC political and military wings fully supported the RAR operations and co-operated with them.[1] Maj. Rawstron sent a report to his brigade commander in July 1979, outlining the success of the SFA in Hurungwe. He also noted limitations from his perspective and I have commented on these. Whether Maj. Rawstron's traditional military thinking would fully grasp and adjust to our revolutionary war remained to be seen. I doubted that the RAR would remain in Hurungwe on a permanent basis. His report was as follows:

To: Bde. Comd' HQ 2 Bde.	From: B. Coy 1 RAR
Cc: Comd HQ Special Forces	Magunje Base Camp
	Major Gavin Rawstron
Urungwe Tribal Trust Land	25 July 1979

SECURITY FORCE AUXILIARIES: HURUNGWE TRIBAL TRUST LAND

Aim

The aim of this report is to bring out the concept of SFA deployment, the successes achieved by them in the TTL, and their limitations.

Introduction

The Urungwe TTL was initially allocated as a 'Test Ground' for SFA under the name of IGF (Interim Government Forces), in August 1978. Initially, it was under the supervision of John Padbury and his team, who until Feb 1979, were responsible for the training, deployment, administration, Command and Control of approximately 200 Auxiliaries recruited from their respective areas.

In Feb 1979, B Coy 1 RAR were given the task of taking over command of all SFA in Hurungwe TTL. A total of 200 SFA's were deployed in Central Hurungwe, another 200 were to undergo training at Chabwino Farm (just outside Karoi) and a further 50 to be trained at Paradys Farm.

A total of 262 recruits were trained between Feb and the elections in April 1979 by B Coy 1 RAR Instructors at Paradys Farm (QL604934) and Penstock Farm (QM 656455)

A total of 700 SFA's were deployed by the elections, covering approx. 90% of Urungwe TTL.

Prior to the deployment of SFA's, all schools had been closed down as a result of CT action, bus services were no longer operating, all dips were closed and only 1 clinic (Magunje) remained open.

All locals in Urungwe TTL were considered subverted and anti-Government.

Deployment

Recruits were initially deployed to Katenhe (QM 599288) as it was fairly

[1] Exemplified by the fact that a senior UANC official, John Mutuve, attended the SFA pass-out ceremony at the RAR base.

central. Once that area was secured and the locals were back on sides, further deployments took place radiating outwards.

By Feb 1979, the following areas were secured under the Padbury Team:

a. Katenhe
b. Magunje
c. Kebvunde
d. Chidzimamoto
e. Kweche
f. Mudzimu

By April 1979, the following areas were secured by both Padbury and B Coy 1 RAR Teams:

a. Chidzimamoto
b. Chitiki
c. Mahwada
d. Kapfunde
e. Kavaya
f. Zvarai
g. Chinyembwe
h. Nyamutora
i. Karereshi
j. Kahonde
k. Chisape
l. Maumbe
m. Nyampfukudza
n. Zvipani
o. Nyamhunga
p. Mashuma
q. Bhururuka
r. Chigede

Base strengths depended entirely on the activity of CT's in the area.

After elections, the whole command, control and administration was passed on to B Coy 1 RAR. The Padbury House in Karoi was closed down and B Coy 1 RAR Base HQ established at Magunje. Chabwino Training Base closed down and Penstock Training Base continued.

John Padbury and the majority of his controllers were withdrawn.

Pre-election Aims

The main objective given to operations in Hurungwe prior to the elections was to mobilise the masses in order to get a high percentage vote and to establish an environment where free-and-fair voting could take place.

This was achieved and statistics reveal that Hurungwe had a 65% turnout, however, these figures were based on the 1969 figures. Since CT incursions into the area, a fairly large percentage of the local population had moved into the built-up areas and local farms. A local estimate is believed to have been in the region of 90% of those physically living in the TTL at the time.

Tribal Administration

As mentioned previously, Tribal Administration had all but collapsed prior to SFA deployments into the area as a result of CT activity.

By the end of Feb 1979, 7 schools had re-opened and bus services restored to Magunje.

By elections, 13 schools had re-opened and bus services to Mudzimu and Maumbe restored.

A total of 18 schools have been re-opened as of this date and a number of clinics under SF and SFA supervision have been established in most areas of the TTL.

The following are schools that have been re-opened:

a.	Charles Clack	QM581363	
b.	Maumbe	QM556434	
c.	Katenhe	QM495377	(Should be QM5928)
d.	Chisapi / Chinembiri	QM634328	
e.	Kebvunde	QM544340	
f.	Nyamtora	QM662185	
g.	Kapfunde	QM565116	
h	Zvarai	QM574052	
i.	Tengwe	QM614015	
j	Mahwada	QM506046	
k.	Mudzimu	QM468095	
l.	Matau	QM355226	
m.	Chidzimamoto	QM517223	
n.	Nyamupfukudza	QM510513	
o.	Kapare	QM638288	
p.	Kavaya	QL533975	
q.	St Gabriels	QM444127	
r.	Magunje	QM580365	

(Author's note: The following schools had also been opened, making a total of 20 schools reopened:

s.	Kweche	QM605194
t.	Nyarumwe	QM623105)

In some cases where schools had been destroyed by CT's, the locals re-built them with the help of SF and SFAs. Pupil attendance far exceeded numbers provided prior to the schools being re-opened. This was partly due to the politicians promising free education during their electioneering campaign.

As there was a shortfall of teachers, schools were having to teach the school children on a rotational basis.

Additional Comments not originally in this paper

Deployment under B Coy 1 RAR

As recruits completed their training, they were then armed and given the necessary uniforms and equipment and deployed to the various areas from which they came.

Attached to them were elements of SF (1 RAR) who provided them with the basic infrastructure of transport, communications, medical, etc.

As they were deployed into the new areas, a number of contacts ensued where unknown numbers of CT's were wounded. Documents recovered from these contacts revealed that some died as a result of their injuries and that the ZIPRA hierarchy were extremely concerned at the turn of events.

ZIPRA tactics then changed, whereas, in the early stages, they would move around in small groups of 10-20, they then moved in groups of 100 plus. They also started to avoid built-up populated areas and were forced to move to the western area where there was no SFA presence. A number of contacts and sightings took place between SF and CT's, but because air support was not available due to external operations taking place in other parts of the country, results were not as good as they could have been. We suspected that ZIPRA had possession of radios and that they were tuning in to SF communications although this was not conclusively proven. Our men found themselves in a number of situations that were detrimental and counter measures had to be implemented. We suspected that one of our callsigns was lured into an ambush by ZIPRA using radios. On 31 March 1979 Sgt. Hamandishe (644775) was leading a callsign and were clearing the roads for landmines. For a split second Hamandishe hesitated when he saw Rhodesian camouflage in the high ground at QM520229 - he shouted out to them for identification and was shot and killed.[1] Capt. Joseph Columbus Smith attended the scene, collected Sgt. Hamandishe's body and surveyed the area. I was away at the time of the contact, but later attended and established that our men were ambushed from a piece of high ground next to the road by about 50 terrs (as I can remember). Spoor leaving the area was initially easy to follow but became more difficult as groups kept on splitting up. As far as I can remember, I deployed a Platoon of my guys the following day into the populated area ahead of where we lost spoor, but they were not able to get any concrete results. An investigation uncovered that an Indian shop had sold the CTs our uniforms, purchased on the black market.[2]

On 28 June 1979 L/Cpl. Richard Maworera, an NCO in 6pl B Coy, was on a patrol in Western part of Hurungwe. During a contact with ZIPRA he was shot in the chest. Unfortunately, there were no helicopters in the area to casevac him out and he succumbed to his wound.[3] I was very angry and deployed with a small team into an OP position at night, overlooking a built-up area. In the morning we sited 20 terrs 3Ks away, too far for us to engage and FF was not available.[4] When we noted that there were no locals in the area, I assumed our position had been compromised and we withdrew under the cover of dark.

On another occasion one of our vehicles took a direct hit from an RPG7, fortunately there were no injuries.[5]

During the period in which B Coy 1 RAR were deployed in Hurungwe, a total of 36 landmines were recovered that had been laid by the enemy. Only 1 was driven over by one of our vehicles, but fortunately did not detonate as the detonators had been placed in upside-down.[6] Those recovered were as a direct result of information from the locals, indicating the extent of co-operation and assistance from them.

There were a number of SFA's that went AWOL, some with their weapons (2) who joined ZIPRA, and the others because they were dead scared of being killed.

Various meetings were held with the headmen and locals and addressed

---

1 Confirmed by Capt. Joseph Columbus Smith (USA) who adds: "This gifted NCO was scheduled for officer training at Gwelo and was a huge loss. He was a Muslim and I remember buying small kapenta fish from Kariba. He couldn't eat regular rations. He was my only loss in the RAR, and I regret his loss deeply." Email 4/4/2017.

2 Karoi Contacts Map Incident 51.

3 Karoi Contacts Map Incident 52.

4 Karoi Contacts Map Incident 53.

5 Karoi Contacts Map Incident 54.

6 Karoi Landmine Map 20.

by myself and some of my senior staff that were very fruitful and showed the amount of support that we had been able to obtain, so much so, that when we were eventually given the orders to move back to Methuen Barracks without replacement, a number of local leaders pleaded with us to remain.

Some of the Disadvantages

Integrating the Company with semi-trained SFA's had a distinct disadvantage in that the junior ranks were subject to the temptations of drink and women. These vices were readily available to them through the local SFA's. Apart from sexual diseases, morale and discipline took a very definite turn for the worse. Being "stood down" from this task could not have happened any later and I was glad to regain what had been temporarily lost. (Author's note: Herein lies the difference between a true people's revolutionary army and the traditional military approach. I believed that the RAR should integrate with the SFAs and not the other way round. The military were not trained for this revolutionary role which was a proven effective counter-revolutionary strategy. In my view, they lacked the capacity, ability and suitable training to adapt accordingly … they could not make the necessary paradigm shift. This was not the fault of the "foot soldiers" but clearly reveals a serious flaw in the Security Forces command machinery, across the board, in their inability to clearly analyse the facts that stared them in the face, and adapt accordingly. Furthermore, it revealed Ian Smith's unwillingness to adapt appropriately for the good of the nation. In reality, it was all about paradigm shift and adaptability. Personally, and importantly, I did not see my command of the SFAs as a task. Rather, it was the solution, an opportunity to defend, liberate and attend to the people's GNA, in order to become one with the people for the good and future of the nation: the only way to win the war!)

I feel that the fact that we were not replaced would have had a detrimental effect on the morale of the SFA's and the local population as a whole. A tremendous amount of time and effort had been put into getting them "on side", only to drop them in the proverbial "Cart". This would have had a negative impact on the final elections prior to independence. (Author's note: This was my major concern from the outset and confirms Com.Ops. complete misunderstanding of counter-revolutionary and mass-mobilisation principles. The military abandoned the people, again!)

That we were not able to carry out our conventional tasks as normal, resulting in minimal number of kills. (Author's note: Herein lies the conflict between the traditional military strategy that success and victory is based on kills, as opposed to the principle of winning the people by attending to their GNA and protecting them, which inevitably leads to kills.)

The collapse of all local administration resulted in no maintenance of roads and upkeep of administration buildings. Accessibility to various areas was therefore difficult and time consuming.[1]

RAR Modus Operandi in Hurungwe

As far as deployments were concerned, I had 1 platoon (33 men) in reserve at HQ and their task would have been reaction standby. The other 2 platoons would have been integrated with the SFA groups and deployed into their respective areas. My Officers and NCO's would have given them the necessary leadership and skills backup as well as continued training in the field. As time went on and the SFA leadership showed that they could continue on their own, my guys were withdrawn and sent to newer areas. White officers were kept at HQ for obvious reasons. SFA areas normally had a minimum of a

[1] Gavin Rawstron email 6/7/2016.

section strength attached. We tried to rotate the platoons as much as possible so as to give them a break as well as re-instill discipline. We were in the area approx. 8 months before being redeployed elsewhere.

The only area that we were not able to cover was the western area. Recruiting from that area was more difficult as well as the terrs were more established there. I remember going in there under cover of darkness with about 10 guys and had a sighting (approx. 4 kms away), of approx. 20 terrs moving NE before 10 a.m. Unfortunately, we had no air support or Fire Force at the time to call in as they were occupied on an external. We decided to sit tight and see what transpired, but there was no further movement for the following couple of days. Unfortunately, I had to return to Base to take care of other issues. I sent my reaction platoon in by vehicle a couple of days later and they were ambushed by RPG, RPD and small arms fire. Fortunately, there were no casualties.

It was obvious that the terrs still had full co-operation from the locals in this area. Unfortunately, we were redeployed before we could sort that area out.

I do remember one of the UANC operatives who was trained overseas was Katima. We had a lot of co operation and assistance from him. I cannot remember the names of the others.[1]

The RAR moved out of Hurungwe at the beginning of September 1979 and, as I initially suspected, were not replaced. Fortunately, the UANC political and military wings had remained active throughout the changes and continued to function with the assistance of Admin. and headed up initially by Tony Coom and later Mike Mingay. As a result, I managed a sense that all was not lost. As I continued to observe the country's deteriorating fabric, beyond Hurungwe, politicians were calling for economic and military aid. Politically, they demanded international recognition and the lifting of sanctions but, in my view, from a platform of defeat, laying the collapse of the country on a variety of factors ignoring their own incompetence. I thought, and I would suspect, so did scores of others, that the country was in an utter shambles, with Ian Smith's "Never in a thousand years" nothing more than a haunting ghost-like comment from the pages of fiction.

Situation at Combined Operations

My brother, Capt. David Padbury, makes the comment:

> Combined Operations was the hub of the command and control for the Rhodesian Bush War. Much has been written about it by various people over years gone by, and many views as to the effectiveness, or otherwise, of this War Office have been aired.
>
> Questions have been raised about the seniority of Lt. Gen. Peter Walls: should he have been made a full General; would it have made a difference in the Command and Control function; would it have made a difference in the outcome of the war; was there agreement among Senior Commanders? Perhaps most interesting, was the question "was Peter Walls the right man for the job"? and many more. My opinion is that Ian Smith's style was to divide and rule, and to have a Supreme Commander was not in his agenda. To have promoted Walls would have vested too much power in one man, and he did not want this to happen. This was equally seen in his policy of refusing to promote black Rhodesians in the various branches of the Armed Services. When he did, it was too little, too late.
>
> Criticism has regularly been levelled at Com.Ops. about the efficiency, strategy, handling and many other aspects of the command over the war effort, some have merit, others do not. However, for me, there are perhaps two major aspects that stood out when it comes to the debate about Com.Ops.:

[1] Ibid.

First, there was no Strategic Aim, Political or Military. This was a critical aspect that caused the Military to be reactionary rather than proactive, the result of the Political masters of the day not really knowing where they were going, and the reliance of the Political leaders on statistics to mislead and draw their constituency into a false sense of security and misguided support. Com.Ops. was dictated to by this political swamp of increasingly desperate politicians who knew that they were on a road to nowhere as early as 1972, and remained in total denial, despite warnings from Com.Ops. General Staff that the war could not be won.

Second, there were severe financial limitations. This aspect was less well known and had a major impact on the conduct of the war.

These two issues had a major impact, imposing severe limitations on the conduct, direction and outcome of the war.

Sitting in the Com.Ops. pub after a particularly stressful period of Operations, I had a typical discussion between brother Officers about various happenings with the Chief of Staff Operations, Major General Bert Barnard. I was a mere Captain at the time but had perhaps one of the privileged appointments in Combined Operations Headquarters, that of Staff Officer 2 Intelligence (Army). It gave me an insight into Com.Ops. that very few saw, and at a level that brought about an understanding of the desperate state of the war. I also had a unique insight into all aspects of Special Operations, which was my dedicated task with regard to my intelligence work. During this discussion I raised the question about Strategy and the Military Aim. In any war, the Strategic Aim is most critical. It goes well beyond this simplistic statement, as every aspect and facet of the military effort must be focused on achieving the Strategic Aim. It goes even further; every aspect and facet of Government must have a Strategic Aim and pursue it. Without it the country, and the security forces, have no direction, becoming reactive as opposed to being proactive, and ending in defeat. The Strategic Aim dictates the way the war is fought, the desired Strategic Outcomes, the tactics employed to achieve it, and the allocation of resources to support it. The Strategic Aim of the Military comes from the Political Strategic Aim and supports the Government in achieving it.

In this discussion the response was that there must be a Com.Ops. Strategic Aim. The debate continued, and it soon became clear that perhaps this should be pursued. It was indeed pursued: various Planning Officers holding the keys of the war machine were gathered together the next morning to answer the question "What is the Strategic Aim of Combined Operations?" There wasn't one. Not only that, it became very obvious that there was no Political Strategic Aim, and if there was, it was not known nor was it obvious or clearly understood. This was February 1979!

Around the same time, I had occasion to present an external target to Lt. Gen. Walls. This particular target was one that we had been building on for a number of months, and it was now at the stage that it could be presented for approval as an Operation. Due to the sensitivity of the target, I gave a preliminary overview to Lt. Gen. Walls, the Deputy Commander of Com.Ops. Air Marshal McLaren and the Chief of Staff Operations Major General Barnard. At the end of this short brief there was a very short discussion which ended with Lt. Gen. Walls commenting: "David, how do you evaluate the importance of this target, will it make a major impact on the war? We have only a week's worth of ordinance left to fight the war internally and are battling to get more in. This target will take all we have left." (Lt. Gen. Walls confirmed this in a post-war interview.) I recall as a young Platoon Commander the many instructions handed down to conserve ammunition, along with other essential resources, but this was the first time that I came face to face with the reality that the war was being greatly impacted by the restricted and limited resupply from beyond our borders.

I must admit that I was pretty shattered. The answer was obvious, and it brought home the stark reality of our precarious situation. There was no hope of sustaining this war, let alone any hope of a favourable political settlement.

Before the end of my tour at Combined Operations, and my move to the SAS as their Intelligence Officer, I had occasion to call Lt. Gen. Walls out of a meeting that was being held in his office to answer a call from Colonel Reid-Daly, Commander of the Selous Scouts. Lt. Gen. Walls was not enamoured with this intrusion, and his words to the Colonel were "Ron, this better be important and not a waste of time. The country is bleeding". It was a short conversation!

Lt. Gen. Walls has been accused by some of selling the country out. The reasons for their argument are varied, and I find no substance to these. In my dealings with Lt. Gen. Walls I found that in all things he placed the welfare of the country, its people and the men and the women of the armed forces first. This is emphasised by a statement he relayed by radio to me when I had occasion to be in a Lynx overhead the battle for Mapai during Operation Uric. My task was to co-ordinate military aspects on the ground. During the early part of the day we had lost a South African Puma helicopter carrying Engineers and RLI troopers into the battle. The battle continued throughout the day, and Mapai proved to be a hard nut to crack. Towards mid afternoon a further bombing run was ordered onto Mapai, and this was duly executed. It was my contention that Mapai could now be taken by the SAS who were tasked with this aspect of the operation. Lt. Gen. Walls intervened and spoke to me personally on the radio, stating that he would like the order to withdraw to be given as the country had already a great deal to grieve over, and he did not want to have to add to the grief by adding any further needless casualties to the day.[1]

The impact of this radio transmission was to be driven home a number of years later when I became aware that the Senior Command element of Combined Operations already knew that the war could not be won, and they had relayed this to Ian Smith in a signed letter. In addition, they had also considered a coup to save the country from further sadness. People may have their personal views on this, but for me it shows the measure of Lt. Gen. Walls, his dedication to the country, its people and in particular the forces that were under his command. The loss of life in the latter years of the war were unnecessary as the war was already a lost cause, and the politicians were intransigent in their sincerity to end it. In the end the Politicians had made the sale, and the sale had no return clause.

The question about the chaotic state of Com.Ops. at the end has been raised: it may well have been so in the eyes of many. However, it is well to take into considerable account the hurried and almost indecent way the hand-over came about. So much had to be done in such a short time, emotions were running high, there was very little account given to those of the forces that took the brunt for a political system that simply collapsed, let them down and discarded them. The never-ending circle of war played itself out… "Thank you Tommy, now go home". The Politician had, once again, used and abused. As the end came Ian Smith meddled, manipulated and castigated others to vindicate himself.[2]

Let down by other parties outside our borders? Yes, but I personally believe that there was a greater let down from failed internal political strategy, or lack of it, as well as a bungling Prime Minister![3]

---

1 Operation Uric (5/9/1979-7/9/1979): Casualties included one Bell helicopter shot down with an RPG-7 with Senior Aircraftsman Alex Wesson being killed and Fl. Lt. Dick Paxton surviving. A South African Air Force Smersh 330 Puma Helicopter 194 was shot down with an RPG-7, killing all three South African crew members and 14 Rhodesian Security Forces personnel. Moorcraft, P., McLaughlin, P. (2008), pp. 62-68.

2 Smith, I. (1997), *passim,* especially Chap. 21.

3 David Padbury emails 5/12/2016 and 10/4/2018; Petter-Bowyer, P. (2005), pp. 298-300.

Forced into an irreconcilable political and military situation, agreement was finally reached at an all-parties conference at Lancaster House, London, England, in 1979. The Lancaster House Agreement was signed on 21 December 1979, leading to recognised independence on 18 April 1980, after another controversial election process. In my opinion, the agreement was a "face-saving" capitulation that avoided the looming reality of military defeat.

ZANU, led by Robert Mugabe, won an overwhelming yet contentious victory. The UANC won three seats, one of which was in Mashonaland West, which included our operational area.

SFAs in training with the RAR.

Physical training.

On the march.

On parade.

Observing events at the SFAs pass-out parade. (L-R) BSAP GC operator, two UANC military wing officials, Maj. Rawstron, senior UANC official, John Muteve, and Manenji.

John Muteve meets the men: (L-R) CSM Jonah Chitcrcka, WO2 Gibson and Maj. Rawstron.

Maj. Rawstron and John Muteve take the salute at an SFAs pass-out parade.

23 ~ CONCLUSION

I believe many governments, organisations and institutions in the world are in a state of perpetual revolution and counter-revolution. Our lives ought to be revolutionary by nature.
John Padbury

The Rhodesian civil war of 1893 simmered in the 1960s, bubbled in the 1970s and boiled over in the spring of 1975. With the stroke of a pen, UDI stoked the smouldering embers of the First *Chimurenga* of 1896, and ignited the indomitable flame of African nationalism sweeping throughout Africa, frankly acknowledged by the British Prime Minister, Harold Macmillan, in his "Winds of Change" speech on 3 February 1960.

With no meaningful progressive political vision for the people, the only SF military strategy possible was to eliminate the enemy, an unachievable goal. Rhodesian Security Forces responded to the escalating war with commitment and determination, with the benefit of complete air superiority. Despite this and the many military successes inflicted on the enemy, the Rhodesian forces had increasing difficulty combating the military onslaught and growing expertise of the ZANLA and ZIPRA forces as they surged into the country. Notwithstanding massive loss of life, the insurgents continued to fight on in pursuit of their politically inspired liberation. The elite Rhodesian forces could no longer win the war by flying around in helicopters and battling isolated sections of insurgents. Completely overlooked was the point that the Patriotic Front, in particular ZANLA, had won the political battle for the hearts and minds of the people and had gained their overwhelming support.

The Rhodesian Government gradually deviated from its ideology of white minority rule to the limited inclusion of Africans. Failure to integrate the races and allow people to vote was a major obstacle to national and international acceptance. A large percentage of the Security Forces were Africans who fought and died alongside their white compatriots. The RF Government fundamentally refused to integrate the forces and denied African members equal opportunity and the same conditions of service, that is until it was too late, as ZANLA and ZIPRA had their sights on the "finish line".

Thrust into a war not of our making, without training, preparation or overall strategy, BSAP Special Branch and Ground Coverage intelligence agencies made rapid adjustments. It was a matter of survival. In the Rusape district, we developed strategies and tactics and were enmeshed in the misplaced principle that "kills win wars". Many victories in isolated battles were achieved but we were being increasingly alienated from the people. We were losing the war, period! In the Rusape district, we initiated and developed a successful *mujibha* system, fore-runner of the Security Force Auxiliaries. Disappointingly, arming local Africans was never a Rhodesian Front Government policy. They opposed the idea of mass mobilisation until the March 3rd 1978 "internal agreement" when, in chaotic desperation, they reversed their policies. It was no longer treasonable to talk to African nationalists, and mobilising and arming the masses became acceptable.

In this last-minute, panic-stricken move, it was thought that the SFAs would finally protect the chiefs, headmen, kraalheads and locals in their rural domiciles. The chiefs were originally part of the Rhodesian Front Government's administration and proposed solution to their political dilemma. Ian Smith stated: "I know of no method which gives more honest and genuine representation, stemming from the 'grassroots' and ensuring that the people's feelings are accurately submitted and explained. The system is devoid of corruption, nepotism, intimidation, propaganda and brainwashing, all those evil and undesirable ingredients which play such an important part in modern government."[1] Unfortunately, these traditionally recognised leaders carefully selected by the RF Government because of their support of it, were abandoned due to RF policies. Many had been violently assaulted and killed by ZANLA and ZIPRA.

One of the SFA objectives was to gain support and votes for the "internal settlement". Regrettably, in my opinion, the SFAs were generally considered an extension of the Security Forces and beneficial to increasing the kill-rate. Nat.JOC's discussions about a military coup in order to oust Ian Smith's Interim Government reflected the dire political and military situation facing the country. The commanders realised that the only political solution was a return to the legality of British rule. However, even this extreme action was complicated by intricate national and international politics. There was no simple solution. As the war raged on and ZANU and ZAPU increasingly gained military ascendancy, they were less inclined to negotiate. These leaders knew that they could win the war. In this abysmal political and military situation, I took command of the SFAs in the Karoi district.

Prior to my arrival in Hurungwe on September 1978, the TTL was occupied by ZIPRA who ruthlessly controlled the masses. I identified that the people were the Vital Assets and the TTLs were both the Vital Ground and the Ground of Tactical Importance. I developed a clear, unwavering political vision and military strategy which was accepted by the people, therefore proving that it was possible to achieve political and military victory by becoming one with the people, defending them and addressing their GNA. I have presented a considerable body of independent evidence supporting our success. The key was identifying that a "kills-win-wars" strategy had failed and realising the people were the key, not the obstacle. Working in conjunction with the military "killing machine", which acted on our intelligence, generally worked well. Another key to our successes was breaking free from the shackles of traditional political, cultural, military and SB strategies, tactics, thinking and prejudices. This liberation allowed me to approach the "Battle for Hurungwe" with a clear mind. I could draw from the experience I had gained in my police career and the war, and so develop relevant, unique strategies and tactics for our specific battles. I needed like-minded staff who had the experience, skills, ability and capacity to fulfil their roles. As a leadership team, we had recruited men such as Ian Suttill to replace staff not suitably qualified and unable to make the necessary paradigm shift, and lacking in capacity. We had no rank structures in the SFA.

The SFA in Hurungwe operated valiantly against initially overwhelming odds, proving a genuine revolution is achievable without the violent oppression of the people. It was a counter-revolution by consensus, secured by consultation. It is important to understand that the people's army never controlled Hurungwe, the people did, which was a complete reversal of traditional military thinking. The political objective ought to be the rallying of the support of the people by attending to their grievances, needs and aspirations, while the military stands to defend and not to rule them. Dr Chakawa's independent PhD research acknowledged our success in the battle for the hearts and minds of the people. He states: "Under pressure, ZIPRA had been compelled to retire to the perimeters of the TTL reportedly thrust back by the hostility of the people and the aggressive efficiency of the auxiliaries as the Rhodesians would have preferred to say." Dr Chakawa continues as he asserts: "the failure of ZIPRA to put up resistance against SFAs who came to re-open the school (Maumbe Primary School in 1978) is still mind-boggling to explain, how SFAs, some of whom hurriedly trained for 3 weeks, could be tactical enough to easily beat seasoned guerrillas."[2]

The greatest problem I foresaw was that meaningful political change needed to be introduced decisively to negate ZANLA, ZIPRA and international propaganda and criticism. This was unlikely as the RF and their white commanders still "held the reins" during the Interim Government, as well as when Muzorewa came to power after the 1979 elections. If the political obstacles were removed, there would be no reason for war. In my opinion, there was an overall lack of understanding of these counter-revolution and mass-mobilisation principles by intelligence officers, the military and white

[1] Smith, I. (1997), p. 74.
[2] Dr Chakawa, J. (2015), pp. 186-187.

political authorities. "Rhodesia's" defeat emphasises this fact. Early in 1979, I wrote a secret Special Branch report for national distribution explaining, in fine detail, our successful strategies and tactics in Hurungwe. The mere fact that I received little feedback of my report leads me to believe that it was either never read or understood. Generally, intelligence officers were busy doing their "own thing", hell-bent on eliminating the enemy. There was so much under way that it was impossible to know exactly what was going on.[1] In my mind, Mac McGuinness was correct when stating: "The final and essential ingredient which MUST be added if we are to control the trained personnel in the field is mature policemen, who, with tact can ensure that law and order are maintained in these so called 'free zones'."

While we were concerned about the SFA's poor conditions of service, particularly salaries, our decision was to address the matter after elections when we anticipated majority rule, placing us in a stronger position to make demands to a more receptive government. This turned out to be another "not to be".

Bishop Muzorewa and the UANC were aware that the SFA were a solution to the war. He understood that he had to "connect" politically to and defend the people in order to gain popular support and military ascendancy. In my view, one way of achieving this end was with the people's army. The bishop saw the potential and necessity to exponentially expand the SFA, but permission was granted for only 16,000. This would have established the path for a successful campaign in the final elections.

I am of the view that the stranglehold of RF policies, reflected by competent, though generally stereotyped military strategies, thwarted the only chance of survival which was left. The demand by Com.Ops. for me to hand over our operation to the military emphasised their lack of understanding of our counter-revolution and mass-mobilisation strategies. This ignorance was reinforced when the RAR withdrew from Hurungwe and, once again, abandoned the people in September 1979. In my outlook this was disgraceful and incomprehensible.

To this day, I cannot comprehend why a company of RAR soldiers was withdrawn from the field and sent to take over our operations. We had control of the situation, continued to gain momentum and had commenced a retraining programme. In my view, there was no limit to our potential.

I also found it beyond comprehension that all the members in the African forces (police, army and internal affairs) were removed from their home districts and deployed into "foreign" TTLs. This took them away from their familiar homeground and forced them to abandon their unprotected kith and kin to ZANLA and ZIPRA, who tortured and murdered them because of their association with the government. In my opinion, these African SF members should have been permanently deployed into their home areas accompanied by mature and seasoned intelligence officers, and members of the UANC political and military wings from the same areas. They would have known how to deal with the enemy! With the right retraining and politicisation for the new dispensation, supported by actual political changes, SFA-type operations could have been quickly developed. They would have rapidly linked directly to their families, relatives and friends, established their own intelligence networks, gained popular support, and occupied and possessed their homelands. Hostile collaborators, many of whom were probably already known, would be easily identified and the enemy pinpointed and eliminated. Large portions of the country could have been successfully mobilised and insurgents overcome by the people and their army. Had common sense been implemented, the white regiments, comprising the RLI, SAS, Territorial Forces and Fire Force, could then have been released for the role they were best suited and trained for: attack and eliminate the enemy in identified locations. The same principle applied to the white farmers who were called up, often to defend other white farms, while abandoning their own farms and families.

The proviso for success would have been rapid political changes and conditioning for the future which were highly unlikely while the RF "held the reins" of power. Ian Smith and the right-wing elements of his RF party would have had to go. There would at least have been a more solid

[1] Flower, K. (1987), p. 179; Cilliers, J. (2003), Chap. 11.

opposition party to oppose Robert Mugabe in the final elections, a benefit to the whole country. This type of strategy was not something new. It had been spoken about at numerous levels of both the Security Forces and elements of the African rural population. A bold and more realistic military strategy needed to be implemented. However, the inability of Security Forces commanders to abandon failing strategies and tactics, along with an incompetent, manipulating and interfering Rhodesian Front party, denied Bishop Muzorewa the opportunity to address an African problem with an African solution.

When Mugabe's strategy of sending *mujibhas* to the assembly points, leaving the bulk of his fighting men in the rural areas to ensure victory in the 1980 elections was revealed, the government politicians and Security Forces commanders resorted to the old gambit of reacting instead of acting, and complained to all and sundry including the British Government. With some ingenuity during the final elections, SFA-orientated *mujibhas* could have been sent to the assembly points and the people's army left in the field to politicise and protect the people from insurgents, many of whom had remained to intimidate and coerce voters. At that stage of the war, all and sundry wanted an end to the bloodshed no matter the cost. In reality, ZANLA and ZIPRA outwitted their adversary with classic guerrilla-warfare tactics. They constantly changed strategies, gained the support of the people and frustrated the might of the Rhodesian Security Forces.

I, like many "Rhodesians", started to count the cost of the war. In a short 15 years, thousands of lives had been lost or destroyed, our heritage was in ruins and many people, both black and white, driven into exile. Such was the intensity of propaganda from both sides that it seemed impossible to remain in the country. I left for South Africa, concerned about reprisals, retributions and an African black-on-white bloodbath. I had become a victim of Rhodesian Front Government propaganda.

In 1979, with the stroke of a pen, the war ended, bringing a finality to a long 15 years of ill-conceived UDI and white rule. A political solution was the answer to the "Rhodesian" crisis from the outset. The African nationalists finally achieved their ancestors' goal of liberty from colonial rule. I wonder what choices many white "Rhodesians" would have made had the concealed, untoward facts and alternatives been revealed prior to, and even during, UDI? Possibly, they would have followed Winston Field's example and declined the offer. The hard fact was that politically Mr Smith had been defeated and his military machine was collapsing. Commanders at Com.Ops. were well aware that they had lost the war and pressed the government to negotiate a settlement, resulting in the Lancaster House Conference being convened.

Ian Smith sat face to face with the same leaders who he detained and failed to negotiate with a decade and a half earlier.[1] He complained bitterly that the world, in particular, the United Kingdom and South Africa, had betrayed him. On 12 December 1979, Governor Lord Soames took up residence in Zimbabwe Rhodesia, returning the country to legality. A settlement was reached at Lancaster House, London, on 21 December 1979, bringing an end to the war. Edgar Whitehead's far-reaching vision to integrate the races over a 10-15-year period in terms of the 1961 Constitution was a distant dream. In my opinion, Ian Smith and his RF Government had no intention of progressing towards majority rule. A rapidly deteriorating military situation forced him to make concessions when it was too late. The expense of the war could have been better spent integrating the country's citizens in the 1960s. That was the time to negotiate, before the nationalists turned to Russia and China for support. In Ian Smith's words: "The most important thing about negotiations is to secure for yourself a situation where you talk from strength, as opposed to a defensive position where you may have to retreat to an inferior situation."[2] Sadly, this was not to be as he led the country into war and mayhem and his government into an ever-declining position. Compromise not consensus is the dynamics of politics. The RF had 17 years to bring about their proposed policies of evolving African advancement, but failed to do so.

It is difficult to establish the exact number of casualties incurred during the war. However, it

[1] Flower, K. (1987), pp. 308-310.
[2] Smith, I. (2008), Loc 3780.

appears that there were 2,618 Security Forces deaths[1] and 57 South African Forces deaths.[2] Inside Rhodesia, approximately 10,050 insurgents, 7,790 African civilians and 468 white civilians were killed.[3] There are no figures for insurgents and civilians killed externally. From 1972 to 1980 there were 2,504 vehicle landmine detonations, killing 632 people and injuring 4,410.[4]

The Patriotic Front, in particular ZANU, would have liked to have fought on and defeated the SF, while the SF believed they were betrayed by foreign governments,[5] and many felt that, had this not been so, they could have fought on and won the war. However, the SF commanders thought differently. NatJOC's approach to the British Government concerning their contemplation of a military coup confirms that the SF commanders knew they were facing defeat. The political settlement saved the country from continued bloodshed and a humiliating defeat in defence of an unachievable dream. In the aftermath, the RF, ZANLA and ZAPU politicians escaped accountability.

The question which needs to be answered with regards to the Rhodesian civil war is this: was there a counter-revolutionary strategy that could have been implemented by the Rhodesian Government, which would have resulted in a different, more amicable outcome that could have led to a peaceful co-existence for all the people? In answering this, it needs to be clearly understood that, while the military and paramilitary forces are responsible for the application of the military aspects of strategy on the ground, it is the political entity which formulates the overall strategy. The answer, in my opinion, and the opinion of most of those who have worked with me on this book, as well as a myriad of others, is a resounding "Yes", there was an alternative. In my opinion, the problem lay with the political factor.

I do not believe that the Rhodesian forces were made aware of the truth behind the unwinnable war that they fought and died for. Unwittingly, theirs was an attempt to stabilise an ever-deteriorating situation, while Ian Smith and his government attempted to manipulate and negotiate a settlement on their own terms. Outright victory was never a possibility and defeat was inevitable. The failure was political. SFA could have produced a better outcome.

Fate of the SFA

Dr Chakawa states: "When Zimbabwe became independent, SFAs were disbanded because they were not needed by the new dispensation. They were informed they would be called when their services were needed. There were generally no cases of direct retributions by members of the public to the returning auxiliaries for wrong-doing in the war to liberate the country from the Smith regime. They were rescued from direct attacks by their popularity during the war, and the need for ZANU-PF to consolidate its hold in areas where ZIPRA had fought. The pre-occupation of the ruling ZANU-PF was to destroy all ZAPU structures and co-opt everyone to the ruling party. In that spirit, ZANU-PF political commissars were stationed at almost every township to welcome everyone into the ruling party. Attacks on former auxiliaries would have compromised the ZANU-PF agenda."[6]

Grey Mutemasango survived and lived out his days at his home. His neighbours were former SF personnel. Happy Marere moved to the United Kingdom and was killed in a train accident in a London underground tube station.[7] Other members of the UANC survived. Ian Suttill joined the South African Defence Force and was killed in action during the Matola Raid into Maputo, Mozambique, on 30 January 1981. His last words to Rich Stannard, also on the raid, were: "We got, them sir." Stannard replied: "Oh yes, Ian, we certainly did."[8] The remainder of the Admin. staff and

[1] J.R.T. Wood email 17/5/2020.
[2] Adrian Hagget email 18/5/2020
[3] Wikipedia: Rhodesian Bush War.
[4] ditto.
[5] Interestingly, ZIPRA also believed that they were betrayed by the West. Dr J. Chakawa email 18/10/2016.
[6] Dr Chakawa, J. (2015), pp. 261-263, email 21/8/2019 and WhatsApp discussion 8/11/2019.
[7] Graham Des Fountain WhatsApp discussion 19/1/2020. To the best of Graham's knowledge, the information is correct.

members of the team survived. Most of them have contributed to this book.

I believe that the SFA and their supporters were genuine revolutionaries who supported their tribes, communities and families against the predominantly Matabele invading forces in Hurungwe. I consider ZIPRA collaborators as traitors to their own people and the blood of so-called "sellouts" is on their hands. The SFA and the men from the UANC were the heroes and liberators of their people in Hurungwe and should have been acknowledged as such.[1]

Reflections on the war

Propaganda isolated the people from a balanced world view, mobilised them, and gained their support to fight and die for the politicians' evolving and often devious agenda. I found myself in a web of propaganda and indoctrination. Generally, white Rhodesians were alienated from the traditions, culture, language and views of the Africans and, in my mind, led by a government determined to maintain their ideological rule and colonial lifestyle: a fertile ground for racial prejudice. Prejudices are formed from people's circumstances, experiences and situations. They erupt spontaneously as preconceptions and appear true because many do not reflect and examine them.

Political and military rhetoric dehumanises the enemy, making it justifiable to kill them, affording little or no mercy for their collaborators. This process brands the enemy as inhuman objects. Actions against military and civilian targets are condemned and those of the Security Forces justified, thereby introducing the cycle of revenge, justification and condemnation from both sides of the conflict. Deaths and injuries to combatants and civilians accentuates the process: the war escalates.

Initially, I trusted leadership and did not look beyond or examine "truths" presented. I developed tunnel vision and identified with the community holding the same beliefs and felt safe in the hands of leadership that would protect us all: "the brotherhood". My beliefs were that we "Rhodesians" had been set apart from the world, alone, silenced, misunderstood and yet committed and determined. We were prepared to fight and die for the country and its alleged stand against communism, the preservation of justice, civilisation and Christianity in Africa. We stood together, guided by a strong nationalistic ethos expressed in our flags, slogans, patriotic songs and symbols. In "safe hands", it was easier to abandon reason and logic, deny reality, the unfolding chaos, and fight on. War seemed the only way to defend my innate fear of a looming massacre of white "Rhodesians" by African nationalists. After five years of war, I perceived I was led by a racist government determined to maintain an ideological rule and colonial lifestyle, regardless of the mounting military and civilian casualties, with no hope of winning.

On examining my prejudices, I found that, generally speaking, I liked Africans. I respected their traditions and culture, and learned to live with and fight for them. My key was entering their community, accepting their traditions and culture, and not demanding they adopt mine. Arriving at this conclusion was a eureka moment which completely changed me: I was at one with the people. While we took precautions, I was never afraid of captured insurgents or *mujibhas* and did not fear them turning a gun on me. Our Security Forces were "omnipotent" and held in great esteem: the "finest in the world". However, our limitations were exposed as the war dragged on. War consumed and obsessed me. I pursued the enemy relentlessly, abandoning my life to "the cause" while working myself to exhaustion for the "greater good", that latent, unspoken agenda justifying and often obscuring motives authenticated by "the cause". I became unemotional about the fate of the enemy and their collaborators killed in battle, but condemned their action against black and white civilians, and the SF. I considered the Makoni TTL a cesspit contaminated by ZANLA and their supporters whom I categorised as the enemy.

Alcohol was the crutch that veiled my fears and celebrated victories. The war provided a complete social world and lifestyle. War then became a personal challenge to outsmart and outwit the enemy:

---

[8] Rich Stannard email 17/6/2016.

[1] Maj. Gavin Rawstron's diaries, p. 5.

a matter of survival, the ultimate hunt, man versus man, where the penalty for a loss or lack of concentration, a wrong choice or simply unlucky circumstances, spelt death or injury. From my perspective, we and the enemy became objects to kill. We did our duty but lost our humanity.

There is a dark side to war. Atrocities were committed by both sides. In war the mind, in progressive, orderly steps, journeys to acceptable, unimaginable depths of depravity. It has to in order to survive. Soldiers and innocent civilians die. Those who escape death face the postwar traumatic journey back to "acceptable social normality", whatever that is: an elusive objective. And what was that death for, and what of the injured and "walking dead", those who never recovered mentally and never adjusted to peacetime? And what of the waste: unlived and unfulfilled lives, skills, talents and love that lay buried in the graves?

So, judge not those you sent to war,
to live or die to defend your lie.
For they have been and seen and done,
protected you who raised no gun,
yet still lived and had fun.

John Padbury

Certainly, I had changed from my first fearful trip to Mukumbura to a well-seasoned, cold-hearted and ruthless Special Branch intelligence operator. The war was a challenging adventure and I held no regrets at the time. However, I was angry with white politicians whom I felt had led the country to ruin with no apparent regard for the men and women on the ground. The political and military hierarchy frustrated me because they demanded respect and obedience to strategies, tactics and decisions that did not make sense. My superiors did not appear to understand what was unfolding on the ground. Their war was theoretical, remote from any actual fighting. This separated them from those tasked with directly confronting the enemy. Relentlessly and nonchalantly they drove operational staff to pursue ever-increasing demands to feed their inflated egos with kills in their rotating nine-to-five, Monday-to-Friday social war.

We would prevail against all odds. Trapped and isolated with seemingly no escape route, winning the war was the only solution. Defeat was non-negotiable. To join the "chicken run"[1] would bring separation from the "brotherhood". However, it seemed to me, nobody really cared beyond their own agendas. I resigned from the BSA Police because I believed our political leadership was incompetent. I had followed a racist, well-intentioned leader, convinced of his own self-righteousness and confident in his powers of persuasion. It seems to me that he did not heed critical, professional advice, and controlled policy and information from an inner circle. Ian Smith displayed several symptoms of hubris, particularly "loss of contact with reality, often associated with progressive isolation".[2] Herodotus explains the downfall of Croesus, King of Lydia (560-546 BC), who lost his entire empire as a result of his hubris syndrome: the pride in one's achievements that provokes the ire of the gods.[3]

When I arrived in Hurungwe, I considered death to be inevitable and I lived each day to the full with an abundance of tension and fun. I worked with Africans who I was meant to "hate and kill", such as Bishop Muzorewa, James Chikerema and all the UANC political and military men. However, I found myself in harmony with them, enjoyed their company and held them in high regard. They were fine men committed to their cause and never showed signs of fear in the face of severe adversity. Living under the threat of death, they still enjoyed and loved life. They were not afraid to travel into Hurungwe without military escorts in order to address the masses. They were visionary and always receptive to changing strategies, tactics and objectives. Their acceptance of me positively

1 Chicken run: A popular adage describing any route taken by those wishing to leave the country because of the war and uncertainties regarding the future.
2 Owen, D. (2016), pp. 275-279.
3 Arnold, J.H. (2000), p. 18.

affected the entire operation and was instrumental in the people of Hurungwe embracing me. We were one!

Likewise, were the many people involved in the UANC intelligence networks operating "behind enemy lines". Many died at the hands of ZIPRA, yet they persevered, undeterred, to remove and eliminate the enemy from Hurungwe. Finally, the men in the field, the people's army, young men prepared to fight and die for what they believed in. These men faced a ruthless, cruel, and well-entrenched enemy who had gained the support of the masses. They attacked the Security Forces at will, had "liberated" Hurungwe and were living the victory, until the people's army deployed. I admired and respected the locals in Hurungwe for their tenacity, courage in the face of extreme difficulties and their ability to live a meaningful life in a rural, subsistence economy.

In my opinion, given the logistical support and full freedom to determine our priorities, there was no limit to what we could have achieved. However, this was not to be. I felt that the UANC Government officials and leadership were constrained by the RF and military ethos lurking in the background, as they attempted to cling to power. I do not recall any white Rhodesian Front politician holding meetings in the TTLs where I was operational. Why?[1] What was the point of talking and appeasing a dwindling population of 250,000 whites when there were five million African Rhodesians to address?

Our operations in Hurungwe were successful. I have a clear conscience fighting to liberate the oppressed people and paving the way to majority rule in terms of the "internal agreement". Even at that late stage, I believed it possible to influence the outcome of the war on a national basis, unaware that Com.Ops. were in survival mode while the politicians squabbled.

I often think and question, more so since writing this book, of those dying in "glory", and those who lost limbs and had other life-changing injuries, in "defence" of their country: mostly young lives snatched away in an unexpected moment. No one really goes to war to die. There are always casualties. Some died instantly, others after days, weeks or months of agony. What of those summoned to war who bypassed youth, lost their identity and only later searched and maybe found it? There again, maybe not!

I agree with Maj. Gen. Smedley Butler: "War is a racket. To hell with war."[2] War indeed is a complete negation of rational thinking! I now see UDI as an act of extreme self-righteous stupidity. Some politicians are by nature strong in voice, weak under pressure and unaccountable, and then walk away unscathed when conflicts arise.

Post-Revolutionary Displacement

I define post-revolutionary displacement as the "enforced or voluntary movement from home, land or country as a direct result of a successful revolution for reasons that include ethnicity, opposition to the revolution and changed political, economic and employment circumstances directly related to the revolution. Grief embodies the pilgrimage. The effects are generational".

As I observed the situation deteriorating, my concerns about reprisals grew. In the end the decision to leave the country was made for me when my position became defunct and the military took over the operation. This was a difficult process. Change is always difficult especially when I was so adamant that in Hurungwe I proved we were right. To leave the BSA Police was a traumatic decision. Originally, I had been a regular-serving career policeman and had passed all the necessary written examinations and respective promotion-board interviews, achieving the rank of detective inspector within a relatively short period of time. This attainment was a sound foundation for a promising future. As was with the majority of the regular and reserve members of the BSA Police and, indeed, the Security Forces as a whole, we were expected to perform our duties in our various roles, accordingly. Having been obsessed with the war, it was extremely difficult for me to leave the operational arena, as my involvement with it had become a way of life.

Leaving the country, my home, was heartbreaking as it seemed to me that I had lost everything.

1 Flower, K. (1987), p. 134.

2 Butler, S. (1935), *passim.*

Families, relatives and friends were separated and scattered throughout the world. Beverley Abrahams captures the trauma: "When people can no longer call a land their own, when they are displaced from the place of their ancestors, and when they lose control of their destiny, they lose a part of their soul. Once the fragile link between people, their land and their ancestry is broken, they become a shadow roaming a land they no longer understand, beset by cultural conflicts and torn between material wealth and loyalty to tradition."[1]

Dr J. Chakawa states: "Some white operatives left the country immediately after the war. There was no reason for them to understand terrorists from a positive perspective. Fighting for the Smith regime strengthened their resolve and many could find no reason to change their line of thinking. If they were in constant fights with insurgents who murdered civilians ruthlessly, it shaped their mindset; there was no provision, place, or room to understand their reasons for taking up arms against such insurmountable odds. They were sometimes not happy that the war came to an end. It meant loss of jobs, purpose, friends, comradeship, ruined marriages and relationships and of course their country was taken away from them."[2]

The abrupt end to the war was devastating for me. Our move to Cape Town, South Africa, in 1979, was full of uncertainties. The transition from a position of authority, purpose, challenge and the ultimate adrenalin rush to that of a salesman where not only did I have to learn new skills and techniques, but also engage in cold-calling, was a harrowing experience. I was out of my comfort zone and my life had been turned upside down! In Cape Town, I went into a deep, dark depression. In exile, I found no colour, no purpose and no meaning to life, except the need to provide for my family. Alcohol and Valium (not a good mix) were my crutch. There was much unfinished business on my mind. Why would they not listen? What happened to the men of the UANC, the SFA and the team that operated with me? All my mates had either remained or left Zimbabwe and settled all over the world. To cap it all, nobody cared, least of all the South Africans, whom I ridiculously thought appreciated what we had stood for in Rhodesia. I felt quite alone. At the rear of our house in Muizenburg, I made an imaginary "operational office", hung up my Rhodesian and BSA Police flags and war mementos, read my diaries and attempted, on numerous occasions, to write them up: anything to keep me involved in the war! With each attempt to write, I was drawn back to the hopelessness of the end, and finally decided to let it all go and concentrate on finding peace with myself, my wife and family, and continue the struggle to live again.

It took four long hard years to come out of depression. At my lowest ebb, I set myself a goal to forsake my lounge chair, walk to the coffee table and muster the courage and determination for work: quite a journey! We did a great amount of travelling throughout the Cape Province. I bought a caravan and Lynette and our two sons, Robin and Joseph, travelled with me. Gradually I learned to enjoy life. We bought our first house in Somerset West. However, for some time, I was unable to move in and we lived in the caravan parked on the driveway, probably a flashback to my war days. I was not alone on my journey. Supt. Louise Ford, Assistant Staff Officer, Welfare and Sports (1976-1978), recalls: "I had to bury many Policemen and Police Reservists and arrange military funerals which I also had to attend. I saw the devastating effects these deaths had on their families and how they cringed when the gun salute was fired. I guess they suffered Post Traumatic Stress Disorder (PTSD) too. I also had to visit wounded Policemen in hospital — and those sick but not wounded. I saw signs of PTSD although it was not called that then. I had one 'patient' who ended up in the psychiatric ward and also one wife who had a breakdown and also needed psychiatric treatment — she and her policeman husband lived in a rural police camp and he spent a lot of time in the bush in the normal course of his duties over and above his PATU stints. It was a traumatic time for us all."[3]

I returned to Zimbabwe for my father's birthday on 12 February 1980 for a short visit. During the trip, I received a phone call warning me that one of my former white BSA Police Special Branch

---

[1] Staunton, I.: *The Experience of Zimbabwe (1)*: postcolonial web.org.

[2] Dr J. Chakawa oral discussions 2017.

[3] Supt. Louise Ford messenger discussion 1/1/2020.

colleagues was "looking" for me. This made the trip rather uncomfortable, as there was a question regarding a missing weapon which I had to answer for. However, my conscience and records were clear and clean. People, circumstances and situations had changed and I decided that it would probably not be safe for me to return again. However, Dan Stannard "cleared" the way for a more memorable visit in 1985. We had another wonderful family holiday in Zimbabwe in 1986. Standing at Cape Town Airport ready to leave for another visit on my own, I realised that I had to let the country go. Finally, I "closed the door" and did not board the plane, and returned home. I missed the rural Africans with whom I had spent so much time. I missed my career in the BSA Police, the comradeship of the force and the war. I missed being close to family, especially my parents. I missed the country I called home. However, in order to progress, I had to forsake the past and embrace the present, which I did.

Gradually, I saw glimpses of "blue in the sky" and held on to the memory that possibly, one day, the "sky and colours" would return to my life. Certainly, alcohol, Valium and cigarettes were of little help as I struggled to come to terms with life. Lynette returned to enemy ground, the Roman Catholic Church, and met a priest who had spent time in Rhodesia. She thought that I would enjoy his company as we "spoke the same language". He had been involved in the Rhodesian conflict. One day she brought home a Catholic newspaper and I was sitting on the toilet on a Sunday afternoon, with a beer in my hand, tranquillisers in my pocket and smoking a cigarette. I read the prayer to St Jude for "hopeless cases" out of interest. When I had completed reading, I stood up, poured the beer down the toilet, followed by the cigarette and tranquillisers, and have never desired to indulge in them again. I felt peace for the first time in many years. The colours returned to my life. I recalled the "little voice" I heard in the Makoni TTL, and the many occasions I had narrow escapes and had avoided serious incidents by what I thought was my intuition. All this occurred outside the established church and religion. I am incredibly grateful that God set me free from my addictions, lifted the depression and kept us safe all these years as a family. In time, I met Dr Edwin Louis Cole, founder of the Christian Men's Network (USA). He imparted to me true fatherhood and taught me the principles of being a husband and father. I am still learning!

We moved seven times in South Africa during our stay of 20 years: it was difficult to settle. In 1996, we spent two and a half years in North America where I did biblical studies, preparing and ultimately achieving a master's degree in Christian counselling. In 2000, we moved to England. My first job was walking the streets of London, mustering business for a courier company. My next job was a concierge in a London block of flats before moving to North Devon and settling in Appledore, a small fishing village. After selling timeshare and working for a double-glazing company, I started a property management and maintenance business which provided for our needs. In 2012, I was offered a job managing an estate on the edge of Dartmoor, which I accepted and we lived and worked in a most beautiful, rural, isolated environment on the edge of Dartmoor National Park. In 2020 our employment ended with the sale of the property and we moved back to North Devon to be near family and settle. We are truly blessed. I joined the BSAP Regimental Association and have made contact with many of my former colleagues. Once I put pen to paper, I realised the necessity and great advantages of social media and have connected with friends around the world, which has been good for me. However, I do miss the simplicity of rural African village life, their traditions and custom, and their welcoming, forgiving nature. The English soil is different to that of Zimbabwe. There is something about taking a handful of soil from the land you had called "home": at times, I miss the sensation.

Living in "exile" offers a safe and stable social environment. I am grateful for the many opportunities that opened up for us as a family in South Africa, North America and the United Kingdom, and the people we have met. Former Rhodesians have experienced successes and tragedies. Many of them struggle with short- and long-term psychological consequences. Where there is justification and condemnation, the war rages on in the mind, possibly unaware or unprepared to consider meaningful reflection and reconciliation. In writing this book, I have come to terms with issues I was aware of in my spirit, and fortunately, acted on during the war. My extensive research and the people I have met has brought a greater understanding of the political, military and personal aspects from both sides of the tragedy. However, there is always a bigger picture, always more. Coming to terms with my acceptance that I was deceived and fought a pointless, unwinnable war, has been a difficult yet liberating experience. Truth pursues the lie. For me freedom lies in knowing the truth. I believe revenge, anger, bitterness and justification are engulfed in and follow the deceit, but knowing and comprehending the truth brings understanding, acceptance and peace. Not that I believe for one minute that I own the whole truth but, certainly now, I know a great deal more than when I set out to write this book.

Ex-combatants reminisce about the battles fought and won, discuss successful or failed strategies and remember their fallen. Some individuals manufacture controversy and cover-ups for financial gain, "Walter Mitty" characters emerge from the scrapheap of polluted, corrupted minds. Fading memories merge battles and incidents recalling the victories and leaving behind the fears overcome by obedience to "the call of duty" which bonded men and women. Some identities are wrapped up in what we were or what we did. Reality is, however, elusive.

My brother, David, recalls: "After the elections, and the inevitable rise to power of Robert Mugabe, I was walking down Second Street, Salisbury, with one of the former Commanders of ZANLA. We had struck up a good working relationship, and as we were walking towards the Anglican Cathedral, he said to me: 'David, I didn't realise that there was such a desire for peace, and such a willingness to try and make it work. We have all been victims of our own propaganda'."[1]

I have found facing reality liberating. In asking the question "Why?" or "Was it worth it?" I have to take into account that UDI lasted a meagre 15 years, caused considerable bloodshed, destroyed lives, marriages, families and relationships, and ultimately destroyed the country we all loved: both black and white. I have to answer emphatically "No!" Both cultures lost out by the segregation, and still do, in a post-revolutionary political environment which continues to propagate the revolution that, by definition, remains separatist, nepotistic, tribal and needs to diversify and embrace all Zimbabweans. Ian Smith's Rhodesian Front had 17 years to bring about meaningful change on the road to majority rule but chose war instead. I lived an exhilarating, adventurous and challenging life, which in the end virtually destroyed me. The 17 years would have been better spent developing the entire nation with equality, by integrating all the country's forces, services, schools, hospitals and so on. By attending to the needs and aspirations of all the people, they would have learned to live harmoniously. I am adamant that we would have still lived a wonderful life in a different manner, because we were and still are all Africans: resourceful, entrepreneurial, enduring, resilient and forever hopeful of better days.

When I met Dr Chakawa, he rekindled in me the fondness I have for the rural Africans. He is a living example of a sophisticated rural African who had been given the opportunity of an education. He is an honest, trustworthy man of integrity. Such were the friends I lost when leaving the country.

The common rural folk who bore the brunt of the war, still face political oppression, yet they just want to live, progress and be able to express an opinion. It seems to me that there were no winners in our war, except the politicians. Zimbabweans, faced with a collapsed economy, ruled by an autocrat and desperate for work, have flooded into neighbouring South Africa and any other country willing to accept them. Corruption continues to dictate personal and national policies, all of which echoes the Rhodesian point of view: "I told you so!" Sadly, we will never know what could have happened had the RF negotiated peaceful agreements with the African nationalists from the outset of their tenure, and implemented progressive steps towards majority rule while in a position of economic, political and military strength.

I have sought to bring understanding as to why both sides took up arms: the whites from an intransigent political position of strength initially, and the Africans against seemingly insurmountable odds with genuine grievances, needs, and aspirations. Both parties fought with resilience, determina-

[1] David Padbury email 5/12/2016.

tion and commitment to the bitter end. That end was settled by the politicians who sent them all to war in the first place and still had to negotiate a settlement, before sending them home again. Without a doubt, the obstacle of UDI intensified the racial divide between the black and white moderates on the one hand and the nationalists on the other.

In my opinion, there was another way. Let the politicians fight and die for their own cause if they feel that strongly about it. There will be no more wars I can assure you. I am extremely grateful that no members from my side of the family were killed during the war. Lynette lost two cousins. Richard Laurent died in a vehicle accident on the Filabusi-Balla Balla road on 7 July 1976.[1] Mark Harris was killed in a battle against a 15-man ZIPRA section during Operation Tentacle in the Chamabonda Vlei in the Victoria Falls National Park, 19 kilometres south-west of Victoria Falls.[2] I have a deep sadness for those killed and injured and their surviving families. One of the saddest memories I hold is that of burying Maxwell and the three SFA killed in action. My former deputy headmaster at Mount Pleasant School, BSA Police Field Reservists Raymond Gough and Basil Calder were both sent to protect a farm called Bar G Ranch near the Lion and Elephant Motel. They successfully beat off a terrorist attack but were killed the following day, 8 January 1977, when the vehicle they were travelling in hit a landmine. Stephen Grobler, the driver, lost both legs in the blast.[3]

Postscript

Having violently overthrown the Rhodesian Government through the "barrel of a gun" in order to achieve majority rule, Robert Mugabe and his cohorts set about establishing a one-party state, eliminating or suppressing all opposition, while subduing the people with the same guns. He became a "non-revolutionary" or a "counter-revolutionary". Mao Zedong states: "If a revolutionary today integrates himself with the masses he is a revolutionary; if tomorrow he ceases to do so or turns around to oppress the common people, then he becomes a non-revolutionary or a counter revolutionary."[4] In 1980 and 1981, at Entumbane, Mugabe crushed his former ally, ZAPU. In 1983, Mugabe's North Korean-trained Fifth Brigade massacred around 30,000 Ndebele, men, women and children in an operation known as Gukurahundi.[5] Mugabe "looked East" and, subsequently, petitioned the Chinese for economic and political support. Harold Macmillan was proven right. The Chinese have their own colonial agenda. This confirmed Mugabe's approach to opposition when, on 16 November 1978, "he issued a death list of more than 50 Africans associated with the Salisbury regime who would be shot unless they resign for the elections".[6]

Victorious veterans unsuccessfully demanded an equal share of the trophies of war that their leadership had promised. The problem with revolution is that triumphant leadership often believe the "cake has been baked" for themselves. They falsely believed it was their right to choose if, and with whom, to share the spoils. War "vets" were marginally appeased yet never gained the promised rewards. The people in the rural areas have remained just that: the people. Their lives carry on as usual with some improvements. They are governed by the *mujibha* system, while carrying on with the routine of their lives. They remain cautious with whom they share their political thoughts. The heavy hand of the Zimbabwe Government hovers ready to pounce.

A referendum was held in 1999 on the acceptability of a new constitution. Mugabe lost, mainly because of the emergence of the Movement for Democratic Change party (MDC). With the support of the working class in urban areas and farm workers, the constitution was rejected. Unfortunately, a video appeared showing a group of white farmers handing funds to the MDC leader, Morgan Tsvangirai. Mugabe was incensed and resolved to break the economic and political power of the

1 J.R.T. Wood email 8/5/2018: Rifleman Richard Laurent (23 yrs), Second Battalion, Rhodesia Regiment.

2 J.R.T. Wood email 8/5/2018: Trooper Mark Harris, Grey's Scouts.

3 J.R.T. Wood email 23/9/2019; Adrian Hagget WhatsApp discussion 3/10/2019.

4 Zedong, M. (1976), p. 292.

5 *Gukurahundi*: Shona, translated as "the early rain which washes away the chaff before the spring rains". Literally, Mugabe was washing away the perceived rubbish: ZAPU dissidents and their supporters.

6 British chronology of events, p. 24.

whites, in particular white farmers whom he saw as wanting to use their economic strength to control the political: a throwback to the Rhodesian Front days. Mugabe said to Dan Stannard: "I have given the white farmers the hand of reconciliation and left them alone. Now they will see my hand of wrath."[1] Thus began the removal of white farmers from the land and Mugabe continued his propaganda against colonialism, and any form of opposition. Corruption has brought Zimbabwe to its knees both morally and economically.

The present government is embroiled in power struggles, corruption and ruled with a conception of democracy which upholds their leader, Robert Mugabe. Does this mean that all officials fall into this category? No, absolutely not! Generalisation is a misguided precept. There is a cry from the vast majority of Zimbabweans, as with the people of the world, for just and fair government, fair distribution of land, wealth and assets. When the people realise they hold power, this cherished dream may become possible. In a military coup during November 2017, Mugabe was ousted by his former friend and colleague, Emmerson Mnangagwa. At the time of writing, military men were posted to most government departments in one capacity or another. There was no money in the banks and a desperate need for the economy to be kick-started: a miserable economic and political outlook for a country ruled by an incapable military dictatorship. In my opinion, the dire situation in Zimbabwe was the direct result of the Rhodesian Front Government failing from the outset of its tenure to integrate its society and prepare its citizens for the future.

Mugabe's anti-British propaganda emphasises and condemns the ills of the imperialist colonial period which, in his opinion, necessitated and justified the military actions leading to its violent overthrow. For Mugabe, it was a successful revolution. Former Rhodesians look at and condemn the disintegration of a once economically stable country (the breadbasket of Africa), the corruption, the one-party state, the tribal infighting and the oppression and murder of opponents, all of which justifies their war. Both sides resort to justification and condemnation. The only winners were the politicians, their cohorts and countries which supported the revolution such as China.

Matters of Moment

My thinking was reflected by the following timeless, damning matters of moment.

Mr Smith remained obdurate to the end. He would have fought on in support of his "lost cause" regardless of the mounting deaths within his Security Forces. In September 1979, while attending the settlement conference at Lancaster House under the new Muzorewa Government, and still clinging to power, he asked Pik Botha for a South African loan of R1 billion in order that "Rhodesians" could fight on. The request was rejected at an extraordinary South African Cabinet meeting. Pik Botha summed up the situation during an interview with Theresa Papenfus on 8 November 2004: "Right up to the last minute – and probably today as well – Mr Smith and his supporters were convinced that they could have won the war, how I don't know. Because by 1979 only a few Rhodesian cities and towns were left where Mr Smith and his forces were in full control.[2] He thought that either he could win the war or he could negotiate for better conditions by continuing with the war. I did not agree and said so flatly: Smith had no chance of winning the war and if the struggle continued he would have to accept worse, and not better, conditions for the transitional phase."[3] Mr Smith's war was over: he had lost, politically, militarily and economically!

Ian Smith was convinced that "Rhodesia" had been betrayed by South Africa. The discussion between Theresa Papenfus and Pik Botha on 6 November 2004 reveals South Africa's position towards "Rhodesia". Pik Botha said: "Ian Smith castigated me because he knew exactly what part I had played in ending UDI and persuading him at Lancaster House to go with a one-man-one-vote election. That really went against the grain with Ian Smith. 'And what of the charge that South Africa

[1] Dan Stannard telephone discussions May 2017; Rook, M. (2018), Loc 6-8%.

[2] ZANLA and ZIPRA did not capture any of the country's towns or cities. Certainly, they controlled a majority of the TTLs, the African rural areas. With typical guerrilla strategy, they attacked towns and cities at will.

[3] Papenfus, T. (2010), pp. 282-283. I came across this book as I wrote my conclusions. It was a fascinating find as it confirmed my research and analysis of the Rhodesian crisis.

had left Rhodesia in the lurch, that Rhodesia was the sacrificial lamb that had to buy time and acceptance for South Africa?' Oh, he'd heard that story so often, said Pik Botha impatiently. The simple truth is that they had already had billions of rand out of us that we couldn't afford. We had advanced them huge sums of money and then we decided that we couldn't carry on. We told Rhodesia that this was threatening our survival, and that the burden had become too heavy. Ultimately it comes down to your own survival. Only a very bad and unpatriotic statesman is so blinded by sentiment that he doesn't care how much devastation he's causing. Pik continued, Many whites read into this an alliance between South Africa and Rhodesia — which in fact never existed. Ian Smith declared independence unilaterally and in isolation. They knew that Britain would be very reluctant to send troops to Rhodesia, because three quarters of the population had English connections. The forebears of almost all white Rhodesians came from England. It was only the other day that Cecil John Rhodes attacked the Matabeles. Twenty to thirty years later the colony was being governed by Britain in true colonial style. That's where they came from. A generation later they decided for themselves that they didn't want to join the Boers — whom they looked down on. But we did help them."[1]

In 1986, Mr Smith was a guest at a dinner at Barbarino's Restaurant, St Kilda Road, Melbourne, Victoria, Australia. About 10 members of the Rhodesian Society attended. When asked why Operation Quartz[2] was never initiated, he stated that Lt. Gen. Walls had "bottled it". He spoke disapprovingly of Walls's decision. There is no doubt that he considered it a betrayal.[3] Clearly, Ian Smith would have fought on for his "lost cause" regardless of Security Forces casualties.

Pik Botha spoke about the political world and said: "Politicians suffer from power hunger, the need to dominate. The bloody job boils down to one thing: a central authority that has to be formed — a state under a head. Everything ultimately depends on dictatorship, even a parliament. In the end the voice of the people counts for nothing, the politicians do whatever they like — whether it is Bush or Thatcher or Hitler. Only some of them don't commit such a terrible number of murders. But nobody really follows Christ's doctrine of love."[4] Once elected, the ruling party and its politicians pursue their own collective and individual agendas.

Robert McNamara correctly states: "Ian Smith died believing that Rhodesia's downfall was entirely down to betrayal by the South African government, aided and abetted by Great Britain and the United States. This most unreflective of men, blind to his own hypocrisy and betrayals, frequently delusional and a rebel when it suited, never quite realised that white domination in southern Africa was unsustainable. Rhodesia's white population was too small and moves towards compromise—the so-called 'internal settlement'—came far too late. Smith rejected favourable settlement terms in 1966 and 1968, which he undoubtedly could have sold to the RF's white electorate. And there is no doubt that Smith grossly overplayed his hand in securing his virtually concession-free 1971 deal with Sir Alec Douglas-Home, which made inevitable the Pearce Commission's conclusion that there was no black support for the agreement. His interviews and memoirs betray no suggestion of obduracy or error on his part."[5]

---

1 Papenfus, T. (2010), p. 284-285; Smith, I. (2008), Loc 8705. Pik Botha refers to the 1922 referendum when mainly white voters decided to become a British self-governing colony and independent of South Africa.

2 Operation Quartz: Top secret operation to eliminate ZANLA and ZIPRA leaderships, and insurgents, gathered in locations for the elections. The operation was to be triggered if Mugabe won. The Security Forces commanders made the right decision to abort the operation. Most of ZANLA's and ZIPRA's fighting men had remained in the field to mobilise and control the people's vote. The so-called insurgents sent to the assembly points were merely mujibhas. Smith's attack would have massively escalated the war and unleashed unprecedented reprisals by the insurgents. The international community would have witnessed Smith's duplicity first-hand and would have been forced to respond accordingly, not to mention the unnecessary deaths within his Security Forces for his "lost cause".

3 Former BSAP Insp. Will Keys email 28/7/2018.

4 Papenfus, P. (2010), pp. 849-850.

5 de Meneses & McNamara (2018), pp. 200-201; Smith, I. (1997), *passim.*

The Politician

To war they said, and so we went.
We youth, yet again sent
to fight for the rights of the nation,
and sacrifice our lives in ultimate dedication.

No time to ask for what we fought,
nor to think of families distraught.
War, kill, maim…leave death and destruction on your trail,
we have tried all other means but to no avail.

Amongst our successes our own men fell.
Enraged, we no longer needed the politician to tell
us what he thought we fought for.
We killed, maimed and revelled in death and gore.

And so they sat, smug, with no perturbation.
"Must raise our salaries to keep up with inflation."
"Must cut down on foreign currency,"
the Minister said whilst on a short vakansie….

But then the inevitable denouement,
the meagre signing of a document,
to bring peace to the land or so they said.
Forget about the bereaved and the dead.

But still the war goes on we fear.
We turn to love, sex and beer,
before we die for the politician.

John Padbury, Salisbury, Rhodesia, 11 June 1979.

The Bridge

Small, comparatively, here lies the foresight of man's dreams.
To bridge nature's gap, regardless of troubles unforeseen.
For time marches on, nature too,
and the problems we create only nature (God) can undo.

The components were carefully selected,
any faults only later to be detected.
These would be replaced — no pain,
the bridge would stay intact.
He was here to remain.

Nature was disturbed at last,
and with a mighty blast,
great holes appeared
from which the bridge was cast.

Beneath, the hungry rapids digested the rocks displaced,
gone from site — but not disgraced.
Eroded to the delta of the promised land,
to be free of man's wild and interfering hand.

Nature's bell had rung,
the reasons are unknown.
But the seeds of revolution
had only just been sown.

"Not I," cried the bridge.
"Never in a 1,000 years."
For I am right and I am strong,
but up pricked nature's ears.

Beneath, the insane and savage tears gnawed.
Their cancerous revulsion grew malignant and clawed
at the roots of seemedly resilient "immovable" pedestals.
But nature knew its course, and nature stands not still.

Resilience with sufferance, man's finest dream,
he knew nothing of this, his mind was unclean.
Across that gap his wealth now freely steamed,
without a care of dreams that never dreamed.

The first crack was a joke, they laughed.
Anew then, in their revelry all bathed.
Alas showed more and more again,
it could not take their greedy strain.

Pieces fell into the gorge,
relieved even to be ignored.
Replaced with parts quite new,
anxious to survive as young hearts do.

Wearily, almost pleased at last,
the bridge collapsed as they all do.
Singly conscienced with love, no past,
nature's delta each soul renewed.

Alas, the tragedy my friend,
this was not the end.
Another bridge has just been cast,
will your part form the past?

John Padbury, Victoria Falls, Rhodesia, September 1979.

I wrote this poem when we visited the Victoria Falls before our emigration to South Africa. The bridge was allegedly closed by Ian Smith in 1975, severing trade ties with Zambia. I was, therefore, surprised that it was, in fact, open. This added to my disillusionment with politicians. I have subsequently learned that trains did not cross over to Livingstone but used to push a load down to the bridge at 11.45 p.m., leaving the last wagon on the dividing line between Zambia and Zimbabwe Rhodesia. Zambian crews would clear it and, if they had a load, would do the same. The goods trains returned 30 minutes later. Railway staff had to be very careful not to cross the white dividing line or else the Zambian army would arrest them. This happened to one of the railways employees who was arrested and released three days later. The same procedure was in place at the Mozambique/Zimbabwe Rhodesia border.

APPENDICES

Inyazura petrol station attack, BSAP Form 36.

B.S.A.P.—12M—24-7-75. **B.S.A.P. FORM 36.**

British South Africa Police

APPLICATION FOR SCIENTIFIC EXAMINATION

Forms to be completed in **quadruplicate**, 3 copies with exhibit and 1 copy to remain in docket.

Station: INYAZURA Ref.: CRs. 20-21/5/76

Lab. Ref.:

Telephone No. CID. RUSAPE (TEL. 468).

Accused: NIL AT PRESENT.

Offence: 1) ACT OF TERRORISM. 2) ATTEMPTED MURDER

Date: 14th MAY, 1976. Time: 7-45PM. Place: BI-PASS WELDERS GARAGE, INYAZURA.

Authority for examination given by: CH/SUPT V.L. SIDNELL. PCIO MAN PROVINCE. Date: 15th MAY, 1976.

Article No.	DESCRIPTION OF EXHIBITS
1	4 green coloured expended cartridge cases (Armour piercing types ??). for A/K.
2	14 expended normal type AK expended catridge cases.
	Above cases in the 1 bag.
3	2 wire toggles.
4	2 pieces alien metal at scene.

Type and quantity of preservative added:

Date: 15th MAY, 1976. Time: 12 Noon. By whom: 6455 DET/INSP MacCALLUM.

Persons handling exhibits: 6455 DET/INSP MacCALLUM and 20241 DET/CST GANGA

How packed and sealed: ALL IN PLOYTHENE BAGS.

Method of forwarding to Laboratory—~~ORDINARY POST/REGISTERED POST/C.I.D. BAG/~~ /or

Conveyed by hand of (No.) 20241 (Rank) DET/CST (Name) GANGA

[P.T.O.

Inyazura petrol station attack, BSAP Form 36.

SUMMARY OF CASE

(This must clearly indicate the circumstances connected with each exhibit)

Friday, 14th May, 1976, 2 armed men in possession AK rifles (Terrorists) came to Bi-Pass Welders Garage, Inyazura Village (Just on main road Rusape to Umtali) with the obvious intention of robbing the Night attendent who was attending to stock records and cash proceeds involving nigh on $88-00. The Terrorists claimed to be from a local Haulage firm and enticed the Attendent out from his locked room. However, upon seeing them with AK rifles he made off with the 2 terrorists firing at him, luckily missing him. Through his line of flight the 18 expended cattridge cases recovered. The 2 petrol pumps and 1 Oil rack blown up and this thought to have been by stick grenades. The 2 wire toggles found nearby thus suggesting the thoughts of stick grenades being used to effect the explosions etc. 2 pieces alien metal found at scene and not proved to be from petrol pumps etc. The building also shot at with very noticeable holes on the walls. However, check to locate expended cartridge cases in this connection was negative.

INVESTIGATION REQUIREMENTS

(Indicate here what facts you intend establishing by means of this examination)

1. Can the 18 expended cartridge cases be checked, identified with a view to proving previous history?
2. Thought that the Petrol pumps etc. blown up by stick grenades. In view of where the wire toggles found--any chance of being identified as resulting from stick grenades?
3. The 2 alien pieces of metal--any chance of this being identified as being f om stick grenades----bearing in mind that it has not been identified as hailing from the scene--at this point though this cannot be overlooked.

Date 1[illegible] MAY 1976 .... [signature] I.O.

No. 6455 Rank D/ Ins Name MacCALLUM.

FOR USE BY LABORATORY STAFF

Exhibits received by .... Date ....

Transfer/Disposal of exhibits ....

AFFIDAVIT/REPORT sent to .... Date ....

Ballistics report for the Inyazura petrol station attack.

59 : 14/5/76 : ATTACK: BI-PASS WELDERS GARAGE INYAZURA. (F.B. (T) 265/76) P 1471 - 1472 : 18 x 7.62 mm (M1943) Fired cartridge cases received. These cases had been fired from 1 A/K/M rifle x 5 cases & 1 A/K rifle x 13 cases. The A/K rifle that fired 13 cases matches 3 cases recovered after BUS BURNING, HONDE B.C., MUTASA TTL., Entry No. 58, dated 2/5/76. The A/K/M rifle x 5 cases does not match any previous scenes.

Subsequent ballistics request and report for the Inyazura petrol station attack.

B.S.A.P.—12M—25-11-74. B.S.A.P. FORM 36.

British South Africa Police

APPLICATION FOR SCIENTIFIC EXAMINATION

Forms to be completed in **quadruplicate,** 3 copies with exhibit and 1 copy to remain in docket.

Station: INYAZURA Ref.: CRs 20-21/5/76

Lab Ref.: /

Telephone No. CID. RUSAPE (TEL. 468)

Accused: NIL (AT PRESENT)

Offence: 1. ATTEMPTED MURDER 2. ACT OF TERRORISM.

Date 14th MAY '76 Time 7-45PM. Place BI-PASS WELDERS GARAGE, INYAZURA

Authority for examination given by CH/SUPT SIDWELL FC10 MAN PROVINCE Date 31st MAY, 1976

Article No	DESCRIPTION OF EXHIBITS
1.	Plastic Bag containing total 14 expended cartridge cases (12 thought to have been fired from AK and the other 2 possibly from AWM).
2.	Plastic Bag containing empty AK Magazine and a total of 23 AK bullets plus possibly 5 AWM bullets.
	These exhibits found some distance from the scene :-
	1) 56 yards from the scene (in vlei).
	2) A further 58 yards from (1) and also in vlei.
	This area was alleged to have been cleared by SAS and these exhibits found in a further routine check of the area.
[illegible]	Telecon Ch/Insptr HOLLINGSWORTH and Det/Insptr MacCALLUM on the morning of 31st May, 1976 refers.
	Previous Reference from Ballistics in connection this case :- F/B (T) 265/76.
	Detective Inspector MacCALLUM.

CRIMINAL INVESTIGATION DEPT.—B.S.A. POLICE
1 JUN 1976
P.O. Box 36
RUSAPE, RHODESIA

Type and quantity of preservative added

Date 1st June, 1976. Time By whom

Persons handling exhibits (1) 8105 DSO CUTTING and 20241 DC GANGA (2) 8282 SO RIEDY and 20241 DC GANGA

How packed and sealed: In Plastic bags.

Method of forwarding to Laboratory—ORDINARY POST/REGISTERED POST/C.I.D. BAG/ /or

Conveyed by hand of (No.) 20241 (Rank) Det/Cst (Name) GANGA.

[P.T.O.

THRASHER

PAGE 14

68 : 14/5/76 : FURTHER CARTRIDGE CASES RECOVERED, BI-PASS WELDERS GARAGE, INYAZURA. (F.B.(T) 359/76) : 14 x 7.62 mm (M1943) Fired cartridge cases received. These cases had all been fired from the same R.P.D. Machine Gun and do not match previous Scenes.

Everitt murder, BSAP Form 36.

B.S.A.P.—12M—24-7-75. B.S.A.P. FORM 36.

British South Africa Police

APPLICATION FOR SCIENTIFIC EXAMINATION

Forms to be completed in **quadruplicate,** 3 copies with exhibit and 1 copy to remain in docket.

Station CID Joc 4 Umtali Ref.: Incident Log 46/76

Lab. Ref.: /

Telephone No. 64212 Ext 276

Accused -

Offence MURDER (On white)

Date 4/8/76 Time 5-30 to 6am Place Ngirazi Kr, Makoni TTL VQ 415286

Authority for examination given by PSBO Manicaland Date 4/8/76

Article No.	DESCRIPTION OF EXHIBITS
1	50/7,62 (Int) Cartridges . Butt piece of AKM Rifle. 1 x 7,62(Int)Round
2	25 X 7,62 cartridge cases (F/N)
	The above 25 cases were fired by the murder victim prior to his death, His F/N rifle was subsequently stolen by terrs and it is believed that they may also have a number of rounds for this weapon which they may use in the future. The attached cases a forwarded for future tie-ups.

Type and quantity of preservative added Nil

Date - Time - By whom -

Persons handling exhibits 8595 DFO ATKINSON

How packed and sealed Plastic bags/Envelope.

Method of forwarding to Laboratory—~~ORDINARY POST/REGISTERED POST~~/C.I.D. BAG/ .... /or

Conveyed by hand of (No.) - (Rank) - (Name) -

[P.T.O.

Everitt murder, BSAP Form 36.

SUMMARY OF CASE

(This must clearly indicate the circumstances connected with each exhibit)

On the date, time, place in question a Mr. EVERITT was working in the Makoni TTL when he was fired upon by terrorists, at the time he was in possession of an F/N rifle which he attempted to use in retaliation before his death. This rifle has since been stolen by the terrorists who had attacked Mr. Everett.

F/N is a Police Reserve Rusape weapon, Number 5865 for which 2 magazines and 40 rounds were issued to the deceased.

INVESTIGATION REQUIREMENTS

(Indicate here what facts you intend establishing by means of this examination)

1) Please advise what type of weapon/s were used.

2) Do the weapons used tie in with any other terrorist incidents.

Date 4/8/76 .... I.O.

No. 8595 Rank DPO Name ATKINSON

FOR USE BY LABORATORY STAFF

Exhibits received by .... Date ....

Transfer/Disposal of exhibits ....

AFFIDAVIT/REPORT sent to .... Date ....

Everitt murder ballistics report.

165 : 4.8.76. : MURDER OF MR.EVERITT.VQ 415286 F.B.(T) 913/76. P.2742 - 2745.

Received 50 x 7.62mm (m1943) fired cartridge cases. These had been fired from 4 different A.K.Rifles (1 x 1, 1 x 6, 1 x 8 and 1 x 27cases). 7 cases were unidentifiable. The A.K. RIFLE THAT FIRED 1 cases matches : (i)4 cases from SELBORNE STORE ATTACK, INYANGA, Entry no. 64 of 8.5.76. (ii) 14 cases from ATTACK ON CHIEF'S HALL, MUTASA KL. Entryno. 60 of 4.5.76. THE A.K. RIFLE THAT FIRED 8 cases matches (i) 6 cases from KATIYO TEA ESTATE FACTORY ATTACK, Entry no.65 of 10.5.76. The A.K.RIFLE THAT FIRED 27 cases matches (i) 3 cases from ATTACK: MAKUNIKE STORE, Entry no.105 of 29.5.76. Also redc. 1 live round, 25 x 7.62 x 51 NATO cartridge cases and 1 E.German A.K.M. Butt plate insert.

Operation Thrasher Incidents Log. Entry 413 refers to the Everitt murder.

THRASHER

359	: S/F CONTACT: 4 TERRS. 1 S/F KILLED. HOLDENBY	VQ 787539	18/7/76
360	: AMBUSH: S/F VEHICLES. JULIASDALE	VQ 944583	18/7/76
361	: LANDMINE: S/F VEH. ROWA PL.	VP 598765	16/7/76
362	: NEW YEAR'S GIFT TEA ESTATE ATTACK. CHIPINGA.	VN 551782	17/7/76
363	: LANDMINE: ROADS DEPT. VEH. SABI PL.	VN 431320	17/7/76
366	: AMBUSH: S/F VEH. MUWUSHU TTL.	VP 517042	19/7/76
367	: MURDER: K/H DIP ATTENDENT CHIKORE TTL.	VR 499463	19/7/76
368	: S/F CONTACT: AVILA MISSION. 2 TERRS. KILLED.	VR 781671	20/7/76
369	: S/F CONTACT 1 TERR. KILLED. HOLDENBY TTL.	VQ 872592	19/7/76
372	: FARM ATTACK. (UNOCCUPIED) INYANGA AREA(MURDER OF A/M FARM EMPLOYEE)	VR 542012	21/7/76
373	: S/F CONTACT: NO CAS. HOLDENBY TTL.	VQ 999581	21/7/76
374	: RAILWAY LIN EXPLOSION: RUSAPE ICA.	VQ 078500	21/7/76
375	: RUDA CAMP ATTACK. HOLDENBY TTL.	VQ 8656	22/7/76
376	: S/F CONTACT: 1 TERR. KILLED. HOLDENBY TTL.	VQ 992608	22/7/76
380	: MURDER: K/H & 2 A/M'S HOLDENBY TTL.	VQ 933575	24/7/76
381	: LANDMINE: S/F VEH. MUTEMA TTL.	VN 435803	24/7/76
382	: LANDMINE: S/F VEH. NDOWOYO TTL.	VN 366050	24/7/76
383	: LANDMINE: S/F VEH. CHISUMBANJE.	VN 301031	24/7/76
384	: LANDMINE: S/F VEH. CHISUMBANJE. NDOWOYO TTL.	VN 352036	24/7/76
386	: S/F CONTACT: 1 TERR. KILLED MAKONI TTL.	VQ 420455	25/7/76
389	: MURDER: A/M. INYAZYRA? MAKONI TTL.	VQ 341348	26/7/76
391	: S/F CONTACT: 3 TERRS. 1 A/M KILLED HOLDENBY TTL.	VQ 991608	26/7/76
390	: S/F CONTACT: HOLDENBY TTL. NO CAS.	VQ 991608	26/7/76
394	: S/F CONTACT: 1 TERR. KILLED. INYANGA NORTH TTL.	VQ 887581	27/7/76
395	: LANDMINE: S/F VEHICLE. INYANGA TTL.	VQ 932692	28/7/76
396	: S/F CONTACT: NO CAS. UMTALI FARMING AREA	VP 572115	28/7/76
397	: S/F FIRED ON FROM MOZAMBIQUE. NGORIMA TTL.	VN 996859	28/7/76
398	: ATTEMPTED MURDER: INTAF. EMPLOYEE. MUWUSHU TTL.	VP 474096	27/7/76
401	: S/F CONTACT: NO CAS. HOLDENBY TTL.	VQ 007574	28/7/76
402	: LANDMINE: S/F VEH. XXSXXXXXXXXX.CHINYAUWHERA	VP 595765	29/7/76
403	: AMBUSH: 1 S/F KILLED. INYANGA. HOLDENBY TTL.	VQ 904567.	29/7/76
408	: MURDER: A/M STOREKEEPER. CHIDUKU TTL.	UQ 968277	29/7/76
409	: TERR. ATTACK ON S/F: INYANGA. HOLDENBY TTL.	VQ 932668	31/7/76
410	: MURDER OF A/M. NDOWOYO TTL.	VM 437970	31/7/76
412	: MURDER: K/H AVILA MISSION. INYANGA NORTH	VR 760679	2/8/76
413	: MURDER E/ ROAD CONTRACTOR. ODZI AREA. MAKONI.	VQ 415288	4/8/76
415	: RUDA BASE CAMP ATTACK. VQ 855558.	VQ 855558	5/8/76
416	: AMBUSH: CIVVY. BUS. MARANKE TTL.	VP 330630	5/8/76
417	: S/F CONTACT: NO CAS. MARANKE TTL	VP 400540	5/8/76
420	: CONTACT: S/F. 1 TERR. KILLED. HOLDENBY TTL.	VQ 945587	6/8/76
421	: LANDMINE: CIVVY. VEH. SABI TTL.	UP 858552	6/8/76
422	: FLEETING CONTACT: S/F SABI [illegible]. PL.	VN 465075	5/8/76

Justice and Peace Commission report on Makoni TTL propaganda leaflets.

Special Branch,

(J.O.C.),

P.O. Box 56,

Rusape.

<u>7th November 1977.</u>

The Officer Commanding,
Special Branch,
<u>JOC Rusape.</u>
Sir,

Re: JUSTICE AND PEACE COMMISSION;
<u>PAMPHLETS DROPPED IN THE MAKONI/MANYIKA TTLS..</u>

During the early part of January 1976 Z.A.N.L.A. terrorists commenced operations in the Manyika TTL, Mutasa TTL and the Makoni TTL..

Those early operations were highlighted by the brutal murders of numerous tribesman particularily those associated in any way to the Government. However, many of those locals murdered were in no way connected to either the Government or Security Forces (as informers).

There was little control over the individual groups of terrorists and the overall commander was LAMECK TEMBO. From interrogations of both captured terrorists and locals from the TTL's, it was learnt that Tembo himslef was a brutal man who kept driving his sections to carry out attacks on Farmsteads, Security Force bases and also encouraged the murder of locals thought to be 'sellouts'.

The lower grade terrorists, (cadres), through fear and general disillisuion, became wary of Tembo and his section leaders and there appeared a split between the lower levels of the sections. Disciplinary actions, such as whippings, began, were taken by the Section leaders, presumeably by order of Tembo, and the stage was set for anti terrorist propaganda.

In view of the apparent terrorist section problems, information started filtering back that the locals in the TTL's were becoming more and more disillusioned with the terrorists themselves, and, on one occassion, a Security Force O.P. actually heard locals scolding the terrorists telling them (the terrorists) to leave the locals and their young girls alone.

In conjunction with Censor, it was decided to drop anti terrorist propaganda over the Mutasa South, Manyika and Makoni TTL's, the area being known to the terrorists as the MAKONI/GANDANZARA DETACHMENT.

The pamphlets were to be dropped from a light aircraft over the entire area and would be so designed as to cover the following points :-

Justice and Peace Commission report on Makoni TTL propaganda leaflets.

....
(1 continued)

(1) Evils of terrorism;
(2) Involvement of locals in terrorism;
(3) Lack of harmony amongst terrorists themselves particularily between sections and between sections and Tembo himself;
(4) Intentions of the Security Forces;
(5) Warning to locals actively assisting terrorists should any Security Force action be taken against the terrorists while these persons were assisting (ie probable death of those persons assisting);
(6) Reassurance to locals on the side of the Security Forces/Government.

In particular the pamphlets were designed to warn all the locals that should they be caught assisting terrorists whilst the terrorists were still there, the probability would be that they would be killed. The point being that they would more than likely be caught by cross fire.

The pamphlet dropping programme commenced in approximately the month of March/April 1977 and extended over the entire Makoni/Gandanzara Detachment area. However, the pamphlets were primarily dropped over areas that were known to have supported terrorists and where terrorist bases had been established.

The pamphlets were dropped at an average of some one per every ten days to fifteen days and on the authority of initially JOC Rusape but on the overall authority of JOC Thrasher.

The pamphlets were assessed, from information gleaned from captured terrorists and the interrogations of locals for the respective areas, to have achieved the following :-

(1) Information from locals in the area was more forthcoming, particularily when spoken to in their home areas. When referred to the pamphlets, the locals would say that they agreed with the information contained within the pamhplets but were being brutally forced by the terrorists to co-operate with them. Information regarding the whereabouts of terrorists was thereafter forthcoming.

(2) The pamphlets caused havoc amongst the terrorists groups to the extent that the cadres were not permitted to read the pamphlets and only the section levels were allowed to read them. In many cases the locals were also banned from reading the pamphlets.

(3) LAMECK TEMBO left this country during the month of June and has not returned. In fact recent intelligence obtained has confirmed that he has been replaced as the Sectorial Commander and that he is no resident in Mozambique.

(4) There was a marked drop in the death of locals which seemed to co-incide with the departure of Tembo and with the concentrated dropping of pamphlets. However, recently there has been an up-surge of murders which is attributed to the replacement of Tembo by the new Sectorial Commando.

Attached is a schedule of terrorist acts which have occurred in the Manyika/Mutasa South and Makoni TTLs during the period the 25/12/76 to the 20/10/77.

DSO Padbury 8315

Inquest report on Reverend and Mrs Kuwana.

Special Branch,

J.O.C. Rusape.

13th January 1977.

The Officer Commanding,
J.O.C. Rusape
(Special Branch).

Sir,

Re : Inquest into the deaths of the Reverend Kuwana and Mrs Kuwana.

On the 14th December 1976 a Support Unit following spoor of eight terrorists, and in conjunction with Fire Force, observed movement ahead of their position and opened fire, killing the above mentioned persons. The incident occurred in dense bush and was, as far as Rhodesian Security Forces are concerned, a legitimate killing.

Bishop Muzorewa issued a press statement the following day alleging the deceased were murdered in their home and that Muzorewa himself had been to the scene of the incident and 'seen it for himself'.

On the 16th December 1976 the International Press were transported to the JOC at Rusape and for a full day and a half this JOC was pestered not only by the press but by the J.P.S. as well.

The problem was that we had to explain away the legitimate killing of two persons during a follow up operation and who, as it later transpired, had been feeding and assisting a group of terrorists based in a camp a few hundred yards away from the deceaseds' house.

The Support Unit stick involved was withdrawn from the field to meet the press and a statement was issued. Supt Painting commenced a full investigation into the circumstances with the overall intention of having an Inquest held by a Magistrate to publically dispel the rumours circulated by Muzorewa and his men.

On the 12th January 1977 the Inquest was held in Umtali and authority was sought, and granted, to have the case held in camera in order to 'protect police witnesses'. The Magistrate will give his findings on the matter in open Court on the 17th January 1977.

................/2

Inquest report on Reverend and Mrs Kuwana.

........../1
(continued)

I wish to point out two matters:-

(i) I do not believe that the holding of the Inquest in camera will throw any further reliance on the facts as issued to the press initially particularily in view of the fact that the Magistrate is a white Government employee. Muzorewa and his friends merely need to say that the Inquest was fixed. So do we then hold a board of enquiry to exonerate the Magistrate?

(ii) The Umtali Post had a small article in their daily paper advising the public that the Inquest was taking place on that day, 12th January 1977. Even though the Inquest was held in camera there was nothing to stop a terrorist agent standing immediately outside the Court and identifying State witnesses. We therefore did not protect our witnesses as we should have!!

I wish finally to suggest that in future similar cases that once the matter has been investigated by either the Special Branch or the CID in the usual manner, that a press statement be issued and the usual SDD booklet be compiled.

I do not believe that we should fall into the Terrorists overall plan of stretching us to our limits by by allowing ourselves to become involved in unnecessary and protracted investigations. No matter what we say there is always a way in which the statement can be turned against us and after all we are trying to fight this war like gentlemen!!

I refer this report for your perusal, pse..

DSO Padbury 8315

PRAW Flight Authorisation provided by Peter Anderson.

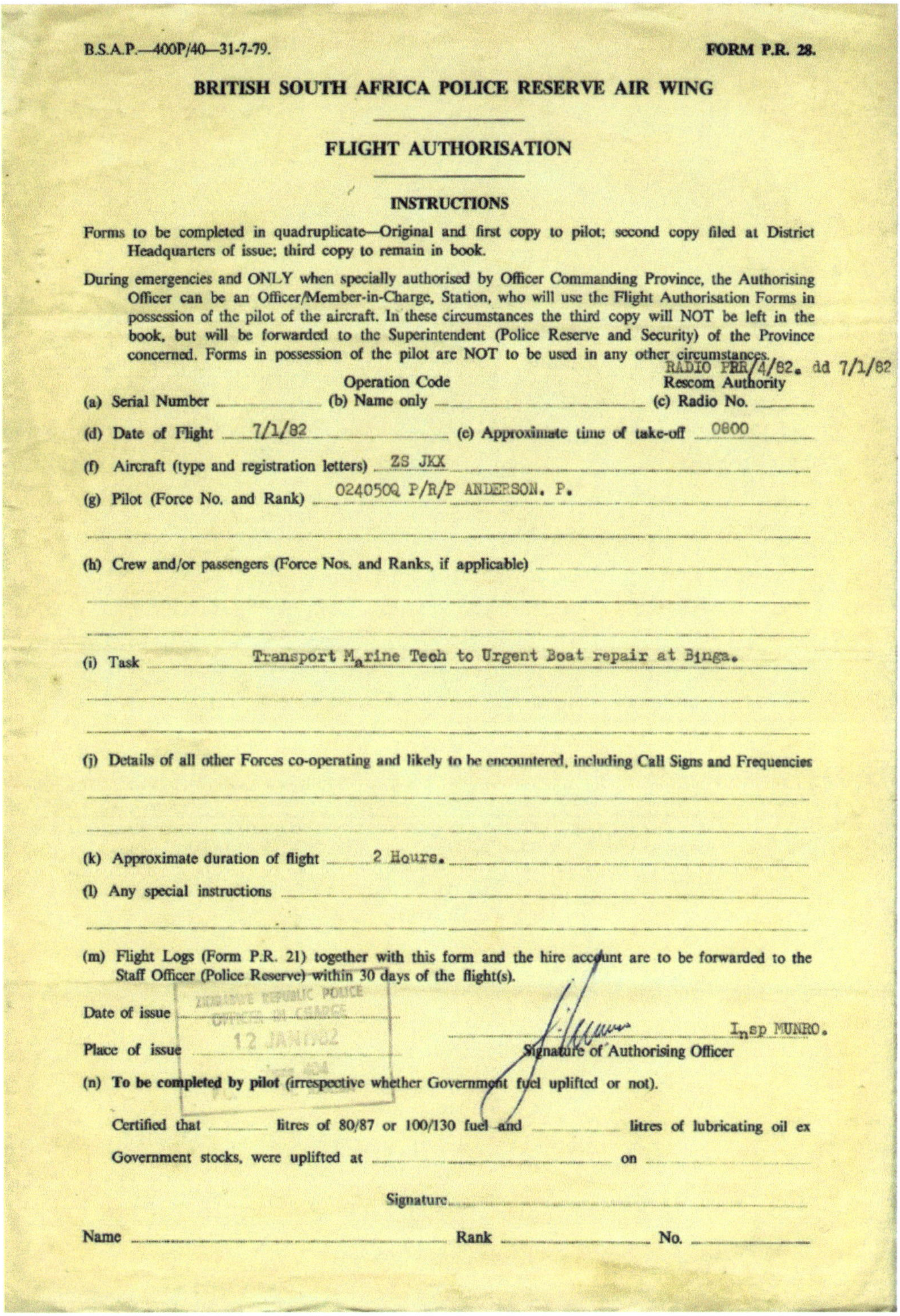

B.S.A.P.—400P/40—31-7-79. FORM P.R. 28.

BRITISH SOUTH AFRICA POLICE RESERVE AIR WING

FLIGHT AUTHORISATION

INSTRUCTIONS

Forms to be completed in quadruplicate—Original and first copy to pilot; second copy filed at District Headquarters of issue; third copy to remain in book.

During emergencies and ONLY when specially authorised by Officer Commanding Province, the Authorising Officer can be an Officer/Member-in-Charge, Station, who will use the Flight Authorisation Forms in possession of the pilot of the aircraft. In these circumstances the third copy will NOT be left in the book, but will be forwarded to the Superintendent (Police Reserve and Security) of the Province concerned. Forms in possession of the pilot are NOT to be used in any other circumstances.

(a) Serial Number ________ (b) Operation Code Name only ________ (c) Rescom Authority Radio No. RADIO PRR/4/82. dd 7/1/82

(d) Date of Flight 7/1/82 (e) Approximate time of take-off 0800

(f) Aircraft (type and registration letters) ZS JKX

(g) Pilot (Force No. and Rank) 024050Q P/R/P ANDERSON. P.

(h) Crew and/or passengers (Force Nos. and Ranks, if applicable) ________

(i) Task Transport Marine Tech to Urgent Boat repair at Binga.

(j) Details of all other Forces co-operating and likely to be encountered, including Call Signs and Frequencies ________

(k) Approximate duration of flight 2 Hours.

(l) Any special instructions ________

(m) Flight Logs (Form P.R. 21) together with this form and the hire account are to be forwarded to the Staff Officer (Police Reserve) within 30 days of the flight(s).

Date of issue ZIMBABWE REPUBLIC POLICE OFFICER IN CHARGE 12 JAN 1982

Place of issue

Insp MUNRO.

Signature of Authorising Officer

(n) To be completed by pilot (irrespective whether Government fuel uplifted or not).

Certified that ________ litres of 80/87 or 100/130 fuel and ________ litres of lubricating oil ex Government stocks, were uplifted at ________ on ________

Signature ________

Name ________ Rank ________ No. ________

PRAW Supplementary Flying Log provided by Peter Anderson.

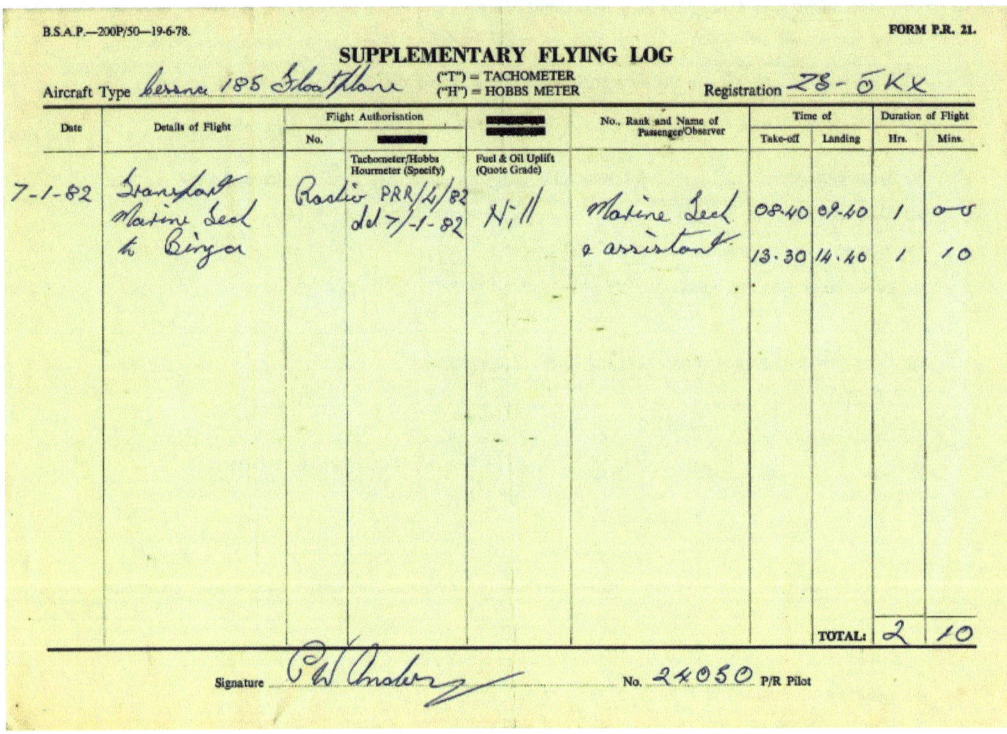

B.S.A.P.—200P/50—19-6-78. FORM P.R. 21.

SUPPLEMENTARY FLYING LOG

Aircraft Type Cessna 185 Floatplane ("T") = TACHOMETER ("H") = HOBBS METER Registration ZS-OKX

Date	Details of Flight	Flight Authorisation		[redacted]	No., Rank and Name of Passenger/Observer	Time of		Duration of Flight	
		No.	[redacted]			Take-off	Landing	Hrs.	Mins.
			Tachometer/Hobbs Hourmeter (Specify)	Fuel & Oil Uplift (Quote Grade)					
7-1-82	Transport Marine Seal to Binga	Radio PRR/4/82 dd 7/-1-82		Nil	Marine Seal & assistant	08.40	09.40	1	00
						13.30	14.40	1	10
							TOTAL:	2	10

Signature P W Anderson No. 24050 P/R Pilot

PRAW Invoice provided by Peter Anderson.

Name and Address: LAKE AIR
to where cheque P.O.Box 102
should be sent: KARIBA

Date..............................

To hire of Aircraft C.185 FLOATPLANE (Type)
ZS JKX (Registration letters), used for
Transport of Marine Tech & assistant
to Binga for urgent boat repairs
for: 2 (hours) 10 (Mins.)
on 7-1-82 (Dates) at
$ 44.00 (Forty-four dollars) : - (Nil cents) cents per hour.

Certified that the above aircraft is my property and was flown on Police duties by me at the above times and date/s.

Certified that the above aircraft is the property of:
LAKE AIR (PTY) LTD. S.A. and was flown by P.W. ANDERSON
at the above times and date/s.

Signed: P.W. Anderson
Rank: PR. Pilot Number: 24050
Name (Block Capitals) P.W.ANDERSON

PSYAC Operations Leaflet 1.

WARNING TO ZIPRA OPERATING IN HURUNGWE

We, the People's Army, wish to advise you that we have declared war on ZIPRA.
As you know we are many in number and we have superior weapons to you.
We control the helicopters in this area and will continue to call them to kill you when we find wherever you are hiding.
We are the People's Army. We are our own Liberators.
We are fighting for majority rule which is coming soon. When majority rule comes, we will be one mighty army … the People's Army.
We do not kill the innocent people who have no guns to protect themselves. We know you are frustrated because the people do not support you. You know the people do not support you that is why you are murdering them.
You know that our spirits support us. The people support us. You are doomed to death. You know that. The spirits of the people you are murdering will rise against you. You know that too.
We are attacking and smashing your bases in Zambia daily. Your supplies are being crippled, daily.
The girls you are raping do not love you. Those that can, are running away from you and we are keeping them in safety in our liberated areas.

IF YOU DO NOT HEED THIS WARNING

1) The war in Hurungwe has not yet started. We are many, we are well armed, we are strong, we are advancing into the areas where you are hiding, and we will kill you when we find you. You know this.
2) The spirits of Hurungwe people have risen now and told us to fight you Ndebele invaders. We will fight to the death because the spirits and the people support us and want us to free them.
3) We are better trained and equipped than you. We have plenty of war material to use to kill you.
4) The war is over for you and you know this. Why do you not go to your own homes where you belong with your families as we are doing?
5) We know there are some of you who wish to join us. We know that your commanders like Moses, Napoleon, Mandebvu, are cruel men and that they have killed their own men, ZIPRA, because they do not want to fight against us and want to join us. If you want to join us, you are welcome, but you had better come soon. Time is running short. We are at war with you and want to kill you because you are killing and harassing our people.
6) The few of you that want to join us come now before it is too late. You know that.

WE ARE INVINCIBLE WE ARE THE PEOPLE'S ARMY WE ARE OUR OWN LIBERATORS

WE OPENLY DECLARE WAR WITH ZIPRA

This message comes to you from the High Command of the People's Army

Pamberi ne hondo (Forward with the war) *Pamberi na Bishop* (Forward with the Bishop)

PSYAC Operations Leaflet 2.

MESSAGE FROM THE PEOPLE'S ARMY HIGH COMMAND TO THE PEOPLE'S ARMY —

We congratulate each and every man for the wonderful work you are doing.

The struggle for the liberation of our people is being won.

ZIPRA are retreating and are hiding from us.

They are murdering our innocent and unarmed people.

ZIPRA are burning kraals.

They are frustrated.

We are finding the landmines they lay to blast innocent civilian vehicles. This is all your work and the work of our people.

We are the People's Army.

We want to warn you that some ZIPRA want to join us. The people will tell us who they are. When they come to join us, they will have hidden their weapons and will be unarmed. When these ZIPRA want to join us, they will fight with our liberation army. We will collect their weapons later.

When ZIPRA join us, you must tell the High Command so that we know how many more of them have joined the People's Army.

Be vigilant. The war has just begun. We are advancing. We are many in number as you know. We are better armed and have more war material than ZIPRA.

We will fight to the finish, until we have liberated our people.

WE ARE INVINCIBLE!

High Command
The People's Army
Hurungwe TTL

PSYAC Operations Leaflet 3.

MESSAGE TO ALL COMRADES

We have received information that the following ZIPRA terrorists are no longer interested in continuing to fight for the ZIPRA forces.
Their names and descriptions are as follows:
(a) Commander Shame.
Description — a short 5′ 4″ man, a short man, with long beard and hair. On occasion, he tied two knots in the front of his hair. He has tribal marks on his face and smokes dagga. He was from the Chiroti area, probably educated at Zvipani, and carries an AK-47.
(b) Comrade Surance.
Description — 5′ 10″ a tall man, of medium build. He has a small beard, short hair and a cut on his right ear. He was from the Badza area near Kapfunde Mission and carries an AK-47. He was probably educated at Kapfunde Mission and smokes a lot of dagga.
(c) Comrade Pearson Looker.
Description — 5′ 9″ tall with a long beard. He has a cut on his lower lip, a wound on his left shoulder and a wound on his stomach. He smokes dagga and carries an AK-47. He was believed to have been educated at Rengwe and Sengwe Schools.
All these three ZIPRAs drink a lot of beer and prefer "seven days' beer".

These ZIPRA were abducted from the schools at which they were being educated and forced to go to Zambia for training.

They do not want to fight for ZIPRA, and they want to fight for Bishop Muzorewa. They know that we are defeating ZIPRA in this area. They are Mashona people and want to join the People's Army.

On Wednesday, 28/2/79, they came to the Murereshi Bridge to surrender and stayed there from 8 a.m. to 12 midday. They became afraid because they thought we would kill them. Again on Thursday, 1/3/79, the group discussed a ceasefire and wanted to join us but became afraid. They have nothing to fear.

WE WILL NOT KILL THEM BECAUSE THEY WANT TO JOIN THE PEOPLE'S ARMY

They know that ZIPRA are killing their own people for nothing. They were forced to fight and now they know that they were wrong. The People's Army is right. We are fighting for our own people in our own areas.

They know that all they must do is to hide their weapons and then they can come to our bases unarmed, or send the people or some mujibhas to tell us about them wanting to join us.

These men must come to us unarmed. You must tell the High Command straight away so that we know how many more ZIPRA have joined our struggle. As you know many ZIPRA have already joined us and are happy to fight for the Bishop in their own homes. They are tired of this war and of dying for nothing.

Pamberi na Bishop (Forward with the Bishop).

Pamberi na ruzhinji rwevanhu (Forward with the masses).

Pamberi ne mauto evanhu (Forward with the People's Army).

Pamberi ne hondo (Forward with the war).

THE PEOPLE'S ARMY IS INVINCIBLE. WE ARE ONE WITH THE PEOPLE!

High Command

The People's Army

Hurungwe TTL.

Karoi SFAs budget.

A		1	**Strengths**			
			a. Field	500 (A)		
			b. Chabwino Farm	13 (A)		
			c. Karoi House	4 (A)		
			d. Regular Army	1 (E)		
			e. S.B.Employed	3 (E)		
		2	**Salaries**			
			a. Field			
			485 men x $20		9700	
	(1)		15 men x $40		600	10300
			b. Chabwino Farm			
			Recruited African Instructors: Jamieson, Albert, Spencer, Jecha, Lucky, Moses,(6 x 100); Harvey, (50); Naison, John, (2 x 55) Marimo, (200)Anonymous, (50) Cook boy, Medic (2 x 20)		1050	1050
			c. Karoi House			
			Cook boy John (55); John (40); Kenny (20)		115	115
			d. Europeans			
	(2)		Coom (Regular Army), Suttill, Meyer, Mingay			
						11465
B			**Ration Allowances**			
		1	**Field**			
			a. 500 men at .50c per day = 250 per day x 31 days		7750	
	(3)		b. Subsidy for remote areas		2000	9750
		2	**Chabwino Farm**			
	(4)		a. 20 recruits @ .50c pd pm		310	
	(5)		b. 150 refugees @ .50c pd pm		2325	
			c. 13 staff at .50c pd pm		201	2836
		3	**Karoi House**			
	(6)		a. 4 European members @ 25 per week (x 4)		400	
			b. 4 African staff @ .50c pd pm		62	
	(7)		c. Allowance for "visitors"		100	562
C			**Other Items of Expenditure**			
	(8)		1.Operational floats 2000			
			2. Travelling - party members, men to towns etc		300	
			3. Compensation - for local deaths, men KIA etc		400	
			4. Payment of informers		200	
			5. Maintenance at Chabwino Farm - repairs, telephone, rates etc		300	
			6. Maintenance of Karoi house as in 5.		200	
			7. Stationary requirements		100	
			8. Bonuses		2000	
	(9)		9. Medical requirements		1000	6500
						31,113
D			**Expenditure on transport, special activity of political instructional staff.**			
	(10)	1	**Transport**			
			a. Cost of petrol, repairs and miscellaneous purchases.		5250	5250
		2	**Special Political Activity**			
			a. UANC float		1000	1000
			b. Salaries of UANC members.			
			Names kept anonymous. 7 men per month		1520	1520
	(11)	3	Accommodation and meals for party members		500	500
		4	Office Rental (UANC) including electricity, water, etc		100	100
		5	House rental party member (anonymous)		40	40
		6	UANC Kariba, controlling Bumi, Makuti, Kariba			
			a. Kariba			
			1. Pay	320pm		
			2. Float	400pm		
			3. Fuel for vehicle including Bumi vehicles	250pm		
			4. Rent of office	45pm		
			5. Lights, water, telephone	75pm	1090	
			b. Makuti			
			1. Pay	400pm		
			2. Float	150pm		
			3. Food	50pm		
			4. Rental of office	60pm		
			5. Lights, water, telephone	50pm	710	
						39,523

		c. Bumi			
		1. Pay	400pm		
		2. Fuel	200pm		
		3. Food	50pm		
		4. Float	200pm	850	2650
(12)	7	Political rallies, visits by party officials, and normal motivation activities		500	
					42,673

The above mentioned figure is approximately (USD) $64,009.5 at the time of the budget.

The following is an itemised explanation of the Budget Forecast (2nd left margin).

1. These are men in leadership capacities such as DCs (Detachment Commanders).
2. These Special Branch European members are accounted for by Salisbury.
3. This subsidy is in line with para B of the Secret Signal HQ Sby 708/79. The subsidy allows each man an approximate allowance of .63c per day, .13c more than the accepted norm.
4. Although this figure of 20 recruits supersedes our allotted figure of man power for the area, they are used to replace man power removed from the field. This man power is removed for such reasons as disciplinary demobilisation, sickness or wounded or killed in action. They are not paid any wages/allowances until such time as they operate in the field.
5. These refugees are from areas in which for various reasons terrorist activity has made it impractical for them to remain in their home areas. As soon as their respective areas are considered "safe" they are rehabilitated. This figure will remain fairly constant so long as there is expansion and terrorist activity in the areas. Refugees at Chabwino Farm are from the area controlled by "B" Coy 1 RAR, as well as our area.
6. No T & S is drawn by these members, consequently in lieu of this the allowance is paid to cover food expenditure.
7. This allowance is to cover the regular visits by either party members or other visitors to our area.
8. This covers all incidental expenses encountered by LOs (Liaison Officers) in the field, such as cultural money and assistance (an important aspect in the type of warfare in which Pfumo reVanhu is engaged), assistance for locals, minor expenses, transport in the T.T.L. and other numerous expenses which occur.
9. The advent of terrorism brought about the closure of clinics in the T.T.L. When Pfumo reVanhu established themselves in the area the locals looked to us for the medical assistance denied them. Because of the nature of our operations and our M.O. it would have been bad policy to deny these facilities to the locals. All major medical cases were naturally referred to Karoi etc, but we still carried the burden of minor cases, and until such time as the clinics re-establish themselves then we must continue to assist where possible.
10. This figure is based on transport costs occurred during our stay in this area. Our transport at this time is, 3 x Land Rovers, 1 x heavy truck, 2 x motorbikes, 1 x Toyota sedan, 1 x pick up. Because of the division of the area for easier control by the command element. The vehicles are constantly/daily commuting in the T.T.L. This naturally involves heavy mileage over bad roads resulting in heavy fuel consumption of some 1,000 gallons of fuel per month. Repairs to the vehicles because of the nature of the roads are at times heavy. Fuel is also provided for the party vehicles and their repair and servicing.
11. At present the UANC members are living at the Rufaro Hotel in Chikangwe Township. Alternative housing in the township is being sought.
12. The amount is required for the continual mobilisation of the people, which includes food and general party activity including maintenance of Spiritual medium factor.

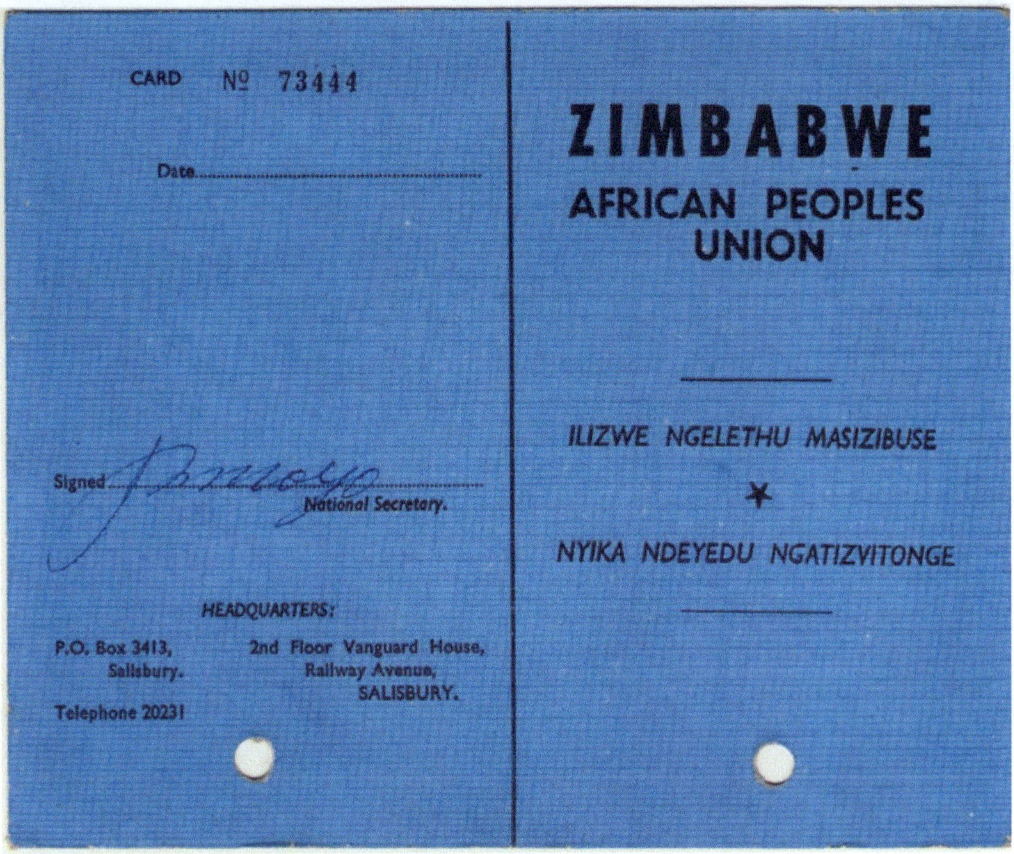

ZAPU membership card. (Courtesy of Brian Perkins)

ZIPRA propaganda card. (Courtesy of Brian Perkins)

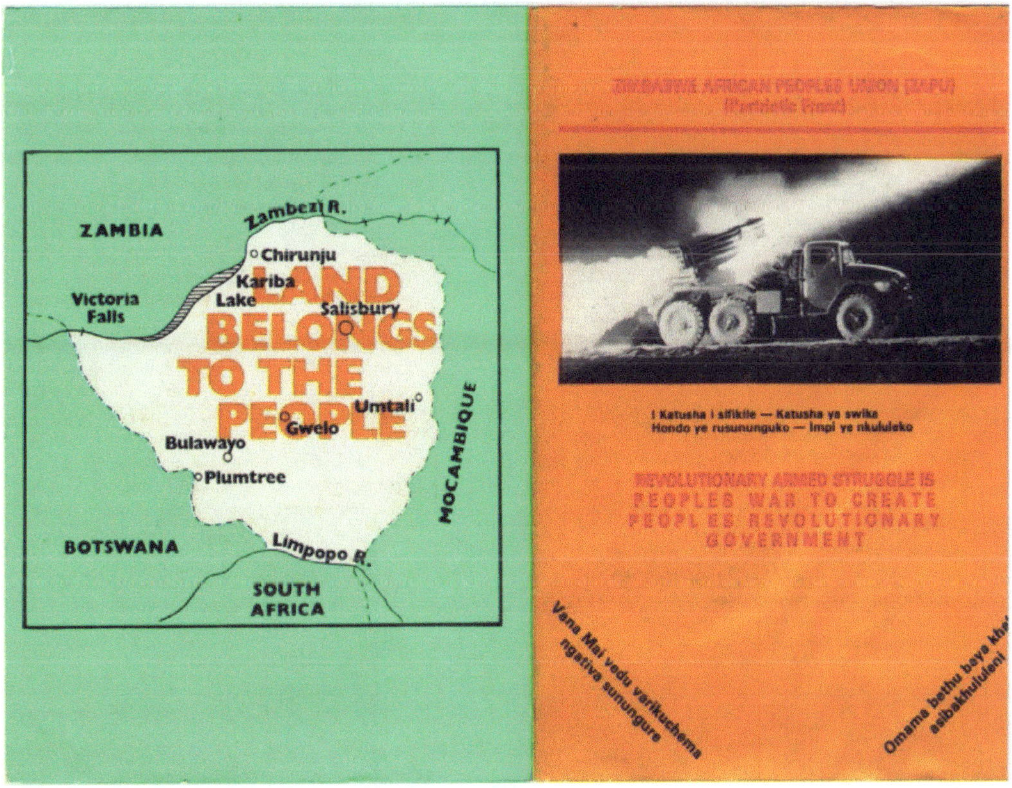

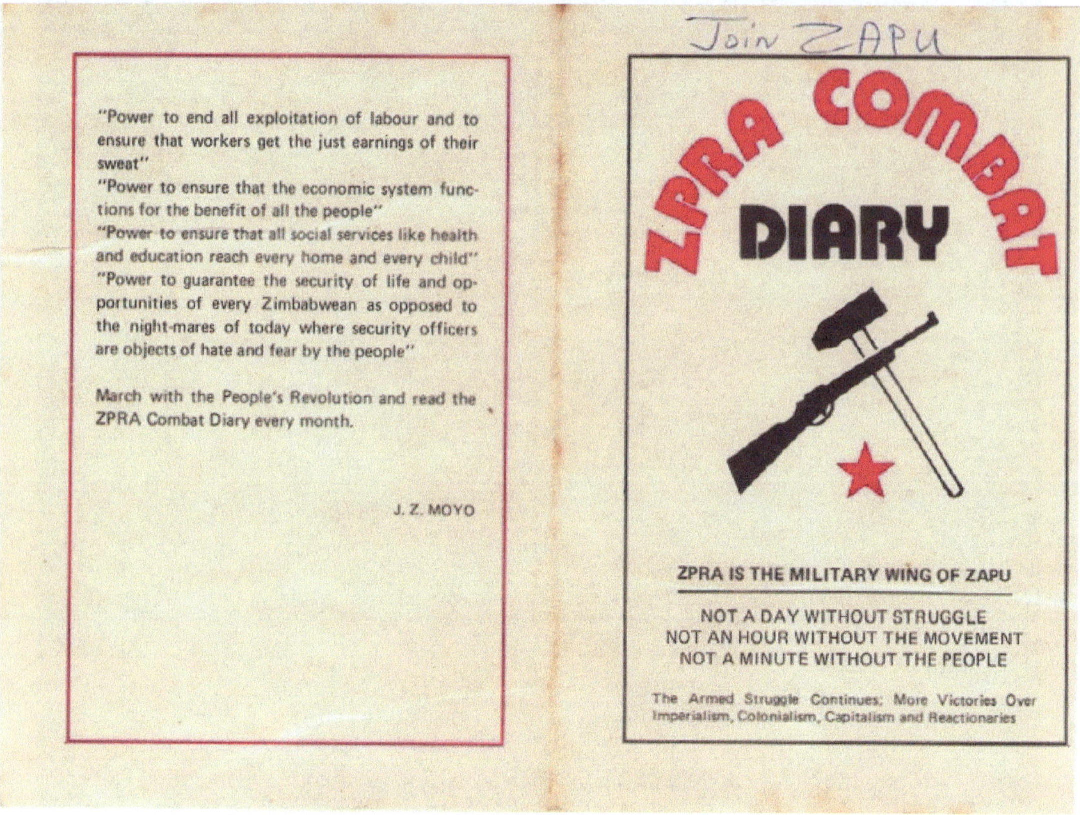

"Power to end all exploitation of labour and to ensure that workers get the just earnings of their sweat"
"Power to ensure that the economic system functions for the benefit of all the people"
"Power to ensure that all social services like health and education reach every home and every child"
"Power to guarantee the security of life and opportunities of every Zimbabwean as opposed to the night-mares of today where security officers are objects of hate and fear by the people"

March with the People's Revolution and read the ZPRA Combat Diary every month.

J. Z. MOYO

Join ZAPU

ZPRA COMBAT DIARY

ZPRA IS THE MILITARY WING OF ZAPU

NOT A DAY WITHOUT STRUGGLE
NOT AN HOUR WITHOUT THE MOVEMENT
NOT A MINUTE WITHOUT THE PEOPLE

The Armed Struggle Continues: More Victories Over Imperialism, Colonialism, Capitalism and Reactionaries

ZIPRA Combat Diary. (Courtesy of Brian Perkins)

FOREWORD

ZAPU our Party and liberation movement has, in the past year 1976, made considerable advances despite many difficulties. In the field of the armed struggle our Party entered 1976 with determination to unify the fighting forces of Zimbabwe with the formation of ZIPA and the opening of a new fighting flank right through the Mozambican border. By April 1976 the presence of our armed wing – ZPRA – in ZIPA had registered its impact with units deployed in the South Eastern, Eastern, and North Eastern border areas and fighting the enemy with completely new tactics to the area.

Sharp administrative problems broke our in ZIPA which forced it to operate as ZPRA-ZIPA on the other hand and as ZANLA-ZIPA (ZANU) on the other. Despite this ZPRA-ZIPA units continue to fight on in several areas of the Eastern front. Thus ZPRA-ZIPA is engaging the enemy at all fronts and has been the first to make a breakthrough in urban guerilla warfare. ZPRA-ZIPA correctly implementing guerilla strategy and daily tested tactics, daily destroys more of the enemy than casualties to itself.

This is because our Party ZAPU ensures that ZPRA-ZIPA is clear as to:

a) Why it is fighting
b) Who it is fighting
c) What the real enemy is
d) How to fight that enemy

Inspired by the victories of 1976 ZPRA-ZIPA enters 1977 upholding the declaration of its Supreme Commander, the President of ZAPU Comrade Joshua Nkomo, who on the 10th October, 1976 declared that: "We are not interested in the prestigious glory of empty ministerial posts or in the display of the glamour and glitter of the wealthy few.

"We cannot either after sacrifice of so many lives and so many years in struggle, allow opportunists and waylayers to slide into the shoes of the priviledged minorities to maintain the same systems but with black faces.
"It must be "POWER TO THE PEOPLE"
"Power to elect a government of their choice"
"Power to end all minority privileges, racism and tribalism"

GLOSSARY

African: Historically a black person living in Rhodesia.
Air Lt.: Air Lieutenant.
AK-47: A selective-fire semi-automatic and automatic, gas-operated assault rifle. Fires 7.62mm x 39mm cartridge. Standard curved magazine holds 30 rounds (also 10-, 20- and 40-round box magazines). Developed in the Soviet Union by Mikhail Kalashnikov.
AM: Air Marshall.
APA: African Purchase Area (Rhodesian Land Tenure Act).
AVM: Air Vice Marshall.
BC: Business centre.
Blue-on-blue: Accidental engagements of friendly forces.
Brig.: Brigadeer.
BSAP: British South Africa Police. The Rhodesian police force, also known as the BSA Police.
Bush: African veld. Generally referring to forests, well-vegetated riverbeds and kopjes.
Cadre: Core members or activists of a communist or other revolutionary organisation.
Callsign: A group of operators with its own radio identification number.
Capt.: Captain.
Casevac: Casualty evacuation.
Cell: A political and intelligence cell is a clandestine group of people operating in an undefined area. A military cell is a group of soldiers operating in a defined area.
Chimbwido: Young African woman, normally single, who actively supported insurgents by gathering intelligence and by cooking and washing for the fighters. Generally had lovers in ZANLA and ZIPRA sections.
Chimurenga: Shona term for the liberation war. Uprising of indigenous Africans against the colonial occupation of their land.
CID: Criminal Investigation Department.
CIO: Central Intelligence Organisation.
CO: Commanding Officer.
Col.: Colonel.
COIN: Counter-insurgency.
Com.Ops.: Combined Operations Headquarters. Centre for joint planning and co-ordination.
Contact: Security Forces armed confrontation with the enemy.
Cpl.: Corporal.
CT: Communist terrorist.
DA: District Assistant. African administration assistant working for the district commissioner.
DC: District Commissioner.
D/Cst.: Detective Constable.
D/Insp.: Detective Inspector.
D/P/O: Detective Patrol Officer.
Doppies: Expended cartridge cases.
D/S/O: Detective Section Officer.
D/Sgt.: Detective Sergeant
European: A white person living in Rhodesia.
FAF: Forward airfield.
FF: Fire Force.
Fire Force: Airborne, airmobile assault group. G-Cars ferried troops into direct confrontation with the enemy escorted by a K-Car.

Flt. Lt.:	Flight Lieutenant.
FN:	Gas-operated light automatic rifle. Magazine holds 20 rounds of 7.62mm ammunition. Manufactured by Fabrique Nationale Herstal (FN, Belgium).
Frantan:	Rhodesian euphemism for napalm.
FRELIMO:	Front for the Liberation of Mozambique.
Frozen:	Declared a no-go area, usually by Selous Scouts, to prevent blue-on-blue incidents (see also proscribed).
G-Car:	Troop-ferrying helicopter which carried the pilot, technician/ gunner and a maximum of four soldiers, called a "stop". Normally an Alouette III armed with twin .303 Brownings, belt-fed at a firing rate of 1,200 rounds per minute.
GC:	Ground Coverage. An operational unit of the BSA Police uniform branch primarily tasked with supplying information to Special Branch for the purpose of intelligence analysis. Int.Aff. had an equivalent scheme for their own resources.
GNA:	Grievances, needs and aspirations of the people.
Gook:	Insurgent (American military slang from the Korean War).
HMG:	Heavy machine gun.
HQ:	Headquarters.
Insp.:	Inspector.
Int.Aff.:	Ministry of Internal Affairs.
JOC:	Joint Operations Centre. Attended by Police Uniform Branch, Special Branch, Army, Air Force and Internal Affairs.
JPS:	Joint Planning Staff.
K-Car:	Helicopter command gunship which carried the pilot, technician/ gunner and Fire Force Commander. Normally an Alouette III armed with a Hispano MG 151 20mm cannon-firing, high-explosive incendiary rounds at the rate of 700 rounds per minute. Colloquially known as a Kill-Car.
KIA:	Killed in action.
Kopje:	A small hill, granite outcrop.
Kraal:	Rural African village, the huts consisting of mud walls with thatched roofs, often surrounded by a stockade.
L/Cpl.:	Lance Corporal.
L/Insp.:	Lance Inspector.
Locstat:	Ordnance survey map reference.
Lynx:	Cessna 337. Aircraft adapted and armed for air-to-ground combat.
Lt.:	Lieutenant.
Lt. Col.:	Lieutenant Colonel.
Lt. Gen.:	Lieutenant General.
LZ:	Landing zone.
MAG:	Gas-operated, belt-fed section machine gun firing 7.62mm rounds of ammunition. Manufactured by Fabrique Nationale Herstal (FN, Belgium).
Maj.:	Major.
Maj. Gen.	Major General.
Mantle:	Appointments code for BSAP Support Unit.
Masses:	A large number of indigenous Africans (see also people and povo).
Mealie meal:	Maize meal.
Mujibha:	Young African male aged 10 to 18 years. Part of insurgents' intelligence networks.
Mutengesi:	Shona for "sellout".
MO:	Modus operandi.
Nat.JOC:	National JOC (see also JOC).
NCO:	Non-commissioned officer.
NGO:	Non-government organisation.
N/S/P/O:	National Service Patrol Officer. Called up for one year's mandatory service. Thereafter, regularly called up.

OAU:	Organisation of African Unity.
OC:	Officer Commanding.
OCC:	Operations Co-ordinating Committee.
OP:	Observation post.
Op.:	Operation.
Paradak:	Dakota carrying paratroopers.
PATU:	Police Anti-Terrorist Unit (BSAP paramilitary COIN specialist unit).
People:	A large number of indigenous Africans (see also masses and povo).
PF:	Patriotic Front alliance between ZANU (Robert Mugabe) and ZAPU (Joshua Nkomo).
PGHQ:	Police General Headquarters.
PKM:	Soviet Pulemyot Kalashnikova Modernizirovany. General-purpose portable light machine gun. Fires 7.62mm x 39mm rounds of ammunition.
P/O:	Patrol Officer.
Pookie:	Light-armoured landmine detection vehicle designed to clear mined roads.
Povo:	A large number of indigenous Africans (see also masses and people).
PRAW:	Police Reserve Air Wing. Civilian aircraft chartered by the BSA Police and flown by police-qualified pilots who were members of the Police Reserve.
Proscribed:	Declared a no-go area to prevent blue-on-blue incidents.
Pseudo:	Purporting to be a terrorist.
PTC:	Posts and Telecommunications Corporation.
R & R:	Rest and recreation.
RAR:	Rhodesian African Rifles.
Recce:	Reconnaissance.
RBC:	Rhodesian Broadcasting Corporation.
RF:	Rhodesian Front (political party).
Rh.AF:	Rhodesian Air Force.
Rh.Art.:	Rhodesian Artillery.
RIC:	Rhodesian Intelligence Corps.
RLI:	Rhodesian Light Infantry.
RPD:	Soviet Rughnoy Pulemyot Degtyaryova. Portable light machine gun, belt-fed or two 50-round belts stored in a round drum and fires 7.62mm x 39mm rounds of ammunition.
RPG-7:	Portable, reusable, unguided, shoulder-launched, anti-tank rocket-propelled grenade launcher. RPG-7 projectile refers to the ammunition. Forerunner was the RPG-2.
RR:	Rhodesia Regiment. White territorial battalions numbering between 1 and 10.
RV:	Rendezvous. Meeting point.
SAS:	Special Air Service.
SB:	Special Branch of the British South Africa Police.
Scene:	A contact. Slang for firefight.
Scotch cart:	A two-wheeled wooden cart hauled normally by a donkey or some other beast of burden.
"Sellout":	Insurgent term for a government collaborator/informer (see also *mutengesi* and *vatengesi*).
SF:	Rhodesian Security Forces.
SFA:	Security Force Auxiliary. Locally recruited and trained soldier deployed into his own residential area to protect his people (local militia).
Sgt.:	Sergeant.
Sitrep:	Situation report.
Sgt. Maj.:	Sergeant Major.
SKS:	Soviet Samozaryadnyj Karabin Sistemy Simonova. Soviet, Eastern Bloc and Chinese semi-automatic carbine, 10-round magazine for 7.62mm x 39mm ammunition.
SNEB:	Air-to-ground white phosphorus attack rocket.
Snr. Asst. Comm.:	Senior Assistant Commissioner.
S/O:	Section Officer.

Sqdn.:	Squadron.
Stick:	Four-man battle group normally armed with one MAG and three FNs. The stick commander carried a radio.
"Stop":	Four-man airborne battle group deployed by the Fire Force.
Strela:	Soviet man-portable, shoulder-launched, heat-seeking surface-to-air missile. Known by the Soviets as Strela-2 (Arrow-2) and by NATO as SA-7, SAM-7 and Grail.
Sub.JOC:	Under command of a JOC (see also JOC).
Supt.:	Superintendent.
TA:	Territorial Army (see also TF).
Terrs:	Terrorists.
TF:	Territorial Force (see also TA).
TTL:	Tribal Trust Land (Rhodesian Land Tenure Act). These areas were reserved exclusively for the domain of indigenous tribal Africans.
UANC:	United African National Council headed by Bishop Abel Muzorewa.
UDI:	Unilateral Declaration of Independence.
Unimog:	2.5-tonne Mercedes 4 x 4 truck.
Vatengesi:	Shona for "sellouts" (see also *mutengesi*).
Vlei:	Low-lying marsh area. Can refer to savannah grasslands.
ZANLA:	Zimbabwe African National Liberation Army. ZANU's military wing.
ZANU:	Zimbabwe African National Union headed by Robert Mugabe.
ZAPU:	Zimbabwe African People's Union. Political party headed by Joshua Nkomo.
ZIPRA:	Zimbabwe People's Revolutionary Army. ZAPU's military wing.
ZSS:	Zipra Strela Section.

BIBLIOGRAPHY

Alderson, E.A.H., *With the Mounted Infantry and the Mashonaland Field Force, 1896*: RareBooksClub.com, 2012.

Alexander, J., *The Unsettled Land: State-making and the Politics of Land in Zimbabwe, 1893-2003*: Ohio UP, 2006.

Arnold, J.H., *History, A Very Short Introduction*: Oxford UP, 2000.

Austen, R., *Racism and Apartheid in Southern Africa, Rhodesia*: The UNESCO Press, 1975.

Baker, D., *Time Suspended: The Quenet Report And White Racial Dominance In Rhodesia*: Zambezia (1979), Vol. II (ii).

Barker, J., *Paradise Plundered*: Jim Barker, 2007.

Barton, F., *The Press of Africa: Persecution and Perseverance*: Palgrave Macmillan, 1979.

Beach, D., *The Shona* & *Zimbabwe 900-1850*: Heinemann Educational Books, 1980.

Bird, E., *Special Branch War*: Helion & Co., 2014.

Binda, A. & Cocks, C., *The Saints: The Rhodesian Light Infantry*: eBook co-published in 2014 by Helion & Co.

Binda, A., Heppenstall, D. & Hopkins, J., *Masodja: The History of the Rhodesian African Rifles and its Forerunner, The Rhodesia Native Regiment*: 30° South Publishers, 2007.

British South Africa Company, *Reports on the Native disturbances in Rhodesia, 1896-1897*: Bulawayo: Books of Rhodesia, 1975.

Brownell, J., *The Collapse of Rhodesia: Population Demographics and the Politics of Race*: Bloomsbury Publishing, 2010.

Butler, S., *War Is A Racket*: Round Table Press, 1935.

Callaghan, J., *James Callaghan Time and Chance*: William Collins & Co. Ltd, 1987.

Cary, R., *Charter Royal*: Citadel Press, 1970.

Chakawa, J., *Abel Muzorewa's Security Force Auxiliaries (SFAs) during and after the War of Liberation in Hurungwe District, Zimbabwe*: Doctoral Thesis, Midlands State University, Gweru, Registration No. R0644595, Gweru, Zimbabwe, 2015.

Cilliers, J., *Counter-Insurgency in Rhodesia*: Routledge, 2015.

Dawson, S., The First Chimurenga: 1896-1897 Uprising in Matabeleland and Mashonaland and Continued Conflicts in Academia: *Constellations* Vol. 2, No. 2, 2011 (DOI: https://doi.org/10.29173/cons10502).

de Meneses, F.R. & McNamara, R., *The White Redoubt, the Great Powers and the Struggle for Southern Africa*: Palgrave Macmillan, 2018, Kindle Edition.

Downes, R., *African Sunrise*: Lulu Press, 2017, Kindle Edition.

Ellert, H., *The Rhodesian Front War: Counter-insurgency and Guerrilla War in Rhodesia, 1962-1980*: Mambo Press, 1989.

Ellert, H. & Anderson, D., *A Brutal State of Affairs: The rise and fall of Rhodesia*: Weaver Press, 2020.

Emerson, S.A., *The Battle for Mozambique: The Frelimo-Renamo Struggle, 1977-1992*: Helion & Co., 2014.

Esterhuysen, P., *Zimbabwe: An Historical Overview*: Institute of Strategic Studies, 2004.

ExecutedToday.com: *1896: Chief Chingaira Makoni, Rhodesian rebel.*

Ferguson, N., *Empire: The Rise and Demise of the British World Order and the Lessons for Global Power*: Basic Books, 2004.

Flower, K., *Serving Secretly: Rhodesia's CIO Chief On Record*: Galago, 1987.

Friedman, H.A., *Psyop 1965-1980*: www.psywar.org/content/rhodesia.

Gallagher, L., *The Catholic Church in Manicaland, 1896-1996*: www.carmelites.ie/Manicaland.pdf.

Geldenhuys, P., *Rhodesian Air Force Operations*: Peysoft Publishing, 2014.

Gibbs, P., Phillips, H. & Russell, N., *Blue and Old Gold: The History of the British South Africa Police, 1889-1980*: South Publishers, 2009.

Hoffman, B., Taw, J.M. & Arnold, D., *Lessons for Contemporary Counterinsurgencies: The Rhodesian Experience*: Santa Monica: Rand Series, 1991.

Horne, G., *From the Barrel of a Gun: The United States and the war against Zimbabwe*: University of North Carolina Press, 2001.

Isaacman, A., Social Banditry in Zimbabwe (Rhodesia) and Mozambique, 1894-1907: An Expression of Early Peasant Protest: *Journal of Southern African Studies*, Vol. 4, No. 1, 1977.

Johnson, D., *World War Two and the Scramble for Labour in Colonial Zimbabwe, 1939-1948*: University of Zimbabwe Publications, 2000.

Keppel-Jones, A., *Rhodes and Rhodesia: The White Conquest of Zimbabwe, 1884-1902*: McGill-Queen's UP, 1983.

Lewis, A., *Too Bright the Vision?*: Covenant Books, 1992.

Lowry, D., *Cold War in Southern Africa: White Power, Black Liberation*: Routledge, 2009.

Martin, D. & Johnson, P., *The Struggle for Zimbabwe*: Faber & Faber, 1981.

Mazungu, E. & Machiridza, R., *African Water Laws: Plural Legislative Frameworks for Rural Water Management in Africa*: projects.nri.org.

Mitchell, N., *Jimmy Carter in Africa; Race and the Cold War*: Stanford UP, 2016.

Mitchell, T.G., *El Salvador: Failure of a Successful Internal Settlement*: pdfs.semanticscholar.org.

Moorcraft, P., *Contact II: Sygma Books, 1981; Mugabe's War Machine: Saving or Savaging Zimbabwe*: Pen & Sword Military, 2011.
Moorcraft, P. & McLaughlin, P., *The Rhodesian War: A Military History*: Pen & Sword Military, 2008.
Moyes, H., *Sacred Darkness: A Global Perspective on the Ritual use of Caves*: UP of Colorado, 2013.
Mushonga, M., *Curfew and the 'Man in the Middle' in Zimbabwe's War of Liberation with Special Reference to the Eastern Areas of Zimbabwe, 1977-1980*: 9-mushonga.pdf.
Owen, D., *Time to Declare*: Penguin Books, 1992; *In Sickness and in Power*: Methuen & Co., 2016.
Pakenham, T., *The Scramble for Africa*: Abacus, 1992.
Palley, C., *The Constitutional History and Law of Southern Rhodesia, 1888-1965 with Special Reference to Imperial Control*: Clarendon Press, 1966.
Papenfus, T., *Pik Botha and His Times*: Litera Publications, 2010.
Parker, J., *Rhodesia—Little White Island*: Pitman Publishing, 1972.
Petter-Bowyer, P.J.H., *Winds of Destruction*: 30° South Publishers, 2005.
Pittaway, J., *Selous Scouts: The Men Speak*: Dandy Agencies, 2015.
Pringle, I., *Murder in the Zambezi*: CreateSpace Independent Publishing Platform, 2017.
Ranger, T., *Peasant Consciousness and Guerrilla War in Zimbabwe*: James Currey, 1985; *Chingaira Makoni's Head: Myth, History & the Colonial Experience*: scholarworks.iu.edu. (1988).
Rook, M., *Farwell Rhodesia—Goodbye Zimbabwe*: Independently published, 2018, Kindle Edition.
Rotberg, R., *The Founder: Cecil Rhodes and the Pursuit of Power*: Oxford UP, 1988.
Rutherford, B., *Working on the Margins: Black Workers, White Farmers in Post Colonial Zimbabwe*: Weaver Press, 2000.
Sadomba, Z.W., *War Veterans in Zimbabwe's Revolution: Challenging Neo-colonialism and Settler and International Capital*: James Currey 2011.
Shaw, B., *Choppertech: A Gunner's Reflection of Fireforce Operations in Rhodesia*: Gordon Bevis Shaw, 2018.
Sibanda, M., Moyana, H. & Gumbo, S., *The African Heritage: History for Junior Secondary Schools*: Zimbabwe Educational Books, 1992.
Sibanda, E.M., *The Zimbabwe African People's Union, 1961-1987: A Political History of Insurgency in Southern Rhodesia*: Africa World Press, 2005.
Smith, I.D., *The Great Betrayal*: Blake Publishing, 1997; *Bitter Harvest*: Blake Publishing, 2008, Kindle Edition.
Spender, S., *The Pylons*: Faber & Faber, 1933.
Stapleton, T., *African Police and Soldiers in Colonial Zimbabwe, 1923-1980*: University of Rochester Press, 2011.
Stocking, M., *Relationship of Agricultural History and Settlement to Severe Soil Erosion in Rhodesia*: sanweb.lib.msu.edu: Zambezia (1978), Vol. II (ii).
Thomson, E. & Bennett, O., *Our Gods Never Helped Us Again*: panoslondon.panosnetwork.org.
Wessels, H., *A Handful of Hard Men: The SAS and the Battle for Rhodesia*: Casemate Publishers, 2015; *The SAS in Rhodesia: We Dared to Win*: Casemate Publishers, 2018.
Windrich, E., Rhodesian Censorship: The Role of the Media in the Making of a One-Party State:*African Affairs*, Vol. 78, No. 313, Oxford UP, 1979 (https://www.jstor.org/stable/721756).
Wood, J.R.T., *The War Diaries of André Dennison*: Ashanti Publishing, 1989; *A Matter of Weeks rather than Months*: Trafford, 2012, Kindle Edition.
Zedong, M., *Quotations from Chairman Mao Tsetung* (The Little Red Book): Foreign Languages Press, Peking, 1976; *The Red Book of Guerrilla Warfare*: El Paso Norte Press, 2010.

INDEX

L - #0082 - 090523 - C498 - 254/178/28 - PB - DID3569555